ADVERTISING
EDUCATION
around the world

Jef I. Richards   Billy I. Ross

Copy Editors:
Tom Bowers
Joe Pisani

This book provided to you by the

AMERICAN ACADEMY
^{OF}ADVERTISING

in association with the

DEPARTMENT OF ADVERTISING + PUBLIC RELATIONS

@

MICHIGAN STATE UNIVERSITY

A Note from the
American Academy of Advertising

The American Academy of Advertising is a community of academics and professionals that stimulates research and advances the teaching of advertising in our society. Every year, we gather at our annual conference to share ideas about teaching and research in both formal and informal ways. I've been attending these conferences for almost twenty years, and have noted several key differences that suggest that this book is highly relevant for those of us involved in advertising education.

First, our membership is decidedly international. A quick look at our membership list shows active and involved members from a variety of countries including Australia, China, Germany, Hong Kong, India, Ireland, Italy, Japan, Korea, New Zealand, the Netherlands, Palestine and Singapore. This increase in international membership has provided all members with new insights and ideas for teaching effectiveness. This wealth of diverse opinions serves all of our members, bringing attention to the fact that advertising is indeed now a global discipline, and American educators must find ways to bring that global importance into the classroom. Connecting with our international colleagues is an exceptional way to do that.

Second, I've seen a curricular sea change where many programs are now requiring (or at a minimum, strongly encouraging) both internships and international experiences. The value of internships for our students is clear: many students need internship experiences to land their first jobs. The value for international experiences is not as direct but still strong. Students are immersed in a new culture, and must be flexible to quickly learn how to adapt in an unfamiliar situation. New business pitch, anyone? Meeting people from new walks of life expands our students' worldview, making them more aware of the need to consider a range of individuals in crafting a message or targeting a consumer. Doing an internship in a country outside of the United States, then, is a big win: students become more aware of the importance of global messaging and can position themselves as even more valuable to the workforce.

This book, then, is a perfect and invaluable resource for the faculty member being asked by a student about an international internship. It also is a handy guide when colleagues or parents question whether students can achieve what they want to achieve. And perhaps most importantly, it will stimulate US members to reach out to colleagues around the world to ask questions, share ideas, and build important bridges.

It is my honor to serve as the 2013 President of the American Academy of Advertising, and I am so pleased to be able to recommend this groundbreaking book to advertising educators and students.

Kim Sheehan
President
American Academy of Advertising

A NOTE FROM THE MICHIGAN STATE UNIVERSITY DEPARTMENT OF ADVERTISING + PUBLIC RELATIONS

The faculty of the Department of Advertising + Public Relations (ADPR) voted unanimously to support the publication and distribution of this book because of its unique international focus. ADPR has a long history of involvement in global issues related to these fields. For example, one of its long-term faculty and former department chair, Gordon Miracle, gained widespread recognition for his leadership in international advertising for several decades.

Today the department possesses an unusually international character, with faculty members from Australia, Canada, China, Greece, Israel, Lebanon, Mexico, Palestine, Poland, Russia, Ukraine and, of course, the United States. Our student body, too, represents a broad sample of the world's people. This is a global marketplace. We have sought to embrace that reality, and to foster understanding across the many cultures. And that is precisely what this book is about.

Its objective is fairly modest, spanning only *advertising education* as it is taught around the world, but a reading of it almost certainly will broaden your appreciation and comprehension of some aspects that make each nationality unique and special. These authors have done a fine job of unearthing so much about each country. And, personally, I am proud to be associated with them. My department and its faculty all hope you like this book, and find it useful.

Jef I. Richards
Professor and Department Chair

Table of Contents

MIDDLE-EAST

NORTH AMERICA

PACIFIC

SOUTH AMERICA

vii

DEDICATION

This Book is dedicated to

KEITH JOHNSON
2/14/50- 7/15/09

IVAN L. PRESTON
12/18/31 - 3/2/11

ELSIE HEBERT
10/23/25 - 3/10/12

MARY ALICE SHAVER
4/9/38 - 10/17/12

MARGARET MORRISON
7/12/63 - 3/12/13

These five names represent the best of advertising education. They all were dedicated professors who loved this field and their students, their contributions were notable, and they all have passed since our last book. Their passing represents a profound loss to advertising education, and they are missed by all of us who continue to work in, and love, this area of academic focus. It is people like these who created the story told in this book.

JIR/ BIR

INTRODUCTION

We now have authored multiple books about advertising education, and probably some of you might wonder what more could possibly be said that hasn't already been covered. Our last book was intended to be the most exhaustive view of ad education, digging much deeper into both the past and the present than we'd ever done before. As we were nearing completion, it suddenly occurred to us that the book was entirely America-centric. It wasn't that we had intentionally made it so, it really was a reflection of our own narrow mindset. We rushed to put together a single, short, chapter on the other 195 countries in this world. As you might imagine, we didn't quite do them all justice.

As we began to discuss "What's next?" we quickly saw the need to flesh out the international perspective on ad education. We had both served as department chairs and in other roles where we encountered students coming to us from other countries, with degrees from universities that were literally and figuratively foreign to us. We had no way of knowing what it meant to have an advertising degree from, e.g., Renmin University of China. In fact, our response might have been, "They teach advertising in China???" So, we decided that our next project really needed to fill that enormous hole in our own knowledge, and hopefully in the minds of others who might read our work.

The problem, of course, is how to write a book about ad education in other countries when we knew little of what happened outside the U.S.[1] We talked about methods of research, but every one of them seemed wholly inadequate. It would be a very short book. Finally, it struck us that the only way to even begin to approach this topic would be to appeal to those from other countries – those who actually know something about the educational system in their own country – to be contributors. This was our epiphany.

We next set out to find those contributors, asking our friends for names and even putting out a general "call" for help. Amazingly, we soon had a large number of potential authors. We then assessed what countries were covered and what other countries needed to be covered. We couldn't

---

[1] Billy actually was involved in a couple of small studies several years ago looking at international students' attitudes toward advertising, so he wasn't entirely ignorant of ad education in other countries.

possibly cover all 200 countries in the world, and the truth is that some of them don't really have any ad education. Our decision was that we wanted a fairly representative sample. To be so, we needed both large and small countries, covering all the continents (well, we could leave out Antarctica). It was especially important to cover most of the large markets that were known sources of advertising talent. We searched for authors until we were satisfied that we had enough covered to give a fairly solid picture of ad education around the world, with about 30 authors from as many countries.

Our marching orders to the authors were minimal. Every culture is different in terms of their normal publishing standards, and certainly every country is different in terms of their history and approach to ad education, so we did not want to tie authors' hands. We simply asked them to write about ad education in their (chosen) country, perhaps including some history, but we left the particulars up to the author. We also put no restrictions on their writing styles, other than to tell them we needed the chapter in English. And we resigned ourselves to doing lots of editing, for which we sought out some help in the form of Tom Bowers and Joe Pisani, who we knew to be outstanding copy editors.

The result is variety. In fact, it's a delightful variety. Our last book was nearly 350 pages about the U.S., alone. So, it's not possible to provide that much depth on 30 countries, unless we intend to publish a multi-volume encyclopedia of ad education. Consequently, every author had to make choices about what they would cover and where they would spend most of their effort, and each author made a somewhat different choice. This, we think, results in a much richer picture of the world of ad education.

Some of the things we have learned by reading these contributions include the striking similarities of approach in teaching this subject matter, despite the equally striking disparities of culture. We also learned a lot about how culture – and politics – affect the development of advertising education, such as where ad education suddenly stalled with the introduction of new political leadership. It also becomes apparent that Western bias has played a big role in some countries. We learned that the lack of native-language textbooks about advertising can frustrate development of this field, and that in some countries there is greater concern for certain aspects of the field, such as a concentration on advertising ethics. And it was an eye opener for us to realize that while ad education in some countries is very young, in others, such as Japan, it is nearly as old as in the United States.

Truthfully, the number of lessons and ideas to be drawn from this material is endless. If you are an advertising educator, anywhere, it would not be a waste of your time to read this book. The lessons here should be learned by everyone who holds theirself out as an ad education expert. If you are a student of advertising, this should give you more of a world perspective. And if you are an advertising practitioner, this may inform your hiring when opening an office in another country.

Of course, like the content, the English and writing styles of our authors varied. Although a great deal of editing was done, we tried to edit with a light hand. We did not want to change the authors' "voices." The stories they tell are their own, as they expressed them.

Jef & Bill

REFLECTIONS

A handful of scholars were invited to write about their own experiences in teaching advertising across national and cultural borders. We asked them to reflect on what they had learned. These authors, Charles H. Patti, Robert Pennington, and Don Schultz, share their own unique insights. One takes a broad perspective on the merits and lessons learned from teaching abroad, another takes us into his own personal experiences and pleasures from his international adventures, and the other takes one lesson learned and makes an argument for change in the way we (Americans, in particular) should be teaching. All of these authors began their careers in the United States.

Learning to be International: One person's journey

Charles H. Patti
University of Denver, USA

Everyone who has ever taught at a university outside the U.S. has a story to share.

My parents were born in Italy, spoke Italian at home (to each other, but not to my brother and me), and they lived their lives like the more than 500,000 other Italians who migrated to the U.S. in the early 1900s—working in construction, the trades, or retail; raising a family; and hoping that their children would finish high school. Sending a child to a university was a far off dream. Unfortunately, by the time I had finished a Ph.D. and was on my way to teach advertising in one of the most prestigious business schools in the world, my parents had passed away. They would have enjoyed seeing the 20+ year international journey I've been on.

Until the summer of 1988, what I knew about Italy and Italians was through my parents and relatives. I had never visited Italy and I didn't speak Italian. One day in early 1988, I was invited to give a few lectures on advertising to undergraduate students at Bocconi University in Milan. This led to a 10-year relationship with Bocconi's Graduate School of Business—a relationship that brought me to Italy two or three times each year. I created and delivered courses in advertising management, marketing communication, and marketing management.

I taught in Bocconi's executive development program and helped several Bocconi faculty members begin their Ph.D. study through arranging for them to spend time at several U.S. universities, including Northwestern, UC-Berkeley, and universities in the California State University System. In time, I learned to speak enough Italian to make my way around restaurants and shops and have simple conversations on the streets of Milan, Florence, and a dozen other cities in Lombardy, Tuscany, Veneto, and the Italian Lakes area. Teaching advertising in Italy reconnected me to my parents' homeland—and it started the most enriching part of my career.

Over the past twenty years, I've taught advertising and other courses in New Zealand, Finland, England, France, Italy, Malaysia, and Australia. Today, teaching outside the U.S. is not uncommon, particularly as U.S. universities seek global partnerships and open off-shore campuses. Also, universities outside the U.S. now regularly seek visiting scholars and offer short-term teaching positions. In the '80s, this was not so common. Gordon Miracle, Wat Dunn, and a few others from the American Academy of Advertising had spent time outside the U.S. earlier, but the idea of living outside the U.S. was—and still is—rare. Here's a quick summary of the major international teaching and administrative positions I've held.

University of Denver's London Study Program (London, England)

This was not my first international teaching experience—that was as Visiting Professor of Advertising at the Helsinki School of Economics—but running DU's London Study Program was my first experience living outside the U.S. We lived in central London and I taught advertising courses to undergraduate students from the University of Denver. Living in London and making connections with some of the top advertising agencies were the pluses of this assignment. However, teaching U.S. students who had traveled to London to take courses from a U.S. professor didn't make much sense to me.

Graduate School of Business, Bocconi University
(Milan, Italy)

As I mentioned above, this was an invited position, and I taught courses at Bocconi for ten consecutive years. Living in Milan, traveling to other cities and regions in Italy, and helping move other faculty members to interactive learning models were highlights of this experience. One of my first Bocconi students, Federico Grayeb, became a close friend. We've built a 20-plus year friendship, and we continue to visit each other at his home in Argentina or my home in Denver.

Graduate School of Business, Otago University
(Dunedin, New Zealand)

I was a Visiting Professor of Marketing at Otago (nine-month appointment), arguably the best business school in New Zealand. I taught a marketing management course, gave seminars in advertising, learned to drive "on the other side of the road," learned how to lawn bowl, played on an amateur basketball team, and was introduced to cricket. I also met one of Otago's new, young faculty members from the U.S., Park Beede. Park went on to complete a Ph.D. at Otago, worked as an advertising executive in New Zealand and Australia, and (who would have guessed?) came to work with me as a faculty member at Queensland University of Technology in Australia—nearly 20 years after we first met in New Zealand.

School of Advertising, Marketing, and Public Relations,
Queensland University of Technology
(Brisbane, Australia)

For nine years (1997-2006), I was the Head of this very large, diverse school. As a full-time, senior administrator, I didn't teach often, but I delivered guest lectures from time to time in a variety of undergraduate and graduate courses. However, I did have the opportunity to help shape the curriculum; develop extensive professional relationships with the advertising and marketing community; build relationships with key articulation partner universities in Singapore and Malaysia; supervise Ph.D. and Masters by Research students; become deeply involved in the Australia and New Zealand Marketing Academy, including hosting that organization's 2006 international conference; and institute a visiting professor program that brought

AAAers Don Schultz, Charles Frazer, Pat Rose, and others to QUT on a regular basis.

I became an Australian citizen in 1999, and I continue to travel to Australia to visit friends, supervise Ph.D. students at QUT, help another Australian university with their AACSB accreditation efforts, and work on advertising-related, expert witness assignments.

The QUT experience is a perfect example of the professional and personal richness we can enjoy through an international assignment. My work at QUT has resulted in many research projects, articles, professional connections, and a large number of new friends.

Other Assignments

Once you get involved outside the U.S. enjoy it, the opportunities are endless. In addition to the above, major assignments, I've been involved at several other schools:

Helsinki School of Economics (Helsinki, Finland)
Visiting Professor of Advertising, sponsored by the advertising industry in Finland. I developed and delivered a university course in advertising research and gave seminars to advertising professionals in Helsinki and to graduate research students at University of Tempera, Tempera, Finland.

Temasek Polytechnic (Singapore)
Two terms (six years) as the External Examiner of their marketing curriculum. Beyond the content of this assignment, I've made strong friendships with several Temasek faculty members, including Geoffrey da Silva, author of *Marketing Introduction: Asian Perspective* (Asia-Pacific edition of the Kotler and Armstrong marketing text), and Lynda Wee, now the CEO of the training and consulting company, Bootstrap.

Universiti Teknologi Malaysia (Johor Bahru, Malaysia)
Visiting Professor giving lectures to students and workshops and seminars to faculty and administrators.

Universiti Tunku Abdul Rahman (Petaling and Kampar, Malaysia)
Two terms (six years) as External Examiner of their advertising curriculum. This assignment has included providing advice on the content, structure, and staffing of their undergraduate advertising program.

Tips from the Journey:

Have you ever seen the TV programs or read the travel books of Rick Steves? Rick is the master of taking you "through the back door" on just about any international trip you might be thinking about. Borrowing from Rick, here are a few "back door" tips on the teaching of advertising outside the U.S.:

It's not really about teaching advertising

Early on, those of us who taught advertising outside the U.S. were asked to show others how advertising is developed and produced in the U.S. But, as the marketplace became increasingly global and virtually everyone has access to information, my international role matured into an advisor and mentor, from university administration matters to curriculum to faculty development to the development of professional partnerships. Even if your assignment is to teach advertising, look for other ways to help your host university.

Short-term assignments have short-term effects

Going to China, the Czech Republic, or any other country to deliver a two-week, intensive course might be where you start—and it's better than no international exposure—but it is unlikely to give you a deep understanding of the culture. Besides, short-term assignments seldom lead to other, longer-range projects and relationships. Whenever possible, try to live in a city for six months or more.

Your family will make a difference

When I was working at QUT in Australia, we were in a growth mode and often had faculty openings. In the nine years I was Head of School, I found exactly one U.S. faculty member who could—or would—move outside the U.S. Living outside the U.S. is a great adventure and appeals to many of us. However, the reality is that our family situations make it difficult to leave the U.S. An international move can disrupt the lives of children, your partner, and perhaps your parents and siblings and life-long friends. The international opportunities that I've been fortunate to experience would not have been possible without the support of my wife and my children.

Fit in and deliver value

I can't even estimate the number of articles that have been written about the importance of "fitting in." Yet, the point rarely sinks in. During the nine years I lived in Australia, dozens of U.S. citizens were hired to work in key positions in Australian universities and businesses. Very few make the adjustment. We're talking about adjusting to a culture that shares a similar language, religion, ethics and values, justice system, etc. The fact is that most countries aren't just sitting around waiting to hear "how it's done in the U.S." At the same time, if you are selected for a full-time, permanent position, you can assume that you have something to offer. Find a way to deliver value within the lifestyle of the country you've moved to.

Build long-term relationships

This is good business advice and it works just as well with international academic assignments. I much value my friends and feel blessed to have so many close friendships with people all over the world. To me, the greatest benefit of an international assignment is developing new, meaningful relationships. If you are willing to move outside the U.S., leave your friends and family, and give up the security and comfort of your current job, take advantage of the personal and professional opportunity of relationship building.

The journey continues

I now live and work in Denver in a college that has modest level of international involvement. Yet, my international journey continues. All of those friendships and connections to universities outside the U.S. assure the continuation of student and faculty exchange agreements, supervision of Ph.D. students in other parts of the world, international research projects and grant applications, consulting, exploring offshore campuses and collaborations with universities outside the U.S, and many other projects that I haven't even thought of yet. As my travel expert, Rick Steves, often warns, "This is not a trip for everyone." But, compared to what the Italian immigrants of the early 20th century went through, being "international" today is as easy as a 14-hour flight on a 747 to a place you've never been to work with people you've never met. Exciting stuff.

Adventures in Taiwan

Robert Pennington
Fo Guang University, Taiwan

On my first visit to Taiwan at the end of spring semester in 1993, I had the pleasure of meeting the chair of the advertising department at a private university. After I returned to the States, we exchanged cordial notes by mail. When I returned to Taiwan at the end of fall semester, I contacted him by telephone to arrange a social meeting. He invited me to speak to a large class of undergraduates the following morning. As much as I wanted to decline the invitation because of jet lag, I could not. So I spent about an hour writing an outline, then got some rest.

The campus is in a beautiful area in the mountains north of Taipei. Clouds often take over the campus, and they did so on that December morning. I still felt the effects of jet lag, so I don't remember very much about breakfast. A couple of students who came to escort me gave me a colorful bouquet of flowers. I had read that such a gift was a common and respectful welcome, so I accepted it gratefully.

The class met in a large classroom, not in a lecture hall, which was full to its capacity. During my lecture, students were quite attentive, I think. I was working hard through my jet lag to improvise from my outline. Every time I looked, though, student eyeballs were looking right back at me. But I wonder how much they understood.

At that time, Taiwan already had a policy of encouraging English-language competence. However, competence on a test often does not reflect competence in practice. When you ask if they understand, quite often students will say "yes" even though they do not understand. I had learned that from dealing with Taiwanese students in the States. At least they listened respectfully. When I finished, they awarded me with a sustained round of applause, and thanked me profusely.

Students had remained silent when I asked for questions during the class. Afterward, they surrounded me with questions. I found this practice to be very common. No matter how curious they may be, most Taiwanese students are reluctant to speak in class. Some of the cause is lack of confidence in their ability to speak English. A greater cause is that in Taiwan classroom communication tends to be one-way, so that when you ask for questions and comments, they think you are being rhetorical. Students also are afraid of saying something wrong among their classmates in the formal classroom setting. To elicit responses in Taiwan, then, you must be especially positive with students when you do get responses. Outside, in informal settings, they tend to lose that fear and let their curiosity take over.

The second time I spoke to a class in Taiwan was eight years later. I had visited Taiwan four or five times in the intervening years and had visited a few more universities. I had also learned to deal with jet lag. (I leave the USA at night, try to keep the same routine on the plane as I would at home, arrive in the early morning and keep going all day.) I had been invited to speak to graduate students at the Institute of Communication Management at a national university in southern Taiwan. My arrival day, though, was dedicated to Taiwanese academic hospitality. This includes meeting as many faculty, administrators, staff and students as possible within three or four hours, exchanging name cards and small gifts, and drinking tea.

Two graduate students greeted me at the airport and escorted me to my on-campus lodging, which featured a small balcony overlooking the ocean with a small beach. After I'd had the opportunity to shower and rest, other graduate students called on me to escort me to lunch. Meals and eating are very important socially. I had already learned that. But this was the first of many episodes in which graduate students would take the opportunity to learn from me and about me.

In my own experience as a student, I recall that most of what I learned from my professors was unrelated to course material. I also recall faculty who joined students to socialize after classes in the afternoon or early evening. This lunchtime experience was similar, because the conversation covered anything but what I'd come to talk about. And I was with many students. In Taiwan, social contact with students tends to include several students at once. I've accepted invitations from one student, only to arrive and find several students. I've extended an invitation to one student, only to arrive and find several students. I expect it.

After lunch with these graduate students, we felt more comfortable with each other. The next day, when I talked about what I came to talk about (integrated marketing communication) the students and I had already established an informal relationship. Such relationships are very important at both graduate and undergraduate level. They determine how receptive students will be during class. They increase the likelihood of student participation during class. However, during the class, even though you acknowledge the informal relationship, the class relationship is formal. You must create a distinct and definite time for the formal relationship to begin and to end, just as teaching coaches advise in the United States.

12

When I lecture, even in the States, if a word play, pun, double entendre, or other humor device occurs to me, I include it without giving any cue that I am using humor. I don't expect anybody to notice. If somebody does, I'm gratified. But I do it for my own amusement. In the States, the one student who noticed most was Canadian. As I spoke about IMC, I used whatever humor occurred to me, as usual. Afterward, my host told me that he didn't think the students would catch very much of my humor. I told him that I used it for my own enjoyment. But I was very surprised that he had noticed it. He must have learned more than economics at the University of Iowa!

A year later, I was teaching full-time at a national university in central Taiwan. Now I am at a private university in the northeastern part of the country. My initial observations have held up. But I have added a few that also would be useful in the States.

I teach in English because the government wants Taiwan students to learn English. (Unfortunately, that slows my further development in Chinese.) At some departments and institutes, all required courses are in English because Taiwan attracts increasing numbers of foreign students who have learned English but not Chinese. For all of my students, English is a second language. So I have to speak carefully and enunciate clearly. I know that I am doing well because foreign-language majors have asked me to teach their conversation course. They said that although other professors speak English, I'm the only one they can understand.

In class, I need to find out whether students understand during class. Because they tend to be too polite to say they do not understand, I have learned to look for subtle cues in their facial expressions and in their eyes. In the classroom this means I cannot teach to a group. I teach to an aggregation of individuals. When I lecture, I speak to specific individual students one at a time. I do not just scan the faces. I make direct eye contact with each student individually. This is similar to social situations outside of class when I speak with students directly and include each individual.

Assessing students' understanding during class is especially important because I am effectively teaching in two foreign languages at the same time. The obvious first foreign language is English. The second is advertising, mass communication, research, media, or whatever the specific course topic. Each of these topic areas has specialized vocabulary that would be new even to those whose native language is English. In each class session, no matter what material I plan to cover, I have to adjust my lecture to meet student needs and challenges for understanding. I stop frequently to ask, "What are your questions?" I allow students to interrupt at any time with comments and questions. I do not continue until the student is satisfied with my explanations or clarifications.

Outside of class, students have come to me with questions from any of their other classes in English. Graduate students who had to present English-language journal articles turned to me for help when they could not understand the articles. Literature students have brought me Shakespeare sonnets and other English poetry. This presents a delicate ethical concern, because I don't want to interfere with another professor's teaching methods. So I have done a quick reading of whatever material the students bring, then I have given them some points to discuss with their professors. I tell them that I will be happy to discuss the readings further after their discussions with the course professor. Apparently, they have been satisfied with those discussions because none has returned for discussion with me.

When speaking English, students tend to begin with the apology, "My English is not very good." Sometimes they are correct. Often they are not. Although their English may not be perfect, it is usually understandable and intelligible. I have noticed that most Taiwanese tend to make the same errors that can be obstacles to understanding. Once I become aware of an error pattern, I can understand its meaning by guessing what they probably mean in that context, then listening for whether that probable meaning conforms to their error pattern. The technique has worked so well that one amazed student asked how I knew which words she wanted to say. I could have taken the opportunity to discuss conditional uncertainty, orders of approximation and all that blahblahblah. But I just told her I picked the word that people would probably use in that context.

One of my graduate students used to make a completely idiosyncratic error. He used the error so infrequently that I had to be alert to catch its occurrence and listen for its context. Finally, when I understood what he meant I told him about it. He had a great sense of humor, so I congratulated him for originating an error that was uniquely his. He was flattered. His example, though, shows why I encourage students not to be shy about making errors: I cannot help them improve unless I hear their mistakes.

My university has cordless microphones in the classrooms. Professors usually stand in the front of the classroom, with students, like their U.S. counterparts, tending to sit toward the back. Professors use microphones to talk to students. I do not. Many times in high school when I was active in theater, I heard the director's voice from the auditorium demanding that we "PROJECT!!!!!!" In the classroom now, I project. But I also move through the desks to get closer to students, so where they sit does not matter. If a student in another part of the room misses what I have said, I go to that part of the room and repeat. At such times, I may hear some murmuring among students, but that is usually discussion in Chinese of what I have said in English. I encourage a limited amount of such discussions because they help students understand the topic. But they are supposed to be learning English, too.

In Taiwan, "teacher" is an honored title. People are curious about me because, clearly, I'm not from around here. When they find out I am a teacher, they visibly demonstrate respect—from a farmer who stops his tractor for a short chat, from a township chief who invites me for tea, from the woman who cuts my hair, and, of course, from the students. They give this honor on credit. I do my best to demonstrate that I deserve it.

The New 80/20 Rule

Don E. Schultz
Northwestern University, USA

A quick look at the table of contents for three of the most widely adopted advertising textbooks in the U.S. reveals much commonality. Sections and chapters on consumer behavior, development of creative or messaging, media planning and implementation all suggest a standard approach to the subject of advertising instruction. Therefore student learning through the Kleppner[1], Belch and Belch[2] and O'Guinn[3] texts is quite similar. These authors, and others, seem to agree on some sort of underlying advertising instructional model.

Apparently, the advertising instructors who use these texts agree with the author's approaches, else why use the text? One would assume that, after instruction, students would agree the approaches used are valid and relevant and will serve them well in their chosen careers. Yet, is all this agreement on how to teach and learn the subject of advertising really a consensus of what is correct or a misconception, that, once started, has been allowed to continue without challenge and has now fallen out-of-date?

In spite of the fact that the overall definition of advertising may have changed, advertising content areas have moved from persuasion to relationships, and delivery systems have fragmented and multiplied[4], we seem to be teaching advertising in the same old way. The traditional, American-inspired view of "how to teach advertising" may be becoming less and less relevant around the world.

In this chapter, I argue for change. Not just for change's sake, but, because basic advertising instructional areas are no longer relevant in a vast majority of the world.

Advertising growth and opportunity are now in emerging markets[5]. So, while we have excellent approaches to advertising in established economies, as illustrated by the texts previously mentioned, those approaches and concepts become less and less relevant as the 80% of the world that is made up of emerging markets, surges ahead.

Advertising instruction is caught in a time warp.[6] It reflects the way advertising perhaps once was, but no longer is. Indeed, the characters in the television series "Mad Men"[7] would likely feel quite at home in many advertising classrooms, even today.

An Inherent Established Market Bias

For the most part, advertising instruction, as it is conducted in most western (meaning North American and Western European) colleges and universities, is biased toward development and use of persuasive mass communication in established economic markets. This model assumes marketplaces are fairly stable, with limited and known competitors, competing in an orderly and well defined way.

Advertising, therefore, attempts to influence and persuade marketwise consumers about useful, relevant products and services being offered by law-abiding marketers whose primary goal is to build on-going brand loyalty through long-term relationships. This occurs, in spite of the fact that much advertising tends to over-promise and the products under-deliver on those promises.[8]

The result? This idealized, western-biased scenario is likely relevant in only about 20% of the world's markets today.[9] The rest of the world consists of emerging markets which lack most of the basic structures that advertising education seems to assume exist. Those emerging markets are commonly unruly, dynamic, filled with unknowing and less educated consumers who have not been trained, nor do they know how to respond to the ploys of sophisticated marketers and advertisers.[10] Therefore, the western advertising approaches are either irrelevant or culturally deficient of meaning.

The New 80/20 Rule

Most everyone who teaches advertising is familiar with Pareto's 80/20 Rule[11], meaning 20% of the buyers make up 80% of the market. We seem to following that same rule in advertising instruction. While 80% of the advertising spending may currently be occurring in 20% of the markets, this is not going to be the future case.[12] The emerging markets of the world will ultimately dominate advertising investments, *i.e.,* China, India, Brazil, Russia, Indonesia, and so on. Yet, we continue to develop advertising instruction not for the future, but for the past.

Here, I have tried to develop the case for a revised view of advertising education. One that is likely more relevant for the majority of the world's population, and, therefore, deserving of research, analysis, innovation and ultimately instructional delivery by faculty. My discussion is about the majority of the world market; that is, the future markets of the world, not the established ones.

Today, those of us in the 20% group are exporting our knowledge and expertise to the 80%. We are preaching a gospel that seems to say "Emulate us and you will be successful." Unfortunately, the advertising instructional products we are exporting may well be irrelevant, or, even culturally unacceptable.

What Needs to be Changed?

In an academic research sense, this paper can be challenged due to lack of theory development, presentation of evidence and quantitative support. Yet, based on my 30 plus years of advertising teaching and research in more than 40 countries, I believe there is substantial face validity to my arguments. It is within this framework that I suggest five basic advertising instructional methodologies should be challenged and most likely changed.

Western Cultural Biases
For the most part, advertising instruction is based on a western-oriented, behaviorist view of how consumers are influenced by advertising, and therefore go to market.[13,14] That is, it is assumed that all consumers around the world are individualistic in nature, behave rationally, and are focused on optimizing their lives within their economic boundaries. While this may be true in developed western markets, it is often culturally irrelevant in the majority of the world. Based on most estimates, approximately 70 to 80% of the world's population live in communal societies, where the views of the group dominate the views of the individual.[15]

These are marketplaces where networks and communities provide the key social glue and which have a major influence in how advertising is perceived and used. Thus, culturally, the western models of consumer behavior, which underlie all advertising instruction, are likely in conflict with the existing norms. The behaviorist models being exported through current advertising instruction must, I believe, be re-thought and made more relevant to the 80% of the market where future growth will occur.

The Death of the "Big Idea"
In many emerging markets, while mass media have existed for some time, new forms of individualized media such as mobile have become the media forms of consumer choice.[16,17] Government technological initiatives have enabled many of these markets to skip generations of communication system development and go from limited-or-no telecommunication to almost unlimited mobile and wireless facilities. This creates major issues for

most western advertising instructional models, since they assume the concept of the "Big Idea." That is, the primary success of advertising is driven by some creative concept or approach that will appeal to the mass audiences generated by mass media; ideas and concepts that successfully knit broad demographic segments into a coherent whole.[1,2,3]

In developing economies, the "Big Idea" may no longer be as relevant as it has been in established markets. Individualized advertising approaches, targeted to specific groups of consumers, which are possible through addressable media, may be more relevant and more effective.

In the current advertising instructional model, "Big Ideas" may have to give way to multiple small promotional ideas that are continuously developed and implemented and followed by additional ideas and executions. Thus, the development of the creative product may have to be radically changed from slowly developing and expanding a single concept to rapidly implementing multiple executions of some basic idea….and, then, moving on.

From Media Distribution to Media Consumption

Today, advertising instruction focuses on optimizing the available resources of the advertiser organization to generate the greatest distribution of product and services messages to the broadest pre-selected audiences.[18] While still relevant in many areas, this outbound distribution system must be complemented by similar models that identify and integrate consumer acquisition of messages on their own, whether that be through consumer "pull models" such as search engines, use of web sites, social media or other, yet-to-be developed technologies, or from the increasingly important consumer-to-consumer networks that are growing exponentially.[19]

Clearly, the message distribution instructional model for the future must be focused on what communication systems the consumer accesses more than on what and how marketers choose to distribute their advertising messages. That means our current descriptions of "audiences" and measurement of message distribution must give way to new models of how consumers access, acquire, and use marketing communication in all its forms.[16,17]

In emerging economies, the use of mobile communications will be pervasive. Yet, today we have limited methods of understanding how consumers use these mobile systems and what their potential for the future might be. Media planning and implementation must be radically changed to reflect the developing media forms in both established and emerging markets.

Research Anomalies

Presently, our advertising instructional methods assume the use of various forms of traditional market and marketing research. These research systems are based on willing consumers who will share their views and feelings with research people at little or no cost. In established economies, consumers are knowledgeable about these research systems and are willing to provide their views. Such is often not the case in emerging markets.

Lacking experience with research systems, gaining marketplace information is often difficult, if not impossible.[20,21] Cultural mores often influence the type of answers emerging market consumers provide. In some cases, consumers are unwilling to speak with interviewers or share their views, simply because of their past political experience. So, while even more research knowledge will be needed in the future, our current research tools are often inadequate for the emerging market needs.

At the same time, vast amounts of market and marketplace information are being generated by various forms of data gathering technologies, such as frequent shopper programs, recruited panels, online research communities and the like.[22] It is this anomaly, the difficulty in gaining consumer information on one hand and being inundated with data on the other, that creates the problems. Thus, major changes are required in how we develop and use research information everywhere. Our present systems appear to be inadequate for either need in both established and emerging markets.

Measurement and Numbers

Today, advertising education, with minor exceptions, avoids the development or use of substantial quantitative analysis. Other than the limited statistical analysis used in media planning, students, with the aid of instructors, manage to either avoid or are not required to develop any but the most rudimentary financial skills. Statistical training is the dreaded enemy of the student population, being put off or avoided as long as possible in the advertising instructional periods.

Thus, when current students who have graduated from advertising programs are put into semi-management situations where advertising expenditures or investments are discussed, they are ill prepared to justify or support their recommendations. Unfortunately, this situation exists not just in the emerging markets, but in most advertising education. Too often we teach advertising as an "art," not as a "science." In truth, it must be a mix of the two.

In the cursory review of the advertising texts mentioned earlier, there is scant mention of the "business side" of advertising. We teach students primarily to "talk" advertising, that is, to create adverting programs in exquisite detail, and then deliver them to waiting consumers. But, too often we ignore measurement and accountability in our advertising instruction as being either too difficult or too challenging for student consumption.

Here again, another anomaly arises. For example, when we consider emerging markets, it quickly becomes obvious they will be heavily influenced by mobile and other forms of direct communication. That means more direct, relevant, and useful measurement and accountability skills will naturally occur than those in the more mass media dominated established markets. Thus, it may be the emerging markets will reverse the knowledge feed. That is, the new concept for interactive advertising may likely be developed in the emerging markets, not the existing ones. Wherever done, however, measurement and accountability are critical issues for advertising instruction.

A Final Thought

One major area of advertising instruction that is often neglected is teaching consumers how to be good consumers. How to understand their new marketplaces. How to make wise purchasing decisions. How to balance wants, needs and requirements. This is an area that seems to be sadly lacking in current advertising instruction. Yet, in developing economies and markets, it may be the most important topic to be taught if advertising is to be a relevant topic globally.

While this brief chapter may seem to be railing against the establishment, that may well be what is needed today. Given the changing composition of the audiences advertising must address in the future, that seems to be one of the most relevant issues we can address.

Advertising instruction, if we take the leading advertising texts as the basis for evaluation, is mired in an academic time warp. The focus of today's advertising education may have been, and may continue to be relevant for established markets, such as those in North America and Western Europe a number of years ago, the 20% of the world's population. The real question of how advertising is being taught, however, is whether it is relevant for the other 80% of the world.

That raises the ultimate question of whether we should continue to focus our efforts on improving what we know or begin exploration of what we don't know? To me, the challenge seems quite clear. But, to others, the solution may not be quite so obvious nor as palatable.

References

1. Lane, R., King, K. and T. Reichert (2010). *Kleppner's Advertising Procedure (18th ed.)*. Upper Saddle River, NJ: Prentice Hall.
2. Belch, G. and M. Belch (2008). *Advertising and Promotion: An Integrated Marketing Communications Perspective (8th ed.)*. Columbus, OH: McGraw-Hill/Irwin.
3. O'Guinn, T., Allen, C. and R.J. Semenik (2008). *Advertising and Integrated Brand Promotion (5th ed.)*. Florence, KY: South-Western College Publishing.
4. Schultz, D.E. and H.F. Schultz (2003). *IMC: The Next Generation*. New York, NY: McGraw-Hill.
5. Schultz, D.E. (2010). Communications between organizations and their markets in emerging economies: A research agenda. *Organizations and Markets in Emerging Economies*, vol. 1(1): 51-67.
6. Kerr, G. and D.E. Schultz (2008). Filling in the gaps or plugging in the holes? Why academic advertising research model needs maintenance. *Proceedings of the ICORIA Conference, Antwerp, Belgium.*
7. http:www.amctv.com/originals/madmen.
8. Edelman (2010). *Edelman Trust Barometer*, www.edelman.com.
9. De Mooij, M. (2010). *Global Marketing and Advertising (3rd ed.)*. Thousand Oaks, CA: Sage Publishing..
10. Dawar, N and A. Chattopadhyay (2002). Rethinking marketing programs for emerging markets, *Long Range Planning*, vol. 35(5): 457-474.
11. Schultz, D.E. and B.E. Barnes (1994). *Strategic Advertising Campaigns (4th ed.)*. Lincolnwood, IL: NTC Publishing Group, 56.
12. Ciochetto, L. (2010). *Globalization and Advertising in Emerging Economies: Brazil, Russia, India and China,* Taylor & Francis, London, UK.
13. Schiffman, L.G. and L.L. Kanuk (2007) *Consumer Behavior, 9th ed.,* Pearson-Prentice Hall, Upper Saddle River, NJ.
14. Solomon, M.R. (2006) *Consumer Behavior: Buying, Having and Being*, Pearson-Prentice Hall, Upper Saddle River, NJ.
15. Koch, R (1999) *The 80/20 Principle,* Currency DoubleDay, New York, NY.
16. Block, M.P. and D.E. Schultz (2009). *Media Generations: Media Allocation in a Consumer-Controlled Marketplace*. Worthington, OH: Prosper Publishing.
17. Schultz, D.E., and M.P. Block (2010). *Retail Communities: Customer Driven Retailing*. Worthington, OH: Prosper Publishing.
18. Sissors, J. Z. and R. B. Baron (2002). *Advertising Media Planning*. Lincolnwood, IL: NTC Business Books.
19. Schultz, D.E., Barnes, B.E., Schultz, H.F. and M. Azzaro (2009). *Building Customer-Brand Relationships*. Armonk, NY: M.E. Sharpe.
20. Schultz, D.E. (2010). Test your brand management skills. *Marketing Management* (in press).
21. Srinivasan, R., Vijayakumar, K., Agarwal, M. and D.A. Stiawan (2010). Premarket evaluation of new consumer durable brands in Asian markets. *Proceedings of the ESOMAR Asia-Pacific Conference, Kuala Lumpur.*
22. Humby, C., Hunt, T. and T. Philips (2004). *Scoring Points: How Tesco is Winning Customer Loyalty*. London, UK: Kogan Page.

AFRICA

Botswana: The Environment of Advertising Education

Eno Akpabio
University of Botswana, Botswana

As in other areas of human endeavor, advertising has had its own fair share of changes. Just as Albert Lasker's definition of advertising as "salesmanship in print" at the beginning of the 20th century (Arens, Weigold and Arens 2008, p. 7) was rendered obsolete by the advent of radio and television, so also has information and communication technologies (ICTs) and other developments in professional practice made advertising a moving target.

From an economic standpoint, Arens, Weigold and Arens (2008) note that advertising has evolved through the preindustrial to industrial, post-industrial, and global interactive age with significant changes in professional practice and more sophisticated approaches to reaching and persuading consumers. Not only have agencies changed in their structure and ways of doing business, even traditional functions such as account planning, copy, production, media planning and buying, traffic, etc., are configured differently to cater for the challenges of the 21st century marketplace.

The constant changes in the marketplace are acknowledged by the authors of the *Online advertising playbook,* who go ahead to insist that they have based their book on "principles and proven strategies" even though they concede that "new tactical opportunities arise daily … [hence] where there is shelf-life issue, we've tried to highlight this with a note" (Plummer, Rappaport, Hall and Barocci 2007, p. 5).

Media planning, for instance, gained greater mileage after it moved from being an isolated activity to one closely related to marketing planning following the significant premium placed on the marketing concept, so much so that "a good media effort is what makes the rest of the advertising campaign work – or not work" (Kelley and Jugenheimer 2008, p. 5). Creative media choice, which involves placing messages on novel media (sheep, bananas, face masks, golf holes, egg shells, elevator panels, etc.), has been found to be positively correlated with more positive ad and brand evaluation, as well as enhanced brand association, than placement in a traditional medium (Dahlén, Friberg and Nilsson 2009).

Print ads now presume a visually-oriented, as well as casually browsing, viewer, unlike older ads that assumed an attentive reader as a consequence of the blitzkrieg of ad messages the modern consumer is exposed to (McQuarrie and Phillips 2008). Some ad agencies are now producing reality commercials that involve real users of the product rather than models, in the hope that such campaigns will resonate more with consumers than traditional ad campaigns. Seamless and hybrid messages through the agency of the Internet, product placement, virtual reality, mobile phones, m-commerce, and viral marketing allow advertisers to reach consumers through a noncommercial appearance ((Frith and Mueller 2007).

The dizzying pace of change in the advertising landscape also raises questions about the value and quality of advertising education. The approach to adopt for the former remains contested, from those who stand opposed to advertising education, insisting that "hands-on experience is the only worthwhile training," to those who prefer to train within the agency environment because universities are not well equipped, to universities who differ in their approach from more applied to more liberal ad education schools/departments (Ross and Richards 2008, pp 336-339). There is also the recurring debate about the best place to house advertising programs, between marketing and communication departments.

Some of these debates are clearly informed by the need to produce job-ready graduates who know their onions. Another reason is the penchant by practitioners who have performed excellently without a qualification in advertising, preferring to hire "bright-but-untrained employees in their own image" (Ross and Richards 2008, p. 337).

However, advertising programs that meet the standards of industry will most likely dispel the mist and convey the impression of job-ready graduates, as well as impress hard on the disbelieving regarding the value of ad education. But do programs which meet this criterion exist in Botswana? How are practitioners adapting to the changing advertising landscape and are they fully in the know as regards the changing nature of the profession? Finally, what does the advertising industry in Botswana bring to the table of global practice?

Rationale and Significance of the Study

This study seeks to make known advertising development and practice in Botswana. In terms of ad education, the study will focus on advertising programs and the intersection between such programs and the needs of the ad industry. A paucity of materials on this is apparent compared to information on other aspects of advertising. There have been efforts to document advertising education and players (*see* Ross and Richards 2008) but this effort is skewed in favor of the United States and, like in most scholarship emanating from the West, Africa is marginalized. The only mention of advertising in Africa references the AAA School of Advertising based in South Africa.

The study, then, will serve the purpose of giving a comprehensive picture of advertising education in this country and position it within the changing ad landscape. It will profile programs and academics and advertising professionals. As a consequence, it will make an important contribution to the advertising literature from a Botswana and African perspective.

Research Questions

1. What is the nature of advertising (comprehensive or partial training in aspects of advertising practice) education in Botswana?

2. Are advertising professionals involved in the design of academic advertising programs and evaluation of students' work?

3. What has been the contribution of practitioners and academics to the development of advertising in Botswana?

Methodology

The study involved intensive interviews, which have the advantage of providing a wealth of information on the topic under focus (Wimmer and Dominick 2006). All agencies listed in the 2010 Botswana Telecommunications Corporation (BTC) Phonebook were contacted. Fourteen ad professionals agreed to participate in the study. Twelve of the interviewees were agency heads, while the remaining two had the designation of Creative Director and Business Development Manager. Four persons involved in ad education were also interviewed. An analysis of advertising course materials and programs also was done.

Botswana Advertising Landscape

Botswana obtained independence from Britain on September 30, 1996. This country of 1.9 million people is widely regarded as a shining example (Hope 1999) in the African continent. A 2007 Gallup Poll attributed the country's success story to diamond wealth, political stability, and sound macro-economic policies.[1] The 2010 Global Peace Index[2] ranked Botswana 33rd, behind Singapore, United Kingdom, and France, and above the United States (85th) as well as all other African countries. The World Bank[3] classifies Botswana as an upper-middle income country with GNI per capita of US$ 6,471.22, and ease of doing business rank of 45 out of 183 economies. To see how this translates in terms of the advertising business, a short history of advertising in Botswana is germane.

Prior to 1990, any advertising in Botswana had to be taken across the border to South Africa.[4] A number of factors created a conducive atmosphere for advertising to take root and flourish in Botswana. Newspapers were set up in the 1990s, and they needed revenue to keep the business going, and advertising was a natural source of financing. The influx of newspapers provided a much needed booster shot to the advertising industry.[5]

Early newspaper advertising which pioneered the ad industry was quite primitive, with the use of electroset and compuset methods.[6] At about this time, also, some Zimbabwean-based companies had invested in the Botswana market and needed advertising support.[7] This gave rise to agencies like Marketing Communication and Diacom Advertising, which initially serviced Botswana Telecommunications Corporation and Mascom Wireless, etc., and then began to look for other clients to which they could provide advertising service.[8] The entrance of cell phone companies into the market changed the advertising landscape, especially because they are big spenders.[9]

The Agencies

There was a consensus among the interviewees that the decent-sized agencies at this time were Marketing Communication, Ogilvy, Saatchi and Saatchi, and Media Communication. These big agencies were mostly white-owned (that is, White South Africans and White Zimbabweans).[10] The pioneers were Alistair Carlisle, Lyn Medeley, Alan Brough (Horizon Saatchi and Saatchi/Horizon Ogilvy), Vic Hanna (Medcom), and Thomas Whitney (Marketing Communication). One informant indicated that some of the brilliant employees at Horizon Saatchi and Saatchi had a tremendous impact on the agency environment.[11] This group was made up of

Gerald Mashonga (CEO of Synergy Advertising and Promotions), Tonderai Tsara and Noma Moremong (Directors of Dialogue Saatchi and Saatchi), as well as the late Mathata Kasinnelwe (former Managing Director, Horizon Ogilvy).

There were also a number of small/medium sized agencies, such as CBS, Diacom, Infinity, Optimum media, OP Design (now OP Advertising), Stiles and Stiles, etc. An influx of Zimbabwean graphic designers provided the much needed skills to keep the wheel of advertising turning[12], especially since South African graphic designers felt that the market was too small.[13] Even though there are a number of trained Batswana graphic designers, they seem not to be making an impact on the industry for a variety of reasons. Batswana designers do not want to pay their dues by coming in at an entry level with a small salary and rising through the ranks, preferring instead to seek their fortunes in other better paying industries, or obtaining citizen empowerment loans to set up on their own shops.[14] Zimbabweans appear to understand the local context better, having been trained in their country as opposed to the mostly foreign-trained Batswanans who have a good grasp of current technology and software but do not fully appreciate and understand the African context[15].

Interviewees credit computers, especially desktop publishing software, as well as the coming of commercial radio stations (RB2, Gabz FM, Yarona FM), and the launch of Botswana Television (BTV) as bringing about a transition from largely print ads to electronic ones. The growth of the SMME sector is also a contributory factor to the development of the local advertising industry, by giving exposure to their products and services.

The Media

The transition to Internet advertising has been slow, especially because of the low level of Internet penetration. Even when this is done, there are mixed results. Instead of the expected interactivity, people just visit the sites and read the material as if it were a brochure.[16] Dialogue Saatchi and Saatchi reports working on a Twitter and Facebook campaign for a client, noting that traffic to the client's website as measured by Google Analytics was "decent."[17] As technology becomes cheaper, and as young people move from telephone calls to SMS to data, this area will pick up.[18] However, the expertise to carry out Internet advertising is unavailable.

There also are developments in the outdoor advertising landscape. Continental Outdoor was probably the first such company in Botswana.[19] According to Sussanah Steenkamp, General Manager of Continental Outdoor—Botswana, the outdoor sector has experienced tremendous growth as a result of the unregulated environment. The indiscriminate erection of billboards results in chaos and substandard outdoor development that does not add value to the aesthetics of the environment.Some of these billboards lack structural integrity and may be a danger to the general public. Billboards are everywhere, and it is sad to note that even big players in the sector are part of the problem. Approval to put up billboards is usually obtained from private individuals as well the city council.[20] But even when boards are erected illegally, the councils lack the manpower to pull them down.[21]

The Trends

There is a growing trend towards international affiliation even though a few interviewees decried this. The rationale for affiliation is to attract international corporations that have a proper appreciation of the role of advertising.[22] Another reason is the growing sophistication of the Botswana market, and the mileage that local agencies obtain from affiliation.[23]

Local agencies are able to get referrals, training resources, and the latest software, which is leveraged to give clients the best.[24] One source cited the example of a memorable Orange TV commercial involving 250 persons from 25 different countries.[25] The consequence of affiliation is reflected in nomenclatures: Marketing Communication is now (Draft) FCB Marketing Communication, Media Communication is TBWA/Medcom, Ogilvy Saatchi and Saatchi has metamorphosed into Horizon Ogilvy, Dialogue Group is now Dialogue Saatchi and Saatchi. The present Continental Outdoors has changed names over the years to reflect various owners: Airport Advertising, to Inter Africa, to Corp Com, to Clear Channel, and INM, in that order.[26]

All interviewees decried the lack of advertising regulation in Botswana as an ill wind that has distorted the sector and stunted professionalism. Many of them look back at their native South Africa and Zimbabwe with nostalgic feelings in this regard. These informants note that lack of regulation has resulted in fly-by-night agencies that come in cheap and get business that proper agencies are supposed to get. Some of these one-man businesses are able to do the required executions, but some are not able and end up taking the job to the regular agencies, thus resulting in higher pricing for services.

This unregulated environment has also been fingered for lots of unethical practices. One informant[27] described how a big player in the telecommunication sector had called for a pitch. One of the conditions for participation was five years' track record, but a newly formed agency got the brief. In the same vein, a big player in the financial services sector had also called for a pitch, and instead of the winning agency getting a two-year contract, it was given one for six months. The suspicion was that the winning agency would develop the campaign, then the job would be passed on to another agency.[28]

Growth of the sector is fine, but in terms of depth, a majority of interviewees see a big problem in almost all areas: photography, copywriting, strategy, and research. A number of untrained people feel that they know enough to set up shop, and this detracts from professionalism. Many agency heads also are involved in other sectors apart from advertising, so the required devotion and drive is absent.

There also is a lot of outsourcing for artwork and illustration, research, and strategy to South Africa and other countries. As a consequence, some clients take jobs directly to South Africa, knowing that the required expertise is not available locally. One interviewee stated that a main reason for this is that agencies cannot afford experienced staff.[29] As people stay longer in the industry they are likely to be pushed out because they would be too expensive. That means experience is lost because those persons go into other sectors. Very few use this experience by setting up ad agencies of their own.

But clients are not adding value to the sector, either. Clients are very price sensitive, so much so that the bigger the agency the more likely it is to go out of business, because the small and cheap players are favoured.[30] And government, which is a big ad spender, accepts shoddy jobs.[31] So to succeed, one has to do what clients dictate, slap it together, and pass it on.[32] Some clients want a job that will take three months done in a week.[33]

The main reason why more sophisticated billboards are not present in the Botswana outdoor advertising landscape is because clients are not willing to pay for it.[34] This is a far cry from what is taking place in South Africa, where the outdoor budget is quite large.[35] The result is uniformity: happy faces, headline, and logo so much so that the ads for the three cellphone companies in Botswana look uncannily alike.[36]

A few interviewees insist, though, that Botswana advertising can compare favorably to international advertising executions, if there is a level playing field, which is often not the case. One informant[37] painted a scenario that brings home the challenges in stark terms:

> To execute a big assignment, if you are in London or New York, you can call up a recruiter and have 10-15 top notch resources at your door step tomorrow morning. This is not possible in Botswana. I can't just pick up the phone and say I need five copywriters, 10 high-level art directors, etc. Talent takes long to find, and one has to hold onto them with both hands, because it is a small market and there is lack of skill out there.

Advertising Education in Botswana

For a long time the University of Botswana was the sole provider of higher education in the country. In 2007, a Malaysian University, Limkokwing University of Creative Technology, set up a Gaborone Campus. There also are smaller institutions offering franchise programs, such as ABM University College, Botho College, etc. In terms of advertising education, two main institutions/outfits are in reckoning.

University of Botswana

There is no specific degree program in advertising at the University of Botswana, but advertising is offered in the Bachelor of Business Administration (Marketing) Degree as an optional course. To qualify to take the advertising course, students are expected to have taken a course in integrated marketing communication. The ad course basically provides an overview of advertising, with particular emphasis on its intersection with marketing. Advertising is also offered in the Department of Media Studies for students studying for the Bachelor of Media Studies Degree. It is lumped together with public relations. The specific courses are as follows: Writing for Public relations/Advertising Copywriting, Introduction to Public Relations and Advertising, Public Relations and Advertising Campaigns Management and Public Communication Campaigns.

In Advertising Copywriting, students are taught about creativity, research, strategy, creative copywriting, as well as how to write copy for print, radio, television, outdoor and point-of-purchase. In Introduction to Advertising and Public Relations, the advertising component involves history and evolution of advertising, classification, roles and functions, formulas, and the industry of advertising.

The Advertising and Public Relations Campaigns course takes an integrated marketing communication approach, with learning centered around analysis of company, consumers, product/brand, competition, setting of objectives, strategy, positioning, targeting and delivering the message, media planning and related marketing communication – personal selling, public relations and direct marketing. Public Communication campaigns take almost the same format as Advertising and Public Relations Campaigns, with the notable difference being emphasis on attitude and behavior change. In the latter course, students are expected to produce campaigns for products and services, while the former addresses pressing social issues, such as HIV and AIDS, drink spiking, road accidents, etc.

Preparatory and complementary courses equip students with the skills to carry out campaigns, and they can choose from other theoretical and practical courses that students can choose from. Students also take the following courses: Computer Animation, DTP and Digital Media, Communication Research Methods, Scripting for the Electronic Media, TV and Video Production, Radio Production, and various programs in print journalism as well as core courses from the Department of English. An AVID, Macintosh, and PC lab allows students to work on and or produce the training newspaper, TV and programs, news, features and documentaries, and PR and ad campaigns.

Limkokwing University of Creative Technology

The Head of the Faculty of Design and Innovation, Mr. Philisani Amos, and program leader for advertising, Ms. Bone Kobua, outlined the advertising program. The program leads to the award of Associate Degree in Advertising, and it is the only one in the country that focuses exclusively on advertising training.

The program used to be housed in the Faculty of Communication Media and Broadcasting, but it was moved to the present faculty (Design and Innovation) to make it more practice-oriented. The modules offered are a combination of general education courses, such as communication and study skills, introduction to research, computer skills, drawing, internship, entrepreneurship, fundamentals of design and creative and innovative studies and specializations such as visualization techniques, creative studies, design studies, photography for advertising, computer graphics for advertising, desktop publishing, principles of advertising, multimedia presentation, typography, advertising studio, copywriting, art direction and advertising publication.

Advertising Professionals' Involvement in Education

The internship program in the two institutions provides work-based training for students. For a period of three months, students learn what the world of work feels like. However, not all students get placed in advertising agencies, as there are a range of options to choose from. In terms of program development, the University of Botswana has advisory boards in place to give input regarding how to make programs relevant to the needs of industry. Since advertising is a component of the marketing and media studies degrees, professionals in various areas of marketing, as well as professionals in every area of media and communication, sit on the two advisory boards. Professionals are invited to critique students' campaigns in the Department of Media Studies, and the feedback is usually well received by the students.

A similar structure exists at Limkokwing University of Creative Technology, but the nomenclature is "Industry Advisers." The Head of Faculty and Program leader for advertising informed me that the chair of the Industry Advisers for the Advertising Program is Mr. Olivier Prentout, who is the managing director of OP Advertising. Advertising professionals also form a panel that critiques student work. Students' ad productions are also placed in exhibition halls within the institution for ad professionals and members of the general public to view. Interviewees also told me that two Limkokwing students recently won an ad award in a competition organized by Elements Advertising, an agency based in South Africa.

From the agency side, the picture was not as rosy. One interviewee[38] said agencies are thirsty for more engagement and wanted educational institutions to be more proactive in engaging ad professionals, as opposed to the present laid back outlook. Another informant[39] acknowledged that Limkokwing University does involve him in judging students' work, but he decried the quality of graduates from the institution. He felt that the lecturers were young and inexperienced, and this reflected negatively on the institutions' graduates. He also was unhappy with the quality of industrial design interns from the University of Botswana, who were not exposed to industry-standard software.[40]

Conclusion

The media studies program at the University of Botswana was designed to give students opportunities to fit into any sector in the media and communication field based on feelers from the market. Students can pick and choose from the available streams – public relations and advertising, print journalism, radio, TV and video. Bachelor of Media Studies graduates, because they are exposed to various aspects of journalism and mass communication, have gotten employment in advertising, public relations, radio, television and film production outfits. The Associate Degree in Advertising program at Limkokwing University of Creative Technology is narrower, but there is also a concern about not saturating the small Botswana market.[41]

Yet the ad industry is still dominated by foreigners. One interviewee felt that the future of advertising is rosy because of the specialized program offered by Limkokwing University of Creative Technology.[42] However, a number of the Associate Degree graduates are in ad agencies, but quite a number of them are also in various companies where they come up with concepts and outsource productions.[43] This is the same approach used by the Business Development Centre, which offers short courses on advertising and branding to players in the small-business sector, so they can be empowered to do their own branding and advertising.[44] How this self-help approach will aid the industry is unclear. There is no doubt that it is a contributory factor to the poor executions in the country, given that persons who are trained but inexperienced, and those who are not trained in the field, all feel they can have a go at advertising and branding.

One of the significant findings of this study is the fact that there is insufficient engagement between the town and the gown. For one informant to mistake industrial design (Engineering and Technology) students for advertising (media studies) students clearly signals a communication gap. What the industrial design students were doing, seeking internship opportunities in an ad agency, communicates poor internship management and begs for answers. Clearly, if players in the advertising sector do not know what is going on in institutions offering advertising courses, graduates of such programs are likely to be passed over in terms of employment opportunities. The present level of engagement should be extended to the entire industry. The downside is that there is no regulatory body or industry association. Until these are in place, ad educators may need to engage each player individually in judging students' work and curriculum development.

Graduates from the two universities can help fill a gap. Limkowing University graduates, due to the hands-on nature of the program, can handle photography while the University of Botswana graduates should be able to add value to the areas of research and strategy, which are identified areas of need. Both programs train students in copywriting, so the dearth of good copywriters should be a thing of the past in the industry. The Bachelor of Media Studies has a very strong new media component, and this should position the graduates to provide expertise in Internet advertising, when the industry eventually turns this important corner. Now that jobs are difficult to come by, these graduates will be willing to stay in the ad agency environment and rise through the ranks while gaining the requisite experience to make them seasoned professionals.

Other programs should be a footnote to advertising education in Botswana: an Advanced Certificate in Multimedia offered by Gaborone Technical College, which has a small component of advertising, as well as short courses in branding and advertising offered by Business Development Centre.

References

1. *Retrieved from www.**gallup**.com/**poll**/.../stability-good-governance-boost-confidence-**botswana**.aspx* - Similar on May 12, 2010.
2. *Retrieved from www.visionofhumanity.org/gpi-data/* - Cached on May 12, 2010.
3. *Retrieved from* http://www.doingbusiness.org/exploreeconomies/?economyid=27 on May 12, 2010.
4. Interview with N. T. (personal communication. May 19, 2010).
5. Interview with V. H. (personal communication May 21, 2010).
6. Interview with V. H. (personal communication May 21, 2010).
7. Interview with T. K. (personal communication May 20, 2010).
8. Interview with T. K. (personal communication May 20, 2010).
9. Interview with O. P. (personal communication May 24, 2010).
10. Interview with T. K. (personal communication May 20, 2010).
11. Interview with L. S. (personal communication May 6, 2010).
12. Interview with T. K. (personal communication May 20, 2010).
13. Interviews with R. V. (personal communication May 27, 2010) and T. K. (personal communication May 20, 2010).
14. Interview with R. V. (personal communication May 27, 2010).
15. Interview with R. V.(personal communication May 27, 2010).
16. Interview with T. K. (personal communication May 20, 2010).
17. Interview with T. T.(personal communication April 30, 2010).
18. Interview with T. T. (personal communication April 30, 2010).
19. Interview with S. S. (personal communication May 24, 2010).
20. Interview with F. W. (personal communication May 10, 2010).
21. Interview with F. W. (personal communication May 10, 2010).
22. Interview with T. M. (personal communication May 11, 2010).
23. Interview with V. H. (personal communication May 21, 2010).
24. Interview with T. T. (personal communication April 30, 2010).
25. Interview with T. T. (personal communication April 30, 2010).
26. Interview with S. S.(personal communication May 24, 2010).
27. Interview with R. V. (personal communication May 27, 2010)
28. Interview with R. V. (personal communication May 27, 2010)
29. Interview with T. K. (personal communication May 20, 2010).
30. Interview with T. N. (personal communication April 26, 2010).
31. Interview with T. N. (personal communication April 26, 2010).
32. Interview with L. S. (personal communication May 6, 2010).
33. Interview with T. T. (personal communication April 30, 2010).
34. Interview with F. W. (personal communication May 10, 2010).
35. Interview with F. W. (personal communication May 10, 2010).
36. Interview with T. K. (personal communication May 20, 2010).
37. Interview with T. T. (personal communication April 30, 2010).
38. Interview with T. T. (personal communication April 30, 2010).
39. Interview with T. K. (personal communication May 20, 2010).
40. I pointed out that these were not Media Studies' students who are exposed to the right software but students of Faculty of Engineering and Technology.
41. Interviews with B. K. and P. A. (personal communication June 8, 2010).
42. Interview with L. S. (personal communication May 6, 2010).

43. Interviews with B. K. and P. A. (personal communication June 8, 2010).
44. Interview with B. S. (personal communication June 9, 2010).

Advertising Education in Egypt

Kevin Keenan
The American University in Cairo, Egypt

As a country only beginning to move toward a private economy since the last years of the twentieth century, and with a media system still largely government operated and controlled, Egypt has a surprisingly long history of advertising education. With the largest population and probably the most influential system of higher education in the Arab world, the teaching methods, curriculum, and outcomes of Egyptian advertising education have an impact on how advertising is taught and practiced throughout the Middle East region.

Efforts to meet "media literacy" objectives in primary and secondary schooling in Egypt usually include mention of advertising's roles and functions. Vocational training programs, provided through the Egyptian national government and non-governmental organizations for teenage and adult students, occasionally touch on topics related to advertising production. However, professional aspects of advertising and its treatment as an academic discipline generally are the exclusive province of universities and university level technical institutes.

Higher Education in Egypt

The oldest university in Egypt, and certainly one of the oldest in the world, is Al-Azhar University, founded over 1,000 years ago, in 975 A.D. (Said, 2003). Established as an institution devoted to Islamic learning, Al-Azhar remains probably the world's leading center for the study of Islam. In recent years, its curriculum has expanded to include nonreligious areas, including some limited attention to advertising as a factor related to economics, though no coursework or degrees focus exclusively on advertising.

In terms of more mainstream higher education, the Egyptian system can be subdivided into 23 public universities and 29 private universities or institutes. The constitution of Egypt provides citizens with access to free education at public universities, which operate under the authority of the Ministry of Education. Egypt's history of occupation, colonization, and revolution is such that the present public university structure has existed only since 1908, with the establishment of Cairo University, the largest and, in most fields, sort of the "parent" university of the public system.

Public universities are scattered throughout the country, but given the barren geography of much of the country and the fact that population density is concentrated around Cairo and a couple of other cities, that is where most schools are located. While certain universities have strong programs in one or two fields, overall, Egyptian public universities are beset with several problems, including overcrowded classrooms, very low faculty salaries, poor facilities, and antiquated methods of teaching and evaluation.

For those who can afford them, private universities tend to provide a more modern quality of education. The oldest private university in Egypt is the American University in Cairo (AUC), which has been operating since 1919, originally in the downtown heart of the city, and since 2007 at a new campus in an outlying suburb. The number of private universities has increased dramatically in recent years, with the majority of such institutions opening since 2002. English is the language of instruction at most private universities, though there also are private schools where classes are taught in German, French, Russian, and, of course, Arabic. Private universities have smaller class sizes and lower enrollments than the public government universities.

The organization and nomenclature of Egyptian universities is similar to that of most western universities, with only a few differences. If large enough, an individual discipline is housed in a *department* that carries its name. Smaller fields are placed as a *unit* within a more broadly named department. At the next level, at least in public universities and the larger private ones, several related departments make up a *school* or in the case of public universities, a *faculty*, with the term "college" not common in reference to either that entity that includes multiple departments *or* the overall institution.

Egyptian universities that use this structure include anywhere from three to 18 schools or faculties. In the case of advertising, no schools or faculties are so named, though there are departments at a number of universities that include advertising in their title. Such departments are most commonly located within a faculty of mass communication. Some advertising classes are offered in faculties and schools of business.

Early Advertising Education in Egypt

It appears that the first advertising course offered in Egypt was in the Faculty of Arts and Sciences at AUC during the 1937-1938 academic year. Listed simply as "Advertising" in the university catalog, it was described as a three-hour course at the senior level. Drawing on data from Ross, Osborne, and Richards (2006), this was at a time when no more than 44 schools in the United States were teaching advertising, quite a surprising finding given the comparative underdevelopment of both advertising and higher education in Egypt.

A fuller description of this first advertising course is found in the 1943-1944 catalog of the American University in Cairo, which indicates that "emphasis is placed upon the business side (advertising, circulation, management) as well as upon purely writing techniques." In 1947-1948, the course was placed in the curriculum of a newly formed Department of Journalism at AUC and renamed "Journalism 305: Principles of Advertising." Catalog copy changed to indicate that it dealt with "organization of the advertising industry; advertising services; advertising media; practice in writing copy and making layouts." It further lists the textbook used as *Principles of Advertising*, by Nixon.

Among Egypt's public universities, advertising was first taught at Cairo University. The exact year and course description is unclear, but interviews with those familiar with this history suggest a general advertising class was begun in the university's Faculty of Mass Communication sometime in the early 1960s.

Clearly, the pioneering universities in advertising education in Egypt were the American University in Cairo, among private institutions, and Cairo University, among public ones. Most other Egyptian universities did not become involved in advertising education until the 1980s or 1990s. Both private and public university offerings in advertising have followed the models used by AUC and Cairo University, even to the extent of copying the class syllabi, readings, and notes existent in their courses. As of 2011, approximately half of all universities in Egypt offer at least some coursework in advertising.

Undergraduate Advertising Degrees and Specializations

Beyond individual advertising classes, over the years a number of Egyptian universities offer concentrations, specializations, majors, and degrees in advertising. At the American University in Cairo, the Department of Journalism evolved into a Department of Mass Communication in 1982. At that time, the AUC major in Mass Communication was divided into two "functional sequences" of Journalism and Public Relations/Advertising (note the order of the two elements differs from the more common stateside major of Advertising/Public Relations). The public relations/advertising sequence required nine credit hours, in the form of three specialized courses: Introduction to PR/Advertising, PR Techniques, and Advertising Campaigns. When AUC adopted an administrative structure consisting of three separate schools in 1993, the department, renamed Journalism and Mass Communication, and the major were placed in the School of Business, Economics, and Communications (along with Department of Economics and Department of Management).

As part of a major overhaul in 1996, the public relations/advertising sequence at AUC was replaced by a specialization in "integrated marketing communication" (IMC). Faculty from the marketing area of the Department of Management collaborated with the Department of Journalism and Mass Communication in developing and seeking approval of the IMC program. While IMC is, and was, administered by Journalism and Mass Communication, and the Bachelor of Arts degree was issued by that department, required course work was drawn from both departments.

The curriculum of the integrated marketing communication major has gone through changes in the 15 years since its introduction. As of 2011 it consists of seven core courses: Principles of Advertising, Mass Communication Research, Introduction to Marketing, Public Relations Theory and Techniques, Creative Strategy and Advertising Copywriting, Consumer-Buyer Behavior, and Integrated Marketing Communications Campaigns.

Since 2009, with yet another wave of administrative restructuring at the American University in Cairo leading to a separate School of Business, the Department of Journalism and Mass Communication and the IMC major have been part of the School of Global Affairs and Public Policy. The rather awkward fit of the program in such a school has weakened the cooperation and links between marketing and communication, formerly together in the School of Business, Economics, and Communications. It remains to be seen what will become of IMC as the primary avenue of advertising education at AUC, what it will be called, and where it ultimately will reside.

Other private universities in Egypt that offer some form of advertising education generally have used the American University in Cairo curriculum as a template for their own programs. Course titles and descriptions commonly are copied verbatim from the AUC catalog, identical class outlines and schedules are used, the same textbooks are adopted (and in some cases illegally reproduced copies are distributed to students), and class notes in circulation from AUC often end up being the primary source of class lectures.

One exception to the straight mimicking of American University is the Advertising and Public Relations major in the Faculty of Mass Communications at Modern Sciences and Arts University (MSA), which also includes a media planning course. The MSA media planning class uses *Media Flight Plan* (Martin & Coons, 2006) software, an ambitious endeavor in a country where audience measurement and basic media planning concepts are, for the most part, nonexistent in the advertising industry.

The advertising courses at Cairo University, and in turn at those other public universities with advertising programs, are different and somewhat more extensive than what is found in private schools. Within the degree in mass communication, the advertising curriculum at Cairo University consists of Introduction to Advertising, International Advertising, Ethics of Advertising, Art of Advertising, Electronic Advertising, Writing for Advertising, Creativity in Advertising, Advertising Media, and Advertising Campaigns. There would seem to be overlap among several of these classes, and advertising is also the topic of courses in the Faculty of Commerce and the Faculty of Arts at Cairo University. Beginning in 2005, the regular Arabic language advertising offerings in the Faculty of Mass Communication at Cairo University have been supplemented with a parallel English Division, where English is the language of instruction, class sizes are smaller, and more stringent admissions criteria are applied.

As is true in many parts of the world, advertising is a popular area of undergraduate study in Egypt. In both private and public universities, whether named Advertising, Advertising and Public Relations, Public Relations and Advertising, or Integrated Marketing Communication, majors in the field attract big numbers and produce many degrees. At the American University in Cairo, an institution with an undergraduate enrollment of just over 5,000, the Department of Journalism and Mass Communication is the largest department on campus, with more than 400 students, the majority of whom are Integrated Marketing Communication majors. Admission to the IMC program at AUC is selective, and fewer than half of the students who apply are accepted.

Among other private schools, approximately 100 students major in advertising at both Misr International University (MIU) and at MSA, with probably another 200 in advertising-related majors at all other private universities combined. The International Academy of Media Sciences (IAMS), an institute devoted entirely to media-related study and careers, has around 100 students whose focus of study is advertising. At Cairo University, where the total student body is over 100,000, there are around 400 advertising majors, and an estimate for all public universities combined is around 1,000 students in advertising.

While such healthy student numbers reflect genuine enthusiasm for the field among Egyptian undergraduates and insure relative security for advertising programs within Egyptian universities, the fact is that fewer than half the majors end up employed in advertising after they graduate. Multinational advertising agency offices and corporations tend to hire the best AUC graduates for entry level positions, and a number of local agencies are staffed by graduates of advertising programs from various Egyptian universities. Persistent advertising students often can find production or government jobs with some ties to their major, but many students who major in advertising never find employment in their area of study, and there are concerns among parents, university administrators, and others that efforts be made to prepare undergraduates for job search and workplace realities.

Graduate Study of Advertising in Egypt

No graduate degrees in Egypt include the term "advertising" in their title. However, students often address advertising topics through coursework, theses, or dissertations in various graduate programs at Egyptian universities. As with undergraduate advertising education, the American University in Cairo and Cairo University provide the models used by other schools and are the primary institutions where students are likely to encounter advertising at the graduate level.

At AUC, the School of Business offers a Master of Business Administration (MBA) degree and the Department of Journalism and Mass Communication offers a Master of Arts (MA), both of which may be designed to include advertising. In the MBA degree, students can designate marketing as their area of concentration and take advanced classes that relate to advertising, including "Marketing Communications Management," a course that might carry "advertising" in its name at other universities.

The AUC mass communication MA consists of four core courses within the department and five graduate level electives from the department, or elsewhere in the university. In the past, MA students interested in advertising have included marketing MBA classes among their electives, and the Department of Journalism and Mass Communication has occasionally offered graduate classes related to advertising on a "special topics" basis, including "International Advertising" and "Advertising and New Media." The MA also requires a research thesis, and most years there are several students whose thesis concentrates on some aspect of advertising. AUC is the only private university in the country where students might pursue graduate work related to advertising.

Cairo University also has MBA and MA degrees that can include an advertising focus. The MBA degree is housed in the Faculty of Commerce and, as with the AUC MBA, students have the option of choosing marketing as their area of concentration. Through a relationship with Georgia State University in the United States, a portion of the Cairo University MBA is offered jointly between the two schools, and in recent years faculty from Georgia State have visited Cairo to teach courses, including one devoted to advertising and marketing communication. Cairo University's MA in mass communication draws on coursework from its undergraduate advertising program, as well as more advanced classes, including some that involve advertising, and a graduation project or thesis that may be based on advertising study. The Cairo University MA serves as the model for the other public universities that have graduate programs in mass communication, including Ein Shams University, Zagazig University, South of Egypt University, and Minya University.

At the doctoral level, Cairo University is the only institution in Egypt to offer degrees related to advertising. In the Egyptian system of higher education, the PhD usually does not involve coursework beyond what is taken for a Master's degree, but includes extensive examinations and the same kind of advanced research, dissertation, and defense as western universities. Doctorates with an advertising focus might be taken in the Cairo University Faculty of Commerce, but they are more commonly from the Faculty of Mass Communication. A very rough estimate is that there have been around 15 to 20 PhD degrees completed at Cairo University involving advertising, at least indirectly, in the past 40 years.

Workshops and Non-Degree Advertising Education

In addition to formal academic degree programs in Egyptian public and private universities, advertising is occasionally the subject of workshops or seminars for different constituencies. The most elaborate of these is the "professional diploma in marketing communications" that is offered by the Institute of Management Development (IMD), a continuing education arm of the School of Business at the American University in Cairo. This diploma, in collaboration with the International Advertising Association (IAA), was introduced in Egypt in 1995 and has been quite popular among undergraduate students majoring in advertising or related areas, as well as mid-career professionals working in the field. It consists of a set of classes prescribed by the IAA, some of which may be transferred from a degree-granting program and the rest taught at the IMD on a non-credit basis. Approximately 300 Egyptian students and professionals have obtained the diploma since it began.

The American Chamber of Commerce in Egypt (AmCham), a network of Egyptian and American business leaders, regularly sponsors speakers and sessions for members and the public on different topics. Especially through the Marketing Committee of AmCham, advertising subjects have been covered in a number of these over the years. Similar, though less developed and less frequent, are presentations and roundtables on issues related to advertising organized by other chambers of commerce, embassies or diplomatic missions, and organizations such as the Rotary Clubs in Egypt.

On an annual basis, the Union of African Journalists holds a set of workshops in Cairo for media professionals from throughout Africa. These usually include one or two sessions introducing attendees to basic advertising principles and offer training in advertising sales, design, or management. In 2007, the United Nations Development Program sponsored a similar gathering in Cairo for Iraqi media personnel, and the United States Agency for International Development also has been involved in media education efforts, though advertising is rarely included.

Advertising Faculty in Egypt

The teaching of advertising subjects in Egypt is done by a mix of full-time and adjunct instructors. Some advertising educators in Egypt have advanced degrees in the field, some are in the process of completing advanced advertising related degrees in Egypt or abroad, and some have degrees in peripheral fields. Most have at least some professional experience with advertising or communication work, but the relatively common western profile of an advertising faculty person who goes into teaching after a successful industry career is quite rare in Egypt, probably due in part to the low salaries paid at public universities.

Nationwide, the number of university teachers in business and mass communication departments whose specialty is advertising is around 50. A much larger number of faculty teach advertising classes, but many come from other areas of expertise, with general business or marketing people often covering advertising courses in business programs, and mass communication advertising classes commonly taught by instructors whose primary interests are journalism or some other area of communication.

Not surprisingly, most full-time advertising faculty are Egyptian. Roughly 15 percent of all faculty are from outside of Egypt, with that number being higher at private universities. Non-Egyptian faculty include those with American, Canadian, French, German, Lebanese, and other nationalities. Part-time faculty, who probably teach a little less than half of the advertising classes offered in the country, are almost exclusively Egyptian. On occasion, Fulbright Scholars from the United States or sabbatical visitors from different countries have spent time in Egypt and have taught advertising classes, usually at Cairo University.

The educational background of advertising teachers in Egypt varies, with a minority having doctorates, but almost all holding a master's degree of some kind. At the two largest and most prestigious programs in the country, Cairo University and the American University in Cairo, senior advertising faculty over the past decade have held PhD degrees from Cairo University, the University of Georgia, the University of Minnesota, Ohio State University and the University of Washington in the United States, and the University of London in England.

At other Egyptian public universities, faculty with earned doctorates typically have the degree from Cairo University, and faculty holding an MA degree usually have it from Cairo or from the institution where they are teaching. At private universities other than AUC, a few advertising teachers have Cairo University doctorates, but the most common credential among such faculty is an MA in mass communication from the American University in Cairo.

It is not unusual in Egypt for a faculty member to teach at more than one university. This practice is prohibited at the American University in Cairo, but among other private schools and with the public universities, faculty who have an advertising specialization often teach courses at several universities during the same term. The concept of a "teaching assistant" is familiar to most Egyptian faculty and is employed at most universities.

The teaching of workshops and classes, such as the Union of African Journalists program or the IMD diploma mentioned earlier, is sometimes done by regular university faculty, including those from AUC, and sometimes by industry professionals. Lectures on advertising to outside groups, such as the AmCham or embassy events, also are usually a mix of academic and industry speakers.

Student Characteristics

Advertising is a topic of interest to a variety of people in Egypt. Unlike many other parts of the world, advertising is a relatively new phenomenon, for the most part coming to the country only with efforts toward privatization during recent decades. Thus, a broad population seeks to learn about advertising topics and practices and investigate careers in the field.

Among those who pursue formal academic study of advertising, certain characteristics distinguish Egyptian students and institutions. Distinctions can also be made between those who attend private or public universities, between undergraduates and graduates, and between full-time and part-time students. Finally, motives differ among Egyptian advertising students.

On a basic level, Egyptian students can be classified socioeconomically into those who go to private schools and those who go to government-supported public schools. In a country with quite real poverty issues, and typical family incomes of less than $500 per month, private universities are simply out of the question for many. At the American University in Cairo, for instance, tuition alone is almost $10,000 per semester. Thus, in advertising as in other fields, there is a dichotomy in which the wealthy attend private universities and everyone else studies at public universities. This difference in background impacts a number of factors in the teaching of advertising, including the technology sophistication and experience of students, the kind of teaching examples students are likely to be familiar with, out-of-class expectations, and several other things.

As is true in many other countries, most undergraduate advertising students in Egypt, at both public and private universities, are female. At Cairo University the percentage who are female is around 75, and at AUC it is even higher. Females also account for a majority of those studying advertising at the graduate level, though the difference is not as extreme as for undergrads, and among doctoral students females are probably the minority.

Other than income and gender, religion and age are demographics to consider for describing advertising students in Egypt. Approximately 90 percent of the population in Egypt is Muslim, with the other 10 percent Christian. No statistics are available concerning the religion of students studying advertising, but over ten years of exposure to ad students in Egypt suggests the ratio of Muslims to Christians is more like 80/20. This disproportionate representation of Christians in advertising classrooms is most evident at private universities. No single factor can explain the phenomenon of Muslims being slightly underrepresented among Egyptian advertising students, but it may be that for the most conservative minority of Muslims, modern media advertising is one of the many things they feel is "haram," or forbidden by their religion.

Egyptian students commonly finish secondary school at 16, so university students tend to be slightly younger than in other countries, and it is not unusual to graduate with a baccalaureate degree at 19 or 20. Although most advertising courses are offered at the junior and senior level, undergraduate advertising classrooms often seem more youthful than their equivalents in the United States.

Graduate students are divided about equally between those who enter an MA program immediately after receiving their undergraduate degree, and others who return for graduate study after working in advertising or in unrelated jobs. This results in a graduate population similar to what is found in the West, ranging from people in their early twenties through some in their forties or older.

Issues and Idiosyncrasies of Advertising Education in Egypt

In some ways, the teaching of advertising in Egypt is no different than in other parts of the world. The subject matter of advertising classes is much the same, and course content and materials are similar or identical to what is found elsewhere. In other ways, circumstances unique to Egypt make advertising education there something of a special challenge.

Although Egyptian marketing and media systems have changed in recent years, with modernization and global approaches increasing, the fact remains that the kind of advertising practiced in Egypt is not the same as in the developed world. Ideas about creativity are different and rather stunted. Regulation is more strict. Audience definitions and measures are generally primitive. The government controls and even owns major media outlets and the largest advertising agencies (Keenan, 2003a). With these and other factors considered, a dilemma for advertising educators in Egypt is whether to teach the existent state of how advertising is done in the country, to teach what might be considered "best practices" of advertising from other parts of the world, or to find some balance between those two approaches.

While most would endorse the balanced solution of covering contemporary best practices within a context of Egyptian realities, some obstacles make such an ideal difficult, though not impossible, to attain. One major problem is the lack of textbooks and teaching materials that have much connection to Egyptian advertising (Keenan, 1998; 2003b). Available texts are almost exclusively American, or less commonly European, in their focus. Books on international topics give almost no attention to Egypt or the Middle East, understandable given the region's admittedly miniscule portion of global ad spending, innovation, and development, but frustrating to advertising teachers and students in Egypt. Textbook publishers' claims to offer "international editions" of popular basic texts used in their home country are misleading or even fraudulent, in that the content of most such books is identical to the home country edition.

Reliance on textbooks from the West has additional problems related to language and culture. That is, for those universities where Arabic is the language of instruction, English language books are clearly inappropriate and, to date, none of the commonly used advertising texts are available in translation. A lot of western textbooks also include content and illustrations that for cultural or religious reasons are offensive to many students and faculty in conservative Egypt.

There is definitely a market for locally written and published advertising textbooks, and in fact such books would likely be adopted in advertising classes at other universities in the Middle East. As advertising education in Egypt looks to the future, development of texts and other materials that relate specifically to Egyptian aspects of the field would provide welcome supplement to or replacement of the largely American textbooks long used.

Advertising education in Egypt would also benefit from closer industry involvement and support. While the number of local graduates working in advertising jobs has grown in recent years, and senior personnel at advertisers, agencies, and media are made up more and more of those with undergraduate or MA degrees from the American University in Cairo and Cairo University, the relationship of those in the advertising business to those in advertising education remains remote, for the most part. As a source of adjunct or full-time faculty, student internships, and contributions in terms of classroom examples, materials, and cases, the Egyptian advertising industry can contribute much to how their field is taught in Egypt. Reciprocally, the industry should benefit from recruitment opportunities and better trained entrants into the field.

While Egypt lags behind the developed world in advertising education, awareness of the points covered here may lead to improvements. Recognizing issues of importance and making efforts to address them should result in the already a popular subject of advertising study growing into a respected and valuable element of Egyptian higher education.

References

Keenan, K. L. (1998). Perspectives on advertising education in the non-western world. In D. D. Muehling (Ed.), *Proceedings of the 1998 Conference of the American Academy of Advertising*. Pullman, WA: American Academy of Advertising, 310-312.

Keenan, K. L. (2003a). Advertising in northern Africa. In J. McDonough & K. Egolf (Eds.), *Encyclopedia of advertising*. New York: Fitzroy Dearborn, 20-22.

Keenan, K. L. (2003b). Teaching international advertising in an era of diversity: A perspective from Egypt. In P. B. Rose, & R. L. King (Eds.), *Proceedings of the 2003 Asia-Pacific Conference of the American Academy of Advertising*. Miami, FL: American Academy of Advertising, 83-87.

Martin, D. G. & Coons, R. D. (2006). *Media flight plan*. Provo, UT: Deer Creek Publishing.

Ross, B. I., Osborne, A. C. & Richards, J. I. (2006). *Advertising education: Yesterday, today, tomorrow*. Lubbock, TX: Advertising Education Publications.

Said, M. E. (2003). Egypt. In D. Teferra & P. G. Altbach (Eds.), *African higher education: An international reference handbook*. Bloomington, IN: Indiana University Press, 285-300.

Advertising Education and Training in Nigeria: Development, Infrastructure and Policies

Olugbenga Chris. Aveni
Eastern Connecticut State University, USA

Gabriel T. Nyitse
Benue State University, Nigeria

Benjamin E. Ogbu
Benue State University, Nigeria

Historical Foundation

Advertising, both at the level of training and practice, is crucial in human activities, particularly as a marketing, selling, promotional or marketing communication tool. Like other management, behavioral, and social sciences, as well as the liberal arts disciplines, advertising hardly can be properly practiced or managed in the contemporary world of business, governance, and other fields of human endeavor, without adequate education and training.

An overview of advertising education and training in Nigeria has to be dissected from the broad perspective of journalism education, which often has been cited as predicated upon a strong American influence. Whereas Nigeria's premier university, University of Ibadan, was established in 1948, the slow pace of journalism/mass communication education in Nigeria, and perhaps in West Africa, could be attributable to the non-inclusion of journalism education in the initial academic programs taught in the university. The university's first communication arts program was introduced almost forty years later at the graduate level.

Two key figures often mentioned in connection with pioneering roles in journalism education, training, and practice in Africa were Kwame Nkrumah and Nnamdi Azikiwe. Both were among the earliest scholars from Africa who underwent training in the United States. While Nkrumah started the first journalism institute in Ghana in 1958, an identical model was introduced to the University of Nigeria, Nnsuka, in the early sixties. American style journalism training started in Cairo in 1935 with the introduction of the American University in Cairo, which was followed by that of Cairo University four years later (Salawu, 2009).

This somewhat episodic take off of journalism education, and by extension the training of advertising professionals, perhaps explains why until recently no Nigerian university offered a complete course at degree level in Advertising, despite its indispensable position in modern society (Nwosu and Nkamnebe, 2006:13). In fact, until 1962 when Nigeria's first journalism training institution at the university level was started at the Jackson College of Journalism, University of Nigeria, Nsukka, no Nigerian university offered any formal journalism training and education.

A few short-term programs catered to journalism training, such as the informal two-week vocational course organized for working journalists at the University of Ibadan in 1954, and a follow up for radio journalists two years later (Akinfeleye, 2003). This was followed by the famous University of Lagos institute of mass communication (now Department of Mass Communication) in 1966. Today, the status of advertising education in Nigeria has relatively improved.

The foregoing overview of advertising education in Nigeria obviously supports the fact that training is critical to practice. Akinfeleye (1996:82) similarly stated that the kind of journalism training is as important as the journalists themselves because the type of training is reflective of the kind of journalistic performance. But the pertinent question here is how an advertising practitioner should be trained. Perhaps the most logical approach to answering this question is to present an up-to-date survey and analysis of the diversities and contrasts that exist in advertising education in Nigeria.

By around the year 2000, close to 50 Nigerian universities were offering courses in journalism/mass communications, with ownership split between mostly the federal and state governments, and structured either along the university model or the Polytechnics. The Polytechnics are similar to two-year colleges in America. Mostly professional and technical courses are offered for an initial two-year period that leads to the award of Ordinary National Diploma (OND), with an additional two years to earn the Higher National Diploma (HND). In many cases people stop at the OND level and enter the work force, while others proceed to earn the HND, giving them four years at the Polytechnics.. The HND is equivalent to the bachelor's degree that is offered after a four-year study at an accredited university.

Currently, 58 institutions in Nigeria offer degree and diploma programs in Public Relations and Advertising in departments of mass communication within faculties of Administration and social sciences of various Nigerian universities and polytechnics (JAMB Brochure, 2010/211 Academic Session). In addition, vocational institutions like the Nigerian Institute of Public Relations (NIPR) and APCON are committed to providing public relations and advertising education in Nigeria. These are treated separately, below, in terms of contents and pedagogy of courses taught and the type of preparation that students receive.

University Training

Most of the journalism/mass communication programs took off as integral parts of other programs, often subsumed under departments like English Studies, Arts, Social Sciences, and so on. That seems to have changed a bit now with the recent bursts of private ownership of universities. Apart from two universities, Igbinedion and Lagos State University (LASU), that offer bachelors degree programs in Public Relations and Advertising, the other 31 universities offer courses in public relations and advertising leading to awards of degrees in Mass Communication and media studies. Table 6.1, below, provides the list of the universities.

Table 6.1: Universities Providing Advertising Education
at a Degree level in Nigeria

No	Name	Course of Study	Faculty
1	Igbinedion University, Olada, Edo State	PR and Ad	Administration
2	Lagos State University, Lagos	PR and Ad	Administration
3	Western Delta University, Ogbara Delta State	Media Studies and Mass Communication	Administration
4	Caritas University, Enugu State	Mass Communication	Administration
5	Cross River State University of Technology, Calaba	Mass Communication	Administration
6	Enugu State University of Technology	Mass Communication	Administration
7	Madonna University, Okija, Anambra State	Mass Communication	Administration
8	Nasarawa State University, Keffi	Mass Communication	Administration
9	River State University of Science and Technology	Mass Communication	Administration
10	Ahmadu Bello University, Zaria	Mass Communication	Social/Management Sciences
11	Anambra State University	Mass Communication	Social/Management Sciences
12	Benson Idahosa University, Benin City, Edo State	Mass Communication	Social/Management Sciences
13	Bowen University, Iwo, Osun State	Mass Communication	Social/Management Sciences
14	Benue State University, Makurdi	Mass Communication	Social/Management Sciences
15	Caleb University, Lagos	Mass Communication	Social/Management Sciences
16	Crescent University, Ogun State	Mass Communication	Social/Management Sciences
17	Delta State University, Abraka	Mass Communication	Social/Management Sciences
18	Ebonyi State University, Abakaliki	Mass Communication	Social/Management Sciences
19	Fountain University, Oke-Osun	Mass Communication	Social/Management Sciences
20	Igbinedion University	Mass Communication	Social/Management Sciences
21	University of Ilorin	Mass Communication	Social/Management Sciences
22	Imo State University, Owerri	Mass Communication	Social/Management Sciences
23	Joseph Ayo Babalola University, Osun	Mass Communication	Social/Management Sciences

	State		
24	Kaduna State University	Mass Communication	Social/Management Sciences
25	Kogi State University, Anyigba	Mass Communication	Social/Management Sciences
26	University of Lagos, Akoka	Mass Communication	Social/Management Sciences
27	Lagos State University	Mass Communication	Social/Management Sciences
28	NOVENA University, Ogume, Delta State	Mass Communication	Social/Management Sciences
29	Redeemers University, Lagos	Mass Communication	Social/Management Sciences
30	RENAISSANCE University, Enugu State	Mass Communication	Social/Management Sciences
31	Tansian University, Oba, Anambra State	Mass Communication	Social/Management Sciences
32	Nnamdi Azikiwe University, Akwa, Anambra State	Mass Communication	Social/Management Sciences
33	Wukari Jubilee University, Taraba State	Mass Communication	Social/Management Sciences

Source: *Joint Admissions and matriculation Board Unified Tertiary Matriculation Examination Brochure (2010/2011 Academic Session)*

Course Contents

Generally, mass communication training in Nigerian tertiary institutions has three sequences in which students can specialize: Print Journalism, Broadcast, and Advertising and Public Relations. Again, it should be noted that there has been a traditional and functional synergy between advertising and public relations, especially in the various training programs in Nigeria. This is anchored on the belief that public relations and advertising maintain a smooth interface with each other as marketing support systems. Two American leading authors in advertising, Bovee and Arens (1986, p. 550), gave a more convincing justification to this relationship when they wrote that:

> Every company, organization and government body has groups of people who are affected by what that organization does or says. These groups might be employees, customers, stockholders, competitors or just the general population of consumers. Each of these groups may be referred to as the organization's publics. To manage the organization's relationship with these publics, the process called public relations is used.

Despite the foregoing, there are specific courses that are taught aimed at providing advertising education in Nigerian universities. For example, the Department of Mass Communication of Benue State University teaches the following advertising courses in the four-year undergraduate program:

- Introduction to Mass Communication
- Basic Mass Communication Skills
- Writing for the mass media
- English and Communication Skills

- Marketing for Advertising and Public Relation
- Introduction to Advertising
- Advertising media planning
- Advertising and Public Relations Research
- Reporting on business and economy
- Creative Advertising Strategies and Tactics
- Organization and management of Advertising and public Relations Agencies
- Communication Law and Ethics
- Economic and social issues in Advertising and Public Relations.
- Data Analysis in Communication Research

It should be noted that all university training programs in Nigeria are accredited by the National Universities Commission upon substantial fulfillment of both physical and academic requirements.

Admission Requirements

Candidates for admission into the four-year degree program in a mass communication department should possess five credits in a senior secondary school certificate or General Certificate of Education, or its equivalent, which must include English and at least a "pass" in mathematics. This is in addition to the candidate passing the University Matriculation Examination with a high score of between 250 and 285 points.

Direct entry admission into a two- or three-year degree program also is available for candidates who possess five credit passes in the General Certificate of Education, or its equivalent, at not more than two sittings. Two of the subjects must be at the Advanced level.

Polytechnic Training

A total of 24 polytechnics in Nigeria provide advertising education in various departments of mass communication, leading to awards of the National Diploma (ND) and Higher National Diploma (HND) upon completion of two and four-year programs in the polytechnic. A one-year industrial attachment is compulsory for all polytechnic diplomas, which, when added, makes their program a five-year full-time course.

The polytechnics are: Akwa-Ibom State Polytechnic, Auchi Polytechnic, DorbBen Polytechnic, Federal Polytechnic Oko, Federal Polytechnic Bauchi, Federal Polytechnic Bida, Federal Polytechnic Offa, Federal Polytechnic Nekede, Rufus Giwa Polytechnic Owo, The Polytechnic, Ibadan

Institute of Management and Technology Enugu, Kaduna Polytechnic, Mallam Usman Polytechnic, Lagos State Polytechnic, Moshood Abiola Polytechnic Abeokuta, Nasarawa State Polytechnic Lafia, Nuen Polytechnic Zaria, Nigerian Institute of Journalism Lagos, Delta State Polytechnic Ogwashiuku, OSISATECH Enugu, Osun State Polytechnic, The Polytechnic Ile-Ife, Wolex Polytechnic Lagos and Yaba College of Technology Lagos.

All 24 polytechnics provide enriching advertising education in their various departments of mass communication. Indeed, most have had their ND programs accredited by the National Board for Technical Education. However, most are equally struggling with accreditation challenges for their HND programs in Mass Communication. The courses offered are similar to those taught at the first degree level of the university. Interestingly, about 40% of course content is on theory while the remaining 60% is practical.

Professional Training

The promulgation of Decree 55 of 1988, otherwise known as the Advertising Practitioners Council of Nigeria (APCON), remarkably altered the landscape of advertising training and practice in Nigeria. With this decree, advertising practitioners in Nigeria must be registered or licensed and, thus are strictly professionals. APCON is therefore at the center of the drive for advertising professionalism in Nigeria. Interestingly, out of the council's five broad functions as presented by the law, three relate to advertising training and education:

1. Determining what standards of knowledge and skill are to be attained by persons seeking to be registered members of the advertising profession and reviewing those standards from time to time.

2. Regulating and controlling the practice of advertising in all its aspects and ramifications.

3. Conducting examinations in the profession and awarding certificates or diplomas to successful candidates as and when appropriate. (Keghku, 2008, p. 5)

It is worth mentioning that APCON has long taken advantage of its training policy to run professional certificate and diploma programs in advertising at various centers in Nigeria. The current status of operation and training contents will be treated much later in this work.

It was decided to focus on APCON separately here, because its training programs relate directly to the subject under study. Interestingly, AP-

CON runs a professional diploma program in advertising at six centers across Nigeria: Lagos, Abuja, Kano, Port-Harcourt, Enugu and Owerri. The institution also provides regular training courses to update professional knowledge and skills required for career growth and development.

Course Contents

Unarguably, APCON certificate and Diploma programs in Advertising provide a more comprehensive training and preparation of students. To this end, Nwosu and Nkamnebe (2006, pg. 13) conclude that APCON Diploma in Advertising provides the richest Advertising training in Nigeria. The APCON program contains core courses designed for professional excellence and, on the whole, contains 31 such courses:

- Introduction to Mass Communication
- General Studies
- Qualitative Analysis
- Advertising Copy Layout I
- Advertising Law Ethics I
- Principles of Advertising
- Advertising Production Techniques II
- Consumer Behavior
- Research Methodology
- Creative Strategies & Techniques
- Account Planned
- Advertising & Society
- Advertising Management
- Art Direction
- Brand Management II
- Special Project
- Communication Skills
- Social Psychology
- Principles of Marketing
- Advertising Production Techniques I
- Quantitative Analysis II.
- Advertising Copy Layout II
- Advertising Law Ethics II
- Integrated Marketing Communications I
- Media Planning
- Advertising Design & Illustration
- Brand Management I
- Integrated Marketing Comms. II
- Media Management
- Account Management
- Advanced Copy Writing

Other Training Institutions

The Nigerian Institutes of Journalism (NIJ), mentioned earlier, and the Time Journalism Institute also offer diploma courses in Advertising and Public Relations. These are privately owned institutions committed to the training of advertising professionals in Nigeria. However, most of their programs are not accredited by the National Board for Technical Education (NBTE,) which is the only accreditation body for all polytechnics and similar institutions.

The Nigerian Institute of Public Relations (NIPR) is another institution that provides advertising education in Nigeria. Expressing the diversity and contrast between APCON and NIPR training programs, Nwosu and Nkamnebe (2006) stated that while the Diploma Program of APCON has no single, full, or independent course in Public Relations, the NIPR's Certificate and Diploma Program contains marketing and advertising practices. However, since APCON has a course in Integrated Marketing Communication, Public Relations knowledge will certainly be taught.

Training Facilities

Training facilities can be divided into two main areas:

1. Media Facilities
2. Physical Facilities

Media Facilities

There is no argument that the landscape of advertising training and practice is being altered daily by the influence of modern information and communication technologies. This is so obvious that the advertising student and practitioner of this age must necessarily be a technician whose competence on the computer must not be in doubt.

Chile (2005) conducted a study on Information and Communication Technologies for learning among students of the Department of Mass Communication, Benue State University, Makurdi. The population of the study was made up of undergraduate students of the Department of Mass Communication, Benue State University. Using the quota sampling technique, the researcher drew 30 students from each of the four levels to provide a total sample size of 120 respondents.

Data analysis on students' access to information and communication technologies shows that 100% of the sampled respondents claimed not to have access to any form of information and communication technologies (ICTs) in the Department of Mass Communication for research and learning. Based on that data and attendant interpretation, the researcher concludes that potential journalists who are largely students of communication in Nigerian universities are not adequately exposed to relevant ICTs needed in the journalism of this digital age.

Indeed, this conclusion gives credence to numerous charges of compromise of international best practices in academic trainings and professional practices in Nigeria. Certainly, much still needs to be done towards upgrading media facilities on advertising training institutions in Nigeria. However, it is important to observe that there has been growing concern for acquisition of media equipment, occasioned by enormous pressure of accreditation requirements. For example, functional Advertising/Public Relations laboratories currently exist at the Department of Mass Communication, Benue State University, Makurdi, Kogi State University, Anyigba, and several other institutions conducting advertising education and training in Nigeria.

Physical Facilities

On comparative bases, the physical structure in all the universities and polytechnics are fairly adequate for media training, but are largely outdated. Of particular concern are classrooms and staff offices which are inadequate and poorly equipped for advertising training and performance. The situation is worse in some institutions, like Benue State University, Federal Polytechnic, Bida, Benue Polytechnic, Ugbokolo and Auchi Polytechnic, where student populations of 200 – 300 usually compete for a classroom accommodation facility meant for 100–150 students.

Conclusion and Recommendation

Illiteracy and lack of expertise contribute to low degree of advertising education in Nigeria. The existing status of ICTs, along with illiteracy in advertising training and practice, has again worsened the chances of quality advertising education in Nigeria. Nigeria has suffered major setbacks in its socio-economic and political development because a proper platform is not created for advertising education, which is supposed to drive the system.

Similarly, most of the curricula of advertising training institutions in Nigeria are outdated. They need to be reviewed in line with modern realities. There also is a need to develop a new philosophy of advertising education in Nigeria. The scope of courses like "Commerce," which is taught at higher (secondary) school level, needs expansion to incorporate the values of advertising earlier. Students need to be caught when young, making good advertising professionals out of them. This begins with equally good training.

References

Akinfeleye, R.A. (2003). Fourth Estate of the Realm or Fourth Estate of the Wreck: Imperative of the Social Responsibility of the Press, inaugural lecture. University of Lagos: Nigeria.

Akinfeleye, R. A. (1996). Journalism Education and Training in Nigeria. In Momoh, T., & Omole, G. (eds.) *The Press in Nigeria*. Lagos: Nigerian Press Council.

Bourgault, L. M. (1995), *Mass Media in Sub-Saharan Africa*, Bloomington, IN: Indiana University Press.

Boyd-Barrett, O. and Newbold, C. (1995). Defining the field. In O. Boyd-Barrett and C. Newbold (eds), *Approaches to Media: A Reader*, London: Arnold.

Bovee, C. L. and Arens, W. F (1986). Contemporary Advertising. Homewood, Illinois: Richard D. Irwin, Inc.

Chile, C. (2006). Computopia and Informatics in Communication Learning: A Study of Mass Communication Students in Benue State University, Makurdi. *International Journal of Mass Communication*, 1(2): 119-134.

Joint Admission and Matriculation Board Unified Tertiary Matriculation Examination Brochure, (2010/2011 Academic Session).

Keghku, T. (2008). Perception of Public Relations, Advertising Professions and Professionals in Nigeria. A. Ph.D Thesis Submitted to the Postgraduate School, Benue State University, Makurdi, Nigeria.

Nwosu, I. E and Nkamneb, A. D (2006). *Triple – P Advertising: Principles, Processes, Practices*. Lagos: Afri-Towers Ltd.

Salawu, A. (2009). The growth and development of African media studies: perspectives from Nigeria. *Journal of African Media Studies* 1(1): 81–90.

Students' Handbook, Department of Mass Communication, Benue State University Makurdi, Nigeria.

The History of Advertising Education and Training in South Africa

Ludi Koekemoer
AAA School of Advertising, South Africa

The Education Landscape

South Africa's higher education is dominated by state-owned (public) Universities, Universities of Technology (also state-owned and previously called Technikons), and private higher academic institutions. Advertising education, pre-1986, was largely in the hands of some Universities who offered Advertising as a major in a Bachelor of Arts (BA) Communications. A small number of Universities offered Graphic Design qualifications, and most Technikons had Graphic Design or Design departments. These Design departments offered a wide variety of design options including textile design, corporate design, architectural design, graphic design etc.

In 1970 the University of Pretoria started offering a B. Com (Bachelor of Commerce) Marketing. This was an initiative of Proff Hennie Reynders and Sieg Marx. Other Universities joined in the 80s and featured Advertising as a module in either the 2nd or final year. At the B. Com Honours level (4th year), Advertising often was an elective subject. Many B. Com Marketing students ended up in the advertising industry as Stratplanners, Media planners and Account Executives. Universities do not offer a B. Com specifically in Advertising.

In 1986 the first privately owned advertising school, called Boston House College of Advertising (BHCA), was founded (Sinclair R. personal communication, November 26, 2009). BHCA became the AAA School of Advertising in 1990, and South Africa currently has three advertising schools. Professional bodies also contributed to advertising education, especially the IAA (International Advertising Association) in New York, USA, ACA (Association for Communication and Advertising), and AMASA (Advertising Media Association of South Africa).

Training is conducted by some public academic institutions that offer Advertising as a specialization, by private Advertising schools, private design schools, and by Advertising industry employers (e.g. ad. agency internship programs). This chapter will focus on Universities, Universities of Technology, and private higher education institutions offering Advertising or Marketing Communications and Graphic Design qualifications.

Public Academic Institutions: Universities

University of South Africa (UNISA)

UNISA is the only distance learning university in South Africa. Its BA Communications became popular in the 1970s and 1980s, and during the 1980s the choice of subjects was rather limited. Students had to successfully pass 12 full-year subjects (Study Guides 1971 – 4):

- Communication Science (1, 2 & 3). Advertising was a year 3 specialization
- Sociology or Psychology (1, 2 & 3)
- Language (Afrikaans Nederland's or English) (1, 2)
- Communication Research (2)
- Communication Law (1)
- General literature science (1 & 2)

Currently this qualification offers a wide variety of options. The curriculum comprises 30 modules (http://www.unisa.ac.za), 10 in year 1, 10 in year 2, and the 10 in the final year include the focus on Advertising and other Marketing Communication tools and New Media:

Third year (10 modules)

- Marketing communication
- Media studies (theories & issues)
- Media studies: content, audiences & production
- New media technology
- International communication
- Communication research
- Advertising & Public Relations
- Political & government communication and media ethics
- Persuasive texts
- 1 x major selected from Cultural, Art, Political, Sociology/Psychology, Development, Languages, Information, and Economic & Management Sciences.

UNISA, from 2010, now also offers a Bachelor of Arts (Culture and Arts) with specialization in Multimedia Studies for prospective Multimedia designers and Web designers. This curriculum comprises 23 modules (see http://www.unisa.ac.za).

UNISA was one of the first universities in South Africa to offer a qualification in Marketing Research & Advertising. Under the able supervision of Prof. Ockie Lucas, this Post Graduate Diploma in Marketing Research & Advertising has been offered since the late 1960s and became popular in the early 70s, as many B. Com graduates wanted to study further in Marketing Research and Advertising. The curriculum consisted of the following (Wiid, J. personal communication, May 13, 2010):

First level	*Second level*
• Economics I	• Business Economics II
• Business Economics I	• Market Research A
• Consumer Behaviour	• Market Research B
• Statistics I	• Advertising

University of Free State (UFS)

According to Mulder, D. (personal communication, February 23, 2010), teaching Advertising goes back to 1971 when the Department of Press Science offered a 3-year BA degree in Journalism. A key player was the Journalism & Communications icon, Das Herbst. In 1973 Herman Engelbrecht joined Das Herbst. They expanded the field of study, and Advertising was offered at the 2nd ear level and the final year level, as part of Communication II and Communication III. In Communication II, Advertising Law was covered, and Communication III included Communication & Advertising research. At the Honours level Advertising was featured as one of the 5 modules.

In the late 1970s Media Science was introduced, and Advertising was offered at the 2nd year level. In the early 1980s the 2nd year module changed to PR & Advertising while Persuasive Communications Research became a separate module. At the Honours level, PR & Advertising was one module, but in 1984 they became separate modules and Advertising became a major at 3rd year level. Students also could now study Advertising at Honours, Masters, and at Doctorate (Ph.D.) levels.

In 1990 Advertising moved to the 2nd year level, and in 1995 it moved to the 1st year level, and until 2000 UFS offered a BA Communications without Advertising as specialization. However in 2001 the curricula changed considerably, and the Department of Communications started offering three BA degrees: (1) BA Media Studies, (2) BA Corporate Communication, and (3) BA Integrated Marketing Communication. Apart from the typical BA subjects like Psychology, Sociology, language, etc., the BA Integrated Marketing Communications also included Introduction to Advertising (1st year), Advertising research, Advertising Law, Advertising Ethics, Advanced Advertising (2nd year), Applied Advertising (3rd year) and Integrated Marketing Communications (3rd year). In 2009 the curricula changed again, when the BA Corporate Communications and the BA Integrated Marketing Communications merged to become the BA Communications (Corporate & Marketing Communications).

Currently, Advertising is no longer a separate module, but it becomes the focus of a variety of first year modules like Marketing, Marketing Communications, and Business Communications. It also is the focus of 2nd year modules like Visual Communication, Brand management, Advertising, Copywriting, and 3rd year modules like New & Social Media, Internet marketing, IMC, Applied Visual Communication and Advertising Discourse.

University of Pretoria (UP)

In the University of Pretoria's Department of Marketing and Communications, the subject of Marketing Communications is one of many 2nd year modules in the B Com (Marketing) degree, but students cannot specialize in Advertising or Marketing Communications (North, E,. Personal Communication, May 7, 2010). This University also has a Department of Information Design offering a 4-year degree in Information design (http://www.unisa.ac.za).

In the 4th (final) year students are exposed to a multitude of design fields. These include Advertising, Branding, Identity and Collateral design, Broadcast design, Design for development, Editorial design & Publishing, Event branding, Information design, Wayfinding and Instructional design, Motion graphics, Animation and Interactive Media, Packaging & Display design, as well as Photography, Image making & styling (Cunningham N., personal communication, March, 16, 2010).

University of Johannesburg (UJ)

UJ used to be RAU (Rand Afrikaans University). This university became UJ after the merger of RAU and Technikon Witwatersrand in 2005. Advertising is taught in two faculties at UJ: the Faculty of Humanities and the Faculty of Art, Design and Architecture.

Faculty of Humanities

According to N. de Klerk, (personal communication, March 19, 2010), the Department of Communication at RAU, one of the first of its kind in South Africa, was established in 1971 by Prof Tom de Koning. The curricula offered a broad foundation in the theory and methodology of Human Communication, from interpersonal to small group to organizational to mass communication and its effects. A three year BA or B. Comm Degree was offered, with Communication as a major, and another Humanities subject (or Economics major for a B. Comm). Honours, Masters and Doctoral degrees in Communication were also offered.

By 1978, students still did a broad degree in Communication, but had to choose 2 of 3 undergraduate specialization courses which were required for the degree. Initially the three were Developmental Communication, Journalism, and Organizational Communication. Organizational Communication consisted of internal communication, and external communication (Advertising and PR).

By 1985, the three specialization courses in Communication became Journalism, Audio-Visual Communication, and Advertising, of which one had to be taken in the second year and one in the third year. Advertising at the undergraduate level still included a module on PR.

At the postgraduate level, however, students were required to specialize exclusively in one of these three specializations. For the first time, an Honours Degree in Communication "with specialization in Advertising", for instance, could be obtained. A prerequisite for doing an Honours with specialization in Advertising was that the student should have also passed the undergraduate specialization course in Advertising (or its equivalent, if from another university). At the honours level, students did a one-year course in Advertising Theory and Research, and another year course required them to apply their Advertising knowledge in an independent major seminar/assignment to be externally examined by advertising industry experts.

In 1998, under the chairmanship of Prof Sonja Verwey, the Department of Communication revisited its curricula and developed 4 (initially 5) fully fledged career-focused degree programs in the Department of Communication. This proved to be a major success and a drawing card for undergraduate learners. These were Journalism, Audio Visual Communication, Corporate Communications and Marketing Communications (of which Advertising was an integral part). A solid foundation in Communications and related subjects as majors was still required, however, and specialization in, for instance, Advertising, only kicked in during the second year. Therefore, a student who did a degree in Marketing Communication did Advertising 2A and B in the second year, and Advertising 3A and B in the third year. Later the subject name 'Advertising' was changed to 'Marketing Communication'.

In 2005 RAU was rebranded as the University of Johannesburg following the merger of RAU with the Technikon Witwatersrand. Specialization in the Department of Communication became complete, and students in Marketing Communication (Advertising) could do Marketing Communication as a major subject from their first year for the three-year degree, with the second major being Marketing Management and Communication as their third major.

In January 2009, the Department of Communication was reconstituted as the School of Communication, and in 2010 three departments came into being: The Department of Strategic Communication, the Department of Film, Television, and Journalism, and the Department of Communication and Media Studies. The Department of Strategic Communication houses two degree programs, namely Corporate and Marketing Communication (Advertising) and the Diploma in PR.

Faculty of Art, Design and Architecture

The history of FADA (Faculty of Art, Design and Architecture) of the University of Johannesburg spans over more than 80 years, covering the Witwatersrand Technical College, which became Technikon Witwatersrand (TW), and TW merged with RAU to become the University of Johannesburg. A major contribution was made since 1926 by these institutions in the field of Graphic Design (Brink, E., 2006).

The De Villiers Street Era. This era (1926 – 1938) could be described as turbulent beginnings when the School of Arts and Crafts (SAC) was founded. Classes in Commercial Art and in Design were offered, in addition to classes in Modeling, Drawing from Life, Anatomy, Still life etc., Commercial Art later became Graphic Design (Brink E. 2006, pp 24 – 40). The Career Guide of March 1934 maintained that there were ample opportunities for art work in the growing advertising industry.

The Eloff Street Era (1938 – 1962). During the Eloff Street Era, the SAC was still an integral part of the WTC. Although Johannesburg was far removed from the battlefields of World War II, the effects of the war were nevertheless felt directly, both in the city and at the art school (Brink, E. 2006, p. 12). During this period the school produced remarkable alumni, many of whom, after studies and travels overseas, returned to the advertising industry and the Art school as lecturers.

The Bok Street Era (1963 – 1976). During the Bok Street Era, major changes occurred at the school between 1963 and 1976, the period of high apartheid in South Africa (Brink, E., 2006, pp 12 + 40). The school's name changed. It became bilingual: the "School of Art, Johannesburg"/Kunsskool Johannesburg, and in the late 1960s the College of Art, Johannesburg/Kollege vir Kuns, Johannesburg. During this period, differences in approaches to art culminated in a split in the school, and the founding of a short-lived "rebel" school. Despite the split, the school continued its community outreach and involvement with the local Johannesburg art world, where its staff and students played an important role.

The Doornfontein Era (1976 – 2006). The Doornfontein Era (1976 – 2006) tells the story of the diaspora of the art school between 1976 and 2006 (Brink, E,. 2006, pp 13 + 120). From 1976, as a result of a severe shortage of accommodation in Bok Street, individual departments of the art school had to move to larger premises elsewhere in the city of Johannesburg. In 1979 control of the school reverted to the Technikon Witwatersrand (TWR). By the mid-1990s student numbers had increased to more than 1000, and the students were dispersed in nine buildings on two campuses. During this period the College of Art became known for its variety of design courses, including Industrial design, Graphic design, Interior design and Fashion design. Student numbers increased dramatically between 1989 –1993, and many Black students joined.

The Bunting Road Era (2006 -). With the merger between the Technikon Witwatersrand (TWR) and RAU (Rand Afrikaans University) the Faculty of Art, Design and Architecture obtained a multi-million rand campus in Bunting Road (Brink, E., 2006, p 141). A key player in the planning of the new campus and the courses on offer was Eugene Hön, the Dean of the Faculty from 2000 to 2006. The number of white students' leveled off, while the number of Black, Coloured, and Indian students continued to increase steadily.

The current National Diploma: Graphic Design (3 years) and B. Tech (4th year) are structured as follows (http://www.uj.ac.za):

Graphic Design

- Graphic Design Drawing 1, 2 & 3
- History and Theory of Graphic Design 1, 2 & 3
- Communications Design 1, 2 & 3
- Professional Graphic Design Practice 1, 2 & 3
- Design Techniques 1, 2 & 3

B. Tech Year

- Theory of Graphic Design and Academic Report 4
- Communication Design 4

The Diploma will be phased out in 2011 and a BA Design degree specializing in Communication Design will be introduced. This new degree will offer the following modules (http://www.uj.ac.za):

- Communication Design 1, 2 and 3

- Communication Design Technology 1
- Design studies 1, 2, and 3
- Professional Design Practice 1 and 2
- Visualization 1 and 2

University of Stellenbosch (US)

The University of Stellenbosch is situated in the winelands of the Western Cape, near Cape Town. According to Kaden, M. personal communication, February 18, 2010), the Department of Visual Arts of the University of Stellenbosch has been offering education in art and design since the 1960s. US currently offers 3 streams: Fine Arts, Visual Communication Design and Jewellery Design.

Although many of its Visual Communication students go into the advertising industry (and some from Fine Arts) its course or training cannot be perceived as mainstream Advertising education. It is a broad education with emphasis on visual literacy, practical craft skills (emphasis on drawing, illustration, typography, layout, photography, video, conducting research, working with materials and computer as a tool), and critical thinking (concept, taking social, cultural, political, economic, environmental contexts into account).

North – West University (NWU)

According to Van der Westhuizen, W (personal communication, May 4, 2010), the Graphic Design subject group within the School of Communication studies of NWU was formed in 2000, to offer a 4 year BA Graphic Design at the Potchefstroom Campus, South Africa. Prior to this, it was a specialization that formed part of the Communications studies curriculum at the University.

NWU's BA degree is unique in its nature, since it encompasses various subject choices within the realm of Graphic Design. This includes a communications-directed field of study or alternatively a more illustration and art history focused field of study. Recent additions to the Graphic Design course include a Multimedia elective that specifically focuses on the creation of digital content for the Internet, mobile devices and high-definition television and film editing.

Public Academic Institutions: Universities of Technology

It must be noted that most Universities of Technology offer a qualification in Design or Graphic Design. Many were approached for this study, but they felt that Advertising is either non-existent at their school or the focus on Advertising is too little for them to contribute to this chapter. A couple did provide information, however.

Central University of Technology, Free State (CUT)

According to Nortje, C. (personal communication, March 19, 2010), the Graphic Design qualification offered at the Central University of Technology, Free State, originated in 1937 at the Free State Technical College under the name of Commercial Art, which was a 3-year course. In 1981 the Free State Technikon was established, and the name of the course was changed to the National Diploma: Graphic Design. Currently it is still called the National Diploma: Graphic Design, and it is still a 3-year course.

CUT also offers the Baccalaureus Technologiae: Graphic Design, Magister Technologiae: Design (3-year course), and then the Doctorate Technologiae: Design in the School of Design Technology & Visual Art. The student can enroll for the 4-year Baccalaureus Degree, but can exit with a National Diploma after 3 years of study.

Curriculum (http://www.cut.ac.za)

The curriculum includes three years of study of each of the following year modules:

- Communication Design 1, 2 & 3
- Design Techniques 1, 2 & 3
- Graphic Design Drawing 1, 2 & 3
- Professional Graphic Design Practice 1, 2 & 3
- History and Theory of Graphic Design 1, 2 & 3

After the first three years (National Diploma), the student can study for one more year and obtain the B. Tech: Graphic Design by successfully completing the following two modules:

- Theory of Graphic Design and Academic Report 4
- Communication Design 4

Vaal University of Technology (VUT)

Although VUT has never offered a qualification majoring in Advertising, it offers Professional Graphic Design Practice: Advertising and Marketing as a 3rd year subject, as part of its 3-year National Diploma and in the B. Tech (4th) year. Students study Art Theory, Research Methodology, and can specialize in Drawing or Multimedia in order to find employment in the South African advertising industry (Chmela, K. personal communication, February 17, 2010).

Private Higher Academic Institutions (PHEIs)

PHEIs could be divided into three meaningful groups, namely Advertising Schools, Design Schools and Marketing Schools.

Advertising Schools

South Africa is blessed with three very good advertising schools, namely AAA School of Advertising (AAA School), Vega The Brand Communications School (Vega), and Red and Yellow School of Logic and Magic (R&Y).

AAA School of Advertising (AAA School)

AAA School is the oldest and largest advertising school in South Africa. Its history actually began in 1986 when the Boston House College of Advertising (BHCA) was established in Cape Town by three ex-advertising executives. During 1986 - 1989 BHCA and AAA (Association of Advertising Agencies), the official professional body of the South African advertising industry, joined forces to educate young talent in Advertising. They received the blessing of the IAA (International Advertising Association) in New York (Barenblatt, M & Sinclair, R. 1989).

At the end of 1989, the AAA decided to buy BHCA and changed its name to AAA School of Advertising. Tuition was then offered at two campuses: Cape Town and in Rosebank, Johannesburg. Bob Rock was the first director of AAA School of Advertising, Johannesburg.

Internal records of AAA indicate that the AAA School offered three diploma programs from 1990 to 1993: the Diploma in Advertising (Marketing) (2 years), the Diploma in Copywriting (1 year), and the Diploma in Advertising (Art) (1 year). From 1994 to 1999 these qualifications became 3-year diplomas (except the Diploma in Copywriting, which remained a 1-year qualification).

In 1999 all Private Higher Education Institutions had to revamp their courses, apply to SAQA (South African Qualifications Authority) for qualification accreditation, and get registered with the South African Department of Education's Council on Higher Education (CHE). Early in 1999, the AAA School contracted Professor Ludi Koekemoer, then Chairman of Business Management at RAU, to obtain the necessary accreditations and CHE registration. Professor Koekemoer joined AAA full-time as Managing Director & Principal in 2000.

AAA School applied for three diplomas in 1999: the 2-year Diploma in Copywriting, the 3-year Higher Diploma in Integrated Marketing Communication, and the 3-year Diploma in Visual Communication. At this stage the Higher Education Act did not provide for private institutions to offer degrees. Degrees were the domain of public institutions.

According to the AAA School 2001 Prospectus (p. 3), the curriculum for the *Diploma in Copywriting* included Copywriting, Popular Culture, Creative writing, Radio & TV production, Campaigns and an Internship.

For the *Higher Diploma in Integrated Marketing Communication*, after having studied Marketing, Economics, Business Management, Advertising, Communications and Popular Culture in years 1 and 2, students had to complete the following modules in year 3:

- Marketing and advertising planning process
- Specializations:
  - Brand Management or
  - Account Management or
  - Media Management
- Campaigns Internships

The first year of the *Diploma in Visual Communication* is a foundation year, with focus on drawing, rendering, illustration, 2D & 3D design while the 2nd year focuses on Art Direction and Graphic Design. In the 3rd year students can specialize in Art Direction or Graphic Design whilst studying Print Production; Marketing and Advertising Planning Process; Creative Process; Campaigns and do an Internship.

Since 2000 a few changes have been made to these diploma courses. In the *Diploma in Copywriting* course students also have to study English Language Proficiency and the Tools of language (due to the deterioration of the teaching of English at high school level). The 2nd year has been brought in line with the requirements of Digital and New Media.

The Department of Education decided in 2006 that the words Higher and Integrated can no longer be used, and it changed the name of the Higher Diploma in Integrated Marketing Communication to the Diploma in Marketing Communication.

The Diploma in Visual Communication, too, is changed. Emphasis is now given to Digital and New Media.

In 2004 the Minister of Education, Professor Kader Asmal, reconsidered the policy of degrees being reserved for Universities and Universities of Technology, and invited PHEIs to apply for degrees. In 2005 the AAA School applied for two 3-year Bachelor of Art (BA) degrees: the BA Marketing Communication, and BA Creative Brand Communication. Approval was granted by SAQA, and AAA School started offering these two degrees from 1 January 2006.

The AAA School prides itself on its knowledge and skills teaching model. Final year Marketing Communication, Copywriting and Creative Brand Communication students work together in simulated advertising agency teams, on a number of real-life briefs. They all go on a 4-week advertising agency internship, as well. Graduates of AAA School are employed by the South African advertising industry as Account Service executives, Stratplanners, Media Planners, Copywriters, Art Directors or Graphic Designers.

AAA will be changing its 2-year Diploma in Copywriting in 2012, to a BA with specialization in Copywriting. This new qualification will be offered at both campuses from 2013.

Vega The Brand Communications School (Vega)

Vega is part of IIE (Independent Institute of Education), owned by ADVTECH (a quoted company on the SA stock exchange). Vega The Brand Communications School, was an initiative of Gordon Cook, Dr. Carla Enslin, Greg Tregoning, and Christian Zimelke. It was launched in 1999, with a brand-centric focus. It now has four campuses (Johannesburg, Durban, Cape Town, Pretoria), and offers the following accredited programs (Cook, G. personal communication, March 1, 2010):

- A three-year BA in Creative Brand Communications, with electives in multimedia, visual communication and copy/creative writing. This undergrad program articulates into a one-year BA Honours.

- A three-year BA in Brand Building and Management. This is a hybrid commercial and arts degree, with a focus on the art and science of branding, and the art and science of business. This program articulates into a BA Honours in Brand Leadership.

- A one-year Higher Certificate in Photography, and a one year Advanced Certificate in Photography.

- A part-time, three-year plus Diploma in Communications Management, soon to become a Diploma in Integrated Brand Communications

- An advanced Diploma in Brand Innovation (pending accreditation for delivery mid 2010)

All Vega programs endeavour to combine both a strategic and creative approach to building brands, and to the designing of integrated communication campaigns.

The *BA Creative Brand Communication* is offered over 3 years. In years 1 and 2 the curriculum includes Creative Development, Digital Media, Copywriting, Brand Strategy and Critical Studies. Students can then in year 3 specialize in Visual Communication, Copywriting or Multimedia Design (see http://www.vegaschool.co.za for the curriculum). In third year students work individually and within simulated teams, on a wide range of brands, and are exposed to real-life brand challenges within the guiding environment of Vega before they experience a 4-week industry internship at a relevant company or agency.

BA graduates from Vega, AAA School, or universities can do a 1-year full-time Honours. For the *Honours in Creative Brand Communication*, Modules One and Two are undertaken by all Honours students at Vega. Module Three however, is designed to train students in their chosen field of creative application:

- Module One: Brand & Brand Building
- Module Two: Alchemy
- Module Three: Creative Application (Visual Communications or Copywriting or Multimedia Design)

The *BA Brand Building & Management* is structured to include Brand Strategy, Critical Studies, Creative development, Economics and Business Communications in years 1 and 2. In the third year students have to successfully complete:

- Brand Strategy 3
- Critical Studies 3
- Innovation & Business Management 3
- Logistics in Brand Building
- New Media in Brand Building

For the *Honours in Brand Leadership*, Modules One and Two are undertaken by all Honours students at Vega. Module Three is designed to train students in their chosen field of application:

- Module One: Brand & Brand Building
- Module Two: Alchemy
- Module Three: Specialization (Brand Management or Brand Communications)

The *Diploma in Communication Management* includes modules like Principles and Practice of Brand Communications, Business Communications, Market Information Management, Media efficiency, and building brands through PR, in the first two years. In year 3 students study The Brand in Action and Creative Tools.

Red and Yellow School of Logic and Magic (Red & Yellow)

According to John Cooney (personal communication, February 23, 2010), Rightford Searle-Tripp & Makin sold part of their advertising agency to Ogilvy & Mather Worldwide in 1993. Two key partners, Brian Searle-Tripp and Allan Raaff, decided on advice from Bob Rightford, the Group CEO of Ogilvy & Mather, Rightford Searle-Tripp & Makin, to start an advertising school. They became founding partners. The Red and Yellow School of Logic and Magic opened its doors in February 1993.

From the day a student arrived at the school, he or she would be regarded as having entered the communications industry. The curriculum would be dynamic and fluid. The pace would be urgent, the tone practical and businesslike. From the first week of the course, students would learn how to formulate, write and work to a tight strategy. Strategies would be structured around "The Logic" (what one wants to say and to whom) and "The Magic" (the creative idea, how it would be communicated and why). Students would be taught how to write and present a creative rationale for every assignment.

In the early years there were no examinations because all projects would be reviewed while in progress and, on completion, marked. The pass mark would be 65%, and failure to meet a deadline would result in a zero mark.

From 1993 to 1999, Red & Yellow offered only creative courses. In 1999, John Cooney and Malcolm Wood joined. Cooney was founding director and chairman of TBWA Hunt Lascaris Cape Town, and Wood former Marketing Director of National Brands. They convinced Searle-Tripp and Raaff to launch the post-graduate, 1-year course in Communications Management.

In 1999 Red & Yellow had to, like other PHEIs, apply to SAQA for program accreditation, and to CHE for registration. It currently offers three accredited diploma programs: the 3-year Diploma in Graphic Design and Art Direction, the 2-year Diploma in Copywriting, and the 1-year post-graduate Diploma in Marketing and Advertising.

The curricula of their qualifications vary (Gordon, L. personal communication, May 4, 2010). The *Diploma in Marketing and Advertising Communications* is a one year, full-time Post-Graduate program that consists of 6 modules:

- Induction to Communications Management
- Strategic marketing and Advertising Communications
- Communication processes and Industry workshops
- CrossOver projects
- Brand strategy

- Specialist skills

Career Facilitation is also done.

The *Diploma in Graphic Design and Art Direction* is a 3year program consisting of the following:

- *First year:* Principles of typography, packaging design, print advertising, editorial, radio and television, campaign advertising, drawing and craft skills, digital design.

- *Second Year:* D & AD International Awards, Self Initiated Advertising campaigns (5), "Live" External Brief, Digital Module 01 (Adobe Indesign, Adobe Illustrator, Photoshop) Digital Module 02 (Web Design, Flash). Principles of campaign Advertising, Visual Diary.

- *Third Year:* D & AD International Awards, Self Initiated Advertising campaigns (8), Digital Integrated Applied Briefs (3), Environmental Design, CrossOver campaign working with copywriters and marketers on "Live" Client Briefs.

The *Diploma in Copywriting* is a 2 year program consisting of the following:

- *First Year:* Assignment work with Art Directors to produce print, radio and television advertisements, an Editorial Feature and a Mixed Media campaign. Individual assignment to write a Category Essay (in preparation for a packaging project with Art Directors), a Weekly Blog (reviewing movies, books and advertisements), a Public Relations campaign (to a live Client brief together with marketers), Web and Brochure writing.

- *Second Year:* Portfolio building through a selection of self-initiated Public Relations, Television and Radio campaigns, a CrossOver Project with Art Directors and Marketers to a "Live" Client brief, a two week mid-year Internship in an Advertising Agency.

Design Schools

Stellenbosch Academy of Design and Photography

Founded as recently as 2002 by Barbara Fassler, it is the new kid on the block, striving to make a name for itself. Originally setting out with a Diploma in Applied Design, the Academy has been accredited with the BA Applied Design, with the choice of either Graphic Design or Photography as a specialization and also offers a one-year Certificate in Commercial Photography.

The Academy's difference is its multifaceted approach to education, whereby subjects are specifically aligned to support the major specialization. Graphic Design majors would engage in courses such as Illustration, Photography, Computer Design Practice and Copywriting, all subjects that feed and inform the advertising specialization. The Photography specialization is supplemented with Graphic Design, Computer Design Practice, Copywriting and Digital Media. The theoretical subject component, a mix of Marketing Communications, Visual Studies, Design, and Photographic Discourse, has been constructed to create both strategic and critical thinking and ensure that there is a balance of content and context, academic and vocational outcomes.

The Academy is a privately-owned institution, and the overall program is headed up by the Academic Head, Clayton Sutherland who was previously Faculty Head of Visual Communication of the well known AAA School of Advertising in Cape Town (Sutherland, C. personal communication, March 30, 2010).

Midrand Graduate Institute (MGI)

Midrand Graduate Institute (Pty) Ltd, established in 1989, is like all PHEIs registered with the Department of Education, and all its programs are fully accredited by the Council on Higher Education (CHE). In the field of Creative Arts, MGI currently offers a 3-year BA Graphic Design degree. The degree was accredited for the first time at the institution in 1999, with classes commencing in 2000.

The first two years of the course cover the fundamentals of design and layout, starting with hand work, drawing, typography, digital design, and building up to Graphic Design Studio, and an introduction to 3D animation. Theory subjects include Communication Science, English, Advertising Theory, and the History of Graphic Design.

In the 3rd year students choose to specialize in either Multimedia or Advertising. The Multimedia course covers Broadcast, Web Design and 3D Animation. The Advertising stream covers print and web-related design. Students make use of industry-related software and are encouraged to develop a considered approach to design, as well as their own unique style. Lecturers are well-qualified, and in many cases are practitioners in cutting edge areas of the Graphic Design industry. Classes are small and students receive individual attention, making interaction and student participation an integral part of the learning experience (Giloi, S. personal communication, December 11, 2009).

The Open Window School of Visual Communication (Open Window)

Open Window was founded in 1989 and provided one-year Diplomas in Art and Design. In 1994 the Department of Education registered the School as a tertiary education institution. In 2002, Open Window received full institutional accreditation by the Council on Higher Education, and the South African Qualifications Authority accredited all its qualifications. Francisca Badenhorst played a major role in this. Over the years, career-orientated courses were developed, and Open Window successfully delivered degree level students with placement of all students in the industry within 3 months of graduation. From 2010 onwards Open Window offers a BA Honours Degree in Visual Communication (Badenhorst, F. personal communication, April 15, 2010).

Open Window offers a 3-year Degree, a 2-year Diploma, and a post-graduate Honours Degree in Visual Communication. The *BA Visual Communication Design* degree is a professional qualification, aimed to produce design experts who are also academically driven. The program ensures technical, academic, and practice-related competencies in traditional and new media.

The degree may lead to post-graduate studies in Visual Communication. Students integrate industry-based competencies with scholarly and applied research methodology. Entrepreneurial skills are developed, as students have to show their ability to plan, operate and manage a project. Experiential training characterizes the third year, when students are given the opportunity to direct and execute projects commissioned by actual clients. The student receives a *BA Visual Communication Design* degree after successfully completing at least 130 credits (note: 1 credit equals 10 notional hours) on 3rd year Degree level (including a Research Skills workshop, Practical workshops and a Work-based learning session).

The *BA (Honours) Visual Communication* program of post-graduate study complements the BA degree by providing graduates the opportunity to specialize in their major. The course consists of a 60% practical and a 40% theoretical component. The practical component consists of industry projects executed under the supervision of a recognized industry partner, and one of the student's choices. The theoretical component consists of a dissertation, visual culture modules and business practice workshops.

The *Diploma in Visual Communication* is a qualification of competence, a qualification providing students with the necessary technical and practical skills to enter the demanding design world. The program ensures industry-related skills in most new media sectors. The 1st-year program forms the foundation of both the Degree and Diploma. Students who en-

75

roll for the Diploma, or any second level subject, must have successfully completed the Foundation level. Applications are considered on a basis of continuing good standard, class attendance and general commitment.

Marketing Schools

IMM Graduate School of Marketing (IMM)

South Africa has only one private School of Marketing, founded by the Institute of Marketing Management, called the IMM Graduate School of Marketing. This PHEI is an examining institution, and it accredits other private academic institutions in South Africa to lecture to students who have registered for their qualifications in Marketing.

Students can, however, enroll at IMM via distance learning. The IMM Graduate School of Marketing introduced its 3-year Diploma in Advertising in January 1990, under the able management of its CEO, James McLuckie. The Diploma in Advertising consisted of 14 subjects: 6 in year 1, 4 in year 2 and 4 in year 3. In year three, students had to pass Creative Strategy, Media Strategy, Promotional Strategy and Advertising Production management (Venter, N. personal communication, April 15, 2010). This Diploma in Advertising will be phased out after 20 years during the 2010 academic year.

Professional Bodies

Three professional bodies played a major role in Advertising education and training in South Africa: IAA, ACA and AMASA. The South African Advertising Research Foundation (SAARF) also offers readership, viewership and listenership research workshops for advertising and media workshops from time to time. The main three bodies are discussed below.

IAA (International Advertising Association)

The IAA inspires excellence in communications worldwide. IAA is an Advertising professional body operating out of New York, USA, and it boasts 4000 members, 56 chapters in 76 countries.

The IAA introduced its Diploma in Advertising in 1974, and between 1974 and 1980 candidates all over the world wrote the IAA examinations in order to obtain this sought after qualification. In 1980 IAA stopped offering this Diploma and introduced the Diploma in Marketing Communication for accredited academic institutions worldwide (Martinez, N. personal communication, April 19, 2010). This meant that graduates of IAA accredited institutions not only received their local qualification, but also received the IAA's Diploma in Marketing Communications.

During the 1970s and early 1980s, South Africa hosted an IAA Chapter, but the activities of its own professional body (AAA at the time) negatively impacted on support for IAA. The Captains of industry did not see any reason to support two advertising organizations.

In 1988 the AAA School of Advertising (then still called Boston House College of Advertising) received IAA accreditation for the first time for its qualifications, and AAA School is still the only IAA accredited PHEI in Sub-Sahara Africa.

ACA (Association for Communication and Advertising)

ACA is the professional body of the advertising industry in South Africa. This body has undergone a number of name changes over the years. In the early 1960s the AAA (Advertising Agents Association) changed its name to the AAPA (Association of Accredited Practitioners in Advertising). In 1971 the AAPA's name changed back to AAA, but this time AAA stood for the Association of Advertising Agencies. In early 2002 the advertising industry decided to change its name yet again, and called it ACA (Association for Communication and Advertising) (Internal records of AAA & ACA). The history of AAPA was captured by Tommy Young (1971) in an unpublished document entitled AAPA 1947 – 1971. The following is his account of the early days.

Pre-1947, much of what happened in advertising was controlled by the NPU (Newspaper Press Union). There was little co-operation between the advertising agencies themselves, leading to a lack of understanding on the part of the Newspaper Press Union. In November 1942, the NPU met with the agency heads of those days with the view to form the AAA (Advertising Agents Association). This association, as a professional body, did not come into being until 1947, when a steering committee was formed. This committee prepared the Memorandum and Articles of Association, and the Advertising Agents Association was formed. In 1951 a private company was registered for the association, and it was called the Advertising Agents Association of South Africa (Pty) Ltd.

In 1947 the NPU proposed that practitioners give consideration to the training of advertising personnel to be coordinated through Technical Colleges, but under the joint control of the NPU and the AAA. Attempts to carry out that idea failed. However, in the next 10 years or more, not all attempts failed. They had some successes. In the short-term the Johannes-burg committee was largely successful in forming, in 1962, the Council for Education in Advertising in South Africa (CEASA). They started with 37 enrollments for a 2-year course. Sadly CEASA ceased to function two years later.

AAA's collaboration with the Advertising Association (AA) and the Institute of Practitioners in Advertising (IPA) in the United Kingdom start-ed early in 1952, when the Advertising Association asked for AAA's co-operation in assisting students who were enrolled to take their examina-tions. The AAA subsequently persuaded these bodies to adopt a South Afri-can Media Syllabus, as well as a revised Law Paper, adapted to South Afri-can conditions.

The AAA has collaborated fully with the IPA and the AA through these years in invigilating examinations, and more specifically by setting and marking the examination papers. The IPA and AA examinations ceased in 1969 in the U.K. AAA then investigated their replacement. This has re-sulted in one of AAA's most conspicuous early successes – the ICS "South Africa" Course. The International Correspondence School agreed to the AAA revising all lecture material to bring it into line with South African conditions. This took some 3 years of painstaking work. What always has been a valuable training effort, then, became more pertinent to the needs of the South African advertising industry.

During the 1970's the then AAPA initiated an internship program for post-graduate students as part of its Manpower Training and Develop-ment Programme. (De Klerk, P. personal communication, February 5, 2010). Dr. Roger Sinclair, Allan Brook, and Peter Rostron designed a di-ploma course which was offered at FCB's offices (then called Lindsay Smithers), and at the Witwatersrand Technical College.

By the end of the 1970s, AAPA was encouraging Black people to study for their diploma, much to the annoyance of the authorities at the time. AAPA clashed with the South African Broadcasting Corporation (SABC), which refused to allow its Black students to eat in the cafeteria with the whites. Dr. Sinclair cancelled the SABC visit in protest.

In the late 1970s AAPA acknowledged that there were more than a few providers of advertising education, including IMM, Damelin, and the technical colleges. AAPA changed from delivering lectures and established the committee as the examining body, setting examinations, recommending textbooks, maintaining a standard of marking and awarding the Diploma of the AAPA.

By the turn of the decade, it had established a new diploma course that was being taught by a variety of institutions around the country. The course was spread over three years and comprised a range of topics which included media, creative, production, the psychology of advertising, law related to advertising, and the principles of economics, among others (De Klerk, P. personal communication, February 5, 2010).

During the late 1970s and early 1980s a select group of students working in AAPA selected advertising agencies, as Interns, while studying the Diploma course or the IAA course. These Interns spent three months at each agency, and rotated between Client Service, Creative, Production, and Media. Agency staff acted as mentors, and at the end of the year the Intern decided in which department he/she wanted to work and for which advertising agency.

In 1980 the IAA held its annual conference in Durban, South Africa. It was at this conference that the IAA announced its own education program. IAA evaluated the South African diploma course and awarded it the world's first IAA accreditation. This accreditation was a great drawing card for young aspiring ad people.

In 1983 Graham de Villiers, of De Villiers & Schonfeldt (now Y&R) and then president of AAA, encouraged Dr. Roger Sinclair to write an Advertising text. AAA agreed in 1984 to contribute financially. It was joined by Nasionale Pers, SABC and Argus Newspaper Group. The first edition of *Make the Other Half Work Too: A text on Advertising in South Africa* was published in 1985. This book was prescribed by numerous universities and technical colleges.

Dr. Sinclair approached Mark Barenblatt to co-write the 2nd edition. This edition was published in 1987. A 3rd edition followed, but it lacked the IMC orientation, and the authors believed it might have been a mistake to change the title under pressure of the publisher to *The South African Advertising Book* because that positioned it firmly in the above-the-line sector. The 4th and final edition (1997) covered the development of brand equity and IMC and, since media buying and choice of media vehicles had changed so radically, had a completely revamped media chapter (Sinclair, R. personal communication, November 26, 2009).

In 1989, the AAA bought Boston House College of Advertising and changed its name, from 1 January 1990, to AAA School of Advertising. AAA (now called ACA) still owns the AAA School of Advertising. Education is in the hands of AAA School, and an ACA Education Portfolio Committee helps to assess training needs for the industry. Executive training is done via part time AAA School courses.

AMASA (Advertising Media Association Of South Africa)

According to Muller, G. (personal communication, December 28, 2009), to benchmark structured training in the modern media planning industry goes back to what is generally referred to as the "British Invasion" of the 1970s. The influx of top media talent from the UK fundamentally altered the status of the industry, in terms of professional standards. The names associated with this "British Invasion" are the late George Smith, Roger Garlick, Ms. Chris Rainford, and media gurus Paul Wilkins, Ian Snelling, Mike Armstrong et al. The legacy of Roger Garlick is recognized in AMASA's annual Roger Garlick Awards. Local South African luminaries added to this list would include Frank Muller (deceased) and Dick Reed, on the agency side, and on the client (Unilever) side the late Eddie Shultze.

Many South African media directors in the 1970s made reference to David Hart (Media Director of Quadrant Advertising, which became Afamal and then McCann Erickson), in their formative years. One of the key names in terms of providing informal training in the 1970s was Claude Dobson. Dobson wrote a series of articles for various trade publications over the years, which were mandatory inclusions in any young Planners' library.

All of these individuals are synonymous with "training" in the early industry. Training, for juniors starting out in the latter half of the 1970s, consisted of paying for drinks and extracting as much insight as possible from the gurus of the day. Invariably that insight was freely and enthusiastically given.

The Media Association of South Africa (MASA) is a registered Section 21 company, and, since its inception as a professional body in 1971, has been at the forefront of media education and training in South Africa. In the mid-1970s, due to the objection by the "Medical Association of South Africa," MASA changed its name to the "Advertising Media Association of South Africa" (AMASA).

The AMASA mandate was to educate people with an interest in media, marketing, and advertising, with a view to improving knowledge and skill in media decision-making techniques and their use. Initially this took the form of relatively informal monthly gatherings, where keynote speakers addressed industry issues in an open forum, but these gatherings soon became the sounding board for some of the big issues which shaped the commercial media industry in the 1970s.

AMASA's first major conference was organized by Brian Nuttley, held in conjunction with the National Development and Management Forum (NDMF) in 1974. The first ever AMASA Workshop was organized by

Ian Snelling and Noel Coburn in March/April 1975 at the old Kyalami Ranch. A 3 – 4 day's intensive learning program, the "Workshop" featured seasoned media practitioners taking young media planners and buyers through the basics of media planning theory and practice. Traditionally, the Workshop culminated with a "group project," which was prepared by the learners through the night and presented to a panel the next morning.

In the mid-1980s it was decided that the AMASA weekend work-shops were not enough to really plumb the depths of the media planning discipline, and so it was decided to have a "media planning certificate course." It was essentially the forerunner of the current AAA School/ AMASA course. The first formal collation of material was Mike Leahy's *Media Year Book 1989.* That was essentially a Guide to Media in RSA and some basics of media planning. This was used to shape the early AMASA media certificate course. Leahy's book became a little outdated, and under pressure from AMASA, Gordon Muller was commissioned to write a more detailed media planning text book. This textbook's first edition, entitled *Media Planning – Art or Science,* came out in 1996. More editions followed and it became the prescribed text for media planning for many years.

In 2009, AMASA launched its "Learnership Programme" in Johan-nesburg, where deserving applicants are selected through a rigorous process as recipients of the AMASA scholarship. The pioneer agency partners to the AMASA Learnership Programme were Starcom (under Gordon Patter-son) and Mediaedge CIA (under Wicus Swanepoel) (Aigner, B. personal communication, May 5, 2010). The objective of the AMASA Learnership Programme is to attract and recruit into the Media Industry individuals trained in non-Media disciplines like Finance, Economics, Marketing etc. The Learnership Programme involves the partnership between AMASA and Media Agencies, who jointly fund, recruit, and mentor the Learners select-ed. From a formal training perspective, the Learners join the AAA School media module as part-time students, attend the AMASA workshop and are also mandated to attend the AMASA monthly forums.

Formal Media planning education in South Africa is done only via the AAA School of Advertising, where full-time students can specialize in Media Management, or industry people can equip themselves with a part-time Module Certificate as a media planner. AMASA is responsible for all the lectures and assessments of the 6-month course offered at AAA School of Advertising's Johannesburg and Cape Town campuses.

In an effort to further widen the net and to ensure that media plan-ning in South Africa is well served by young talent from all communities, AMASA created a number of bursaries over the past years which are made available to deserving students. All profits from advertising courses and the sale of the textbook go towards maintaining this bursary fund, which is a key focus for AMASA (http://www.amasa.org.za).

Conclusion

Pre-1990 education in Advertising was the task of the Communications departments of Universities, and Graphic Design was taught at Technikons. Advertising's academic location then slowly but surely shifted from public institutions to private Advertising Schools and Design Schools. In recent years public institutions, especially Universities of Technology, started to focus again on offering Graphic Design, in an effort to increase their student intake.

Communication departments at Universities offer a more general degree in Advertising, and cannot compete with the three Advertising Schools in South Africa. They also are offering Advertising as one of many Communications specializations, or merely as a module, not as a specialization. This resulted in fewer post-graduate (MA & Ph.D) students studying Advertising. Those who do are likely to pursue an academic career rather than a career in the advertising industry.

The current situation is therefore characterized by the diminishing role of public institutions, and the dominating role of Advertising Schools and Design Schools. In the past 20 years these private schools offered 1- or 2-year diplomas, then 2- or 3-year diplomas, and since 2005 BA or BA Hons. degrees. They do not offer MA or Ph.D degrees, as their staff members are ad industry experts, and they simply do not have the required academic staff (i.e., with MA or Ph.D degrees). Advertising Schools are career-focused, while Design Schools are multi-option design focused. Graphic Design is but one of many design specializations at the Design Schools. The focus of these private schools is on theory and application, and their objective is to deliver a career-ready graduate to the Advertising industry.

Due to the worldwide economic crisis since 2008, the South African advertising industry was hard hit, both in terms of pressure on the bottom line and in terms of employment opportunities. Public institution graduates are finding it difficult to get jobs, as the perception is that their qualifications are too theoretical. More than 80% of Advertising School graduates will either find a job at an advertising agency or become an Intern at a Seta (Sector Education & Training Authority) funded Internship program. Salaries are relatively low, there is little career planning for these young graduates, and many leave the ad industry to go to the broader communications, media and marketing industries.

Student intake in Copywriting qualifications has diminished over the past three years, due to poor language education at the high school level, the emphasis on sms language, young people no longer reading, and the fact that English is a second language to all Black, and most Afrikaans-speaking, scholars. This trend will continue and it is a real challenge for public and private academic institutions.

The most popular courses at private Advertising Schools are Brand Management and Graphic Design. Universities teach Brand management as part of a Marketing specialization, while Advertising Schools teach Brand management as part of an Advertising Stratplanning specialization. Graphic designers and Art Directors often move on to Multimedia and the new lucrative world of Digital marketing.

Even though ACA, the professional body of the South African advertising industry, has actively promoted advertising as a career, student numbers have been static in the past 3 years. This trend is likely to continue in the next 3 to 5 years, due to the economic recession and the slow recovery forecasted by economists. The advertising industry is still retrenching people, not employing people.

What about the future? International (IAA) accreditation (offered only by AAA School of Advertising) will remain important, as graduates will want to work in other parts of the world. Due to Black empowerment pressures, Black talent will have to be found, trained, and educated, but they prefer to study Marketing. Few Blacks enroll in the creative arena. There will be less post-graduate focus, as being career-ready (knowledge and skills) is demanded by the ad industry. Instead of studying for post-graduate degrees, many graduates will join multi-national ad agencies' Internship programmes funded by SETAs, where the focus is on acquiring skills and getting a job.

Finally, the current and immediate future challenge for all academic institutions is to fully embrace the Digital Media Marketing world at graduate and post-graduate levels, to teach language graduates Copywriting at the post-graduate level, and to liaise closer with professional bodies (like ACA, AMASA etc) to do specialized training. In the longer term, academic research is essential at MA and Ph.D levels, and universities should take up this challenge. There is also a need for an Executive MBA in Advertising Agency management.

References

AAA School of Advertising. (1990 – 1993). Internal records. Johannesburg.

AAA School of Advertising. (2001). *Prospectus.* Johannesburg.

AAA School of Advertising. (2010). *Prospectus.* Johannesburg.

Aigner, B. (brada@fgi.co.za). (5 May 2010). *History of AMASA and Education.* E-mail to Koekemoer, L. (ludik@aaaschooljhb.co.za).

AMASA. Retrieved April 23, 2010 from http://209.85.135.132/search?q=cache:_ U9mEgRtGm0J:www.amasa.org.za/about.asp+amasa&cd=2&hl=en&ct=clnk&gl=za

Association of Advertising Agencies (AAA). (1971). Internal records. Johannesburg.

Association for Communication and Advertising (ACA). (2002). Internal records. Johannesburg.

Badenhorst, F. (fran@openwindow.co.za). (15 April 2010). *The Open Window School of Visual Communication.* E-mail to Koekemoer, L. (ludik@aaaschooljhb.co.za).

Barenblatt, M., Sinclair, R. (1989). *Make the other half work too.* 2nd edition. Southern Book Publishers.

Brink, E. (2006). *FADA: A History 1926 – 2006.* Faculty of Art, Design and Architecture. University of Johannesburg. Johannesburg.

Central University of Technology. Free State. Retrieved April 13, 2010 from http://www.cut.ac.za/web/academics/faculties/eng/sdtva/bgd.

Chmela, K. (kate@vut.ac.za). (17 February 2010). *History of Advertising education in South Africa.* Email to Koekemoer, L. (ludik@aaaschooljhb.co.za).

Cook, G. (Personal communication, 1 March 2010).

Cooney, J. (john@redandyellow.co.za). (23 February 2010). *International Advertising Education.* E-mail to Koekemoer, L. (ludik@aaaschooljhb.co.za).

Cunningham, N. (nicole.cunningham@up.ac.za). (16 March 2010). *Advertising education history.* Email to Koekemoer, L. (ludik@aaaschooljhb.co.za).

De Klerk, N. (ndeklerk@uj.ac.za). (19 March 2010). *History of Advertising education in South Africa.* Email to Koekemoer, L. (ludik@aaaschooljhb.co.za).

De Klerk, P. (peter.deklerk@neotel.co.za). (5 February 2010). *Advertising Ed History.* Email to Koekemoer, L. (ludik@aaaschooljhb.co.za).

Giloi, S. (sueg@mgi.ac.za). (11 December 2009). *Graphic Design course history final. pdf.* Email to Koekemoer, L. (ludik@aaaschooljhb.co.za).

Gordon, L. (liezel@redandyellow.ac.za). (04 May 2010). *Red and Yellow Course Outlines.* E-mail to Koekemoer, L. (ludik@aaaschooljhb.co.za).

Kaden, M. (mjkaden@sun.ac.za). (18 February 2010). *History of Advertising education in South Africa.* Email to Koekemoer, L. (ludik@aaaschooljhb.co.za).

Martinez, N. (nubia.martinez@iaaglobal.org). (19 April 2010). *IAA in South Africa.* Email to Koekemoer, L. (ludik@aaaschooljhb.co.za).

Mulder, D. (mulderd@ufs.ac.za) (23 February 2010). *Advertising Education in SA.* Email to Koekemoer, L. (ludik@aaaschooljhb.co.za).

Muller, G. (gsmquadrant@iafrica.com). (28 December 2009). *History of Advertising education in South Africa.* Email to Koekemoer, L. (ludik@aaaschooljhb.co.za).

North. (personal communication. May 7, 2010).

Nortje, C. (mnortje@cut.ac.za). (19 March 2010). *History of Advertising education in South Africa.* Email to Koekemoer, L. (ludik@aaaschooljhb.co.za).

Sinclair, R. (rogers@brandmetrics.com) (26 November 2009). *Ludi Koekemoer advertising education book.doc.* Email to Koekemoer, L. (ludik@aaaschooljhb.co.za).

Stellenbosch Academy of Design & Photography. Retrieved on April 13, 2010 from http://www.stellenboschacademy.co.za/course/ba-degree-applied-design-specialising-graphic-design.

Sutherland, C. (clayton@stellenboschacademy.co.za). (30 March 2010). *Articles post haste.* Email to Koekemoer, L. (ludik@aaaschooljhb.co.za).

University of Johannesburg. Retrieved on April 13, 2010 from http://www.uj.ac.za/graphic.

University of Pretoria. Retrieved on April 14, 2010 from http://www.up.ac.za.

University of South Africa. Retrieved on April 13, 2010 from http://brochure.unisa.ac.za/brochure/showprev.aspx?d=1_2_33&f=p_0233X

University of South Africa. Retrieved on April 13, 2010 from http://brochure.unisa.ac.za/brochure/showprev.aspx?d=1_2_33&f=p_02305MMD

University of South Africa. (1981). BA Communications Study guides. Pretoria.

Vaal University of Technology. Retrieved on April 13, 2010 from http://www.vut.ac.za/visual

Van der Westhuizen, W. (wessie.vanderwesthuizen@nwu.ac.za). (4 May 2010). *Advertising education in SA.* Email to Koekemoer, L. (ludik@aaaschooljhb.co.za).

Vega The Brand Communications School. Retrieved on April 13, 2010 from http://www.vegaschool.co.za/full-time/BA-creativecommunication.

Vega The Brand Communications School. Retrieved on April 13, 2010 from http://www.vegaschool.co.za/full-time/BA-honors-creativecommunication.

Vega The Brand Communications School. Retrieved on May 11, 2010 from http://www.vegaschool.co.za/full-time/BA-brandbuilding.

Vega The Brand Communications School. Retrieved on May 11, 2010 from http://www.vegaschool.co.za/full-time/BA-honors-brandleadership.

Vega The Brand Communications School. Retrieved on May 11, 2010 from http://www.vegaschool.co.za/part-time/diploma.

Venter, N. (nina@imm.co.za). (15 April 2010). *IMM GSM Feedback.* Email to Koekemoer, L. (ludik@aaaschooljhb.co.za).

Wiid, J. (May 13, 2010). Unisa. *Post Graduate Diploma in Market Research & Advertising.* Fax to Koekemoer, L.

Young, T. (1971). AAPA 1947 – 1971. Unpublished document entitled *Advertising in South Africa. The History of the Association of Accredited Practitioners in Advertising.* Johannesburg.

ASIA

Advertising Education in Cambodia

Sela Sar
Iowa State University, USA

Lulu Rodriguez
Iowa State University, USA

Cambodia is located in Southeast Asia and shares borders with Thailand, Laos, and Vietnam. It has over 139 miles of coastline along the Gulf of Thailand. Advertising education in Cambodia is still in its infancy. Its development can be divided into two stages. The first stage began in the 1960s; the second started in the early part of the 21st century.

Stage 1

Advertising education in Cambodia began during the so-called "Golden Age" of the Cambodian movie industry in the 1960s. In the early part of that decade, at the Royal University of Fine Arts, under the direction of then King Norodom Sihanouk, French instructors developed and offered eight courses with some advertising content. According to documents retrieved from the Royal University of Fine Arts,[2] the courses were intended to develop basic skills in arts and display, creativity, and advertising design, in support of the emerging movie industry and other creative venues. The courses were offered through the School of Humanities and Arts at the Royal University of Fine Arts in Phnom Penh.

This was part of the School's degree programs in Acting, Arts and Design, Movie Production, Sociology, and French Literature. Because advertising courses, offered as electives, were taught by French instructors, the

---

[2] Between 1975 to 1979, many official documents were destroyed as part of the Khmer Rouge's objective of implementing a totalitarian and agrarian-based form of communism.

language of instruction was French[3]. The number of advertising courses grew from eight in the early 1960s to 11 by the early 1970s. These were offered by a number of academic departments, including Arts and Design, Sociology, Acting, and Literature. The growing number of students interested in advertising arts and design provided the impetus for new courses (Royal University of Fine Arts documents).

This momentum ceased, and advertising education came to halt as a consequence of the pervasive civil and political unrest between the mid-1970s and the early 1990s. Under the reign of the Khmer Rouge, the entire Cambodian education system was abolished.

When the socio-political system began to stabilize in the mid-1990s, the government laid the foundations of a free market economy by opening its borders to the outside world. Direct foreign investments began to flow into the country, a phenomenon that triggered the demand for professional skills in promotions and branding. This economic transformation encouraged international advertising agencies from around the world to establish offices in the country. As a result, the demand for skilled advertising professionals became more urgent, prompting universities and colleges throughout the country in the early 2000s to once again offer various courses in advertising, including strategic communication. Today, these courses are offered through the departments of Humanities and the Social Sciences.

Stage 2

In 2001, the Department of Media and Communication at the new Royal University of Phnom Penh offered courses in Advertising Research, Strategic Communication, and Marketing Communication, which were attended by about a dozen students. Advertising and Strategic Communication courses were developed and taught by a German professor, Caroline Schmidt Gross, and a Cambodian instructor, Tung Tithanu. The language of instruction was English.

By 2005, with the support of the Konrad Adenauer Foundation (Germany), the Ateneo de Manila University (Philippines), and Ohio University (USA), the Media and Communication Department has grown to 150 students and 15 full-time instructors. The Department has an additional 15 part-time instructors and lecturers (working practitioners) every

---

[3] Cambodia was a protectorate of France from 1863 to 1963, administered as part of French Indochina. At that time the official language in schools and universities was French (Chandler, 1993).

academic year who deliver lectures and seminars (Tieng, 2009). Today, the Department boasts of three emphasis areas: Public Relations, Print and Design, and Media Management. But as of 2010, no full- service Bachelor of Arts or Bachelor of Science program in Advertising can be discerned.

By 2002, advertising strengthened its presence at various universities around the country. For example, the departments of Marketing, Accounting, Tourism, Economics, and Human Sciences at the National University of Management began offering courses in Advertising. According to the National University (2003), six courses had some advertising content: Advertising Principles, Advertising Strategy, Advertising Sales, Advertising Management, Advertising and Promotional Strategy and Strategic Marketing Communication.

The Advertising and Strategic Communication courses offered at the Royal University of Phnom Penh and the National University of Management both have an almost exclusive focus on one aspect of advertising— advertising *strategy*. None of those courses emphasizes *creative* advertising. However, in early 2003, Limkokwing University of Creative Technology, a private university in Malaysia with a satellite campus in Cambodia and known for its program in graphic design, saw the need for instruction in both creative advertising and advertising strategies.

In 2004, Limkokwing University's Cambodian campus began offering various advertising courses. Its Faculty of Communication, Media and Broadcasting developed courses in Advertising Graphic Design, Media Audience Analysis, Advertising/Public Principles, Advertising Creativity, Advertising Art and Display and Advertising Copywriting, Advertising Management, Strategic Advertising, Advertising Campaign, Media planning, Advertising Agency Management, Advertising Regulations, Issues and Ethics, and Strategic Communication.

Limkokwing is the only university in the country that offers a comprehensive advertising program with all types of courses, except Advertising Theory and Psychology of Advertising. Ironically, it does not grant an Advertising degree, but rather a Bachelor of Arts in Professional Communication. The university also exposes students to advertising research strategies in addition to the creative courses. The Cambodian campus of Limkokwing University also offers courses in Computer Animation and Interactive Communication. It requires students to work with those from other disciplines on joint projects.

In 2006, in response to the continuous demand for skilled advertising professionals, the International University of Phnom Penh, a small private university, began offering an Associate Degree in Advertising through the

Department of Journalism, under the School of Humanities and Social Sciences. The program focuses on the vocational aspect of advertising (i.e., Advertising Copywriting, Advertising Display and Design, Advertising Arts, and Principles of Advertising). The School was fully accredited by the Ministry of Education and the Accreditation Committee of Cambodia (ACC) in 2006.

To expand its program, the Department of Journalism plans to offer a Bachelor's Degree in Advertising by 2011. Currently, it employs 12 full-time instructors and 10 part-time instructors and lecturers. A large majority of the part-time instructors (around 90 percent) are working practitioners.

There is no doubt that the advertising industry's growing demand for skilled professionals has encouraged other universities to offer more advertising and related courses. In 2008, several universities, including the University of Cambodia, Norton University, Build Bright University, and the Pannasastra University of Cambodia began to offer a total of 25 advertising courses, most of which (about 60%) were in the business schools, and about 40% through the departments of Communication and the Social Sciences.

Another driving force behind the development of advertising education in Cambodia is the demand for skilled professionals who speak the Cambodian and/or Khmer languages, by non-governmental organizations (NGOs) and international groups such as the United States Agency for International Development (USAID), the United Nations Children's Emergency Fund (UNICEF), the World Health Organization (WHO), and Family Health International (FHI) to assist with their public information campaigns. Some of these include disease control (i.e., HIV-AIDS and malaria prevention, housing and public works, and poverty alleviation. Other campaigns address issues such as land and water resource development, the preservation of cultural heritage and historical sites, and wildlife protection.

Because of the shortage of Cambodian advertising professionals, some of these organizations employ university instructors to offer short courses with a vocational approach (i.e., courses in advertising production, creative advertising, advertising art, advertising display, advertising graphic design, and advertising copywriting). According to USAID Cambodia (2007), some trainees continued their career with various advertising agencies after their stint with these organizations.

Conclusion

Advertising in Cambodia is taught in different schools and organizations following different approaches. Some schools offer advertising courses that focus on strategy and creativity; others offer only creative courses. Only recently has one school started to offer comprehensive undergraduate training. Some schools and non-government organizations take a more vocational approach. However, not a single program employs a plan of course work that is steeped in theory and the psychological aspects of advertising. As demand for skilled professionals continues to grow, these two aspects of advertising are expected to be included in the curriculum.

References

Chandler, D. P. (1993). *A history of Cambodia (2nd ed.)*. Boulder, CO: Westview Press.
Chhay, B. (3/11/2010). E-mail, Accreditation Committee of Cambodia (ACC), Phnom Penh.
Royal University of Phnom Penh research document.
Tieng, S.V. (12/17/2009). E-mail, Royal University of Phnom Penh.
US Agency for International Development. Cambodia report.

China's Advertising Education

Guangzhi Chu
University of China, China

Generally speaking, the level of development of advertising education is closely related to the level of the development of advertising industry in a given country. China's advertising industry was born in the early 20th century, and it has developed rapidly since China's reform and opening-up policy was implemented in 1978. China's advertising education has become an important part of the world's advertising education, in light of China becoming one of the largest markets in the world.

The history of China's advertising education

China's advertising education began in the early 1920s, as one course in the department of Journalism of some Universities or Institutes. Based on some important historical events, China's ad education history can be roughly divided into four periods: [1] period of germination (1918-1949), [2] period of stagnation (1950-1978), [3] exploratory period (1979-1991), and [4] period of rapid development (1992 until now).

Period of germination (1918-1949)

In 1918, the Journalism Research Institute of Peking University was founded. The chairman was Professor Xu Baohuang. This is the beginning of China's journalism education. In 1920, a Department of Journalism was established in Saint John's University. In the following ten years, Xianmen University, Peking Mass University, Yanching University, Shanghai South University, and Fudan University created their own departments of journalism, respectively. After 1930, more and more Universities and Colleges did this.

From the beginning of journalism education, as a required course, advertising was taught in Universities or Colleges. Among these programs, two notable schools were Yanching University and Fudan University.

The Department of Journalism at Yanching University

As a part of Chinese Language & Literature College in Yanching University, the Department of Journalism was founded in 1924 in Beijing. *The Principles of Advertising* was among the required courses. This class aimed at exploring the function and importance of modern advertising from an economic perspective, especially focusing on the significant role of advertising in newspapers and magazines, and briefly discussing all aspects of advertising. It also paid more attention to the practice of newspaper and magazine advertising production.

From 1929 to 1932, Group, who came from the U.S., taught courses in advertising in Yanching University. He also was the first journalism researcher selected by Missouri University. In 1931, he gained his Master's degree from Yanching University and became an assistant professor. He also was in charge of marketing for *Pingxi* newspaper and *New China* magazine, run by faculty and students. In 1932, he went back to the U.S.

The Departments of Journalism at Fudan University

The Department of Journalism was founded in 1929 at Fudan University, Shanghai. "Newspaper and magazine advertising" was one of the core courses. This class included the principles and function of advertising and design and production of newspaper and magazine advertisements, and it focused on advertising management. It would take a semester to finish this class. Students also had opportunities to be interns in some newspapers and news agencies, with the guidance of Professors and adjunct lecturers.

In addition, the China Professional Journalism School, the Department of Journalism of the Business school at Hujiang University, the Department of Journalism of University of the Republic of China, and the Correspondence School of Shen Newspaper also offered advertising courses. These classes were taught by some managers or executives of advertising agencies and some senior journalists, such as Meizeng Lu, Youwu Huang, and Junhao Zhao.

In this period, advertising was still being taught as a single course. Advertising education was a part of journalism education, and it relied heavily on the development of the journalism industry. Its mission was to meet the demand of that industry. Most journalism programs that were offering an advertising course were located in Beijing and Shanghai, where the level of development of the economy, and the journalism and advertising industries, was higher. However, there was no independent advertising program yet.

Period of stagnation (1950-1978)

After the foundation of the People's Republic of China, the new government regulated the advertising market and strengthened its management. Small and private advertising agencies were merged together and transformed into state-owned advertising agencies. Advertising became the part of the new political and economic system.

In the period of Great Cultural Revolution (1966-1976), a commodity-based economic system was replaced by a planned economic system. Therefore, as a marketing communication tool, commercial advertising was banned. In fact, during these ten years, advertising for foreign trade was nearly the only remaining form of commercial advertising.

Under such unique political and economic circumstances, all the departments of journalism were closed down. Accordingly, advertising courses disappeared in journalism education. Only in some art institutes, such as Luxun Art Institute, Xian Art Institute, and Sichuan Art Institute, a few of advertising design courses remained.

Exploratory period (1979-1991)

In December 1978, The Third Plenary Session of the Central Committee of the Communist Party of China (CCCPC) made a strategic decision to shift the focus of the whole party to socialist modernization, thus initiating China's reform and opening-up policy. As a barometer of the economy, the advertising industry has an opportunity to recover.

On January 4, 1979, *Tianjing Daily* kept ahead in rehabilitating commercial advertising in China's newspapers. Ten days later, *Wen hui bao*, an official newspaper in Shanghai, published the article, "*Restoring Reputation for Advertising.*" Yunpeng Ding, the author, noted that advertising should be regarded as an academic discipline that can promote trade and improve business management. It was seen as a clear signal of the recovery by the advertising industry.

In the same year, some newspapers, TV, and radio stations resumed their advertising business. Advertising agencies also started to operate one after another, nationwide. The advertising industry grew rapidly. As a result, trained advertising professionals were in demand.

From 1978 to 1983, Guangxi Arts Institute and Shanghai Light Industrial Higher Junior College started to offer some advertising courses in their Upholster & Design Majors. However, these far from met the demands for advertising professionals. Because advertising education was still limited to a few courses, it is undeniable that the lack of a focused advertising curriculum hampered the development of advertising education.

In August 1983, The Propaganda Department of CCCPC and Ministry of Education of the People's Republic of China co-issued a document, aiming to promote journalism education, including advertising programs and related curricula. In fact, the preparation process had already begun in Xiamen University. Advocated by two alumni in Hong Kong, named Jibo Liu and Yelu Yu, this University applied to establish a journalism and communication department, including an advertising major in Mainland China. In May, 1983, the application was approved by the Ministry of Education. This became the first department with the title of "communication," and the first advertising major in Mainland China.

The next year, the advertising major of Department of Journalism and Communication at Xiamen University formally enrolled 15 undergraduate students. The mission of this major was to train advertising professionals with all-round development of morality, intelligence, and physique for advertising research, teaching, publicity, management, design, and production. The program length was four years. In the following years, some institutes of finance and economics and institutes of arts started to offer courses in advertising. But, in July 1988, the first students majoring in advertising gained their Bachelor degree.

Figure 9-1: The first graduation class of advertising students at Xiamen University, July 1988

In the same year, a TV advertising major was set up in the Department of Communication at Shenzhen University. This program was only two years long. It was a non-Bachelor degree program.

Then, in September 1989, the Beijing Broadcasting Institute (BBI, Now named Communication University of China) began to enroll undergraduate students. This was a four-year program. The mission of this major was to train advertising professionals with a high level of theory and practical skills, including advertising management professionals, as well as professionals in production and research. The curriculum of BBI combined the advertising, marketing, and art design together. It was different from the advertising major of Xiamen University, which focused more on courses oriented toward journalism and communication.

By the end of 1992, six Universities already had established an advertising major. These Universities are pioneers of China's advertising education. They did a lot in exploration in major positioning, structure of curriculum and teachers' improvement.

Period of rapid growth (1992 till now)

In 1992, the 14th Congress of the Communist Party of China decided to build China's socialist market economic system. Over the next year, the State Development Planning Commission (SDPC) and the State Administration of Industry and Commerce (SAIC) co-issued the development plan to promote the advertising industry. In this plan, advertising education played an important role. The government also would provide the place, funds, and teachers to support the establishment of advertising majors and training bases. Given these circumstances, some Universities and Institutes were eager to create advertising majors or departments.

In 1994, Beijing Broadcasting Institute established the first advertising *department* in Mainland China. This department included both the advertising major and the art design major. According to an incomplete record, by the end of 1997, more than eighty Universities and Institutes already had created advertising majors or departments. The increasing demand of the advertising industry was the main driving force. Most of these majors and departments were located in journalism departments or schools and in developed cities.

In June 1999, the State Development Planning Commission (SDPC) and the Ministry of Education decided to increase the enrollment numbers in China's higher education. In doing so, it further promoted the development of advertising education.

In February 2000, Beijing Union University set up an advertising *college*. This is the first college in China with "advertising" in the title. It was co-run by Beijing Union University and the Noble advertising agency, which belongs to *The People's Daily* newspaper. This college was aimed at training advertising professionals, thereby promoting vocational advertising education. In 2002, a School of Advertising at the Communication University of China (former Beijing Broadcasting University) was founded.

According to *China's Radio and TV Year book 2009*, by the end of 2008, 338 Universities, Institutes and Colleges enroll undergraduate students majoring in advertising, covering all provinces, autonomous regions and municipalities in Mainland China. Among these Universities, Institutes and Colleges are 105 independent colleges.

The rest includes 81 Universities; 64 institutes of technology; 36 normal Universities; 28 institutes of business, finance and economics; 6 institutes of foreign languages; and 8 institutes of agricultural and forestry, 9 institutes of arts, 1 institute of political science and law. Qidi Wu, former vice minister of the Ministry of Education, estimated the number of undergraduate and graduate students is about 40,000. During this period, with the rapid growth of the number of advertising programs, the multi-level advertising education system has been developed.

In 1993, Journalism Department of Beijing Broadcasting Institute took the lead to enroll graduate students majoring in advertising. In 1994, the Advertising Department of Beijing Broadcasting Institute took the lead to enroll undergraduate students majoring in advertising as a second bachelor degree. In 2000, Beijing Broadcasting Institute took the lead to enroll doctorate student majoring in advertising.

Till June 2010, there are nine Universities enrolling doctoral students majoring in advertising, including Communication University of China (former Beijing Broadcasting Institute), Xiamen University, Wuhan University, Renmin University of China, Peiking University, Fudan University, Huazhong University of Science & Technology, Shanghai University and Shanghai Normal University. Advertising education system covering higher junior, undergraduate, graduate and doctorate program was formed.

Notable Advertising Educators

Zhongpu Tang

In 1981, Mr. Tang participated in editing the first Chinese advertising book, *Advertising Practice*. The next year, he began offering a class titled "The Introduction to Advertising" to undergraduate students in the Journalism Department at Renmin University of China, as an adjunct teacher. In 1984, he became an Adjunct Professor in the Journalism and Communication Department at Xiamen University. In 1991, Mr. Tang edited the *Modern Advertising* classic book series (8 books). In 2008, he was honored with a "Historical contribution in the 30 years development of China's advertising," set up by the China Advertising Association (CAA).

Dajun Pan

Beijing Technology and Business University (former Beijing Institute of Business)

The late Professor Pan was one of the earlier advertising educators. In 1980, he and Shuping Zhang co-wrote *Advertising Senses and Skill*, the first book specialized in advertising, since the recovery of advertising in China. In 1987, he created the first vocational college advertising education in China. In 1989, he edited the *Modern Advertising* series (10 books). Professor Pan also is the founder of the advertising major at the Beijing Institute of Business.

Hanzhang Fu
Jinan University

In 1985, Mr. Fu co-wrote *The Principles of Advertising* with Tiejun Kuang. He also co-wrote *Advertising Psychology* (1988) and *Measurement of Advertisement Effectiveness* (1990) with other scholars. He took the lead in establishing marketing courses in Mainland China, and did a lot to promote marketing research and teaching.

Yuechang Zhu
Sanda University

From 1983, Zhu started to teach advertising in Xiamen University. He was one of the founders of the Advertising major and the Journalism and Communication department of Xiamen University, and former vice director of that department. Professor Zhu led a key research study supported by National Philosophy and Social Science, titled "Research on the Advertisements in Mass Media."

Peiai Chen
Xiamen University

Professor Chen is chairman of Academic Committee of the CAA. He was the former chairman of China Advertising Education Society (CAES). He was one of the founders of the Advertising major at Xiamen University. Professor Chen edited *The 21th Century Advertising Series*, and wrote some books including, *The Principles and Practices of Advertising, Advertising History of China and the World,* and *The Introduction of Advertising.* He led a research study supported by National Philosophy and Social Science, titled "Research on Advertising Communication." In 2008, he was honored with the CAA's "Historical contribution in the 30 years development of China's advertising."

Junjie Ding
Communication University of China

Professor Ding is the chairman of ASEC, vice president of CAAC and Vice President of CUC. He was one of the founders of the advertising major, department and school at Beijing Broadcasting Institute and former chairman of Academic Committee of China Advertising Association. He wrote several books, including *Theories and Operations of Modern Advertising Activities* (1996) and *General Studies on Modern Advertising* (1997). Professor Ding led a research study supported by National Philosophy and Social Science, called "The Current Situation and the Future of Advertising Communication Research in China." In 2008, he received an "Excellent Contribution in the 30 years development of China's advertising," from the CAA.

Shenmin Huang
Communication University of China

Professor Huang is Dean of the Advertising School at CUC, and the chief editor of *Media* magazine. In 1990, he began teaching advertising at Beijing Broadcasting Institute. Professor Huang is one of the founders of the Advertising Department and the school at Beijing Broadcasting Institute. He co-edited *The Comparative Study on Advertisement in China and Japan,* along with *Accelerated Growth of China's Advertising Industry,* and he wrote *Empirical Analysis in China's Advertising Activities,* as well as *The Attitudes to Advertising,* among others. In 2008, he was honored with an "Excellent contribution in the 30 years development of China's advertising."

Jinhai Zhang
Wuhan University

Professor Zhang is the chairman of CAES. In 1993, he established an advertising major at Wuhan University with his colleagues. He edited the *Luojia Advertising* series and wrote several books, including *The Theories of Advertising Communication in 20ᵗʰ Century, The Practice and Regulation of Advertising Communication,* and *Advertising Business.* Professor Zhang led a research project supported by National Philosophy and Social Science, called "The Regulation of Advertising."

Yumin Wu
Shenzhen University

Professor Wu is Dean of College of Mass Communication at Shenzhen University. In 1990, he established the advertising major at Shenzhen University with his colleagues. He wrote several books, including *Modern advertising and marketing* (1991). Professor Wu led key research study supported by China's Ministry of Education.

Ad Education Support Organizations

In the developing process of China's advertising education, professional associations played and are playing a significant role. When there was no independent advertising program in China, associations took charge of training advertising professionals. Notable associations involved were the China Advertising Society, China Advertising Association, China Advertising Association of Commerce (formerly the China Advertising Association for Foreign Trade and Economic Cooperation), China Advertising Education Society, and The Advertising Specialty Education Committee of the Chinese Association of Higher Education.

China Advertising Society (CAS)

CAS was founded in February 23, 1982. The chairman was Ding Zhang, a famous painter and former vice president of The Central Academy of Arts & Design. In August 7, 1982, the first national academic conference was held. The hot topics included whether advertising was needed in a socialist country or not, what are the characters and function of advertising, what is the difference between socialist advertising and capitalist advertising, and so on.

In May 1983, CAS and the General Corporation of China Advertising Co. held a training class in the Qindao, Shandong province. Three months later, the second national academic conference was held in Beizhen city, Liaoning province. Participants discussed the position and role of advertising in the period of socialist modernization, the direction and principles of advertising industry, the relationship between advertising and journalism, advertising education, and how advertising serves the material and spiritual civilizations of socialism.

Beginning in 1985, the national academic conference was held by CAA. In 1987, the Academic Committee of China Advertising Association took its place. As the first academic advertising association in China, China Advertising Society played a very important role in the earlier years of the development of advertising industry as well as advertising education in China.

China Advertising Association (CAA)

CAA was founded in December 1983. The mission was to advocate truthful, scientific advertisements, improve the artistic quality of advertisements, and work out a developing plan of advertising industry in order to advise the government. As the biggest advertising association in China, CAA took charge of the training of advertising professionals.

In February 22, 1986, China Advertising Correspondence College was founded by CAA. At that time, 4100 students enrolled. CAA invited experts from the academy and industry to edit a series of textbooks. This series included *Brief History of Advertising, Measurement of Advertisement Effectiveness, Advertising Planning, Ten Tactics of Advertising Design, Advertising Design, Advertising Psychology,* and *Advertising Management and Copywriting.* All of these textbooks were published in March 1989 by Industrial and Commercial publisher of China. This series was the earliest systemic advertising textbooks in Mainland China.

In 1987, the Academic Committee of CAA was founded. Its mission included academic research for government decision-making; organizing academic seminars and experience exchange; introducing the newest and advanced theories, methods and techniques; selecting excellent advertising and papers; editing academic books; supporting and guiding the training of advertising professionals; developing international academic exchange, and so on.

After that, CAA did a lot of work to support advertising education in China. For example, in February 1988, a training class for executives of advertising agencies nationwide was co-held by this committee and CAA for Foreign Trade and Economic Cooperation in Shenzhen, Guangdong province. From 1989 to 1990, the Committee and the Department of Journalism at Beijing Broadcasting Institute co-held three training classes. More than 400 students received the professional certificate. Then, in 1990, the Committee of the Department of Journalism and Communication at Xiamen University co-held the first advertising teaching seminar in Xiamen, Fujian province (Figure 9-2).

Figure 9-2: The first advertising teaching seminar, 1990

Some other examples include, in 1991, the TV committee of CAA and Beijing Broadcasting Institute co-held national training class focusing on creativity and design of TV advertisements. In 1998, the Academic Committee of the CAA, along with Beijing Broadcasting Institute and Xiamen University, established a graduate training program. In 2000, the first students of that program finished their study and received course-completion certificates (Figure 9-3). Finally, in June 2005, CAA held the "Worldwide Chinese Advertising Education Forum" in Beijing.

Figure 9-3: Course-completion ceremony at Beijing Broadcasting Institute, in 2000

China Advertising Association of Commerce (CAAC)

CAAC is the former China Advertising Association for Foreign Trade and Economic Cooperation (CAAFTEC). As the first national advertising association, it was established in 1981 under the Ministry of Commerce of the People's Republic of China. In earlier years, this association was aimed at using advertising to promote the import of China's products, in order to increase foreign currency exchange.

Being familiar with international markets, CAAFTEC introduced an exhibition of foreign advertisements, invited advertising experts from developed countries, along with the Hong Kong, Macao, and Taiwan regions, to give lectures. It jointly sponsored the Third World Advertising Conference with CAA, and promoted international business exchange.

In 1985, *International Advertising* Magazine belonged to this association. It was launched in Shanghai.

In November 2005, China Advertising Association for Foreign Trade and Economic Cooperation changed its name to China Advertising Association of Commerce. Aimed at rendering service for commercial interests, CAAC focused on brand building for Chinese marketers. It established the Business Brand Institute and the Creative Industry Institute. These two institutes also regularly publish the periodical, *Reference of Brand Management* and *Reference of Creative Industry.* In addition, CAAC and Communication University of China have published several books, including, *IAI Chinese Advertising Works Yearbook* and *IAI Terminal Marketing Yearbook.*

CAAC has organized several local, joint-venture, and foreign advertising agencies to form a top-line organization called the Association of Accredited Advertising Agencies of China (abbreviated as the "Chinese 4A"). In recent years, the Chinese 4A has played an active role in the industry. From 2007 to 2009, the Chinese 4A invited 100 advertising specialists to give lectures or speeches in Chinese universities.

China Advertising Education Society (CAES)

China Advertising Education Society, the full name being "China Advertising Society of The Journalism and Communication Specialty Education Committee of Chinese Association of Higher Education," was founded in 1999. This organization was co-lunched by Xiamen University, Communication University of China, Renmin University of China, Wuhan University and Shenzhen University.

Figure 9-4: The first conference of CAES, in 1999

In the same year, CAES held the first annual national academic conference (Figure 9-4). Beginning 2005, the academic conference was held twice each year. In each conference, the training of advertising professionals and the construction of advertising programs were the main topics.

CAES provided three platforms for China's advertising education, including (1) teacher training, (2) the publishing of academic papers, and (3) research in teaching and academic exchange. After more than ten years' development, CAES has become influential. Now it has more than 200 unit members, and it has made a significant contribution to the development of China's Advertising Education.

The Advertising Specialty Education Committee of the Chinese Association of Higher Education (ASEC)

In November 2009, the Advertising Specialty Education Committee of the Chinese Association of Higher Education was founded in Beijing (see Figure 9-5. It is an academic society aiming at promoting research in advertising and advertising education. The members include teachers from advertising and related majors nationwide. The primary mission of ASEC is to promote an exchange within the advertising field, to hold advertising education research conferences or forums regularly, to upgrade advertising education in the higher education system, to publish academic books, to support advertising research, and to arbitrate serious problems related to advertisements.

Figure 9-5: The opening ceremony of ASEC, in 2009

In the first conference of ASEC, Junjie Ding from Communication University of China was elected as the president. The vice presidents are Gang Chen from Peking University, Ning Ni from Renmin University of

China, Jinhai Zhang from Wuhan University, Dinghai Jin from Shanghai Normal University, Yumin Wu from Shenzhen University and Ruiwu Liu from Beijing Union University.

Dentsu Group and China's advertising education

http://www.dentsu.com/vision/index.html

In addition to advertising organizations, advertising agencies and media agencies have done much to support advertising education. Among them, a notable one is the Dentsu Group, one of the biggest advertising organizations in the world.

In 1996, the Japan-China Advertising Educational Exchange Project was launched as a five-year project commemorating the 95th anniversary of the foundation of Dentsu, in coordination with the Chinese Government and six universities in China. This included Beijing University, Renmin University of China, The Central Fine Arts Academy (now the Academy of Arts & Design, Tsinghua University), the Beijing Broadcasting Institute (now the Communication University of China), Fudan University, and Shanghai University. The project consisted of establishing advertising courses at those six universities.

All courses were taught by leading advertising executives at the department director level or higher, along with a study exchange system that gave temporary positions at Dentsu to teachers involved in teaching advertising at the six universities. Students who attended these classes are currently active in media/advertising companies and university, making a huge contribution to the advancement of the Chinese advertising industry.

This project ended in 2001. But in order to respond to the requests from China's Ministry of Education for further exchanges and celebrate the Dentsu centennial anniversary, the former project was renewed in an improved form, as the Japan-China Marketing Study Exchange Project, with the support of the Chinese Government, the six universities, along with the endorsement of the China Advertising Association.

The aim of this project has been to promote Japan-China cultural and economic exchanges and deepen mutual understanding and friendship through education in the field of advertising. The project was run for four years, starting in 2001, and covered four areas: the Dentsu Joint Advertising Class, Dentsu New Study Abroad Program, Japan-China Corporate Exchange Seminar, and Advisory Assistance provided to facilitate a research project to be funded by the Yoshida Hideo Memorial Foundation.

In July 2006, to continue the exchange, Dentsu signed an agreement with China's Ministry of Education. Its purpose was to promote the Japan-China Advertising Class, Study Abroad Program for China's teachers, Research and publication, and marketing consultation. This program includes Dentsu Abroad researchers Program, Training seminar of China's advertising professionals, research supporting program. The new agreement covered more than 140 Universities with advertising departments or majors and doctorate candidates.

Select University Advertising Programs

Xiamen University (XU)
School of Journalism & Communication
http://comm.xmu.edu.cn/

Xiamen University is recognized as the pioneer of China's advertising education. In 1983, the first advertising major in China was created there. XU established a basic model for China's advertising education, and trained many ad educators for other Universities or Institutes. Some textbooks, edited or co-edited by the faculty of XU, were widely used in China, including *The 21th century advertising series* and *Advertising textbooks series of Tenth Five-year plan*, supported by China's Ministry of Education.

In 1994, XU began graduate degree specializations under the journalism major, including Journalism, Radio and TV Journalism, and Advertising specialty. In 2002, the graduate degree discipline of Communication was founded, including Communication, Advertising, and Public Relations specialties. In 2006, the doctorate discipline of Communication was set up, and it now includes advertising specialties.

In 2008, the advertising program at XU became the "Brand Major,"[4] supported by China's Ministry of Education, with a purpose of training high quality Account Executives who are familiar with advertising practice, including advertising planning, brand planning, media planning, PR, creative, copywriting, production of commercial, design, advertising management, marketing research, and event marketing.

Communication University of China (CUC)
School of Advertising
http://ggxy.cuc.edu.cn/

Advertising education began in Communication University of China (former Beijing Broadcasting Institute) in 1989, when its first undergraduate students majoring in advertising enrolled. This is the second accredited advertising major in China.

---

[4] A "Brand Major" in China means that it is recognized as an exemplary version of such programs.

In 1993, the first two postgraduate students majoring in advertising in China were enrolled. In 1994, the Department of Advertising was founded. This is the first advertising *department* in China. At the same time, the first undergraduate students for a second degree in China were enrolled. In 2000, China's first doctoral students in advertising enrolled.

The *School* of Advertising was founded in 2002: the first School to create China's first ad training system covering undergraduate education all the way to doctoral programs. It now includes an Advertising Department, a Art Design Department, a Public Relations Department, and a New Media and Advertising Department, with 6 research institutions and 3 laboratories.

In 1993, the faculty prepared the "Training Program for a Professional Certificate in Advertising," edited textbooks, and produced the TV training series *Modern Advertising*. From 1996, the Department of Advertising has edited and published *IMI Consumer Behaviors and Lifestyle Patterns Yearbook*, the *IAI China Advertising Works Yearbook*, the *Accelerated Growth of China's Advertising Industry*, and *Media* magazine. Since 2002, the Department has been in charge of the annual "Research about the Ecological Environment of China's Advertising Industry," that was entrusted by the Academic Committee of China Advertising Association.

In 2005, the School of Advertising became the organizer of *Yong Creative Competition & Workshop Annual in China*, supported by the One Club. And in 2006, the "Introduction to Advertising" course, offered by Professor Junjie Ding, was selected as a National Brand Course. In recent years, students at the School of Advertising at CUC won nearly all of the gold awards in student competitions, including Times Advertisement Golden Calf Prize, the One Show, and Academic Award of Advertising Festival for Chinas' Universities' Students.

Wuhan University (WU)[5]
School of Journalism & Communication
http://journal.whu.edu.cn/

The Advertising program in Wuhan University was established in 1993. Through the years a relatively integrated system of advertising training has been created. In 1994, the first undergraduate advertising students were enrolled, and in 1998 the first graduate students were added. Then, in 2002, doctoral students joined.

The number of undergraduate and graduate students is about the same. Since its beginning, the advertising program at WU has trained more

---

[5] This section contributed by Xi Yao.

than 1000 professionals for China's advertising industry.

With continuous innovation and improvement, a unique and scientific professional approach was formed. The advertising teaching system at Wuhan University was ranked the top in the Hubei province. The advertising major was selected as a "Brand Major" by the Education Commission of the Hubei province. Also, "Advertising business" was selected as a National Brand Course.[6] The *Luojia Advertising Series* and *Advertising series for the 21th century* were published at WU.

Peking University (PU)
School of Journalism and Communication
http://sjc.pku.edu.cn/English.aspx

PU's advertising program was founded in 1993, in the Department of Arts, as a major. In 1999, the Institute of Modern Advertising was founded. This institute is aimed at promoting communication and cooperation through various forms of research and communication activities. And on May 28th, 2001, became part of the School of Journalism and Communication, as an independent department.

During the intervening years, the PU program gradually formed its approach, combining theory and practice, while focused on the leading edge of advertising industry and training highly qualified professionals. The purpose of the bachelor's degree is to train students with systematic knowledge and skills of advertising and broad cultural and science knowledge, while making them familiar with the related law and regulations in China, and prepared for work in Journalism, Publication, Film and TV, Advertising and Cultural Industry, and so on. Degree programs include the BA in Advertising, MA in Advertising, and Advertising Ph.D. in Communication.

Renmin University of China (RUC)
School of Journalism and Communication
http://jcr.ruc.edu.cn/

Advertising as a major was founded in 1996. Advertising design and production, especially the computer-assisted advertisement design and advertising photography, are the focuses.

The undergraduate curriculum in advertising is composed of foundation courses and specialty courses. In addition, a range of selective courses are offered by other teaching and research sections of the School of Business and School of Economics at Renmin University of China.

---

[6] This indicates the course was one of China's best such courses.

For undergraduate students, a whole semester in the first half of their fourth year is scheduled for a formal internship in advertising companies or advertising departments of media outlets. For the two-year term post-graduate students, three months is scheduled for an internship. They are all encouraged to do hands-on practices in their spare time during the semester period, or in summer, either on- or off-campus. Most graduates of this major are working at different positions of advertising companies or ad departments in media companies.

In September 2009, the Department of Advertising and Media Economics was founded. The advertising major is one of the two majors of this department.

Tsinghua University (TU)
Academy of Arts & Design
http://ad.tsinghua.edu.cn/qhmy/index.jsp

The Advertising Design major was the former Art Design major that was one of the earlier majors of The Central Academy of Arts & Design (Now Academy of Arts & Design of Tsinghua University). Now it belongs to Department of Visual Communication. The courses related to advertising include advertising strategy, advertising planning and design, brand design, and sales design. This program's emphasis is on integrating theory with practice, so it focuses on case studies and skills training. The purpose is to teach the combined talents of creative thinking, sound professionalism, broad theoretical attainment, and rich design experiences.

The Academy of Arts & Design of TU grants both Master's and Doctoral degrees in Design and Theory of Arts, along with a post-doctoral specialty in Theory of Art. Faculty and students have attained remarkable achievements in major art design activities, both at home and abroad and successfully completed many national and international major art design projects. They have won many domestic and international awards.

Fudan University (FU)
School of Journalism
http://www.xwxy.fudan.edu.cn/index/node_101.htm

Advertising education arrived at FU in 1994. The purpose was to train advanced professionals in marketing communication planning and management. Students should be familiar with the history, current situation, and the trends of the advertising industry in China and the world, have total marketing communication planning knowledge and ability, proper knowledge structure and practice skills, foreign language, and art design ability.

The "marketing communication" orientation embodied three teaching parts, including the basic knowledge of economics, knowledge of communications, and knowledge of advertising. In addition, two internship opportunities are available for all undergraduate students.

In 2004, the Department of Advertising began offering a Master's degree in advertising. In 2005, it expanded to offer a doctorate in mass communication with an advertising specialty.

Jinan University (JU)

College of Journalism and Communication
http://xwxy.jnu.edu.cn/

The history of advertising education can be traced back to 1984 when JU took the lead to organize an "Advertising practitioner training class" in Guangdong province. More than 40 students attended.

In 1994, an advertising major was officially founded. Since then, the system has expanded to cover the undergraduate, graduate, and doctorate disciplines with an advertising specialty, a PR specialty, and a marketing communication specialty. This is currently one of the most important sites for teaching and research in advertising in Southern China.

The advertising major trains high quality professionals in advertising planning, design, and production, with training in business and management. Students are prepared for comprehensive advertising agencies, marketing departments of power companies, the organizations of Administration of Industry and Commerce, and the advertising departments of media. There is also a "Brand and Strategic Communication Institute" related to advertising in the College of Journalism and Communication at JU.

Zhejiang University (ZU)[7]

College of Media and International Cultural
http://www.cmic.zju.edu.cn/index.php

An advertising major was created at ZU in 1993, and it began to enroll undergraduate students the next year. In 1999, ZU started enrolling graduates in its advertising specialty in the discipline of communication. Since then, ZU has trained more than 600 undergraduate and more than 100 graduate students in advertising.

The program's innovative model of education guarantees both quality and quantity of students. It trains students with cultural ability, creative ability, and communication ability. Therefore, unique skills and strategic thinking are given as much attention as possible. This innovative model fo-

---

[7] This section contributed by Xiaoyun Hu.

cuses on skill training. It includes a tutor system, forming program and research teams for undergraduate students, interacting with advertising magazines, and so on.

Shenzhen University
College of Mass Communication
http://cmc.szu.edu.cn/Article/

In 1990, the Mass Communication Department of Shenzhen University started enrolling four-year undergraduate students in an advertising major. That major now belongs to the Advertising Department of the College of Mass Communication. It enrolls undergraduate students majoring in advertising and advertising design and graduate students majoring in communication.

The mission is to cultivate professional talents in the fields of Advertising Strategies and Advertising Design. Students learn IMC, the theory and practice of advertising planning and creative, have marketing research, data analysis, creative and design, copywriting and so on. Those basic courses enable students to work in the field of advertising management, marketing, advertising regulation, advertising planning and design, and other related fields.

Research projects focus mainly on brand and advertising concerns directly related to the key issues of China's advertising industry, as well as to its social and cultural development. In recent years, the Department of Advertising has presented several comprehensive regional studies.

Shanghai University (SU)
School of Film and TV Arts & Technology
http://www.suftv.shu.edu.cn/

The advertising major was founded at SU in May 1993. It was the first advertising major in Shanghai. As of this writing, the department of Advertising has 580 undergraduate students, 45 graduate students, and two doctoral students. The department also cooperates with The World Federation of Advertisers, along with teacher and student exchange programs with University of Oklahoma, University of Tennessee, and University of Missouri, every year.

Some institutes are related to advertising research, including "China brand Institute, Shanghai Advertising Database Center and Academic Information Center." The students of the Department of Advertising won gold awards in a variety of competitions such as the One Show and the "Academy award" of the Advertising Festival for China's University students.

Shanghai Normal University
College of Humanities and Communications
http://renwen.shnu.edu.cn/

Advertising education has more than ten years' history in Shanghai Normal University. The Department of Advertising includes an advertising and photography major with advertising creative and planning, event planning and multimedia design specialties. Shanghai Normal University was also the first to establish a specialty called event planning in Mainland China. More than 400 undergraduate and graduate students are now in the Department of Advertising.

The purpose of advertising education here is to provide high quality professionals in advertising planning, design and production, business and management for comprehensive advertising agencies, marketing departments of power companies, the organizations of Administration of Industry and Commerce, advertising departments of media.

Though long-term development, the progressive teaching model that includes innovation, creative and business starting-up and skill training platforms were gradually formed. This Department facilitates the interaction between teaching and market and society. In recent years, the number of student competition winners ranks No. 1 among Shanghai's Universities. The department also has the *Research Center of China's New Advertisements* and *China Creative Industry Institute*.

Beijing Technology and Business University (BTBU)[8]
School of Communication and Art
http://yc.btbu.edu.cn/

Advertising courses began at the Beijing Technology and Business University (former Beijing Business Institute) in the early 1980s. In 1993, the first undergraduate students were enrolled in an advertising degree program. In June 1998, a Department of Advertising was established, with a marketing orientation that focused on advertising business and brand communication. Today this department includes two specialties: the advertising planning and business management specialty, and the advertising design specialty. The advertising major at BTBU was selected as a "Brand Major" by the Beijing Municipal Education Commission.

---

[8] This section was contributed by Xiang Zhang.

Najing University of Finance and Economics (NUFE)
College of Marketing and Logistics Management
http://yxwl.njue.edu.cn/

The advertising major of NUFE was founded in 1993. It is the first junior college ad major in Jiangsu province. In 1999, the major began enrolling undergraduate advertising majors from the entire country. Since that time, nearly 500 vocational college students and 600 undergraduate students have trained there. It currently has 290 undergraduate students.

In 1999, the advertising program of NUFE started training professionals especially for the Jiangsu Advertising Association. In 2004, a graduate degree majoring in marketing and advertising planning was added.

Vocational Education

Besides formal, full-time programs in Universities and Colleges, there also are vocational education programs in China. The most influential programs are Correspondence and Online advertising education.

Correspondence Advertising Education

In 1985, Changchun Radio & TV University took the lead to enroll Correspondence students majoring in advertising. It offers a 3 year vocational junior college level education.

On February 22, 1986, the China Advertising Correspondence College, founded by the CAA, held its opening ceremony. Forty-one hundred students were enrolled. The mission of this college was to train professionals in advertising account management, creative, design, and production fields which were urgently needed by advertising industry. The length of study was 3 years. The curriculum included 17 courses. Students regularly received textbooks and guidance materials. In some places, guiding sections adopt face-to-face teaching or audio-visual teaching methods.

In August 1989, the first students finished their study and received a diploma or certificate. In the following years, some universities with advertising majors also began offering correspondence advertising education.

Online advertising education

In July 2000, China's Ministry of Education issued a document aiming at supporting some Universities in starting modern long distance education via the Internet. This document gave the Universities greater autonomy in operation. China's online education witnessed rapid growth as a result.

The next year, CUC took the lead to enroll undergraduate students with a vocational college diploma. Online education involved a point system, where the length of study could be adapted to the students' schedules. Students could select courses, self-study textbooks and multimedia courseware and online resources, according to their ability and schedule.

Today, the online advertising education of Communication University of China includes vocational college education and undergraduate education. More than 300 students are enrolled every year. The length of study ranges from 2.5 years to 7 years.

The courses include introduction to advertising, advertising design, advertising psychology, advertising planning, advertising shutting, advertising media, advertising regulation and law, copywriting, and so on.

So far as is known to this author, Peking University also is enrolling undergraduate advertising students for a vocational diploma. The length of study is from 2 to 2.5 years.

Outstanding Alumni

Guoying Feng
Xiamen University: (1989)
> Chairman and founder of TEAM, a brand management agency. She also is the adjunct supervisor of advertising major graduate students for Xiamen University. TEAM was selected as one of the top 10 planning organizations and one of the top 30 local advertising agencies in comprehensive strength.

Lucy Lv
Xiamen University: (1992)
> Chairman of CC& E. Her agency has served Nice Group for 15 years, helped Nice brand to become a well-known brand in China, and helped Huawei and TCL to build brands in the international market. This agency continues to hold a top-10 position in China, according to *Campaign Brief*, for the past 6 years.

Hongbo Xia
Xiamen University: (1999)
> Vice president of advertising business for Phoenix Satellite Television Holdings Limited. He was the director of Advertising Department of China Central Television (CCTV) from 2005 to 2009. During this period, he changed the CCTV bidding model, which lead to continuous growth in ad revenue for CCTV.

Yi Wang
Communication University of China: (1993)
> Managing Director of Leo Burnett Beijing. He established W&K Communications in 2002, and worked as its Managing Director until 2008, when W&K Communications joined Leo Burnett. He provided many valuable communication services to

numerous clients, including Yili, Mengniu, Parmalat, PICC, Sinopec, Yutong Bus, etc.

Jason Zhao

Communication University of China: (1993)

> Chief Operating Officer and Executive Creative Director for Cheil Worldwide Greater China. He worked for Saatchi & Saatchi, BBDO, Lowe, D'Arcy, and Publicis. The clients that he served include Coca-Cola, P&G, HP, Microsoft, Mars, Bank of China, China Mobile, etc.

Wensheng Luan

Communication University of China: (1996)

> Brand management director of Mengniu Dairy Group. He successfully planned and executed the "Everyday 0.5 Kilo milk, make Chinese stronger" public service campaign and Olympic marketing campaigns for Mengniu Dairy Group. His "Go to Beijing in 2008" dome design received the gold award in outdoor media section in 38th The Mobius Advertising Awards.

Quan Fan

Wuhan University: (1998)

> Media planning director of GDAD, the biggest local advertising agency in China. The successful campaigns that she did include the creative media planning of the 5th Season beverage, the launch of the Accord car of Guangzhou Automobile in China's market, and the launch of Swellfun liquor.

Yong Xiao

Wuhan University: (1998)

> Vice director of the advertising business center for Guizhou News Daily Group and standing director of Guizhou Advertising Association. He has been involved with newspapers for 12 years, did much to promote changing the business model, and planned and established "Ranking list of the city cars," that has become one of the most influential promotion platforms in Guizhou Province.

Xuhua Sun

Wuhan University: (2003)

> Director of *Fengshang Week* of *Nanfang Daily*. He is in charge of advertising, marketing, and publishing. Before March 2010, he was the manager of sales teams and engaged in the business of automobile and real estate advertising for the newspaper. He received many awards from *Nanfang Daily*.

Lingbing Yu

Zhejiang University: (1998)

> Director of the marketing department of alibaba.com. He has been involved in many businesses, including household electrical appliances, apparel, communication, and E-business. In 2009, his campaign called "Alibaba-Chengxintong Partner Plan" received "China Marketing innovation award."

Jianfeng Le

Zhejiang University: (2000)

> He worked in the creative department of several 4A and famous local advertising

114

agencies, including Ogilvy China and Saatchi & Saatchi Great Wall. He received many awards, including a gold award in the Asia-Pacific Advertising Festival. He also was an adjunct lecturer at the Zhuhai Branch of the School of Beijing Normal University, and wrote a book called, *Copywriting: The Power of Words.*

Zeyi Weng
Zhejiang University: (2008)
> Copywriter in Dentsu-Top. He holds both Bachelor's and Master's Degrees from ZU. In 2009, he was one of the 10 winners of Longxi Chinese Advertising Competition.

Jing Jing
Beijing Technology and Business University: (1997)
> Executive editor of *BAZAAR Jewelry.* She did account service work in the Beijing Advertising Agency prior to establishing her own advertising agency. She also was planning director of *Harper's BAZAAR* (Chinese edition) of Trends Group.

Xiaolong Lu
Beijing Technology and Business University: (1998)
> Executive director of IMNEXT advertising agency. He was creative director of Charm Communications Inc. Over ten years he helped this agency to become one of the biggest private advertising groups and the earliest local agency to win the gold award in Asia-Pacific Festival. In 2008, he established IMNEXT.

Zhi Zhao
Beijing Technology and Business University: (1998)
> He is running a communication group named HIZONE. His awards include the copper award of China EFFIES, and he served many well known clients. HIZONE is member of China AAAA and has branches in Chengdu, Fuzhou, and Hangzhou.

Jing Li
Jilin University: (1998)
> Founder and vice executive director of a cultural communication firm, People's Posts and Telecommunications News (PPTN). She did services of corporate culture building, corporate image and brand communication for some Tele-communication companies.

Shizhou Li
Jilin University: (2003)
> Executive of the client service team for the Advertising department of China Central Television. She worked on the communication team and promotion team in the department and planned dozens of forums.

Student Opinion Study

Even though it has been more than 20 years since the first advertising education program was founded in Xiamen University, there are few surveys of student opinion. Notable is a survey conducted by Professor Shuting Zhang, from the Department of Advertising of Beijing Broadcasting Institute in 2003.

The questionnaire targeted graduate alumni majoring in advertising and advertising design working in advertising and related fields. Eleven Universities, including Xiamen University and Beijing Broadcasting Institute, participated in this survey. The questions covered basic information about these alumni, their perception of the advertising major before going to study advertising, their study processes in Universities, the essential qualities for a job, the manner of learning after graduation, and the opinions of advertising education in Universities.

After analyzing the 122 questionnaires, researchers concluded that regarding the motivation to study advertising, 83.5% respondents expressed advertising was an interesting major, and 58.2% said advertising work is challenging. Other reasons included loving advertising and being interested in it (35%), and excellent advertisements (26.3%). Meanwhile, art-related courses (38%), advertising planning (29.8%), advertising research (28.1%), and marketing (26.4%) ranked as the most useful courses to these alums. They also suggested the university should provide more courses related to marketing, media, and advertising psychology.

Besides school education, respondents thought the most useful way to learn advertising is to read professional magazines and books, view and analyze award-winning advertisements, and work in the field. Most graduate alumni thought advertising education was behind professional practice and advertising programs should interact with industry more.

Courses, Programs, Students, Faculty and Student Competitions

There have been few in-depth investigations of national advertising education over the past 20 years. In September 1996, the Academic Committee of CAA did the first national study. The questionnaire covered basic information about each program, its faculty, students, courses and textbooks. After analyzing 30 valid questionnaires, *Analysis on the current situation of advertising education in 30 Universities and suggestions* was published.

In 2003, Shuting Zhang from CUC conducted a survey of departments of journalism and communication (sample size was 144), along with 10 art departments of different universities and colleges. The questionnaire covered the basic information of advertising programs, faculty, and so on.

In the end, 111 valid questionnaires were collected.

In 2006, the Academic and Training section of CAA, *Modern Advertising* magazine, and one School of Journalism and Communication conducted a sample survey. Based on this survey, *Report of the Current Situation of China's Higher Education of Advertising* was published. In 2007, Yinhe Cui from East China Normal University wrote *Report on Current Situation of the Development of Higher Education of Advertising and Programs*. This survey covered 208 Universities and Institutes which have advertising programs. In 2008, Heshui Huang and his students from Xiamen University conducted a national survey of advertising education among 322 Universities and Institutes.

Courses

The 1996 study revealed that the curricula of most advertising programs focused on skills training. The common core courses were Introduction of Advertising, Copywriting, Basic Design, Advertising Production and Outdoor Advertising. In addition, Advertising Photography, Print Advertisement, TV Advertisement and Advertising Planning were offered. However, there were few courses related to theories such as Psychology, Communication, and Sociology, with the exception of Marketing. There were also no appropriate textbooks.

From Professor Zhang's survey in 2003, the common curriculum model was "basic courses plus core major courses and selected major courses" or "core major courses and selected major courses." The major courses include Introduction of Advertising, Advertising Planning, Copywriting, Advertising Psychology, Advertising Media, The History of Advertising, Advertising Management, Advertising Law and Regulation, Advertising Expression and Production, Case Studies, Advertising and Culture, Advertising Industry, Advertising Design, Training of Creative Thinking, Communication, Statistics, Branding, Economics, Sociology, Public Relations, Marketing, Consumer Behavior, Advertising English, Photography and filming, TV Editing, Multimedia Design, and so on.

The 2006 survey found that some Universities and Institutes offered Communication, Advertising Business and Management, Brand Planning and Management, Public Relations, Strategic Branding, Integrated Marketing Communication, New Media, and other advanced courses.

In 2007, Professor Cui's survey indicated that Introduction of Advertising, Copywriting, Marketing, Advertising Planning and Creative, and Advertising Media had been offered by the Universities and Institutes participating in this survey. Eighty-six percent of advertising programs provided Advertising Law and Professional Ethics, Marketing Research, the History of Advertising, and Public Relations. Fifty-seven percent of advertising programs offered an Advertising Psychology class.

In 2008, Professor Huang's survey found that more than half of 322 Universities and Institutes were offering Print Design, Advertising Planning, Introduction of Advertising, Communication, Advertising Creative, Advertising Media, Marketing, Advertising Management, Marketing Research, History of Advertising, Copywriting, Advertising Psychology, and Basic Advertising Design. In the curricula of most advertising programs, professional skill training courses were prominent.

Programs

The 1996 survey found 49 advertising programs that enroll undergraduates majoring in advertising. *More than half of these programs were founded in 1993 and 1994.* Most advertising programs were established in colleges or departments of liberal arts, while 44.8% of them belonged to colleges or departments of journalism. Business schools, Radio and TV schoosl of Universities, and art institutes, normal institutes, print institutes, even institutes for nationalities were also eager to establish advertising programs. These programs tended to be located in Beijing, Shanghai, and economically developed cities.

The survey in 2003 found that 71.2% of advertising programs belonged to provincial governments and 22.5% belonged to China's Ministry of Education. In addition, there were two independent colleges that were run by Universities belonging to China's Ministry of Education and private capital. There was also a private University that can enroll undergraduate students. Among these advertising programs, 38.2% belonged to colleges or departments of journalism and communication, 24.5% to departments of Chinese language and literature, 15.5% to departments of art design and 8.2% to departments of business management.

The survey in 2006 indicated that about half of advertising programs were established during the period from 2000 to 2004. After 2005, the development of advertising education was sustainable and stable. Forty-four percent of advertising programs belonged to colleges or departments of journalism and communication, and 24% to colleges or departments of art design.

The survey in 2007 found that 59 advertising programs located in colleges of journalism and communication of Universities and Institutes, 47 in art colleges, 23 in colleges of Chinese language and literature, 44 in colleges of humanity or cultural communication, 3 in colleges of management, and 3 in colleges of business. The remaining 29 programs resided in other colleges. There were 61 departments of advertising, 145 majors of advertising, and 2 colleges of advertising at that time.

The 2008 study found 234 undergraduate advertising programs and 88 vocational college programs. Among the total 322 advertising programs, 39 were located in private Universities, while 35 were located in independent colleges running by government and private capital.

Students

The 1996 survey discovered 2216 students majoring in advertising in Universities or Institutes. Most of those students were male. In the 2003 survey, 50.5% of advertising programs had 101-250 undergraduate students majoring in advertising, while 6.9% had more than 400 students; 13% of advertising programs had vocational college students and 22.9% had graduate students majoring in advertising. There were 3 doctoral advertising programs. In 2006, the average number of University and Institute students majoring in advertising was 226, growing at 11.8% per year.

Faculty

In the survey of 1996, half of the advertising programs had 6-10 full time teachers and 28.6% had no more than 5 teachers. Fully 69.8% of teachers were male. The average age of teachers was 37.3 years, 68.5% had Bachelor's degrees as a final degree, 25.9% graduated with majors in Chinese language and literature, 23.2% graduated from art design, while only 10.3% graduated with advertising majors.

In the 2003 survey, the percentage of male teachers was 56.7%. Their average age was 35 years, 37% held Master's degrees,10.3% had a Ph.D. as their final degree, 29.5% graduated with degrees in art design, 24.9% in Chinese language and literature, and only 6.5% of teachers graduated from economics or management. Sixty-sevenpercent of advertising programs had adjunct teachers. The average number of adjuncts was 4.8, about same as full-time teachers.

In 2006, the average number of teachers was 11. Among these teachers, 38% were 20-29 years old, 41% had Master's degrees, and 9.8% had a Ph.D. In the 2007 study, the lack of teachers remained a problem. Among 208 Universities and Institutes, only 63 teachers were professors with "advertising" in their title. More than 60% of advertising programs had no "professor."

In 2008, the percentage of male teachers was 56.17%. The average age of teachers was 37, while 48% had Master's degree and 10.93% had a Ph.D. Of those, 32.8% of teachers graduated from art design programs, 24.6% from Chinese language and literature, and 21.6% graduated from journalism and communication (includes 13.6% of teachers graduated from advertising majors).

Student Competitions

The most famous awards are the "Times Advertisement Golden Calf Prize," the "Academic Award of Advertising Festival for Chinas' Universities' Students," the "Advertising Competition for Chinas' Universities' Students," and the "One Show China Young Creative Competition & Workshop." Each is discussed below.

Times Advertisement Golden Calf Prize

This prize was established in 1992, targeting Chinese students majoring in advertising all over the world. In 2001, the competition expanded to Mainland China, and Award Ceremonies were held in Taiwan and Mainland China simultaneously. In the following years, the type of competition and the range of participants gradually expanded. In addition, the *First Advertising Education Forum of Both Sides of the Straits* was held anda scholarship was funded.

Academic Award of Advertising Festival
for China's University Students

This award, established by CAA in 1999, aimed at college students and professionals with no more than three-years' work experience. This festival is held every two years. The competition involves a creative campaign for China's most famous companies. This competition has covered more than 500 Universities and Institutes, involving 270,000 students. In 2007, Adman magazine began hosting this festival.

Advertising Competition for China's University Students

This competition was established by the Department of Higher Education of the Ministry of Education of the People's Republic of China in May 2005, targeting all students in higher education programs. This festival is held every two years. The competition includes print, TV, radio, Internet advertisements, and advertising planning.

One Show China Young Creative Competition & Workshop

The ONE CLUB was founded in 1975. In 2001, ONE CLUB started to hold an advertising forum and *One Show Young Creative Competition & Workshop* in China. In September 2005, ONE CLUB set up a branch in China and established *One Show China Young Creative Competition & Workshop*. China's partner is Communication University of China.

Concluding Comments

China's advertising education began in the early 1920's as a single course in the departments of journalism of some Universities or Colleges. From the late 1960s to 1978, for about ten years, advertising education stagnated. After executing the policy of reform, opening to the world, along with the recovery of China's advertising industry, independent advertising programs were founded and began to enroll undergraduate students.

From about 1992, advertising education in China grew rapidly. At that time an advertising system that covered vocational, bachelor's degree, second bachelor's degree, master's degree, and doctoral degree levels was formed. The system also included programs run by government and private capital, and encompassed professional and vocational programs.

Today there are three different models of advertising education. One model is represented by Xiamen University, where the advertising program is centered in journalism and communication. A second model is represented by Communication University of China, which uses a combination of journalism and communication, business management, and art design. The third model is represented by Academy of Arts & Design of Tsinghua University, which involves only advertising design.

The government is the dominant factor affecting advertising education in China. The development of advertising education is also tightly related to the development of the advertising industry, and with education in journalism and communication. The advertising specialty is still a third-level specialty under the Journalism and Communication disciplines.

Associations related to advertising played, and continue to play, an essential role in the field's development. With the evolution of China's socialist market economy system, more and more business and management courses are being offered in advertising programs. With the rapid growth of China's economy, China's advertising education will become an important part of the world's advertising education system.

References

Chen, G (2010). *The contemporary history of China's advertising: 1979-1991*. Peking University Press.

China Advertising Association (1989). *China Advertising Yearbook 1988*. Xinhua Publishing House.

China Advertising Association (1992). *China Advertising Yearbook 1989-1991*. Xinhua Publishing House.

China Advertising Association (1999). *China Advertising Yearbook 1998*. Xinhua Publishing House.

China Advertising Association (2009). *Big events of China's Advertising Industry in the past years*. China Industrial and Commercial Press.

Cui, Y, H (2007). Report on Current Situation of the Development of Higher Education of Advertising and Programs. *Modern Advertising*, 2007 (6).

Ding, Y, P (1979). Restoring Reputation for Advertising. *Wen Hui Bao*, January 12, 1979.

Huang, H, S (2008). Report on the Current Situation of Advertising Education. *Advertising Research*, 2006 (6).

International Advertising Magazine, School of Advertising of Beijing Broadcasting Institute, and International Advertising Institute (2004). *Accelerated Growth of China's Advertising Industry: 1979-2003*. Huaxia Publishing House.

Journalism Research Institute of Chinese Academy of Social Sciences (1984). *China Journalism Yearbook 1984*. People Daily Press.

Journalism Research Institute of Chinese Academy of Social Sciences (1985). *China Journalism Yearbook 1985*. People Daily Press.

Long, W., Ren, Y, Z., Wang, X, A., He, L. and Wu, H (2010). *Selected works of the history of journalism education in the period of the Republic of China*. Peking University Press.

Modern Advertising magazine, School of Journalism and Communication of Renmin University of China (2007). Report of the Current Situation of China's Higher Education of Advertising. *Modern Advertising*, 2007 (1).

Shuting Zhang (2005). *Advertising Education and Brand Position*. Communication University of China Press.

The Advertising Specialty Education Committee of Chinese Association of Higher Education (2009). *Newsletter of ASEC*. December 6, 2009.

The editor board of China Radio and TV yearbook (2009). *China Radio and TV yearbook 2009*. China Radio and TV yearbook publisher.

The introduction of China Advertising Association. *http://xh.cnadtop.com/about/about.html#*.

The introduction of China Advertising Association of Commerce. *http://baike.baidu.com/view/1575369.htm?fr=ala0_1*.

The introduction of Times advertisement golden calf prize. *http://www.ad-young.com/about.asp#*.

The introduction of Advertising Competition for China's Universities' Students. *http://www.sun-ada.net/html/history_file.html*.

The introduction of ONE CLUB. *http://www.oneshow.com.cn/*.

Advertising Education in India

Mukesh Bhargava
Oakland University, USA

Alan D'Souza
Mudra Institute of Communication Research, India

Introduction

Advertising education in India faces multiple contradictory demands on the curriculum and skill development. Some of the issues include resolving the balance between managing communication budgets, as a part of a global network, versus creating "local" brand identities and communications; reaching existing markets in urban areas, versus learning/experimenting with creating new markets in rural areas; managing commercial versus social communication programs, and working with data/facts, versus dealing softer issues (Bijapurkar 2007; Singhal and Rogers 2001; Prahalad 2010).

Advertising education in India has its foundation in mass communication, with most of the development taking place in the post-independence (1947) era. India has been the site for a number of ambitious mass communication experiments. Among these was the use of television programs to rural villages via satellite, diffusion of innovation of high yielding varieties of corn, and ongoing campaigns on family planning (Chander and Karnik 1976; Rogers 2003). Government sponsored media, such as the All India Radio and Doordarshan[9] (television), have over 90 percent reach and are among the largest global broadcasting networks.

While the "social" function of mass communication has a long history, the "commercial" or "advertising" function of mass communication has gained momentum in the last two decades. Advertising expenditures in India have increased from $138 million in the mid-1980's to an estimated $5.1 billion by 2010 (Leff and Farley 1980; Balsara and Agnihotri 2010). The opening of the economy to global competition led to a number of multinational brands competing with local companies in the Indian market place. The size of the market, coupled with strong economic growth, has led to double-digit growth in most industries (Indian Brand Equity Foundation 2010). The result has been a rapid and profound change in the prac-

---

[9] Doordarshan is the public television broadcaster, by the Government of India.

tice of advertising in India. Advertising education has witnessed a similar growth in demand for skilled personnel.

Surprisingly, there is a paucity of research on the advertising education sector in India. Given the rapid expansion of the number of programs in recent years, this is an important gap that this chapter begins to address. We first provide a brief review of the advertising market, along with some of the recent changes that provide the drivers to growth. This is followed by a description of a advertising programs and a critique of various facets of the programs. The chapter ends with recommendations about emerging issues of advertising education.

Brief History of Advertising in India

The history of modern advertising in India can be traced to the creation of B. Dattaram and Co., the first advertising agency of Indian origin, in 1905. Today, it remains the oldest functioning Indian advertising agency. Subsequently, the 1900's saw the creation of more advertising agencies, both national and foreign. Initially, most of the advertising agencies, such as Lintas, J Walter Thompson, and McCann Ericsson, were founded to service multinational brands such as Levers, General Motors, Coke, etc. Many of these were headed by expatriates who recruited Indians and taught them the skills of the trade. Thus advertising education, in that sense, already began pre-independence through "on the job learning" (Chaudhri 2007).

At that time most advertising agencies were not full-service agencies, but merely brokers for advertising space. In 1934, Bobby Sista, one of the well-known names in Indian advertising, set up his own full-service Indian advertising agency, called Sistas Advertising and Publicity services. Later, many advertising professionals broke away from the foreign advertising agencies they were working with to set up ad agencies of their own. Notable among them were Chaitra, Ulka and Trikaya Advertising. The coming of age of Indian advertising was formalized by the creation of the Advertising Club, Mumbai, by some of the well-known professionals in advertising, media and marketing organizations in 1954.

The 1960's saw an upsurge of creativity, inspired by the transformation of advertising at the international level, into a more modern and scientific approach. Al Reis and Jack Trout brought in new concepts, such as positioning, as opposed to the Unique Selling Proposition (USP), which led to a completely new approach to building brands. ITC's launch of the "Made for Each Other" campaign for Wills cigarette in 1963, Lifebuoy's memorable "Tandurusti ki Raksha" campaign in 1964, and Amul's "Utterly, Butterly Delicious" campaign for Amul butter (Figure 10-1) are notable milestones during that era and have continued to this day.

Figure 10-1: Recent Amul outdoor advertisement
(Originally posted to Flickr as Butter Nano! Mumbai, India.JPG)

The 1970's saw a further boost in advertising with the availability of advertising research. Until then, research played a minimal role in the advertising process. For example, the data on consumer reading habits were available for the first time through National Readership surveys. This helped in the media planning process. Further excitement spread through the industry when the first television commercial hit the screen in 1978. However, it was in the 1980's that, coinciding with the Asian Games, Doordarshan introduced color transmission, and Bombay Dyeing became the first color television commercial.

The 1990's were marked by a media explosion. Cable and satellite television grew, print media became niche, and the Internet explosion began in India. The economy was deregulated and led to the entry of many multinational organizations competing with domestic brands. With the relaxation of foreign ownership, domestic agencies were taken over by global partners like Chaitra Advertising (now Leo-Burnett), Ulka Advertising (now FCB-Ulka) and Trikaya Advertising (now Grey Advertising). Today, the top 20 agencies are either a part of or have strategic global partnerships (Patwardhan, Patwardhan and Vadavada-Oza 2009).

In addition to the commercial advertising agencies, the Directorate of Advertising & Visual Publicity (DAVP) is the model agency to undertake multi-media advertising and publicity for various ministries and departments of the Government of India for over six decades. As a service agency, it communicates at grass roots levels on behalf of various central government ministries. Some of DAVP's advertising and publicity are campaigns on rural development programs, health and family welfare, AIDS awareness, road safety and energy conservation among others.

The demands on advertising have increased considerably, with stakes in building brands becoming higher, thanks to increasing competition, globalization, proliferation of media channels etc. Spending on advertising has also increased and stands at around $5,100 million today. While this may be small in comparison to other markets, it is one of the fastest growing advertising regions in the world. The demand for good advertising professionals in every area, therefore, is increasing, be it account planning, creative, or media. Coupled with the changes in the advertising market, numerous challenges shape the skills that professionals need to operate in this environment.

Changes in the Advertising Market

The Indian marketplace presents several unique challenges that make advertising decisions complex. The sheer size of the market (with an estimated population of over 1 billion) and over 22 official languages lead to an increasingly heterogeneous marketplace (*Statistical Pocket Book of India 2008*). The development of rural and urban markets, and the interplay of a variety of media ranging from organized media such as newspapers to video vans, wall posters, point-of-purchase materials, etc. (Figure 10-2), are facets that advertisers have to deal with on an ongoing basis (Bhatia 2007; Kashyap and Raut 2007).

One of the major drivers of advertising is the size and growth of the Indian market. India's retail market, the fifth largest globally, has been ranked as the most attractive emerging market by AT Kearny. The passenger car segment is expected to grow from 1.89 million units to 3.75 million units by 2014. Fast-moving consumer goods (FMCG) are poised to grow by 10-12 percent over the next decade, to reach $74 billion by 2018 (India Brand Equity Foundation 2010). All of these industries require active advertising support, both by multinationals entering the market as well as existing domestic brands.

Figure 10-2: Street view of outdoor and wall posters

While past advertising support simply meant changes in the language of the advertising, the emerging competition requires applying knowledge and skills to the current market conditions. Many of the local brands (such as Nirma and Rasna) have successfully competed with the multinational brands. Other local brands that were largely regional have adopted new packaging, advertising, and retail support to become successful national brands (e.g., Pan Parag, Lijjat Papads etc.), an issue of strategic importance globally (Kumar 2003; Eckhardt 2005).

Companies like Nestle and GlaxoSmithkline Consumer Healthcare (GSK) are taking a different route and launching products specifically for rural markets. GSK (maker of Horlicks), for instance, launched Asha, a low-cost variant (40 per cent cheaper than Horlicks) for rural markets only. Nestle recently launched Rupee 2 and Rupee 4 products (approximately 5 cents and 10 cents) -- Maggi Masala-ae-Magic and Maggi Rasile Chow products, which will be first marketed in areas with low purchasing power.

Finally, there has been a dramatic shift in media use with budgets moving from print (40%) to television (46%) (Balsara & Agnihotri 2010). Traditional print media have dominated the industry. Given the diversity of the country in terms of the number of states and regional languages and dialects, India has a proliferation of newspapers and magazines that serve different parts of the country. It is estimated there are 635 daily and 9364 other periodicity English newspapers, along with 7453 daily and 61, 870 other periodicity Indian language newspapers (*Statistical Pocket Book of India 2008*). The penetration of print in India in the urban areas is 42.6% and in rural areas 15.4%, as per the Indian Readership Survey (IRS). Indian print media and advertising have come a long way. Although the first Indian advertising was primitive in nature, it gradually created a new breed of advertising professionals, like artists, illustrators, copywriters, visualizers, photographers, etc.

While the first television channel, Doordarshan, was Government owned and run, it is only with the opening of the private satellite channels, with Zee Telefilms being the first entrant, that television really took off. Today, thanks to the opening of the skies and the technological advancements in this area, television reach of all India is estimated by the IRS as 46.3%, and satellite as 26.1%. This development requires skill in programming, content creation and business management.

All of these factors, combined, have led to the growth of the advertising business and the concomitant demand for people to manage the business. We now provide a review of the "supply side" of advertising education in the following sections.

Advertising Education in India

The University System

Education in India is governed by the Ministry of Human Resource Development, Government of India. This is the policy-making body which has set up several Institutions, such as The Central Board of Secondary Education, Council of Indian School Certificate Examination, University Grants Commission (UGC), All India Council of Technical Education, etc., to manage School, Graduate and Post Graduate Education in India. There were 355 Universities and 18,064 colleges, with an enrollment of 11.02 million students (UGC 2005). Of these, 45.1% were enrolled in arts program and 18.0% in commerce/management courses.

Advertising education in India so far has been seen as a subset of education in mass communication. Mass communication education in India is defined as education in journalism, advertising, and public relations, the prime focus being on journalism. Though journalism education had its beginnings in the early 1940's, it was only in the 1960's and 1970's that several Indian universities began teaching journalism classes. In addition it was during these two decades that course content, degree nomenclature, and departmental reorganization of faculties in universities underwent drastic changes. The global strides in curricula, changes in areas to be covered, and practical needs of the national and mass media prompted the universities to affect wide ranging changes in mass communication education.

In the first instance, several students who had gone to the U.K., U.S.A., and Canada for higher education in journalism, on their return to India, suggested several curriculum revisions. Some American universities also offered collaboration for the advancement of Journalism programs to their Indian counterparts. Osmania University at Hyderabad and Nagpur University are two good examples of such programs.

The rapid expansion of the media industry in India prompted the inclusion of advertising and public relations as an integral part of mass communication courses, both at the undergraduate and graduate level. The concept of mass communication education was widened to include other fields, and not only the study of journalism. Media and economics, politics, sociology, management and administration began to be recognized as important areas of mass communication education.

This led to departments of journalism being renamed after the mid-seventies to Departments of Journalism and Mass Communication, Departments of Communication, and Departments of Journalism and Communication. This trend was started by Bangalore University and soon Osmania, Mysore, Banaras, and many others followed. Now more than 69 Universities and 98 other institutions teach this subject at the undergraduate and graduate levels (Table 10-1)[10].

Apart from these institutions, in 2007 *Outlook* (a weekly magazine) and CFore (a market research firm) conducted a survey to rank the top 10 mass communications institutes in India. To rank the colleges, the *Outlook*-C Fore researchers asked faculty and professionals to rank the Institutes on a 10 point scale against 4 parameters: faculty, pedagogic systems, infrastructure, and placements. They then multiplied the average ratings by weight in order to rank the top 10 mass communication institutes in India (*see* Table 10-2).

These programs show a variety of support raging from government sponsorship to those supported by advertising and media companies. The best mass communication colleges are also spread over various cities in India.

---

[10] There are multiple but conflicting directories of various mass communication programs now available online. Unfortunately, these do not report the dates or source of the data. In compiling this table, we consulted the National Network of Education (State directories); Indiaedu and the websites of various universities.

State	Number of Universities	Other Institutions	Diploma	Undergraduate	Graduate
Andhra Pradesh	7	8	R	R	R
Arunachal Pradesh	1		R		
Assam	3	1	R	R	R
Chattisgarh	1			R	R
Delhi	3	28	R	R	R
Goa	1			R	
Gujarat	3	5	R	R	R
Haryana	4	2	R		R
Himachal Pradesh	1	1	R	R	
Jaharkhand	1				R
Jammu and Kashmir	1	1	R		R
Karnataka	5	4	R	R	R
Kerela	2	2	R		R
Madhya Pradesh	4	2		R	R
Maharahtra	6	18	R	R	R
Orissa	4	3	R		R
Meghalaya	1				R
Punjab	4	2	R	R	R
Podicherry	1				R
Rajasthan	2	1	R		R
Tamil Nadu	2	5	R	R	R
Tripura	1			R	
West Bengal	4	4	R	R	R
Uttar Pradesh	6	9	R	R	R
Uttarachal Pradesh	1	2	R		R
Total	69	98			

Table 10-1: Statewise Availability of Program in
Journalism/Mass Communication by Academic levels

Name of Institution and Website	Courses Offered
Indian Institute of Mass Communication, New Delhi http://www.iimc.nic.in/index1.html	Post-graduate Diploma in Journalism (English and Hindi), Radio & Television Journalism and Advertising & Public Relations. Publishes a research journal, Communicator.

Xavier Institute of Communication, Mumbai, Maharashtra http://www.xaviercomm.org/home/default.htm	Journalism & Mass Communication, Public Relations & Corporate Communications, Advertising & Marketing, Digital Animation and Television & Video Production.
International School of Business and Media (ISB&M), Kolkata, Pune, Bangalore and Noida http://www.isbm.edu.in/isbm.htm	Undergraduate and Postgraduate programs in Business Management, Media management, Advertisement, Public Relations, Event and Corporate Communication, TV & Radio production, Broadcast and Journalism
Symbiosis Institute of Mass Communication, Pune, Maharashtra http://www.simc.edu/	MBA in Communication Management (Advertising, Public Relations. Masters in Mass Communication (Journalism and T.V and Radio Production)
Asian College of Journalism, Chennai, Tamilnadu http://www.asianmedia.org/index.asp	The Master's Degree course includes reporting, writing, and editing, modern issues in journalism, history of the media, law of media.
Mudra Institute of Communications, Ahmedabad, Gujarat http://www.mica-india.net/	Executive Diploma Program in Media Management. Certificate Program in Managing Integrated Media, Retail Communications, Crafting Creative Communication and Visual Merchandising. Post Graduate Program in Communications Management and Entrepreneurship.
Film and Television Institute of India, Pune, Maharashtra http://www.ftiindia.com/index.html	Direction, Acting, Cinematography, Art Direction and Production Design. Audiography, Animation and Computer Graphics, Editing, Feature Film Screenplay Writing.
AJ Kidwai Mass Communication Research Centre, Jamia, New Delhi http://ajkmcrc.org/#	Ph.D. and M.A. in Mass Communication. Post Graduate Diploma in Development Communication, Journalism and Broadcast System Maintenance.
Manorama School of Communication, Kottayam, Kerela http://www.manoramajschool.com/index.htm	Post Graduate Diploma in Journalism
Indian Institute of Journalism and New Media, Bangalore, Karnataka http://www.iijnm.org/overview.html	The Post-graduate programs offer courses on Reporting and Writing for Radio and Television, Ethical and Legal Issues in Journalism, Advanced Media Concentration and Business and Financial Reporting.
Times Center of Media and Management Studies, New Delhi http://www.tcms.in/index.html	Post-Graduate Diploma in Business Journalism

Table 10-2: Details of the Leading Mass Communication programs (2007)

If one were to take a look at the courses offered by these institutes of communication, we can classify them broadly into the following categories:

Category 1: Institutes with pure Journalism as a thrust area, such as Asian College of Journalism, Chennai and Times School of Journalism, New Delhi.

Category 2: Hybrid Institutes with Courses in Journalism and Mass Communication, Public Relations and Corporate Communications, Advertising and Marketing Digital Animation etc such as Xavier Institute of Communication, Mumbai and Symbiosis Institute of Mass Communication, Pune.

Category 3: Vocational Institutes offering courses in Acting, Direction, Cinematography, Art Direction, Audiography, Animation, and Computer Graphics, such as the Film and Television Institute in Pune.

Category 4: Pure Advertising schools in Management offering courses in Account Planning, Media Planning, Market Research such as the Mudra Institute of Communications, Ahmedabad (MICA).

Category 1 and category 2 are the most prevalent types, and category 3 and 4 the least prevalent.

The early sixties saw the emergence of Management Education in India. The Indian Institutes of Management (IIM's) were created to cater to the needs of industry for managers to manage various sectors of business. Recognizing that the advertising sector, too, was emerging as an important domain, the Business Schools introduced Advertising Management as an "elective" course in the second year of the 2-year post-graduate program in management.

Typically this course gave a broad overview of advertising from a manager's perspective and was run over 30 classroom sessions of 90 minute durations each. Today the over 2500 Business Schools in the country offer this elective course in advertising as part of their regular curriculum. Assuming on average that around 30 students opt for this course, about 75,000 students are being exposed to advertising annually as part of their MBA program.

If one were to consider where the advertising industry gets its intake of professionals, one could safely conclude that most of the professionals who get into the Account Management or Account Planning and Media Planning streams come from Institutes such as MICA, or the typical Business Schools. Similarly, those in the creative function come from the Art Schools, such as the J. J. School of Fine Arts, Mumbai, the National Institute of Design, Ahmedabad, and the Baroda School of Fine Arts, Baroda.

Curriculum

Recognizing the importance of mass communication education in the country and the need for a uniform system across all Universities, UGC appointed a curriculum development committee in October 2000, consisting of senior professors in mass communication and journalism from various leading Institutions across the country. This group, under the chairmanship of Professor M.R. Dua, came up with a model curriculum for the B.A.

(Honors) (Table 10-3), as well as one for the M.A. (Honors) degree in mass communication (Table 10-4).

First Year:
        Paper 1 Introduction to Mass Communication
        Paper 2 Reporting and Editing -1
        Paper 3 Writing for Mass Media
        Paper 4 Indian Government and Politics and International Relations
        Paper 5 Computer Applications for Mass Media

Second Year.
        Paper 6 Introduction to Audio Visual Media
        Paper 7 Reporting and Editing -2
        Paper 8 Advertising
        Paper 9 Public Relations/Corporate Communications
        Paper 10 Economic Development and Planning in India

Third Year:
        Paper 11 Reporting and Editing-3
        Paper 12 Photo-Journalism
        Paper 13 Design and Graphics
        Paper 14 Indian Constitution and Media Law
        Paper 15 Developmental Communication

Table 10-3: Recommended Course Curricula –
B.A. (Honors) Mass Communication

First Semester
- Principles of Mass Communication
- Development of Media
- Print Media-1 (Reporting and Editing)
- Electronic Media (Radio and Television)
- Advertising and Public Relations/ Corporate Communications

Second Semester
- Development Communication
- Communication Research
- Media Law and Ethics
- International Communication
- Media Management

Third Semester
- Print Media 2
- Radio
- Television
- Advertising
- Public Relations/Corporate Communications.

Fourth Semester
- New Media Applications
- Inter-Cultural Communication
- Elective course
- Dissertation
- Attachment/placement

Table 10-4: Recommended Course Curricula –
M.A. (Honors) Mass Communication (2 Year Program)

Faculty Resources

Faculty to teach the courses in the schools outlined above come from three sources.

1. Pure Academicians. These faculty normally come with a PhD. degree in the relevant stream, be it Journalism, Mass Communication, Advertising or Public Relations. They find jobs in the typical University framework or in private schools.
2. Vocational Teachers. These are highly qualified technical people who teach the crafts of Communication, such as Photography, Video Filming, Editing, Animation etc. They teach primarily in the vocational institutes.
3. Industry Professionals. These normally are employed as Adjunct Faculty or Visiting Faculty in their respective areas of specialization. They work on a part-time basis and are appreciated by students for the practical aspects they bring into the classroom.

There is a shortage of qualified faculty, especially among the smaller and lesser known programs. To the best of our knowledge, there are no programs geared to address the manpower needs of the industry in India.

As of now the research output in India has not risen to international standards in the advertising area. However, an increasing emphasis is now being given to research in most of the communication schools. Faculty are encouraged to write cases and present papers at national and international conferences. Research journals are being produced by schools, such as MI-CA, to add to the body of original work being produced in the country. MICA also has set up an Institution called MICORE, specifically devoted to Research work.

Advertising Literature

Until recently most advertising books that were prescribed to students were authored by foreign authors. However, several advertising books by Indian authors have emerged. These books have the advantage of citing relevant Indian cases and students are better able to relate them to the Indian context. One of the pioneers in this area was Professor Subroto Sengupta, an industry professional who moved into academics in the later part of his life. A list of the textbooks in advertising by Indian authors which currently find favor with different schools in mass communication are listed in Table 10-5.

Batra, Rajeev (2008). *Advertising Management* (5th Edition). Singapore: Pearson Education (Singapore) Private Ltd.

Bhatia, T.K. (2007). *Advertising and Marketing in Rural India* (Second Edition). Noida, India: MacMillan Publishers India Limited.

Chaudhuri, Arun (2007). *Indian Advertising: 1780-1950 AD*. New Delhi: Tata McGraw Hill.

Chunawalla, S.A. (2006). *Foundations of Advertising: Theory and Practice*. Himalaya Publishing House: Mumbai, India.

Imam, Syed (2002). *The Making of Advertising: Gleanings from Subhas Ghosal*. Noida, India: Macmillan Publishers India.

Jain, Gautam Raj and Raunika Ahluwalia (2008). *Marketing Communications Industry: Entrepreneurial Case Studies*. Thousand Oaks, California: Sage Publications Inc.

Kashyap, Pradeep and Siddharth Raut (2007). *The Rural Marketing Book*. New Delhi: Biztantra.

Manedra Mohan (1989). *Advertising Management: Concepts and Cases*. New Delhi, India: Tata McGraw-Hill Publishing.

Mathur, U.C. (2002). *Advertising Management : Text and Cases*. Delhi, India: New Age International Private Limited.

Rangenekar, Sharif D. (2004). *Realizing Brand India*. New Delhi, India: Rupa and Company.

Shah, Kruti and Alan D'Souza (2009). *Advertising and Promotions: An IMC Perspective*. New Delhi, India: Tata McGraw-Hill Publishing.

Singh, Raguvir and Sangeeta Sharma (2003). *Advertising: Planning and Implementation*. New Delhi, India: Prentice Hall India.

Tellis, Gerard J. (2003). *Effective Advertising: Understanding When, How and How Advertising Works*. Thousand Oaks, California: Sage Publications Inc.

Valladares, June A. (2000). *The Craft of Copywriting*. Thousand Oaks, California: Sage Publications Inc.

Vilanilam John V. and A.K.Varghese (2004). *Advertising Basics: A Resource Guide for Beginners*. Thousand Oaks, California: Sage Publications Inc.

Table 10-5: Textbooks by Indian Authors

A limited number of journals provide outlets for advertising research in India. Some examples are the *Journal of Creative Communication* (MICA), *The Communicator* (IIMC, Delhi) and *Vikalpa* (IIMA). Many of the faculty members in the leading institutes publish in the leading international academic journals.

Over the years, several magazines on Indian advertising have emerged and provide information about the industry. Prominent among them are *The Brand Reporter, Impact, Pitch, Brand Equity, 4 P's*, etc. The advertising business has led to the development of some good professional websites catering to advertising professionals. These websites provide current information on industry happenings, creative work, comments on campaigns, etc. Prominent among them are www.agencyfaqs.com, www.magindia.com, www.exchange4media.com, and www.indiantelevision.com.

Advertising Industry/Academics Interaction

The advertising industry has long felt the need to contribute to the academic field, and this is being done in several ways. Industry professionals go as visiting faculty to teach in various mass communication schools across the country. They also employ graduates from these Institutions and offer them internships.

The Advertising Clubs across the country conduct various kinds of programs for advertising professionals, thus helping them keep their knowledge and skills updated constantly. Very often, prominent advertising professionals and academicians from abroad are invited to participate. The advertising industry also offers consultancy projects to faculty of various schools. Sometimes even students get engaged in this activity.

Some advertising agencies have invested financial and other resources in setting up their own advertising schools. Mudra Communications Ltd., one of the large advertising agencies in the country, has set up Institutions like MICA and MICORE. Lintas has set up a school called Northpoint at

Khandala, on the Mumbai-Pune Highway, primarily to train media professionals.

Conclusion and Recommendations

In completing the research for this chapter, it became evident that there is very little systematic and verifiable information about advertising education currently. The information from government sources is outdated by at least five years and is often at the aggregate level. With the mushrooming of academic institutions created by the private sector, this gap becomes even more critical. It is clear that a systematic and regular effort at collecting data about existing programs, student enrollment, faculty and productivity and placement would provide a foundation for developing policy issues in the future.

In a recent review of advertising education in Australia, Kerr, Waller, and Patti (2009) identify a number of critical issues which can be applied to the Indian context. Among these are defining the role of advertising, funding, program choices, faculty workload, accreditation, and research. We believe that an accrediting body could be instrumental in developing an agenda for the appropriate development of advertising education.

The Accrediting Council on Education in Journalism and Mass Communication (ACEJMC), American Advertising Federation, and the American Academy of Advertising provide templates that could be modified for the Indian context. Working with local advertising clubs, both in India and Asia (e.g., Asian Federation of Advertising Association), would ensure that the appropriate issues are developed and addressed.

With exciting development in a variety of sectors such as retail, telecommunication, FMCG and consumer durables, advertising is poised to play a critical role in the economic development in India. Patwardhan, Patwardhan, and Vasavada-Oza (2009) provide a theme that has become critical – the need for Indianization. Historically, advertising executives tended to be "English" educated, with more comfort and knowledge about the western world than the Indian environment. It is encouraging to see that the leading advertising agencies, such as McCann India and JWT India, have now developed indigenous proprietary tools for planning. Clearly this limitation of knowledge about the "Indian customer" should be addressed and form a part of the core curriculum.

References

Balsara, S. & Agnihotri, A. (2010). *Road to recovery*. 7th Annual Pitch Madison Media Advertising Outlook accessed on May 12, 2010, at http://www.pitchonnet.com/Pitch MadisonMediaAdvertisingOutlook/Outlook-2010-Intro.asp.

Bijapurkar, R. (2007). *Winning in the Indian market: Understanding the transformation of consumer India*. Singapore: John Wiley & Sons (Asia) Private Ltd.

Bhatia, T.K. (2007). *Advertising and Marketing in Rural India* (Second Edition). Noida, India: MacMillan Publishers India Limited.

Chaudhuri, Arun (2007). *Indian Advertising: 1780-1950 AD*. New Delhi: Tata McGraw Hill.

Chander, R. & Karnik K. (1976). *Planning for satellite broadcasting: The Indian instructional television experiment*. Paris: UNESCO Press.

Eckhardt, G.M. (2005), "Local branding in a foreign product category in an emerging market," *Journal of International Marketing*, 12 (4), 57-79.

India Brand Equity Foundation (2010). *Quick Facts*. Accessed on May 20, 2010, at http://www.ibef.org/resource/quickfacts.aspx

Kashyap, P. & Raut, S. (2007). *The Rural Marketing Book*. New Delhi: Biztantra.

Kerr, G.F., Waller, D. & Patti, C. (2009), "Advertising education in Australia: Looking back to the future," *Journal of Marketing Education*, 31 (3), 264-74.

Kumar, S.R. (2003), "Branding strategies in a changing market environment (Indian context)," *Journal of Brand Management*, 11(1), 48-62.

Leff, N.H. & Farley, J.U. (1980). Advertising expenditures in the developing world. *Journal of International Business Studies* 11 (2), 67-79.

Patwardhan, P., Patwardhan H. & Vasavada-Oza, H. (2009), "Insight on account planning: A view from the Indian ad industry," *Journal of Current Issues and Research in Advertising*, 31 (2), 105-21.

Prahalad, C.K. (2010). *Fortune at the bottom of the pyramid. Eradicating poverty through profits*. (5th Edition). Upper Saddle, New Jersey: Wharton School Publishing.

Rogers, E. M. (2003). *Diffusion of innovations* (5th ed.). New York: Free Press.

Singhal, A., & Rogers, E. M. (2001). *India's communication revolution: From bullock carts to cyber marts*. New Delhi: Sage.

University Grants Commission (2005). *Annual Report*. Extracted on May 10, 2010. http://www.ugc.ac.in/pub/index.html#report

Advertising Education in Japan

Kazue Shimamura
Waseda University, Japan

Janusz Buda
Waseda University, Japan

Preface

From 2001 to 2002 one of the authors (Shimamura) spent a sabbatical year at the Department of Advertising of the University of Texas at Austin, visiting similar departments at other universities and interviewing faculty members. As a teacher of advertising studies at a Japanese university, Shimamura was particularly interested in the existence of departments of advertising providing education for students wishing to establish careers in the advertising industry.

Hitherto, very few Japanese universities, especially at the faculty level, have offered education or designed curricula to facilitate career opportunities in specific professions. Medical schools for students aiming to become doctors, or universities of education for those wishing to become teachers, are exceptions to this general tendency.

In recent years, *manga* (graphic novels) and *anime* (animated movies) have become world-wide symbols of modern Japanese culture. With the growth in the number of fans of these genres has come a growth in the number of people considering careers in these fields. The establishment of departments of *manga* and animation in some universities (mostly those specializing in art) has attracted media attention, but this trend has not extended to most Japanese universities. The creation of new departments in fields popular among young people, and the establishment of specialized departments linked to specific professions, is more evident in vocational colleges than universities.

Conversely, it would appear that a significant number of universities in not only the United States, but also in Asian nations such as China, Korea, and Taiwan, include departments of advertising. Why is it that Japanese universities have not created similar departments, and what kind of advertising education are those universities providing?

Some of the largest and most successful advertising agencies in the world are based in Japan. It is, therefore, not surprising that many Japanese students aspire to careers in the advertising industry. The following study examines the education such students are offered in Japanese universities and the characteristics of advertising education in Japan from a historical, contemporary and future perspective.

Advertising-related Courses in Universities

The Nikkei Advertising Research Institute 2009 Survey

In 2009, the Nikkei Advertising Research Institute conducted its first "Survey of Advertising-related Courses in Universities" in three years. This survey had been conducted annually from 1989 to 2006. No official explanation was given for the two-year hiatus, but it may be surmised that the recession in the Japanese advertising and mass-communication industries had an adverse effect on the budget of the Research Institute and the *Nihon Keizai (Nikkei) Shimbun,* with which it is closely associated.

In the years prior to this temporary suspension, the survey attempted to identify the extent to which advertising-related subjects were taught in Japanese universities by focusing on three areas:

1. Courses with advertising as their main subject.

2. Seminars or practicums with advertising as their main subject.

3. Courses that included advertising among other topics.

The much simpler survey of 2009 abandoned these three categories, listing only the titles and instructors of advertising-related courses, the names of the undergraduate and postgraduate faculties of the universities offering them, and brief summaries of course content.

This survey was far from comprehensive and did not encompass all universities in Japan. Consequently the number of courses listed cannot be taken as a precise indicator of the status of advertising education in Japan.[11] However, if supplementary data, such as course instructor membership of academic associations, and anecdotal network information, are taken into

---

[11] According to Ministry of Education, Culture, Sports, Science and Technology statistics for 2009, there were 773 four-year universities in Japan (86 national, 58 public, and 595 private) and 406 two-year colleges (2 national, 26 public, and 378 private).

account, a picture does emerge of which courses are taught in which universities. This supplementary data would indicate that, for all its shortcomings, the survey's results are not fundamentally flawed.

Compared with twenty years ago, it is evident that, while the number of courses incorporating advertising-related material has grown significantly, no new departments of advertising have been founded at the university level. In contrast, a few new departments of marketing, public relations, and publicity have been created, and some of these no doubt include advertising-related courses. However, the prospects for the foundation of new departments of advertising are not promising.

According to the survey, 246 universities offered a total of 1,778 advertising-related courses taught by 870 instructors. In the titles of these courses, the most frequent keywords were "Marketing" (30% of 1,778) and "Advertising" (15.2% of the same number). These figures suggest that, in many cases, advertising is perceived as a subsidiary element of marketing studies.

The course titles suggest very few differentiated specific aspects of advertising, such as Creative Advertising Strategy, Advertising Research, Advertising Effectiveness, and Advertising Regulations. Where taught, advertising was either included under the generic term "Marketing Studies" or, if offered as a separate course, was limited to introductory-level courses such as "Advertising Studies."

A ranking of university faculties (departments) according to the number of advertising-related courses they offer produced, in descending order, the following list:

Management,
Commerce,
Economics,
Fine Art,
Social Studies,
Literature, and
Literature and Human Studies

The first three faculties have consistently offered the greatest number of advertising-related courses, but recently there has been an increase in the number of faculties of fine art, social studies, and literature offering such courses.

It should be noted that Japanese universities do not impose any regulations or guidelines on the content of advertising, marketing or, indeed, any other courses. Taking advertising as an example, the selection of course content, the order in which it is presented, the choice of textbooks and reference works, the use of supplementary materials such as advertisements and commercials — all these are left to the discretion of the course instructor. The focus of course content often will depend on whether the instructor has a professional or academic background, or even on his or her personal interests.

Whether a course carries two or four credits will also have a direct influence on the depth and scope of course content. Be that as it may, it can be said that the level of advertising courses in Japanese universities that do not offer specialized advertising education is equivalent to the "Introduction to Advertising" courses offered in the departments of advertising of U.S. universities.

"Introduction to Advertising" would normally provide only the most basic general coverage of the subject, but some faculties of fine art offer both theoretical and practical classes in graphic design, computer graphics, and Web design. Likewise, some faculties of literature examine advertising from psychological and cultural perspectives. Occasionally, seminar courses will require students to carry out advertising planning.

Changes in Advertising-related Courses over the Past 20 Years

The Nikkei Advertising Research Institute Survey has its origins in a survey carried out by Akihiro Kamei, *et al.* (1989), as a research project of the Japan Academy of Advertising (JAA). Kamei's independent survey found that Japanese universities were offering 93 advertising courses, 28 advertising seminars, and 24 advertising practicums: a total of 145 courses.

Almost each year after Kamei's pioneering research, the Nikkei Advertising Research Institute conducted a nearly identical survey, chronicling the development of advertising education in Japan. That no such systematic surveys had been carried out before 1989 reflects the contemporary lack of interest in advertising education.

The following graph, based on data from approximately 20 years of Nikkei Advertising Research Institute surveys, shows the number of lectures, seminars and practicums with advertising as their main topic. In 2006 the number of such courses was 3.8 times larger than that in Kamei's survey.

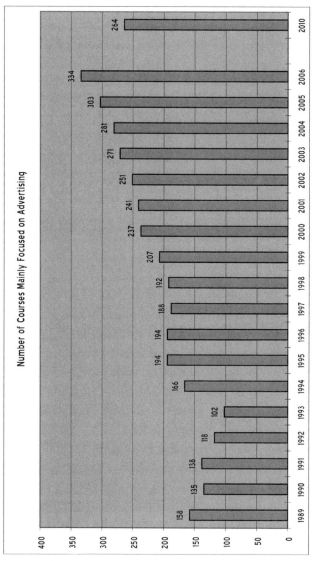

Figure 11-1: 1989–2009 Advertising Courses

The survey data give detailed information on course titles, faculties, departments, instructors, and course content in a format that makes it difficult to analyse statistically. Leaving aside such analysis and focusing only on a summary of the results of the survey, two salient points emerge.

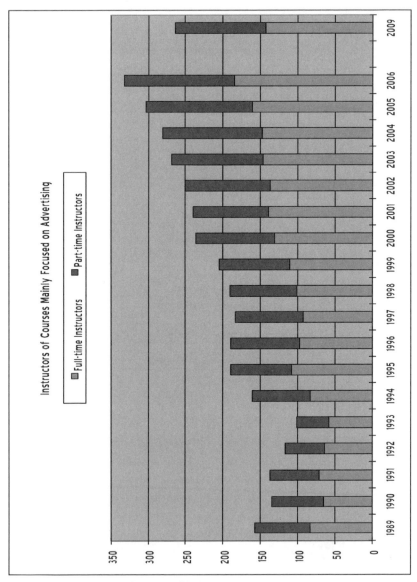

Figure 11-2: Ratio of full-time to part-time instructors

First, faculties offering courses which concentrate on advertising as their main theme can be divided into four groups:

1. Management, commerce, economics, etc.
2. Literature, communication, social studies, etc.

3. Art and fine art.
4. Liberal arts, international liberal studies, information technology, human sciences, etc.

Advertising-related courses have a tendency to incorporate inter-disciplinary elements, and the faculties offering them are many and varied. Consequently, the title "Advertising" or "Advertising Studies" is often applied to courses with profoundly different content. Currently, faculties of management, commerce, and economics offer the greatest number of advertising courses, but the number of faculties of art and fine art, as well as faculties of literature, communication, and social studies that offer such courses is growing steadily.

Second, a large percentage of advertising-related course instructors are part-time faculty. Looking only at those courses with advertising as their main theme, the number of part-time instructors is between 40–50% (*see* Figure 11-2). The survey does not provide details of the background of course instructors, but it can be assumed the part-time instructors include tenured faculty teaching part-time outside their own faculty or university, and advertising industry professionals. Whatever the case, it is evident that while the need for advertising-related courses has been recognized and the number of such courses is increasing, they are often entrusted to part-time instructors rather than tenured faculty.

The History of Advertising Education in Japan

The Origins of Advertising Education in Waseda University
The Nikkei Advertising Research Institute survey has been conducted for twenty years, but the origins of advertising education in Japan go back to the 1910s — to a period spanning the end of the Meiji Period and the beginning of the Taishō Period. It is widely recognized that Waseda University was one of the first universities to offer advertising education, but the education of that time differed significantly from that of the present. In other words, the university did not conduct advertising education in the form of courses with names such as "Advertising" or "Advertising Studies." Rather, advertising education can trace its origins to the activities of an in-formal study group formed by students with an interest in advertising.

In October 1913, to mark the 30th anniversary of the founding of Waseda University, several departments, such as those of Politics, Literature, and Commerce (the precursor of today's School of Commerce), staged a commemorative exhibition. The Department of Commerce's contribution was an advertising exhibition. Classrooms were adorned with realistic displays of consumer goods reminiscent of department stores, advertisements from newspapers and magazines around the world, and real advertising posters, drawing the interest and attention of many visitors and receiving high critical acclaim as a concrete example of Waseda University's academic ideal of the practical application of learning.

In January 1914 the students and faculty who had taken part in this exhibit founded the Waseda Advertising Society. It is reputed to have been the first advertising study group formed by students themselves. The first chairman of the Society was Hozumi Tanaka, the Dean of the Department of Commerce.

The Society's primary aim was to conduct an academic study of advertising. Between one and four hours of lectures were given each week by instructors, including: Jūjirō Itō of the Department of Commerce; Yōichi Ueno, a young researcher majoring in psychology at Tōkyō Imperial University; and Jūjirō Izeki, editor-in-chief of the industry journal *Jitsugyōkai* and later professor at Meiji University.

In addition to lectures such as Principles of Advertising, Overview of Advertising, History of Advertising, and Psychology of Advertising, published materials were read and discussed, and presentations of research findings given. The reading and discussion sessions were led by Jūjirō Itō, and among the texts studied were Walter D. Scott's *Psychology of Advertising*. It must be noted, however, that Itō was not an advertising specialist who taught formal courses in Transportation Policies and Commercial English.

The second aim of the Society was the promotion of the results of its research by holding public lectures and exhibitions. The third aim was the training of persons who would play a significant role in the advertising industry of the future. To this end, the Society held meetings with members of the advertising industry, organized visits to advertising companies, and sponsored practicums at department stores. Such activities could be said to be the forerunners of today's internship programs.

Although the Society was a student initiative, its activities extended to lectures by professors and lecturers, and to seminars, practicums and internships. As if in response to this initiative, in 1920 the Department of Commerce introduced an official though extra-curricular course in advertising. As an extra-curricular course, it did not offer credit toward graduation. However, permission was granted to hold it in regular classrooms, and the university paid the instructors an honorarium. It can thus be said that the roots of advertising education in Japan lie in the activities of the Waseda Advertising Society and the extra-curricular course offered by the Waseda University Department of Commerce.

Initiatives in Other Universities

From that beginning, the number of students interested in advertising grew steadily, and in many universities the first steps towards the creation of advertising study groups were taken. Soon after the establishment of the Waseda Advertising Society in 1914, similar groups were founded at Rikkyō University in 1915, Kōbe Higher Commercial School (now Kōbe University) in 1919, Meiji University in 1920, and Keiō University in 1925.

Although the foundation of an advertising research society at Keiō University came a little late, in the following year the society broke new ground with the publication of *Mita Kōkoku Kenkyū* (Mita Advertising Studies). Not to be outdone, in 1927 the Waseda Advertising Society brought out its own journal, *Kōkokugaku Kenkyū* (Advertising Studies). In 1925 the University Advertising Studies Federation was established, and student interest in the subject continued to grow (Yamamoto & Tsuganezawa, 1985).

In his *Kōkoku to Senden* (Advertisement and Propaganda) published in 1924, Shizuka Nakagawa notes that an advertising seminar was introduced at the Kōbe Higher Commercial School in 1921, and a formal advertising studies course was created at Meiji University in 1922. Nakagawa was one of the most influential figures in the advertising studies and education field of the time. He graduated from the Tōkyō Senmon College (the precursor of Waseda University) in 1883. After teaching at commercial high schools in Nagasaki and Kumamoto, he became a professor at Kōbe Higher Commercial School in 1921, where he himself taught the above-mentioned advertising seminar.

The Meiji University advertising course Nakagawa records as starting in 1922 is not mentioned in the *Centennial History of the Meiji University*

School of Commerce (School of Commerce 100th Anniversary Commemorative History Committee, 2007). However, the curriculum for 1929 lists a course called "Advertising and Selling" taught by Jūjirō Izeki, who had formerly offered a similar extracurricular course at the Waseda University School of Commerce.

In 1947 a new advertising course taught by Takizō Matsumoto made its debut. Although this course continued to be a part of the Meiji University School of Commerce curriculum, subsequent instructors are not named and it can be assumed that it was taught by part-time faculty.

The First Official Courses at Waseda University and Postgraduate Education

Although the Waseda University School of Commerce pioneered the introduction of advertising education, it was not until 1953 that "Advertising" was instituted as an official course (Kobayashi, 1975). It took the form of a seminar taught by Tasaburō Kobayashi, who, after studying sociology at the School of Literature and management at the Graduate School of Commerce, devoted himself to advertising research.

Course content consisted of "A study of advertising campaigns and the effectiveness of advertising, supplemented by research into related topics such as consumers, products, advertising media, advertising copy and design, advertising-related legislation, advertising ethics, and the organization and activities of advertising departments and advertising agencies" (Kobayashi, 1975, p. 67). No such course had ever been offered before, and student familiarity with the subject was minimal. One student of the time admitted, "I thought that Advertising had something to do with commercial art." (Kobayashi, 1975, p. 68). It is symbolically appropriate that this course began in the same year as Japanese commercial television broadcasting.

In 1955 a new course called "Advertising Management" was introduced. Sponsored by a donation from the Japan Federation of Employers' Associations, the course aimed to promote advertising research and education. The course instructor was Fumio Uekuri, head of the advertising department of the *Reader's Digest* Japan Office. The course covered the marketing of advertisements, advertising techniques, media characteristics, budget setting, problems besetting advertising agencies, advertising surveys, measurement of effectiveness, overseas advertising, advertising and publicity, public relations, and so on. In essence, the curriculum of this course differed little from the advertising course of today. In an age when commercial radio and television broadcasting had just begun and was still relatively unfamiliar, the study of advertising must have provided the students of the time with intense intellectual stimulation.

In 1955 Kobayashi changed the name of his seminar from "Advertising" to "Advertising Management," and in 1959 added another seminar called "Advertising Media," which continued until 1962. Along with the explosive growth of television came calls for a thorough examination of advertising media. Despite this tumultuous background, the number of students able to take Kobayashi's two seminar courses was severely limited, as was the number of School of Commerce students able to study advertising theory.

At Waseda University, many official lectures are given in classrooms seating from 300 to 400 students. In 1962 "Advertising" was finally recognized as an official commercial science course, allowing hundreds of students to enroll. In the same year, Kobayashi began teaching an Advertising Major Program in the Graduate School of Commerce. The introduction of this program laid the foundation for the education of students wishing to pursue careers as university researchers and teachers of advertising.

In 1973, Akihiro Kamei, one of Kobayashi's students in graduate school, took charge of "Advertising Research," the second of the School of Commerce's two advertising seminars. (The course name was changed to "Basic Principles of Advertising" in 1975.) With this addition, the number of faculty members teaching advertising at the School of Commerce grew to two. In 1980 Kamei began teaching "Advertising," allowing a large number of School of Commerce students to study the subject.

Although the Waseda University School of Commerce led the way in introducing student-led research into advertising, another 40 years were to pass before the subject was formally recognized in the form of an advertising seminar.

What caused this delay? One possible reason is that while student interest in advertising studies had grown steadily from the 1910s onwards, the subject was taught as an extra-curricular course by faculty members with an interest in advertising but a specialization in other areas of research, and by instructors from other institutions. It is not clear how long advertising continued to be taught as an extra-curricular course, but what is certain is that no attempt was made to hire tenured faculty specializing in advertising research, and a valuable opportunity to establish advertising education on a firm and permanent basis was lost.

Traditionally, the two most important subjects taught at the School of Commerce have been bookkeeping and accounting. Advertising and marketing were considered subsidiary, or marginal, fields of academic research. In comparison with accounting and other fields boasting a large number of faculty members, marginal academic fields with, at best, one specialist teacher must have appeared of little interest or significance to the students of the time. However, the remarkable changes in Japanese media in the 1950s, and the revolution in distribution technology epitomised by the introduction of American-style supermarkets, turned the attention of students to the effects that these changes were exerting on society. In retrospect, Tasaburō Kobayashi's interest in advertising and his unflagging research into the subject bear ample witness to his perspicacity and foresight.

Kobayashi's graduate-level Advertising Major Program was probably the first of its kind in any Japanese university. Among the first group of students taking the course were Akihiro Kamei (later professor at the School of Commerce) and Yasuhiko Kobayashi (later professor at Aoyama Gakuin University). Although the primary aim of the course was to educate scholars who would pursue academic careers in advertising research and education, a majority of students chose to find employment in advertising and other industries after obtaining their master's degree. Few went on to become researchers or university teachers.

It was not until 2005 that Kamei himself began supervising research at the Graduate School of Commerce. This long hiatus was not conducive to the training of a significant number of specialists in the field. It had been hoped that the alumni of the Graduate School of Commerce who had been taught by Kobayashi would go on to teach advertising and related subjects at other universities, but such was not the case.

Again, 40–50% of the faculty teaching the Advertising course were part-timers. There is little doubt that the paucity of postgraduate students going on to teaching careers, coupled with the perception that advertising courses could be adequately entrusted to part-time instructors, raised serious doubts among undergraduate students regarding the advisability and future prospects of studying advertising at the graduate school level.

Other Institutions Offering Advertising Education

Having covered the history of advertising education in Japanese universities, this section concludes with an overview of the advertising education being conducted currently in other institutions. A significant number of university students wishing to obtain professional qualifications or pass external examinations enroll in courses offered by specialist vocational schools or colleges. In Japan this is commonly referred to as "double-schooling." Many of the students who choose to double-school are hoping to gain certification as accountants or lawyers.

It would be wrong, however, to assume that students aiming at a career in the advertising industry follow the same path and enroll in vocational colleges of advertising. Such cases are extremely rare. Most so-called vocational colleges of advertising draw their students from the ranks of high-school graduates and concentrate on such technical aspects as design and photography rather than advertising, as such.

Although few in number, there are students who, after graduating from university departments of management or commerce, decide to aim for careers as art directors or web designers and continue their studies in vocational colleges. However, the education offered in such vocational colleges is mainly of a technical nature and differs fundamentally from that offered in universities. Cooperation and reciprocal recognition of credits between universities and vocational colleges is almost non-existent.

In addition to publishing advertising-related periodicals, a Japanese firm called Sendenkaigi Co. Ltd. offers training for copywriters, art directors and other specialists. Lectures are given by advertising-industry professionals, and the courses attract students with clear career goals such as copywriting, commercial planning, or art direction. Very few of the students enrolling in such courses are studying advertising at the university level. Rather, the majority are students wishing to work in the advertising industry but belonging to university faculties that do not offer advertising-related courses. It is often said that among former students of the Sendenkaigi courses are some of the most famous copywriters in Japan, but it does not follow that taking these courses will necessarily guarantee future employment in the industry.

An organization based in Kyōto, and known as the International Academy, offers a series of courses taught by famous copywriters and art directors under the name of *Kyōto-kōkoku-juku* (The Kyōto Advertising

School). Summaries of these courses, given in a series of books published in 2007, suggest that the focus is less on practical training in advertisement production and more on listening to production professionals discussing various aspects of their work.

The education offered in advertising-related vocational colleges differs fundamentally from that offered in universities, concentrating as it does on the needs of students hoping to find jobs in advertising companies, or providing supplementary education for those already working in advertising or related fields.

Organizations Supporting Advertising Education in Japan

Student Organizations

A simplified overview of the history of advertising education shows that student interest and enthusiasm in advertising generated *ad hoc* study societies that, in turn, stimulated the introduction of formal courses in educational institutions. Today, a number of organizations exist to support the activities of both students and researchers. The following is a brief account of the organizations that influence and support advertising education in Japan.

The earliest such organization exists to this day, and under the same name. The Waseda Advertising Society is approaching its one-hundredth anniversary. From an informal group devoted to studying advertising with the assistance and advice of faculty members, it has grown into a much larger multifaceted organization, creating advertising campaign proposals, advertisements and commercials, and cooperating with the advertising circles of other universities in holding regular Advertising Festival events.

Currently, advertising study circles exist in the following Tōkyō Metropolitan Area universities: Aoyama Gakuin University, Atomi Women's University, Daitō Bunka University, Gakushūin University, Hitotsubashi University, Hōsei University, Jissen Women's University, Keiō University, Kokugakuin University, Meiji University, Meiji Gakuin University, Meisei University, Nihon University, Rikkyō University, Seikei University, Sophia University, Tama Art University, Tōkyō Institute of Technology, Tōkyō Keizai University, Tōyō University, the University of Tōkyō, and Waseda University.

Research Organizations

The Japan Academy of Advertising (JAA), an organization for advertising researchers, was founded in December, 1969. Its first chairperson was Shikamatsu Mukai. Mukai was a professor at Keiō University, lecturing in trade management, commercial planning, the stock exchange, management and economics, monetary banking and other subjects. Advertising was not his speciality, and at the time of his election he was already over eighty years old. The JAA did not begin to function as an active academic organization until the election, in 1976, of Waseda University professor Tasaburō Kobayashi as its second chairperson. He was succeeded in 1998 by Akihiro Kamei, and Yasuhiko Kobayashi in 2004. In 2010 Shizue Kishi, of Tōkyō Keizai University, was elected chairperson. Kishi obtained her Ph.D. at the University of Illinois, and her international perspective promises to lead the JAA into new and broader fields of research.

JAA membership consists of university faculty and postgraduate students, advertising industry professionals, and corporate members. As of September 2010 the number of members was 636, of whom 60% were connected with universities and 40% with the advertising industry. The university membership includes not only specialists in advertising, but also teachers working in fields such as marketing, psychology, art and fine art, and linguistics. Many of the advertising industry professionals who belong to the academy also teach advertising courses as part-time lecturers at universities and other institutions. There are many instances of advertising industry professionals with both practical and academic experience filling full-time positions as university faculty.

Currently, the JAA holds an annual conference at which members present the results of their research, and it publishes a biannual peer-reviewed journal called *Kōkoku Kagaku* (Journal of Advertising Science). Within Japan are four local chapters of the JAA, each holding several study meetings every year. In 2008, the Academy added a Creative Forum study group to further research into the hitherto neglected field of creativity in advertising.

Representative Support Organizations

The Yoshida Hideo Memorial Foundation

The Yoshida Hideo Memorial Foundation was created in 1965 to commemorate the achievements of Hideo Yoshida, the fourth president of Dentsū Inc. Among the many activities of the Foundation, several are of particular relevance to students studying advertising and advertising researchers.

ADMT (Ad Museum Tōkyō) http://www.admt.jp/en/index.html

The ADMT is a unique museum created to further research into advertising and marketing and promote a better understanding of advertising in society. It was opened in December 2002 to mark the one-hundredth anniversary of Hideo Yoshida's birth. In addition to a permanent advertising-related exhibit, each year the museum holds twelve smaller exhibits with special themes. Its convenient location and free admission draw not only students but also visitors from the provinces.

Ad Library http://www.admt.jp/en/library/about.html

A specialist library associated with the ADMT was founded much earlier, in 1966. As of 2008, its holdings included 12,100 Japanese books, 2,900 foreign books, and approximately 170 different periodicals. Computer terminals with search functions allow the viewing of an extensive digital archive of advertising materials.

The library's comprehensive collection of specialized materials and the excellent condition of its books and periodicals attract both students studying advertising and industry professionals. Admission to the library is free.

Research Aid http://www.yhmf.jp/activity/aid/index.html

The foundation also provides financial research aid to university researchers and Ph.D. students. Grants are allocated on the basis of a fair and open evaluation, and are awarded to not only Japanese researchers but also researchers throughout the world. The results of sponsored research are available for inspection in the library and regular compendia of summaries are published.

Nikkei Advertising Research Institute
http://www.nikkei-koken.gr.jp/

Despite the inclusion of 'Nikkei' in its name, this institute is an independent organization founded in 1967. Affiliate members include advertisers, advertising agencies, production companies, research companies, newspapers, periodicals, broadcasting companies and many others. It conducts independent surveys such as "Advertising and Promotion Expenditure of Major Companies" and the previously mentioned "Survey of Advertising-related Courses in Universities," publishes the "Bulletin of Nikkei Advertising Research Institute" and the "Advertising White Paper," and offers courses and seminars in advertising-related subjects. It also sponsors a number of study groups made up of faculty members and graduate students from many universities. A notable feature of these groups is the comparative youth of the group leaders.

Issues Facing Advertising Education in Japan

Low Interest in Advertising Education

As can be seen from the above overview of advertising education in Japanese universities, the inauguration of such education in the late 1910s and early 1920s was by no means tardy. On the other hand, in contrast to the creation of departments of advertising at Michigan State University and the University of Illinois in the late 1950s, no such department ever has been created in a Japanese university.

Why should this be? There is no simple answer to this question but several reasons may be posited.

1. Advertising is taught in a number of different faculties, each bringing to the subject its own distinctive perspective. In other words, the content of advertising education will differ markedly in accordance with the characteristics of the faculties offering relevant courses.

The curricula of American departments of advertising cover essential subjects such as Introduction to Advertising, Advertising Research, Advertising and Society, Media Planning, Creative Advertising Strategy, and Advertising Campaigns. In addition to these core subjects, universities strive to differentiate their advertising education with varied courses such as History of Advertising, Account Planning, Global Advertising, and Interactive Advertising. The advertising courses offered in Japanese universities differ little from the Introduction to Advertising of American universities, while those that do differ tend to pick up one of the many other courses offered in American universities and teach them under the generic label of "advertising."

2. The curricula offered by American departments of advertising represent, from the Japanese point of view, a conglomeration of courses that would normally be taught separately in different faculties. Advertising is, of necessity, an interdisciplinary field of study that transcends faculty boundaries. In the United States, departments of advertising are often found within faculties of journalism or faculties of communication. Were a department of advertising ever to be founded in a Japanese university, the problem would inevitably arise of choosing the most appropriate faculty for such a department: management, commerce, art, and so on. Without first overcoming the strict lines of demarcation between faculties, the formation of a department of advertising in Japan remains intractably difficult. If the number of interdisciplinary or liberal arts faculties continues to grow and generates stiffer competition, there is still a possibility that one or more of them may create a department of advertising to differentiate itself from the others.

3. However, perhaps the most salient reason for the absence of departments of advertising in Japan is that there is no common agreement as to what constitutes advertising education. Hitherto, there has been almost no serious discussion or debate among researchers or educators regarding the content of advertising education. Of the forty annual conferences held by the JAA, only one was devoted to the theme of advertising education. Any improvement in the quality of advertising education in Japan is conditional upon researchers and educators taking a more active interest in defining the nature of advertising education itself.

The Necessity for Training New Researchers

There is an urgent need to increase the number of researchers specializing in advertising, marketing, and communication. Even if the desire to provide content-rich advertising education is there, the number of qualified instructors is not. This shortage of researchers inevitably will be reflected in the lack of postgraduate programs offering an opportunity to conduct advertising studies.

156

Currently, the number of Asian students enrolling in Japanese graduate schools is growing significantly. While it is gratifying that so many talented foreign students should choose to study in Japan, most of them will end their studies when they have obtained their master's degree, going on to find education-unrelated jobs in Japan or their home countries. Serious consideration needs to be given to ways of increasing the number of students, both foreign and Japanese, who wish to progress to Ph.D. courses and eventually become researchers and educators.

Although much of this chapter has focused on advertising education at the undergraduate level, advertising education at the postgraduate level also merits close examination, and it is hoped such a study will be conducted in the near future.

References

Kamei, A., Suzuki, Y., & Lee, S. (1989). *Wagakuni kōtōkikan ni okeru kōkoku kyōiku no genjō to shōrai ni okeru mitōshi* (The current state and future prospects of advertising education in Japanese higher education). *Kōkoku Kagaku* (Journal of Advertising Science), 19, 37–53.

Kobayashi, T. (1975). *Kōkokukyōiku no kei'i to tenbō* (The history and future prospects of advertising education). *Waseda shōgaku* (The Waseda Commercial Review). 249, 67-74.

Kobayashi, T., Shimamura, K., & Ishizaki, T. (1997). *Nihon no kōkoku kenkyū no rekishi* (The history of advertising studies in Japan). Tōkyō: Dentsū.

Nakagawa, Shizuka. (1924). *Kōkoku to Senden* (Advertisement and Propaganda). Tōkyō: Hōbunkan.

Nikkei Advertising Research Institute. (1989). *Daigaku kōkoku kanren kōza chōsa* (Survey of advertising-related courses in universities). *Nikkei kōkoku kenkyūjohō* (Bulletin of Nikkei Advertising Research Institute), 126, 78–88.

———— (1990). *Daigaku kōkoku kanren kōza chōsa* (Survey of advertising-related courses in universities). *Nikkei kōkoku kenkyūjohō* (Bulletin of Nikkei Advertising Research Institute), 132, 80–95.

———— (1991). *Daigaku kōkoku kanren kōza chōsa* (Survey of advertising-related courses in universities). *Nikkei kōkoku kenkyūjohō* (Bulletin of Nikkei Advertising Research Institute), 138, 72–89.

———— (1992). *Daigaku kōkoku kanren kōza chōsa* (Survey of advertising-related courses in universities). *Nikkei kōkoku kenkyūjohō* (Bulletin of Nikkei Advertising Research Institute), 144, 76–91.

———— (1993). *Daigaku kōkoku kanren kōza chōsa* (Survey of advertising-related courses in universities). *Nikkei kōkoku kenkyūjohō* (Bulletin of Nikkei Advertising Research Institute), 150, 75–91.

———— (1994). *Daigaku kōkoku kanren kōza chōsa* (Survey of advertising-related courses in universities). *Nikkei kōkoku kenkyūjohō* (Bulletin of Nikkei Advertising Research Institute), 156, 78–109.

———— (1995). *Daigaku kōkoku kanren kōza chōsa* (Survey of advertising-related courses in universities). *Nikkei kōkoku kenkyūjohō* (Bulletin of Nikkei Advertising Research Institute), 162, 57–98.

———— (1996). *Daigaku kōkoku kanren kōza chōsa* (Survey of advertising-related courses in universities). *Nikkei kōkoku kenkyūjohō* (Bulletin of Nikkei Advertising Research Institute), 168, 70–120.

———— (1997). *Daigaku kōkoku kanren kōza chōsa* (Survey of advertising-related courses in universities). *Nikkei kōkoku kenkyūjohō* (Bulletin of Nikkei Advertising Research Institute), 174, 67–120.

———— (1998). *Daigaku kōkoku kanren kōza chōsa* (Survey of advertising-related courses in universities). *Nikkei kōkoku kenkyūjohō* (Bulletin of Nikkei Advertising Research Institute), 180, 65–130.

———— (1999). *Daigaku kōkoku kanren kōza chōsa* (Survey of advertising-related courses in universities). *Nikkei kōkoku kenkyūjohō* (Bulletin of Nikkei Advertising Research Institute), 186, 58–128.

———— (2000). *Daigaku kōkoku kanren kōza chōsa* (Survey of advertising-related courses in universities). *Nikkei kōkoku kenkyūjohō* (Bulletin of Nikkei Advertising Research Institute), 192, 79–154.

———— (2001). *Daigaku kōkoku kanren kōza chōsa* (Survey of advertising-related courses in universities). *Nikkei kōkoku kenkyūjohō* (Bulletin of Nikkei Advertising Research Institute), 198, 58–136.

———— (2002). *Daigaku kōkoku kanren kōza chōsa* (Survey of advertising-related courses in universities). *Nikkei kōkoku kenkyūjohō* (Bulletin of Nikkei Advertising Research Institute), 204, 1–84.

———— (2003). *Daigaku kōkoku kanren kōza chōsa* (Survey of advertising-related courses in universities). *Nikkei kōkoku kenkyūjohō* (Bulletin of Nikkei Advertising Research Institute), 210, 1–96.

———— (2004). *Daigaku kōkoku kanren kōza chōsa* (Survey of advertising-related courses in universities). *Nikkei kōkoku kenkyūjohō* (Bulletin of Nikkei Advertising Research Institute), 216, 1–102.

———— (2005). *Daigaku kōkoku kanren kōza chōsa* (Survey of advertising-related courses in universities). *Nikkei kōkoku kenkyūjohō* (Bulletin of Nikkei Advertising Research Institute), 222, 1–104.

———— (2006). *Daigaku kōkoku kanren kōza chōsa* (Survey of advertising-related courses in universities). *Nikkei kōkoku kenkyūjohō* (Bulletin of Nikkei Advertising Research Institute), 228, 1–110.

———— (2009). *Daigaku kōkoku kanren kōza chōsa* (Survey of advertising-related courses in universities). *Nikkei kōkoku kenkyūjohō* (Bulletin of Nikkei Advertising Research Institute), 248, 1–85.

School of Commerce 100th Anniversary Commemorative History Committee. (2007). *Meiji daigaku shōgakubu hyakunenshi – shiryō o chūshin ni* (Centennial History of the Meiji

University School of Commerce: From historical records). Tōkyō: Meiji University School of Commerce.

School of Commerce Centennial History Editorial Committee. (2004). *Waseda daigaku shōgakubu 100-nenshi* (Centennial History of the Waseda University School of Commerce). Tōkyō: Waseda University School of Commerce.

Shimamura, K. (2002). *Amerika no kōkoku kyōiku – genjō to kadai* (Advertising education in America: present status and future prospects). *Nikkei kōkoku kenkyūjohō* (Bulletin of Nikkei Advertising Research Institute), 205, 2–8.

Waseda Advertising Society. (1962). *Sōritsu 50-shūnen – kōken 50-nenshi – kai'in meibo* (Celebrating the fifty-year history of the Advertising Society. Membership directory included). Tōkyō: Waseda Advertising Society.

Waseda University School of Commerce Alumni Association. (1996). *Waseda daigaku shōgakubu 90-nenshi* (Ninety-year history of the Waseda University School of Commerce). Tōkyō: Waseda University School of Commerce Alumni Association.

Yamamoto, T. & Tsuganezawa, T. (1986). *Nihon no kōkoku – hito, jidai, hyōgen* (Japanese advertising: The people, the period, the expression). Tōkyō: Nihon Keizai Shimbunsha.

Korea's Advertising Education

Jang-Sun Hwang
Chung-Ang University, Korea

Hyun-Jae Yu
Sogang University, Korea

Overview

A Brief Summary of Korea's Advertising Industry

Korea has one of the largest advertising industries in the world. The volume has sharply increased in last three decades, and is now ranked 10th in the world. In the early 1970s, the country spent 3.5 million dollars on advertising, and it increased by 20-30% every year during the 1980s. In 2009, the size of the Korean advertising industry reached approximately 6 billion dollars, which is about 1% of the country's gross national product.

The structure of the Korean advertising industry is very similar to that of the U.S. Four major media have traditionally played critical roles in the industry, and television (TV) has been the most influential, followed by newspapers. However, as experienced in other advanced countries, the Internet rapidly spread throughout the country, now accounting for more than 15% of the industry. More than 80% of the population now uses the Internet, which makes Korea one of the top five connected countries in the world. Other new media, including IP-TV, DMB, Satellite TV, Digital cable TV, and mobile devices, also are widely used.

Among advertising media, three national broadcast TV channels – KBS2, MBC, and SBS – account for all television broadcasting, and more than ten nationwide newspapers (i.e., *Chosun, Joong-Ang, Dong-A*) account for the majority of the newspaper advertising market.

In the Internet market, unlike other countries, domestic portal brands, including Naver, Daum, and Nate, account for the entire search engine industry and are top high-traffic sites. Global brands such as Yahoo and Google have not yet succeeded in this market. Major advertisers are companies in electronics (i.e., Samsung, LG), mobile (i.e., SK Telecom, KT), and automobiles (i.e., Hyundai, Kia).

The market characteristics that make the Korean advertising market differ from other countries (i.e., U.S.) should be emphasized. First, due to Korea's limited geographical size, mass media have held a great deal of power. For example, some popular soap operas achieve more than 50% ratings, and they are the so-called "nation's soap operas."

Second, the client-agency relationship is strongly bonded. In-house agencies, such as *Cheil Communication,* one sub-company of *Samsung Conglomerate*, have dominated the whole market, and independent agencies have not been successful in the market.

Third, with Korea's smaller population of 50 million people, and its collectivistic culture, the so-called "Big Model" strategy of employing popular celebrities has been widely and successfully adopted. The effectiveness of using celebrities in advertising is one of the most popularly researched topics among the country's advertising scholars.

Advertising Education Overview

In Korea, advertising has been one of the most popular career fields for the last two decades. Most intelligent young adults search for such creative employment, and once employed dedicate their lives to their profession. Recruiting efforts by advertising agencies and advertisers are extremely high. Therefore, many college students and job applicants are eager to learn skills in advertising. Advertising education has become extremely popular in Korean universities, and the classes are full of students from non-major fields, in addition to those in the major department.

Approximately 40 independent programs for advertising are found in more than 45 universities out of 200 in Korea. In other words, one of five of the country's universities offer advertising programs.[12] Enrollment in each program ranges from 30 to 100 or so students, and double-majors and transfers are abundant in most advertising programs.

Most programs are located in Seoul's metropolitan area, where 40% of the population resides and where the country's advertising industry is concentrated. However, some programs are in other metropolitan areas, including Busan, the second largest city in the nation, and every region has a college-level advertising program. Since the need for college education is quite high in Korea – more than 80% of the country's high school students advanced to college in 2009 – every college attempts to have popular programs, and advertising is one of them.

History
Since the inception of Korea's Fourth century Confucian traditions

---

[12] There were approximately 200 four-year universities in Korea in 2009.

in the Chosun Dynasty, advertising as a part of commercial business was long underestimated. Because of the Confucian cultural legacy, advertising was regarded as a shallow affair. However, along with the process of modernization in the 20th century and dynamic industrialization in the 1960s through the 1970s, advertising and commercial business became more highly esteemed. Advertising education ran a similar course. Among advertising scholars, there are three distinct stages in the development of advertising education in Korean colleges.

Early Era (1974-1988)

College-level advertising education in Korea was established in 1974. The first advertising program opened at Chung-Ang University (CAU) and was named the Department of Advertising & PR. Before the CAU program opened, only a few advertising classes in business colleges taught advertising curricula in Korea. In the mid 1960s, advertising was adopted as a credited course at a few universities. Nonetheless, the CAU program was the first independent advertising program at the department level in a university.

The CAU program was established by two tenure-track professors, Dr. Dae-Ryong Lyi and Dr. Woo-Jin Lee. Each year, 20 to 30 undergraduate students enrolled in this department, and several adjunct professors from the advertising industry, in addition to the two major professors, participated in the program. The program was included in the College of Political Science & Economics, and it still operates under that college.

In its early years CAU's advertising program included political communication, which encompassed public relations in part, as well as commercial communications. Since the Korean advertising industry's infancy in the early 1970s, the academic program was less oriented towards commercialism. However, as professional advertising agencies, including Oricom and Cheil Communications, started their businesses in the mid to late 1970s, college programs gradually adopted commercial aspects, such as advertising effectiveness.

The major courses taught included advertising planning, copywriting, advertising management, advertising effectiveness, etc.. About 150 advertising majors graduated from the program, and more than 70% of them started their professional careers in major advertising agencies and with clients in the late 1970s through 1980s.

CAU's advertising program eventually closed and merged into the Department of Mass Communication, incorporating a change in educational policies due to the country's political upheaval. Specifically, the new government, which was dominated by military authorities in 1980, tried to merge a variety of college-level programs into a handful of programs. From 1981 to 1988, the volume of advertising courses taught in the program was gradually reduced to three to four advertising classes offered to undergraduate students. In the 1980s, advertising education in Korean colleges was generally neglected.

Blooming Era (1989–mid 1990s)

With the dynamic change of Korea's social environment in the late 1980s, which is commonly referred to as "The Fever of Democratization," a more liberal atmosphere pervaded universities. Most universities could afford to establish new programs, and advertising was one of the most attractive fields, considering the industry's enormous growth, which consisted of 1% of the GNP during the 1980s.

Four college-level advertising programs were opened in 1989. The CAU program was re-opened, and three new advertising programs were established at Hanyang University, Hongik University and Kwangju University. The names of those departments were somewhat different, as indicated in Table 12-1. The size of freshmen enrollment in these four programs totaled up to 190 each year (Chung-Ang U.: 30, Hangyang U. & Hongik U.: 40 for each, Kwangju U.: 80).

Table 12-1: Early Advertising Programs in Korea

University	Name of Program	Established	Region	Major Professor [13]
Chung-Ang U.	Advertising & Public Relations	1974 / 1989 [14]	Seoul	Lyi, Dae-Ryong
Hanyang U.	Advertising & Public Relations	1989	GyeongGi-Do [15]	Cho, Byung-Ryang
Hongik U.	Advertising Design	1989	ChungCheong Nam-Do	Kwon, Myung-Kwang
Kwangju U.	Publishing & Advertising	1989	Jeolla Nam-Do	Seo, Bum-Seok

Among these four programs, Chung-Ang University and Hanyang University resembled each other in terms of curricula. Their programs were strongly oriented toward commercial advertising planning, as well as practi-

---

[13] "Major Professors" denoted are scholars who are regarded as "founders" or one of the first faculty members in each program.

[14] As noted earlier, Chung-Ang University's advertising program was established in 1974, and re-opened in 1989 after eight-year closing during 1981-1988.

[15] "Do" represents a Korean regional province, which resembles the state in the U.S. There are nine Do's in South Korea.

cal courses. These programs adopted some courses taught in CAU's 1970s program, but they also included some newly established classes, such as advertising and society, international advertising strategy, and advanced copy writing. Both programs were established within the social science fields. Although the name of the department was a little different, Kwangju University's program was not much different from these two major programs.

Hongik's advertising program was much different from the others in terms of their orientations and curricula. As shown by the name of the department, Hongik's program was much more focused on execution and production. In contrast to the other programs that were taught by social scientists, especially from mass communication studies, the majority of Hongik's program consisted of creative, design, and copywriting fields.

In this second birth of advertising education, an academic association for advertising was also established. The KAS (Korean Advertising Society), which is equivalent to an AAA (American Academy of Advertising) in Korea, was founded in 1989 with scholars from relevant areas. Among the founders were Boong-Noh Yoo, Chang-Gyu Hwang, Won-Soo Kim, Yong-Seob Song, Dae-Ryong Lyi, and Myong-Kwang Kwon. In its early years, KAS was an association of professors teaching advertising courses in marketing, art design, mass communications, and advertising (in social science). Their contributions to advertising education, as well as research, are much acknowledged in the society.

Since the mid-1990s, advertising programs in universities, especially in suburban and metropolitan regions, have sharply increased. More than twenty independent programs were established in this period, and the names generally adopted "advertising." Due to the popularity of the advertising field in Korean society during the 1990s, many universities tried to establish advertising programs. Thanks to this drastic increase, most programs recruited professors from both academic and practical areas.

Along with the growth of undergraduate programs, graduate-level advertising programs were also gradually established. In 1981, Chung-Ang University established the first master's degree in advertising in the College of Mass Communications, which is a kind of professional school enrolled mainly with practitioners.

During the 1990s, general graduate programs for advertising began to be established for full-time students. Currently, approximately 20 graduate programs offering advertising majors operate in Korea, and two of them, Chung-Ang and Hanyang, also offer a doctoral program.

Restructuring Era (mid 1990s-Present)

After the country's economic crisis in 1999, the Korean advertising industry fell into a recession. In this environment, the number of advertising programs declined from the previous era. However, in contrast to the preceding period, a relatively large number of advertising doctorates came forth. Although there were some in the 1990s, Koreans with American-awarded Ph.Ds have increasingly returned to the country, and more advertising doctorates were conferred in Korea, as well.

In this period, advertising programs at major universities – both departments and majors – systematically reconstructed their programs. Many large universities in major cities, including Seoul, established advertising-minor programs in mass communication programs. The year 1995 should be noted as the third milestone of advertising education in Korea (with the preceding milestones being CAU's 1974 program and the four programs that opened in 1989). More than five universities opened their advertising programs by establishing departments for advertising and public relations in 1995, including Dongkuk, Se-Myong, Mokwon, Hyub-Sung, Hanshin, Cheong-Ju, and Nam-Seoul Universities.

The Programs

There are approximately 40 departments that mainly focus on advertising, and an additional 45 universities that have smaller advertising programs within relevant departments such as Mass Communications and Business. Moreover, the need for advertising education from a practical perspective also increased. As such, some valuable advertising programs also exist outside of colleges.

Advertising Education at the College Level

Basically, the Korean programs for advertising education (i.e., about principles, theories, planning, and execution) could be divided into two categories: programs in established colleges and programs in related professional organizations.

First, regarding programs in colleges, there are diverse units which use different titles (i.e., departments, schools, colleges, majors), where college students can learn advertising-related knowledge. The majority of programs have departments with titles that simultaneously use the words "advertising" and "public relations" (e.g., Chung-Ang University, Hanyang University, Nam-Seoul University). These programs usually offer 30 to 50 credits for advertising majors in each semester.

In some universities, advertising-related courses are offered under the auspices of a School of Communication (e.g., Korea University, Sogang

University). These have several faculty members in the units who regularly teach advertising-related courses. Therefore, it is wise to check if there are advertising-related courses for students in every unit (similar in terms of the units' titles) indicated above to determine the current situation of advertising education at the college level in Korea.

Many specific colleges have changed or varied their titles and specific courses over the years. First, across Korea, there are about 30 to 40 universities that contain departments using the word "advertising" in the title, such as the Department of Advertising or the Department of Advertising and Public Relations, including that at Chung-Ang University, which houses the oldest college-level advertising program in the country. In addition, there are about 45 more universities that have departments with titles that include the word "advertising." Table 12-2 shows the list of the colleges/universities belonging to this category.

University	School Unit	Department	URL
Cheongju University	School of Journalism & Information	Advertising & PR Major	http://www.cju.ac.kr
Chung-Ang University		Dept. of Advertising & PR	http://www. CAU.ac.kr
Chungwoon University		Dept. of Advertising & PR	http://www.chungwoon.ac.kr
Daegu Catholic University	School of Journalism & Advertising	Advertising & PR Major	http://www.cu.ac.kr
Dankook University	School of Journalism & Communication	Journalism & Advertising Major	http://www.dankook.ac.kr
Dong-Eui University		Dept. of Advertising & PR	http://www.dongeui.ac.kr
Dong-Guk University		Dept. of Advertising & PR	http://www.dongguk.edu
Dongseo University	School of Mass Communication	Advertising & PR Major	http://www.dongseo.ac.kr
Ewha Woman's University	Division of Media Studies	Advertising & PR Major	http://www.ewha.ac.kr
Gwang-Ju University	School of Mass Communication	Advertising & PR Major	http://www.gwangju.ac.kr
Gye-Myung University	School of Broadcasting, Journalism & Advertising	Advertising & PR Major	http://www.kmu.ac.kr
Halla University		Dept. of Advertising & PR	http://www.halla.ac.kr
Hallym University	School of Journalism & Information	Advertising & PR Major	http://masscom.hallym.ac.kr
Hankook University of Foreign Studies	School of Journalism & Information	Advertising & PR Major	http://www.hufs.ac.kr
Hansei University	School of Media & Information	Advertising & PR Major	http://www.hansei.ac.kr
Hanshin University		Dept. of Advertising & PR	http://www.hanshin.ac.kr
Hanyang Cyber University		Dept. of Advertising & PR	http://www.hanyangcyber.ac.kr
HanYang University	School of Advertising & PR	Advertising Major	http://www.hanyang.ac.kr
Honam University		Dept. of Advertising, PR, & Event	http://www.honam.ac.kr
Hongik University	School of Advertising	Advertising & PR Major	http://www.hongik.ac.kr

		& PR	
Hyupsung University	School of Business	Advertising & PR Major	http://www.uhs.ac.kr
Inje University	School of Journalism & Political Science	Journalism & Advertising Major	http://www.inje.ac.kr
International University of Korea		Dept. of Media Advertising	http://www.iuk.ac.kr
Jeonju University	School of Business	Advertising & PR Major	http://www.jj.ac.kr
Jung-Bu University		Dept. of Advertising & PR	http://www.joongbu.ac.kr
Kookmin University	School of Journalism & Information	Advertising Major	http://www.kookmin.ac.kr
Ko-Shin University		Dept. of Advertising & PR	http://www.kosin.ac.kr
Kyung-il University		Dept. of Advertising & PR	http://www.kiu.ac.kr
Kyung-Ju University		Dept. of Advertising, PR & Media	http://www.gju.ac.kr
Kyungsung University		Dept. of Advertising & PR	http://www.ks.ac.kr
Mokwon University		Dept. of Advertising & PR	http://www.mokwon.ac.kr
NamSeoul University		Dept. of Advertising & PR	http://www.nsu.ac.kr
Pyeongtaek University		Dept. of Advertising & PR	http://www.ptu.ac.kr
Sang-Ji University	School of Journalism & Advertising	Advertising & PR Major	http://www.sangji.ac.kr
Se-Myung University		Dept. of Advertising & PR	http://www.semyung.ac.kr
Seowon University		Dept. of Advertising & PR	http://www.seowon.ac.kr
Sin-Ra University		Dept. of Advertising & PR	http://www.silla.ac.kr
Sookmyung Women's University	School of Journalism & Information	PR & Advertising Major	http://www.sookmyung.ac.kr
Soongsil University		Dept. of Journalism & PR	http://www.ssu.ac.kr
Sunmoon University	School of Journalism & Advertising	Advertising & PR Major	http://www.sunmoon.ac.kr
Tongmyung University		Dept. of Advertising & PR	http://www.tu.ac.kr
Woo-Suk University		Dept. of Advertising & Event	http://www.woosuk.ac.kr
Young-San University		Dept. of Advertising & PR	http://www.ysu.ac.kr

Table 12-2: Advertising Programs in Universities with the Department Unit.

However, a few universities also have colleges with the word "advertising" in their title, including Kyung-Ju University, Sang-Ji University and Hong-ik University. Although many units in Korean universities do not use the word "advertising" in titles, many departments and colleges offer diverse advertising-related courses For example, in one department called "Department of Mass Communication," students may take several advertising–related courses. About 50 departments do not use the word "advertising" in official titles for their units, but it was confirmed that each offered some advertising-related courses (see Table 12-3).

Universities	Source
Changwon U.	http://www.changwon.ac.kr
Cheju U.	http://www.cheju.ac.kr
Chosun U.	http://www.chosun.ac.kr
Chungnam U.	http://www.cnu.ac.kr
Daegu U.	http://www.daegu.ac.kr
Daejeon U.	http://www.dju.ac.kr
Daejin U.	http://www.daejin.ac.kr

Gongju U.	http://www.kongju.ac.kr
Hanseo U.	http://www.hanseo.ac.kr
Incheon U.	http://www.incheon.ac.kr
Inha U.	http://www.inha.ac.kr
Jeonbuk U.	http://www.chonbuk.ac.kr
Jeonnam U.	http://www.jnu.ac.kr
Kangwon U.	http://www.kangwon.ac.kr/
Konkuk U.	http://www.konkuk.ac.kr/
Korea Cyber U.	http://www.knou.ac.kr/
Korea U.	http://www.korea.ac.kr
Kyungbuk U.	http://www.knu.ac.kr
Kyunghee U.	http://www.khu.ac.kr/
Kyungnam U.	http://www.kyungnam.ac.kr
Kyungwooon U.	http://www.ikw.ac.kr/
Mok·po U.	http://www.mokpo.ac.kr
Paichai U.	http://www.paichai.ac.kr
Pukyong U.	http://www.pknu.ac.kr/
Pusan U.	http://www.pusan.ac.kr/
Sejong U.	http://www.sejong.ac.kr/
Seoul National U.	http://www.snu.ac.kr
Seoul Women's U.	http://www.swu.ac.kr/
Sogang U.	http://www.sgcomm.ac.kr
Sunchenhyang U.	http://www.sch.ac.kr
Sungkyunkwan U.	http://web.skku.edu
Wonkwang U.	http://www.wonkwang.ac.kr/
Woosjuk U.	http://www.woosuk.ac.kr/
Yonsei U.	http://www.yonsei.ac.kr
Youngnam U.	http://www.yu.ac.kr/
Youngsan U.	http://www.ysu.ac.kr/

Table 12-3: The Universities Offering Advertising
Courses under the Independent Units of which
Titles Include the Words "Mass Comm.", "PR,"
or "Information."

Traditionally, the most popular title of a unit in this field has long been the Department of Newspaper and Broadcasting, which has been used in many colleges in the country. However, some departments use only the words "public relations," as well. Those units may have several advertising-related courses and advertising major professors. But most universities mainly have undergraduate programs, with few colleges having graduate programs in advertising. Only a handful have doctoral programs.

Advertising Education Outside the Colleges
KOBACO

One of the most prestigious and oldest organizations for running non-college level advertising education in Korea is KOBACO (Korea Broadcast Advertising Corporation), which was established in 1981. KO-BACO had several sub-organizations responsible for diverse tasks, including selling specific vehicles for TV commercials. It also had a full-sized advertising education program called "The Institute for Advertising Education," which was established in November, 1987. The Institute was a non-profit subsidiary of KOBACO, and its major purpose was to upgrade the advertising industry in Korea by re-educating advertising practitioners. However, not only advertising practitioners but also college students who wanted to enter advertising agencies in the near future could be educated in this Institute if they passed some qualifying tests.

In a joint program with IAA (International Advertising Association), the Institute has run special advertising education programs for 22 years, and the institute has had close to 230,000 graduates, as of 2009. IAA officially certified KOBACO's program as the official advertising education program that educates professionals and students to be international advertising experts (the second-highest acknowledgement among Asian countries).

Among diverse sub-programs conducted in the Institute, the IAA-KOBACO programs are offered for advertising professionals and college students separately. For about a year, this program teaches basic principles of advertising, professional theories, and up-to-date trends in advertising. For participants who complete the program and successfully pass the graduation test, IAA grants the IAA AD Diploma I (students) or II (advertising practitioners). These diplomas acknowledge that the participants have undergone all required courses to be international advertising experts.

In addition to the IAA-KOBACO program, KOBACO has run several joint advertising education programs, as well, including units in other colleges nationwide (a total of 27 universities, including Seoul Women's University and Kyungwon University). The students from these schools can obtain credits by taking the advertising-related courses from KOBACO.

KFAA

The second major advertising education institute for non-advertising professionals is KFAA (Korea Federation of Advertising Associations), which also houses what has been considered to be one of the most popular databases regarding diverse characteristics in Korean advertising business: www.adic.co.kr (Korea Advertising Information Center).

In 1999, KFAA opened the website for the first time, and it has been one of the most popular and helpful information sources for Korean advertising professionals and students. It has been used by both for more than 10 years. In addition, KFAA has sponsored several advertising festivals, awards, and competitions among college students, so that it has provided several opportunities for students to experience the advertising planning process by competing with other teams in the nation.

In 2005, the KFAA held the first "Korean College Students AD Challenge." A more developed and bigger scale-competition called KOSAC (Korea Student Advertising Competition) was started by KFAA in 2008, providing important motivation for students who want to enter the advertising industry after graduation. This is the biggest advertising competition among college students in the nation, and academics, practitioners and government officials participate as staff members and judges. Many colleges in the nation participate, with college student teams under the lead of major professors, and they are required to plan campaigns from marketing research, situation analysis, concept development, idea brain-storming, producing actual advertisements, and professional presentations. The colleges go through regional competitions in designated areas, and winners from each area compete in the final competition. Members of the winning team generally are recruited to start as advertising professionals upon college graduation.

Others

In addition, the C&A Expert (the Institute for Advertising Education in KOBACO) and Korea Association for Advertisers (KAA) have also made efforts to educate advertising-related professionals and college students. In the case of C&A Expert (Ad college), about 7,000 graduates have taken marketing and advertising-related courses from about 300 experts. However, the KAA mainly focuses on re-educating advertising professionals by holding several workshops such as "media strategy workshops," " public relations strategy workshops" and "Internet advertising strategy workshops." Besides the organizations indicated above, several advertising agencies have their own educational programs for insiders, such as those offered by Cheil Communications, Ino-cean, and TBWA.

History of Advertising Education in Malaysia

Teck Hua Ngu
Mara University of Technology, Malaysia

Introduction

The history of advertising education in Malaysia began not in colleges or universities, but with the advertising industry itself. In 1952, the Malaysian Advertisers Association (MAA) was formed. Since its inception, it has had a vision of educating advertising professionals. Its foray into advertising education had humble beginnings, in the form of Tea Talks on the advertising industry organized for industry personnel.

Professional body involvement

In the early 1970s, the MAA and the Association of Accredited Advertising Agencies (4As) set up the Joint Education Committee (JEC) to offer advertising courses at both the certificate and diploma levels. Courses were industry-oriented, and industry professionals taught the courses. The courses were funded by the MAA/4As. It was successful in attracting and graduating a few hundred students, both at the certificate and diploma levels. Many of the students were young executives in advertising, marketing, and the media industries (Fernandez, 1990).

At the certificate level, the courses offered were related to the advertising field. They included introductory courses in marketing, advertising, public relations, sales promotion, media, market research, and behavioral studies. At the diploma level, the courses delve deeper into similar subjects, with more orientation to application and practice.

Most of the instructors were senior managers from the advertising and media industries. The academic parts of the courses were supplemented by periodic seminars and workshops presented by industry experts from overseas and locally.

In 1981, the JEC succeeded in securing a franchise with the Communication Advertising and Marketing Education Foundation of the U.K. (CAM) to offer the CAM Diploma Course in Malaysia. However, this franchise agreement was terminated a few years later. This was followed by an-

171

other short duration of cooperation with the International Advertising Association of New York (IAA), whereby several students successfully completed and graduated with the IAA Diploma in Advertising.

Birth of the Advertising, Communication, Training Committee (ACT)

In 1990, the JEC was replaced by a new entity: the Advertising, Communication, Training Committee (ACT). Similar to JEC, ACT consisted of professionals from advertising, communication, marketing, and media. It began by offering professional courses in the evenings, followed by certificate and diploma courses. To further enhance the academic training of the graduates, an internship program was established to place graduates in member agencies of the 4As.

Institute of Advertising Communication Training (IACT)

The ACT eventually became the Institute of Advertising Communication Training (IACT) as a full-fledged education institution in 1993 to train advertising professionals in the country. Today, IACT is known as IACT College. It is the only education institution in Malaysia accredited by IAA Global. Its slogan is proudly presented as "Founded, Endorsed & Taught by Industry Professionals." Today, it is a full-fledged private higher education institution offering the following courses:

- Certificate in Communication Studies,
- Diploma in Advertising/Marketing Communications,
- Diploma in Marketing Communication,
- Diploma in Broadcasting,
- Diploma in Graphic Design,
- Diploma in Creative Multimedia, and
- Diploma in Sales & Marketing.

One unique feature of the IACT College is that it has entered into twinning agreements with foreign universities, whereby its students could choose to proceed to bachelor's degree programs offered at those universities. To date, it has partner universities in Australia (RMIT University; Charles Sturt Univeristy; University of Canberra), New Zealand (AUT University), England (University of Hertfordshire), and the United States (Hawaii Pacific University; Northwood University).

Other Advertising Professional's foray into Education

One of the original members of JEC, local advertising guru Lim Kok Wing, also ventured into the education business by setting up the Limkokwing Institute of Creative Technology (LICT) in 1991. The Institute offered a wide range of courses, mostly creative and design-based. The Institute enjoyed phenomenal growth, and it was upgraded to a full-fledged university named after the founder, the Limkokwing University of Creative Technology (LUCT) in 2007. Today, it has established overseas campuses in the U.K., Botswana, Lesotho, Swaziland, China, Cambodia, and Indonesia. It will soon set up a campus in New York City in the United States.

The Role of Public Universities

The Science University of Malaysia (USM) was the first public university in Malaysia to offer a communication program in 1970. However, it offered only two courses in advertising: Advertising I and Advertising II (Adnan, 1993).

The second university to offer advertising courses was the School of Mass Communication, Mara Institute (now University) of Technology (UiTM) in 1972. It was the only university offering advertising as a field of specialization, with several advertising subjects (detailed description of the program below).

The National University of Malaysia (UKM) is the third public university in Malaysia to offer advertising courses. However, only two courses, Advertising I and Advertising II, are offered in the Communication Department under the Faculty of Social Sciences and Humanities.

In 1977, Malaysia's premier public university, the Malaya University (UM), offered advertising as an optional subject in the Creative and Descriptive Writing Program, under the Department of Malay Studies, Faculty of Arts and Social Sciences (Adnan, 1993).

At the Agricultural (now Putra) University of Malaysia (UPM), the only advertising course offered was Principles of Advertising. This course was offered by the Center for Extension and Continuing Education, in 1979, as an optional subject under the auspices of the Department of Development Communication (Adnan, 1993, Hamdan, 1986).

Focus: Advertising Program at UiTM

Advertising studies as a field of specialization began in 1972 at UiTM with several advertising courses, including Principles of Advertising, Principles of Marketing, Marketing Research, Media Planning, Copywriting, and Advertising Campaign Project. In recent years the advertising curriculum has expanded to include Online Advertising and International Advertising.

Today, Adnan Hashim, one of the earliest graduates of the Advertising Program of UiTM, has become the Dean of the Faculty of Communication and Media Studies at UiTM. The advertising program at UiTM is the largest in the country. The faculty consists of 10 lecturers in various areas of specialization. About 360 students are enrolled in the program. There are two intakes each year, with about 60 students each intake.

Students are enrolled in a three-year program and will graduate with Bachelor of Mass Communication (Advertising) degree. The last semester of their studies is an 18-week internship in advertising agencies as well as clients' marketing departments. The students submit a report after their internship ends, and some are directly employed by the agencies where they do their internship.

Outstanding Graduate: Azizul R. Kallahan

Azizul was among the first cohort of advertising students (1975-1978) to graduate from UiTM. He worked in some of the biggest international and local advertising agencies (SSCB Lintas; Ted Bates; Union 45; McCann) before setting up his own agency in 1985. He partnered with Spencer Wing to set up the SpencerAzizul Sdn. Bhd. (Pte. Ltd.), a totally integrated agency. He has become one of the most successful and illustrious graduates of the Advertising Program that UiTM has produced. Many other graduates have also set up smaller agencies.

References

Adnan, Hashim. 1993. Advertising Education in Malaysia: Present Status and Future Directions, in Mat Pauzi Abd. Rahman and Mazni Buyong (Eds.) , *Advertising and Promotions: Trends and Reflections*, Bangi, Selangor: Jabatan Komunikasi, Universiti Kebangsaan Malaysia. 61-70.
Fernandez, Oscar. 1990. "The Story of Advertising in Malaysia." *Ad Asia 1990 Memorabilia*. Kuala Lumpur: Malaysian Advertisers Association.
Mohd. Hamdan, Adnan. 1986. "Mass Communication and Journalism Education in Malaysia." *Journal Komunikasi*. 4, 67-76.

Advertising Education in Singapore

May O. Lwin
Nanyang Technological University, Singapore

Rebecca Ye
University of Oxford, UK

Tim Clark
Nanyang Technological University, Singapore

History and Development of Advertising Education in Singapore - Milestones

1938   The Nanyang Academy of Fine Arts was founded in 1938 with an inaugural class of 14 Fine Art students

1969   Baharuddin Vocational Institute started operations in 1969, offering several courses such as Graphic Design

1984   LASALLE College of the Arts started a specialist tertiary program

1990   Establishment of the Institute of Advertising Singapore (IAS)

1992   The first public university program offering full-time degree programs (bachelor's, master's and PhD) in advertising and public relations, amongst other communication fields, commenced at the Wee Kim Wee School of Communication and Information (WKWSCI), Nanyang Technological University

2001   The Crowbar Awards, a student competition accepting entries in advertising, design, photography, interactive and film, was created by the Association of Accredited Advertising Agents Singapore

2002   The Singapore Government announced the Creative Industries Development Strategy

2005   The launch of the School of Art, Design and Media (ADM), Singapore's first comprehensive professional Art School

2008   IAS hosted the World Effie Festival in Singapore

2010   Launch of the Asia Pacific Advertising and Marketing Congress (APPIES), a marketing and advertising congress reaching out to marketers, practitioners and students

Before the 1980s, international advertising agencies were ruled by expatriates (expats), mostly from the UK, USA or Australia. Education to prepare Singaporeans for a career in advertising was almost non-existent. And the expats were mostly too busy learning the ropes of their jobs to provide much in the way of in-house training.

Allein Moore, publisher of *AdAsia Magazine*, started as Creative Director of Batey Ads in 1979. Here's how he remembers the scene then:

Allein Moore

> My art directors within the ad agency were all trained at an institution called Baharuddin Vocational Institute. I volunteered to speak to the students on design and advertising. I was most surprised when I walked into the classroom to find the students dressed in uniform. From my teaching experience in the UK, I was used to students with long hair and tattoos! These students were also quiet as church mice!
>
> I soon realized that the students were attending a vocational course and therefore were being trained as "artists" to go into the advertising industry (there were few real branding or design groups in those days, so this was the source of employment). Back then, agency art directors were not involved in conceptualization, but were there to execute the copywriter's ideas. The students needed to learn how to paste up artwork and order typesetting, and such basics.

One illustrious beneficiary of that basic education system, Patrick Low, went on to become one of Singapore's best-known creative directors, with countless international creative awards to his name. Patrick was voted Creative Director of the Year in 2007, when he was serving his 21st year at Y & R. He currently is the creative partner of his own advertising consultancy, Goodfellas. He still finds time to give students at polytechnics and universities the benefit of his experience. He remembers with a smile how tough it was in the old days. For someone interested in art and design, there was really only one choice: Nanyang Academy of Fine Arts (NAFA). But here he could only learn how to draw and paint. Patrick recalls the following:

Armed with a few oil paintings and charcoal sketches, I went about looking for a job as a Commercial Artist, a term used to describe Visualisers and Art Directors in those days. Everywhere I went, I was told that my qualifications were not relevant to the job I was required to perform.

Eventually, a gentleman who I showed my paintings to, advised me to enroll in an Advertising Art course at Baharuddin Vocational Institute. The government in those days did not value right-brain thinkers. There weren't any colleges, polytechnics, or universities teaching Design and Visual Arts.

To study Graphic Design, I had three choices – England, Canada, or the United States of America – none of which was feasible, since my parents weren't wealthy and it would have blown their life savings just to pay for my tuition. So, for my two years effort at Baharuddin, I was finally rewarded with a Trade Certificate. Design and Advertising wasn't a profession, but a trade, in those days. And to add salt to injury, I had to don a school uniform and attend a flag raising ceremony every morning.

Patrick Low

But I learned one thing at Baharuddin. That is, if I wanted something real bad in life, I would have to swallow my pride and persevere. After all, if I could make it through National Service, what's two more years in a uniform?

The writing side of the creative departments had even less opportunity for training. Tim Clark, currently a lecturer at Nanyang Technological University's Wee Kim Wee School of Communication and Information, remembers this well. In 1983 he was recruited in London to join Grant Kenyon & Eckhardt (GK&E) as Creative Director. He recalls:

GK&E was the third biggest agency in Singapore and this was my first job as Creative Director. Actually, many of my contemporaries were also learning on the job how to be creative directors, including Neil French, over at Ogilvy & Mather. Little did we all know then that Neil would help to raise the creative profile of this advertising backwater to one of international renown.

One thing that struck me about the creative departments of agencies in Singapore was that the English-

Tim Clark

177

language copywriters were nearly all female. It was explained to me, then, that this was because the education system placed high value on science and technical subjects especially for males looking to carve a "serious" career in life. The softer option and luxury of studying arts and social sciences naturally fell to female students. To make matters worse, the nascent advertising industry was regarded as rather an offbeat career choice, so educated young women were steered towards teaching and administration. This resulted in a serious dearth of local copywriting talent.

One person who did a great deal to organize the much-needed training for the advertising industry was (and still is) David Teo Keng Hock. His

David Teo Keng Hock

career began in teaching, so when he was working at the Straits Times, he was asked to be their representative on the Joint Education Committee founded by the three advertising trade bodies – Singapore Advertisers Association (SAA), Association of Accredited Advertising Agents Singapore (4As), and the Advertising Media Owners Association of Singapore (AMOAS). In his words:

The committee was set up to upgrade the training for advertising practitioners offered by the Adult Education Board, which later became known as the Vocational and Industrial Training Board (VITB). Through association with the CAM Foundation of the UK, this organization offered Certificate and Diploma courses in Communication Studies. It was from this humble beginning that the Singapore Institute of Management (SIM) (now UniSIM) and the Management Development Institute of Singapore (MDIS) sprang up. But there was no organization totally dedicated to the training of advertising practitioners until 1990, when the Institute of Advertising Singapore (IAS) was established, and I was invited to be its founding president.

Patrick Mowe

Another veteran of advertising education, who began his career as a teacher and who also found his way into the Straits Times, is Patrick Mowe. He went on to make waves in book publishing and distribution, and he founded two of Singapore's best-known publications: *Silver Kris* and *Female Magazine*.

He can testify to the improvements made in vocational training by David Teo and his associates, because he himself was an early beneficiary of a CAM diploma in Communications Studies. When IAS needed help to revive its activities in 1998, Patrick came out of retirement to join Dr. Donald Ee, former president YP Chan, and returning president David Teo to expand the scope of its operations. As executive director of IAS, Patrick explored ways of bringing an interest in advertising to a broader audience:

> I started the events side of IAS in 1998. We began by launching the Singapore Advertising Hall of Fame Awards (replacing the Max Lewis Awards) to recognize the best campaigns and most outstanding individuals contributing to the Singapore ad industry. We also conceptualized the Singapore International Advertising Congress in order to engage the advertising industry and educate the general public about the advertising profession. And both these events took off in 1999.

Patrick's efforts to educate the broader public made an international breakthrough in 2003, when he went to New York to pitch for, and win, the chance for Singapore to host the EFFIE Singapore Awards. This was followed by IAS organizing the World Effie Festival and the Asia Pacific Effie Awards event, designed to recognize effectiveness in advertising, in 2008. High profile advertising industry leaders gathered in Singapore from all over the world, and with none other than M.M. Lee Kuan Yew appearing as guest speaker. In 2010, Patrick launched the Asia Pacific Advertising and Marketing Congress (APPIES), reaching out to marketers and practitioners as well as students of marketing communications.

Advertising education in Singapore has certainly come a long way and students now come here from Europe and North America, as well as from around the region, to study marketing communication at every level from a professional certificate at IAS, to a PhD at Nanyang Technological University (NTU). Here is how Tim Clark sums up his experience:

> When I arrived in Singapore in the early 1980s, the writing was on the wall. The absolute domination of expats couldn't last. Locals had to be groomed to take over. My first boss, London-trained Y.P. Chan, was the first Singaporean to be made M.D. of an international advertising agency. Patrick Low, at Y & R, was one of the first Singaporeans to become Creative Director of an international agency. And he was locally trained. Education was the key, and veterans like me had a duty to contribute. For that reason I began lecturing part-time at IAS in 1990, and later at Ngee Ann Poly. Today I'm a

full-time lecturer, joining the many for whom advertising began or ended with teaching. And I now realize that the advertising and teaching professions have much in common.

Advertising Education Programs in Singapore

The Singapore Landscape

The Creative Industries (CI)[16] in Singapore is anticipated to be a key growth sector for the Singapore economy. CI currently hires about 110,000 workers in more than 8,000 establishments, and there will be an estimated demand of more than 10,000 creative workers by 2012 (Singapore Workforce Development Authority, 2010).

In 2002, the Singapore government announced the Creative Industries Development Strategy. As part of the push for creativity, the "Design Singapore" Initiative was the first national collaborative strategy to spearhead the promotion of design and tap into Singapore's business, artistic, cultural, and technological resources and capabilities (Economic Review Committee, 2002). The initiative sought to bring together the different players in the design ecosystem: enterprise, expertise and education.

The Media Development Authority (MDA) announced its "Media 21" vision in 2003--to invest S$100 million over five years, in order to cultivate a vibrant media industry. MDA also introduced the Media Education Scheme in 2003, to fund the education and training for existing students and professionals in the media industry (Media Development Authority, 2003).

These governmental initiatives propelled the economic contribution of the creative cluster and compelled various educational institutions to initiate or strengthen their existing visual arts and design programs. Vis-à-vis established programs like Medicine and the Arts and Social Sciences (the former celebrated its centennial anniversary in 2005 and the latter turned 80 in 2009), advertising education in Singapore could be considered a

---

[16] In Singapore, the Creative Industries (CI) is defined as "industries which are inspired by cultural and artistic creativity and have the potential to create economic value through the generation and exploitation of intellectual property." This definition is adapted from the UK definition in the Creative Industries Mapping Document (Nov 1998) by the UK Creative Industries Taskforce. In Singapore, the Creative Industries are broadly classified into the arts, media, design and software & IT services (MICA, 2009).

relatively new kid on the block, the discipline making its debut into local educational institutions at the later part of the twentieth century.

Since its entry, however, advertising programs have grown in popularity and have been delivered in degree-granting institutions, polytechnics, and vocational institutions across Singapore. These advertising modules are typically tied to the school's communication or design programs, resulting in a focus in either the management or creative aspect of advertising.

To date, there are close to twenty institutions in Singapore that provide advertising education programs. These schools, and the type(s) of academic qualifications they offer for the various advertising-related programs, are listed in Table 14-1.

	University / Institution	Cert.	Dipl.	B	M	D
1	Wee Kim Wee School of Communication & Information (Nanyang Technological University)		√	√	√	√
2	Nanyang Academy of Fine Arts	√	√	√		
3	La Salle College of the Arts		√	√		
4	Raffles Design Institute		√	√	√	
5	School of Art, Design and Media (Nanyang Technological University)			√	√	
6	Management Development Institute of Singapore	√	√	√	√	
7	Singapore Institute of Management			√		
8	Curtin Singapore			√		
9	Kaplan Singapore		√	√		
10	Shelton College International		√			
11	TMC Academy for Advanced Education		√	√		
12	Temasek Design School (Temasek Polytechnic)		√			
13	School of Film and Media Studies (Ngee Ann Polytechnic)		√			
14	Centre for Culture & Communication & School of Technology for the Arts (Republic Polytechnic)		√			
15	School of Design (Nanyang Polytechnic)		√			
16	School of Communication, Arts and Social Sciences (Singapore Polytechnic)		√			
17	First Media Design School		√			

18	Institute of Advertising, Singapore	√	√			
19	Chatsworth Medi@rt Academy School of Communication and Design	√	√			

Table 14-1: Institutions in Singapore offering certificates, diplomas, or degrees in advertising.

Leaders in Advertising Education: Degree Granting Institutions

Wee Kim Wee School of Communication and Information, Nanyang Technological University

The Wee Kim Wee School of Communication and Information (WKWSCI) has its roots in the Department of Mass Communication, situated in the National University of Singapore. One year after it was established, it relocated to Nanyang Technological University, where a freestanding School of Communication Studies was established in 1992.

The school enrolled its first class of 96 undergraduates and master's degree students in 1993. In 2006, the school received an endowment named after the late president Wee Kim Wee and was thus renamed to WKWSCI. By 2010, WKWSCI's student population (undergraduate and postgraduate) stood at approximately 1,300.

WKWSCI endeavours to be the premier school of communication and information in Asia, with international eminence. Its vision is to educate and nurture communication and information professionals and academics, to advance knowledge, and to serve society. The institution offers the Bachelor of Communication Studies (with Honours), Masters in Mass Communication, and Degree of Doctor of Philosophy.

The Division of Public and Promotional Communication grooms students in the fields of public relations, advertising, marketing communication management and media planning. Upon graduation, graduates can find careers as public affairs managers, media planners, account executives, creative directors, consultants, marketing specialists, and publicists in corporate communication settings, government roles, and advertising and public relations agencies.

Nanyang Academy of Fine Arts

The Nanyang Academy of Fine Arts (NAFA) was founded in 1938, with an inaugural batch of 14 Fine Art students. NAFA has since been widely recognised as Singapore's pre-eminent tertiary institution for artistic studies. Between 1999 and 2009, 11 of NAFA alumni were awarded Cultural Medallions, the prestigious national accolade for artistic achievements conferred by the President of the Republic of Singapore (Nanyang Academy of Fine Arts, 2010).

NAFA offers Diploma, BA (with Honours), and part-time Specialist Certificate programs. The BA in Visual Communication with Business, delivered in collaboration with SIM University, provides students at NAFA the opportunity to pursue advanced study in visual communication and acquire skills and knowledge in business. The visual communication aspect of their learning will provide them with essential skills in visual arts, digital media, design and communication and prepare them for careers in the design and advertising industries.

LASALLE College of the Arts

Founded in 1984 by De La Salle educator, Brother Joseph McNally, LASALLE College of the Arts is a specialist tertiary institution leading contemporary arts education in fine art, design, media, and performing arts in the Asia Pacific (LASALLE, 2010). The Diploma and BA (Hons) in Design & Communication programs offer three different specializations, including Advertising Communication, which fosters the idea of communication and the media as important cultural mechanisms in reflecting everyday life. The program requires students to understand good advertising concepts and design communication principles, and its teaching philosophy focuses on practice-based learning, which allows students to discover and be enriched in an interdisciplinary environment.

Raffles Design Institute

Raffles Design Institute was founded in 1990 through a private initiative between "Raffles LaSalle Limited" and "LaSalle College Group" (founded in 1959), with the help of the Singapore Economic Development Board and the Canadian International Development Agency. In conjunction with the change of name, Raffles LaSalle Colleges have since been rebranded as Raffles Design Institute (RDI) in and around the region (Raffles Design Institute, 2010). The vision of Raffles is to be the premier creative arts, design, lifestyle and business management education Group in Asia Pacific.

At RDI, the study of graphic design involves an in-depth under-standing of a graphic designer's role in history, society, and research. Students have the opportunity to explore issues of culture, economics, and social implications of graphic design solutions. Students hone their multi-disciplinary skills through major practical projects, to offer creative and practical solutions. This training seeks to prepare students for challenging careers combining creativity, concepts and computer software skills in the highly competitive advertising and publishing industries.

Management Development Institute of Singapore

The Management Development Institute of Singapore (MDIS), founded in 1956, is Singapore's oldest not-for-profit professional institute for lifelong learning (MDIS, 2009). The MDIS School of Media and Communications was one of the first schools to offer mass communications degree programs and the first institution in Singapore to collaborate with an American university –Oklahoma City University – to offer mass communications programs.

Its full suite of advertising-related programs includes the Master of Arts in Mass Communication, Graduate Certificate in Mass Communications, BA (in Liberal Studies with concentration in Mass Communication), Professional Certificate in Marketing and Communications Management, Advanced Diploma in Mass Communications, and a Diploma in Mass Communication.

School of Art, Design and Media, Nanyang Technological University

The School of Art, Design and Media (ADM), founded in 2005, provides unique educational experiences that facilitate students gaining a deep understanding of the arts, design, and media fields, in dialogue with the humanities, social sciences, natural sciences and technology. Interdisciplinary learning underlies the majors offered by ADM. The School also aims to develop communication and management skills at the highest levels, while refining skills necessary to engage the field professionally, both independently and through teamwork, in the realization of experimental and professional art, design, and media projects (Nanyang Technological University, 2010).

Although relatively young as a school, ADM has attracted faculty members with significant contributions to arts and design education, or with significant professional experience in the creative industries. The school offers the Bachelor of Fine Arts and Master of Fine Arts, and was to launch a Doctor of Philosophy program in academic year 2010 – 2011.

Other Qualifications

Temasek Design School, Temasek Polytechnic

Once better known as the Baharuddin Vocational Institute, Temasek Design School started operations under the Vocational and Industrial

Training Board in 1969 at Kim Keat Vocational School. It offered several courses from Graphic Design to Dressmaking, mainly to serve the design and tourism industry (Temasek Polytechnic, 2010). In 1990, with the establishment of Temasek Polytechnic, 192 students from Baharuddin were absorbed into the Polytechnic's School of Design.

Temasek offers the Diploma in Visual Communication. The school endeavours to train students to master the fundamental skills and knowledge relating to creative thinking, drawing, digital media, graphic design, and design studies. It grooms students to gain an intellectual understanding of visual information and messages, how to manage, and turn these abilities and knowledge into memorable and effective solutions. Through this program, Temasek aims to prepare its students for design professions in advertising, graphic design, branding, and multimedia agencies.

School of Film and Media Studies, Ngee Ann Polytechnic

The School of Film & Media Studies (FMS) was established in 1989. It was the first tertiary institution in Singapore to offer a full-time Diploma in Mass Communication (MCM) and subsequently, the Diploma in Advertising and Public Relations in 2009 (Ngee Ann Polytechnic, 2009).

The FMS learning experience hinges on the application of theoretical and practical knowledge. The Diploma in Advertising and Public Relations – the first polytechnic diploma course in Singapore to offer combined specialisations in Advertising and Public Relations – allows for practice-oriented, agency-based learning that offers real-time campaigns planning for external clients under the mentorship of industry experts.

Chatsworth Medi@rt Academy School of Communication and Design

Chatsworth Medi@rt Academy (CMA) School of Communication and Design prides itself in being the only marketing, advertising and design integrated school in Singapore. The School provides professional and in-dustrial oriented courses and programs to equip participants with the rele-vant knowledge and skills to engage in communications and creative design. CMA offers the Professional Diploma in Advertising & Design, Diploma in Communication Design, and Professional Certificate in Communication Design.

The Industrial Orientation Program at CMA provides opportunities for students to come into contact with the creative industries, interact with professionals and veterans of the industries and gain work-relevant experi-ence. The program is delivered via the following activities: (a) Adman Talk

Profile, (b) Experiential Learning, (c) Creative Networking, (d) Apprenticeship, and (e) Internship.

Support from the Advertising Industry

Professional Internships / Industrial Attachments

Educators can do so only much in the knowledge-transfer process to enrich the learning experience of students (Frith & Chen, 2006). In their 2006 Singapore study on *Insights on the Education Needs of Aspiring Advertising Professionals,* Frith and Chen concluded that the most apparent implication from their findings of interviews with practitioners was that schools should ensure that a formal internship program is in place for students to receive on-the-job training as well as learn skills not commonly taught in schools. Local industry practitioners are also of the view that practical education experience is a key factor for students to secure a job in the advertising industry, eventually (Frith & Chen, 2006).

Institutions like WKWSCI have a mandatory six-month professional internship program built into the four-year curriculum. Students head out for six months to intern at advertising agencies that range from the world's major international agencies to boutique firms. At FMS, students get to participate in internship opportunities with local and overseas agencies over a 20-week duration. The support and participation of advertising agencies in these professional internship programs have therefore been crucial in ensuring that students receive real-world learning opportunities.

AWARD School Asia

AWARD School is a special course run by the Australasian Writers and Art Directors Association for people who want to become copywriters or art directors in advertising. The 16-week part-time course runs across Australia, New Zealand, and Asia, including Singapore. Led by AWARD Committee executives and senior creatives across the Asia Pacific, AWARD School offers amazing opportunities for budding advertising art directors and copywriters to learn from the industry's finest (AWARD School Asia, 2009). Top agencies in Singapore have been involved in tutoring on Thursday evenings, and on Monday evenings lectures are delivered by the industry's top creative leaders and innovators.

Professional Organizations

The Institute of Advertising Singapore (IAS) has been actively promoting and assisting the upgrading of advertising practitioner standards since 1990. Its vision is to see Singapore acknowledged internationally as an influential "diffusion hub" of world class advertising people, professionalism, practice and product (Institute of Advertising Singapore, 2007).

With a comprehensive range of educational and training programs, the Institute has endeavoured to bring relevance to education, by ensuring that IAS' programs are taught by industry professionals. These lecturers and speakers include creative directors from established advertising firms. IAS offers both professional certificate and diploma programs.

The Association of Accredited Advertising Agents Singapore, better known as the 4A's, was founded in 1948. The 4A's represents advertising and marketing communications practitioners, agencies and related businesses in Singapore. It works in close co-operation with other related trade associations, schools and government bodies (Association of Accredited Advertising Agents Singapore, 2009).

Student Competitions

Launched in 2001, the Crowbar Awards, Singapore, highlights the best emerging talent in creative communications and design. Leading creative practitioners judge entries from across six categories – advertising, design, interactive, photography, film, and the Crowbar Challenge. Organized by the 4A's in Singapore, it is an annual platform for emerging young creatives to showcase their work and learn from their peers.

Speaking on the value of the Crowbar Awards in the industry, Troy Lim and Jon Loke, Creative Director and Head of Art at Ogilvy & Mather Advertising, respectively, commented:

> Creative candidates looking for a foot-in would do well to have a Crowbar award in hand. It demonstrates a person's level of talent, passion and initiative more than any resume or CV ever could. Students also get the opportunity to see how respected industry doyens respond to their work. A Crowbar Award serves as a mirror that never lies: if you're great, you go home with the spoils. If you play it safe, you're ignored - welcome to the business of creativity! (Association of Accredited Advertising Agents Singapore, 2010).

Continuing Education and Training for the Practitioner

The Creative Industries Workforce Skills Qualification (CI WSQ) is an initiative to upgrade the capabilities of Singapore's creative workforce. Working in collaboration with economic agencies, employers, and creative practitioners in the industries, Singapore's Workforce Development Agency (WDA) and the Ministry of Information, Communications and the Arts (MICA) developed the CI WSQ to encapsulate workplace competencies for the Creative Industries (Workforce Development Agency, 2010). There is no academic pre-requisite for admission into the CI WSQ training program and progressive qualification pathways can be created to facilitate career advancement prospects.

WSQ training courses are competency-based and practice-oriented; they include attachments to companies and real projects to reinforce learning (MICA, 2010). CI WSQ training has provided an avenue for mid-career switchers, fresh graduates, and existing media professionals to acquire new skills to switch into the creative industries.

The Institute of Advertising Singapore offers WSQ Professional Courses in three areas: (i) preparing a design presentation; (ii) developing and managing business development strategies to enlarge clientele; and (iii) promoting and publicising creative work and services. Since 2007, when the first WSQ course for the CI was introduced, over 1,000 CI professionals have taken part in such training (MICA, 2010).

Future of Advertising Education in Singapore

DesignSingapore (2009 → 2015)

The strategy for the DesignSingapore Initiative in the first five years of its inaugural phase, from 2004 to 2009 (Dsg-I), was to level up both the "supply" and the "demand" for quality design (DesignSingapore Council, 2009). The initiative focused on design capability and appreciation of design, seeding of "upstream" and "downstream" activities, and strengthening designers' professional standing locally and internationally.

For the DesignSingapore Initiative Phase 2, 2009-2015 (Dsg-II), a new set of strategies will be implemented. One of the chief objectives of these strategies will be to accelerate the transformation and growth of the design cluster (DesignSingapore Council, 2009). Capability development will thus be key as educational institutions play a crucial and important role in delivering the quantity, quality, and "right type" of professionals to support these aspirations. DesignSingapore will also work jointly with the International Advisory Panel (IAP) and relevant agencies, such as the Singapore Ministry of Education and the Workforce Development Agency, to review policies and initiate projects that will redefine design learning.

Conclusion

In a short span of time, advertising education in Singapore has advanced tremendously. There are now educational opportunities for all facets of advertising work locally, and for the different levels of expertise required in the industry. Singapore has positioned itself well as a regional educational hub. And with the government having identified the potential for creative industries, initiatives and support are growing in the educational arena. The way forward for advertising education in Singapore certainly is bright in terms of attracting regional and international educators and students, as well as in terms of the widening number of opportunities for Singaporeans.

References

Association of Accredited Advertising Agents Singapore. (31 March 2010). Duo from Ogilvy to helm Crowbar Awards 2010. Retrieved May 10, 2010 from http://4as.org.sg/resources_media.htm

Association of Accredited Advertising Agents Singapore. (2009). About Us. Retrieved May 10, 2010 from http://4as.org.sg/resources_media.htm

AWARD School Asia (2009). Overview. Retrieved May 15, 2010 from http://www.awardschoolasia.com/index.php?p=94

DesignSingapore Council. (2009). Dsg-II: Strategic Blueprint of the DesignSingapore Initiative. Retrieved May 12, 2010 from https://www.designsingapore.org/pdf/Dsg_II_Strategic_Blueprint.pdf

Economic Review Committee. (2002). Creative Industries Development Strategy - Chapter 3: Design Singapore. Retrieved May 10, 2010 from http://app.mti.gov.sg/data/pages/507/doc/ERC_SVS_CRE_Chapter3.pdf

Frith, K. & Chen, J. (2006). Insights on the Education Needs of Aspiring Advertising Professionals. *Media Asia, 33 (1&2)*, pp. 79 – 86.

Henry, C. (2007). *Entrepreneurship in the Creative Industries: An International Perspective.* Edward Elgar Publishing Limited, UK.

Institute of Advertising Singapore. (2007). IAS Vision and Mission. Retrieved May 10, 2010 from http://www.ias.org.sg/about/vision_mission.html

LASALLE College of the Arts. (2010). About Us. Retrieved May 11, 2010 from http://www.lasalle.edu.sg/index.php/about-us

Ministry of Information, Communications and the Arts. (2010, May). Opening Speech by Mr Lui Tuck Yew, Acting Minister For Information, Communications And The Arts, at The Opening of the Creative Industries Fair 2010, 21 May 2010, at Marina Square Shopping Centre Atrium

Management Development Institute of Singapore (MDIS). (2009). Overview. Retrieved May 10, 2010 from http://www.mdis.edu.sg/About/Overview

Media Development Authority, Singapore (2003). MDA awards S$560,000 to groom media talents 14 recipients get opportunity to pursue their passion and nurture their media

skills. Retrieved May 10, 2010 from
http://www.mda.gov.sg/NewsAndEvents/PressRelease/2003/Pages/25072003.aspx

Ministry of Information and the Arts (MITA). (June 2002). Addendum to the MITA Green Paper on "Investing in Cultural Capital: A New Agenda for a Creative and Connected Nation", Retrieved May 10, 2010 from
http://www.mda.gov.sg/NewsAndEvents/PressRelease/2003/Pages/25072003.aspx

Ministry of Information, Communications and the Arts (MICA). (2009). Creative Industries. Retrieved May 12, 2010 from http://app.mica.gov.sg/Default.aspx?tabid=66

Nanyang Academy of Fine Arts (NAFA). (2010). About Us. Retrieved May 10, 2010 from http://www.nafa.edu.sg/aboutus.htm

Nanyang Technological University. (2010). ADM - Mission and Vision. Retrieved May 10, 2010 from http://www.adm.ntu.edu.sg/AboutADM/Pages/MissionandVision.aspx

Ngee Ann Polytechnic (2009). About Film and Media Studies: Introduction. Retrieved May 10, 2010 from http://www.np.edu.sg/fms/aboutus/Pages/introduction.aspx

Raffles Design Institute. (2010). About Us. Retrieved May 10, 2010 from http://www.raffles-design-institute.edu.sg/about_us/about.asp

Singapore Workforce Development Agency (2010). Creative Industries – Industries Overview. Retrieved May 12, 2010 from
http://app2.wda.gov.sg/web/contents/contentms.aspx?contid=875

Temasek Polytechnic. (2010). Temasek Design School: Our History. Retrieved May 10, 2010 from http://www-des.tp.edu.sg/des_home/des_aboutus/des_ourhistory.htm

Wee Kim Wee School of Communication and Information (WKWSCI). (2010). History of the Wee Kim Wee School of Communication and Information. Retrieved May 10, 2010 from http://www3.ntu.edu.sg/sci/about/history.html

Thailand's Advertising Education

Chompunuch Punyapiroje
Burapha University, Thailand

History of Advertising Business and Education in Thailand

In the mid-1840s, the first Thai advertisement (*see* Figure 15-1) for quinine appeared in the first Thai newspaper, *The Bangkok Recorder*, published by Dr. Dan Beach Bradley, an American missionary (see Figure 15-2). Later, many products, both local and imported, were advertised in various newspapers. In the early 1940s, an American advertising agency, Groake Advertising, first entered the Thai advertising industry, followed by Grant Advertising in 1948 and the Cathay Advertiser in 1953. The development of advertising in Thailand has tended to follow the media industries' developments, and that, in turn, has led the development of advertising education.

Recently, Senarak (2004) conducted a study related to the development of advertising education in Thailand. She classified modern Thai advertising education into four periods, as described below.

Figure 15-1: First Advertisement in Thailand

The Establishment Period
(1948-1975 A.D.)

The beginning of television as a national medium in Thailand made the advertising business flourish. Several U.S. and Japanese transnational advertising agencies (TNAAs) started their business in the Thai marketplace, serving advertisers or transnational corporations (TNCs) who invested their own businesses in Thailand. All the practitioners, from "creative" persons to top executives, were foreigners. This was the beginning of a significant era, the so-called "foreign era" (1943-1974) in the Thai advertising business (Chirapravati, 1996), as seen in Table 15-1.

191

Meanwhile, advertising education in Thailand began in the period of Field Marshal Plaek Piboonsongkram, a Thai prime minister who was interested in mass communications, with a particular interest in radio and newspapers as a means to promote nationalism and build the new culture. Thus, he set up a policy to support professional journalism education.

Figure 15-2: Dr.Dan Beach Brad-

Established	Agency	Parent Company
1943	Groake Advertising	Thailand
1948	Grant Advertising	United States
1953	Cathay Advertising (Ted Bates)	United States
1963	Chuo Senko	Japan
1964	Far East Advertising	Thailand
1965	McCann-Erickson	United States
1968	Asia 21 (Thailand) Co.,Ltd.	Japan
1969	Mayford	United Kingdom
1970	Lintas: Bangkok	United Kingdom
1973	CP&Co.,Ltd.	Thailand
1973	Thai Hakuhodo	Japan
1973	Ogilvy & Mather (Thailand) Ltd.	United States
1974	Bay & Ben Ltd., Partnership	Thailand
1974	Diethelm/Leo Burnett Ltd.	United States
1974	Dentsu (Thailand) Ltd.	Japan

Table 15-1: Foreign Era Advertising Agencies in Thailand, 1943-74 [17]

Chulalongkorn University was the first university to offer the journalism diploma degree under the Faculty of Arts and Sciences, in 1939. Later, in 1948, a course related to the Theory of Advertising was first introduced by the Faculty of Arts and Sciences, Chulalongkorn University, as a two-year certificate journalism curriculum.

In 1953, the Thai government paid a great deal of attention to the field of journalism and mass communication, and it requested Thammasat

---

[17] Source: Annual Report & Membership Directory: The 25th Anniversary Issue, 1991 cited in Chirapravati, V., "The Blossoming of Advertising in Thailand," in Katherine Toland Frith (1996), *Advertising in Asia: Communication, Culture and Consumption*. Ames, Iowa: Iowa State University Press (pp.223-240).

University offer a journalism undergraduate major, which was run under Political Science Department. The program concentrated on publishing and advertising, and had one advertising course, "Principles of Advertising." This course examined the relationships among mass media, the owners, consumers, and distributors. Later, the program was moved out of the Political Science Department to the new Department of Journalism, housed in the Faculty of Social Administration.

Figure 15-3: Field Marshal Plaek Piboonsongkram

The popularity of higher education in journalism received increasingly significant interest among public and private universities. For example, in 1965 the Department of Mass Communication and Public Relations of Chulalongkorn University offered a journalism undergraduate program, including a number of advertising courses.

In 1972, Chiang Mai University, a public university located in the northern part of Thailand, also offered a number of courses in advertising. This was the first time that advertising courses had been introduced by a public university located outside of Bangkok. In addition, the Faculty of Commerce and Accountancy of various universities started offering students a number of advertising courses, particularly "Advertising and Promotion" (offered at Chulalongkorn University, Thammasat University, Bangkok College of Technology and Rajamangala University of Technology, Phanakhon).

In 1970, a vocational diploma concentrating in advertising was created at Rajamangala University of Technology, Phanakhon. A year later, Bangkok Commerce College (now called Bangkok University) was the first private university that offered a vocational diploma degree with a major in advertising. It can be said that the beginning of advertising education in Thailand occurred primarily in journalism schools, as it did in western countries, particularly in the United States (Senarak, 2004).

The Rapid-Growing Period
(1976-1987 A.D.)

From 1977 to 1987, most transnational advertising agencies in Thailand employed and trained Thai advertising practitioners, teaching them western advertising practices. After gaining significant experience, these Thai practitioners decided to establish their own advertising agencies. For example, Mr. Prakit Apisarnthanarax (chairman of Prakit and Associates, *see* Figure 15-4), Chalerm Vatcharatanond (CVT & Bercia), Vinit Surapongchai (Damask, *see* Figure 15-5) and among others decided to found their own advertising businesses. As a result, the number of Thai-owned advertising agencies substantially increased (Chirapravati, 1996). See Table 15-2.

Figure 15-4: Mr..Prakit
Apisarnthanarax

Established	Agency	Parent Company
1977	Patterson and Partners Thailand	United States
1977	Indrayuth Co., Ltd.	Thailand
1978	Prakit and Associates	Thailand
1978	Amex Team Advertising	Thailand
1978	Patterns Advertising Co., Ltd.	Thailand
1979	Plan Grafik Co., Ltd.	Thailand
1980	Thai Image Advertising Co., Ltd.	Thailand
1980	The Ball WCRs Partnership	United States
1980	Isco Advertising Co., Ltd.	Thailand
1981	Spa Advertising Co., Ltd.	Thailand
1982	Major Advertising	Thailand
1982	PK Advertising	Thailand
1982	The Media	Thailand
1984	CVT & Bercia	Thailand
1984	DDB Needham Worldwide	United States
1986	Dai-Ichi Kikaku (Thailand)	Japan
1987	Damask Advertising	Thailand

Table 15-2: Thai Era: Advertising Agencies in Thailand, 1977- 1987 [18]

---

[18] Source: Annual Report & Membership Directory: The 25th Anniversary Issue, 1991 cited in Chirapravati, V., "The Blossoming of Advertising in Thailand," in Katherine Toland Frith (1996), *Advertising in Asia: Communication, Culture and Consumption*. Ames, Iowa: Iowa State University Press (pp.223-240).

Figure 15-5: Mr. Vinit Surapongchai

During this era, many Thai universities such as Chulalongkorn University, Thamasart University, and Bangkok University, offered bachelor's degrees in advertising. For instance, the program at Chulalongkorn University was designed by Associate Professor Dr. Pana Thongmeearkom, a pioneer of advertising education in Thailand (Figure 15-6). This curriculum's objective was to produce students for the advertising labor market. It later became an archetype for many universities, helping spread the advertising major.

In the meantime, Associate Professor Dr. Seree Wongmonta (Figure 15-7), Associate Professor and the dean of Faculty of Journalism and Mass Communication at Thamasart University, was another key person in the development of the bachelor's degree in advertising. His curriculum was geared toward having students gain hands-on experiences through real world applications.

Additionally, mass communication education was set into the education policy statement of Thai government between 1977 and 1981. Many advertising courses were offered through open university [19] (Ramkhamhaeng University) and local vocational teaching colleges (Rajabhat University, presently) in Lumpang, Phuket, and Chiang Mai.

Additionally, there was cooperation between advertising educational sector and the industrial sector. The Advertising Association of Thailand, established in 1966, had offered many schools to its members, who were advertising professionals, to educate stu-

Figure 15-6: Associate Professor Dr. Pana Thongmeearkom

---

[19] An open university typically refers to one that has no entrance requirements, being open to anyone irrespective of their background. Open universities often heavily rely on distance learning methods.

dents in various universities. It also opened three training courses (New Account Executive, New Creative, and New Media courses) for new advertising staffs.

In addition, there was an advertising competition in this period, called the TACT Awards (Top Advertising Contest of Thailand Awards) (Senarak, 2004), held by three major universities: the National Institute of Development Administrator, Thamasart University, and Silpakorn University. *KooKhang Magazine*, which belonged to Media Focus Company, was a famous magazine to provide advertising and marketing knowledge in terms of practice, for students and professors.

Figure 15-7: Associate Professor Dr. Seree Wongmonta

The Leaping Period (1988-1997 A.D.)

Between 1988 and 1997, the Thai advertising industry entered the golden age, as indicated by high advertising expenditures. However, several Thai-owned advertising agencies encountered difficulty due to rapid growth of the industry, forcing them to partner with several transnational advertising agencies (TNAAs) such as J. Walter Thompson, Saatchi & Saatchi, and Backer Spielvogel Bates (Thailand). More than 200 advertising agencies were established in Thailand during this time (Chirapravati, 1996). As a result, careers in advertising gained popularity.

Many professors at Thai universities responded to this growth. Both private and public educational institutions in local and metropolitan areas began offering advertising programs. Consequently, the number of students seeking advertising as their concentration area increased (Anantachart, 2002; Senarak, 2004). Moreover, an advertising major at the graduate level was found in four major universities: Bangkok University, Sripratum University, Chulalongkorn University, Dhurakij Pundit University, and Suan Dusit Rajabhat University.

In Warren and Khotanan's article (1991) and Sherer's article (1995), three Deans of Communication – Associate Professor Dr. Darunee Hirunrak (Figure 15-8), Associate Professor Laksana Satawedin (Figure 15-9) and Associate Professor Dr. Seree Wongmonta – were interviewed about Thai students' interests in studying advertising and communication. They shared similar views, indicating that the major reason for these students choosing a major in advertising and communication might come from pragmatic and

Figure 15-8: Assoc. Prof.
Dr. Darunee Hirunrak

idealistic student motives. Thai students see opportunities to possess a well-paid job with prestige.

Among Thai students, those working in mass communication areas (e.g., television, radio) have been well received as "celebrities" in Thai society. Associate Professor Dr. Wongmonta added that those who work with advertising agencies generally got paid better than those who work as an accountant. In addition, Mr. Chanarong Tangsakulkraiang, an art director of Dentsu, Young Rubicam Ltd., stated that Thai students are interested in working in advertising because of the opportunities offered (e.g., working outside and meeting new people), which excite them (Sherer, 1995). Presently, many advertising programs have opened in both public and private universities, including Rajabhat Universities, in the colleges of education and teaching.

Present Period
(1998-Present)

Since the Asian financial crisis in 1997, the Thai government has tried to improve the economy in every aspect, including changing the quality of advertising education in order to better serve the workforce. As a result, Thailand has ranked sixth in the world in terms of advertising expenditures. Compared to other Asian countries, excluding Japan, Thailand was ranked third as the country with fastest growing advertising expenditures ("Global Adspend Trends," 1998).

According to Nielsen Media Research, Thai advertising expenditures in 2008 reached

Figure 15-9: Assoc. Prof.
Laksana Satawedin

89.5 billion baht ("Advertising Spending," 2009). The advertising business has grown. Consequently, the academic sector has designed various curricula to produce the needed qualifications and knowledge for the advertising business. Some universities offer courses about marketing communication perspectives in their advertising curricula, while other universities separate the marketing communication curriculum from the advertising curriculum.

Kaewsuwan (2009) researched the factors influencing the choices of communication arts students at Chulalongkorn University by surveying the junior and senior students in 2008. Her research revealed that about one-third of students entering in the Faculty of Communication Arts chose advertising as their major, out of seven offered majors in each academic year. This finding confirms that the advertising major is still popular among Thai students. Presently, advertising education in Thailand can be summarized as follows:

Institutes Offering an Advertising Curriculum

In Thailand, advertising programs range from a two-year vocational diploma to doctor of philosophy degrees. However, this paper mainly concentrates on advertising education in the undergraduate and graduate levels in universities.

A search via the Google search engine reveals that Thai Universities offering advertising, market communications, or related fields as a major at the Bachelor Degree level involve four public universities, two open universities, 22 private universities, 24 Rajabhat Universities (used to be teaching colleges), and two Rajamangala Universities of Technology. Most advertising programs are housed in the Faculty of Communication Arts in public, private, and open Universities, while some belonged to the Faculty of Management Sciences in Rajabhat Universities (*see* Table 15-3).

Type	Name	Faculty/Major	Degree level		
			Bachelor	Master	Ph.D.
Public Universities	Burapha University	Faculty of Humanities and Social Sciences	✓	✓	
	Chiang Mai University	Faculty of Mass Communication	✓	✓	
	Chulalongkorn University	Faculty of Communication Arts	✓	✓	✓
	Thammasat University	Faculty of Journalism and Mass Communication	✓	✓	✓
Open Universities	Ramkhamhaeng University	Faculty of Business Administration	✓	✓	
	Sukhothai Thammathirat Open University	Faculty of Communication Arts	✓	✓	✓
Private Universities	Assumption University of Thailand	Faculty of Communication Arts	✓		
	Bangkok University	Faculty of Communication Arts	✓	✓	✓
	Chaopraya University	Faculty of Communication Arts	✓		
	Dhurakij Pundit University	Faculty of Communication Arts	✓	✓	✓
	Eastern Asia University	Faculty of Communication Arts	✓		
	Far Eastern University	Faculty of Communication Arts	✓		
	Hatyai University	Faculty of	✓		

			✓		
		Communication Arts			
	Huachiew Chalermprakiet University	Faculty of Communication Arts	✓		
	Kasem Bundit University	Faculty of Communication Arts	✓	✓	
	Krirk University	Faculty of Communication Arts	✓	✓	✓
	Payap University	Faculty of Communication Arts	✓		
	Pathumthani University	Faculty of Communication Arts	✓		
	Ratchaphruek College	Faculty of Communication Arts	✓		
	Rungsit University	Faculty of Communication Arts	✓	✓	✓
	Saint John's University	Faculty of Communication Arts	✓	✓	
	Siam University	Faculty of Communication Arts	✓	✓	
	Sripatum University	Faculty of Communication Arts	✓	✓	
	University of the Thai Chamber of Commerce	Faculty of Communication Arts	✓	✓	
	Thongsook College	Faculty of Communication Arts	✓		
	Vongchavalitkul University	Faculty of Communication Arts	✓		
	Webster University	Unknown	✓		
	Yonok University	Faculty of Communication Arts	✓		
Rajabhat University	BanSomdejchaopraya	Faculty of Management Sciences	✓		
	Chiang Mai	Faculty of Management Sciences	✓		
	Chiang Rai	Faculty of Management Sciences	✓	✓	
	Kanchanaburi	Faculty of Management Sciences	✓		
	Loei	Faculty of Management Sciences	✓		
	Mahasarakham	Faculty of Management Sciences	✓		
	Nakhon Pathom	Faculty of Management Sciences	✓		
	Nakhon Rajasima	Faculty of Management Sciences	✓		
	Nakhon Si Thammarat	Faculty of Management Sciences	✓		
	Piboonsongkram	Faculty of Management Sciences	✓		
	Phetburi	Faculty of Management Sciences	✓		
	Phetchabun	Faculty of Management Sciences	✓		
	Phranakhon	Faculty of Management Sciences	✓		
	Phranakorn Si Ayutthaya	Faculty of Humanities and Social Sciences	✓		

	Rajanagarindra	Faculty of Management Sciences	✓		
	Rambhai Barni	Faculty of Management Sciences	✓		
	Suan Dusit	Faculty of Management Sciences	✓		
	Suan Sunandha	Faculty of Management Sciences	✓		
	Sisaket	Faculty of Management Sciences	✓		
	Thepsatri	Faculty of Management Sciences	✓		
	Ubol Ratchathani	Faculty of Management Sciences	✓		
	Udon Thani	Faculty of Management Sciences	✓		
	Uttaradit	Faculty of Management Sciences	✓		
	Yala	Faculty of Management Sciences	✓		
Rajamangala University of Technology	Tawan-ok: (Chakrabongse Bhuvanarth Campus)	Faculty of Business Administration	✓	✓	
	Thanyaburi	Faculty of Mass Communication Technology	✓	✓	

Table 15-3: Thai Universities that offer advertising, market communications or related fields as a major in Undergraduate and Graduate Degree[20]

Curriculum, Course Content and Degree
Undergraduate Level

Most faculties that offer an advertising major are similar in terms of their study plan. Generally, students begin their freshman or sophomore year with fundamental advertising courses, such as "Principles of Advertising" or "Introduction to Advertising." When they are sophomores, they need to choose their major. They usually take more advanced advertising courses during their junior and senior years. The number of total credit hours students must complete to earn their Bachelor's degree in Communication Arts (B.Com.Arts.) ranges from 135 to 145 credit hours.

Other advertising courses that students must take include "Advertising Media and Planning," "Advertising Creative Strategies," "Advertising Research," "Advertising Campaigns," "Copy Writing," "Advertising Management," "Consumer behavior," and so on. These courses are offered at both private and public institutions. However, most of the public universities or autonomous universities[21] still have a limited budget to provide high-

---

[20] This table was compiled through a query on the Google Search Engine, and is subject to the limitations of such a search.

[21] An "autonomous" university is one not governed by the Higher Education Comission. There currently are eleven autonomous universities: Suranaree University of Technology, Walailak University, Mae Fah Luang University, King Mongkut's University of Technology

technology equipment, such as cameras, computers, and/or studios, for teaching their advertising students. Consequently, some private universities take advantage of this as their own unique selling proposition by offering courses related to marketing, management, and advertising production to draw students to their universities.

In addition, most schools that offer an advertising major also require students to take an internship, for students to gain real-world experiences. They are required to complete approximately 135-160 hours for their internship, under supervision of on-site practitioners. Their grades for an internship course are be assigned as either pass or fail, based on their reports and portfolios. However, some universities allow students to substitute an internship course by taking an independent study, if that student already has had an internship experience.

An analysis of course content and structure reveals two types of curriculum structures, generalists and specialists, in Thailand. The generalist advertising curriculum prepares students with general advertising knowledge, and provides them training to be able to work any positions within advertising agencies. Students can then discover for themselves what kinds of positions within the agencies best suit them. On the other hand, specialist advertising programs, aimed to produce students with particular skills for, e.g., creative departments or account executive departments, are intended to prepare students to more quickly begin work.

Course content of Thai advertising curricula is influenced by the western educational system because the majority of Thai professors with advanced communication degrees (e.g., M.S. and Ph.D.) graduated from western universities.

Graduate Level

In Table 15-3, the data show that 18 Thai universities offer a Master's degree in Communication Arts. Seven universities that offer a Ph.D. Program in Communication Arts are Chulalongkorn University, Thammasat University, Sukhothai Thammathirat Open University, Bangkok University, Dhurakij Pundit University, Krirk University, and Rungsit University. Bangkok University offers a Doctor of Philosophy in Communication in cooperation with Ohio University in the U.S.A.

At the master's level, most students take some core subjects before choosing their own specific areas of interests. Thus, if the students want to

---

Thonburi, Burapha University, Chaing Mai University, Chulalongkorn University Mahidol University, Thaksin University, King Mongkut's University of Technlogy Ladkrabang, and King Mongkut's University of Technology North Bangkok.

be specialists in advertising or marketing communications, they need to study more advertising courses. Students have an option to choose either a thesis or non-thesis track for their master's degree. The degree they obtain is the Master of Communication Arts, either in Advertising, Communication Arts, or Marketing Communications. The degree that Ph.D. students obtain is Doctor of Philosophy in Communication Arts.

Instructors & Instruction for Undergraduate and Graduate Programs

Most advertising instructors are Thai, with a master's degree in advertising, marketing communications, or a related field. Thai language is mainly used in classroom teaching, with an exception in some international programs where classes are taught in English. Most introductory courses are mainly in lecture format, while the courses related to production and strategies allow students to be involved with hands-on activities. Senior-level classes are sometimes taught in seminar format or small group discussions.

Punyapiroje (2009) studied the current status of advertising education in Thailand. Professors' opinions about advertising program administration in both private and public universities were sought. Some of the findings suggest:

- Most advertising programs set the curriculum philosophy and objectives congruent with the college's vision and mission ($\bar{x}$ =4.11 from 5 point scales).

- Committees manage the advertising programs ($\bar{x}$ =3.68).

- In curriculum development and evaluation, the professors valued an instructional process ($\bar{x}$ =3.93) and an learning evaluation process ($\bar{x}$ =3.89) higher than others.

- There are both short and long term budget plans for managing resources ($\bar{x}$ =3.79), as well as an audit system ($\bar{x}$ =3.61).

- Most advertising programs have a database related to the students and graduates, academic, research, personnel, budgets, depot and workplace information ($\bar{x}$ =3.25).

- Most advertising programs set appropriate criteria for admission, to select qualified students. These criteria were the qualification of applicants, the number of students to be accepted in the program, and timetable ($\bar{x}$ =3.67).

- Internships ($\bar{x}$ =4.26) and providing academic advisors for students were among the most important features of the programs ($\bar{x}$ =4.04).

- For instruction and research, course syllabus and teaching plan ($\bar{x}$ =4.36), student-centered instruction ($\bar{x}$ =4.25), instructional evaluation by students to improve teaching ($\bar{x}$ =4.19), media, technology and innovation usages for teaching ($\bar{x}$ =4.00) were commonly found in most advertising program.

- Regarding the learning environment, activities that create learning atmosphere ($\bar{x}$ =3.85), and resources that support students' learning, such as libraries, computers, equipment, and workplaces, were seen as critical to the student learning process ($\bar{x}$ =3.82).

- For assessment of program graduates, programs tend to conduct a survey and other follow-ups regarding their graduates' satisfaction of the curriculum and instruction, based on their work experiences ($\bar{x}$ =3.86).

- Allowing students to transfer course credits to other faculties and universities within the country was common ($\bar{x}$ =3.54). There was less cooperation with universities outside the country.

When professors were asked about the most suitable advertising courses (see Table 15-4), they said the 10 most suitable courses in advertising programs were (1) Advertising Creative Strategy, (2) Advertising Production or Management of Advertising Production, (3) Consumer Behavior, (4) Advertising Principles, (5) Advertising Media Planning and Advertising Media Strategy, (6) Internship or Cooperative Education, (7) Principles of Marketing, (8) Advertising Research, (9) Seminar in Advertising, and (10) Computer Graphic for Design.

However, advertising practitioners said the most suitable advertising courses were (1) Consumer Behavior ($\bar{x}$ = 4.56), (2) Advertising Principles ($\bar{x}$ = 4.53), (3) Presentation Techniques ($\bar{x}$ =4.36), (4) Brand Building ($\bar{x}$ =4.30) or Advertising Creative Strategy ($\bar{x}$ =4.30), (5) Analysis of Audience Behavior ($\bar{x}$ =4.24), (6) Internship or Cooperative Education ($\bar{x}$ =4.22), (7) Integrated Marketing Communication ($\bar{x}$ =4.18),(8) English for Communication and Advertising and New Media ($\bar{x}$ =4.16), (9) Introduction to Business Communication ($\bar{x}$ =4.14), and (10) Brand Communication ($\bar{x}$ =4.12)

For recent graduates currently working with advertising businesses, the top 10 courses were Consumer Behavior ($\bar{x}$ = 4.00), (2) Advertising Principles ($\bar{x}$ = 3.90), (3) Advertising Campaign Planning ($\bar{x}$ =3.78), (4) Principles of Marketing ($\bar{x}$ =3.68), (5) Analysis of Audience Behavior ($\bar{x}$ =3.67), (6) Advertising Creative Strategy ($\bar{x}$ =3.58), (7) Advertising Media Planning and Advertising Media Strategy ($\bar{x}$ =3.56), (8) Advertising Research ($\bar{x}$ =3.54), (9) Introduction to Business Communication ($\bar{x}$ =3.52), (10) Advertising Management ($\bar{x}$ =3.50).

When comparing the opinions of advertising professors, advertising practitioners, and these recent graduates, toward the forty-two courses in advertising curriculum (*see* Table 15-4), the findings revealed that advertising practitioners' opinions were higher on 31 advertising courses than the opinions of recent graduates (p-value< 0.05). Also, there was a significant difference between advertising professors and practitioners' opinions related to the Seminar in Advertising (p-value< 0.05). But there were no significant differences among these three groups in eleven courses such as the Principles of Marketing, Advertising Campaign Planning, Advertising Management, Photography in Advertising, Advertising and Society, Personality and Manners, Portfolio, Marketing Management, Marketing Information Management, Advertising for Service Business, and Marketing Public Relations courses.

Courses in Advertising Curriculum in Thailand	Professors (N=28) Group 1		Administrative Practitioners (N=50)Group 2		Graduates (N=50) Group 3		F	p
	$\bar{x}$	S.D.	$\bar{x}$	S.D.	$\bar{x}$	S.D.		
Advertising Principles	4.30	0.72	4.53	0.99	3.90	0.82	8.19	0.001*
Introduction to Business Communication	3.77	0.81	4.14	0.99	3.52	0.89	5.73	0.004*
Principles of Marketing	4.22	0.75	4.12	1.12	3.68	0.96	3.62	·
Consumer Behavior	4.31	0.79	4.56	0.70	4.00	0.95	5.76	0.004*
Analysis of Audience Behavior	3.87	0.92	4.24	0.99	3.67	0.98	4.53	0.014*
Presentation Techniques	4.00	0.65	4.36	0.85	3.46	1.22	10.56	0.000*
Business Psychology	3.14	0.73	3.74	1.23	3.02	1.23	5.12	0.011*
Advertising Research	4.21	0.79	3.67	1.10	3.54	1.09	3.99	0.025*
Advertising Media Planning/Advertising Media Strategy	4.29	0.81	3.92	1.11	3.56	1.20	4.11	0.021*
Advertising Campaign Planning	4.29	0.66	4.06	0.98	3.78	1.02	2.81	·
Integrated Marketing Communication	4.15	0.88	4.18	1.05	3.42	0.99	8.60	0.011* 0.001*
Brand Building	4.04	0.77	4.30	0.81	3.47	1.04	9.01	0.000*
Writing for Advertising or Copy Writing	4.04	0.72	3.92	1.00	3.32	1.15	6.09	0.016* 0.016*
Advertising Management	3.92	0.64	3.70	1.02	3.50	0.91	1.84	·
Client Service Management	3.59	0.91	3.82	1.14	2.92	1.02	9.49	0.048* 0.000*
Art Appreciation or Principles of Design or Ad Design	4.00	1.06	3.96	0.92	3.26	1.29	6.25	0.025* 0.008*
Advertising Creative Strategy	4.36	0.68	4.30	0.81	3.58	1.23	4.15	0.004* 0.002*
Photography in Advertising	3.75	0.85	3.43	0.94	3.28	1.34	1.47	·
Advertising Production or Management of Advertising Production	4.33	0.64	3.81	0.98	3.23	1.22	9.63	0.000* 0.027*
Computer Graphics for Design	4.16	0.90	3.75	1.00	2.83	1.48	12.26	0.000* 0.001*
Seminar in Advertising	4.20	0.58	3.47	1.14	3.10	1.11	9.34	0.019* 0.000*
Internship or Co-operative Education	4.26	0.90	4.22	0.98	3.49	1.42	6.19	0.024* 0.009*
Advertising and Society	3.56	0.87	3.42	1.15	3.06	0.99	2.41	·

Persuasive Communication	3.72	0.89	3.96	1.00	3.36	1.17	4.03	0.021*
Personality and Manners	3.48	1.08	3.71	1.11	3.14	1.19	3.01	·
International Advertising or Global Advertising Culture Comparative	3.36	0.95	3.47	1.10	2.83	1.26	4.04	0.027*
On-line marketing	3.18	0.96	3.81	1.16	2.54	1.22	14.62	0.000*
Event Marketing and Sponsorship	3.55	0.60	3.56	1.07	2.96	1.12	4.84	0.018*
Portfolio	3.45	0.86	3.44	1.18	2.94	1.22	2.74	·
Strategy of Integrated Organizational Communication	3.68	0.72	3.60	1.01	2.84	1.01	9.85	0.004* 0.001*
Exhibitions and Events Media	3.48	0.73	3.31	0.98	2.88	1.12	3.62	0.050*
English for Advertising	3.57	1.08	4.16	1.05	3.27	1.41	6.81	0.002*
Direct Marketing/ Strategy for Direct Marketing and Sales Promotions	3.23	0.92	3.38	1.10	2.69	1.21	4.82	0.013*
Communication and Retail Business	3.39	0.78	3.13	1.10	2.65	1.12	4.59	0.024*
Marketing Management	3.52	0.73	3.73	1.05	3.31	1.07	2.06	·
Marketing Information Management	3.39	0.78	3.48	1.15	3.04	1.11	2.14	·
Brand Communications	4.04	0.81	4.12	0.97	3.49	1.08	5.56	0.008*
Advertising for Service Business	3.39	0.66	3.59	1.00	3.15	0.90	2.97	·
Advertising and New Media	3.57	0.73	4.16	1.09	3.40	1.38	5.62	0.006*
Case Analysis of Advertising Problems	3.63	0.93	3.90	1.25	3.19	1.23	4.32	0.016*
WWW Design for Advertising	3.36	1.05	3.25	1.02	2.51	1.32	6.42	0.019* 0.009*
Marketing Public Relations	3.39	0.84	3.57	1.12	3.21	1.11	1.40	·

Table 15-4: The comparison of opinions toward the courses in advertising curriculum of professors, practitioners working in administrative positions and graduates working in Advertising Agencies

For opinions about the actual qualification and expected qualification of advertising students (see Tables 15-5 and 15-6), the findings revealed that both advertising professors and advertising practitioners evaluated actual student qualifications lower than they expected.

The student qualifications that the professors expected were (1) Be punctual ($\bar{x}$ =4.56), (2) Be able to work as a team ($\bar{x}$ = 4.50), (3) Good in human relations, Enthusiastic to gain new information, and Be able to communicate with people very well ($\bar{x}$ = 4.46), (4) Have creativity, Self-Confidence to express their opinions, Have countenance, Be flexible in working, and Have ethical in work ($\bar{x}$ = 4.42), and (5) Open minded to other's opinion ($\bar{x}$ =4.40).

The student qualifications that the practitioners expected were (1) Be careful in the assigned work ($\bar{x}$ =4.42), (2) Enthusiastic to gain new information, and Be Honest ($\bar{x}$ = 4.41), (3) Have creativity, Be punctual, Self-Confident to express their opinions, and Have ethical in work ($\bar{x}$ =4.38), (4) Be observant ($\bar{x}$ = 4.36), (5) Good in human relations ($\bar{x}$ =4.29).

When comparing the opinions of advertising professors and advertising practitioners about their perception of the recent graduates' actual qualification in advertising field, most of the findings revealed that there were no significant differences between professors' and practitioners' opinions related to their perception of recent graduates' actual qualifications, except on two qualifications that revealed significant differences. That is, professors rated the recent graduates' qualifications related to their "strategically thinking" higher than practitioners (p-value< 0.05). On the other hand, practitioners rated the recent graduates' qualifications related to "foreign language knowledge" higher than professors (p-value< 0.05).

When comparing opinions of advertising professors and advertising practitioners related to their expectation of the recent graduates' qualification that they should posses for a career in advertising, the findings revealed that there were no significant differences.

The actual qualifications of graduates in advertising field	Professors (N=28) Actual qualifications		Practitioners (N=50) Actual qualifications		t	df.	Sig.
	$\overline{x}$	S.D.	$\overline{x}$	S.D.			
1. Have academic knowledge about his/her job	3.43	0.69	3.16	0.77	1.51	75.00	0.137
2. Good Personalities	3.43	0.96	3.38	0.75	0.25	76.00	0.805
3. Good in human relations	3.79	0.74	3.80	0.99	-0.07	76.00	0.947
4. Enthusiastic to gain new information	3.32	0.98	3.39	1.10	-0.27	75.00	0.792
5. Have creativity	3.54	0.79	3.56	0.99	-0.11	76.00	0.912
6. Open minded to other's opinion	3.61	0.83	3.40	0.86	1.04	76.00	0.304
7. Self-Confident to express their opinions	3.68	0.98	3.52	0.91	0.72	76.00	0.475
8. Be sagacious in solving problems	3.29	1.01	3.10	1.03	0.76	75.00	0.450
9. Have countenance	3.46	0.65	3.18	0.83	1.58	76.00	0.119
10. Have information-analytical skills	3.14	0.65	2.86	0.90	1.46	76.00	0.149
11. Be able to communicate with people very well	3.32	0.67	3.16	0.93	0.81	76.00	0.423
12. Be careful in the assigned work	3.04	0.69	2.88	1.12	0.76	75.13	0.451
13. Have a presentation skills and sense of salesman	3.21	0.88	2.96	0.98	1.14	75.00	0.257
14. Be flexible in working	3.46	0.74	3.28	0.97	0.87	76.00	0.386
15. Be punctual	2.89	0.99	2.98	1.02	-0.37	76.00	0.716
16. Have strategic thinking	3.14	0.93	2.62	0.99	2.29	76.00	0.025*
17. Be Honest	3.54	0.79	3.78	0.91	-1.19	76.00	0.238
18. Have ethics in work	3.57	0.79	3.71	0.92	-0.66	74.00	0.513

19. Have foreign language knowledge	2.57	0.96	3.04	0.92	-2.12	76.00	0.037*
20. Be able to work as a team	3.54	0.84	3.66	0.94	-0.58	76.00	0.562
21. Be observant	3.18	0.86	3.31	1.08	-0.57	67.00	0.573

Table 15-5   The comparison of opinions toward the graduates' actual qualifications in advertising field of professors and practitioners working in administrative positions

The expected qualifications of graduates in advertising field	Professionals (N=28) Expected qualifications		Practitioners (N=50) Expected qualifications		T	df.	Sig. S.D.
	$\bar{x}$	S.D.	$\bar{x}$	S.D.			
1. Have academic knowledge about his/her job	4.27	0.53	4.18	0.67	0.57	4.27	0.53
2. Good Personalities	4.35	0.63	4.06	0.79	1.60	4.35	0.63
3. Good in human relations	4.46	0.65	4.34	0.75	0.70	4.46	0.65
4. Enthusiastic to gain new information	4.46	0.76	4.41	0.64	0.32	4.46	0.76
5. Have creativity	4.42	0.70	4.38	0.67	0.26	4.42	0.70
6. Open minded to other's opinion	4.40	0.58	4.30	0.68	0.63	4.40	0.58
7. Self-Confidence to express their opinions	4.42	0.70	4.38	0.67	0.26	4.42	0.70
8. Be sagacious in solving problems	4.31	0.79	4.26	0.80	0.25	4.31	0.79
9. Have countenance	4.42	0.64	4.23	0.78	1.08	4.42	0.64
10. Have information-analytical skills	4.38	0.64	4.16	0.68	1.39	4.38	0.64
11. Be able to communicate with people very well	4.46	0.71	4.08	0.91	1.85	4.46	0.71
12. Be careful in the assigned work	4.35	0.69	4.42	0.73	-0.43	4.35	0.69
13. Have presentation skills and sense of salesman	4.27	0.72	4.15	0.85	0.63	4.27	0.72
14. Be flexible in working	4.42	0.64	4.26	0.72	0.97	4.42	0.64
15. Be punctual	4.56	0.77	4.38	0.85	0.89	4.56	0.77
16. Have strategic thinking	4.20	0.76	4.00	0.83	1.01	4.20	0.76
17. Be Honest	4.38	0.70	4.41	0.73	-0.14	4.38	0.70
18. Have ethics in work	4.42	0.70	4.38	0.73	0.27	4.42	0.70
19. Have foreign language knowledge	4.08	0.95	4.30	0.71	-1.13	4.08	0.95
20. Be able to work as a team	4.50	0.76	4.32	0.71	1.02	4.50	0.76
21. Be observant	4.27	0.83	4.36	0.78	-0.47	4.27	0.83

Table 15-6   The comparison of opinions toward the graduates' expected qualifications in advertising field of professors and practitioners working in administrative positions

Advertising Education Support Organizations

The Advertising Association of Thailand (AAT)
The Advertising Association of Thailand was established in 1966. Its major goals are to establish a good relationship among members, to negotiate advertising-related issues with governmental agencies, and to promote the advancement of professionalism in the advertising profession and the industry. The AAT has its own code of ethics, which serves as a voluntary set of guidelines for the advertising industry in Thailand. However, the enforcement of this code of ethics does not include punitive power. The only penalty for violating the code is expulsion of the member from the association. Even though the AAT is a private organization, it works and coordinates with the government regulatory agencies.

In 2004, AAT held the first Adman Award & Symposium providing a competition related to marketing communication campaigns. This included not only advertising work, but also public relations, graphic designs, and media strategies.

The Bangkok Art Directors Association
The Bangkok Art Directors Association was established in 1985. Its major goal is to promote quality creativity by organizing seminars and workshops to train young creative people, as well as sponsoring the annual Bangkok Art Director Awards competitions, i.e., "BAD" Awards.

Summary

Programs across Thailand tend to be quite similar. Most are housed in the Faculty of Communication Arts. Most of their professors employ similar teaching techniques, such as lectures, group discussion, seminars and hands-on activities. They tend to invite advertising practitioners to share their working experiences with students. Most of the undergraduate programs require students to take an internship as a part of curriculum, to enhance students' learning experience outside the classroom. Such internships can take place with advertising agencies or business organizations related to an advertising field.

It is evident that course content and structures of Thai advertising curricula were adopted from those offered in western countries (e.g., USA). This may be due partly to the fact that many Thai advertising professors obtained their graduate degrees from western universities, particularly from the United States (Anantachart, 2006). Thus, it is suggested that Thai advertising professors may need to reassess their advertising curricula, and might consider applying their unique knowledge about Thai culture to further develop their own advertising curriculum.

References

"Advertising Spending down 2.77% in 2008," The Nation, January 23, 2009, available at: http://www.nationmultimedia.com/2009/01/13/business/business_30093114.php.

Annual Report & Membership Directory: The 25th Anniversary Issue 1991. Bangkok: The Advertising Association of Thailand.

Anantachart, S. (2002). Public Relations in Thailand: A Review on Its History, Recent Research and Practices. *Journal of Communciation Arts, 20(4),* 49-66 (in Thai).

Anantachart, S. (2006). Integrated Marketing Communication in Globalization: Current Status and Body of Knowledge. *Journal of Communciation Arts, 24(1),* 94-118 (in Thai).

Anantasomboon, K. (2000). *Undergraduate Curriculum in Advertising and Workforce Demand in Thailand.* Unpublished master thesis, Chulalongkorn University (in Thai).

Chirapravati, V. (1996). The blossoming of advertising in Thailand. In K. T. Frith (Ed.), *Advertising in Asia* (pp. 223-241). Iowa: Iowa state university press.

"Global Adspend trends: Asian Adspend, A review of its development & future prospects." *International Journal of Advertising,* 1998 17(2), 255-263.

Kaewsuwan, N. (2009). Factors Influencing Major Selection of Communication Arts Students of Chulalongkorn University. *Journal of Communication Arts, 27 (3),* 140-155 (in Thai).

Punyapiroje, C. (2009). The Current Status of Advertising Education in Thailand in the 2000s. Presented at the *2009 Asian conference of the American Academy of Advertising* (May 27-30), Beijing, China.

Senarak, P. (2004). *The Development of Advertising Education in Thailand.* Unpublished master thesis, Chulalongkorn University (in Thai).

Sherer, P. M. (1995). Selling the sizzle: Thai advertising crackles with creativity as industry continues to grow. *The Asian Wall Street Journal Weekly,* 1, 6-7.

The Advertising Book: Thailand 1994-1995 Advertising, Marketing and Media Guide, 1995, Bangkok: AB publications.

Warren, J. and Khotanan, A. (1991). Communication education at Thai universities. *Journalism educator, (winter),* 28-33.

EUROPE

Germany's Advertising Education

Olaf Werder,
University of Sydney, Australia

History and development of advertising education

To truly understand the diverse approaches to advertising education in Germany, one has to take a quick excursion into Germany's dual education system, that combines on-the-job training with theory taught in public vocational schools one or two days per week (Soskice & Schettkat 1993). It is interwoven with the different tracks students go into at high-school age:

> German students are separated into different tracks at age 10, when their parents place them into one of three levels of secondary education: Hauptschule, Realschule, and Gymnasium. The lowest level, Hauptschule, is designed for students who plan to begin apprenticeship programs starting at age 16. Similarly, the Realschule focuses attention on providing students with the skills necessary for an apprenticeship, though it provides slightly more advanced academic theory than the Hauptschule. Students who plan to attend universities generally attend Gymnasia, the highest level of the secondary educational system. Upon graduating from Gymnasia, students receive a university entry certificate, known as an Abitur (Petrosky 1996).

It is primarily (but not exclusively) the first two education levels that, after completion, lead a student to participate in an ongoing on-the-job training, while being hired by an employer. To offset the lack of scientific training for those levels, so-called *Berufsakademien* have grown with an aim to provide an alternative to institutions of higher education. These professional academies have taken the principle of the dual system of vocational education and training, and applied it to the tertiary education sector (International Association of Universities 2006).

Advertising education's origin in Germany as a technical skill (creative/design and sales, primarily) has put it in the mix for a non-university education track. If it involved university training, it was primarily a course as part of a marketing or business degree, or the nature of a project in a design degree.

There typically are three educational pathways for advertising and strategic communication (GWA 2010a):

1. A standard apprenticeship in the dual system combines on-the-job training with a basic education at vocational schools (similar to community colleges in the United States). This usually leads to entry-level or lower-level jobs, after being hired full-time by the apprenticeship agency or any other agency to which the graduating student may apply.

2. An advanced training combines the on-the-job training with more rigorous advertising training at special academies that lead to a recognized title upon graduation. The principal degree for those following this scheme is the "Kaufmann/Kauffrau für Marketingkommunikation" (roughly "merchant of marketing communication"). Offered primarily by the slightly more than 25 private professional academies (e.g., the AfAK – Akademie für Absatzwirtschaft Kassel, the DAMK – Düsseldorfer Akademie für Marketing-Kommunikation, or the IMK - die Internationale Akademie für Marketing, Kommunikation und Werbung in Berlin), the curriculum is tailored to those holding permanent employment (or apprenticeships) in the advertising industry. Courses are offered in the evening, and taught mostly by professionals in the industry (Schwaller 2010).

The study program takes about three years, requires a secondary degree (see above) and follows a federally sanctioned education plan with final tests to be taken at the regional chambers of commerce (Industrie und Handelskammer, or IHK). It leads to a federally recognized title, according to Germany's vocational education law (Bundesinstitut für Berufsbildung 2006).

While this more practically oriented "Kaufmann" degree seems more suited to attract primarily those students who graduated from the two lower-level tiers of high school, increasingly "Gymnasium" graduates (8 out of 10 as of 2006) appear to choose this route. Whereas these programs are more well-rounded in all aspects of advertising and media communication than, say, a design or arts program, they resemble in their overall structure private art and design schools in the United States, such as the Miami Ad School or Creative Circus in Atlanta.

3. Despite the popularity of the practical approach to advertising ed-

ucation, it has become relatively difficult for German advertising professionals to climb to leadership positions in the industry without scientific basic knowledge in such areas as mass communication, business administration, pedagogy, or sociology (Schwaller 2010).

A university education has therefore become an almost indispensable foundation to those aspiring to a high-flying career in the advertising industry (Vieregge 2009). As in any country, leadership roles in German advertising require more profound knowledge of business and economic contexts than technical skills in design or media buying. While many university degrees can lead to a career in advertising in Germany, the classic degree according to most hiring managers in agencies is still business administration with an emphasis in marketing (ZAW 2007).

The website *medienwissenschaft.de* (Barth 2007) lists about 45 universities that offer a degree in media or strategic communication. Those are often overlapped to a large extent by degrees in journalism and media management, and one has to research a program carefully to find one that focuses on advertising. About 60 fine art academies offer the degree of design, with an average study time of 3-5 years. Finally, at about 100 universities in Germany, advertising is a research and study area within the marketing degree. However, only a few, e.g., the Pforzheim Academy and the Academy of the Arts in Berlin, offer a direct degree in advertising or marketing communication.

Profiles of a variety of advertising programs

Duale Hochschule Baden-Württemberg (DHBW) in Ravensburg

The advertising degree at the DHBW is a major of the course of studies in media and communication sciences in the College of Business. It focuses on the areas of marketing, consulting and design (Ottler 2010). Overall, the courses are systematically adapted to the requirements of the advertising industry. Students are confronted with all phases of advertising from consumer research and advertising planning, advertising design, production and dispersion to measuring advertising success.

Business subjects form the solid basis of the studies. This is supplemented in every semester with a wide range of courses on media and communication. Research, specializing in advertising, especially the areas of consumer media research and usability testing, is the backbone of the program. Close cooperation with the *Steinbeis Research Center* at DHBW on the topic of promotion and communication guarantees a permanent transfer of knowledge between the school and the industry.

As is standard for a professional academy, admission requirements include a training contract with an appropriate company, besides a high school degree (usually from a Realschule or Gymnasium).

Zeppelin University in Friedrichshafen

Zeppelin University is a state-recognized private institution of higher education in the state of Baden-Württemberg. Named after Graf von Zeppelin, one of the most important German pioneers of aviation, Zeppelin University's mission is the education of pioneers who can make the improbable probable in business, culture, and politics.

zeppelin university

Bridging Business, Culture and Politics

Advertising industry professionals are involved heavily in advertising education at the university. It offers a Bachelor and Master of Arts in communication and cultural management. Students can choose from different majors, among them a major in strategic communication.

The teaching and research of the Department of Strategic Communication is built on three content areas: corporate communications, consumer behavior, and managerial decision making (Lipper 2010). Besides advertising and advertising psychology, the curriculum includes courses in public relations, media relations, corporate brand management, and corporate design and identity.

Rheinische Fachhochschule (RFH)
in Köln (University of Applied Sciences)

Calling itself a place for practical studies, this university offers degrees that have clear job descriptions and are integrated in broad professional networks, where faculty, students, and professionals collaborate in research and practical projects. Resembling adult or continuing education courses, seminars are small, with 20-50 students Compact and short courses are part of the curriculum. The RFH offers a bachelor of arts in media management that includes advertising as an emphasis (Gutzeit & Nell 2010).

What makes this program unique is (a) a dual qualification as strategic media economists (basically a business administration degree plus media competence), a growing desirable field in Germany with 350,000 employees in the university's home state of Northrhine-Westphalia, and (b) an emphasis on media technology and design, which not only is a separate bachelor of arts degree (BA in Media Design), but an important component of the media management curriculum, as well. It resembles the growing emphasis of digital media and media management at U.S. universities.

Professional organizations that support advertising education

Equivalent to the American Advertising Federation (AAF), the German Association of Communications Agencies (abbreviated GWA, for *Gesamtverband der Kommunikationsagenturen*) is the umbrella membership organization for German advertising. The leading agencies in Germany, such as BBDO, Grey, Jung von Matt, JWT, Saatchi & Saatchi, Scholz & Friends, and Springer & Jacoby, are in the GWA.

In 2002, the association launched an initiative to promote young researchers and interdisciplinary cooperation, titled GWA Junior Agency (GWA 2010b). Quite similar to the AAF's National Student Advertising Competition (NSAC), it is Germany's most demanding academic competition for students of marketing communication, and the only junior competition in Germany that judges the strategic and creative services simultaneously. Marketing and design students work out long term strategies and concepts of communications for a real client. Slightly different from the NSAC, briefing and coaching  is permitted by GWA agencies who each partner with a student team.

After working with and presenting to their agency partner, the GWA invites all participating teams to the final presentation of the developed case studies (during the GWA Junior Agency Day). Parallel to the NSAC routine, a team of no more than five people presents the strategic and creative concepts in 25 minutes. An independent panel of judges evaluates the presentations and awards the "Junior" in Gold, Silver and Bronze. The participating student teams also vote on their own favorite (the participants' choice award), which is awarded as a trophy (GWA 2010).

References

Barth, C. (2007). *Auflisting medien- und kommunkationswissenschaftlicer Studiengänge* (List of programs in media and communication sciences). Universität Trier, Retrieved on March 22, 2010 from http://www.medienwissenschaft.de/studium-lehre/studiengaenge.html.

Bundesinstitut für Berufsbildung (2006). *Verordnung über die Berufsausbildung zum Kaufmann für Marketingkommunikation* (regulation about the vocational training for "Kaufmann" of marketing communication). Federal legal paper, 2006, Part 1, No. 17., Bonn, Germany: Bundesinstitut für Berufsbildung (BIBB).

Gutzeit, C., & Nell, P. (2010). *Admissions Advisors – short profile of the degree in media management and media design.* Köln, Germany: Rheinische Fachhochschule Köln. Retrieved on May 20, 2010 from http://www.rfh-koeln.de/studium/studiengaenge/medien/medienwirtschaft/.

GWA (2010a). *Job and Career.* Website of the "Gesamtverband Kommunikationsagenturen GWA e.V." Frankfurt, Germany. Retrieved on March 15, 2010 from http://www.gwa.de/job-karriere/uebersicht/.

GWA (2010b). *GWA Junior Agency.* Website of the "Gesamtverband Kommunikationsagenturen GWA e.V." Frankfurt, Germany. Retrieved on March 15, 2010 from http://www.gwa.de/job-karriere/gwa-junior-agency/.

Lipper, T. (2010). *Program director for CCM: A short description of bachelor and master studies in communication and culture management.* Friedrichshafen, Germany: Zeppelin University, gGmbH. Retrieved on May 20, 2010 from http://www.zeppelin-university.de/deutsch/lehrstuehle/strat_kommunkation/Strat_Kommunikation_Profil.php.

No author (2006). Germany – Structure of education system. International Association of Universities: *World Higher Education Database.* Retrieved on April 21, 2010 from http://www.euroeducation.net/prof/germanco.htm.

Ottler, S. (2010). Program Director Advertising Track: A profile of the studies in the business of media and communication with an emphasis in advertising. Ravensburg, Germany: Duale Hochschule Baden- Württemberg. Retrieved on May 20, 2010 from http://www.dhbw-ravensburg.de/de/fakultaet-studiengang/wirtschaft/bwl-medien-und-kommunikationswirtschaft/werbung/.

Petrosky, J. (1996). The German dual educational system: Evolving needs for a skilled workforce. *Perspectives on business & economics, Vol. 14,* 59-69.

Schwaller, T. (2010). Kommunikarriere.de: An initiative for job starters. Frankfurt, Germany: Gesamtverband Kommunikationsagenturen. Retrieved on April 10, 2010 from http://www.kommunikarriere.de/.

Soskice, D., & Schettkat R. (1993). West German labor market institutions and East German transformation. In: L. Ulman, B. Eichengreen, & W. Dickens, (Eds.). *Labor and an Integrated Europe* (pp. 102-127). Washington, D.C.: The Brookings Institution.

Vieregge, H. von (2009). Tips from the professionals: Avenues toward advertising jobs (translated). GWA working papers. Frankfurt, Germany: Gesamtverband Kommunikationsagenturen.

Zentralverband der Werberwirtschaft in Deutschland (2007). ZAW-Jahrbuch „Werbung in Deutschland" (ZAW Yearbook "Advertising in Germany"). Berlin, Germany: Verlag edition ZAW.

Sixty Years of Teaching in Italy

Edoardo Teodoro Brioschi
Catholic University of the Sacred Heart, Italy

The Evolution of Italian Advertising and the Teaching Issue

The quantitative development of Italian advertising in the post World War II period had immediately raised an important question: that of the recruiting of newcomers in this sector who should already have been trained in an appropriate way. During this period different generations of advertising experts co-existed in Italy. Many people who had found advertising as an alternative means of employment, after that they were forced to give up due to political reasons in the 1920s and 1930s, made up the first generation. However, many of them took up their original jobs in post war democratic government, and thus this first generation count further reduced.

Immediately after the war, and during the fifties, a second generation of advertising experts grew up with the first one. However, they often thought that their training was not satisfactory: they were "men who were born to communicate, who looked up to their jobs with enthusiasm rather than with a technical training" as we pointed out in the past (Mengacci & Brioschi, 1972, p. 388).

Their arrival marked the transition phase of Italian advertising, from practical experience to technique, which lasted until the mid-fifties. However, they represented the last group of versatile advertising experts who were able to face and analyze thoroughly, any aspect of advertising. This distinguished the advertising expert - the professional - from those with a limited set of skills - the collaborators - who were dependent on the professionals (La Manna, 1951, p. 84 and following).

The lacunae encountered in the training of most of the advertising experts – which were to be remedied for the forthcoming generation (the third one) – were strictly interconnected to teaching (the well known advertising course held at the Chamber of Commerce, Milan, during 1920-1922 and the birth of an Italian branch of the Ecole Supérieure de Publicité Pratique of Paris at the publishing house L'Ufficio Moderno in 1928).

From the fifties onward, the teaching issue was constantly discussed at national congresses, both to clarify and officialize the formulation of the problem, and to examine in real terms training courses conducted and their results in order to suggest new solutions.

In this respect, there were essentially two trends related in a specific manner to different aims: On one hand the completion of the training of the future managers of companies operating in different sectors (industry, commerce and services), on the other hand the specific qualification of those who should have worked exclusively on advertising in both pertinent companies and in those companies which used advertising.

The first aim suggested to integrate both the standard curriculum of senior high schools, highlighting some courses, and that of the university essentially referring to the Faculty of Economics. The second one, that of the training of the future advertising experts, favored the institution of a relatively complex school outside of the standard organizations after the completion of the senior high school, rather than the choice of a specific curriculum in an academic faculty.

However, notwithstanding the risks associated with the creation of a special advertising school outside the standard organizations, and the existence of some first solutions in the academic courses of the University[22], the advertising sector chose the first solution to train its newcomers following French and German advertising trends. This led to the establishment of the new advertising schools in Milan (1952) and Turin (1953).

The School in Milan, born to be a leader among institutions belonging to the same genre, got off a good start as a daytime two-year program, which was made famous by some university lecturers who took up the advertising phenomenon with great dexterity.[23] A further ten-year follow-up period, as an evening three-year course, then had to be completed.

Since 1954 the presence of one of the most well-known advertisers, Campari, guaranteed the School of Milan a much more satisfactory life full of good prospects. This lasted until the School had to reduce its activity and close down indefinitely in 1973, because there wasn't any location at its disposal anymore. In the meantime, the School joined an international association –the International Association of Schools in Advertising (I.A.S.A)

---

[22] The two-year course dedicated to the methods of propaganda and advertising held at the Istituto Superiore di Giornalismo e di Scienze dell'Opinione Pubblica of the International University "Pro Deo" in Rome and the Media two-year course at the Statistics faculty of the Rome University belonged to these academic courses. To these courses which dated back to post World War II and which corresponded essentially to a two-year course in any faculty of the University was added the extensive Scuola Superiore di Giornalismo e Mezzi Audiovisivi, established by Università Cattolica in 1961.

[23] "The list of the teaching staff – it is stated in this period- includes prestigious names belonging to economic and sociological sciences as those of the Professors Siro Lombardini, Gaetano Kanitza, Francesco Brambilla and Luigi Guatri. A. Valeri, *Appunti per una storia della pubblicità in Italia*, X, in "I prodotti di marca," p. 342, 5/1970.

– and its executive director, Adriana Ferrari Battaglia, was the President of this Association.

The Teaching of Advertising:
An Appropriate Approach to the Problem

As mentioned, from the nineteen fifties the teaching issue was constantly discussed at the national congresses (Brioschi, 1966, p. 290 and following). From that period onwards the lively discussion about the teaching of advertising marked the existence of two trends: (1) the teaching to train young people for their future advertising job with any advertiser, advertising agency, or media company (*professional training*), and (2) the teaching with the aim to educate, both at senior high school level and at University and postgraduate courses.

The first trend, that of the professional training, gave rise in Italy to pioneering organizations in the early fifties. After a start-up period, these organizations transformed into paracademic institutions or postdiploma organizations. Even though these schools had the unquestionable merit of training newcomers, and that of improving course material, they could not shed their pioneering nature. The reasons were not related to the evolution of the job, which required certain institutional flexibility or periodic revision, but to inherent faults which existed at the beginning.

In the Sixties and the mid-Seventies, notwithstanding the most advanced and prestigious School – that operating in Milan – expressed a wish to be renewed in a real and proper way (La Manna, 1963), the teaching situation with the aim to educate for the advertising jobs seemed inadequate. This was confirmed by the decision taken by the national association which represented the advertising professionals (A.I.T.P.), when it believed (1968) it was suitable to conduct entrance tests (grade 1 of basic knowledge, and grade 2 of in-depth and applicative knowledge) to guarantee an appropriate qualification of its members in the perspective of a possible future legal status for them.

The grade 2 exam was irreplaceable, because it was considered comparable to the ones required for officially entering the old and traditional professions. Instead, the grade 1 exam would be progressively replaced by the accreditation of institutions, considered adequate to this purpose (Brioschi, 1972, p. 14).

The introduction of these exams leads to some considerations. In this respect it is necessary to highlight that the type of teaching instituted until then, to train young people to their future advertising job, gave rise -

as I have repeatedly remembered - to specific schools outside the context of the university, which followed the French model. The introduction of the exams was primarily put in action drawing inspiration from the English model, which was one of the leading models in Europe. By this model, teaching was conducted by already existing institutions or universities.

In particular, the introduction of the grade 2 exam helped to define better the different professional roles which represented the professional activity. Specifically speaking, they distinguished the "generalists" who could manage and develop initiatives and advertising campaigns in every aspect, from the "specialists" who belonged to the creative sector (like copywriters, art directors, and audio-visual specialists) or to other sectors (planners and researchers).

The need to define clearly these two professional roles led, on one hand, to finding basic and common knowledge between them, and on the other to identifying some specific necessities of training. Thus, for some, the attempt to optimally satisfy the needs of both led to the creation of two distinct *types* of schools for the two professional roles, for others it led to the creation of a single school, really much more complex, with a common learning foundation and two specialized courses distinguished for professional roles. Generally, giving these courses to the already existing universities would supposedly avoid the creation of complex, but probably less functional, institutions.

The Involvement of the Università Cattolica del Sacro Cuore

I dwelt on the problems concerning the teaching of advertising and the development of advertising jobs in Italy, first of all, because I wanted properly to include the Scuola Superiore di Giornalismo e Mezzi Audiovisivi in this scheme. This School was set up by Professor Mario Apollonio, who also was its first director at the Università Cattolica, during the academic year 1961-1962. It was a postgraduate school, which offered dedicated courses in the advertising specialization, with the aim to train future communication or advertising professionals whose profiles would be clearly demarcated by their jobs.

The original plan of study (Apollonio, 1963, p. 306 and following) focused on general courses such as psychology, sociology, history of modern culture, history of modern church, catholic social teaching, vocational courses, and basics of courses such as history, theory and practice of journalism, advertising, television, film and theatre.

The School, which was later called Scuola Superiore delle Comunicazioni Sociali, was officially recognized five years later (1966). This official recognition helped to better define its structure.

In particular, in the second year students were required to study, in-depth, fundamental topics that covered the core area of the specialization. They were also required to choose other subjects among the additional courses, to assist in fulfilling the advertising graduation requirement.

The course of theory and technique of advertising represented the fundamental course in this field, and it was interconnected with the ones of the first year. This course covered topics such as psychology and sociology of advertising, as well as market research. The additional courses focused on the diverse types of advertising (press advertising, film, radio and television advertising), as well as on the graphic visualization of advertising (we refer to it as "graphic adverting").

After many years of experience, the best the School could do to meet the interests of any learner was to group general subjects at the first year of the two-year course. With the reduced number of courses better satisfying the School's aim, the School became a school of specialization, and the number of courses from a single specialization area generally increased.

In particular, with regard to the advertising section, the business economics course – among the others introduced - completed the curriculum. This course allowed consideration of advertising as a tool of a business activity and with a marketing perspective.

In Pursuit of Scientific and Ethical Fundamentals of Teaching Advertising

At the Scuola Superiore delle Comunicazioni Sociali advertising was not considered on its own, but it was included in a much larger theoretical model referring to the increasingly evolving social communications (more frequently studied under the title of mass communications), whose foundations were focused on psycho-sociological sciences.

In general its aim was to contend and overcome an artisanal practice, which didn't lay down a solid scientific foundation, even if it dealt both with an ancient art, such as journalism or theatre, and with a less ancient practice as in the case of advertising. To overcome this artisan's practice meant also to overcome those myths which governed this practice, and which were able to fascinate youth.

However the myth referred to here was not the one of the business leader, but the one of the hidden persuader, as it was defined in a well-known work of a bad popularization (Packard 1958), and which was much more dangerous. In this respect we could observe that also some autobiographies by famous workers in the field of advertising[24] had a subtle influence, above all, on the youth. We could cite – one for all – David Ogilvy's autobiography (Ogilvy, 1963). More precisely, these autobiographies gave a sense of adventure and improvements on which lay the foundations of the professional practice.

A second essential aspect related to the approach followed by the Scuola Superiore delle Comunicazioni Sociali, with reference to advertising, was the specific care for ethics. As it was stressed by its founder: "The School will allow students to pursue diverse professional careers. They will be able to get a job with much more responsibility; they will be experts of technique and science and even more of ethical and religious values; without these values every attempt appears to be useless" (Apollonio, 1964).

The concepts of the respect for man, the communication media as tools, the use of these tools to take part in the world, as expressed by Second Vatican Council's *Inter Mirifica* Decree and later by *Communio et progressio*, which pervade the work by Apollonio, also affected advertising.

Although these principles traditionally provided the foundation for the Università Cattolica's learning and teaching, it's also true that they clearly reflected the desire of the advertising industry in those times. In fact, the advertising industry approved and enacted a set of rules, of an ethical value, in 1966. The Code – originally defined "Codice della Lealtà Pubblicitaria" – was the result of a long and comprehensive study which spanned more than ten years of debates. It was intended to influence both the advertising expert and, consequently, the practice of the profession, ever more deeply as new editions of the Code (today it is called Codice di autodisciplina della comunicazione commercial) were published.

I outlined the role of a modern advertising professional, according to this perspective, at the beginning of the seventies:

---

[24] We refer to the well-known work by Claude Hopkins, *My life in Advertising*, which was translated in Italy in 1932 and which was entitled *I miei successi in pubblicità*. It played an important role to promote the American school, which was founded at the beginning of the last century. The same role was played by his second book *Scientific advertising*, Moore Publ. Co., New York 1923. I have to observe that in 1968 appeared a new edition of this book with an introduction by David Ogilvy.
The autobiography by the most famous and historical representative of Italian advertising: D. Villani, *Cinfessioni di un «persuasore»*, Ceschina, Milano 1972, is also related to the first book by Hopkins. Actually the author, as Hopkins, belongs to the first generation of advertising experts.

The man of communication will have to take on new undertakings and assume further responsibilities, and to handle them it is required a technical education more and more developed as well as an increasingly human comprehension.

Actually man is at the heart of every event, and he must be there, irrespective of any technological evolution and of any economical and social development.

If I could think about the future of my son, as a man of communication, I would think of him as someone who should have been trained by a school of a high culture, as someone who has been trained to communicate with his fellows in any sector and for any aim the society sets. (Mengacci & Brioschi, 1972, p. 388)

However, the theme of responsibility, and particularly the theme of social responsibility with reference to advertising, is very important. It marked about twenty years which span the second half of the Sixties to the mid-Eighties, in a periodization which goes from the beginnings to modern advertising (Brioschi, 1984, p. 17 and following).

These responsibilities can be fulfilled only with a deeper and more extensive professionalism. The first element of professionalism is ethics: "ethics," I insisted, "is not *a* component of this professionalism, but it is *the* essential component... so that if there is not ethics we cannot actually talk about professionalism, at the most we can talk about of a job which does not contribute to the progress of advertising in Italy."[25]

Now, if I wanted to remind the fundamental contribution which Mario Apollonio gave to the birth of an Italian theory of advertising, I could summarize it as it follows:

- a proposal of ethics which gives sense to advertising and which promotes its social recognition. This is in perfect agreement with the concept of "modern advertising" in general, and with that of the "new directions of Italian advertising," promoted by the National Congress of Advertising held in Rome in 1971 (Brioschi, 1974);

- the definition of a communicational theory of advertising to be integrated with the business and economic advertising theory, which was in fact formulated on a basis of a quite marginal consideration of the communicational nature of the activity under consideration;

- the formulation of this communicational theory as part of a much more extended theory of social communications, as in the case of the economic theory,

---

[25] E. T. Brioschi, *T.P. Basi etiche per la professione*, in «Pubblicità & Successo Annual 1985», Milano 1986, p. 23. I affirmed this concept as a president of the Associazione italiana tecnici pubblicitari AITP (Italian Association of Practitioners in Advertising), and I stressed it still further in *Presentazione degli Atti del Convegno nazionale per il 40°anniversario* of the Association under consideration, held in Milan, 25 october 1985.

advertising appeared to be part of a much more extended business economics theory.

Teaching Advertising at the Faculty of Economics

I should note that, in the meantime, advertising teaching also had been introduced in the faculty of Economics of Università Cattolica as a specialized course. Starting with the academic year 1968-1969, principles of economics and technique of advertising were outlined in this faculty, in an appropriate way, specifically inside the industrial and commercial technique course held by Giordano Caprara.

At the beginning of the Seventies only two universities in Italy had officially introduced this course: the Università Cattolica and the Università Bocconi, both based in Milan, which is properly defined as the Italian capital of the advertising industry. In these courses advertising was considered, first of all, as a tool for business management. More specifically, these courses outlined advertising objectives, its related problems, and a planning model. They also made general reflections (of ethical, juridical, economic aspects, etc).

The aim was to make students - who would get responsible jobs within the different classes of businesses - aware of advertising, and of its potential, but at the same time of its limits. This was so they could clearly understand its function and properly judge its application within their companies. The evolution in the teaching of advertising within the faculty of Economics clearly led to the enrichment of the proposed framework of such an activity, and to its integration with multiple and meaningful experiences.

In conclusion, let me briefly mention also the general issue of updating, which not only refers to advertising professionals. In this respect, there are fundamentally two essential aspects to be considered. On one hand is the need of the business management, at any levels, to be informed about the progress in the use of tools of advertising and its related problems. It needs to be underlined that advertising represents one of the most effective, but also one of the most delicate and complex forms of that *non–price competition* involving an increasing number of markets, specifically referring to consumer goods and services.

On the other hand, we can't forget the verified opportunity to transfer the techniques of advertising in other industries (I think of the so-called social interest campaigns in favour of blood donation, the conservation of forest wealth and other aspects and values of social life, which were developed from the beginning of the Seventies in Italy). This should also lead to introducing these techniques in training programs for the staff of the involved social institutions.

The Università Cattolica started with a pioneering spirit, also in the updating field, by organizing some wide-ranging conferences starting in 1963. These encompassed subjects as "Wealth and advertising" or "The human factor in advertising."

From the Mid-Eighties to the New Millennium

Until the mid-eighties teaching advertising in Italy was characterized, *first*, by a very limited number of universities involved in such a teaching. Among them is the Università Cattolica, which continues to be the leader. In this respect I need to remember the contributions of IULM, of some curricula belonging to the Faculty of Sociology at Federico II in Naples, La Sapienza in Rome and Urbino, and of some curricula belonging to the faculty of arts and philosophy of a few other universities.

IULM has special importance with respect to its contributions in the field of communication, beginning with public relations. It was founded in 1968 as a University Institute for Modern Languages. Later, in 1998, it was called Free University of Languages and Communication IULM. This name strikingly underlines its mission in the field of education of future professionals with a deep knowledge of languages and business communication.

Second, this period was notable for the rise of a very limited number of private and well-qualified non-university institutions. Among them was the Istituto Europeo di Design (IED). This institution was established in 1966, and it would play a significant role in the field of teaching, even if its contribution in the area of advertising would have been gradually defined in the following decades. In particular, this happened through the establishment in the eighties of Istituto Superiore di Comunicazione (Higher Communication Institute), which gave rise to IED Comunicazione in 2000.

Besides these, the Accademia di Comunicazione, was founded and became operational in 1988, in Milan. Its plan was to create a project on education, research, and innovation in visual and persuasive communication (marketing, advertising, public relations, graphic design and all the technologies related to these professional sectors). In particular, the project on education was based on the "bottega" concept, where students could learn the essential skills for their future job.[26]

---

[26] Also "Fabrica," founded in 1994 in Treviso by Benetton Group, one of the most famous Italian companies to use communication, appears to draw inspiration from this concept.

The introduction in Italy of study programs and diplomas launched by the International Advertising Association (IAA), during its Congress in Durban (1979), ends the landscape of the first half of the eighties. This association was concerned that each country have teaching institutions able to offer adequate training for future professionals. The first Italian university to be IAA accredited in Italy was Università Cattolica, in 1983. Several years later the same accreditation would was granted to some courses held by IED.

In the second half of the eighties two important initiatives, connected with the university world, were launched:

• The Master[27] Publitalia, promoted by the Fininvest group in 1988 in collaboration with the main universities in Milan.

• The Master in business communication, promoted in 1989 by UPA, the association of the most important companies which invest in advertising, in collaboration with the Department of Economics and Business Administration of University Ca' Foscari of Venice.

The most relevant event of this period, probably the greatest one, was the launch of graduation courses in communication sciences, which included a major in business communication. The foundation of these courses was built on the observation that the study of communication events (either individual or social, private or public in nature) involved a multidisciplinary approach including, in particular, sociology, psychology, and semiotics.

These courses began in the academic year 1992-1993 at a very limited number of universities (first of all Salerno, Siena and Turin). Two universities of Rome, La Sapienza and LUMSA, followed them. Later, other universities followed, until the beginning of 2000.

The courses raised great hopes for their vocational nature, but then proved to be below expectations, in particular, with regard to the teaching of business communication. While the demand decreased, the universities followed different strategies to uncap job opportunities. However, faculties of Communication Sciences also were established. The first one was at IULM University of Milan, in 1999. The first public university to inaugurate this faculty was the University of Rome La Sapienza, in 2000.

Starting with the nineties, three-year diplomas were introduced in the communication field. They referred to advertising, and even more generally

---

This group didn't intend to give birth to a school or a "university" which supported its group, but to an international creativity lab.

[27] In didactic terms, the word "Master" in Italy means a postgraduate course, which is attended by graduates whose aim is to specialize and qualify themselves.

to business communication, often interconnected with marketing. However, these diplomas were later included in the three-year degree course introduced by the national university reform in academic year 2001-2002. Following this reform, a large number of first and second level Masters (in the Italian meaning) were introduced after the third and fifth year of university courses, respectively.

In my opinion what is the most interesting steps in the progress and evolution of above mentioned aspects, for our aim, is:

> • The increasing involvement of universities in the field of teaching advertising, or rather in business communication, both for basic training purposes (the first three years) or vocational purposes (following two years of study). Thus, the approach to the teaching issue which was proposed in the fifties was gradually being modified, if we don't take into account the strict creative aspects of advertising and business communication.

> • The absorption of university studies on advertising into the wider field of business communication according to that concept of total communication, which I shall discuss below.

Such an evolution is understandable when one considers the increasing complexity and articulation of business communication, and the reduction of the role played by advertising, as it is traditionally intended in the field of such communication.

In this respect I have to finally underline that the development of institutions and initiatives involved in advertising teaching in the period 1985/2000 was strictly connected to the increasing competitiveness on the Italian advertising market, as it is shown in the following table:

Mezzo	1985	1990	1995	2000
Televisione	54,70%	51,20%	62,10%	57,10%
Radio	2,60%	1,70%	1,80%	4,90%
Stampa	42,70%	42,20%	33,30%	34,20%
Affissione*		5,00%	2,90%	2,80%
Cinema*		0,00%	0,00%	0,90%
Internet*		0,00%	0,00%	0,00%
Direct mail*		0,00%	0,00%	0,00%
Grand Total	1.522.718	3.289.151	4.024.008	7.121.963

not evaluated

Table 17-1: the evolution of advertising investments in Italy ('000 euros)

From Advertising to Business Communication

To deal with the business communication it is absolutely necessary, first of all, to define the concept that I am referring to in using this expression. The concept under consideration is that of the "total business communication." This expression refers to the entirety of the communication process of a business. In fact, any business elements, aspects, and activities can influence the process of communication, and then the business corporate identity and the related image.

Management can be aware of this influence at different levels. It can be completely aware, or not sufficiently aware, or even, in a number presumably even higher, absolutely unaware. Moreover, this process of communication involves both implicit aspects, typical of the nature and structure of a business, and aspects that can explicitly influence its identity and its corporate image, which is a quite complex concept.

The corporate image is not the exclusive and predominant result of an explicit communication activity promoted by the business. This image exists even if the mentioned communication activity is not carried out. On the contrary, it is a much more complex consequence of the presence of the business itself, in its entirety, of the various forms of communication activated by that presence (interpersonal, non-personal or mass communication) and, finally, of the different communication processes promoted by the business.

With reference to this, I have to remark that the traditional four areas which form the total business communication (corporate communication, internal communication, external marketing communication – obviously including advertising – and economic and financial communication) are the subject of debates, in order to revise partly these areas and consequently their roles (for example, the internal communication has been extended to the organizational communication including the distributors, and the economic and financial communication has been extended to the communication addressed to those who hold strategic resources in general, whether financial, technological, etc). On the other hand, these areas appear to be the subject of an increasing integration that involves the values and the principles of the business communicationin general.

Now, the business communication in the sense of a total communication can be considered under different profiles and at different levels:

> • The *communication as a culture* whose aim is primarily to suggest and affirm
> the permanent and strategic character of the communication as a business production factor. It follows that not only is it essential for the business itself to

look at this factor, but also that the communication – used in an efficient and effective way - represents a value for the business (as it is the development of the human resources or the conservation of the environment);

• The *communication as a business approach*, that is as a general rule of the business governance in order to offer the business identity and image - or, as it is also said, the reputation - to the different audiences in the best way;

• The *communication as a business function*, whose aim is directed to promote, create and control the variety of the communication initiatives of the business. In this connection I recall a survey completed in the mid-nineties at a European level, which involved most of the sectors of the economic activity and represented a group of six countries including Italy (Brioschi, 2007). This research revealed that only 1% of the businesses belonging to the sample reported the absolute absence of any explicit communication activity. Seventy-seven percent of the businesses had an organizational unit essentially dedicated to communication, whereas five years before it was only in 52% of the businesses. Therefore, had the percentage increased at the same rate in the following years, today this organizational unit would have been present in an overwhelming majority of the businesses, particularly in those involved in the consumer goods and services; even if it is always advisable to distinguish between the reality of the small and medium enterprises and that of the large ones.

With respect to the development of the total business communication, according to the three previously cited categories (as culture, in terms of governance and as an operational function), it appears that the evolution of theory in this field and the relation between theory and practice are considered highly relevant. In this respect, there is more than one reason to talk about the myth and the reality of business communication.

Undoubtedly the development of this theory has been guided by a dominant American school, which has effectively given a century worth of contributions and experiences (Brioschi, 1984, 104 and following). As we know, this theory has been applied not only in the United States, but also across continents, including Europe and Asia.

It deals specifically with a school which has been able to theorize the indispensability of the integration between the different activities, and the multiple instruments of business communication which gave birth to the concept of "integrated marketing communications" (IMC)." This development, an important goal for the theory, started at the end of 1980s. At the same time, this theory is in a continuous evolution as frequently advocated by one of its eminent theorists, Professor Don Schultz from Northwestern University (Schultz, 2005).

Besides the American school, however, we also need to consider the emergence of two others: the European and the Japanese schools. These schools have undoubtedly, and profitably, drawn inspiration from the American one, but they increasingly consider the peculiarities of each action area beginning from its culture. In fact, the European school devises the concept of the "total communication," towards which the concept of the "integrated marketing communications" (Brioschi, 2006, p. 101 et seq.) can be compared, even if its premises and assumptions are partly different from the ones of the European concept. The Japanese school highlights the holistic nature of business communication, based on its national culture which has to be deeply reconsidered, and the need to elaborate concepts partly different from those which have been used until today to guide and conduct the communication activity (Brioschi – Kobayashi, 2008, p. 211 et seq.).

Whatever is the school one belongs to, regarding theory, I will note that the practice does not still appear, at an international level, predominantly and sufficiently inspired by the aspects of permanence and strategies of the business communication, upon which I previously dwelt. As I have remarked (Brioschi, 2005, p. 22 et seq.), "The theoretical principles underpinning the business communication appear to be clearly developed, even though they require further checks and above all deepenings. Then instantly arises the question of why the application of these principles is still very limited even in the highly developed countries."

The Obstacles to Principles' Application: the Professionals of the Future

The above-mentioned application of theoretical principles is not so easy, as the business reality shows us concrete difficulties to putting these principles into effect. The difficulties we are talking about are specifically caused by:

• The disparity between the specific objectives which each area of business communication pursues, even though they share a single final objective;

• The dispersion of the governance of these areas between different organizational functions, with the consequent difficulty of pursuing that final shared objective, also because this objective ends up by reducing the power of the individual functions in terms of the responsibility for communication attributed to each;

• The increasing richness, complexity and specificity of the means and instruments of communications, which may make it more difficult, even extremely difficult, to pursue the objective of a unified use, which theory refers to;

• The different levels of importance attributed to the different areas of business communication in the sector where the business operates, in the individual business examined in a particular phase of its existence and, finally, in the business considered in its development.

On a more general level, the approaches suggested by the different theoretical schools require business and its top management to overcome many types of obstacles: cultural, organizational, technological, and financial.

The term "culture," in the case of the cultural obstacles, specifically refers to the field of communication. Now, the culture of communication still seems to be quite inadequate in the great majority of firms. It can be summed up simply as caused by a "lack of people who understand the total business communication." The first obstacle for the development of such a culture and, hence, the management or governance of business communication in the modern sense is a mental look. This was shown by research into the same subject that were carried out in Italy in the second half of the nineties. These studies showed that the change in the mentality of management was the first and fundamental problem to be dealt with on the level of general business management itself, and not simply in the case of communication. But just considering the change of this mentality and, on the whole, the appropriate education of those who are and will be responsible for communication at different levels, the well-known role of education appears relevant.

The results of one of the studies already mentioned, conducted at the European level, outlined the role of an ideal professional. The results can be summarized as: "The goal is to train the future professionals in the field of total business communication." It was also underlined that, "This approach should allow to satisfy the existing needs of the professionals, and consequently to develop an [education] which implies the knowledge of theory and practice of each area of communication...." Moreover, it was affirmed, "Today, both professionals and academics of every country included in the research study acknowledge the existence of a high level of the general basic education..., in spite of the remarks that education is too frequently restricted to this .... However this represents a fundamental basis not only to acquire in the future more specific professional skills through a practical experience, but also to acquire cultural openness and international exposure."

Before considering the needs of education for the field, and consequently the characteristics to be adopted by education, it is advisable to make two general observations. The first is related to the type of business for which communication is used. The second is related to the size of the market in which the company operates. Let me start from the first one.

Communication in small and medium enterprises is distinguished by a set of needs different from the ones of larger enterprises, even if they both share common basic principles, methods, and techniques of business communication. The Research Lab which I oversee conducted a thorough study on these needs at the beginning of this decade. This analysis revealed that, in order to accomplish the predicted growth prospects in the field of communication, small and medium enterprises need to adopt an ad hoc communication model. This model should take into account the peculiarities and the specific needs of these enterprises, and should succeed in covering any form of communication favouring a network of enterprises located within a supply chain or an industrial district.

If we better identify the functional approach of these businesses we can differentiate two fields of communication. One is *communication with the market*, which often applies to activities and means different from conventional advertising. The other is *communication with other enterprises belonging to the same network*, whose methods and intensity go beyond the traditional relationship between supplier and client, just as it is done at an international level.

Beyond the definition of an appropriate communication model, the following conditions are required for the growth of small and medium enterprises in the communication field: (1) the definition of clear methods of strategic planning for optimizing resources through an appropriate coordination of the tools of communication, and (2) the education of professionals able to assist the entrepreneur, who often directly manages the business communication, even if he or she has neither good knowledge nor the required skills. These assistants should allow the entrepreneur to become aware of the needs of his or her company with respect to communication.

Taking now into account the size of the market in which the business operates, it is evident that international markets should get appropriate attention irrespective of the phase of development of the considered company, whether the company is multinational or international, global or transnational. In this regard, we should not forget that even small and medium enterprises are interested in international markets, even though they use multiple approaches.

Thus those people who work in the field of communication at an international level are required to have, first of all, a set of complex skills to appreciate the different country cultures and enter the field of international research (I refer to the deep work of Professor Miracle (Miracle, 2009, p. 66

and following), and that of the diverse markets with their own characteristics and own models, the market of communication among them.

The Evolution of Total Business Communication: Technology and Research

Another important argument is the role played by technology in the field of communication, and its innovation relative to any business, any market, or any sector in which the company operates. The Italy Chapter of the IAA conducted a study on this topic at an international level, from December 2006 to February 2007, involving IAA members. The findings suggest respondents believed the most innovative media are Internet, online communication, search engine and new media in general. It also revealed the growing importance of advertising online and of mobile communication, but that regardless of the level of innovation of the media, the budget will always dictate the rules of the game (*see* Tables 17-2 through 17-5).

Please rank the degree of your personal "perceived innovation" of each of the following media using a scale where 5=Highly innovative / 4=Innovative/ 3=Stable / 2=Low innovative/ 1=Very low innovative

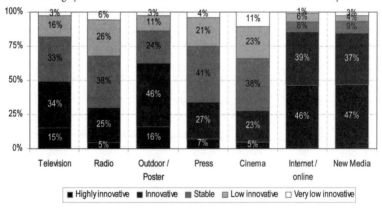

Table 17-2: Perceived innovation

Please rank the degree of your personal "perceived innovation" of each of the following media using a scale where 5=Highly innovative / 4=Innovative/ 3=Stable / 2=Low innovative/ 1=Very low innovative

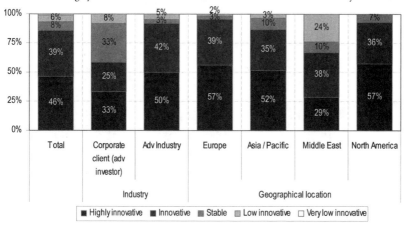

Table 17-3: Perceived innovation – Internet/online

Please rank the degree of your personal "perceived innovation" of each of the following media using a scale where 5=Highly innovative / 4=Innovative/ 3=Stable / 2=Low innovative/ 1=Very low innovative

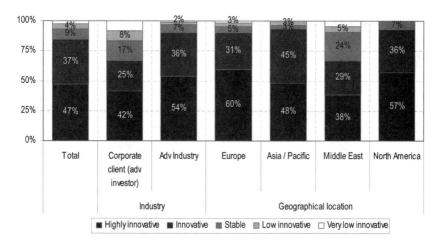

Table 17-4: Perceived innovation – new media

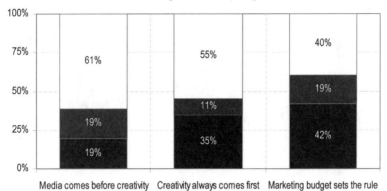

Table 17-5: Perceptions on media assets

On the other hand, the evolution in technology does not necessarily coincide with a corresponding evolution of business behavior, as was highlighted by a study conducted by the Research Lab mentioned above (Gambetti, 2005, p. 233). That study reveals the companies which make use of the Internet can be divided into three clusters. For the first, and least populated (27% of respondents), the Internet does not play any particular role. It is hardly ever used and its usage is restricted to basic functions.

The second cluster (30% of respondents) believes the Internet primarily is an important means of building relationships to optimize business processes and information exchanges within the enterprise. The third and largest cluster (43% of respondents) pursues a web development and online strategy based on a widespread use of the Internet-based technologies to manage processes and relations, and based on the online integration of the primary functions of business operations. This behavior creates value for all the interconnected parties (Table 17-6). Let me now address education, its features and its problems.

Education: Importance, Types and Components

The Italy Chapter of the IAA conducted a national education survey (17 October - 7 November 2007) to be successively extended to all of Europe. A sample of 500 qualified representatives in the field of communication was then selected. This represented users of communication, specialized agencies, and the media, with 203 respondents.

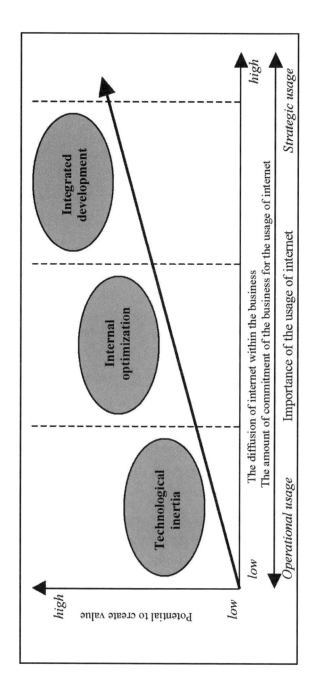

Table 17-6: The internet approach of the businesses

I should note that the role of communication in companies where the interviewees worked appears to have, on average, a high amount of importance (4 on a scale of 1 to 5), at least on a strategic level. But there were considerable differences, depending on the class to which the company belonged (user company, communication agency, media), as reflected in Table 17-7.

Let me analyze the importance, *desirable and actual,* of education within those companies (Tables 17-8 and 17-9). The importance of education appears to be slightly higher than was attributed to communication (4.07 against 4 as mentioned above), with the highest peak for communication agencies. Paradoxically the importance *actually* attributed to education by the companies fell drastically, at 2.9. That is why we could probably speak about education as a myth and in the reality.

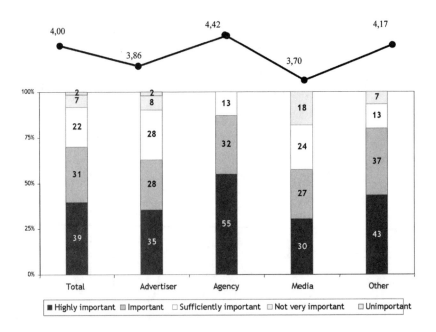

Table 17-7: The importance to be attributed to communication

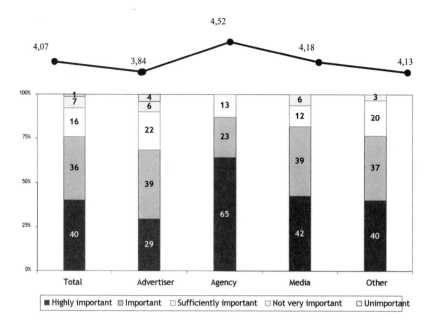

Table 17-8: The desirable importance attributed to
education in business communication

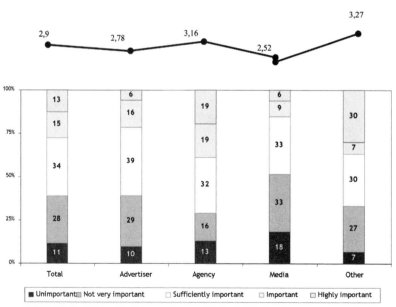

Table 17-9 – The actual importance attributed to business communication

Let me now analyse the type of education that is considered more useful and effective (Table 17-10). The existence of a *general* culture and connected skills, combined with a specific knowledge, appears clearly predominant (49% against 17%) over the existence of a highly *specialized* culture and consequent skills. This result is connected to the one of a survey conducted at the European level, cited above.

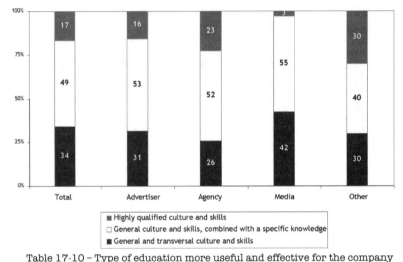

Table 17-10 – Type of education more useful and effective for the company

And let me specifically consider those skills which are believed to be important for a communication manager (Table 17-11). The survey took into account twelve types of skills, to which one or more skills could also be added. The first three skills are the following:

- the inclination towards interpersonal relationships (88%)
- the ability to get into relations at interfunctional level (86%)
- the ability to work in teams (84%)

The third skill was followed by a mastery of a strong general culture, which peaks at 97% in the case of communication agencies. In short, we could say that an inclination towards interpersonal relationships appears to be successful, irrespective of the sector and beyond a strong general culture. The list includes:

1. the inclination towards interpersonal relationships,
2. ability to get into relations at interfunctional level,
3. ability to work in teams,
4. strong general culture,
5. sharing knowledge,
6. analysis and estimation,
7. public speaking,
8. management of the diverse culture,
9. foreign languages,
10. creativity,
11. technology skills,
12. economic education

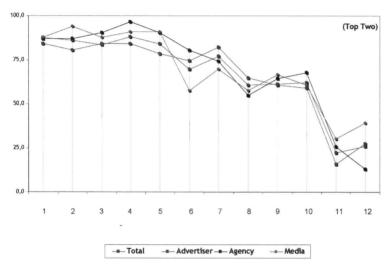

Table 17-11 – The importance of skills for a communication manager

As for the improvements in the field of education in business communication, with respect to 6 parameters discussed below (Table 17-12),
the control management (72% of the cases) and the strategic planning
(64% of the cases), followed by an increasing openness to the research (57%
of the cases) appeared to be of significant importance. These were followed
by media, creativity and production/implementation as possible areas of
improvement. Concerning this we could say that the ability to consider the
communication in functional terms, that is in terms of planning and control, appears to be successful with respect to expanding fields of knowledge
of basic character.

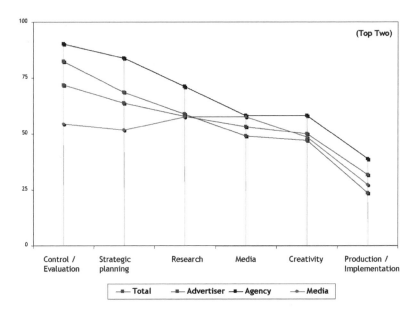

Table 17-12 – Improvements in the field of education

As for the job profiles (Table 17-13), those of the generalists such as communication/PR experts appear to be the most needed in the next five years, followed by different types of managers: strategic, marketing, and knowledge managers. The last one represents a new professional role, a person who should be able to manage the complexity of the information flow inside the company. Moreover there are two more roles: new media web expert and researcher.

These results concerning the professional roles can be integrated with the ones of the cited international research, conducted by the Italy Chapter of IAA at the beginning of 2007 (Table 17-14) which highlighted on one hand the importance of planning represented by the roles of the media planner and the digital planner and on the other the importance of creativity represented by the roles of the copywriter and the graphic designer.

The final aspect of the research was concerned with the role of the employer within the context of education and training in the field of business communication. Thus according to the survey conducted in Italy not only should the employer show interest in education but also he should be involved in continuous training courses (Table 17-14).

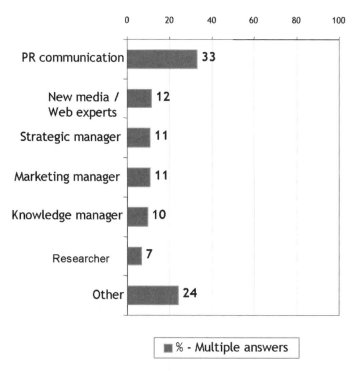

Table 17-13 - Professional job profiles most requested in next 5 years

This expectation expressed by the interviewees is the most striking result of this survey. This result is even more surprising if we consider that the education of future communicators given by the employer was not without some concern following the research frequently cited, conducted at a global level.

Thus the challenge of education continues not only for the needs of our times but also for the medium and long term needs in the field of business communication. Even if in the direction of this challenge, it sounds limiting the assertion made in the course of a often cited study, that "trainers are aware that their mission is to meet not only the present needs, but also the needs of the future, but with a view to bet on the immediate future."

In summary, I would say that the challenge of education is related to the short and medium term future and its goal is something which involves company, market and environment – beyond the communication. In fact, education must deal with the change of the multiple aspects of our economy and society.

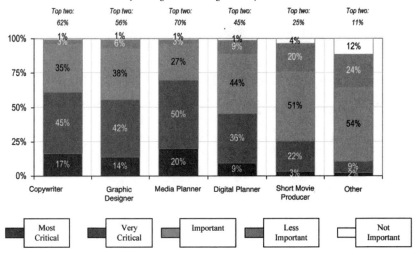

Which are the most requested job profiles in the media / advertising industry among the following? Could you rank them?

Table 17-14 - The most requested job profiles in the media /advertising industry

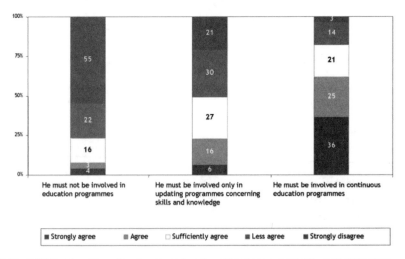

Table 17-15 - Employer involvement in education in the field of communication

242

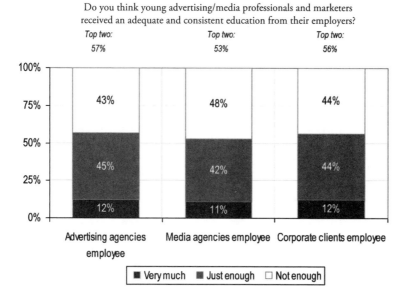

Do you think young advertising/media professionals and marketers received an adequate and consistent education from their employers?

Top two:	Top two:	Top two:
57%	53%	56%

Table 17-16 - Evaluations about young advertising/media professionals and marketers education

The Current Teaching Situation

This brings me to highlight the circumstances of teaching advertising and moreover business communication at the end of this decade (2010). The teaching under consideration involves two types of platforms: (1) universities, and (2) non-university institutions.

Notably, these two platforms are interconnected, at least at the level of teaching. As a matter of fact, the university requires highly specialized professionals to teach various specialization courses, whereas the non-university institutions need the university teachers to formulate the structure and contents of certain courses.

In my opinion, good theory and good practice reciprocally encourage and reinforce each other. In our subjects, the theory, when it is abstract in an exaggerated way, does not conform to the practice, and even less is reflected in practice. However, empiricism, which is an end in itself, does not provoke approval and insight into the theory. In that context, the seminars conducted as a part of the study at various university courses and internships, both at the national and international level, enable the students to come close to theory and practice, and to facilitate comparison and insight.

Having said that, it should be noted that 703 courses conducted in 57, of the approximate 90, Italian universities have communication titles (Table 17-17). This refers to the teaching of any type of communication (interpersonal, mass, business, scientific etc.)

Universities faculties	Number	Subtotal
Humanistic area		66
· Lettere e filosofia (Arts and Philosophy)	32	
· Scienze della Formazione (Education Sciences)	23	
· Scienze Linguistiche (Foreign Languages)	11	
Economic, legal and political area		46
· Economia e commercio (Economics)	21	
· Giurisprudenza (Law)	9	
· Scienze politiche (Political sciences)	16	
Engineering and mathematics related areas		24
· Ingegneria (Engineering)	12	
·Scienze matematiche, fisiche e naturali (Mathematics, Physics and Life Sciences)	12	
Social area		21
· Psicologia (Psychology)	10	
· Sociologia (Sociology)	6	
· Scienze della comunicazione (Communication sciences)	5	
Other faculties		28
Total		185

Table 17-17: Present Distribution of Communication
Courses in Italian Universities

Looking specifically at business communication, the situation appears to be much more concentrated. Moving on to graduate programs which offer a degree in business communication, totally or partly, the following situation is depicted:

- Looking at the three-year, i.e., the first-level of graduate programs, there are 83 degree courses available at 56 different Italian universities entitled to business communication. Most of these degree courses belong to the class of Communication Sciences.

- Analyzing the two-year, i.e., the second-level of graduation programs, there are 28 degree courses in 22 Italian universities entitled to business communication. Almost all these degree courses belong to the class of Public and Business Communication and Advertising.

You must further add six PhD degrees referring to business communication, which may also be combined with marketing. Furthermore, in this field of teaching, there is a high number of the first-level and second-level masters, which are managed directly by the university or promoted by associations, businesses and more generally by public or private institutions. The business communication teaching area is terribly crowded.

At this time the Italian Association of Advertising Professionals (A.I.T.P) has accredited 13 institutions, in order to replace the examinations of grade 1, mentioned above. More specifically, these accreditations include:

- Two were given to universities (Università Cattolica and IULM).

- Two were given to the Association (Master in Communications promoted by UPA) or Business groups working in the communications sector (Master in Business Communication and Marketing by PubItalia-Fininvest).

- Nine were given to non-university institutions including IED Comunicazione ed Accademia di Comunicazione.

The term "master" occurs in six out of 13 accreditations, several of which were granted to non-university institutions so that they could prepare professionals in the creative sector (copy writing, art direction, graphic design etc.). Each of the above-mentioned institutions has evolved differently during the first decade of 2000.

The Università Cattolica established an interdisciplinary second level degree course in Business Communication, Media and Complex Organizations involving the Colleges of Economics, Humanities and Sociology in 2009. The curricula are several, among which the historical one in Business Communication.[28] Following the foundation of the Research Laboratory in Business Communication in 1998, the Università Cattolica has further developed studies analysing the communication policies of more than 1000 companies operating in several industries. In 2008 this University has also launched a publication, "Communicative Business. Italian Research Review on Business Communication," with an international editorial board.

IULM University has established in 2007 the IULM Communication School, operating in the field of education into different sectors, among

---

[28] In 2002, the Alta Scuola in Media, Comunicazione e Spettacolo was established by the College of Humanities of the same Università Cattolica. This school - deriving from the preceding Scuola di Specializzazione in Comunicazioni Sociali - trains the new professionals for the strategical sectors of the communication and performance arts.

which Communication and Relationship Systems, including the business and public communication as well as public relations and advertising, and Media and Creativity.

In addition, IED – operating in different disciplinary fields other than Communication (Design, Fashion and Visual Arts), has continued with its internationalization program in Europe and South America. As far as the Accademia di Comunicazione is concerned, this became a Foundation in 2008. It has continued in its activity of education, while it devoted itself to the research and in the spreading of a communication culture.

A Profile of Two Leaders in Italian Advertising Education

Dino Villani (1898-1989)

Belonging to the first generation of Italian advertising experts, he began working in the thirties of the twentieth century. He took soon the direction of advertising of two historical businesses, Motta (1934) and GiViEmme (1939), operating respectively in the food and toiletries industries. In this role, he organized advertising campaigns, contests, public relations events and more in general initiatives in the business communication, characterized by a great innovativeness that led him to become the creator of integrated communication in Italy.

After the end of World War II, he was co-founder and president of advertising associations (Asssociazione Italiana Tecnici ed Artisti della Pubblicità – 1946 to 1950 – and Federazione Italiana della Pubblicità – 1950 to 1970 – of which he also became honorary president). Starting from the thirties, he also dealt with journalism, while starting from the fifties he increasingly was involved in teaching advertising in the advertising School of Milan, as well as in the training course for Italian managers held in the Università Bocconi in Milan for 14 years. He summarized his various work experiences (professional, teaching, cultural etc.) in his last book *Confessioni di un persuasore* (1972), Milano: Ceschina.

Mario Apollonio (1901-1971)

Professor of Italian Literature at Oslo, Urbino and Cattolica Universities in Milan. At the Università Cattolica he taught from 1942 until 1971. He was a passionate expert of theatre becoming in 1955 the first Italian Professor of History of Theatre. He wrote an extraordinary History of Italian theatre (Firenze: Sansoni 1943-1950), edited again in 2003 in Biblioteca Universale by the publisher Rizzoli and he was co-founder of Piccolo Teatro in Milan with Strehler, Tosi and Grassi, an innovative initiative in the Italian theatre field.

In 1961, he established in Bergamo the Scuola Superiore di Giornalismo e Mezzi Audiovisivi of Università Cattolica: this School moved to Milan in the seventies and became the Scuola di Specializzazione in Comunicazioni Sociali. In 1965, he asked Edoardo Teodoro Brioschi to cooperate with him in the Advertising Section of the School in order to enrich its scientific foundation. In 1971, Brioschi became Professor of Advertising Theory and Technique and from 1980 director of the same Advertising Section serving about 20 years.

References

Apollonio, M., (1963), Relazione sulla Scuola Superiore di Giornalismo e Mezzi Audiovisivi in Bergamo, *Annuario dell'Università Cattolica del Sacro Cuore*, 306-308.

Apollonio, M., (1964), Scuola Superiore di Giornalismo e Mezzi Audiovisivi in Bergamo, *Annuario dell'Università Cattolica del Sacro Cuore*, 394-397.

Brioschi, E.T., (1966), Speech at VIII Congresso Nazionale della Pubblicità, *Official Proceedings*, Firenze, 290-291.

Brioschi, E.T., (1972), Università Cattolica e professioni nuove: l'insegnamento della pubblicità, *Vita e Pensiero*, 5, 82-90.

Brioschi, E.T., (1974), La pubblicità italiana ed il suo nuovo corso. Impieghi, effetti e prospettive, Milano: *Confederazione Generale Italiana della Pubblicità*.

Brioschi, E.T., (1984), Elementi di Economia e Tecnica della Pubblicità, Vol. I, Dai primordi alla pubblicità moderna, Milano: Vita e Pensiero.

Brioschi, E.T., (2005), La comunicazione totale d'azienda: profili e problemi per il nuovo secolo, in E.T. Brioschi (Ed.), La comunicazione totale nel contesto internazionale, a special issue of Comunicazioni Sociali, 1, 22-29.

Brioschi, E.T., (2007), Business Communication: myth and reality at the beginning of the new millenium, Paper at the International Advertising Association European Education Conference, Milan, manuscript being printed.

Brioschi, E.T., (2008), Communicative Business. Il governo dell'azienda e della sua comunicazione nell'ottica della complessità, Milano: *Vita e Pensiero*.

Brioschi, E.T. & Kobayashi, Y., (2008), A comparative study in business communication. Integrated Marketing Communication, Total Business Communication, Koukoku, Milano: *Vita e Pensiero*.

Gambetti, R.C., (2005), Le relazioni internet-based nei mercati industriali. Premesse strategiche e modalità di governo, Milano: *Vita e Pensiero*, 229-233.

La Manna, G., (1951), Definizione delle categorie pubblicitarie, Paper at II Congresso Nazionale della Pubblicità. In Proceedings of the II Congresso Nazionale della Pubblicità, 83-93.

La Manna, G., (1963), Progetto per l'istituzione di una Scuola tecnica di pubblicità, off-print from *L'Ufficio Moderno – La Pubblicità*, 9.

Mengacci, G., & Brioschi, E.T. (1972). Il pubblicitario: evoluzione di un uomo dalla intuizione alla professione, paper presented at the National Advertising Congress "*La pubblicità per lo sviluppo economico e sociale degli anni '70*". Confederazione Generale Italiana della Pubblicità, Milan, 386-395.

Miracle, G.E., (2008), Historical perspectives on International Advertising. Communicative Business. Italian Research Review on Business Communication, I, 54-73.

Ogilvy, D., (1963), Confessions of an Advertising Man, New York: Atheneum.

Advertising Higher Education in Romania

Anca Cristina Micu
Sacred Heart University, USA

Madalina Moraru
Bucharest University, Romania

Evolution from Communism to Free Market

Romania, a former communist country in Eastern Europe, saw the iron curtain lifted in 1989, and started at that time the transition to a free market economy. The past couple of decades encompass extraordinary changes in the economic structure and environment, with state monopolies being dissolved and private companies entering the market and competing in western manner. The Romanian conversion from central planning to a market-oriented economy provides a fascinating laboratory for research in economic theory and practice (Hefner and Woodward 1999). With the advent of a free market economy and a competitive environment, advertising exited its dormant communist stage and started playing increasingly important economic and societal roles.

In this chapter, we briefly present the evolution of the Romanian advertising industry, followed by a description of the higher education institutions that aim to train the talent needed today by a mature Romanian advertising industry. The enrollment, curriculum, and faculty qualifications are presented. We close the chapter with a look at how the local advertising practitioners view the qualifications of students who graduate with a degree or concentration in advertising in terms of meeting advertising agency hiring needs.

Brief History of the Romanian Advertising Industry

Romanian advertising originated in the 19th century, along with the first promotional and commercial activities in the Romanian capital, Bucharest. Cliché statements like "Advertising is the soul of commerce" (coined by George Albert Tacid, manager of the Romanian Advertising Office in 1886) were published at that time in newspapers, to point out the connection between business and advertising and the main purpose of promotional efforts: to sell the product.

The first advertisements appeared in the local paper, "Curierul romanesc" (i.e., "The Romanian Courier") in 1829. The newspaper advertised a book titled, "The Philosophy of Words and Vices," published in the Romanian language in Pest, Hungary. After 1840, text advertisements became more common in Romanian periodicals. No sooner than 1886, ads began to include images. Each company had its own slogan or unique message to promote its products or services.

In 1879, a law referring to a company/business "identity" was passed, and lead to publishing "The Marketing Almanac" by the Romanian Advertising Office, which was in charge of the legal aspects. In 1918 The General Advertising Society took over this responsibility.

The first Romanian advertising agency, the David Adania Agency, appeared in 1880. Two years later, in 1892, The French-Romanian Advertising Agency began publishing announcements in different languages, and after 1900 supported publishing foreign advertisements in Romania. By 1924, a number of important multinational advertising agencies had opened branch offices in Romania, among them: J.W. Thompson- New York, Rudolf Mosse-Berlin (specialized in posters/banners) and Siegfried Wagner (specialized in the promotion of spa vacations) (Petcu 2002). Advertisements were increasingly attractive and significant after 1906.

In 1925 J.W. Thompson invited Queen Maria of Romania to appear in an ad for Pond's Cold Cream, after she visited the USA, bought creams of Pond's, and was delighted by the quality of the products. Subsequently, she wrote a letter to the company granting permission to be quoted in the advertisement (see Figure 18-1).

Between the First and Second World Wars most ads were claiming "the best" product in the category (e.g., best soap, best face cream, most artistic photographs). In addition, during the 30's and 40's, the first international brands started being promoted in Romania (e.g., Nivea, Scwartzkopf - known as Tête Noir at that time) (Bunea 2010).

Later, during the communist era (after 1955), advertising activities were increasingly restricted by the government and the Romanian Communist Party. A single state-owned agency ended up remaining active. Advertising media were limited to simple ads in the two newspapers of the communist regime: the "Romania Libera" and the "Scanteia."

As a consequence of this too-long period of restriction, the year 1990 brought an advertising renaissance to Romania and all Central and Eastern European emerging free-market economies that were aspiring to become part of the newly-formed European Union (EU). Although Romania lagged behind the tier-one EU accession countries (i.e., Hungary, Czech Republic and Poland) in its transition process, the country held much promise as an attractive market for many western goods and services.

Figure 18-1: Queen Marie of Romania in a Pond's Cold Cream Advertisement

It has the second largest land area and population among the emerging market economies of Central and Eastern Europe (largest is Poland), boasts ten cities with populations over 200,000 (compared to three in Hungary and Czech Republic), and has low levels of ethnic and language diversity and a high literacy rate. Even so, advertising agencies followed their clients to Romania rather than proactively pursuing a market-expansion strategy (Rhea 1996).

On the Romanian higher education front, the prospective EU integration acted as a major trigger of change, affecting the disciplines covered as well as the structures and promotional efforts of universities themselves (Chiper 2006). Advertising is one of the new disciplines that started being included in the higher education curriculum after 1990, and progressed to dedicated undergraduate and graduate degrees that are being offered today.

The next section of this chapter presents the enrollment, history and structure of a variety of institutions offering courses in advertising. Then, we describe the curricula and faculty qualifications followed by a relevance assessment from the advertising practice side.

Higher Education Institutions Offering Advertising Courses

The complex discipline of advertising is taught within a variety of institutions. With its business, communications, and sociological roots, advertising is taught in journalism schools and business schools, as well as (maybe specific to Romania only) in political science and public administration schools, and even at the academy of theatre and film.

We group schools in PhD-granting versus non-PhD-granting ones, as far as advertising courses are concerned. Some of the schools we included under non-PhD-granting may offer doctorates, however the doctoral programs are not related to advertising. All schools included here are public, as opposed to private higher education institutions. Before delving into each school's details, we will justify our choice of including public universities, to the detriment of private ones, because Romania is a special case.

Why Public Universities?

Romanian public higher education is free and is available each year for a limited number of candidates supported by public money. In addition to these subsidized spots, the Department of Education offers a limited number of fee-based spots. Each public university organizes its own admissions exam, in order to fill both subsidized and fee-based spots. These admissions exams are highly competitive, as the number of candidates always outnumbers the spots available.

Romanian private higher education started being developed after 1990, as a new profit-generating business sector. Many private colleges entered the higher education market and became an attraction for future students due to their educational offering, which was similar to that of the public universities. For a while, they organized admissions exams in the same manner as the public institutions, hence, at the time they acted as real competitors.

However, employers clearly differentiated between diplomas obtained from public as opposed to private institutions, favoring the former and considering private education less rigorous (Coman 2007). In addition, as the number of private institutions boomed to 127 in 2006 (Danaila 2006), serving the same market of applicants, the admissions exams at private colleges became a mere formality as the only necessary document was a high school diploma. By 2009, only 32 private institutions remained active in Romania (Mihai 2009).

Year	School of Journalism and Communication Sciences			School of Letters		
	Number of subsidized spots	Number of applicants taking admissions exam	Number of applicants per subsidized spot	Number of subsidized spots	Number of applicants taking admissions exam	Number of applicants per subsidized spot
2003	100	1100	11.18 applicants/ position	85	974	11.46 applicants/ position
2004	100	1110	11 applicants/ position	65	837	13 applicants/ position
2007	85	890	10.48 applicants/ position	73	765	10.47 applicants/ position
2008	120	983/770	6.42 applicants/ position	60	551	9.19 applicants/ position
2009	120	1238	10.31 applicants/ position	115	964	8.38 applicants/ position

Figure 18-1: The number of applicants per subsidized spot at Bucharest University

To conclude this brief explanation, contrary to many Western countries, Romanian public universities attract the better students and graduate better-qualified job candidates, thanks to the competitive allocation of subsidized spots. Students at public institutions are motivated to study, as the thorough admissions exam only guarantees free tuition during the first year to those who ranked high enough to obtain a subsidized spot. In subsequent years, student ranking is determined by the GPA during the prior academic year (i.e., freshman year GPA counts for sophomore year ranking, sophomore year GPA counts for junior year ranking and so on).

The level of competition for subsidized spots is illustrated in Table 18-1, showing the number of applicants per subsidized position who took the admissions exams at the two schools within Bucharest University that offer advertising courses.

Now that we explained the inclusion of public universities alone in this chapter, we take a look at the institutions offering advertising courses. A full list of universities and schools with the degrees each grant as well as the number of students starting each specific degree in 2010 (per each university's web site) is presented in Figure. The numbers in Table 18-2 should help gauge the level of enrollment at each institution and compare the programs by size.

University	School	Undergrad. Degree	Master's Degree*	Ph.D.	Students starting in 2010		
					Sub-sidized	Fee-based	Distance Learning
Bucharest University, Bucharest	School of Journalism and Comm. Sciences	Comm. Science (specializing in Journalism, Advertising or Public Relations)			120	60	250
			Communication Science		120	200	
				Communication Science	12		
	School of Letters	Communications and PR			70	80	
		Consulting and Expertise in Advertising			45	70	
Academy of Economic Studies, Bucharest	School of Marketing	Marketing			212	104	64
			Marketing management		78	110	
			Marketing research		32	18	
			Managing client relationships		10	8	
				Marketing	12	4	
National School of Political and Administrative Studies, Bucharest	School of Communication and Public Relations	Communication sciences (incl. Comm. & PR and Advertising)			200	220	200**
			Comm. Sciences (incl. Advert.)		186		
				Communication Sciences	7		
Babes-Bolyai University, Cluj-Napoca	School of Political, Admin. and Comm. Studies	Advertising			24	73	
		Comm. & PR			44	77	31
			Advertising		25	6	10
				Comm. Sciences (Adv. & Comm.	3		

		only)			
Lucian Blaga University, Sibiu	School of Journalism	Communications & PR		25	40	
		Advertising / Comm. & PR	14	66	
Petre Andrei University, Iasi	School of Comm. Sciences	Communications & PR			60	
		Communication Sciences				
West University, Timisoara	School of Political Sciences, Philosophy and Comm. Sciences	Comm. & PR, Comm. or Advertising		1	12	
National University of Theatre and Cinematography, Bucharest	School of Film	Specialization: Audio-Visual Communication		16	2	

* - Master's Degree names are what schools list on their promotional materials as specializations

** - The National School of Political and Administrative Studies organizes nationwide admission exams in several local centers across the country for its distance-learning program (at the time this chapter was written there were 200 admitted students who had passed the exams however still had to decide whether to start the program)

Table 18-2. The number of students starting degrees that include advertising courses in 2010

There are few institutions in Romania that state "advertising" on a diploma. However, advertising courses, concentrations, and specializations abound in degrees that name communications or business as the major. An additional clarification we would like to make is that the various schools within one university are called "faculties" in Romania (i.e., Faculty of Journalism and Communication Sciences within Bucharest University). We refer to these "faculties" as schools throughout the document. We reiterate here that we grouped schools in two groups based on whether they offer a PhD on an advertising-related topic (e.g., Communications or Marketing).

Schools that Offer Advertising Courses at the Doctoral Level

The schools presented in this section belong to the oldest and most respected universities in Romania. These universities carry a long history that permeates the culture of each institution and is felt in the size of the library and the passion for research of both the faculty and graduate students. These are the "research one" universities in Romania that offer advertising courses up to the doctoral level.

Bucharest University, Bucharest
School of Journalism and Communication Sciences

Bucharest University (BU) is Romania's oldest higher education institution, founded in 1864. The School of Journalism and Communication Sciences within BU was established on January 19, 1990, only one month after abolition of the communist regime, thereby joining the other 6 colleges at BU (whose number, during the following years, increased to 19). From those early years, the School's dean, Dr. Mihai Coman, opened it to Western influence by establishing international connections and attracting foreign lecturers (King and Gross 1993).

The School was a pioneer in its domain, soon setting the bar for communications higher education and becoming a model for other schools that adopted its structure and curricula. The School offers advertising-related specializations (concentrations) to undergraduate communication science majors, as well as those studying in Master's and doctoral programs.

A look back at the efforts to include advertising (and public relations) in the curriculum pinpoints the school year 1997-1998 as the one when the BU Senate formally approved the creation of the Public Communications Department. The department was created to address the needs of students interested in public relations and advertising. Due to market-driven expansion, on January 24, 2000, the School made an application to modify the department name to the Department of Public Relations and Advertising. Unsuccessful in terms of including the advertising label, the effort resulted in the new name Social Communications and Public Relations Department. Hence, the advertising specialization was not yet formally recognized, even though advertising courses were included in the public relations specialization curriculum.

In 2004, a second wave of accreditation papers for the Social Communications and Public Relations department dedicates many pages to the advertising curriculum and enrollment. At this time, advertising becomes a formal area of specialization for communication science majors, and students' diplomas spell it out. At the time this chapter is written, the process for the formal creation of an Advertising Department is under way. The process is driven by the Master's degree numbers, as well. At the Master's level, the School accredited in 2007 a specialization called Public Relations and Advertising Communications Campaigns.

At the doctoral level, the School offers a doctorate in communication science. As the School's website lists, out of the twelve doctoral candidates currently in the program, at least three are completing dissertations on advertising-related topics such as "branding," "new product strategies," and "communications campaigns."

Bucharest University, Bucharest
School of Letters

A second school within BU that offers both public relations and advertising courses is the School of Letters. The School houses the Department of Communications and Public Relations, formally created in 1993. While the main discipline of the School is philology/literature, the School offers a formal specialization in Communications and Public Relations to its undergraduates who seek a writing-related strategic communications job. The School also offers a Master's specialization titled Services and Expertise in Advertising. This School does not offer advertising courses at the doctoral level, however we included it here because of its affiliation with Bucharest University.

Academy of Economic Studies, Bucharest
School of Marketing

The Academy of Economic Studies (AES) is Romania's first business higher education institution, founded in 1913. While the two schools presented from Bucharest University started offering advertising courses based on their journalism and communications expertise, the AES added advertising to its business and marketing foundation.

Housed within the School of Commerce (later School of Commerce and Marketing), the Marketing Department has been in place since 1971, offering the first marketing courses in Central and Eastern Europe. In 1975, the Academy published the first marketing textbook, and in 1983 the first Romanian-authored paper (by two professors at the Academy) was presented at the annual academic conference of the American Marketing Association.

Just after 1990, marketing was formally recognized as a separate academic specialization. By 1995, a course titled Promotional Techniques was added to the expanding list of marketing courses. The first marketing Master's program was offered in 2000-2001. After that, the educational offerings at the Master's level became more diverse and now include three distinct specializations in: Marketing Management, Marketing Research, and Managing Client Relationships.

Given the level of interest in the market for marketing graduates, and the number of students enrolled, the Academy formally approved the creation of a separate School of Marketing in 2003. The school admitted sixteen new students to its doctoral program in 2010.

National School of Political and Administrative Studies, Bucharest
School of Communications and Public Relations

The National School of Political and Administrative Studies (NSPAS) is an autonomous public institution founded on April 11, 1991. It opened its doors with areas of emphasis in: Political Sciences, Administrative Sciences, Preparation and Improvement of the Magistrates, International Affairs, Management, and Mass Communications Studies. In this context, mass communications was initially studied from an administrative and political perspective.

In 1995, the Social Communications and Public Relations Department is accredited and offered a 2-year program at the postgraduate level. Starting with the school year 1998-1999 the School of Communications and Public Relations was formally created within NSPAS. In the following years, the School of Communications and Public Relations succeeded at building the name of its advertising programs, both nationally and internationally.

At the undergraduate level, in addition to its subsidized and fee-based spots, the School added a distance learning program for which it organizes thorough admissions exams in a number of cities across the country. In addition, it started collaborating with the advertising agency, Ogilvy, and its curriculum started being known as the Ogilvy school. The School also collaborates with the Romanian chapter of the International Advertising Association (IAA) to bring guest speakers and expertise (Toma 2005).

In 2003, the School started offering a Master's program in advertising. The Master's program was recognized by the IAA in 2008, alongside programs offered in US universities (e.g., Emerson College, University of Florida, and Michigan State University). Today, the advertising programs at the School of Communications and Public Relations within NSPAS are known for their practice-oriented curriculum, and many of the courses are offered in English as well. Among the twelve Master's programs offered, three deal specifically with advertising topics: Advertising, Brand management and corporate communications, and Communications and Advertising (in English). Active on the research side too, the School houses a Center for Research in Communications, and offers a doctoral program that enrolled seven new students in 2010.

Babes-Bolyai University, Cluj-Napoca
School of Political, Administrative and Communication Studies

Located in the Transylvania region of Romania, "Babes Bolyai" University in Cluj-Napoca is one of the oldest and most respected Romanian universities outside of the country's capital of Bucharest. Specific to Babes-Bolyai University is that (in addition to Romanian language courses) it offers courses in both the German and Hungarian languages to the two respective minority groups in Romania.

The University was restructured in 1993, and the number of specializations offered increased to eleven. Within the School of Political, Administrative and Communication Studies, advertising courses are offered to undergraduates specializing in either Communications, Advertising or Public Relations.

The School offers a distinct specialization in advertising at the Master's level, as well. The Master's program was first offered in 1993, in German, under the title of Advertising and Public Relations. The Master's program finished its accreditation process in 2008, and by now has an established tradition and is offered in Romanian, as well. In 2010, the School admitted three new students in advertising at the doctoral level.

Schools that do not Offer Advertising Courses at the Doctoral Level

In this section we present the most-recently created schools and programs that offer advertising courses. Even if housed within older/established universities, the schools have lower enrollment, do not offer doctoral programs, have a short history in offering advertising curriculum, and mostly follow the curriculum structure from the schools presented in our previous section. In addition, most of these Schools are located in cities that do not house the headquarters of any advertising agencies or other potential employers, as is the case with Cluj-Napoca, and especially the capital city of Bucharest.

Lucian Blaga University, Sibiu
School of Letters, History and Journalism

The School of Letters, History and Journalism was founded in 1995 within "Lucian Blaga" University in Sibiu. The School offers an undergraduate degree in Communications and Public Relations that includes advertising courses. Advertising has a stronger presence at the Master's level, where students can specialize in either Communications and Public Relations or Advertising.

Petre Andrei University, Iasi
School of Communication Sciences

The School of Communication Sciences within the University "Petre Andrei" from Iasi follows the curriculum structure from the School of Journalism and Communication Science within Bucharest University. It offers an undergraduate degree in Communications and Public Relations and a master's program in Communication Science.

West University, Timisoara
School of Political Sciences, Philosophy and Communication Sciences

The West University in the city of Timisoara created a specialization in Advertising in 2009, within the School of Political Sciences, Philosophy and Communication Sciences. The School offers undergraduate specializations in Communications, Communications and Public Relations, and Advertising. The advertising specialization is functioning on a temporary authorization until the formal authorization process is complete.

National University of Theatre and
Cinematography "I.L. Caragiale," Bucharest
School of Film

The National University of Theatre and Cinematography has a long history and tradition in offering theatre and film higher education programs. The School of Film offers Advertising courses within its Audio-Visual Communications specialization. No advertising curriculum is present in either the Master's or doctoral programs offered by the School.

We conclude here the presentation of schools offering degrees that include advertising courses. In the next section we cover the curricula/plans of study focusing on the top four PhD-granting institutions.

Curricula

All public higher education institutions in Romania are authorized by the Ministry for Education, Research and Innovation, and accredited by the Romanian Association for Quality Assurance in Higher Education (ARACIS). ARACIS was founded in 2005, and is an autonomous public institution. Its mission is to evaluate the quality of higher education in Romania. In 2009, as part of the European integration process, ARACIS became a member of the European Association for Quality Assurance in Higher Education (ENQA), and is listed in the European Quality Assurance Register for Higher Education (EQAR).

A more important EU integration effort is the adherence to the Bologna Declaration, which promotes the offering of "easily readable and comparable degrees" throughout the European Union, so as to help with "European citizens' employability and the international competitiveness of the European higher education system." (Bologna Declaration 1999) The declaration stipulates that undergraduate degrees shall be completed in no less than three years and can be followed upon completion with graduate degrees at either master's or doctorate levels. As a consequence of this adherence, starting 2005, all undergraduate programs are three years long rather than four, as they were previously. A three-year undergraduate program can be followed by a two-year master's.

We present in Table 18-3 the curriculum of the four Schools that cover advertising courses. All courses listed are to be completed within the three years of study for the completion of an undergraduate degree.

Bucharest University	Academy of Economic Studies	National School of Political and Administrative Sciences	Babes-Bolyai University
School of Journalism and Comm. Sciences	School of Marketing	School of Communications and Public Relations	School of Political, Administrative and Communication Studies
Communication Science majors - Advertising specialization	Marketing majors	Communication Science majors - Advertising specialization	Advertising majors
Year 1	Year 1	Year 1	Years 1-3**
Semester 1 Intro to communication theory	*Semester 1* Microeconomics	Communication Theory Intro to Public Relations	Intro to comm. and PR theories Verbal and non-verbal communications
Intro to mass media Elaboration/Framing techniques	Accounting Fundamentals Management	Imagology Intro to organizations' theory	Intro to political science Research methods in comm. and PR
Intro to public relations Elaboration/Framing in written press Conversation strategies (French/English) Journalism and reflecting current news	Applied Mathematics in Economics Finance English/French for business communication 1 Psychology	Computer science I Computer science II Intro to Advertising History of communications	Computer science Negotiations and decision making Writing scientific papers Advertising
Semester 2	*Semester 2*	Management and marketing	Public communications
Intro to mass media Intro to interpersonal comm.	Computer science for business Statistics	Intro to sociology Research methods in social sciences	Intro to public relations Mass media communications

Col 1	Col 2	Col 3	Col 4
Information gathering techniques	Business Law	Electives:	Conflict management Organizational communications
Intro to advertising	Macroeconomics	Digital media	
Internet techniques Conversation strategies (French/English)	Marketing English/French for business communication 2 Design and Aesthetics of Goods	Photography English I English II	Advertising and PR techniques Branding and brand mgmt.
Typing			Visual communications
Journalism and reflecting current news		French I	Marketing
		French II	Graphic design

Year 2	**Year 2**	**Year 2**	Semiotics
Semester 3	*Semester 3*	PR Techniques and Strategies	Promotional techniques in mass media
Communication social structures	Consumer Behavior	Elaboration techniques in advertising Advertising management	Media planning
Intro to semiotics Journalism investigative techniques	Promotional Techniques Marketing Information Systems	Consumer behavior and persuasion	Radio and TV advertising
Multimedia	Econometrics English/French for business comm. 3	International marketing Semiotics - language theory	Event planning Ethics
Working in television (lab) Research methods in comm. sciences	European Economy	Advertising campaigns Culture and communications	Political advertising
Ethics Media discourse (French/English)	International Trade		Copywriting
	International Negotiation Fundamentals of Science Goods	Electives: Print advertising	Mass media and society
	Geopolitics	Audio-video advertising	Online advertising Advertising language and representation
	Databases	Digital advertising	Intro to persuasion theory Methods of scientific data collection
Semester 4	*Semester 4*	Advertising rhetoric	Collective mentalities Culture and civ. in the 20th century
Communication law	Public Relations	Computer science III	Persuasion strategies
Professional deontology	Marketing Research	English III	Art history
Intro to semiotics	Direct Marketing	French III	
Types of written press	Logistics English/French for business comm. 4		Advertising projects Public relations and evaluation
Internet (lab) Communication with the press	Economic Geography of the World		Advertising and art
Advertising management Elaboration/Framing techniques (French/English)	Project Management Technics Operations of Tourism Human Resources Management		European governance Communications philosophy
Politology	Negotiation and Techiques for Foreign Trade		

World Economics

Year 3	Year 3	Year 3
Semester 5	*Semester 5*	
		Mass media and society
Creativity in advertising	Services Marketing	
Advertising management	International Marketing	Advertising planning
Successful techniques in comm.		Image crisis management
	Cybermarketing	
	English/French for business comm. 5	
Below-the-line advertising		Corporate culture
French/English culture and civilization	Sales Techniques	Communications Law and Ethics
Advertising semiotics	Marketing Projects	Electives:
Research methods in advertising	Food products and consumer safety	Non-verbal communications
	Multimedia	Communication pathologies and therapies
	Tech. for Hotels and Restaurants	
	Economic and Financial Analysis I	Public image of leaders and institutions
	International Capital Markets	Sociology of public opinion
		Project management
		Human resources management
Semester 6	*Semester 6*	
	Social and Political Marketing	
Persuasion techniques	Business to Business Marketing	
Advertising lab		
Consumer behavior	Tourism Marketing	
French/English culture and civilization		
	Agro-food Marketing	
Gender in advertising	Data Analysis using SPSS	
	English/French for business comm. 6	
Negotiation techniques		
	European Union Law	
	Public Services and Utilities	
	Comparative management	
	Operational Management	
	International Tourism	

*- The study plans included here are per the schools' web sites, not including optional courses or practice/internship credits.

**- Babes-Bolyai University does not post a plan of study broken down by year of study; these are the courses listed to be offered in 2010-2011

Table 18-3. Undergraduate plans of study
that include advertising (Curricula)*

The roots of the advertising discipline are in business, communications, sociology and psychology, and, last but not least, visual and verbal creation. This perspective induces a certain direction of the academic curriculum organization, reflected in the courses the students are offered to study. The school that houses the advertising program has a strong influence on the foundation courses. Hence, communication schools start with introductory courses to communication theory, while the school of marketing starts with economics, finance, and marketing courses.

It is worth noting that even though a school of journalism would include more journalism-oriented courses in its program of study for students specializing in advertising, all four schools presented cover a blend of all aspects relevant to advertising. Hence, we see management and marketing courses offered to advertising students at the School of Communication and Public Relations within the National School of Political and Administrative Studies, as well as public relations and psychology courses offered to marketing majors at the School of Marketing within the Academy of Economic Studies.

All courses presented in Table 18-3 are undergraduate courses and build a strong theoretical base as well as an introduction to the practical side. Most students decide to continue on with Master's level courses that include more skills-oriented courses.

Faculty

All schools presented in this chapters feature a mix of faculty that combines pure "academics" who hold a PhD degree, as well as practitioners who also work (many full-time) in advertising agencies. The qualifications of these instructors vary widely just as the roots of the advertising discipline itself are diverse. We start by addressing the structure of the faculty from a formal final degree perspective. Then, we follow with details on international collaborations that helped refine the expertise of advertising faculty members.

The academics who first taught advertising-related courses in Romania did not have, back in 1990, a specific educational background in this domain. Backgrounds ranged from a Bachelor or PhD in Letters/Literature, Psychology, Philosophy, Foreign Language or even Engineering. This is why, the first step these educators took was their own professional conversion, because each chose a research area close to the new curricula and they focused on their professional improvement by enrolling in doctoral programs.

For example, in 1990 at the School of Journalism and Communication Sciences at Bucharest University there were only three professors who held a PhD. The number increased to twenty-two in 2009 (from a total of 39 permanent employees). In some cases, qualified professors are teaching for more colleges as collaborators, because the number of qualified professors still does not meet market needs.

In addition, practitioners teach a number of skills-based courses. These are people who currently work for advertising agencies (i.e., not retired) and who teach courses such as Account Planning, Media Planning, Creative Writing, Advertising Campaigns, Branding. The School of Journalism and Communication Sciences, mentioned above, collaborates with many practitioners from known advertising agencies: McCann Ericsson, Leo Burnett, Graffiti BBDO, and the local Grapefruit and Headvertising.

The School of Communications and Public Relations, within the National School of Political and Administrative Studies, has a similar situation. From a number of 41 teaching staff, 36 are permanent employees, among whom 24 have a PhD and the rest are still working on their dissertations. This School also collaborates with practitioners for some of their skills-based courses.

At Babes-Bolyai University in Cluj, the advertising program within the School of Political, Administrative and Communication Studies benefits from the collaboration with Hannover University and "Hochschule Mittweida" from Germany which grants the involvement of foreign teachers into the educational process for classes such as online marketing and audio-video advertising. From the 18 instructors teaching in the advertising program at the undergraduate level only 3 have not yet finished their doctoral dissertations. At the graduate level, all professors (9) have their doctoral title.

The School of Political Science, Philosophy and Communication Sciences within West University of Timisoara developed its advertising study program with 23 permanent professors. Among them, 15 have a PhD. This was one of the aspects that helped this School receive the authorization to start its advertising program.

In addition to earning a doctorate, many professors participated in academic exchange programs and benefited from the expertise of prestigious universities around the world. For example, the School of Journalism and Communication Sciences within University of Bucharest sends its faculty to either Europe (e.g., 12 faculty members to École Superieure de Journalisme from Lille, France) or the United States (e.g., Gaylord College School of Journalism and Mass Communication Studies at Oklahoma University, and the College of Communication and Information at the University of Tennessee).

The faculty at the School of Communications and Public Relations within the National School of Politic and Administrative Studies have either completed graduate studies abroad (e.g., Lille School of Management, France or Georgia Institute of Technology, Atlanta, Georgia, US) or participated in academic programs such as Fulbright (e.g., Fulbright scholar at the College of Communication and Information Science University of Alabama, US) or other specialization programs in a number of countries (e.g., Italy, Belgium, France). In addition, the educational partnership with the International Advertising Association (IAA) provides opportunities to permanent faculty to participate in events and seminars where they meet foreign professionals or even gain practical experience within the advertising agencies belonging to this organization.

The School of Political, Administrative and Communication Sciences within Babes-Bolyai University benefits from a prestigious collaboration with German advertising academia and practice. The School offers a Master's degree in Advertising and Public Relations which is taught in German (in addition to Romanian). Delia Balaban, who coordinates of the Master's program, explains: "The particularity of our programs is to cooperate with the most important local agencies and also to facilitate the presence of some foreign specialists with wide experience in advertising, such as German advertising professionals."

The Transylvanian School is also part of the Social Science Curriculum Development program, supported by the United States Information Agency and coordinated by the International Research and Exchange Board and the American Council for Learned Society. This program provides the collaboration with a number of American universities to develop new courses and to improve the curriculum (i.e., Michigan State University, University of Pittsburgh, Florida State University, University of California Irvine, University of Virginia, and Delaware University).

After embracing the European system of education and the Bologna Declaration, Romanian higher education institutions were involved in the development of ERASMUS exchange (The European Community Action Scheme for the Mobility of University Students). While the Erasmus program dedicated to students (they can attend courses for 3, 6 or 12 months at universities from the European Union), faculty members can benefit from it as well. Professors have the opportunity to be guest lecturers and collaborate with peers from EU institutions.

Besides earning graduate degrees and gaining international exposure and experience, faculty members are active in research centers present at their respective institutions. From the schools offering advertising courses, examples include the Sparta Research Center from Bucharest University focused on research of the role communication plays in public space, The Centre for Fundamental and Applied Research in Marketing from the Academy of Economic Studies, and the Center for Research in Communication from the National School for Political and Administrative Studies.

In conclusion, Romanian advertising higher education benefits from highly qualified instruction from both academics and practitioners who are well-grounded and stay current in their fields.

In the last section of our chapter, in order to gauge how the industry views advertising higher education, we interviewed three practitioners (two of whom are Ph.D-holders and one is ABD) who teach at institutions described above in addition to their full-time jobs.

Advertising Practitioners' View

No assessment of the quality of higher education can be done without including the opinion of employers. We wanted to determine how practitioners view the various degrees and the level of preparedness of recent graduates.

One of our interviewees is Lucian Georgescu, a local advertising celebrity, who has been active in the advertising industry since 1992 as a copywriter, creative director and then President of BBDO Romania and who founded his own advertising agency, GAV Balkanski, in 2005. The agency client roster includes Reiffeisen Leasing and Mercedes Benz Romania. Dr. Georgescu holds a Ph.D in Audio-Visual Communication from the National University of Theatre and Cinematography, Bucharest, and is an associate professor at the same institution.

Our second interviewee is Sorin Psatta, Director of Research and Strategy at BBDO Romania. He has been on the faculty of the School of Journalism and Communication Sciences within Bucharest University since 1996, and is now completing his dissertation in advertising.

Lastly, our third interviewee is Dan Petre, also on the faculty of the School of Journalism and Communication Sciences within Bucharest University. Dr. Petre holds a Ph.D in Sociology and is the managing partner of D&D Research, a market research company that includes the following advertising agencies among its clients: FCB Advertising Romania, Saatchi & Saatchi Romania, Ogilvy & Mather Romania and Leo Burnett Romania.

With an eye on academia and one on the industry, our three interviewees answered the same questions about advertising higher education in Romania.

Popular majors with the industry – well, it's a mix

Asked about the educational background of employees within each of their companies, our respondents agree: there is no standard background for an advertising agency employee. Dr. Georgescu stresses the fact that none of his employees have a degree in advertising. Majors present in his agency include business, arts, architecture, and philology.

Which majors are represented within BBDO Romania? "You name it" answers Mr. Psatta. Then he adds that prior experience is more important when hiring as well as whether the candidate has a portfolio (for creative positions). Dr. Petre lists marketing and communications followed by arts, sociology and psychology as majors present within his company.

Advantages of hiring someone with a specialized degree – skills highly valued

When asked about the upside of hiring someone with the appropriate degree, BBDO's Psatta states it is highly advantageous especially for the creative department as the candidates would have acquired the necessary skills in college. Mr. Psatta names arts as an appropriate major for art director positions and letters or audio-visual communications for copywriting candidates.

Dr. Petre has a similar opinion, hiring graduates from the appropriate field brings you employees who have the basic knowledge, have already had contact with practice and practitioners via internships and practitioner-taught courses. Dr. Georgescu is skeptical about the level of preparedness of students from either communications school in Bucharest where his agency is headquartered.

How DO practitioners view advertising higher education? - They are skeptics

This is a question where we see similar responses from our three interviewees. They agree that practitioners are still skeptical about the level of preparedness of advertising graduates. All three name the lack of stronger ties with the industry as the cause of this skepticism.

Dan Petre believes the root cause of this opinion from the side of practice is the disconnect between theory and practice. "Specialized [advertising] coursework is still focused on accumulating knowledge and information rather than skills and competencies. Because of this, practitioners' perception is that higher education needs to include the bridging of theory and practice," he states.

From Lucian Georgescu, we learn that such disconnect is likely to come from not enough contact between academia and industry. "Universities do not account for industry realities. This is specifically the reason why we [practitioners] have doubts about specialized [advertising] higher education – there is a lack of constant and coherent contact with the industry," says Lucian Georgescu. Hence, "Practitioners have a lack of interest [in specialized degrees], they are even ironical about them," believes Sorin Psatta.

We do not believe Romania (or the advertising discipline) is a lonely case where there is a perceived disconnect between academia and industry. Romania has a burgeoning advertising higher education market with high quality programs.

No statistics are available on the percentage of advertising majors who are employed in advertising agencies or advertising-related companies. Nor are there statistics available on how many graduates from the institutions we presented find a job when they leave college. What we can say for sure is that advertising has become more and more important to companies present on the Romanian market in the past couple of decades and this demand is reflected in an increasingly complex advertising higher education offer. The growing popularity of the discipline can be tracked in the number of programs and the increases in enrollment.

References:

Bunea, Iulia (2010), "Agonie si extaz in "copilaria' publicitatii" ("Agony and ecstasy in advertising's childhood") *Adevarul* newspaper, April 27, 2010.

Chiper, Sorina (2006), "The discourse of Romanian universities," *Journal of Organizational Change Management, 19(6)*:713-724.

Coman, Mihai (2007), "Patterns and Experience: Journalism Education in Romania", Media Industry, Journalism Culture und Communication Policies in Europe (Festschrift for Professor Dr. Gerd G. Kopper), published in Hans Bohrmann/ Eliasabeth Klaus/ Marcel Machilleds. Berlin, Vistas, 2007.

Danaila, Aida (2006), "Inflatie de universitati in Romania" ("University Inflation in Romania") *Romania libera* newspaper, September 28, 2006.

Hefner, Frank and Douglas Woodward (1999), "A better red: The transition from communism to Coca-Cola in Romania," *The Quarterly Journal of Austrian Economics, 2(2)*:43-49.

King, Stephan and Peter Gross (1993), "Romania's New Journalism Programs Raise Old Questions", *Journalism Educator, 48(3)*.

Mihai, Adelina (2009) "700.000 de studenti dau anual 250 mil de euro la facultatile private", ("700 000 Students Pay Every Year an Amount of 250 mil euros to Enroll in the
Private Univeristies") *Evenimentul Zilei* newpaper, July 14, 2009.

Petcu, Marian (2002), O istorie ilustrata a publicitatii romanesti, (An Illustrated History of
Romanian Advertising) *Ed. Tritonic, Bucuresti*, 2002.

Rhea, Marti J. (1996), "The emergence of an advertising industry in Romania," *Journal of
Euro-marketing, 5(2)*:53-76.

Advertising Education in Slovenia

Vesna Zabkar
University of Ljubljana, Slovenia

Mihael Kline
University of Ljubljana, Slovenia

Zlatko Jancic
University of Ljubljana, Slovenia

Historical background into how advertising education developed in Slovenia

Even though Slovenia is a relatively young country, its nation has a much longer history. Losing its kingdom of Karantania in the 8th century, to Charlemagne, caused a thousand years of foreign rule, mostly Austro-Hungarian. After the World War I, Slovenia briefly regained its freedom and, due to the pressures from the neighboring countries, formed an alliance of Slovenians, Croats, and Serbs. This entity was later joined to the Kingdom of Serbia and became known as the Kingdom of Serbs, Croats and Slovenians, later called Yugoslavia.

After the World War II, the name changed to Federal Peoples Republic of Yugoslavia and finally to Socialist Federative Republic of Yugoslavia. After the short war and the collapse of the federal state in 1991, Slovenians finally regained their long awaited independence (Slovenia Cultural Profile, 2010).

During these permutations, Slovenians also discontinuously changed their political and economic system for several times. In the last hundred years they had to thrive in the capitalist system, central planning system, system of self-management and again back in the market economy after the independence (Feldmann 2006).

This brief introduction is needed in order to explain the context of advertising development in Slovenia. In our wish to be as precise as possible we will split the history into the following three parts:

1. Austro-Hungarian period (18. century until 1918)

2. Yugoslav period (from 1919 until 1991)

3. Slovenian period (after 1991)

Austro-Hungarian period (18. century until 1918)

The history of advertising in this period is similar to its development in the rest of Europe. Gutenberg's invention of printing presses enabled the dawn of printed books and later newspapers, especially in the countries with the intensity of manufacturing and trading activities. And newspapers, as we know, quickly adopted advertising into their contents. Slovenians were among the first in Europe with the printed book, in 1550, but lagged behind in their newspapers due to the oppression of Austro-Hungarian monarchy better known as the "prison of nations" (Bucur, Wingfield, 2001).

Slovenian advertising first appeared in bilingual form in German newspaper, in Ljubljana Kundschaftblatt des Herzogthums Krain, in 1776. After Napoleon's conquest of Austria, the first Slovenian newspaper *Lublanske novice* appeared in 1797. Worthy of mentioning is the fact that it presented the ads with persuasive, not only informative, content in a manner of brief classified ads as usually used at that time. The first copywriter was Valentin Vodnik, editor and the first Slovenian poet (Hudalist 1997; Korošec 2006).

Further development was slowed down due to weak industrialization of the region, and also because the only Slovenian newspaper was discontinued after the Napoleon's defeat. The next newspaper appeared almost 50 years later, together with the "spring of nations" in the 1848. Soon, the number of newspapers increased and the need for advertising middlemen became evident.

According to some testimonials, the first Slovenian advertising agency Aloma Company opened as early as in 1897, but did not fully develop until the 1920s (Matelič, in Erjavec 2007). In the period before the First World War, several dozens of small agencies also appeared, mostly dealing with the distribution of print ads, poster printing, photographic services etc. Restricted in their creative, especially copywriting, potential they prepared ads for local businesses only. They were not able to produce advertising campaigns for foreign companies, so these were made in Germany, Austria, and Czech Republic. Advertising agencies handled the correspondence with domestic and foreign media. They also offered the translation of original messages (Lavrič, in Erjavec 2007).

Many experts at that time propagated the importance of advertising for craftsmen and predominantly small firms in Slovenia. The knowledge of even the basic principles of advertising was mostly absent in the underdeveloped industrial region, and followed the method of learning-by-doing. Thus, the plea for higher standards in advertising was in place. An article on the importance of seeking the professional help when in need for advertising is detected as early as in 1909 (Höfler, in Erjavec 2007). Despite the problems, no formal education activities were present during this period.

Yugoslav period (from 1919 until 1991)

In presenting this period, we will have to bear in mind the drastic changes that happened in political and economic system during these 70 years. There are three parts of this period: market economy, planned economy and self-management system with market-planning economy.

Market economy with a high proportion of foreign
owned businesses and few domestic ones (from 1919 until 1945)

The south Slavic community of nations was, in a way, some boost for Slovenians, especially in a language and cultural sense. The nation established in the capital, Ljubljana, its basic institutions such as its first National gallery, in 1918, and its first University, in 1919. But the fact remains that relatively industrially under-developed Slovenia formed a new state with other nations that were even less developed.

So the development of advertising after the "great war" was slow and, if there was any, it was mainly though the inputs of foreign companies and foreign managers from Germany, Czech Republic, France etc. A majority of domestic managers didn't really understand the importance of effective and quality advertising, so they relied on their "in house" forces and many advertising amateurs around the industry. Advertising was being done as part-time job by painters, graphic technicians, and architects. They learned their skills abroad in Vienna, Munich, Prague, Milano, Florence and Zagreb. Mainly it was a process of using some implicit theories and a process of learning by doing, and no formal education seemed to be needed.

Advertising was seen as salesmanship in print, and it was assumed all that was needed was a bit of talent and a lot of practice. There also were no known copywriters at that time, since the text was considered of secondary importance to the dominance of visuals (pictures). As a consequence, Omahen in 1929 (Erjavec 2007) appealed to advertisers to hand over all advertising activities to advertising agencies that were masters of the trade. He further claimed that the development of advertising was slow in Slovenia and should follow the examples from the western countries where the outburst of professional schools, seminars and faculties for advertising could be found at the time (Erjavec 2007: 20).

Among the agencies we should again mention the biggest one Aloma Company (acronym of the owner Alojzij Matelič) that handled the most important account, Ljubljana Fair, the biggest annual gathering of Slovenian business community at that time. The other agency worth mentioning is

Reklama Saturn Ljubljana (Kordiš 2005). Connected with this fair, and also with promotion of Slovenian tourism, some excellent work did develop, especially in the area of poster design (Kordiš 2005).

Centrally planned economy (from 1945 – 1965)

After the Second World War, advertising in the socialist Yugoslavia, as in other socialist countries, should not have had any role whatsoever. Analysis shows, however, that some of the practices were constantly present. The only exception was the first seven years after the war, mainly due to the system of rationing, where very few ads would have had any meaning (Zupančič 2000).

During this time and in the following years of rapid industrialization we can, however, detect an interesting breed of corporate ads with strong elements of state propaganda. After this period a rise in consumer advertising is evident, in spite of prevailing Marxist skepticism toward advertising and marketing (Patterson 2003).

The center of advertising development in former Yugoslavia was not in Slovenia, but in Zagreb, Croatia, and Belgrade, Serbia. Already in 1954, the Zagreb advertising agency Ozeha had over one hundred employees (Patterson, 2003). However, its development at that time was largely connected with political propaganda. Nevertheless, the efforts to form an advertising profession already were present by the late 1950s. The leading industry figures in Belgrade and Zagreb launched the first specialty publications and first comprehensive manuals for training a new cadre. Technical training was offered by 1958 at one of the "workers universities" in Zagreb (Patterson 2003).

At that time, two important books were written in the Serbo-Croatian language, Josip Sudar's *Ekonomska propaganda u teoriji i praksi* in 1958, and other in 1959 by Josip Mrvoš: *Propaganda, reklama, publicitet: teorija i praksa* (Patterson 2003). Beside these books, several others were written or translated at that time, accompanied with numerous other publications, papers in journals, etc. However, the Yugoslav educational system at that time completely underestimated the importance of university education for advertising experts. Table 19-1 provides an overview of textbooks and trade books that were written between 1950 and 2000 to support the country's university-level and vocational advertising education in the three centers of influence: Zagreb (now Croatia), Belgrade (now Serbia), and Ljubljana and Maribor (now Slovenia).

Zagreb:

Sudar J. (1958), Ekonomska propaganda u teoriji i praksi, Zagreb

Mrvoš J. (1959), Propaganda, reklama, publicitet: teorija i praksa, Ozeha, Zagreb

Sudar, J. (1971), Ekonomska propaganda [Advertising], 3d ed. Zagreb

Dinter, Č. (1974), Utvrdivanje djelotvornosti ekonomske propagande", Vjesnik-Agencija za marketing, Zagreb

Petz B. (1974), Psihologija u ekonomskoj propagandi, Društvo ekonomskih propagandista Hrvatske, Zagreb

Keller Goroslav (1975), Design-dizajn; Vjesnik, Zagreb.

Hitrec, M. (1981), Temelji i učinci promocijskog komuniciranja. Zagreb : Udruženje propagandista SR Hrvatske.

Belgrade:

Barton R. (1964), Uspješna ekonomska propaganda, Privreda, Beograd

Jovanović B. (1965), Funkcija i strategija ekonomska propagande, Beograd

Laird D.A. and E.Ç. Laird (1965), Prktična psihologija prodaje, Panorama, Beograd

Henry H. (1966), Što potrošač želi?, Privredni pregled, Beograd

Trfunović M. (1969), Psihologija kupaca, Sportska knjiga, Beograd

Fruht M. (1975), Kreacija privredne propagande, Savremena administracija, Beograd

Fruht M. (1981), Industrijski dizajn, Privredni pregled, Beograd

Ljubljana, Maribor:

Deželak B. (1966), Ekonomska propaganda, Višja ekonomsko komercijalna šola, Maribor

Deželak B. (1965), Organizacija in politika blagovnega prometa, Višja ekonomsko komercijalna šola, Maribor

Deželak B. (1969), Teorija in praksa raziskave tržišča, Založba Obzorja, Maribor

Deželak B. (1971), Marketing, Založba Obzorja, Maribor

Deželak B. (1969), Marketing v nabavni politiki, Založba Obzorja, Maribor

Vezjak D. (1969), Izbiranje tujih tržišč, Založba obzorja, Maribor

Vreg F. (1973), Družbeno komuniciranje, Založba Obzorja, Maribor

Možina S. (1975), Psihologija in sociologija trženja, Založba Obzorja

Radonjič D. (1977), Pospeševanje prodaje, Delo GV, Ljubljana

Lorbek F. (1979), Osnove komuniciranja v marketingu, Delo GV, Ljubljana.

Snoj B. (1982), Embalaža, Delo GV, Ljubljana

Jančič Z. (1990), Marketing: strategija menjave, Gospodarski vestnik, Ljubljana

Sfiligoj N. (1993), Marketinško upravljanje, FDV, Ljubljna

Ule M. in M. Kline (1996), Psihologija tržnega komuniciranja, FDV, Ljubljana

Table 19-1: Advertising-related books in Yugoslavia/Slovenia, 1950-2000

Planned-market economy (from 1965 – 1990)

After liberal economic reforms in the 1960s that ended the Yugoslav planned economy and changed it into market-planning system, together with the system of workers self-management, the importance of market activities became obvious. Kline (1985), in his study of marketing research in Yugoslavia, described the situation at the time. Borders were opened and many foreign firms signed license agreements with domestic firms. With the inflow of technology, there was also the inflow of managerial, marketing, and advertising knowledge. New products started to pile up and needed the help in promoting them. The competition became the game of the day, especially for the firms that operated in the industries with too much supply for the autarchic economy of Yugoslavia such as food, beverages, furniture, domestic appliances, fashion etc.

Important influence also came from domestic exporting firms that had to adapt to the more demanding market circumstances abroad. One characteristic of this new development in advertising was the effective use of the new television medium, where Slovenian firms especially excelled. So local experts in advertising were needed, opening significant employment opportunities.

With no university advertising education at that time in Slovenia, the criteria for employment were extremely low and undemanding. Besides, this growing profession had to constantly present its work as contributing to the common good and fitting the prevailing ideology, or face the consequences.

This game lasted until the collapse of the socialist system at the end of the 1980s with ups and downs for the advertising profession. The worst situation that the advertising profession had to tackle was a crisis that started in the early 1970s, when the communist party purged "liberals" deemed too friendly to the market (Patterson 2003). This crisis lasted for more than ten years, and severely hindered the development of advertising profession in Yugoslavia, especially in Croatia.

The first official textbook for "economic propaganda" was written by Deželak at the University of Maribor, Faculty of Economics and Business (at the time still a college called VEKŠ) in 1966 (see Table 19-1). It concentrated on "producing messages." The first academic, university-level course on advertising in Slovenia started in 1969, at the University of Ljubljana, Faculty for Sociology, Political Sciences and Journalism. This early start, compared to other socialist countries, was a reaction to the liberalization of the economy, and embracing western standards of management and marketing in the mid-60s.

The pioneering work began with Prof. Nada Sfiligoj, who taught an elective course titled "Economic Propaganda." The term was uniquely used in the former Yugoslavia, meaning propaganda necessary for companies, as opposed to political propaganda. However, the syllabus was quite contemporary, similar to courses on advertising principles, with the emphasis on economics of advertising. Among the topics covered were the marketing background of advertising, market research, consumer behavior, advertising media, advertising message structure, advertising copy, advertising organization in the firm and advertising testing.

That course was taught twice a year until 1976, when it was replaced with "Political and Economic Propaganda." The emphasis also changed into mainly propaganda topics with more critical attitude towards advertising (Sfiligoj 2004). Another course, Sociology of Consumer Behavior, was offered in 1971, but was part of the journalism curriculum only once again, in

1976. After a decade of downturn in advertising education a single advertising course, Economic Propaganda and Contemporary Market, finally was offered in 1988 (Sfiligoj 2004).

A similar history can be found in the Faculty of Economics, also at the University of Ljubljana (Damjan & Jancic, 1997). Its class on Organizational Psychology covered parts of advertising, led by Stane Možina. But it started and ended in 1971. With support from VEKŠ he published a book on psychology and sociology of marketing in 1975 (*see* Table 19-1), used in graduate studies at Faculty of Economics. Later this course changed its name and emphasis. Some topics were dimly covered in many other courses, such as Market Research taught by Drago Kotnik, or courses on the trade economics.

One of the good signs in these hard times was the opening of Slovenia-based advertising agency, Studio Marketing, in 1973, now a partner to JWT group. By diligent, politically smart and professional work, this agency escaped the anti-liberal crisis and helped to establish the huge reputation of regionally well-known corporate brands such as Fructal, Radenska, Mura, Unior, Lek, etc. Studio Marketing was initially led by the first creative director in the country, Jure Apih, now a retired president to Golden Drum Advertising Festival. Later, and to this day, the agency is led by Jernej Repovš.

An important contribution of this agency was the dissemination of knowledge of the western-style strategic, as well as creative, adverting. It was no longer a so-called "socialist advertising" (Patterson 2003), but was global in its approach and performance and, of course, always ethically and socially responsible. Its competitive edge was in excellent creative skills, where creative figures such as Jaka Judnič, Meta Dobnikar, Jani Bavčer, Jure Apih, Jernej Repovš, Zlatko Jančič, etc. excelled, while using scientific methods in advertising.

Pioneering work in this field was done by Mihael Kline, now a professor at University of Ljubljana, Faculty for Social Sciences. He was educated in advertising, and especially consumer behavior, during his many visits to prominent professors in the U.S.A. He taught an elective course on Consumer Psychology in the Department of Psychology, University of Ljubljana, where he was able to include research on advertising effectiveness as applied to packaging, as well as motivation, perception, emotions, research on perceptual mapping, experimental design, conjoint analysis, etc. (Kline, 1976; 1977).

Thanks to politics, new equipment donated to the Department of Psychology by the American government sat unused at the time, as if waiting to enable the start of experiments in the field of consumer behaviour – solving problems such as emotional response of consumers to the package elements (four channel lie detector), eye movement over visual surface (eye movement camera), and the tachistoscope for measuring perception and defining benchmarks of advertising stimulus at the selling point. The first results from these devices were encouraging and a strong motive and initiative for the beginning of practising an elective course Consumer Psychology in 1977 as a part of the educational program Industrial Psychology at the University of Ljubljana, Faculty of Arts, Department of Psychology. Interest shown by the students in this course and potential market opportunities for the graduates proved the correctness of such development (Kline 1977, 1998).

Kline's role as an employee of Studio Marketing, and later as an external partner to the agency, always pushed contemporary advertising knowledge in the agency. Under his influence, executives were present at the majority of important advertising events in Europe and the U.S.A., usually the only delegates from the so-called socialist block. The knowledge they brought home was then first disseminated internally through workshops, publications, and internal conferences, and later externally to the clients and members of advertising profession.

Studio Marketing became the hub of advertising knowledge for decades in Slovenia. Needless to say, many of its executives in the late 1980s and early 1990s left the company and opened their own advertising agencies that are, even today, on the top ten list in the Slovenian advertising agency scene.

Kline also was one of the organizers of early educational seminars on marketing communications, known as SETEK, in 1979 that somehow tried to bridge the gap in the knowledge among members of Slovenian advertising industry. These seminars were vocational education, organized for employees in advertising agencies and advertisers without adequate education that were prevalent in the advertising industry at the time. The seminars prematurely ended and again showed the hardship that advertising education have to face in Slovenia.

Slovenian period – free market economy (after 1991)
After the collapse of Yugoslavia, Slovenia became a sovereign state in 1991. A few years later it became a member of NATO and EU in 2004, adopted Euro currency in 2007 and in 2010 became a member of OECD countries. Most importantly, the market-economy enabled political changes.

The independence of Slovenia finally brought deeply needed changes also in the curriculum of our universities. Similarly to the American situation (Ross and Richards 2008), there were three pillars of advertising education: psychology, journalism, and business schools. Specific to Slovenian situation is the fourth pillar, namely design schools which followed from bases in the previous periods (e.g., Fruth's and Keller's books, *see* Table 19-1).

In 1991 Nada Sfiligoj became the first head of marketing and advertising at the now renamed Faculty for Social Sciences. A boost in students and related courses happened when Zlatko Jancic left his long and successful career in the biggest advertising agency, Studio Marketing, and became a university professor.

In 1993, the first study program of marketing communication started, consisting of courses such as Basic Marketing, Strategy and Technology of Advertising, Market Research, Psychology of Marketing, Language and Style of Advertising and Public Relations. Among other pioneers of marketing communication study program we also need to mention Marko Lah and Mihael Kline, who joined the faculty in subsequent years. In the mid-1990s, this program began to produce graduates and post-graduates with advanced knowledge of marketing and advertising.

The only specialized study of marketing communications at the Faculty of Social Sciences soon became a kind of elite study program in Slovenia with high requirements for new student entry. In order to successfully trespass the period of economic transition to market economy in Slovenia in the 1990s, this marketing communications chair responded with the ever-improving curriculum and new courses (Jancic, 1997).

Faculty of Economics joined with the opening of its marketing major in 1991. Among the courses was also the renewed course on Consumer Behavior, taught by Stane Možina. The first Marketing Communication course started in 1994, taught by Iča Rojšek and Danijel Starman and later, after 2001, by Vesna Žabkar. Zlatko Jančič contributed in development of the course in the early years.

Up until the year 1984, when a new Design Department at the Ljubljana Academy of Fine Art was established, painters, graphic artists, architects/educational programs at the Faculty of Architecture played the role of the main designers in advertising agencies. It represents a start of a visual communication design study, at first in undergraduate programs, and in 15 years also in Masters and PhD degrees, which filled a large gap in the development of advertising in Slovenia up to that point.

Besides planning, technical and artistic courses, two or three marketing courses are also included into the program: Fundamentals of Marketing, Consumer Psychology and Basic of Visual Communication. This makes it easier for designers, strategists and creative directors, who are taking courses at business and journalism or communications schools to work as a team and to learn about teamwork. Of course, their results range much wider than just the narrowly understood field of advertising. They cover the whole field of Marketing Communications, as well as the field of designing new products, which is covered in Industrial Design major.

Besides the efforts in formal advertising education in this period we have to mention also other sources that disseminate the knowledge of good theory and practice in advertising. These are materials of the Slovenian Advertising Association, *MM Akademija* scientific marketing journal, MM trade journal, Festivals and seminars such as Slovenian Advertising Festival advertising awards, Golden Drum Festival, EFFIE competition, many student's organized seminars, conferences and festivals etc.

Overview of Advertising Education in Slovenia Today

After presenting the historical background of advertising education in Slovenia, it is about time to bring the reader up to the present condition of this field. There are no full-service programs that teach every aspect of advertising in Slovenia, to date. However, there are several programs that specialize in one or more aspects of advertising (art direction or account management), or offer only selected courses in advertising. Profiles of a variety of programs will be presented to highlight where advertising education stands as of 2010. Before we present leading programs, as well as smaller and less prominent programs, in journalism, business, and art schools, a short overview of the higher education system in Slovenia is needed.

Higher education studies in Slovenia are provided by public and private universities, faculties, art academies and professional colleges. Starting in 2005, the three-cycle higher education system, in accordance with the Bologna declaration, was introduced. *First cycle* study programs are academic and professional study programs (three to four years programs) and credit points (180 to 240 ECTS, 1 ECTS consists of 25 to 30 hours of a student's work). *Second cycle* study programs are Master's study programs (Master's professional degree, 60 to 120 ECTS, one to two years). *Third cycle* includes doctoral study programs (three years; 180 ECTS, two thirds of which is acquired by research).

In public higher education institutions students pay tuition fees only for part-time studies, while full-time studies are free. For doctoral (third-cycle) studies, tuition fees are paid. Students in private higher education institutions also pay tuition fees (Ministry of higher education and science, 2010).

An access requirement to academic study is the general matura examination, or the vocational matura examination plus an additional exam from one general matura subject. In the case of art study programs, specific requirements include a test of talent of artistic skills. Graduates are granted the diploma and the professional or academic title.

The majority of courses are offered in Slovenian language. More and more frequently, higher education institutions offer consultations and courses to foreign students also in English.

High school level education (for school kids from 15 to 19) includes a range of vocational schools, e.g., a high school of design and photography in Ljubljana, a high school for design in Maribor, as well as a range of business high schools (called "ekonomska šola"), or more general high school programs. At age 19, students can enroll in a higher education institution.

Future students can choose among three public universities (University of Ljubljana, University of Maribor and University of Primorska); two private universities (University of Nova Gorica and EMUNI University) and several independent schools. These universities and independent institutions offer several arts, journalism, and business programs that cover different aspects of advertising: management, art direction, copy writing, or planning (media), and will be explained more in detail below.

Advertising management is included in marketing and advertising courses at a range of business schools. Copy writing and media planning are part of educational programs at journalism schools, while art direction programs is in art schools.

Starting with journalism schools, there are three possibilities for studies in Slovenia: (1) University of Ljubljana, Faculty of Social Sciences; (2) University of Nova Gorica, School of Humanities and (3) Faculty of Media, Ljubljana. All three will be presented more in detail.

Specific Programs

University of Ljubljana Faculty of Social Sciences was established in 1961. The school is one of the largest members of the University of Ljubljana. It has over 5,100 students in 30 undergraduate and graduate study programs. The Faculty of Social Sciences is housed in a modern, state-of-the-art facility.

The head of department of communication is Zlatko Jančič. The department consists of three chairs: Chair of Media Studies, Chair of Journalism, and Chair of Marketing Communications. Seven full-time faculty members teach in Marketing Communications: Golob Urša, Jančič Zlatko, Kamin Tanja, Kline Mihael, Kropivnik Samo, Lah Borut Marko and Podnar Klement. They offer a widest selection of advertising related courses of any educational institution in Slovenia: advertising strategy, marketing communication of innovations, corporate communication, introduction to visual communications, advertising and society, introduction to communication research, social cause advertising, integrated marketing communications, business to business marketing communication, and consumer psychology.

At the graduate level, they offer journalistic studies, communications, media and society studies, public relations and strategic marketing communications. Some of undergraduate courses are taught in English (e.g. Communication Management by Dejan Verčič).

The University of Primorska Faculty of Humanistic Studies Koper (UP FHŠ), offers Media Studies, the undergraduate degree program that provides students with an understanding of the media and the modern media culture. The program educates also for work as a technical assistant or adviser in media companies in the field of communication services and in the area of event management, marketing, and promotion or public relations. The program covers media studies and communication theories, social history of mass media, epistemology and methodology of media research, marketing and marketing communication, and communication and politics.

Faculty of Media (FaM) was founded in 2008 in Ljubljana and is one of the newest higher education institutions in Slovenia. The school offers media and journalism study programs at undergraduate and Master's levels, and enrolls 60 students in each level annually. Both study programs offer students a combination of knowledge and skills in social sciences and technical fields, so as to qualify students to create quality media contents. The studies are organized as part-time studies only for which students have to pay tuition. The school does not reveal the names of its professors.

Moving on to business programs, there are several options, since the competition in business programs is very intensive: (1) University of Ljubljana, Faculty of Economics; (2) University of Maribor, Faculty of Economics and Business; (3) University of Primorska, Faculty of Management Koper; (4) Faculty of Applied Business and Social studies (DOBA) Maribor and (5) GEA College of Entrepreneurship, (6) International School for Social and Business Studies, Celje (MFDPŠ), (7) School of Business and Management, Novo mesto (VŠUP). Because advertising in most schools is limited to a few lectures, only schools with courses in advertising/marketing communications are presented.

The University of Ljubljana Faculty of Economics (FELU) was founded in 1946. It is the largest faculty of the University of Ljubljana, with almost 8000 full-time and part-time undergraduate and graduate students. The school's graduates can be found in the highest positions in Slovenian and international companies, while professors have been on supervisory boards of key Slovenian companies and ministers in government administration.

At the undergraduate level, the school offers two different study programs: University Degree - Business and Economics Program in Marketing, and Professional Degree - Business Program in Marketing. The FELU offers marketing programs also in the English language (University degree in Marketing in undergraduate programs, Master in International Business, and International Full Time Master Program in Business Administration) as well as doctoral program in Economics and Business. Each year, in total 160 -200 marketing students learn about principles of marketing communications (undergraduate level) and advertising (graduate level). The courses are taught by prof. Vesna Zabkar.

The University of Maribor Faculty of Economics and Business (FEB) celebrated its 50th anniversary in 2009. It is the second largest business school in Slovenia. During that fifty years more than 26,000 students graduated from the school, acquiring different professional and scientific titles.

The academic staff is organized in 13 departments, including a department of marketing. The department has 7 members, including Bruno Završnik and Aleksandra Pisnik Korda that teach Marketing Communications and Strategic Marketing Communications courses (in Slovenian language), and Damjan Mumel who teaches Art of Communication.

The International School for Social and Business Studies, Celje (MFDPŠ), offers professionally-oriented higher education undergraduate study program Business in Modern Society with interdisciplinary knowledge in the fields of economics, business, management, organizational sciences, informatics, technologies, communications, ethics and foreign languages. One of the elective programs in the third year is also Multimedia & Design in Business. The school does not reveal the names of teachers, however the web pages of the program promise local, national, and international field experts and guest lecturers.

The DOBA Faculty of Applied Business and Social Studies Maribor (DOBA Faculty) is the largest distance education and e-learning provider in

Slovenia, targeting people in full-time employment. Part-time study takes 3 years. Mode of study is both on-site study and distance learning.

The schools offers bachelor program in marketing management and public relations management. In the 2009/2010 academic year, there were more than 130 students enrolled in this program. The main focus of the program is on knowledge and skills for performing marketing activities, knowing and mastering media markets and new media, and planning media communications, as well as with applied knowledge of management. The school does not reveal the names of its professors.

GEA College of Entrepreneurship, Piran (VŠP), offers the International Bachelor Study of Entrepreneurship and serves as "a springboard for young people who are aware of the necessity for international activities and the opportunities offered." Advertising/communication courses are elective, including Principles of Contemporary Mass Media Operations and Market Communication, Market Communication, Marketing strategies, and Principles of Contemporary Mass Media Operations, taught by practitioners like Darko Števančec, Vinko Zupančič and Tomaž Perovič.

To complete the picture of business programs in Slovenia that offer courses in advertising/communications, also the *School of Business and Management, Novo mesto (VŠUP)* should be mentioned, which offers marketing communication as part of its undergraduate program. However, not much information is available about this program or the school.

From business schools we move on to art schools. These institutions offer a different set of knowledge and skills:

University of Ljubljana Academy of Theatre, Radio, Film and Television: Department of Film and Television Directing offers courses in film directing, television directing, film history and film theory. Students carry out number of exercises in film and television directing, cinematography and editing. The department closely collaborates with Television Slovenia, the Slovenian Film Fund, and other media institutions.

The school has been awarded several prizes for student films at various international film festivals including Bucharest, Montpelier, New York and Sarajevo, as well as at numerous student film festivals. It was awarded the best European film school at the 2007 Anima & Etuida Film Festival in Krakow.

The University of Ljubljana Academy of Fine Arts and Design: Department of Design was established in 1984 and has two branches: industrial design and visual communications. Future designers are offered a broad professional education and analytically define and creatively solve designing problems.

The first year of study enables development of the abilities of artistic and spatial expression and recognizing the basis of the designing process. The project work in later years is organized in seminars under the individual guidance of different mentors. Seminars graphic design cover techniques of typography and photography combined with the use of a computer. Formally, the graduates from the department of design are either graphic or industrial designers. Some graphic designers specialize in advertising.

The University of Nova Gorica, School of Applied Sciences: School of Arts offers a bachelor's program in digital arts and practices that is, at present, in the process of acquiring the consent of the Council for Higher Education of the Republic of Slovenia. According to the information provided at its web page, the program is in line with conceptual and structural basis of the existing three-year program Digital Media School of Applied Arts Famul Stuart.

The program builds on creative use of digitalization of media and technologies. The program structure will be divided into four supporting optional modules, which will be supported by historical-critical and creative-technical parts: animation (animated film animation in the creative industries); videos (fiction, documentary, experimental videos, video art); photo (copyright, functional photo) and new media (creative use of new technologies).

The College of Visual Arts, Ljubljana (VŠRS) offers painting and other basic art genres: visual-spatial design, graphics, photography and film, as well as video, performing art, body art, land art visualization, and other artistic ideas. Graduates also work in design and advertising bureaus and TV media as video directors or graphic designers. The program is 4+1 years. Other details are not evident to the outside observer.

The Academy of Design, Ljubljana (VSD) is an independent institution of higher education that offers education in the field of interior design, visual communications, textiles, and fashion. Visual communications design is responding to growing needs for professional staff in all fields of visual communications in print or digital media. The school enrolls 30 students in visual communications annually. Not much is known about educators at the school besides that they are "constantly taking part in advanced study-courses in order to improve their knowledge and skills" which should provide "the guarantee that the education is always modern and that it is adapting to the latest technological and substantial demands in the field of visual communications."

The College of Services, Ljubljana (VIST) was accredited in 2008 as an undergraduate program for photography (three-year study). The program promises that "well-trained students to work in practice - individually or in teams so that they will handle all phases and aspects of photographic production including aspects of marketing communications with clients, of multimedia, design, etc." Some of the lecturers are established photographers, such as Arne Hodalič, Borut Furlan, Rajko Bizjak et al.

A few more important facts

Having presented the range of journalism, business and art schools that offer formal education related to advertising, some more words need to be said about the involvement of the advertising business people in ad education. There is a professional organization that supports advertising education: Slovenian Advertising Chamber (SOZ 2010), a non-govern-mental organization representing the interests of advertisers, advertising agencies, and media, and advocating for high standards and advertising ethics in advertising. SOZ is a member of European Advertising Standards Alliance (EASA) and the International Advertising Association (IAA).

The Slovenian Association of Advertising Agencies is a member of the European Association of Communication Agencies (EACA), Slovenian member of the World Federation of Advertisers (WFA), Section on the Internet for SZM, a member of the Interactive Advertising Bureau Europe (IAB-Europe). SOZ contributes to education of professionals through events, seminars (Effie Academy) and such.

For several years, industry supported students in InterAd, IAA's annual student advertising competition which provided hands-on marketing communications experience for undergraduate students. With participation in this case-history style projects, students got a chance to apply their marketing theory in practice and experience real-world marketing environment. And since 2008, students from University of Ljubljana Faculty of Economics participate in the EACA AdVenture competition. Some larger Slovenian companies support students' research and thesis work with rewards (Krka, 2010, Trimo, 2010). Also, international exchanges of students show that there is high quality of advertising related education in Slovenia in the programs offered in the country.

Another, student based competition should be mentioned, since it offers additional educational opportunities for all participating: established in 1999, Magdalena is a non-profit festival of creativity, organized and managed by young people for the young people in Maribor. It is a response to expensive and formal advertising festivals, focused on creative manifestations of marketing communication, and takes a more critical stand toward irresponsible practices in this field. It offers low fees for entry registration and attendance to festival lectures and parties (more than 3,500 visitors and 4,200 entries presented in last nine years). Magdalena has become "an important meeting point for those who seek their future in the world of design, advertising, media and other fields of public communication." (Magdalena 2010).

However, there is a concern that needs to be presented since it is related to the present state of advertising industry in the country. There are around 200 advertising agencies in Slovenia at present (Marketing magazin, 2010). Interestingly, the situation does not resemble the situation in other ex-socialist countries, where the dominant agencies are all multinationals. Slovenian agencies do cooperate with multinational advertising agency groups, but remain owned by locals (Jancic & Zabkar 1998).

One reason for this local focus is the relatively low percentage of foreign investment and ownership in the Slovenian economy does not attract multinational agencies. Another reason is presented above in the unique history of advertising that is much different than in other ex-socialist countries. Advertising, as practiced by advertising agencies, developed in professionalization. However, these advertising agencies now predominantly work on adaptations of standardized campaigns for multinational companies, and less on development of brands for domestic advertisers. Domestic advertisers are predominantly small and medium-sized companies where marketing is losing a "seat at the table," being evicted from the company boards (Zabkar & Jancic, 2008).

We believe that advertising has a reduced role on the side of domestic advertisers, being considered as a cost, rather than an investment, which has important consequences for advertising education as well. This creates less demand for students with advertiser-centered knowledge. It is not clear whether students who enroll in advertising-related courses at present will be able to fully use the knowledge they gain from formal education. The odd question arises at the end of this study: Are they overqualified for the contemporary Slovenian job market?

References

Academy of Design, Ljubljana (VSD): http://www.vsd.si.
Bucur, M., & Wingfield, N. M. (2001). *Staging the past: the politics of commemoration in Habsburg Central Europe, 1848 to the present.* Purdue Univ Press.
College of Services, Ljubljana (VIST): http://www.vist.si.
DOBA Faculty of Applied Business and Social Studies Maribor: http://www.vpsm.si/.
College of Visual Arts, Ljubljana (VŠRS): http://www.arthouse-si.com.

Damjan, J. & Jancic Z. (1997). Great Marketing Education for Small Countries, 7th International Marketing Conference: European Marketing Challenge, Budapest, Nov. 21.

EMUNI University: http://www.emuni.si

Erjavec, A. (2007). *Zgodovina slovenskih oglaševalskih agencij*, FDV Ljubljana (History of Slovenian advertising agencies).

GEA College of Entrepreneurship, Piran (VŠP): http://www.gea-college.si/visoka-sola-zapodjetnistvo/.

Faculty of Media (FaM): http://www.fame.si/fame/index.php.

Feldmann, M. (2006). Emerging Varieties of Capitalism in Transition Countries: Industrial Relations and Wage Bargaining in Estonia and Slovenia. *Comparative Political Studies* *39(7)*, 829-854.

Hudalist, M. (1997). 200 let prvega slovenskega časopisnega oglasa, *Marketing Magazin*, February, p. 7.

International School for Social and Business Studies, Celje (MFDPŠ): http://www.mfdps.si

Jančič, Z.(1997). V popotnico prvi generaciji, Prvi, Magazin absolventov prve slovenske generacije študija komunikologije, smer trženje in tržno komuniciranje na Fakulteti za družbene vede. Ljubljana, p. 2.

Jancic, Z. & Zabkar, V. (1998). Establishing Marketing Relationships in Advertising Agency Business: A Transitional Economy Case. *Journal of Advertising Research*, November-December, pp. 27-36.

Kline, M. (1977). Doprinos psihologije k razvoju ekonomske propagande v Jugoslaviji. SEPJ. Kladovo.

Kline, M. (1976). Kontrolisani eksperiment kao merilo uspešnosti ekonomske propagande u OUR, in Milanović R. and B. Tihi, (Eds.), Ekonomska propaganda: Društveni i poslovni aspekt, Udruženje ekonomskih propagandista BiH, Sarajevo, pp. 246-253.

Kline, M. (1985). *Marketing Research in Yugoslavia.* Working Paper. University of Florida, Miami.

Kline, M. (1998). Consumer Psychology in market oriented organizations. *Panika*, 3, 3: 22-25.

Kordiš, M. (2005). Gospodična vi ste lepa kot plakat: Plakat v Ljubljani med obema vojnama, Filozofska fakulteta, Ljubljana.

Korošec, T. (2006). Jezik in stil oglaševanja, Univerza v Ljubljani.

Krka (2010): Krka Awards. http://www.krka.si/sl/o-krki/krkine-nagrade.

Magdalena (2010): http://www.magdalena.org/.

Marketing Magazin (2010): http://www.marketingmagazin.si/.

Ministry of higher education and science: http://www.mvzt.gov.si.

Paterson, P. H. (2003). Truth Half Told: Finding the Perfect Pitch for Advertising and Marketing in Socialist Yugoslavia, 1950 – 1991. *Enterprise & Society*, 4. pp 179-225.

Ross, Billy I. and Richards, Jef I. (2008). *A Century of Advertising Education*, American Academy of Advertising.

School of Business and Management, Novo mesto (VŠUP): http://www.visoka-sola.com

Sfiligoj, N. (2004). Kronološki pregled nastanka dodiplomskega študija tržnega komuniciranja na FDV, unpublished memoars, Ljubljana.

Slovenia Cultural Profile: http://www.culturalprofiles.net/Slovenia/Directories/Slovenia_Cultural_Profile/-6792.html.

SOZ (2010): Slovenian Advertising Chamber, http://www.soz.si/.

Trimo (2010): Trimo research awards. http://www.trimo-researchawards.com/

University of Ljubljana: http://www.uni-lj.si.

University of Ljubljana, Academy of Fine Arts and Design: Department of Design: http://www.alu.uni-lj.si

University of Ljubljana, Academy of Theatre, Radio, Film and Television: Department of Film and Television Directing (http://www.agrft.uni-lj.si/departments_and_sections/ department_of_film_and_television_directing/)

University of Ljubljana, Faculty of Economics: http://www.ef.uni-lj.si

University of Ljubljana, Faculty of Social Sciences: http://www.fdv.uni-lj.si

University of Maribor: http://www.uni-mb.si

University of Maribor, Faculty of Economics and Business: http://www.epf.uni-mb.si/

University of Nova Gorica: http://www.p-ng.si

University of Nova Gorica, School of Applied Sciences: http://www.ung.si/.

University of Primorska: http://www.upr.si

University of Primorska, Faculty of Humanistic Studies Koper: http://www.fuds.si/.

Zupančič, M. (2000). Razvoj tiskanih oglasov v osrednjih slovenskih časnikih od leta 1945, FDV Ljubljana.

Zabkar, V., & Jancic, Z. (2008). Marketing decision-makers in Slovenia: Empirical evidences of the importance of marketing function. *Naše gospodarstvo, 54.*

Teaching Advertising in Spain

David Roca
Universitat Autònoma de Barcelona, Spain

Daniel Tena
Universitat Autònoma de Barcelona, Spain

Jean Grow
Marquette University, USA

Spanish Advertising Education History

Advertising education in Spain has a rich, nearly 100-year, history. Its foundation is framed by pioneering advertising practitioner and educator, Pere Prat Gaballí, whose influence was significant. Another significant factor in advertising education, and post-secondary education generally, is the influence of formal government legislation on educational models. Thus, the authors frame much of the historical aspects of this study within a political lens.

Following Gaballí's initial work, the growth of Spanish advertising education was curtailed by the Spanish civil war (1936-39) and World War II, which Spain endured under dictator Francisco Franco. Franco's influence lasted until November 1975, and severely truncated Spanish economic, cultural, and social development, as well as Spanish post-graduation education.

That said, in 1961 Franco's government formalized the study of advertising, but not at the university level. On the heels of Franco's death, the transitional period (1975-78) laid the groundwork for renewal of the educational system overall. It included advertising education, this time at the university level. Following this, Spanish advertising education entered the democratic period and began to expand at a rapid pace, eventually becoming one of the premier systems in all of Europe. Today, the Bologna process frames all European post-graduate education, with the Spanish advertising education representing a hybrid of the Bologna model.

Prat Gaballí: the pioneer

Advertising seminars began to be taught Barcelona around 1911. They were informally structured and sponsored by *La Cambra de Comerç*,

Indústria i Navegació de Barcelona[29] (Barcelon's Commerce, Industry and Navigation Chamber). In 1917, Pere Prat Gaballí (1885-1962)[30] became the director these seminars, and created a formalized structure based on his book *Publicitat Científica* (*Scientific Advertising* 1917), which predated Claude Hopkins' book of the same title (1923). Gaballí's focus was a new rational perspective. "These days of plentiful advertising, visibility is harder to get day after day and needs a growing sum of technical resources and observations" (1917:23).

In 1932 a program, which focused on marketing and advertising research, was established at *Escola d'Alts Estudis Mercantils* (*School of Commercial Studies*). This technical school was the precurser to Universitat Autònoma de Barcelona, which would later become the home of a leading advertising program in Spain (www.elmundo.es). Pere Prat Gaballí, already teaching at *Escola d'Alts Estudis Mercantils,* was appointed the first chair in the summer of 1936. Upon his appointment, he began to consolidate and formalize advertising education. However, this position never came into existance, and the seminars were terminated due to the onset of the Spanish civil war.

After the Spanish civil war and World War II, and despite highly constrained economic conditions, Gaballí returned to work as an advertising professional. He also continued to teach and published articles and books on advertising. His last book, *Publicidad Combativa* (Combative Advertising) was published in 1953. However, due the difficult economic conditions under the Franco dictatorship, advertising and advertising education remained stymied. Gaballí died in 1962.

---

[29] Barcelona's Chamber of Commerce is one of the most representative institutions of Catalan society and a first order's point of reference for the country's socio-economic arena. The Chamber of Barcelona works to improve the results of companies: it offers services that companies can use individually and carries out general interest actions to encourage the promotion of the country's economic and business activity which, indirectly, also favor each company. The Official Chamber of Commerce, Industry and Navigation of Barcelona was founded in 1886, although its history goes back to the Middle Ages as the Consulate of the Sea or the Royal Assembly of Commerce (http://www.cambrabcn.org/).

[30] Gaballí started his career as a writer (poems, tales and translating). He studied at *Escola Superior de Comerç* de Barcelona between 1897 and 1901. In 1911 he discovered System Magazine, this magazine deal with advertising and selling. After this, he found *Pinter'sInk, Advertising World,* first theoretical treatises from Daniel Starch and Walter Dill Scott and books from Hamilton Institute. From that moment he started to write articles at the magazine *Comercio and* the journal *El Día Gráfico* (1914). He started a successful career in the First World War Word, when Spain developed thanks to its neutrality (at Tena& Roca 2009).

The importance of Gaballí's influence cannot be overstated. His work was formally recognized by the Spanish advertising industry. In 1992 *La Cambra* reprinted his groundbreaking book, commemorating its 75th anniversary. Then in 2007, the *Collegi de Publicitaris i de Relacions Publiques* de *Catalunya*[31] (association of advertising and public relations professionals holding college degrees) established the Prat Gaballí's Award to promote advertising and public relations research.[32]

Pre-University Period: Constraints of Dictatorship

During the 1940s and much of the 1950s, Franco's government pursued a policy of autocratic rule. Spain turned inward with a focus on economic self-sufficiency, without foreign trade or investment.[33] Much like the isolation Spain experienced politically and economically, advertising, too, was isolated. Thus advertising educations also was curtailed.

During these strained times Barcelona, which was the creative heart of Spanish cultural life, remained the center of advertising production in Spain. However, there was little activity as the economy was in a severe downturn. Further, Franco's policies did not encourage expansion of advertising, nor its educational components. More than 20 years would pass before the Spanish economy, and Spanish advertising education, began to develop.

With the government Stabilization Plan (1959-74)[34] a very important change of strategy came about in Spanish economic policy. This policy opened the economy to foreign goods and capital. Tourism began to boom during the 1960s, spurring Spain's development. In turn, advertising activity began to pick up pace, spreading consumption of goods and services and the advertising of some new brands. With this came a renewed interest in advertising education. Within this context two laws come into existence: *El Estatuto de la Publicidad* (Advertising Statute, 1964), the first law in the country to regulate advertising industry; and *La Ley General de Educación* (General Education Law, 1971), the law which formalized advertising education at universities.

Three years prior to *El Estatuto*, and under the supervision of Information and Tourism Ministery, *El Instituto Nacional de Publicidad* (National Advertising Institute) was established in 1961. Its goals were "to drive

---

[31] Authorized by Catalan parliament.
[32] More information can be found at: http://www.colpublirp.com/_premi-prat gaballi/premi.php?idioma=CAS
[33] http://www.megaessays.com/viewpaper/201370.html
[34] http://sispain.org/english/economy/stabilit.html

technical and artistic advertising progress, and to promote education to qualify for the professional practice of advertising in its different specialities."

To accomplish these goals *Las Escuelas Oficiales de Publicidad* (Official Advertising Schools) were created around the country from 1964 to 1970. These schools depended on *El Instituto de la Publicidad* (National Advertising Institute) and offered training to educate young people as advertising professionals. Students had to prove their "technical capacity to run or to plan/program the advertising activity of a client, agency and media" to become *Técnicos de Publicidad* (advertising technicians). Though the degree was not a formal university degree, it gained great popularity.

University Period: Democracy Coming

El Instituto de la Publicidad's schools functioned for six years. Then, in 1971, *La Ley General de Educación* (Education General Law) moved advertising education to the university level, under the supervision of Education and Science Ministry. During this time students studied courses common to communication and journalism. Three years later, in 1974, public relations was formally linked to advertising. The linkage between advertising and public relations education remains today.

In addition, new Schools of Information Sciences (*Ciencias de la Informacion*) were born with the *La Ley General de Educación* (Education General Law). Schools were now officially able to provide education in advertising, broadcasting [cinema, television, radio], and journalism. The official degrees would refer to the different three branches as: journalism, broadcasting (*comunicación audiovisual*), and advertising.

The first university to begin offering advertising degrees in Spain was Universidad Complutense de Madrid, in 1971. The Universitat Autònoma de Barcelona and Universidad de Bilbao where the next, in 1972. All three were public, state funded, universities.

The next law to be approved was *Ley de Reforma Universitaria (LRU)*, in 1981. This formalized the educational structure, which was based on three coursework years focused in communication, journalism, and liberal arts (sociology, economy, literature, languages, etc.). This was followed by two years focused exclusively on advertising and public relations. This law formalized the degree, "information sciences: advertising and pubic relations," which lived under communication sciences along with journalism.

The law mandated three subjects or classes for advertising and public relations studies. First was advertising creativity, involving the creation and realization of advertising messages for different communication media. Second was advertising media, encompassing analysis and media selection for advertising activities. The third was public relations techniques, involving establishment and development of strategies in public relations.

Ten years later, in 1991, the Decree 1386 approved the official degree in advertising and public relations (*Licenciado en Publicidad y Relaciones Públicas*). This formally established it as independent from broadcasting and journalism. With this change advertising and public relations courses began to be taught in the freshman year, establishing an intensive study of advertising at the entry level.

Classes were now organized in two semesters rather then one yearlong, as was previously done. The first semester began in October, and second in February, with the academic year concluding in June. There were generally around 40 credits per year. However it varied from university from university. One credit is understood as 10 hours of classroom instruction. Upon completion of this degree, students could apply for master programs. Thanks to the Decree 1386 a specialized Masters in Advertising and Public Relations emerged in Spain, and became more and more popular among students.

Period	Law	Results/Degree	Stuctural Outcome	Degree Timeline
Pre-University				
1964-70 Dictatorship	61/64 Advertising Statute	Advertising Technician	*Advertising Institute*	3 advertising
University				
1971-72 Dictatorship	Decree 2070/1971 *Ley General de Educación y Financiamiento de la Reforma Educativa*	*Licenciado en* Communication Sciences: Branch, Advertising and Public Relations	Information Sciences Schools (*Facultades*)	3 communication 2 advertising & public relations
1981 Democracy	Ley de Reforma Universitaria (LRU)	*Licenciado en* Communications Sciences: Branch, Avertising and Public Relations	Information Sciences Schools (*Facultades*)	3 communication 2 advertising & public relations
1992 Democracy	Decree 1386/1991	*Licenciado en* Advertising and Public Relations	Information Sciences Schools (*Facultades*)	4 advertising & public relations
2010 Democracy	Decree 1393/2007 Bologna	*Grado en* Publicidad y Relacions Publicas Official Master	Communication Sciences Schools (*Facultades*)	4 advertising & public relations 1 Masters

Note: Bachelor = Licenciatura o Grado.
Source: Adapted from Tena & Roca (2009).

Table 20-1: Legislation Impacting Advertising Education

The 1393/2007 Decree was the last significant advertising education legislation. This decree stated that Spain would officially adopt the Bologna process. The 1393/2007 Decree was approved in 2007 and universities were given three years to adopt the Bologna process. Thus, as of 2010, all of Spanish advertising education is in compliance with Bologna. While the credit structure will be uniform, in order to allow for credit transfer, different universities have been implementing Bologna in a very different ways. Thus, is can be said that Bologna offers uniformity with autonomy.

European Academic Systems

Bologna: The European Standard

The Bologna Declaration of 19 June 1999 began the process of creating the European Higher Education Area (EHEA). The goal of EHEA was to standardize and unify European higher education under a single credit structure. The process involved cooperation between government ministries, higher education institutions, students, and staff from 46 countries. In the end, the hope was that EHEA would facilitate mobility of students, graduates and higher education staff by creating standardized credits.

Specifically, Bologna accomplished five things. First, degrees would now be more comparable and easily understood, organized in a three-cycle structure: bachelor, master and doctorate.[35] Second, quality assurance would be in accordance with the Standards and Guidelines for Quality Assurance within the EHEA. Third, there would be equitable recognition of degrees across all European Union countries, in accordance with the Council of Europe/UNESCO Recognition Convention.[36] Fourth, Bologna unified different European credit systems through the European Credit Transfer System (ECTS). The effect of ECTS was that one ECTS in Spain would correspond to one ECTS in the rest of the European Union. Students would be able to transfer easily all around Europe. Fifth, the ECTS system was based on students' work, not on professors' time. One ECTS is the equivalent of 25 student hours of working time. Around 50 percent of this time, or even more, was considered non-lecture time.

Thus, ECTS is student driven, which is a significant departure from the previous structure and a significant difference from the American model. The results of this mean that lecture time is reduced, but student engagement is greatly increased.

---

[35] Some degrees, such as medicine, dentistry, veterinary science, pharmacy and architecture, are called long programs and do not fit within the structure of three cycles.

[36] http://www.ond.vlaanderen.be/hogeronderwijs/bologna/

Spanish System versus European

The Spanish university system is grounded in three different cycles as the Standard European Guidelines indicates (*see* Figure 20-1): Bachelor, Master and Doctorate. However, there are some differences between Spain and most European countries.

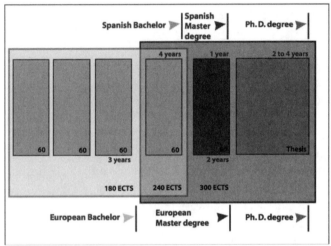

Source: *Adapted from Tena & Roca (2009).*
Figure 20-1. Cycles when studying advertising in Spain

Bachelor Degrees

In Spain, a Bachelor's degree in advertising is earned after four years of education that prepares students for the profession. Students need to study 60 ECTS each of the four years, for a total of 240 ECTS. Students take between six and eight classes per semester. The degree which they earn is called *Grado en Publicidad and Public Relations*[37] (Bachelor of Advertising and Public Relations). By contrast, Bachelor's degrees in Europe generally are earned in three years, with 180 ECTS.

Advanced Degrees

Master's degrees are an advanced education. Students may specialize in one of two tracks: professional or research. The research track allows

---

[37] Bachelor of Advertising and Public Relations. It is important to mention that Spain uses the word *Bachillerato* for High School level and not for university. Bachelor of Advertising and Public Relations were known as *Licenciatura* from 1971 to 2010, before Bologna started. Now they are called *Grado*.

them to apply for doctoral programs, while the professional track prepares them at a more advanced level within the professional world.

Advertising Masters can be official or non-official. Official Masters are accredited by *Agencia Nacional de Evalución de la Calidad y Acreditación* (ANECA), a Spanish governmental agency that verifies education quality. Official Masters are granted by the government only within public universities. On the other hand non-official degrees are granted through the university without governmental oversight. At least sixty ECTS are usually needed to complete the official master degree in Spain, which is a one-year program. The non-official Master's degrees have more variance, as they are not under government control.

However, throughout the rest of Europe, 120 ECTS are needed, as European Master's programs are mainly two-year programs. This variation reflects the fact that an undergraduate degree is obtained in four years in Spain, but in only three years throughout Europe.

Non-official Masters are more industry-oriented. Rather than writing a research project, they complete a campaign-based project, including a formal presentation. Additionally, the courses for the non-official Master's degree are more commonly taught by industry professionals.

After earning a Bachelor and an official Master, students may apply to a doctoral program. While Spanish students need four years of undergraduate education and 240 ECTS, and one graduate year and 60 ECTS. Most European spend only three years with undergraduate programs earning 180 ECTS and thus spend two years completing Master's with 120 ECTS. At least fifteen methodological ECTS are taught, and a research project has to be written in an official research oriented master degree program. In both cases, 300 ECTS are needed to apply for a doctorate program.

Masters	Tracks (orientation)	Who teachs?	How do they guarantee quality?	What is its purpose?	University
Official	Research	Ph.D	ANECA certificated	Persue Ph. D.	Mainly public
	Professional	Ph.D & Industry pros		Go into industry	Private & Public
Non-official	Professional	Industry pros	University board under provost supervision	Go into industry	Private & Public

Source: Adapted from Tena & Roca (2009).

Table 20-2: Types of Masters in Spain

To sum up, advertising education at Spanish universities unfolds as follows: undergraduate level teaches general advertising knowledge, Master's teaches specific advertising skills when on a professional track (creative, planning, accounting, design, art direction, interactive media…) and advertising research when on the research track. The final academic step is, of course, the doctoral degree.

Doctoral Programs

An official Master's degree is needed to apply for a doctoral program in Spain. Doctoral programs last between two and four years. For example, an advertising and public relation doctoral program is offered at *Universitat Autònoma de Barcelona*, and broadcast and advertising doctoral programs are offered at *Universidad Complutense de Madrid*. Many doctorate programs in communication often have students who complete advertising related dissertations. Advertising related dissertations are also often found in economics and psychology programs. Advertising dissertations can be found online in two databases: TESEO (www.educacion .es/teseo) and TDX (www.tesisenxarxa.net).

Publication of Spanish advertising research is just beginning to take root. There are two main academic journals: *Questiones Publicitarias*[38] (Advertising Matters), established in 1993, and *Pensar la Publicidad,*[39] (Thinking About Advertising), which was founded in 2007. Some Spanish scholars also publish in Spanish communication journals, and a few sometimes publish in European communication and advertising journals.

Questiones Publicitarias (Advertising Matters) is a peer-reviewed journal. Its main goal is to promote academic advertising research in advertising. The journal was print based from 1993-2007. Starting in 2007 it moved online. The journal is published annually through the *Universidad de Sevilla*.

Pensar la Publicidad (Thinking About Advertising) is also a peer-reviewed journal. Its main goal is to promote empirical and theoretical research on Spanish language advertising from across the globe. The journal was born in 2007 and can be found both in print and online. It is published twice every year through the *Universidad de Valladolid* and *Universidad Complutense de Madrid*.

---

[38] Volumes can be checked free on line at http://www.maecei.es/questiones.html
[39] Volumes can be checked free on line at
http://revistas.ucm.es/portal/modulos.php?name=Revistas2_Editorial&id=PEPU

Non-university education system around advertising

Alternatives to public or private universities falls into four different categories: undergraduate or master, pre-university, continuing education and industry's interaction with universities

Undergraduate or Master's Level

Another way to study advertising after High School or after obtaining a university degree is going to business or commercial art schools (*escuelas de diseño*). Some of them are related to universities, which allow the outside schools to use the university logo and they also supervise the programs. However, the courses are taught by professionals and the university faculty generally does not teach in these programs. These degrees are generally not accredited by the Quality Spanish Government Agency *Agencia Nacional de Evaluación de la Calidad y Acreditación* (ANECA).

Other business and design schools do not have any relationship with universities. Portfolio schools are a common example of this type of program. Portfolio schools often have their alumni teaching within their programs. Yet other traditional commercial art schools (*escuelas de diseño*)are linked to universities.

Pre-University Level

Another approach to studying advertising as an alternative to the university is called *Formación Profesional* (professional education).[40] Professional education is divided into two cycles: First, *Ciclo Formativo en Grado Medio*[41] (Half Level Professional Education, CFGM) and, second, *Ciclo Formativo de Grado Superior*[42] (Full Level Professional Education, CFGS). These cycles provide skills based education.

The CFGM degrees are for students that have finished what might be called a pre-high school, *Obligatory Secondary School, Educación Secundaria Obligatoria* (ESO). After completion of the CFGM degree students may obtain a CFGS, which completes their skills training.

---

[40] Professional Education. A student has to study what follows to reach university: *Educación primaria* (Elementary school, 6 to 12 years), *ESO* (Obligatory Secondary School, 12 to 16) and *Bachillerato* (≈ High School Diploma, 16 to 18). As alternative to attending University, student may apply to Professional Education (CFGM & CFGS).

[41] **CFGM**: *Formative Cycle Medium Degree-Half Level Professional Education.* At least ESO (*Educación Secundaria Obligatoria*, Compulsory Secondary Education, 16 years old) is required to apply for GFMG. Specific test may be required depending on the school.

[42] **CFGS**: *Full Level Professional Education.* At least CFGM or *Bachillerato* (Upper Secondary Education ≈ *High School*) is required.

There are 26 different professional areas in Spain. Some are related to advertising: graphic arts and printing, commerce and marketing, image and sound, and artistic education.[43] Contents may slightly vary depending on the area, but the orientation is always skills based. The Diploma students get is *Técnico Superior* (Superior Technician). There were 37.335 students in professional education related in somehow to advertising[44]. Students can apply for a university program after finishing a CFGS.

Continuing Education

There are also continuing education programs , which are organized by an institution called *Fundación Tripartita*[45] (Tripartita Foundation). As the focus is for workers the organization's board has people from public administration, business organizations[46] and unions. Continuing professional education programs are funded by Social Security fees, European Social Fund[47] and Spanish Government through *Servicio Público de Empleo Estatal,* (Public National Program for Employement, INEM).

Industry's interaction with universities

Finally, beyond the options discussed above, some associations organize seminars (ex. Academia, *Club de Creativos*), small conferences (ex. *Chill Out Laus, Dijous de la Comunicació…*), big conferences (ex. Rethink) and visits to the university to share professional knowledge.

As is common and most countries, advertising creativity is promoted and maintained through competitive awards. For students the main awards are *Drac Novell International Awards,* which is Barcelona based, and *Students Laus,* which is based in Barcelona. For professionals there are three main awards competitions are: *Versus Awards* and *Day C* from *Club de Creativos* (Creatives Club), which are Madrid based. Clients promote different contests, one of the most well-known is *Notodopublifest.*

---

[43] http://www.educacion.es/educacion/que-estudiar/formacion-profesional/que-puedo-estudiar/grado-superior.html
[44] 2007-08 year data: graphic arts and printing (4.040 students) , commerce and marketing (21.574 students), image and sound (11.721 students).
[45] More information can be found at www.fundaciontripartita.org
[46] Associations are: AEACP (Spanish Communication Advertising Agencies Association, based in Madrid); AEP (*Associació Empresarial de Publicitat,* based in Barcelona).
[47] More information can be found at
http://ec.europa.eu/employment_social/esf/index_en.htm

Type of education	Center	Level	Orientation	Years
Official	Public or Private University	Bachelor Master Ph. D.	Professional Research/professional Research/professional	4 1 or 2 2 to 4
Non-official	Public or University	Master	Professional	1 or 2
Non-official	Business and design schools Portfolio schools	Bachelor Master Other	Professional Professional Professional	4 1 or 2 Varies
Official pre-university education	Public or private centers	CFGS CFCM	Professional Professional	2 2
Continuing Education Credits	Associations	Seminars	Professional	Days or weeks

Source: Adapted from Tena & Roca (2009).

Table 20-3: Forms of Advertising Education in Spain

Concluding Data and Final Thoughts

As we look across Spain, there are 33 universities teaching official advertising and public relations programs, with an enrollment of 16.377 students in a Bachelor level (2007-08). Of that, 68.37 percent belong to public universities and 31.63 percent to private universities. The top advertising and public relations programs usually have students come from the best humanities track high schools.[48] Public universities select the students from the public system entrance test called "selectividad," which is quite rigorous. On the other hand, private universities can use this test or an alternative.

One year at public university costs around 700 euros. The cost at private university starts at 5.000 euros and can reach to 8.000 euros. Five to eight classes are taught each semester, regardless of public or private. Both students get the same degree: *Grado en Publicidad y Relaciones Públicas* (Bachelor of Advertising and Public Relations).[49]

El Mundo, one of the leading Spanish newspapers based on Madrid, publishes an annual ranking of advertising and public relations programs. Over a nine year period, 2001-2009, the following universities are ranked at the top: first, Universitat Autònoma de Barcelona; second, Universidad de

---

[48] High schools teach three different tracks: Arts, Humanities & social sciences, and Sciences & technology.

[49] The Degree was called *Licenciatura en Publicidad y Relaciones Públicas* from 1992 to 2010 (date when all universities should have implemented Bologna system). Before 1992, Degree was called *Licenciatura en Ciencias de la Informacion, branch: Publicidad y Relaciones Públicas.*

Navarra (Pamplona); third, Universidad Complutense de Madrid; fourth, Universitat Ramon Llull (Barcelona); and fifth, Universidad del País Vasco (Bilbao), Universidad de Sevilla and Universidad Antonio Nebrija (Madrid).

Public (18)	School	Private (15)	School
Alicante	Economics & Business	Abat Oliba[cat] · CEU (Barcelona)	Social Sciences
Autònoma de Barcelona	Communication	Antonio Nebrija (Madrid)	Social & Communication
Barcelona	Escola Superior de Relacions Públiques (associated center) Superior School of Public Relations	Camilo Jose Cela · SEK (Madrid)	Communication
Cádiz	Social & Communication	Cardenal Herrera[cat] — CEU (Elche y Valencia)	Social and Law
Complutense Madrid	Information Sciences	Católica San Antonio[cat] (Murcia)	Social & Communication
Girona	Tourism	Europea Miquel de Cervantes (Valladolid)	Humanities & Information
Jaume I (Castello)	Humanities & Social	Europea de Madrid	Communication & Arts
Málaga	Communication	Francisco de Victoria[cat] (Madrid)	Communication
Miguel Hernández (Elche)	ESIC Valencia (asociated center)	Internacional de Catalunya (Barcelona)	Communication
Murcia	Communication & Documentacion	Pontificia de Salamanca[cat]	Communication
País Vasco (Bilbao)	Social and Communication	Navarra[cat] (Pamplona)	Communication
Pompeu Fabra (Barcelona)	Communication	Ramon Llull[cat] (Barcelona)	Communication
Rey Juan Carlos I Madrid	Fuenlabrada, Vilcalvaro and online ESIC Madrid (asociated center)	San Jorge[cat] (Zaragoza)	Communication
Roviri i Virgilia (Tarragona)	Humanities	San Pablo[cat] — CEU (Madrid)	Communication & Humanities
Sevilla	Comunicacion	Vic[cat] (Barcelona)	Business & Communication
Valladolid	Social, Law & Communication		
UOC (Barcelona) Catalan Open University	Communication (online based)		
Vigo	Social & Communication		

[cat] *Indicates Catholic University*
Source: Adapted from Tena & Roca (2009).

Table 20-4: Universities Teaching Advertising degrees 2010 (33)

Final Thoughts

Spanish advertising education has a rich and diverse history. It origins are tied to Pere Prat Gaballí, but its history is rooted in legislative processes often highly influenced by political and economic turmoil. Considering this, it is not surprising to see that much of advertising education is defined by its official or non-official status. In that sense, Spanish advertising education might be considering a reflection of an overall governmental welfare structure. Amidst this structure a diverse, dynamic, and at times bewildering, array of advertising programming models flourish.

As a market economy began to take hold and the economy grew, advertising in Madrid, the industrial center, flourished. So too did advertising education. Today Madrid now controls about 60 percent of the advertising market, while Barcelona controls about 20 percent. Yet, the area in and around Barcelona has ten advertising programs while Madrid has seven, with others spread across other regions of the country. It can be argued that while Madrid is the economic heart of Spain, Barcelona remains the creative soul of Spain, just as it did in the time of Gaballí.

References

Batxillerat i curriculum at April 28
    http://phobos.xtec.cat/edubib/intranet/index.php?module=Pages&func=display&pagei
    d=22. Accessed April 28, 2010.
Business in Barcelona. April 25, at
    http://www.cambrabcn.org/web/cambra/business_bcn/institutional_information. Accessed April 25, 2010.
Datos y cifras. Curso escolar 2009/10. Gobierno de España. Ministerio de Educación. May7,
    at http://www.mepsyd.es/horizontales/prensa/documentos.html. Accessed May 7, 2010.
Dónde estudiar las más demandadas 50 carreras, at April 25
    http://www.elmundo.es/especiales/2008/05/cultura/50carreras/43.html. Accessed April
    25, 2010.
Eguizábal, Raúl. April 10, at http://www.academiadelapublicidad.org/index.php/nombres-
    para-recordar/132-pedro-prat-gaballi-. Accessed April 10, 2010.
El Premi Prat Gaballí de foment de la recerca en publicitat i relacions públiques at April 25
    http://www.colpublirp.com/_premi-prat gaballi/premi.php?idioma=CAS. Accessed
    April 25, 2010.
Gaballí, Pedro (1917, republished in 1992). *La Publicidad Científica* {Scientific Advertising}.
    Barcelona: Cámara de Comercio y Navegación de Barcelona.
Hopkins, C. (1980). *Publicidad científica* {Scientific Advertising}. Madrid: Eresma
Spain and the Marshall Plan at Arpil 25.
    http://www.megaessays.com/viewpaper/201370.html. Accessed April 25, 2010.
Stability and Economic Development, 1959-1974 at Arpil 25.
    http://sispain.org/english/economy/stabilit.html. Accessed April 25, 2010.
Tena, Daniel and Roca, David (2009) *Publicitat i Relacions Públiques cap a l'Espai Europeu*

d'Educació Superior {Advertising an Public Relations: towards European Higher Education Area }. Barcelona: Anguiroda.

Welcome to the website of the European Higher Education Area at April 28. http://www.ond.vlaanderen.be/hogeronderwijs/bologna/. Accessed April 28, 2010.

Online sources
    http://dialnet.unirioja.es
    http://ec.europa.eu/employment_social/esf/index_en.htm
    http://ec3.ugr.es/in-recs
    http://revistas.ucm.es/portal/modulos.php?name=Revistas2_Editorial&id=PEPU
    http://www.cindoc.csic.es
    http://www.educacion.es
    http://www.fundaciontripartita.org
    http://www.ine.es
    http://www.latindex.unam.mx
    http://www.maecei.es/questiones.html

Advertising Education in the Nordic Countries: Sweden-Denmark-Finland-Norway

Mary Alice Shaver
Jönköping International School of Business, Sweden

Advertising as a subject at the university level is not common in the Nordic countries. A total of 52 universities were contacted and 18 university programs were identified and studied for inclusion on advertising education. Still, only a very few had what could be considered as an advertising major as commonly understood in the U.S.

Looking at Communication and Business programs, it is clear that, while some courses may contain a module or project relating to advertising, formal courses – if found at all – are likely to be spare in offerings. Even at the prestigious School of Business, Economics and Law at the University of Gothenburg (Sweden), advertising is just one topic in two different courses. One is in English and is a critical discourse analysis class; the other, which carries 15 credits, is titled Media, Journalism and Global Studies. Again, advertising is just one of several topics covered.

This would be typical throughout Scandinavia. Several of the universities offer the courses both through the Business and the Communication areas. (A rough comparison to the new EU credit system is 7.5 credits for a three hour credit in countries not using the EU system. This may seem like a lot, but the requirements also call for a higher credit limit.)

Sweden

Of the universities reviewed in Sweden, looking at both Schools of Business and Schools of Communication, seven had separate courses in advertising. The offerings are quite different in each. Only three of them offered more than one course, however, and only one of these programs was titled "advertising and public relations." One offers a course that is designed for exchange students, one has a diploma program, and the other has a separate Department of Advertising and Public Relations, offering three levels of Advertising and PR studies, as well as a marketing program designed for working professionals.

Linnaeus University

A course entitled "Advertising Campaign Planning" is offered as part of the program for exchange students. The course is built around a project and students work in groups to produce an integrated campaign for an assigned client. The course is full-time for a four-week period, in the short term that takes place after the regular semester. Students entering the class must have some background, but the primary prerequisite is that they are exchange students. Students must also have proficiency in the English language (level B) and have had the equivalent of 30 ECTC hours in business studies.

Stockholm University

This university has a separate Department of Advertising and Public Relations. As noted above, three courses are offered at progressive levels. The first is basic and covers the historic development of the field as well as current trends and target audience analysis. The second course is focused on planned communication and has both a theoretical and practical point of view. Course material includes art direction and copywriting and brings in elements of consumer behavior, agenda setting and media planning. The third course offers a focus on brands and commercial, legal, ethical, cultural aspects. At the completion of the three-course sequence, students are prepared to write a thesis. There is no internship or practical work in the field required.

There is a separate marketing program that is training for management. The course is for full time students over a year's time.

Lunds University

A two-course sequence titled "The Rhetoric of Advertising in the Modern Media" I and II is offered. These courses are affiliated with the Communication area. Open to students with some background in business or communication skills.

Luleas University

This is the only program that requires an internship. A course in creative advertising is scheduled only every two years. A basic marketing course is suggested for preparation, but it is not required. .

Berghs School of Communication

This is the closest thing to what students majoring in advertising in the U.S. would study. Berghs is a private school that enrolls 5000 students each year. This number includes the professional students. Overall, there are 200 students who study full-time during any given year. Berghs also offers short-term studies such as online, executive training courses.

There are four main areas of study at Berghs: advertising, public relations, media, and design. There are opportunities for students to work across the individual area of studies. At the beginning of each term, students from all disciplines, all working toward solving an advertising problem for a client. This one-week seminar is repeated after two more months of regular classwork. Berghs students work for many different types of businesses.

Beyond the undergraduate or Bachelor Program, Berghs offers Professional Diploma Programs which include work in advertising, marketing communication, strategy, and interactive. The emphasis is on real world problems, businesses and solutions.

Berghs is well known in the profession. The School itself claims that 70 percent of those working in the advertising field did some study at Berghs.

Bechmans College of Design

This program began teaching advertising in 1939. It is a three-year program that offers practical and theoretical instruction. In order to be admitted, prospective students must present a collection of their work. Bechmans is the closest to what would be termed a portfolio school in the U.S.

Vrkeshögskolan Göteburg

This program has courses titled Advertising and Project Management and Advertising and form/text which concentrates on message and presentation. Students just have basic qualifications for university studies, with special competence in both English (B-level) and Swedish (B´level).

Denmark

Aarhus School of Business

Both undergraduate (Bachelor's) study and graduate study are offered. Although none of the undergraduate courses have the title of "advertising," the course descriptions show that the program is about corporate communication and marketing communication.

The graduate program is more focused on advertising in some of its course offerings. International marketing, marketing communication, customer relations relationships, international business communication are all areas of study. In the Master's and MBA courses, such as "Advertising: industry organizations," "Internet Marketing and Advertising," and "Advertising/Promotion" appear in listed courses for Aarhus. Courses are taught in both English and Danish.

Danish School of Journalism

This school stresses Branding and Broadcast, Print and Ambient. Students must have completed at least one year in a B.A. advertising program and must know the principles of advertising and graphic communication. A portfolio must be presented as part of the application process.

Finland

Turku School of Economics

There is no real sign that advertising is taught. It is mentioned, along with other topics such as marketing communication, corporate images, brands, and customer orientation.

Helsinki School of Economics

At the master's degree level there is an introduction to marketing and a consumer behavior course. This school, as the one at Turku, offers marketing courses, but no actual advertising emphasis at all.

There are no schools of communication in Finland that offer any type of advertising course.

Norway

Trondheim Business School
(a part of Sør-Trøndelag University College)

There is an emphasis on consumer research, segmentation attitude formation and change, and some related areas, but no courses that specifically deal with advertising. One course in marketing includes central concepts of marketing, segmentation and communication. Aside from these areas, the course presents basic marketing subjects.

Norwegian School of Economics and Business Administration

Housed in a department of strategy and management, there are several courses that focus on advertising. Examples would be: Advertising and Marketing Communication, Brand Management, Consumer Behavior.

Merkantilt Institute

This program concentrates on advertising and brand communication. It requires a satisfactory school record, a letter of motivation, a score of 500 points minimum on a Norwegian test similar to an ACT or GRE. This appears to be a practical course for those who want to pursue advertising as a career choice.

Assessment of Nordic Programs

Taken as a whole, universities in the Nordic countries do not offer an emphasis on advertising. Those who want to go into the field would have a narrow choice for career preparation. However, few as they are, the courses do offer a beginning to the field. Actual work in the advertising business is likely to be a far more inclusive preparation. The field of advertising as an academic standard to not recognized in the Nordic universities. However, the importance of advertising and promotion is seen in the actual workplace.

The History of Education in Advertising in the United Kingdom

Patrick Mills
Institute of Practitioners in Advertising

Jonathan Taylor
London Metropolitan University

Introduction

At the time of writing the economy in the UK is not in the best of health, the imminent and promised recovery put on hold. The last few years have been very tough and agencies in the UK have found their budgets squeezed and revenues reduced. No doubt a familiar story around the world.

This has had an inevitable knock on effect on learning and development, mostly in reining back the budgets allocated to it. However, it is pleasing to note that the commitment to learning and development is at an all time high amongst UK advertising agencies.

The IPA (The Institute of Practitioners in Advertising) make participation in their Continuous Professional Development (CPD) program mandatory, over 80% of practitioners (15,054) in all IPA member agencies participate with the average number of hours learning per head per annum being 31 (the recommended minimum is 24.

And evidence from the 2011 CPD submissions from IPA member agencies shows that the increase in pressure on the bottom line and employee's time goes hand in hand with an increase in the innovation in training programs and the ingenious methods employed to make sure agencies keep ahead of the competition through the education of their staff. So the good news is that despite economic gloom, learning and development has never been healthier.

How Advertising Education Developed in the UK

Key Milestones:

Chartered Institute of Marketing (CIM) Founded	1911
Incorporated Practitioners in Advertising Founded	1917

First IM examinations	1928
Communications and Marketing Foundation Founded	1970
1st Marketing Postgraduate Degree (Lancaster)	1971
1st Marketing Undergraduate Degree (Strathclyde)	1972
50th University to offer Marketing degree	1992
CIM Royal Charter granted	1998
100th University to offer Marketing Degree	2003
IPA introduce first Qualification exam	2004

Chartered Institute of Marketing (CIM)

It started with E. S. Daniells, who was the first President of the Incorporated Sales Managers Association (ISMA),
met with 11 other senior managers including
Pierce Wyatt and decided that their profession
need professional representation. The meeting
took place at the Inns of Court Hotel in London, on 16th May, 1911, when these experienced
and senior managers shared a common goal to
improve sales techniques and bring greater professionalism to their chosen careers. ISMA, the
precursor of CIM, was formed.

E. S. Daniells

Over time ISMA grew both in terms of
members and the services offered. It first began
to offer examinations in the late 1920's, at about
the same time it changed its name to the Insti-
tute of Marketing and Sales Management (IMSM). With the company
growing, more employees were needed to emphasize the company's image.
Formal education was first provided in 1928, when Certificate examinations
were held. Examinations are now taken in 146 countries worldwide, and as
many as 118,000 professionals now hold the organization's qualification.

As of 1931, the Institute's magazine was renamed *Marketing* to reflect
its focus on one of the most important of the business social sciences. It's
scope was widened to produce "a well balanced journal, interesting and au-
thoritative, worthy in every way to represent the Association."

In 1934 a new 3-year education syllabus was introduced, to reflect
the new practices being undertaken within the industry. It had two levels of
exam: intermediate and final.

To help the war effort, in 1940 the ISMA introduced the first ever
correspondence courses for serving soldiers and by the end of the war, over
6,000 men and women had participated across 82 prisoner of war camps.

In 1961, the Institute's exams were revised and renamed the "Diploma in Marketing," and successful candidates were allowed to use the letters DipM after their name. Then in 1965, the College of Marketing was founded, giving the organization a permanent residential base for its education programmes.

The year 1968 was notable, as the name changed again, to the Institute of Marketing, which was granted Chartered status in 1989 and has been known ever since as the Chartered Institute of Marketing.

In 1992, the European Union recognized the CIM Diploma as the gold standard for Marketing, as a qualification across all the member nations. And 1993 saw launch of the first Continuous Professional Development (CPD) programme, adding post-graduate qualifications in 1996.

The CIM continues to develop overseas links and associations with other Marketing bodies across the world. In 2008 it completely relaunched its qualifications programmes and website, and included for the first time a range of digital modules.

The CAM Foundation

The Communications Advertising and Marketing Education Foundation (CAM) is a not-for-profit organization. It began around 1970, with a mission to help advance the training of professionals in marketing communications. CAM joined forces with CIM in 2000, such that all qualifications awarded by CAM now are funneled through and presented by CIM. Courses involve both CIM and CAM classes.

CAM classes currently include: Mobile, Digital Marketing, Metrics & Analytics, and Media & Branding. The aim is for professionals to be able to attain a Diploma in Marketing Communications, or one of the other diplomas or certificates offered by CIM, even up to a graduate education.

Degree Courses at Universities

The first universities in the UK to establish any form of Marketing study at a degree level that included some modules on Advertising were the University of Strathclyde and University of Lancaster.

Lancaster was the first into the UK market when it introduced a Post graduate degree in 1971 under the leadership of Professor Michael Thomas, who had established the Marketing department and led it for its first 10 years. In Glasgow, Michael J. Baker was the first Professor of the Strathclyde Marketing Department, and that school was the first to introduce an Undergraduate degree programme within its Business School. Professor Baker built up a very strong department and by 1979, he led a team of over 50 academics.

These two universities led the way in terms of Marketing degree education for a number of years, before other universities such as Warwick, Bath, City (London), Durham, and Manchester introduced a Marketing option to their business degree programmes. The number of Marketing degree options continued to grow rapidly throughout the 1990's and 2000's, and as of 2009 there were 114 universities offering some form of Marketing degree at Undergraduate level.

Specific degree titles called "Advertising" were developed much later, with Bournemouth University being the first to develop a degree with this title in 1998, and even in 2012 there were only 9 degrees offered specifically called Advertising at the Undergraduate level across the UK. If you include all options that include the term Advertising, such as London Metropolitan's Advertising and Marketing Communications degree, the total offered rises to 28. The most recent development has been the development of Digital Advertising modules within these degrees, and the first Digital Advertising *degrees* were expected to be introduced to the UK in the next year.

The Background to Industry Training

The last few years has seen a proliferation of media opportunities on an unprecedented scale. This has made for a complex and difficult to navigate professional landscape for advertising practitioners. However, the industry is used to change and the last 50 years has seen remarkable innovations in the ways in which brands can communicate with their audiences. This has had a tremendous impact on the way in which agencies go about learning and development (L&D), and the importance of effective L&D is more critical than ever before.

50 years ago agencies had larger numbers of staff on their books and much of the training was given by senior practitioners, imparting their wisdom to the junior members of the agency (we are seeing a significant return to this method at the moment, though formalized through mentoring and coaching). In the 1970's the industry sought to provide more formal standards and the theory based Certificate in Advertising and Marketing (CAM) was developed with help from the IPA and ISBA. This remained as the industry standard until the late 70's when experiential training, pioneered by the IPA.

It is interesting to note at this point that much of the early years in the world of training in the advertising industry is dominated by initiatives from the IPA and D&AD. It is hardly surprising when one considers that

IPA member agencies are responsible for over 85% of all advertising spend in the UK.

Charles Channon, a planner and the father of the IPA Effectiveness Awards, was appointed as the first IPA Director of Studies. He was responsible for launching the course that has now become a rite of passage for young account handlers and planners: IPA Stage 2, Campaign Planning.

In its heyday around 120 people attended this course annually. The aim of the course was (and is) to take a young account handler or planner and put them into a pitch situation, help them gain confidence in their own ideas and thinking and work as an effective team with people they may have never met together. Delegates leave the course with a real sense of achievement and empowerment and it remains one of the pillars of IPA training today.

Charles Channon (left) was the architect of the famous IPA 7 stages program, which could effectively take an individual from graduate trainee to the board (even Managing Director) in seven years. Most have taken the program at a marginally more leisurely pace (though the speed in which high achievers can rise through the ranks in advertising can be dramatic).

We are very lucky in the UK (possibly unique), in that agency people are prepared to collaborate in developing and delivering programs for the industry as a whole, not just their own companies. This remains a USP of IPA courses and qualifications.

The opportunity to meet people from other agencies, with different perspectives is one of the most valuable aspects of IPA training, which cannot be replicated by in-house training, no matter how good it is. The continuing commitment to these methods despite the squeeze on time and budgets will continue to help the IPA stand out.

D&AD, founded in 1962, also has contributed enormously to the heritage and culture of learning and development in the advertising industry. Its Workout Program is now the benchmark training program for creatives (shorthand for creative people in advertising agencies).

In more recent times other trade associations and third parties have supplemented the IPA and D&AD offerings, filling in the specialist gaps like direct marketing, digital, sales promotion, PR and marketing. We will discuss these organizations in greater detail later on in the chapter.

Most agencies, despite being small to medium enterprises (SMEs with less than 250 employees), employ a specialist training manager who works alongside human resources. And the industry has now widely adopted Continuous Professional Development – training is of huge concern at board level (the IPA Chief Executive Survey reports annually that IPA training is the most important offer from the Institute), and the competitive advantage of training in new business pitches, as well as the benefits to talent attraction and retention is well documented.

The Characteristics of Agency Practitioners

People in advertising come from a wide variety of education backgrounds, and it is usual for new graduate entrants to have no previous training or directly relevant degree in the discipline of advertising. This is changing with the proliferation of marketing and communications degrees being offered, however agencies still err on the side of those without the direct relevant experience.

The industry thrives on strong teamwork, both to manage projects requiring a broad range of skills but also to come up with lateral problem-solving ideas. Teams that can approach problems from different perspectives tend to be more productive. The IPA has developed a test to help agency recruiters understand the lateral and logical thinking traits of their prospective employees, Diagonal Thinking (www.diagonalthinking.co.uk).

As I mentioned above, agencies tend to employ from a graduate pool without specific experience, using personality traits as a guide to their future success. The agencies believe that the knowledge can be provided through training programs and professional development.

Agency practitioners tend to have the following characterisitics:

- Good communicators
- Excellent problem solvers
- Team builders
- Good time management skills

In addition, they tend to have passion, curiosity, tenacity and integrity. They need to understand that creativity and commerce can go hand in hand and work effectively together.

Why? Here are a few examples that explain why these characteristics are vitally important:

1. Good communicators are required as agency staff interact with all sorts of different people on any one day, being able to communicate effectively makes it much easier to get the job done.

2. Advertising strategies always start with identifying a client's business problem and then finding solutions to solve that problem. Traditional communications solutions may not always be the right answer so agency staff will need to be lateral thinkers to identify the most effective solutions and advise their clients as well.

3. Every project requires agency practitioners to work with a wide range of people from suppliers (photographers, studios, printers) to partners (web site developers, media agencies, data specialists etc), as well as their clients and internal agency staff, so the ability to build a good team is vital.

4. Most people in agencies work on more than one piece of client business at a time, which means that almost inevitably they'll be doing two things at once. The ability to manage ones time effectively and pay attention to the detail are critical to the success of a project.

5. Communication of strategies and ideas is key to the job, and a passion for the job and the ideas being sold will help dramatically.

6. While being a creative business, it isn't art for arts sake. The industry uses creativity as a powerful business tool to solve problems, make brands famous, sell more product and overall contribute to the financial success of the agency's clients.

7. The best advertising solutions often come out of agencies with strong client relationships, these are built on trust and respect. That's why so many people in the industry enjoy getting on with each other (and having fun doing it).

The Industry Approach Today

The advertising industry has changed dramatically in the last five years, there are more media channels and more agencies vying for the client budgets, all claiming their specialism is the one that will solve all the client's problems. How does an account handler or planner negotiate through this morass of media and help their clients come up with the right solutions?

Consider the types of agency in the UK at the moment (with some examples):

- Creative (JWT, Ogilvy, Leo Burnett, Beattie McGuiness Bungay, Mother, BBH, Weiden and Kennedy, Fallon)

- Media (Starcom MediaVest, Mediacom, Maxus, Mindshare, Zenith, MEC)

- Digital Creative (Dare, Glue)

- Digital Media (Unique Digital, Agenda 21)

- Marketing & Technology Agencies (LBi, Sapient Nitro, Syzygy)

- Search (iCrossing, Trade Doubler)

- Direct Marketing (RAPP, Partners Andrews Aldridge)

- CRM agencies/email marketing (CMW)

- Experiential (Lime, Arc)

- Integrated (most traditional creative agencies now recognise that they have to have an integrated approach)

- Brand consultants

- Broadcast agencies (TwoFour, Endemol)

- Web site developers

- Data suppliers and managers

- Database businesses

- Recruitment agencies

- Healthcare agencies (Wooley Pau, VCCP Health)

- Business to business agencies

- PR consultants (Brunswick,)

The list is extensive, consider for a moment the range of job types, in terms of level of seniority, specialism, discipline and agency type. This presents the industry with a significant issue for training and development, which will explain the massive proliferation of suppliers in recent years.

Add to this the effects of the recent recession which has depleted agency staffing numbers, meaning employees are time-starved. This has led to a sharp decline in demand for residential courses, but an increase in one and half day courses. Though as one senior FMCG Marketing Director stated, short courses are no longer half days, they are one hour or less. The net result of this is that many residential courses are split into shorter modules, which are no less effective in imparting knowledge to the delegates, but lack the networking that longer experiential residential courses offer.

Recent IPA research, however, suggested that agencies no longer have time to be out of the office for three or more days, and that their preferred mode of education was through shorter courses, online qualifications, online resource and evening events.

The following section deals with offerings of some of the key suppliers in today's industry. We start with IPA (Institute of Practitioners in Advertising), who are responsible for professional development of some 270 agencies representing approximately 85% of advertising spend in the UK.

The IPA is the UK trade body for advertising, media, and marketing communications agencies. The role of the IPA is to serve, promote and anticipate the collective interests of member agencies. In particular to define, develop and help maintain the highest standards of professional practice. The key goal is to raise standards of professionalism, improve client / agency working relationships and thus improve agency profitability.

The aim of the learning and development provided by the institute is therefore focused on this target. As such the IPA has determined that training should be build around the essence that binds all agencies together, best described in Figure 22-1.

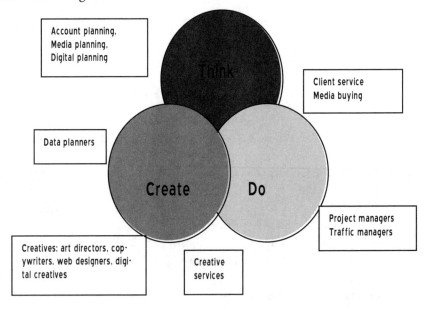

Figure 22-1: The Essence that Binds Agencies Together

The learning is divided into 3 levels targeting junior staff, middle tier and senior levels, and at each level the IPA aim to provide education in People and Management, Business and brands, commercial skills, and creative inspiration. These are delivered through IPA qualifications, residential courses, One day Accelerator courses, half day Energizer courses, web based video content, approved practitioner reading listings and IPA events.

Examples of courses would include Campaign Planning (a five day residential course targeting the Foundation level, spanning the leadership and business and brands columns), Understanding Client Business (run as a one day accelerator and a three day course at the IPA), and TV Production Knowledge (a ten week course of evening seminars, with a residential weekend and an exam at the end).

D&AD is an educational charity and its mission is to promote creative excellence through the global awards (which are the most coveted creative awards worldwide). It works to nurture, inspire, and give practical assistance to the next creative generation, feeding the industry with the best talent and it aims to build understanding of the contribution of creativity, ideas and innovation to business success.

In 2001 D&AD launched Workout (Figure 22-2), the first continuous professional development program specifically for creatives. For the full story, the best place to find out more is at http://workout.dandad.org/. In brief, the workout Program is made up of 27 workshops designed for people in and around the creative industries. They are unusual, uncommon, occasionally unnerving professional development sessions. The courses cover Craft Skills, Survival Skills, Super Powers, Mastercraft Sessions and The Wider Workout.

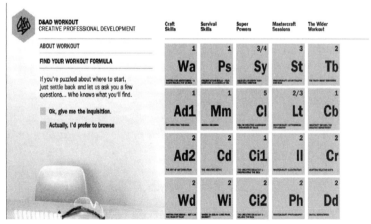

Figure 22-2: The D&AD Workout program

The Institute of Direct Marketing (IDM) is Europe's leading body for the professional development of direct, data, and digital marketing. It was founded in 1987. It is an educational trust and registered charity. The late Derek Holder, then Managing Director of the IDM states, "The IDM has a worldwide reputation for the quality of its training and qualifications programs. Our services – for individual marketers and corporations – are in demand worldwide as more and more businesses seek best practice accountable marketing."

The IDM has trained more than 45,000 marketers on open courses, and more than 10,000 through in-company programs across 28 countries. It has tutored more than 8,000 through professional qualifications.

As an organization it advocates lifelong learning, and as such the IDM maintains an up to date training and education portfolio designed to meet the needs of marketing practitioners throughout their careers – at every stage from college student to senior marketer.

Like the IPA the IDM's curriculum is delivered by leading practitioners, with the network drawn from today's marketing community. IDM marketing training covers direct, data, and digital (internet) marketing. It seeks to assure that the training is relevant, applied and consistent with modern marketing. The marketing training portfolio includes introductory and foundation training courses for those who are new to marketing, as well as more advanced and in-depth training courses for experienced marketers who seek to broaden their knowledge or extend their capability.

The MAA (Marketing Agencies Association) also offers a full program for agencies, under the guidance of Suzanne Barnes, the MAA offers the People First initiative which aims to engage, develop and inspire agency people of all disciplines. The MAA offers a full training program to support the initiative which includes MAA Excellence Training Courses for career development, one day clinics that focus on workplace issues, and bitesize/free training, which are practical two hours sessions.

The Account Planning Group (APG, website www.apg.org.uk) specializes in providing world class training to foster excellent strategic thinking across the advertising industry. It is a not for profit organization run by and for its membership whose aim is to promote the role of excellent strategic thinking and planning in generating profit, and aims to further improve the quality of talent attracted to the planning discipline. As well as training opportunities the APG has a comprehensive collection of strategic case studies through the biennial APG Creative Planning Awards.

Practitioners are offered courses, amongst others, in qualitative research and moderating, The Creative Brief – Writing and Briefing, Leading and Influencing Strategy, Integrated Communications Planning, Inspirational Brainstorming and Cross-media Evaluation.

IAB (Interactive Advertising Bureau) runs regular courses for beginners in the world of digital, through to those with experience. Courses include Digital Brand Building, Project Management, Metrics and Optimization and Digital Strategy.

NABS (the support organization for the communications industry) runs a course called Fast Forward, a practical course in developing "Integrated Communications." It brings together the hottest young talent from across the industry to learn from some of its most respected figures. Over the course of 8 weekly sessions, delegates will hear from leading exponents of the communications craft and, in mini-agency teams, be challenged to apply what they have learned to a live client brief culminating in an integrated 'pitch' to a panel of senior figures.

Jeremy Bullmore and Sir John Hegarty
contributors to NABS Fast Forward

Fast Forward is designed to fast track the skills of the industry's best young people beyond their existing discipline to the benefit of them, their agencies and the industry as a whole. Other organizations offering highly regarded training programs include the Chartered Institute of Marketing, the Chartered Institute of PR and The Institute of Promotional Marketing.

Industry Professional Qualifications

Industry qualifications were introduced after calls from senior executives to professionalize the industry. In an increasingly competitive sector, agencies needed to add weight to their commercial discussions with the evidence that their staff had superior training and qualifications to their competitors.

Members of the IPA repeatedly cite that the qualifications available through membership give them a competitive advantage in pitches, enable them to charge higher fees and therefore become more profitable. Clearly the clients value fully qualified teams working on their business. In addition, the provision of qualifications has enabled the advertising industry to compete actively with other, historically better paid professions like law and accountancy in terms of attracting and retaining the best talent.

Stephen Woodford, DDB London

In 2003, Stephen Woodford (CEO, DDB London) the then President of the IPA saw the need to introduce qualifications to advertising agencies, the process started with the Foundation Certificate which saw its first cohort take the exam in 2004. Since then the IPA have added The Advanced Certificate, The Excellence Diploma and LegRegs (a mandatory qualification for account directors in agencies that generate creative content, dealing with the legal and regulations surrounding the production of ideas).

According to Stephen Woodford, DDB London:

> The IPA qualifications meet a clear desire from our young talent to learn more quickly and gain broader expertise, demonstrated by the fact that over 22% of individuals in IPA member agencies have taken one or more of the exams, adding value to our agencies and their clients.

In May 2010 the IPA launched a specialist qualification for the fastest growing sector of its membership: Search. The Search Certificate targets those new to the industry and provides them with a solid grounding in Search Engine Optimisation and Pay Per Click Search. So far it is the only true independent qualification with collaboration from Google, Yahoo and Bing. It was written by Reform Digital and produced by e-learning specialist, Willow DNA.

In September 2010 the IPA launched a new qualification for junior planners called the Eff Test. Its aim is to provide them with a grounding in evaluation techniques and how to measure the effectiveness of the campaigns they produce for their clients. It is a product of the Value of Advertising Group and is being written by Les Binet (DDB London), Lucas

Brown (Total Media) and Lorna Hawtin (TBWA Manchester) with additional content and overall editing by Peter Field (independent marketing consultant).

And in Autumn 2012 the IPA launched a new qualification in understanding agencies and client finances, and developing commercial relationships, it is written by members of the IPA Finance Policy Group. In addition, the IPA has successfully exported the Foundation certificate to 30 countires across Europe in partnership with the EACA (European Association of Communication Agencies).

The delegate feedback from IPA qualifications is extremely positive, as shown below:

> "The IPA Foundation Certificate has proved extremely useful. Its content is thoroughly applicable to my everyday work and has given me a grater insight into the theory and processes of the wider media industry. Completing the exam has fostered my enthusiasm to build upon my existing knowledge through further qualifications", Clare Conway JWT.

> The IPA Advanced certificate was challenging, insightful and enjoyable. It allowed me to explore the industry in much greater depth and apply new learnings in an environment that has helped me to develop my knowledge in the media industry". Tommy Wong PHD Media.

The IDM is also committed to providing a wide range of qualifications for the direct and digital industries, having tutored over 8,000 people through its professional qualifications. The portfolio of marketing qualifications is recognized worldwide. Each qualification gives a comprehensive grounding in the important concepts, techniques and practices. Every syllabus is underpinned with the principles that will make your marketing measurable, accountable and more effective. Certificates are offered in Email marketing, digital marketing, Business to Business marketing and Direct & Digital Marketing. Diplomas are offered in Digital Marketing and Direct & Digital marketing.

The Chartered Institute of Marketing offer marketing professionals professional qualifications accepted by 95 per cent of UK employers as they are the only ones mapped to the new Government Occupational Standards in Marketing. Some examples include the Introductory Certificate in Marketing Professional Certificate in Marketing Professional Diploma in Marketing Chartered Postgraduate Diploma in Marketing Diploma in Digital Marketing Diploma in Managing Digital Media CAM Diploma in Marketing Communications .

Continuous Professional Development

The Institute of Practitioners in Advertising (IPA)

In 2000, at the request of its members, the IPA introduced a people accreditation standard, based on the key elements of the Government's service industry's Investor in People (IiP) standard. The impetus lay in the recognized need to raise and maintain the minimum standard of people development amongst IPA member agencies in order to attract top graduate talent, retain staff and to provide clients with the most effective service.

Since 2008 it has been a mandatory requirement for all IPA member agencies and every year they must provide evidence in a CPD submission  that they have a training plan based on their key business objectives, thus linking training to bottom line performance.

In addition all new members of staff must go through a comprehensive induction program, all staff must have at least one appraisal each year that reviews training needs, every member of staff must evidence learning through a CPD Diary, in which they have to record a minimum of 24 hours training per annum. Agencies that produce creative content have to ensure that anyone who is seeking promotion to Account Director should have passed LegRegs.

Leslie Butterfield
Principle architect
of IPA CPD

Since 2008 the IPA has awarded Gold Standards of accreditation for excellence in CPD, this reflects innovation in developing staff and successful outcomes. In the first year 11 agencies achieved the standard and in 2011 29 agencies achieved the standard.

There is significant support for the Continuous Professional Development program. Debbie Morrison, Director of Membership Services, ISBA, states:

> Many service sectors have Continuous Professional Development and it is fantastic that the IPA have pioneered CPD within their agency membership. Clients want the best talent working on their business and to be sure that the people they employ look after and build their brands are continuously refreshing their skills. The world of communications is moving so fast that everyone working in the sector needs to constantly ensure that they are up to speed with the latest tools, techniques and thinking, the IPA's CPD programme should deliver this knowledge to all who participate.

Peter Buchanan, Deputy Chief Executive, Central Office of Information, adds:

> Anything that improves the professionalism of agencies is good for their clients, both marketing and procurement, and I see the IPA CPD as an excellent programme of its type.

Figure 22-4: An example page from the IPA CPDzone

And Simon Perryn, Chief Executive, Chartered Institute of Purchasing and Supply, remarks:

> CIPS recognize the IPAs CPD programme as a big step forward in terms of the professionalism of agencies and their staff. Client companies invest significant sums on advertising and marketing communications, and with the impact that this has on brand assets and valuations, it is essential to know that the people responsible for spending this money are properly trained.

Of course, the IPA is not the only body that provides its members with Continuous Professional Development.

The Institute of Direct Marketing (IDM)

The IDM Continuing Professional Development (CPD) Award scheme is an important means of ongoing recognition and advancement for marketing practitioners. CPD provides the systematic means to maintain, improve and broaden knowledge, experience and skills.

Maintaining IDM CPD helps marketers acquire the personal qualities required throughout their professional life by supporting and recognising their ongoing professional advancement. It can increase the personal satisfaction they gain from their work and help improve the contribution they make to the success of their organisation.

Professional, work based activities, self directed and informal learning, personal activities outside direct work responsibilities, formal training and tuition are all good ways to accumulate new knowledge and skills in advancing a career, and it all counts towards CPD.

Chartered Institute of PR (CIPR)

The CIPR's Continuous Professional Development is a practical way for CIPR members to increase their skills and knowledge. Continuous Professional Development (CPD) helps them to identify and plan their skills and development needs. As a PR professional, commitment to CPD demonstrates to others that they are continually updating their skills and developing new expertise.

CPD points can be accumulated in many different ways, including formal training and events, reading, pro bono work, study and mentoring or advising others. All of these activities are eligible for CPD points and can be recorded in the scheme. All CIPR members can join the CPD scheme free of charge.

The Rapid Rise of Digital

This is perhaps the fastest growing area of training in the advertising industry at the moment, agencies have seen the need to acquire skills urgently as vital to the success of their businesses. Entire agency groups have invested in getting their staff up to speed on everything from online display advertising, to website builds, to search, to mail marketing and social media.

The IDM has a wide selection of courses and qualifications for specialists in this sector, but one of the interesting trends is that everyone wants some knowledge: it is an area with significant skills gaps and severe staff shortages, as the sector expands so quickly and clients become more interested in running campaigns using digital media.

The IPA offers a course on the basics of digital, with a follow up day on project management of digital campaigns, and half days on social media and search for beginners. Most training providers are now offering similar services.

There also are many independent bodies and individuals offering fabulous courses in understanding pretty much every area of the sector, examples include UTalk Marketing, Econsultancy and eMarketeers.

As well as courses, there are many qualifications including Google's introduction to search and, as noted above, the IPA Search Certificate. It is extremely likely that more courses and qualifications will develop in this area in the future, though it is interesting to note that many digital agencies are seeking the skills that traditional agencies have in terms of client service, planning, processes and creativity.

This was borne out in the IPA research study conducted in 2009, and was instrumental in defining the new IPA training strategy, "it is vital to engage all member agencies and promote best practice, there are plenty of specialist courses for digital agencies, but no one giving them the sort of skills that will get them sitting at the top table in terms of client business strategy. The IPA does this." Nigel Gwilliam, IPA Digital Consultant.

A recent addition to the IPA curriculum is a two day course featuring some of the most groundbreaking thinkers in the industry titled How technology is changing behavior (and what you can do about it), this is not a course to determine how to do digital, more about identifying the behavioral trends and changes that have occurred, and continue to occur in our digital society.

Support services for agency training managers

As the industry falls back on its own resources in times of recession, so the beleaguered training personnel need support in producing training program in house that maintain the quality set out by the IPA, IDM, D&AD, etc. Therefore, many of the providers of training programs also give best practice advice. For example, the IPA have recently published a best practice guide for CPD and training managers to enable them to create and run the best possible continuous professional development program, including advice on inductions, appraisals, training for internal trainers, getting CPD accreditation and on how to achieve the Gold Standard. The guide is available online though www.ipa.co.uk and was written by Gwyn March of March On Training, in conjunction with Jill Fear of the IPA, Sarah Baumann of Leo Burnett and Howard Nead of PHD Media.

In 2010 the IPA launched a short online module on measuring the effectiveness of training to enable agencies, to prove the impact of their CPD programmes on business performance, a key metric in attaining CPD Gold Standard.

Alongside this the IPA has developed a search engine of member recommended trainers, so that training managers can quickly and easily find trainers recommended by their peers across a wide variety of subjects. And, as is common amongst trade associations the IPA has a Training Forum, a self help group for training managers which meets once every six weeks, with an industry speaker and then key topics for debate. Recently the forum has produced guides on free or nearly free training in the UK, training senior management, best practice in using Myers Briggs, and advice in running digital training programs.

What is so exciting at the moment is the sheer volume of content available online, with valuable training modules and video content being widely available. The talks on TED.com are widely consumed, while information from the Internet Advertising Bureau, The Advertising Standards Authority, Clearcast, www.creativeskillset.org, to name but a few are invaluable in enriching in house training.

And What About the Next Generation?

We have learnt about the importance of maintaining education in our industry, but how do we ensure that there is a steady flow of talented, curious, tenacious, passionate problem solvers and team builders? The industry has been extremely lucky in having no shortage of applicants, but as the industry changes and the types of jobs in the industry evolves it is clear that the industry needs to safeguard its future.

Luckily the UK Government has invested in the Creative Sector as one of huge potential in the future, both in terms of economic growth for the UK but also as an employer. As such it has invested in providing young people with a pathway into creative businesses.

Creative and Cultural Skills, a sector skills council responsible for the music and design industries has produced a detailed site full of useful information about how to get into creative businesses. There is a significant section on the advertising industry, which provides some useful hints and advice. A quick visit to www.creative-choices.co.uk shows just how much resource there is for students interested in getting a foothold in the creative industries.

In addition Skillset, the sector skills council that is responsible for Advertising, Broadcast, Digital Industries including gaming, and Publishing has accredited 28 courses at UK universities in discrete areas deemed a priority by the sectors involved with the scheme. At the moment these include Screenwriting, Computer Games and Animation. Advertising and marketing communications courses are sure to be added once the best courses have been evaluated. These will all fall under the title of Skillset Media Academies. More information can be gleaned at www.skillset.org

Under the leadership of IPA President, Nicola Mendelsohn of Karmarama, and in partnership with Skillset and Creative Process the industry's first ever apprenticeship program was launched. The first apprentices will start in agencies on 1st September studying the Apprenticeship in Creative and Digital Media through Creative Process. In March 2012 the first advertising specific apprenticeship learning program for Level 4 (equivalent to first year at University) students will go live, the National Occupational Standards have been created by Creative skillset in conjunction with a panel of industry experts drawn from agencies of all disciplines and size.

As the pace of change in digital technology gets faster and faster Goodle, in partnership with Hyer Island and the IPA, pioneered a programme for graduates in their first year of employment. With aims to create a generation of digital experts in communications agencies, the first cohort finished the programme in May 2012, made up of individuals in leading media, creative and search agencies. They have described the programme as 'game changing.'

D&AD operates a universities and colleges program which develops relationships between them and the creative practitioners in the industry. It ensures that students, graduates ad teaching staff develop close ties with leaders in their fields and learn from the best in the business. The program has been running for over 20 years.

The program has been designed to complement all higher education courses involved in creative practice. It keeps course content ahead of the game and relevant to current and future student and industry needs.

John Gillard (centre), founder of the
School of Communication Arts

The annual D&AD New Blood Exhibition provides graduates with the opportunity to be seen by the worlds leading agency practitioners. This and a huge amount of additional resource for aspiring creatives is available through www.dandad.org/education.

The School of Communication Arts, founded by the late John Gillard who educated such creative greats as Graham Fink, John Hegarty and Tiger Savage has recently been re-launched as SCA2.0. A large part of the school's program is dedicated to increasing the diversity of potential entrants into the advertising industry. School of Communication Arts (SCA) accepts 50 students a year into an 18-month creative apprenticeship. 12-months of this is spent in SCA's studio, followed by 6 months of placements.

The IPA has a comprehensive advice section for aspiring advertising executives on its website www.ipa.co.uk, with information on applications for graduate schemes the types of jobs available and advice on how to go about applying. The IPA runs an annual Summer School for students aspiring to join the industry, which includes placement in agencies. During their placements, the students will be given a full introduction to agency life and the opportunity to work on real client business. They will also get to see other agencies and meet industry experts through a series of special evening seminars and social events.

Chris Whitson, Chairman, IPA Direct Marketing Futures Group and Planning Partner at Stephens Francis Whitson, remarks:

> The Summer School is now in its third year and we had a record number of entries and the standard was the highest yet. The successful candidates should be immensely proud of their achievements in securing their place. The school is reliant on three things; the agencies who take a student, the speakers who give up their evenings to run the evening classes and the IPA staff who make it all happen.

To apply for a place on the Summer School, the students had to complete the "Diagonal Thinking" self-assessment and answer the following two questions:

1. What is effective communication?

2. Is multi-tasking possible?

To help students understand whether or not they are right for the industry the IPA has developed a tool called Diagonal Thinking (www.diagonalthinking.co.uk): The free Diagonal Thinking Self-assessment is an online tool, designed to aid recruitment into the advertising and communication industries. It tests the hypothesis that the most successful individuals working in the business are both Linear and Lateral Thinkers – they think "diagonally."

People who work in the industry want to do work that is creative, but want it to have a practical impact too. Those who are successful all share the special skill called Diagonal Thinking. Oscillating effortlessly between logical or rational thinking, and creative or lateral thinking, they are able to analyze a company's business and then make creative leaps based on their findings.

Conclusion

As we struggle to break free from the shackles of recession it is pleasing to note how comprehensive the learning and development opportunities are in the advertising industry. The fast pace of change in technologies, media channels and communications opportunities mean we cannot stand still in the sphere of learning and development. However, the education providers in the UK advertising are well placed to keep up with (or even stay ahead of) the changes.

The industry in the UK is creating world class education that is comprehensive, professional and fleet of foot. And it has proved that innovation is often born out of adversity.

References

Account Planning Group
Chartered Institute of Marketing
Chartered Institute of PR
D&AD
Institute of Practitioners in Advertising
IPA Professional Development Research, November 2009
Institute of Direct Marketing
MCCA
The Practice of Advertising, edited by Adrian R. Mackay, chapter 22

Training for a career in advertising, Ann Murray Chatterton

Useful websites
    www.diagonalthinking.co.uk
    www.ipa.co.uk
    www.creative-choices.co.uk
    www.dandad.org
    www.skillset.org
    http://schoolcommunicationarts.com/
    www.theidm.com
    www.iabuk.net
    www.theipm.org.uk
    www.cipr.co.uk
    www.cim.co.uk
    www.apg.org.uk
    www.mcca.org.uk

Middle-East

Advertising Education In Lebanon

Joseph Ajami
Notre Dame University, Lebanon

Lebanon: An Overview

Lebanon is a small country in the Middle East. It has common borders with Syria on the North, Israel on the South, and it sits on the eastern shore of the Mediterranean. Lebanon has an area of 4,035 square miles (four-fifth the size of Connecticut, the second smallest state in the United States of America. No official census has been taken in the country since 1932, but its population is estimated at nearly four and a half million. Because of its diversified linguistic, religious, racial, and social groups, Lebanon is considered as a cosmopolitan and mosaic society. Arabic is the official language but almost every Lebanese is adept in at least one other language such as English, French, Armenian, and others.

Beirut, the capital, has been dubbed the commercial, cultural, and political hub of the Middle East. Lebanon gained its independence from France in 1943, and the Lebanese established a rather unique political system known as the Confessional system whereby various religious groups share power. In its hey day, and before the 1975 Civil War, Lebanon was known to many as "the Switzerland of the Middle East," and the capital, Beirut, was often referred to as the "Paris of the Middle East."

Currently Lebanon enjoys considerable stability in spite of a series of assassinations that claimed the lives of several political leaders, journalists, high-ranked army officers, and former war chieftains and militia leaders since 2005. Other internal skirmishes and the one-month Israeli war on Lebanon in 2006 also proved that complete stability is still a far-fetched dream of many Lebanese.

Higher Education in Lebanon

Due to its multi-cultural and multi-lingual nature, Lebanon has a multitude of colleges, universities, and institutions that provide a variety of educational programs in a variety of educational systems. Since the end of the Civil War in 1989 (it began in 1975), the country has witnessed a remarkable increase in the number of higher institutions. The Lebanese Directory of Higher Education (retrieved 30 January, 2007) lists forty-one nationally accredited universities, several of which are internationally recognized. Others operate without any governmental licensing or are pending governmental approval.

The top six universities are: The American University of rut (AUB), the University of Saint Joseph (USJ), the Lebanese University, the University of Balamand, the Lebanese American University (LAU) and Notre Dame University. The AUB, LAU, and NDU are the top schools that adopted the American system of education in Lebanon, and use English as the language of instruction. Several other universities of lesser quality also use English as the language of instruction.

Some universities in Lebanon offer doctoral programs in several areas, while many others offer only under-graduate degrees in many disciplines. The average time-span needed to graduate with a Bachelor's degree (known in Lebanon as "license") is between three and four years.

The United Nations assigned Lebanon an educational index of 0.871 in 2008. The index, determined by the adult literacy rate and the combined primary, secondary, and territiary gross enrollment ratio, ranked the country 88th out of the 177 countries participating. (Human Development Indicators Lebanon., Development Program, retrieved 11/17/2008)

Advertising in Lebanon

The history of advertising in Lebanon can be traced to 1935, when ads were printed in specialized publications. According to Darouny (2006, p. 35), some advertising agencies were operating in Lebanon in that year, but they did not continue long in the business and their contributions to the evolution of advertising is hardly traceable. One example is Levant company, a sister agency to the French publication Le Commerce du Levant (Ibid). Other examples are al Nil (The Nile) and Gabriel Brenas Agency. The latter lasted from 1935 till 1939. Fouad Pharaon, owner of Publicitie Pharaon, stands out as the pioneer of advertising in Lebanon. According to Darouni (Ibid), Pharaon's prominence is justified by his ability to create proper advertising agencies, and to introduce as early as 1935, practices and regulations that proved invaluable to the advertising business. He was one of the founders of the Lebanese Advertising Agencies' Association (LAAA). In the early 1960s, Pharaon's picture occupied the front cover of TIME magazine in recognition of his successful efforts in promoting Ford cars in Lebanon.

Among other pioneer advertising people were Chafic Hadaya, who used story-telling techniques in his ads. His famous campaign for Continental cash registers netted him and the advertising industry in Lebanon a growing reputation. Hadaya entered a partnership with Fawaz Sultan in 1944 to form SNIP (Societe d'Impression et de Puiblicite.).

It was not until the 1960s, the golden age of the Lebanese economy, that numerous advertising agencies sprung up, several of which have prospered and continue to operate successfully to this day. It was also during the 1960s and 70s that international advertising agencies set their feet on Lebanese soil by establishing their regional offices in Beirut, which enabled them to enter the rest of the Middle Eastern and Arab countries. They, in turn, were benefitting from a huge economic boom, thanks to a prosperous oil industry.

Advertising Education in Lebanon

As early as the 1950s. Lebanese universities began to introduce specialized programs geared to serve the advertising business. In an interview with Muhammad Chucair, the Head of the LAAA (first published in L'Orient Le Jour, on August 27, 1987, and later appeared in the October 1994 issue of Arab Ad) the advertising sector was able to attract an impressive interest of large number of people.

Universities Making Significant Contributions

In the late 1960, the Lebanese University (LU) the country's public University, established the "Faculty of Information and Documentation," and Advertising & Public Relations was one of three sequences offered by the new unit. The other sequences were "Archive & Documentation," and "Journalism."

The establishment of the "Advertising" major, albeit in tandem with "public relation," coincided with the growth stage of the "Advertising" business in the country, and the expansion of international advertising agencies into the Arab world through the Lebanese gate. Unfortunately, for many years the "Advertising" sequence proved to be less attractive to potential students than the "Journalism" Concentration. Teachers of the "Advertising" sequence were brought in from the growing advertising industry. Until this day, LU's Faculty of Information and Documentation has not been able to produce the solid and influential core or rather generation of advertisers as had been anticipated or hoped.

The beginning of the civil war in Lebanon in April of 1975 clearly slowed down both the advertising industry and the advertising education in the country. Education, in general, was one of the early victims of the country's civil strife. Classes in schools, colleges, and universities were interrupted for most of the 1976 academic year. The Lebanese University itself, home of more than 60,000 students, was split into two units or branches: one in the Christian section of Beirut and the other in the predominantly Muslim side.

The 1980s was the decade when numerous new colleges and Universities were given licenses to operate in the divided Country, a trend that continued well into the 1990s, and even into the first ten years of the twenty- first Century. More on these nascent universities will come later in this chapter.

The American University of Beirut, famously known as the AUB, and the oldest educational institution in Lebanon (established in the late 1850s), has not had an advertising major in its storied history. It does have what is described as an "Advertising and Marketing Communication Cluster" that includes four Marketing courses, two of which are required for the marketing concentration. This cluster of courses falls under the Management and Marketing, and Entrepreneurship Track: The AUB offers a couple of "Journalism" courses as a part of its "Social Science" program.

University of Saint Joseph (USJ) is another academic institution with a remarkable history. USJ was founded by the French when Lebanon was under what was called the "French Mandate" in the country, following the Sykes-Picot treaty which divided several Middle Eastern Countries among the French and the British Colonialists.

USJ offers a degree in "Advertising and Sales" (publicite et vente) that it is housed under the Faculty of Business, known as the "Institut de Gestion des Entreprises" (IGE). Students need nearly four years to finish the B.A., and a year for the so called "Maitrise" in the field. The courses cover a wide array of subjects that include: Communication, Art, Music, Graphic Design, Photography, Psychology, Business, Statistics, Sales, Creativity, General Culture, Law; E-Commerce, Human Resources, Marketing, Management, as well as Advertising.

The University of Balamand (UB) is another Top educational institution in Lebanon. It was founded by the Greek Orthodox religious Community in the country. The Department of Mass Communication is a part of the Faculty of Art & Social Sciences. The Department offers a degree in Mass Communication, and the list of courses required to finish the degree includes only one "Advertising" course called "Media and Advertising." A total of 92 credits is required to obtain the degree.

Notre Dame University (NDU) is currently ranked number six among Lebanese Colleges and Universities. The Department of Mass Communication is the second largest single Department at NDU (second only to the Department of Business Administration), and it offers three sequences. One of these is the Advertising and Marketing concentration, with an enrollment of 370 students according to NDU's official stabilities of 2010 (Admission Office, NDU, July 2010). The two other sequences are "Journalism," and "Radio and Television."

The Advertising and Marketing major is a rather unique combination of three Marketing courses and six Advertising courses, in addition to core courses from the Department of Mass Communication and a variety of General Education requirements courses. The Department offers a B.A. in Advertising.

Students must finish 102 credits towards their undergraduate degree and 39 credits towards their M.A. in Media Studies/ Advertising. The latter includes a 6- credit thesis. The M.A. program was officially licensed by the Lebanese government on November 30, 2001, and it began operation in Spring 2002. The official degree is called an M.A. in Media Studies with three concentrations: Advertising, Electronic Media, and Journalism. The university itself, which is owned and run by the Christian Maryamite Order, was established in the year 1987.

Until 2008, M.A. students in Advertising had the option to write a thesis or take two courses instead, in addition to having to take both a written and oral comprehensive exams. The M.A. program includes courses in Integrated Marketing Communication, Advertising & Marketing Management, Advanced Creativity, Advanced Media Planning, Advertising & Society, and other courses in Public Relations, Media Research Methods, and Theories of Mass Communication.

The Undergraduate degree in Advertising and Marketing requires students take the following Advertising & Marketing courses: Principles of Advertising, Media Planning & Analysis, Creativity & Copywriting, Global Advertising; Internship in Advertising, and senior Study in Advertising.

The three Marketing courses, offered by the Faculty of Business, are Fundamentals of Marketing, Consumer Behavior, and Promotional Strategy.

NDU graduates between sixty and seventy-five students every year with a degree in Advertising and Marketing, and it serves as the pipeline for several local and Arab Advertising agencies. NDU'S Advertising and Marketing students end up working in one of the following areas: Traffic Department, Research, Creative, Media Planning, Client Service, and other advertising-related areas. Like several other Universities in Lebanon, the majority of NDU'S Advertising & Marketing professors come from both the Advertising industry and from American and French higher educational institutions.

The American University of Science Technology (AUST) is barely twenty years old, but has made a name for itself in various areas and concentrations. AUST'S School of Business and Economics offers a B.S. in Marketing and Advertising. The degree is offered jointly with the Department of Communication Arts. The Marketing and Advertising program, modeled to a large extent, after the NDU'S program, is designed to prepare students for careers in both Advertising and Marketing domains.

According to its 2010 Catalogue, courses in the Marketing Department are oriented toward Creative problem-solving in marketing and advertising decision-making process. To graduate with a B.S. in Marketing and Advertising, a student must complete, in addition to the general, liberal arts, and business requirements, a minimum of 33 credits from a pool of Advertising and Marketing courses.

AUST'S School of Liberal Arts & Sciences also offers a B.A. in Advertising. This Communication Arts program offers degrees in Radio and Television, Journalism, Public Relations, and Advertising. Students must complete 106 Credit hours to earn a B.A. in those areas. Advertising students are prepared to become advertising copywriters, art directors, graphic artists, media planners, account executives, market researchers, and business managers (http://www.aust.edu.lb/).

American University of Technology (AUT) is another post-civil war higher institution. Like several Lebanese Universities, it also adopted the American system of education and it uses English as the language of instruction. Its Faculty of Business offers an Undergraduate programs in Marketing and Advertising, and graduate programs in both fields. The Marketing and Advertising program requires students to finish a total of 99 credits. All its "Advertising" courses are under the MKT (Marketing) reference titles. Sixty-seven credits constitute the "major" requirements.

AUT'S Masters of Science in Advertising requires students to take a total of 39 credits, including a 6-credit Research Project in Advertising. All the students must complete the Research Project. Their Core requirements include courses in Creativity, Marketing, Research, Advertising Strategy, Integrated Marketing Communication, Advanced Media Planning, & Marketing Management. The degree's "major" requirements are Advertising Design, Web Design & Programming, Multimedia Presentation, and Digital Studio Lab (http://www.aut.edu.academics.aspx).

The last of the significant colleges and Universities of Lebanon is Université Saint–Esprit De Kaslik (USEK), another Church-affiliated University. USEK, which has four branches in various parts of Lebanon, offers only Marketing courses in its B.A. in Business (Licence en Gestion) and its Masters in Business and Enterprises. The Marketing courses in both Undergraduate and graduate programs are offered in English and in French in this University that uses French as the dominant language of instruction. It is useful to mention that USEK does offer a Ph.D Program in Business, with Concentrations in Management and Finance.

Other Colleges and Institutions

As mentioned above, there is a total of nearly fifty higher education institutions in Lebanon. Some of these Colleges and Universities have small student populations, and some are no more second or third-tier institutions that cater to the needs of those who were rejected by major Universities, as well as the needs of local students in various branches or campuses throughout the Country. Some other vocational schools in the country also offer two-year programs or trainings in the field of Advertising.

Lessons and Recommendations

As we have seen above, at least 40 *accredited* Colleges and Universities operate in Lebanon. Advertising education is growing in this small Mediterranean Country, just like in many other countries in the world. This surge in advertising interest is no fluke since it coincides with the economic, cultural, political, and technological changes that are taking place in the world today.

Advertising education has indeed become a tangible manifestation of a truly globalized world. The new means of advertising are numerous and are accessible. The emergence of online advertising especially on social networks has made advertising more fascinating to advertising agencies, advertisers, consumers, and academicians.

The basic question that has baffled researchers, academicians, and observes for many years remain unanswered: Where does advertising education really belong? Is it in Schools and Department of Communication, Journalism, and other Social Sciences, or is it in Faculties and Department of Business and Marketing?

Lebanon proved to be no exception in this debate and the advertising discipline is still teetering between Business and Communication schools. In some instances the Advertising/ Marketing combination is housed in the two corresponding faculties such as the courses at Notre Dame University. Advertising, in some ways, is still seeking a "full" recognition as a true, independent major that can stand on its feet alone, so to speak.

Also noticeable is the fact that advertising education in Lebanon is closely linked to advertising education in advanced countries, such as the United States of America. The U.S. continues to serve as the most desirable and, hence, most imitated model for advertising education. The technological and cultural changes that are taking place in the "developed" world are being emulated in the developing world, known as "The Third World," which includes the country of Lebanon. Local regulations, influencers, needs, and value systems are taken into concentration, however.

Another related point has to do with the extensive use of English in teaching advertising Courses in Lebanon. The Public university of Lebanon (LU), as well as some colleges that have been historically linked to The French language and culture, are now using English in teaching advertising Courses. Some might venture to say that this is another example of what is known now as "Cultural imperialism."

Finally, it is no coincidence that the increase in the role of advertising in the economies of the Arab Countries – especially those in the Gulf region – is also felt in the academic programs that offer advertising majors, where we are witnessing a solid increase in the numbers of those seeking careers in advertising and related areas. Lebanon's advertising industry may have witnessed a remarkable slip in the amounts of money spent on advertising, especially, since 2005 (Assassination of Prime Minister Hariri & Other notables), and since the 2006 brief but destructive War between Israel and Hizbullah. But other Arab countries are in continuous demand for Lebanese talents and skills in various fields, particularly in the field of advertising.

It should be interesting to mention how advertising education develops in the next few years in Lebanon knowing that the volatile and unpredictable political and economic situations are very fragile. For the time being, however, advertising education in Lebanon is both healthy and progressing, coupled with the fact that the Telecommunication and Advertising Industries in the rich and expanding Gulf Countries continue to absorb hundreds of Lebanese workers, managers, and creative people in this beautiful domain that we call Advertising.

References:

Books:
Boutros, Adel (2009) Al Shamel in Kadaya el Nashr wal Iilam (In Arabic.) (Comprehensive In Publishing and Communication) Dar El Manahel, Beirut.
Darouny, kamal ((2006) Advertising and Marketing Communications in the Middle East., Notre dame University Press, Louazie.
Darouny, Kamal (1996) Advertising and Marketing Communications in Lebanon and the Middle East. Infomarket Advertising Agency, Beirut.

Newspapers and Magazines:
Arab Ad, October 1994.
L'Orient Le Jour, August 27, 1987.

Directories:
The Lebanese Directory of Higher Education, 30 January 2007.
The United Nation's Human development Indicators: Lebanon, 17 November, 2008.

Catalogues:
American University of Beirut, 2010
Notre Dame University, 2010
American University of science and Technology, 2010.
Al Balamand University, 2010.
University of saint Joseph, 2010.
American University of technology, 2010.
Lebanese American University, 2010.
Al Kaslik University (USEK) , 2010.

Personal Interviews:
Dr. George Kallas, Dean of Communication, The Lebanese University
Dr. Carol Kfoury, Dean, Faculty of Humanities, Notre Dame University
Dr. Ghadir Saade, the Lebanese University
Dr. Ali Kanso el Ghori, Professor of Communication, University of Texas, San Antonio

Advertising Education in Turkey

Yonca Aslanbay
Istanbul Bilgi University, Turkey

Ozlem Hesapci-Sanaktekin
Bogazici University, Turkey

A Brief History of the Advertising Industry in Turkey

The invention of the printing press in 1450 was one of the major forces that helped advertising rapidly prosper in Europe. But in the Ottoman Empire, from where Turkey inherited a past, texts had to wait for the 18th century to be printed, when Ibrahim Müteferrika set up the first printing house in 1726 (Gevgilili, 1983). Yet, it was hard to talk about advertising Ottoman products and services. It was not before the first Ottoman newspapers Takvim-i Vekayi, Ceride-i Havadis, and Tercüman-ı Ahval, founded in 1831, 1840, and 1860 respectively, contained classified ads and certain official announcements (Koloğlu, 1998; Çakır, 1997). The first professional Ottoman advertising agency, İlancılık Kollektif Şirketi, was established not before 1909 (Nebioğlu, 1983).

With the establishment of the Republic in 1923, Turkey witnessed a period of social and economic reforms through the adoption of a new constitution. Promoting a product or a service was not a simple activity during those periods. Neither television existed at the time, nor there was a national radio network before 1927 that had started its broadcasts (Sandıkçı and Ger, 2002).

İhap Hulusi Görey, who was a graphic artist, played a significant role in the advertising history of Turkey (http://ilef.ankara.edu.tr; Uluengin, 2003). Görey worked also on posters for private foreign brands, such as Kodak, Bayer, Pirelli and Ford (www.ihaphulusi.gen.tr). Such efforts by advertisers were vital in the progression of Turkish advertising industry (Nebioğlu, 1983). But in 1944, advertisers Eli Acıman, Vitali Hakko, and Mario Began established the second Turkish advertising agency: Faal Reklam Acentası (Çetinkaya, 1992).

In the 1960s, after a massive industrialization process, Turkey underwent a transformation in its economic, as well as in its cultural, environment (Sandıkçı and Ger, 2002). In 1964 Turkish Radio and Television Establishment (TRT) was instituted, and in 1968 the broadcast media started to reach masses (Kocabaş and Elden[50], 1997). Thereafter, with the increase of TV programs, consumption patterns, desires, expectations, and life-styles of the Turkish citizens were greatly affected (Oktay, 1993).

Certain regulations and developments took place within the communication industry in the 1960s. Basın İlan Kurumu (Agency for Print Advertising) was established in 1961, and a number of advertising agencies were established.

HOFFER, SAMANON ve HOULİ
İLÂNAT ACENTASI
İstanbul, Kahraman Zade Han, Ankara Caddesi

Radar, Ankara Reklam, İstanbul Reklam, Reklam Moran, and Grafika were among the agencies that started operating during the 1960s.

Turkey's process of globalization started at the beginning of the 1980s, along with the liberalization reforms that dominated the agenda almost everywhere around the globe. Turkey's economic structure has been reformed in parallel with the integration process into the global market economy (Esen, 2000). Right after, a series of governmental programs that paved the way to capitalist economy were launched. With the adoption of the principles of a market economy and westernization movement, social life in Turkey rapidly changed and began integrating to the global consumer culture (Toprak and Çarkoğlu, 2007).

Oker[51] summarizes the development of advertising industry in Turkey:

> The history of Turkish advertising is very exciting. Not so by the fact that advertising itself is an exciting industry, but by the brisk progress it has achieved in founding, building competency, interaction with its global milieu, self regulation and regenerating in a so short time scan not commonly seen in other areas of Turkish development process. To put it short, Turkish advertising matured in almost half the time it took American advertising to become what it is. What makes this specially interesting is the incomparable economic bases these two industries stand on.
>
> The first Turkish agency was founded in 1909, just one year after the proclamation of the Ikinci Mesrutiyet, which tried to solve certain personal freedom issues and reinstate a parliamentary regime for the collapsing Ottoman Empire. Like their counterparts in American advertising, the Turkish pioneers were mainly focused on selling space in newspapers, which flourished by the relative freedom of press conditions. We must mention that the

---

[50] Müge ELDEN; Professor of Advertising and Promotion; the head of Advertising Department at Ege University.
[51] Celil OKER; the instructor of "History of Advertising" course at İstanbul Bilgi University.

first attempts to increase the impact of ads visually came from journalists, not unlike Benjamin Franklin.

The young Turkish Republic, with its nibble economic conditions, established a number of state owned institutions, banks, insurance companies, factories, mining enterprises which almost all delegated their creative advertising to İhap Hulusi. Educated in graphic design in Germany, İhap Hulusi was almost a one man agency. He wrote, art directed and illustrated countless ads, at the same time shaping the modern visual outlook of Turkey.

After the WWII, Turkish modern advertising greeted its founder, Eli Acıman. After his first attempt with some partners, Acıman went to the United States in 1957, spent time in J. Walter Thompson to acquire the know how, gist and culture of American advertising. He returned home to found Man Ajans, rightfully known as the "school" of modern Turkish advertising. Countless managing and creative people worked in Man Ajans, later to establish their own agencies. Among Acıman's first clients was the Koç Group, the emerging leader of Turkish private sector enterprises. By the 1960s, behind walls of preventive customs tariffs, local capitalists had managed to produce various household items to be bought by the again emerging middle class. This led to prolification of advertising agencies, which mostly based their strategies on a "reason why" attitude, teaching masses of consumers to lead a modern life among numerous appliances, self care products, new services. By 1975, Turkish advertising celebrated its own "creative revolution". Ajans Ada, founded by veterans of Man Ajans, acquired a rightful fame by creatively using the facilities of the Turkish language and the opportunities of TV commercials, then was a very recent development in Turkish media. Their followers jumped right in the path that they expended. In the second half of the 1980s, everything changed. Turgut Ozal gained power after the elections following the coupe and introduced a extensively liberal economic program. Brand after brand piled on the Turkish market, selling to an aspiring and psychologically hungry mass of consumers, "educated" by the prolific and diversified new private TV channels. Just by the side of these brands, came their agencies. Thus all kinds of international affiliations emerged, bringing in the latest creative, strategy and business tactics practiced globally. These days, with the ever increasing institutions on advertising education, struggling with the never ending regulation attempts of the state utilizing self regulation and most importantly fighting the effects of economic crisis after economic crisis, Turkish advertising goes on with its exciting journey with unending hopes and self confidence.

The degree of development in communication channels in Turkey has never been as dramatic as it was during the 1980s, and especially the 1990s. The press and broadcast media in the meantime continued to flourish (Bir[52] and Ünüvar, 2000).

The advertising industry, not surprisingly, reacted to the rapid progress in the communication industry. As multinational companies entered

---

[52] Ali Atıf BİR is Professor of Communication and the head of Advertising Department at Bahçeşehir University.

the market, many products that were foreign to Turkish citizens became more usual (Sandıkçı and Ger, 2002). As a result of opening up the market to global brands, advertising industry has developed very rapidly (Aksoy[53], 2005). Foreign brands, as well as domestic ones turned out to be advertisers in this new market economy. Consequently, new advertising agencies were established, such as Cenajans/Grey, Manajans/Thompson, Pars/McCann-Erickson, Y&R/Reklamevi, Güzel Sanatlar/Saatchi & Saatchi.

Advertising Industry in Turkey

Today there are approximately 100 institutionalized agencies, including approximately 30 film production companies. Eighty-four of these agencies are the members of the Turkish Association of Advertising Agencies (TAAA). Among them, 57 were founded after 1980. Twenty-three either became partners with a foreign agency by assigning shares or established a cooperative agreement with such an agency (www.rd.org.tr).

The number of total employees in the advertising agencies is estimated to be around 3000. There are 12 companies providing media planning and purchasing services. There are also many public relations, direct marketing, advertising photography, research and computer companies and printing houses that give support to advertising industry (www.rd.org.tr).

The media extend of 260 television channels (53 of them broadcasting by cable) of which 16 broadcast on a national level, while 15 on a regional level and 229 on a local scale; 1200 radio stations of which 30 broadcast on a national level and 1062 on a local scale; 32 newspapers and 85 magazines distributed throughout the country having a huge potential for advertisements. The publication fees to all these media institutions rose from 635 million USD in 1995 to 1,9 billion USD in 2006 (www.rd.org.tr).

The contraction in the Turkish economy in 2009 affected the ad market adversely. Turkish ad market contracted by 14% in 2009 and amounted to TL 2.971 million (USD 1,9 billion); compared to TL 3.440 million (USD 2,7 billion) in 2008 (www.hurriyet.com.tr). The advertising expenditure allocation among media is shown on Figure 24-1.

---

[53] Atilla AKSOY; the former head of Advertising Department at İstanbul Bilgi University.

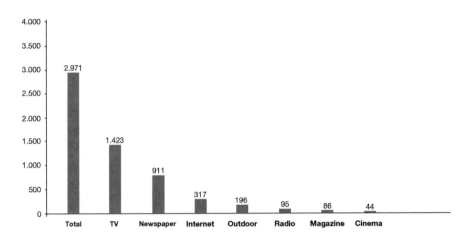

Source: http://www.hurriyetkurumsal.com/eng/advertising.asp, data retrieved 24 May, 2010.

Figure 24-1: Advertising Industry in Turkey - million TL (2009)

In 2009, the industries with the highest ad spending have been food, finance and telecommunications (Table 24-1). The construction industry is the industry that reduced its ad spending less than others and, hence, increased its share among the top 10 advertising industries.

Industry	%
Food	11
Finance	9
Telecommunications	10
Automotive, Transport Vehicles	6
Publishing	6
Cosmetics and Personal Care	5
Retail Trade	5
Beverages	4
Construction and Decoration	5
Home Cleaning Products	4
Other	34
Total	100

Source: http://www.hurriyetkurumsal.com/eng/advertising.asp, data retrieved 24 May, 2010.

Table 24-1: Ad Spending by Various Industries (2009)

Substantial growth in industry gave way to opportunities on the education side. This new way of competing necessitated not only general business education, but also specific marketing, marketing communication, advertising, and the like, education. The rapid internationalization of Turkey[54] even fostered this dynamic. Many new branches about these fields were opened under the universities. Internationalization also imposed the adaptation of curriculums and teaching methods according to the global orientations.

Higher Education in Turkey

Turkey is a populous country, with a high population growth rate having reached to 72.5 million in 2009, from 67.8 million in 2000. The country has a very young and a growing population, with a growth rate of 1.45 % in 2009. In 2009, population at the age 14 and below constituted 26.35 %, whereas those at ages between 15 and 64 constituted 67 % of the total. In the same year, 50 % of the population was aged under 28,8 (www.tuik.gov.tr). As a consequence of such a young population, the demand for higher education institutions is quite high.

In Turkey, higher education is primarily provided by means of state and private foundation universities. The Turkish higher education system has changed significantly in recent years (Eser and Birkan, 2004). The Council of Higher Education (YÖK) was established in 1981. In 1982, after the constitution of the republic was changed, new provisions were made for higher education. YÖK became a constitutional body, responsible for planning, coordination, governance and supervision of the higher education in Turkey.

Certain provisions were also made for non-profit foundations to establish higher education institutions in Turkey. Private foundation universities have been allowed to operate since 1984. Prof. Dr. İhsan Doğramacı founded Bilkent University, the first private university of Turkey in 1984. Bilkent University started to accept students in 1986 (www.bilkent.edu.tr).

After the new higher education law went into effect, institutions were reorganized. Several state institutions merged to form new universities, and all vocational schools were affiliated with universities. In the year 1982, the

---

[54] Direct foreign investment rose from 18 million USD in 1980 to 12.129 million USD in 2006 (Turkish Central Bank statistics; www.tcmb.gov.tr). Exports rose from 2910 million USD in 1980 to 132.027 million USD in 2008 (Turkish Statistical Institute; www.tuik.gov.tr).

higher education system comprised of 27 universities. Since then the system has continued to expand with the establishment of private universities founded by non-profit foundations, as well as newly founded state universities (Harcar and Torlak, 2002).

Currently there are in total 132 universities in the Turkish higher education system. Thirty-eight of these universities are privately owned, where 94 are state universities. YÖK announced that in the 2010-2011 education year the total number of universities would reach to 146, with the creation of one state and 13 private new universities (www.yok.gov.tr).

Students seeking to receive higher education are placed in university departments at pre-bachelor's and bachelor's levels according to their respective scores they receive as a result of a yearly made, nation-wide, central placement examination held by The Student Select and Placement Center (ÖSYM). In 2008, 1.646.376 high school graduates applied for this examination, however quota levels announced by universities stood at about one sixth of such number of applicants (265.230) (www.yok.gov.tr). The young and dynamic population of Turkey is one of the major elements that increased the number of applicants.

Even though it is possible to suggest that more prosperous students prefer state universities, the fact that where in state university's annual fees charged to students are approximately between 40 USD and 300 USD, such fees are at a level ranging approximately between 4,500 USD and 15.000 USD in private universities. This difference in tuitions plays a significant role in making preferences, and in variations within percentage ranking.

Advertising Education in Turkey

Professional education in Turkey has begun to grow rapidly since the beginning of the 1980s. Yet, while engineering, law, and certain sciences are well established in the curricula, marketing and advertising are relatively newcomers to the universities. As a result of a highly growing competition after the liberalization of markets in 1990, business, marketing, advertising, and public relations education gained importance in Turkey. The demand for human resources in this area stimulated the universities to open up departments in the related fields.

Unfortunately there is no specific research on advertising education in Turkey, thus this study will be a pioneering one. The current study includes an analysis of 32 Communication Faculties, as well as the curricula of 6 individual programs in advertising.

Historically in Turkey, advertising education has been directly connected with two academic fields: Journalism and Business, like it is in the U.S. (Ross, Osborne and Richards, 2006). Though in general advertising education is provided by communication faculties, because of this interrelationship, this study analyses both educational fields in Turkey. *Traditionally, public relations departments were established before advertising departments, and advertising education was first introduced within the public relations departments.*[55]

In Turkey, public relations education has older roots than in many European countries (Okay, 2003). The first "Journalism School" set up by Yahya Fehmi Tuna in 1948 is the genesis of this educational field. Afterwards, this school formed into the "Journalism Institute," then to the "Journalism and Public Relations Institute," then to the "Press and Broadcasting College," and finally to the "Communication Faculty." But, the first curriculum program of public relations education in Turkey started as a separate department in 1966 in the School of Journalism, affiliated with the Political Sciences Faculty, Ankara University (Okay, 2003; Yıldırım-Becerikli, 2004).

Then, schools of journalism continued to open one after another. Public relations courses started to be included in the curricula of journalism schools (Yıldırım-Becerikli, 2004). Starting from 1987-1988, YÖK decided to separate Journalism and Public Relations departments into Journalism Departments and Public Relations and Promotion Departments (Tokgöz, 2003; Yengin, 2004).

With the amendment of the law in 1992, names of all "Schools of Journalism" have been changed to "Communication Faculty" (Okay, 2003; Peltekoğlu, 1998), and new communication faculties were established in Anadolu University and Selçuk University (Yengin, 2004). The same year within Anadolu University, Turkey's first Communication Arts and Advertising department was established (Tokgöz, 2003; Yengin, 2004).

In Turkey, advertising education at the university level is basically provided in the Communication Faculties (Okay, 2003). At the time of this study there are 32 communication faculties. In 30 of them (17 in state- 13 in private universities) Advertising and Public Relations programs are offered.

Now there are different departments in various universities providing partial or full advertising education. Very recently a new trend can be seen:

---

[55] Editor's emphasis.

advertising departments are being placed under the Faculty of Economics and Administrative Sciences in three newly established private universities. The remaining programs provide advertising instructions under the name of "Communication Art" and "Communication Science" programs. (See Table 3)

Bachelor of Arts in Advertising

The education in the field of advertising is either a four-year education, giving a Bachelor of Arts (BA) degree or a two year education, giving an associate of arts (AA) degree. In total, currently there are 6 Advertising, 10 Public Relations and Advertising, and 23 Public Relations and Promotion Programs offered in various universities providing Bachelor's degrees in Turkey. (See Table 3)

In Turkey, there is not a ranking system of universities or specific departments to determine which school is the best. Table 2 lists the universities that offer Advertising and Advertising related BA degrees.

	BA in Advertising	BA in Public Relations and Advertising	BA in Public Relations/ Public Relations and Promotion
State Universities			
Akdeniz University			X
Anadolu University		X	
Ankara University			X
Atatürk University			X
Cumhuriyet University			X
Ege University	X		X
Erciyes University			X
Fırat University			X
Galatasaray University		X	
Gazi University			X
Gümüşhane University			X
İstanbul University			X
Karadeniz Technical Uni.		X	
Kocaeli University	X		X
Marmara University			X
Mersin University		X	
Selçuk University			X
Private Universities			
Atılım University		X	
Bahçeşehir University	X		X
Başkent University			X
Beykent University		X	
Çağ University			X

Haliç University			X
İstanbul Arel University		X	
İstanbul Aydın University			X
İstanbul Bilgi University	X		X
İstanbul Ticaret University			X
İzmir Ekonomi University		X	
Kadir Has University	X		X
Maltepe University			X
Yaşar University		X	
Yeditepe University	X		X
Yeni Yüzyıl University		X	

Source: OSYM reports & University Web Pages; data retrieved 15 May, 2010.

Table 24-2: Four-Year Bachelor of Arts in Advertising

Kocaeli University, Ege University as state universities, and Bahçeşehir University, İstanbul Bilgi University, Kadir Has University and Yeditepe University are private universities offering individual four-year advertising programs. In 2009 the total student quotas of these universities were 434; 31, 52, 91, 135, 60, 65 students respectively. However, four state universities and six private universities offer four year integrated programs in public relations and advertising. There now are 13 state universities and 10 private universities public relations and promotion programs in which advertising courses are included in the curricula are offered.

	Communication Faculties		Faculty of Economics and Administrative Sciences		
	State University	Private University	State University	Private University	Total
BA in Advertising	2	4	0	0	6
BA in Public Relations and Adverting	4	5	0	1	10
BA in Public Relations and Promotion	13	8	0	2	23

Source: OSYM reports & University Web Pages, data retrieved 15 May, 2010.

Table 24-3: Number of Universities Offering 4-Year Bachelor of Arts in Advertising

Three private universities, Atılım University, Çağ University and Haliç University offer Public Relations and Advertising program, Public Relations and Promotion programs under the Faculty of Economics and Administrative Sciences. Overall the number of integrated programs is more than individual programs in advertising. However, the number of individual public relations and promotion programs is much greater than individual programs in advertising.

	Communication Faculties		
	State University	Private University	Total
BA in Journalism	15	5	20
BA in Cinema-Radio-TV	17	11	28
BA in Media & Communication	2	5	7
BA in Visual Communication Design	3	11	14

Source: OSYM reports & University Web Pages, data retrieved 15 May, 2010.

Table 24-4: Other Bachelor of Arts Degrees offered by Communication Faculties

In general, Communication Faculties carry out educational programs under three major departments: Journalism, Public Relations and Advertising, and Radio-Television-Cinema. The newly rising departments of Media and Communication and Visual Communication Design are observed more in private universities, and the numbers are expected to increase in the following years.

Advertising Curriculum

Advertising courses were added in some of the university curricula, before individual advertising departments were opened. Dr. Dilber[56], as one of the pioneering Turkish professors in this area, taught his first advertising course at Pennsylvania State University. Upon joining to Boğaziçi University in 1968, he taught one of the first advertising courses in Turkey, alternating with his colleague Dr. Koç.[57] Dr. Dilber tells about those days:

> Advertising is a topic I enjoy the most among numerous other marketing and organization courses. Advertising agencies in the modern sense hardly existed in Turkey at that time. I remember with gratitude some of the Turkish advertising agency greats who showed their practical experiences to the students. Since the course was taught in English, I was also able to acquaint the students with American and British Advertising. A high point was Al Ries' introduction of the positioning concept in my class during his visit to Turkey in 1979.

---

[56] Mustafa DILBER; Professor of Marketing and Organization.- Received "Distinguished Leadership Award, 2005" from the University of Minnesota where he received his PhD in 1967. – Currently teaches at various private and state universities on a part time basis.

[57] Ahmet KOÇ; Professor of Marketing.

Dr. Mustafa Dilber

This may have been the birth of advertising education, but it was not yet a trend on the country's universities. As mentioned previously Anadolu University was the first to offer an advertising major in 1992. Advertising education, as with most other types of professional education, has its ups-and downs in the past 30 years that it has been a part of the curricula.

The curriculums of the six advertising programs (*see* Table 24-2) were analyzed through the websites of the universities. Courses taught in advertising departments can be grouped as follows:

1. Courses related to advertising
2. Courses related to brand management
3. Courses related to interactivity
4. Courses related to public relations
5. Courses related to communication and media
6. Courses related to research
7. Courses related to writing
8. Courses related to accountability
9. Courses related to creativity
10. Courses related to social sciences

Along with theoretical courses, there are courses designed for student practicing. Most of the programs have campaign lectures that the students find opportunity to practice their knowledge on real life or simulated cases. In these universities this wide range of courses are instructed not only by the academics but also by industry professionals. Advertising education in Turkey maintains close industry ties for internships, entry-level employment, and guest speakers.

Generally all BA programs in advertising include psychology, sociology, business and media courses in their mandatory course list. And all programs include at least a course that covers accountability issues. Very recently İstanbul Bilgi University became an international partner in a project on "Advertising Ethics Education" with the Advertising Self Regulatory Organization of Turkey (RÖK), and European Advertising Standards Alliance (EASA).

Courses Covering Advertising	Courses Covering Accountability
Account Planning	Advertising Ethics
Advertising Agency Management	Advertising Law
Advertising Analysis	Communication Ethics
Advertising Campaign Management and Agency Operation	Communication Law
Advertising Campaigns	Communication Law and Intellectual Property Rights
Advertising Campaigns Project	Introduction to Law
Advertising Case Studies	Issues in Advertising
Advertising Strategy	Media Ethics
Case Studies in Advertising	
Creative Thinking	**Courses Covering Creativity**
International Advertising	Advanced Advertising Layout
Media Planning	Advertising and Music
Positioning Strategy in Advertising	Advertising Layout and Design
	Advertising Layout and Production
Courses Covering Brand Management	Advertising Photography
Advertising Strategy	Advertising Scenario
Brand Management	Basic Graphic Design in Advertising
Customer Relationship Management	Communicationscapes
Image Branding in Advertising	Creative Strategy in Advertising
Integrated Marketing Communications	Creative Thinking
Introduction to Marketing	Design Culture
Marketing Communication	Desktop Publishing
Marketing Strategy	Introduction to Creative Communication
Principles of Advertising	Photography
Principles of Marketing	Portfolio Management
Readings in Marketing	Project and Production Management For Communicators
	Text and Image in Publishing
Courses Covering Interactivity	TV Advertising
Advertising in the Digital world	Understanding Image
Advertising Studio	Visual Appreciation
Design in Publishing	Visual Communication Design
Digital Media	Visual Communication
Editing Sound and Image	Visual Culture
Graphic Design in Digital Environment	
Interactive Advertising	
Internet and Computer Concepts	**Courses Covering Social Sciences**
Introduction to Computer and Information Technology	Advertising and Arts
Web Design	Advertising and Consumption
	Advertising and Society
Courses Covering Public Relations	Advertising History
PR Campaigns	Advertising in Cultural Studies
Public Relations	Art Culture and Society
Sponsorship and Promotion	Cognitive Psychology

354

	Communication Psychology
Courses Covering Communication & Media	Communication Science
Communication and Media	Communication Theories
Communication and media history	Conflict Management and Negotiation Techniques
Communication Theories	Consumer Behavior
Culture Communication and Society	Critical Thinking
Digital Media	Fashion, Design and Consumption
Introduction to Mass Communication	Human Resources Management For Communicators
Media Analysis	Interpersonal Communication
Media Planning and Strategy	Introduction to Business
New Media: Internet and Mobile Communication	Introduction to Economics
Principles of Communication and Media	Introduction to Psychology
	Keywords in Social Sciences
Courses Covering Research	Persuasion
Dissertation Writing	Philosophy
Qualitative Research	Political Advertising
Quantitative Research	Political Communication Campaigns
Research in Advertising	Principles of Economics
Semiotic Analysis	Social Anthropology
Social Research Methods	Social Psychology
	Sociology
Courses Covering Writing	
Advanced Copywriting	
Copywriting	
Communications Skills & Academic Writing	
Creative Writing	
Written Communication	

Table 24-5: Curricula of Advertising Programs

Associate of Arts in Advertising

In Turkey, besides the faculties providing four-year advertising education, various universities offer two-year vocational training programs. Two-year vocational training schools are institutions established for the purpose of providing vocational education to meet the practical needs of various fields. There are currently 97 programs offering advertising and marketing related majors (*see* Table 24-6).

	State University	Private University	Total
Public Relations and Advertising	1	2	3
Public Relations and Promotion	16	11	27
Marketing	51	10	61
Marketing and Foreign Trade	4	0	4
Retail Management	1	0	1
Brand Communication	1	0	1

Source: OSYM reports & University Web Pages, data retrieved on 15 May, 2010.

Table 24-6: Two-Year Vocational Education in Advertising Related Fields

Among those, 80 universities (64 state - 16 private) offer two-year vocational training schools that provide advertising related education. Marketing programs dominate the two-year vocational education.

Student Selection and Placement Center provides a special central exam for the purpose of completing an Associate degree to a Bachelor's degree in a related field of study. Thus, students who have completed their two-year vocational study are given the chance to continue their education to get a four-year Bachelor's degree.

	State University	Private University	Total
MA in Advertising	2	2	4
MA in PR & Advertising	1	0	1
MA in Marketing	9	9	18
MA in PR and Promotion	10	4	14
MA in Communication Sciences	3	5	8
PhD in Advertising	2	0	2
PhD in Public Relations and Advertising	1	1	2
PhD in Public Relations and Promotion	7	0	7
PhD in Communication Sciences	2	1	3

Source: OSYM statistics, www.osym.gov.tr, data retrieved 15 May 2010.

Table 24-7: Graduate Education in Advertising and Related Fields

Graduate Education in Advertising

Various postgraduate and doctoral education opportunities are provided after completing four-year educational programs in Turkey (*see* Table 24-7). Being a new educational field, postgraduate programs specialized in advertising are quite limited. As an individual graduate subject, advertising is taught at five different universities. Those universities are İstanbul Bilgi

University, Bahçeşehir University, Marmara University, Ege University, and Anadolu University. Four MA degrees in Advertising, one MA degree in Public Relations and Advertising, two PhD in Advertising, and two PhD in Public Relations and Advertising programs are offered. The number of MA programs in marketing and public relations and promotion areas is quite high.

BA in Management

In Turkey, after the 1990s, business education became very popular. Recently more than 76 state, and 35 private universities offer Bachelor's degree in Business. When the curricula of Management departments are analyzed, a financial education emphasis is observed. Most of the programs have only a few basic marketing courses such as Introduction to Marketing, Principles of Marketing, Marketing Management, International Marketing, Consumer Behavior, and Sales Management.

Students Studying Advertising

The number of students placed in the advertising and related departments by the Student Selection and Placement Center in 2008 is listed in Table 24-8.

	Undergrad B.A			Vocational School AA			Grad	PhD
	Women	Men	Total	Women	Men	Total		
Advertising	533	366	899				198	51
Public Relations & Advertising	622	515	1137	2217	966	3183		
Management	26517	34074	60591	23701	22381	44082	9845	1493
Marketing				7536	11612	19148	901	140
Journalism	1927	2680	4607				276	159
Journalism & PR				1925	4632	6557		
Public Relations & Promotion	2587	2675	5262	2196	801	2997	645	200
Communication Sciences	140	218	358				159	37
TOTAL	32326	40528	72854	37575	40392	75967	12024	2080

Source: OSYM statistics, www.osym.gov.tr, data retrieved 15 May 2010.

Table 24-8: Number of Students Placed in Advertising and Related Programs (2008)

In general, there is not much difference in the total number of female and male students enrolled in B.A. degrees in Advertising, Pubic Relations and Promotion, and Public Relations and Advertising departments. But, number of females enrolled in the same departments in vocational schools is much higher than male student enrollments. When compared to the number of students in various other departments, the enrollment number in the Management field is much higher.

Students who managed to enter Communication tend to fall within the achievement range of 1% and 17.1% on the university entrance exam. Such range is between 1% and 4% for the state universities, while the private foundation universities admit students achieving to fall within the range of 3.7% and 17.1%. As for the two-year vocational training schools, the percentage achievement range is between 4.3% and 9% for the state universities, while it ranges between 22.5% and 37.4% in the case of private foundation universities (Okay 2003).

Evaluation and Accreditation of Advertising Programs

Turkish university system is totally in the process of adapting to the European Union Bologna accreditation system. The aim of the Bologna Process is to create a European Higher Education Area (EHEA) based on international cooperation and academic exchange that will facilitate mobility of students, graduates, and higher education staff, and prepare students for their future careers and life as active citizens in democratic societies, while supporting their personal development. It is designed to offer broad access to high-quality higher education, based on democratic principles and academic freedom (http://www.ond.vlaanderen.be/hogeronderwijs/bologna/about/). Therefore all the departments conform to the requirements of this accreditation process.

Advertising Education Support Organizations and Student Competitions

Advertising education is informally supported by Turkish Association of Advertising Agencies. In addition, the Turkish Foundation of Advertising (http://www.rv.org.tr), advertising agencies, and advertisers provide full-time or guest lecturers to share their experiences and practices. There is no formal financial support to higher education institutions that offer advertising degrees. Research and teaching collaborations usually take place between stakeholders of the advertising industry and the educational foundations. The foundation of advertising, for example, organizes summer schools that offer advertising workshops.

There are different student competitions offered by associations of advertising agencies, advertisers, advertising creatives, media and student clubs of universities. These include:

- "IAA" competition is a global student advertising competition, and part of InterAD competition (www.iaaturkey.com/home.html).
- "Genc Kirmizi" is a print ad competition offered by one of the biggest media institutions in Turkey (www.kirmiziodulleri/genckirmizi.com).
- "Genc Iletisimciler-Young Communicators" is offered by a media foundation, with the aim of educating the media leaders of future (www.aydindoganvakfi.org.tr).
- "Adventure" is the competition organized by Bogazici University student club, targeting the production of creative ideas (www.adventure.org.tr).
- "Just Marketing" is organized by Middle East Technical University, aiming at preparation of a marketing campaign (www.just-marketing.org).
- "Ders arası" student competition is designed by Association of Copy Writers (www.dersarasindayiz.biz).

Summary and Conclusion

The history of advertising education in Turkey is not long. Starting with individual lessons in the curricula, advertising education was departmentalized first within public relations departments. It is very recently that the joint programs of advertising and public relations moved to separate advertising and public relations programs.

In the last decade, with the increase in the number of private universities in Turkey, there is a steady move in the number of advertising education offering institutions. The opening of private universities made the education in this field more competent. This transformation was reflected in the curricula, bringing changes in the content and title of the courses offered by advertising departments.

The practice of advertising shifted into a multidisciplinary area that requires global business and marketing knowledge, embedding creativity and advancements in technology. In our research we found that advertising departments constantly update their syllabuses, and such findings may purport that they keep up with the developments across the world.

Though it is a new area, advertising education is growing quickly, while raising some issues. From the academic side, the increase in number of advertising departments is fed by rising numbers of graduate and doctoral education in advertising, and related new fields like communication sciences. But still the capacity of graduate education is not sufficient to raise the required number of academics. In particular, there is shortage of academics in creativity and technology areas.

Advertising departments attempt to stem this shortage by hiring practitioners on a part-time lecturer basis to teach those courses. On the demand side, each year, many students are admitted to large number of advertising and public relations departments to receive two-year and four-year advertising education.

On the other hand, a large number of advertising related department graduates are compelled to work in different occupational fields since the need for advertising practitioners in agency and advertisers side is less than the number of graduates. But the development of Turkish market and business is an important potential to set the balance. Advertising education is expected to flourish in the coming years.

References

Books, Articles and Periodicals

Aksoy, A. (2005) *Yeni Reklamcılık* (New Advertising). İstanbul Bilgi University Publications, İstanbul, Turkey.

Bir, A. A., & Ünüvar, K. (2000). *Bir Reklam Ajansının Öyküsü Cenajans Grey 1970-2000.* History Foundation of Turkey Publications, İstanbul Turkey.

Çakır, H. (1997). *Osmanlı basınında reklam* (Advertising in the Ottoman press). Ankara: Elit Advertising.

Çetinkaya, Y. (1992). *Reklamcılık* (Advertising). İstanbul: Agaç Publications.

Esen, Oguz. (2000). Financial Openness in Turkey. *International Review of Applied Economics, 14 (1),* 5-23.

Eser, Z., & Birkan, I. (2004). Marketing Education in Turkey: A comparative study between state and private universities. *Journal of Teaching in International Business, 16 (2),* 75-101.

Gevgilili, A. (1983). Türkiye Basını (Turkish Press). In M. Belge (Ed.), *Cumhuriyet Dönemi Türkiye Ansiklopedisi* (pp.202-215), Vol.1, İstanbul: İletişim Publications.

Harcar, T., & Torlak, O. (2002). Perceived instructor quality in marketing education: A comparative study between new and well-established Turkish universities. Proceedings of the Impact of Globalization on World Business in the New Millennium Conference, 346-352.

Kocabaş, F., & Elden, M. (1997). *Reklamcılık: Kavramlar, kararlar, kurumlar* (Advertising: General concepts, decisions, institutions). İstanbul: Iletisim Publications.

Koloğlu, O. (1998). Reklamcılığımızın ilk yuzyılı 1840-1940 (The first century of our advertising 1840-1940). Foundation of Advertising Publications, İstanbul.

Nebioğlu, S. (1983). Reklamcılık (Advertising). In M. Belge (Ed.), *Cumhuriyet Donemi Turkiye Ansiklopedisi* (pp. 1656-1669), Vol. 6. İstanbul: Iletisim Publications.

Okay, A. (2003). Public Relations Education in Turkey. *European PR News*, 2 (3).

Oktay, A. (1993). *Turkiye'de populer* kültür (Popular Culture in Turkey). İstanbul: Everest Publications.

Peltekoğlu, F.B. (1998). *Halkla İlişkiler Nedir* (What is Public Relations). İstanbul: Beta Publications.

Ross, B., Osborne, A., & Richards, J. (2006). *Advertising Education: Yesterday, Today, Tomorrow*. Advertising Education Publications: Louisiana US.

Tokgöz, O. (2003). Turkiye'de İletisim Egitiminin Elli Yıllık Bir Geçmisinin Degerlendirilmesi (An evaluation of the fifty year of communication education). *Kultur ve Iletisim-Ki Dergisi*, Ankara Universitesi Iletisim Fakultesi Yay, 6.

Toprak, B., & Çarkoğlu, A. (2007). *Religion, Society, and Politics in a Changing society*. İstanbul: TESEV Publications.

Sandıkçı, O., & Ger, G. (2002). In-between modernities and postmodernities: Theorizing Turkish consumption space. *Advances in Consumer Research*, 29, 465-470.

Uluengin, M. (2003). Consumption in Turkey: A journey through the republic's economic policies, media channels and advertising (1923-1999). Unpublished Manuscript, University of Texas at Austin, USA.

Yengin, H. (2004). The Public Relations Education and its Problems in Turkey. Proceedings of the 2nd International Symposium, Communication in the Millenium, 1, 173-191.

Yıldırım-Becerikli, S. (2004). Turkiye'de Lisans Duzeyindeki Halkla İliskiler Egitimine İliskin Bir Degerlendirme (An evaluation of the undergraduate level public relations education in Turkey). Proceedings of the 2nd International Communication in the Millennium, 1, 193-219.

Websites

Aydin Dogan Foundation, www.aydindoganvakfi.org.tr, (May 1, 2010).

Association of Copy Writers' Competition, www.dersarasindayiz.biz, (May 1, 2010).

Bilkent University, www.bilkent.edu.tr, (May 11, 2010).

Bogazici University's Competition, www.adventure.org.tr, (May 1, 2010).

Bologna Process, http://www.ond.vlaanderen.be/hogeronderwijs/bologna/about/, (May 10, 2010).

Central Bank of the Republic of Turkey, www.tcmb.gov.tr/yeni/eng/, (May 1, 2010).

Council for Higher Education, www.yok.gov.tr, (May 15, 2010).

Faculty of Communications, Ankara University, http://ilef.ankara.edu.tr/reklam/yazi.php?yad=6007, (May 10, 2010).

Foundation of Advertising, www.rd.org.tr, (May 15, 2010).

Hurriyet Newspaper, http://www.hurriyetkurumsal.com/eng/advertising.asp, (May 15, 2010).

Ihap Hulusi Görey; www.ihaphulusi.gen.tr, (May 23, 2010).

International Advertising Association, www.iaaturkey.com/home.html, (May 1, 2010).

Kirmizi Advertising Awards, www.kirmiziodulleri.com, (May 21, 2010).

Middle East Technical University's Competition, www.just-marketing.org, (May 21, 2010).

Student Selection and Placement Center, www.osym.gov.tr, (May 11, 2010).

Turkish Statistical Institute, www.tuik.gov.tr, (May 1, 2010).

North America

Canada's Approach to Ad Education

S. Scott Whitlow,
University of Kentucky, USA

The razzle-dazzle of advertising. The allure of advertising. The commerce-centric soul of advertising. The advertising industry touted these traits proudly as it lit its own spotlight at 2009's launch of Advertising Week. That week, advertising sparked the news cycle all across Canada. And students with a yen to find their niche in the Canadian advertising world welcomed a new door opening for them.

In bustling cities from coast to coast – Halifax, Montreal, Toronto, Calgary, Edmonton and Vancouver – advertising luminaries touted the contribution advertising makes economically and socially across Canada. Industry-created and produced PSAs shared this message with the Canadian business community and the public-at-large. Through Advertising Week, the industry was ratcheting up its visibility, claiming center stage for a few days and providing students a chance to share that stage (Canada's First Advertising Week 2009).

A feature of Advertising Week was its inaugural Youth Day, carefully crafted to inspire and attract young talent to the industry. The irresistible draw for these industry hopefuls was the chance to develop a campaign promoting a benefit concert for Virgin United's RE*Generation program – with Sir Richard Branson selecting the winner. Student teams, apprenticed for Youth Day to 15 notable Toronto communications firms, shaped and refined their campaigns. With their campaign tagged "Your ticket in is their ticket out," a team of nine students mentored by Due North Communications earned Sir Branson's nod. Also irresistible to team members was the support offered by Astral Media to launch the winning campaign across Canada (Soares 2009).

Like many countries with robust national and international commerce, Canadian advertising is a pivotal force to link buyers with sellers.

Second by second, its endless permutations stream across media, both traditional and cutting-edge, seeking to connect with targeted consumers. Invariably, the stream of advertising draws attention of its own. For those who are at the point of exploring future career possibilities – or those seeking a career switch – the 360-surround of advertising fires the imagination. The path to a successful career in Canadian advertising has a bounty of starting points.

To begin, it helps to have a grasp of the geography of Canada. In a word: vast. Spread from the Atlantic to the Pacific oceans, and from its 5,525-mile southern border with the United States north to the once assuredly frozen Arctic, Canada has a land mass of more than 3.5 million square miles, second only to Russia (Canada 2009). Its sprawling beauty is organized into 10 provinces: Newfoundland and Labrador, Prince Edward Island, Nova Scotia, New Brunswick, Québec, Ontario, Manitoba, Saskatchewan, Alberta, British Columbia, and the three territories of Nunavut, Northwest Territories, and Yukon.

Yet, with approximately 34 million people, much of that land is sparsely populated (9 persons per square mile compared with the United States' 84) (World Almanac 2007). However, it is estimated that approximately 90% of Canada's population resides within 100 miles of the southern border, with concentrations along the northern banks of the Great Lake and at other water-access points. These heavily populated areas are places where communications firms thrive, as do a mixture of higher education options. Here, starting points for a career in advertising-related fields are in abundance. That same mix of options, on a smaller scale, awaits students across Canada.

Higher Education in Canada

Universities: Mostly Business

For over 140 years, each province in Canada has been charged with oversight of the education system of its own citizens. When Canada became self-governing in 1867, the Constitution Act of 1867 established total decentralization of the Canadian education system. Its Article 93 declares constitutional responsibility for education to be the exclusive domain of the provincial governments (AUCC 2009).

With this historic decision, the opportunity was set for distinct differences in educational philosophies and structures among the provinces. Even so, at the post-secondary level, it's typical across most of the provinces to designate degree-granting institutions as universities.

Universities, thus, crown the higher education system in Canada. Currently, 95 of these are members of the Association of Universities and Colleges of Canada (AUCC). Acceptance as a member confers merit-based recognition on a university for AUCC serves as a *defacto* trans-Canadian accreditation organization. It notes on its web site, "There's no federal ministry of education or formal accredit system. Instead, membership in the Association of Universities and Colleges of Canada, coupled with the university's provincial government charter, is generally deemed the equivalent" (AUCC, 2009).

One of AUCC's services for its member organizations and for the Canadian public is its rich on-line database, which provides click-through leads to over 10,000 undergraduate and graduate degree programs, professional degree programs, and certificates. The order of these programs follows the Classification of Instructional Programs (CIP) system of grouping devised by the USA's National Center for Education Statistics (the 2000 edition of CIP was adopted by Statistics Canada as their standard field of study taxonomy). On this database, a search for "Advertising" yields only two results:

> Ontario College of Art & Design Executive Master of Design (EMDes) in Advertising. Master's degree English Advertising Commercial and Advertising Art

> Université de Sherbrooke (Québec) Baccalauréat-maètrise en communication marketing. Bachelor's degree French Advertising Marketing/Marketing Management, General

Almost exclusively, in Canadian universities, advertising courses are folded into the menu of courses that support the marketing function, a core program area in many universities' business or commerce division. At some institutions, advertising's presence is ethereal. Several faculty at such institutions were asked about the absence of dedicated advertising courses. The perspective expressed by most can be summarized in the words of one professor:

> We offer marketing and strategy courses, where advertising is a part of each course, but no course devoted only to advertising or to the broader marketing communication. (Confidential personal communication, August 20, 2009)

More typically, however, the integral role advertising plays in commerce is acknowledged in advertising-specific courses – again within the context of business or commerce programs. Many university level marketing programs offer one or two advertising-specific courses in undergraduate and/or graduate programs. A sampling of these courses and the programs with which they're associated appear in the Province Vignettes section of this chapter.

This almost total absence of identifiable advertising programs at the university level appears to be a mix of tradition, perception and pragmatism. Advertising, and the range of career-related paths it feeds, is regarded as a trade. As such, it's seen as most logically fitting into education settings geared toward "trades" preparation. Dr. Barbara J. Phillips, Rawlco Scholar in Advertising/Edwards School of Business, University of Saskatchewan, a professor with experience in both the American and Canadian university systems, offers a perceptive observation.:

> [T]he American system started out with Journalism schools, which then eventually broadened into housing all kinds of communication, including advertising. In Canada, we have almost no Journalism schools housed in Universities …; journalism was the domain for community colleges, where it existed. So advertising, as an academic discipline of study, was part of marketing (business schools) because we didn't develop the journalism stream. (Barbara J. Phillips, personal communication, September 18, 2009)

Community Colleges

Rather than at the university level, it's at all the other post-secondary institutions that advertising education flourishes from province to province. Differences abound among these provincial institutions – differences in classification of the institutions, types of certification, number of program semesters, etc. – leading to enormous variety in the advertising programs. Essentially, these are community colleges which the Association of Canadian Community Colleges (ACCC) points out, may be identified as "institute, institute of technology, technical college, regional college, cégep (in Québec), university college or simply college" (ACCC 2009).[58]

An explosive trans-Canada spurt of community college launches began in 1965, with a ripple effect that lasted a decade. A number of related factors coalesced to spark this growth of community colleges. The physical and emotional drain of World War II had subsided and Canada's economic engine was surging. Skilled workers were needed to sustain economic growth in the industry and business sectors, to support their communities

---

[58] The Association of Canadian Community Colleges (ACCC) began in 1972 as a national, voluntary membership organization "to represent colleges and institutes to government, business and industry, both in Canada and internationally."

in the public service sector and, by extension, to enrich their communities' arts and culture development.[59]

Across Canada, each province looked to the community college concept as the pragmatic answer to their needs. Each grew its own community college system – either by creating a wholly new system or by amalgamating existing institutions into a coordinated system. Many of these were dual purpose: concentrated career training and, for students looking to their community college as a launch pad for university studies, a general post-secondary education. First and foremost, the community colleges "... share the primary functions of responding to the training needs of business, industry, the public service sectors and the educational needs of vocationally oriented secondary school graduates" (ACCC 2009).

Across the mid-60s to mid-70s window of community college expansion, public perception of them grew increasingly positive and their geographic access made them welcome destinations as a way to prepare further for career success. With the vast career-training options available to students as a function of each college's distinct emphases, a community or region's broad spectrum of worker needs could be met. It was also during this window of time that many of today's robust, veteran advertising programs began.

Degrees and Certification

University Level

Across Canada many universities base their awarding of a Bachelor of Arts degree on completion of a four-year course of studies. Other universities base it on a three-year program with the degree regarded as a pass, ordinary, or general degree. At some of these institutions, there's an option for eligible students to cap their three years of study with one additional year, with heightened requirements. This advances the student's degree to an Honors degree, the "B.A. (Hons)."

---

[59] A comprehensive review of these factors can be found in "Vocational Education in Canada," John E. Lyons, Bikkar S. Randhawa, Neil A. Paulson. *Canadian Journal of Education 16:2* (1991), pp. 137-150. In reviewing the forces which fueled vocational training, the article looks at the impact of the WWII bombing of England on Canada's industrial priorities, the state of Canadian vocational training in the years after WWII, and the companion outreach by Canada to attract a skilled labor force of immigrants, among other forces.

College Level

From province to province, there is variety in the way colleges certify completion of a program, but the similarities are sufficient that it is possible to grasp the general approach by examination of one province's system. In the province of Alberta, for example, there are seven different post-secondary programs. The Alberta government helps students sort out their options by stating the purpose of each of the programs, the length and nature of time commitment, the type of institution(s) offering the program, and how one program may feed into another program. A condensed version of the Alberta system is summarized in Figure 25-1.

Association of Canadian Community Colleges (ACCC)

ACCC member institutions provide the information about their programs which constitutes ACCC's searchable database (ACCC, 2009). Since it's a member-sourced database, the ACCC reminds users that currency and accuracy of the information are not confirmed. Searches using a core of advertising related terms (direct response, media planning, advertising design, interactive marketing) yielded no matches.

A search for "Marketing Communications" yielded identification of a single institution: St. Lawrence College, Advertising - Integrated Marketing Communications. A further search for "Advertising" identified 15 institutions and "Graphic Design" listed 31 institutions. These are summarized in Table 25-1a and Table 25-1b.

Institution	Curriculum Offered by	Length	Earns
Algonquin Col (Ottawa, ON) www.algonquincollege.com	Sch of Media & Design	3 yrs	Ont Col Adv Diploma
Cambrian Col of App Arts and Tech (Sudbury, ON) www.cambriancollege.ca	Sch of Communication Studies	2 yrs 4 sem	Ont Col Grad Certificate Ont Col Degree
Canadore Col of App Arts and Tech (North Bay, ON) www.canadore.on.ca	Communication Arts, Advertising - Creative Media	4 sem	
Centennial Col of App Arts and Tech (Toronto, ON) www.centennialcollege.ca	Sch of Communications, Media and Design	3 yrs	Ont Col Adv Diploma
Conestoga Col Inst of Tech & Adv Learning (Kitchener, ON) www.conestoga.on.ca	Sch of Media & Design •Advertising •Integrated Mkt Comm (post-grad)	2 yrs I yr	Ont Col Diploma Ont Grad Certificate
Durham Col (Oshawa, ON) www.durhamcollege.ca	Sch of Media, Art & Design	3 yrs	Ont Col Adv Diploma

Georgian Col of App Arts and Tech (Barrie, ON) www.georgianc.on.ca	Business Studies	2 yrs	Ont Col Diploma
Holland College (Charlottetown, PE) www.hollandc.pe.ca	Business Studies	2 yrs	Diploma Marketing & Advertising Management
Humber Col Inst of Tech & Adv Learning (Toronto, ON) www.humber.ca	Sch of Media Studies & Info Tech •Advert Media Sales •Advert & Graphic Design •Creative Advert	2 yrs 2 yrs 4 yr	Diploma Diploma Bach App Arts
Lethbridge College (Lethbridge, AB) www.lethbridgecollege.ab.ca	Communication Arts: Advert/PR	2 yr	Diploma
Loyalist Col of App Arts and Tech (Belleville, ON) www.loyalistcollege.com	Sch of Media Studies Advertising Advert & Promotion for Retail Art & Design Foundation	2 yrs 1 yr 1 yr	Ont Col Diploma Advert Ont Col Diploma Ont Col Certificate
Mohawk Col of App Arts and Tech (Hamilton, ON) www.mohawkcollege.ca	Sch of Arts, Science & Communications	3 yrs	Ont Col Adv Diploma
Seneca Col of App Arts and Tech (Toronto, ON) www.se-neca.on.ca	Sch of Communication Art •Creative Advert	2 yrs	Ont Col Diploma
Sheridan Col Inst of Tech & Adv Learning (Oakville, ON) www.sheridaninstitute.ca	Sch of Business	2 yrs 3 yrs	Ont Col Diploma Ont Col Adv Diploma
St. Claire Col of App Arts and Tech (Windsor, ON) www.stclairecollege.ca	Centre for the Arts	3 yrs	Ont Col Adv Diploma
St. Lawrence College (Kingston, ON) www.sl.on.ca	Advertising - Integrated Marketing Communications	3 yrs	Ont Col Adv Diploma

Table 25-1a: Summary of College and Institute Programs, Curricula in Advertising

Institution	Curriculum Offered by	Length	Earns
Algonquin Col (Ottawa, ON) www.algonquincollege.com		3 yrs	Ont Col Adv Diploma
Cambrian Col of App Arts and Tech (Sudbury, ON) www.cambriancollege.ca	Sch of Art & Design	3 yrs	Ont Col Adv Diploma
Canadore Col of App Arts and Tech (North Bay, ON) www.canadore.on.ca	Communication Arts	3 yrs	Canadore Col Graphic Design Diploma

Col Communautaire du Nouveau Brunswick (Bathurst, NB) www.ccnb.nb.ca	Arts et Culture •Conception Graphique	80 wks	
Col of North Atlantic (St. John's, NF) www.cna.nl.ca	Sch of Applied Arts	2 yrs	Diploma
Conestoga Col Inst of Tech & Adv Learning (Kitchener, ON) www.conestoga.on.ca	Sch of Media & Design	3 yrs	Ont Col Adv Diploma
Dawson Col (Montreal, QC) www.dawsoncollege.qc.ca	Creative & Applied Arts	3 yrs	
Durham Col (Oshawa, ON) www.durhamcollege.ca	Sch of Media, Art & Design	3 yrs	Ont Col Adv Diploma
Fanshawe Col of App Arts and Tech (London, ON) www.fanshawec.ca	Sch of Design	3 yrs	Ont Col Adv Diploma
George Brown Col (Toronto, ON) www.georgebrown.ca	Sch of Design (Major in Advert Design)	3 yrs	Ont Col Adv Diploma
Georgian Col of App Arts and Tech (Barrie, ON) www.georgianc.on.ca	Design & Visual Arts Studies Graphic Design Production Graphic Design	2 yrs 3 yrs	Ont Col Diploma Ont Col Adv Diploma
Holland College (Charlottetown, PE) www.hollandc.pe.ca	Media & Communications	2 yrs	Diploma, Graphic Design
Humber Col Inst of Tech & Adv Learning (Toronto, ON) www.humber.ca	Sch of Media Studies & Info Tech Package & Graphic Design Graphic Design	3 yrs 3 yrs	Adv Diploma Adv Diploma
Kwantlen Polytechnic University (Richmond, BC) www.kwantlen.bc.ca	Applied Design	3 yrs	Diploma In Graphic Design for Marketing
Mohawk Col of App Arts and Tech (Brantford, ON) www.mohawkcollege.ca	Graphic Design Production •Digital •Packaging •Creative •Integrated Media Arts	2 yrs 2 yrs 2 yrs 2 yrs	Ont Col Diploma Ont Col Diploma Ont Col Diploma Ont Col Diploma
New Brunswick Community Col (Miramich, NB) www.nbcc.ca	Business/IT	2 yrs	Diploma
Nova Scotia Community Col (Halifax, NS)	Sch of Applied Arts & New Media	1 yr	Diploma
Red River Col of App Arts, Sci & Tech (Winnipeg, MB) www.rrc.mb.ca	Applied Arts and Communications	2 yrs 3 yrs	Diploma Post Diploma
Sault Col of App Arts and Tech (Sault Ste. Marie, ON)		3 yrs	Ont Col Adv Diploma

Seneca Col of App Arts and Tech (Senaca, ON) www.seneca.on.ca	Sch of Communication Art	3 yrs	Ont Col Adv Diploma
St. Claire Col of App Arts and Tech (Windsor, ON) www.stclairecollege.ca	Centre for the Arts	3 yrs	Ont Col Adv Diploma
St. Lawrence College (Kingston, ON) www.sl.on.ca		3 yrs	Ont Col Adv Diploma
Vancouver Community Col (Vancouver, BC) www.vcc.ca	Centre for Design	9 mos	Certificate: Digital Graphic Design

Table 25-1a: Summary of College and Institute Programs, Curricula in Graphic Design

Province Vignettes

Post-secondary education that focuses on advertising and its companion subjects varies widely from province to province. In the province of Ontario it seems to be almost the coin of the realm, while in other provinces its presence is marginal. Many factors contribute to these differences and have become interwoven within a province over time: the geographic character of a province, the cultural priorities of its citizens, population density, priorities in education, economic thrust, and vitality. A rare fusion of these factors is needed to spark a thriving advertising industry. And typically, that thriving presence casts a geographic ripple effect on demand for advertising education.

This section tours each province and offers a brief summary of the scope and nature of educational opportunities found there that bear on preparation for an advertising career. It's not a census of each institution offering some aspect of ad education, rather a view of the varied approaches to this particular subject within a province. Indeed, some noteworthy institutions may simply have escaped the author's netting efforts.

In most province tours, some universities are included where but one advertising-themed course is offered (in a business, commerce, or marketing program). This is done to document the acknowledgment given in the program to advertising's integral strength to the marketing process. Too, while many of these universities' ad-course presence is slim, often they reference "advertising manager" or "advertising executive" as a career possibility for the program's graduates. That's also true in some provinces' colleges and institutes.

The tour also shows that, more so than advertising, education and training in graphic design is firmly rooted across Canada. Its flexible utility to the business sector, government, education and numerous other sectors opens career doors to students for whom advertising-related doors are more scarce.

The historical context of the birth and evolution of specific programs is elusive. Beyond a general awareness, for example, that "our program began some forty years ago," institutional memory about a program, whether advertising or graphic design, is rare. Faculty who were present at the creation of a program are largely gone.

The province tour moves from the west coast (British Columbia) to the east coast (Newfoundland and Labrador), and then makes a brief companion tour of Canada's territories stretched across the upper northwest. A greatly more elaborated version of this tour is available from the chapter author upon request.

British Columbia

Capilano University
www.capilanou.ca

The Creative Intensives summer program offers seven or 14 week courses focused on art, design or media. Representative offerings include magazine publishing, computer animation and visual effects along with a certificate program course titled Foundations in Illustration and Design.

Thompson Rivers University
www.tru.ca

Through both its undergraduate major and minor programs in marketing, Thompson Rivers offers a course in Integrated Marketing Communication as a business elective.

Kwantlen Polytechnic University
(Centre For Design & Communications: Graphic Design for Marketing (GDMA))
www.kwantlen.ca

Kwantlen's Center for Design & Communication admits students to its GDMA program once a year, in September, following a two-tier selective entry process. Students can opt for either a four-year Bachelor of Applied Design in Graphic Design for Marketing or a three-year Diploma in Graphic Design for Marketing. Field studies and a professional practice mentorship augment an extensive lineup of GDMA courses.

University of the Fraser Valley
www.ufu.ca

Marketing is one of three specialized options available in the Bachelor of Business Administration. Within that option, students select more-focused specialization in ether Professional Selling or Marketing Communications, the latter of which includes course work in advertising, public relations, document design (e.g., training with Adobe's InDesign software), web publishing, and integrated marketing communication.

University of Northern British Columbia
www.unbc.ca

Marketing majors in the School of Business begin their program with an introduction to Canadian Business. The program's upper division includes an elective in Marketing Communication, where advertising and sales promotion are studied both in a communication theory context as well as their utility in marketing strategy decisions. Students earn a Bachelor of Commerce.

Vancouver Island University
www.viu.ca

The Marketing concentration is one of seven programs offered through the Bachelor in Business Administration program. Two course focus on advertising's role in marketing: (1) Marketing Communications, where the integration of marketing tools – advertising, sales promotions, public relations, direct marketing and personal selling – is explored; (2) Advertising and Promotion, structured as a hands-on, campaign experience.

British Columbia Institute of Technology
www.bcit.ca

BCIT offers two programs of potential interest – Marketing Management and Graphic Design.

Marketing Management:

This two-year selective admission program leads to a Diploma in Technology. The first year includes work in statistics, accounting, and economics as well as integrated marketing. The second year of the Marketing Communications option is positioned as a time to acquire job-ready skills with a focus on planning, managing, and executing campaigns.

Graphic Design:

Students interested in the graphics aspect of advertising head for the Design Elements program in the Digital Arts department. The program is offered in partnership with Emily Carr University whose courses are an integral part of the program. A selective admission process involves interviews and portfolio reviews. Design Element students learn creative thinking fundamentals and develop design skills using current technology and software.

University Canada West
www.UCan.ca

University Canada West, a for-profit, private university, offers a five-term Bachelor of Arts in Media and Communications.

College of New Caledonia
www.cnc.bc.ca

College of New Caledonia offers an eleven-month Certificate program in Advanced Professional Communications.

Langara College
www.langara.bc.ca

The School of Management offers a Marketing Management program that includes several courses focused on communications and promotions. Students may work toward a Certificate, a Diploma, or a Bachelor's of Business Administration.

North Island College
www.nic.bc.ca

At its main Comox Valley campus, NIC offers a three-year Advanced Communication Design Diploma that features a rich offering of advanced technology courses.

Camosun College
www.camosun.bc.ca

The Marketing Option in the Business Administration division is a two-year program leading to a Diploma in Business Administration. Included is a course in Marketing Communications focused on planning integrated marketing campaigns.

Douglas College
www.Douglas.bc.ca

The Marketing Management Certificate program includes a comprehensive IMC course dealing with promotional planning from the firm's point of view.

Alberta

University of Alberta

University's Department of Art & Design (*www.ualberta.ca/artdesign*) offers a Bachelor of Design that prepares students for visual communication work in advertising as well as other sectors. The School of Business offers coursework in Marketing Communications and Branding, which can be incorporated in the Bachelor of Design, or pursued separately.

University of Calgary
www.ucalgary.ca

The Haskayne School of Business (*haskayne.ucalgary.ca*) offers a four-year Bachelor of Commerce that includes a Marketing Communications course. An upper division version of this is also offered through Haskayne's Master of Business Administration.

Grant MacEwan University
www.macewan.ca

The Center's School of Communications (*www.macewan.ca/web/pvca/centre/home/index.cfm*), offers a Bachelor of Applied Communications in Professional Writing that, among other things, prepares students to "write winning ad copy." The Bachelor of Applied Communications in Design Studies prepares for careers in print design, corporate identity, logo design, advertising production, and campaign conceptualization.

Mount Royal University
www.mtroyal.ca

A Bachelor of Communication in Information Design intends to create "experts at finding the most effective words, images and media to target a specific audience." The Business Administration department offers both diploma and Bachelor's programs in marketing, each with a strong emphasis on advertising.

Northern Alberta Institute of Technology
www.nait.ca

The Business Administration division offers a two-year diploma Marketing program during the second year of which students may choose to focus on coursework in the Advertising and Promotions Stream.

Southern Alberta Institute of Technology Polytechnic
www.sait.ca

Marketing is one of four majors in SAIT's two-year Business program leading to a diploma in Business Administration. Marketing majors can choose courses in advertising and integrated marketing communications. The Diploma is designed to lead to professional designation in the Canadian Institute of Marketing.

Alberta College of Art + Design
www.acad.ab.ca

The Bachelor of Design program's Visual Communications Design major is a four-year programs with admission based on GPA and portfolio review. In the third year, majors focus either on advertising, graphic design, illustration, or character design. The Advertising Stream is designed to prepare students for careers in the advertising industry as designers, art directors, and creative directors. Many courses in the Graphic Design Stream build insight and skills that are uniquely valuable in the advertising context.

Keyano College
www.keyano.ca

A Business Diploma from the Business Administration and Computer Information Systems department includes a course in advertising fundamentals. Keyano places special emphasis on working with regional industries.

Lethbridge College
www.lethbridgecollege.ab.ca

The two-year Communication Arts Diploma program fuses news reporting and advertising. Students complete a 150-hour industry-based practicum in their area of specialization.

Medicine Hat College
www.mhc.ab.ca

In it's Visual Communications area, Medicine Hat a three-year Bachelor of Applied Arts program and two certificate programs, with core courses in Visual Studies and Graphic Design. Electives are available in marketing, advertising and promotion. Philosophically, Visual Communications hopes to fine art, design and technology to prepare students for the "contemporary design workplace."

Saskatchewan

University of Saskatchewan
(Edwards School of Business)
www.usask.ca

Marketing is a restricted access major (based on cumulative grade average) in the Bachelor of Commerce of the Edwards School of Business. Most Marketing majors select a fourth-year elective course in Integrated Marketing Communications, currently taught by Dr. Barbara Phillips and Dr. David Williams.

Dr. Phillips offers this description of the course: "The focus of the class is on IMC strategy, with an emphasis on advertising; we also cover Sales Promotion and PR. We teach the class as a 'campaigns-type' class where students work on creating an IMC campaign for a local business or not-for-profit group. They take the campaign through objectives, target audience, creative strategy, media strategy, sales promotion strategy and PR strategy. They do not create the final ads, as we do not teach Photoshop or design courses. Although the students only get a brief taste of advertising in this one course, I have had three students over the years open up their own advertising agencies, and several more work in the advertising industry. We place quite a few students with media suppliers." (Barbara J. Phillips, personal communication, August 28, 2009).

Saskatchewan Institute of Applied Science and Technology
www.siast.sk.ca

This is Saskatchewan's primary public institution for skills training and technical education. It works on a First Qualified/First Admitted basis for most of its programs, and employs an eclectic array of modes of instruction including classroom, online, the Saskatchewan Communications Network, and work-based training.

At SIAST's Moose Jaw campus, Business Marketing is offered as a two-year diploma program with second-year, course options that include Professional Selling, Marketing Research, Event Planning and Public Relations, Advertising and Promotion, and Design Concepts.

A two-year Graphic Communications diploma program is offered at SIAST's Regina campus. The program embraces both the artistic and the technical sides, with its website advising prospective students: "... you will develop skills in software applications used in advertising, design and publication. ... [O]ur training program addresses the pressing needs of the industry through strict adherence to the national skills standards set out by the Canadian Printing Industries Sector Council." Students build a creative portfolio as they progress through their courses and participate in a four-week industry work experience at the end of the second year.

Manitoba

University of Manitoba
www.umanitoba.ca

The School of Art offers programs leading to Bachelor degrees, Bachelors Honors degrees and diplomas. The School of Art's Graphic Design program guides students in bridging the connection between the origins of typography and visual messaging and their application in rapidly evolving media platforms. The website notes "[t]opics may include semiotics, Gestalt psychology, digital technology, Web design, visual hierarchy, corporate design, marketing, typography, illustration, and structural explorations. Design that is effective, ethical, and appropriate to the context is a general objective."

University of Winnipeg
www.uwinnepeg.ca

The Business and Administration Department of the Faculty of Business and Economics offers majors one course specifically in advertising. Topics include: "...the role of advertising agencies; the function and benefits of advertising and sales promotion for business and other institutions, including not-for-profits." (Dallas Hull, personal communication, August 21, 2009).

Brandon University
www.brandonu.ca

An Advertising Principles course is offered in the Business Administration program, where a student may pursue a Bachelor of Business Administration, a three- or four-year Bachelor of Arts or a Certificate.

Red River College
www.rrc.mb.ca

A Graphic Design program is targeted to those interested in becoming "a graphic designer for print, electronic media and various advertising in the graphic communications industry." Course work is available in advertising and campaigns. Students can earn a two-year diploma or continue for a third year to earn a post diploma. Due to high demand, admission to any of the two-year diploma majors in the Creative Communications program (Advertising, Broadcast Production, Journalism, Public Relations) (*me.rrc. mb.ca/Catalogue/ProgramInfo.aspx?RegionCode=WPG&ProgCode=CRECF-DP*) is currently limited to Manitoba residents.

Ontario

McMasters University - DeGroote School of Business
www.degroote.mcmaster.ca

The DeGroote School of Business offers undergraduate and MBA programs, with an emphasis on experiential learning. Undergraduates, for example, can choose an 8 to 16 month internship in marketing with such industry leaders as Procter & Gamble and IBM.

The experiential emphasis is evident in the annual Canada's Next Top Ad Exec advertising campaign competition (*www.topadexec.com*), managed by members of the DeGroote Marketing Association student organization. The competition offers strong challenges and great rewards. For example, the winning team in developing a non-traditional media pre-launch campaign for the 2011 Chevrolet Cruze was awarded one of the client automobiles.

Ontario College of Art & Design University
www.ocad.ca

Undergraduate programs leading to Bachelor of Fine Arts or Bachelor of Design are joined with graduate level programs, including an Executive Master of Design in Advertising. This program spans three years as well as the globe. Students are banded into teams that, in addition to course attend six four-day international seminars during two of the three years, meeting in advertising hubs such as New York, Montreal, London and Rio de Janeiro to pitch campaigns to agency professionals. Each summer, for three years, students are in residence in Toronto for a concentrated two-week program.

At the Undergraduate level, advertising is one of twelve undergraduate majors and is structured and taught with a uniting philosophy of "Concept before execution. Strategy before style. Solutions that combine powerful language and compelling imagery."

Queen's University
(School of Business - Bachelor of Commerce)
www.qmac.ca

The School of Business offers a Bachelor of Commerce – a four-year Honours program that boasts one of the "highest entrance standards of any undergraduate program in Canada. *BusinessWeek* has ranked the MBA program #1 among non-US programs, and consistently ranks it among the world's top 25 business programs.

Queen's Commerce Society (*comsoc.queensu.ca*), the undergraduate student government for Queen's commerce students, oversees 14 high-profile conferences and competitions under the direction of numerous student committees, working with "a budget of over a million dollars." The organization and all of its events are entirely student-run. One of the 14 conferences/competitions taps into students' advertising smarts. For the 2010 competition, Unilever prepared a case study for its Sunsilk hair care product. Strategic and tactical decisions – including how to deploy the bulging toolkit of promotion options – were up to student teams. Finalist teams presented to judging panel that included Unilever Canada president Christopher Luxon" (Krewen 2010).

Trent University
www.trentu.ca/businessadmin/courses.php

Through its program leading to a Bachelor of Business Administration, Trent University provides a third year introductory advertising course. John Bishop, who teaches the course, characterizes it as "more of a liberal arts approach to advertising ... we are a program within the liberal arts faculty and try to take a liberal arts look at business; we do not see ourselves as just training students for a career." (John Bishop, personal communication, November 15, 2009).

Wilfrid Laurier University
www.wlu.ca

Laurier's School of Business and Economics offers a concentration in Brand Communication & Management. Developed with support by Canada's Institute of Communication Agencies (ICA) and its agency associates the concentration received a Chair in Brand Communications from the Marketing Communications Educational Trust. (Jani Yates, President ICA, personal communication, August 21, 2009).

Algonquin College
www.algonquincollege.com

The School of Media and Design offers a three-year advertising program with the first two years devoted to foundations in advertising and marketing and the third year providing specialization opportunities and an industry internship. Concepts and skills learned in courses are put to work in the student-run advertising agency, Leg Up.

Centennial College of Applied Arts and Technology
www.centennialcollege.ca

The Centre for Creative Communications houses the School of Communications, Media and Design, the site of programs in Advertising, Design, and Integrated Media in a high-tech learning environment with 300 multimedia workstations. The three-year undergraduate advertising program includes courses in administration and finance, as well as an Introduction to Agency Advertising, Two post-graduate advertising programs are also offered – one in Account Management and one in Media Management.

Representative of the post-graduate programs, students in the Fall 2009 Communication Agency Primer spent an intense seven days developing a campaign to raise relief money for an Asia ravaged by a chain of natural disasters, an effort that earned press in *Marketing* (Lloyd, 2009). In 2010, the school introduced a course in Media Engineering Design Integration embrace the reality of rapid changes in the ways people receive and respond to messages, while advancing delivery systems. Nate Horowitz, Dean, says, "This program is about inventing what's next, engineering with media and combining these two disciplines to create the future of information and entertainment products."

Conestoga
www.conestogac.on.ca

Conestoga offers a trio of advertising-related programs: Advertising, a two-year Ontario College Diploma program; a post-graduate, one year Integrated Marketing Communications program yielding an Ontario Graduate Certificate; and the Graphic Design program, a three-year selective admissions course of study leading to an Ontario College Advanced Diploma. The school boasts a 90%+ record of job placement within six months of graduation.

Durham College
www.durhamcollege.ca

The Media, Art & Design division offers a three-year advertising program. with the final semester devoted to in-field placement. Students progress through a series of courses that ready them for allied areas, such as interactive, sales promotion and media sales, and build an array of skills, ranging from PowerPoint and Excel to digital media production and portfolio development. (Dawn Salter, personal communication, October 29, 2009).

Humber College Institute of Technology & Advanced Learning
www.humber.ca

In 2004, the School of Media Studies & Information Technology launched its four-year Bachelor of Applied Arts, Creative Advertising degree program, described as unique in Canada *(www.mediastudies.humber.ca)*. The curriculum is structured to parallel the industry tradition of writers and designers working in tandem. At the fifth semester, students plan and execute solutions for *bonafide* clients through the program's on-campus agency, Ad Centre; and the seventh semester includes a 14-week paid on-the-job stint, facilitated by the school's networking outreach.

The School also offers three other advertising-centered programs. Two of these are diploma programs running four semesters: Advertising and Graphic Design and Advertising and Media Sales. The first of these develop the student's visual, strategic, conceptual, typographic and computer skills, while the later emphasizes the central importance of media to advertising effectiveness and builds skills in the computer systems used by the media. The third is a two-semester postgraduate program in Advertising Copywriting leading to an Ontario Graduate Certificate; this program accepts graduates from virtually any discipline, and sees itself as preparing writers for entry-level jobs in a diverse range of sectors, from agency to corporate to government.

Mohawk College
www.mohawkcollege.ca

The School of Arts, science & Communication offers a three-year Advanced Diploma program with a broad array of advertising-keyed courses. Students branch off into a creative or business trajectory after their first year with a selective admission on the creative side. A student-run agency adds experience in serving clients. In a decade plus, students have won 15 national Canadian Marketing Association awards. A separate two-year Mohawk program, Graphic Design Production – Integrated Media Arts, readies students for graphic arts careers.

Niagara College of Applied Arts and Technology
www.niagaracollege.ca

The Business Administration--Marketing program provides three courses in advertising, including a third year capstone course where students develop campaigns keyed to the Canadian marketing environment. Students earn an Advanced Diploma (Beth Pett, personal communication, October 28, 2009). A two-year Sales and Marketing program includes the Integrated Marketing Communications course, and earns an Ontario College Diploma.

Seneca College of Applied Arts and Technology
www.seneca.on.ca

Seneca's School of Communication Art is home to a two-year program in Creative Advertising leading to an Ontario College Diploma. The first year emphasizes creative concept development and the writing of persuasive advertising copy. In the second year, students develop campaigns and focus their final semester on a 'stream' in either creative development or business management. Through Seneca's joint program with York University, students can go on to earn a York University Bachelor of Arts degree.

Sheridan College Institute of Technology and Advanced Learning
www.sheridaninstitute.ca

Advertising studies are available in three program levels through the School of Business. A two-year program earns an Advertising Diploma. The enriched three-year program results in an Advertising Advanced Diploma. In both, course offerings incorporate current industry-specific software to assure students' market readiness. An optional unpaid four-week on-site experience in the industry is available to student in either of the programs. The three-year program essentially adds a two-semester capstone course focused on campaigns and teaming advertising students with media arts students to create and produce television commercials. The third advertising program at Sheridan's Business School, leads to a Post Graduate Certificate in Advertising Management. This one-year program is structured as an immersion experience that builds and hones account-based decision making skills across the full spectrum of the advertising process.

Through Sheridan's School of Animation, Arts and Design, students can pursue a Bachelor of Design (Honors) a four-year program is offered jointly with York University. The program prepares students for careers such as graphic design, product design, and digital design accelerates in the students' fourth year. (Peggy Bramwell, personal communication, November 9, 2009).

St. Clair College Centre for the Arts
www.stclaircollege.ca

A three-year advertising program (*www.stclaircollege.ca/programs /postsec/advertising*) prepares students in career areas of Media, World Wide Web and Mobile Marketing, Copywriting, and Design and Production. St. Clair notes its Advertising majors win consistently in competitions of the Advertising Educators Association of Canada, and reports, "Our employment rate six months after graduation is over 90%."

Also offered is a three-year graphic design program leading to an Ontario College Advanced Diploma (*www.stclaircollege.ca/programs/postsec /graphic*). The program emphasizes that designers' creativity must support clients' needs Graduation from this program provides the first step in professional accreditation as a Registered Graphic Designer (Association of Registered Graphic Designers of Ontario).

St. Lawrence College
www.stlawrencecollege.ca

The Advertising-Integrated Marketing Communication program is based in the College's School of Business. The three-year program features training in both creative and media and includes two field placements to assure exposure to a range of IMC applications and business contexts. Students "have excelled in numerous video competitions and are consistent winners at the annual Ontario Colleges' Marketing Competition, where expertise in advertising and marketing is recognized by marketing professionals." St. Clair students have won the competition six times in the last nine years (John Conrad, personal communication, October 28, 2009). Graduates receive an Ontario College Advanced Diploma.

An Advanced Diploma is also available from the three-year Graphic Design program (*www.slcgraphicdesign.ca*). The program addresses work contexts from design studios to advertising agencies to new media production units. Students also build mastery of the most current versions of graphics software including InDesign, Photoshop, Illustrator, DreamWeaver and Flash. The program qualifies graduates for future certification by the Association of Registered Graphic Designers of Ontario.

Québec
HEC Montreal
www.hec.ca

HEC Montreal is an independent business school affiliated with the University of Montreal and offers a Graduate Diploma in Marketing Communication developed in conjunction with the Association of Québec Advertising Agencies. A key architect of the program was Cossette's Patrick Beauduin, Chief Creative Officer the Cossette Agency. Prospective students bring at least one year of experience in the field prior to beginning the 2-year program, which is conducted in French.

McGill University
www.mcgill.ca

The Desautels Faculty of Management offers marketing communication courses at the Bachelors and Masters levels. Its undergraduate course takes a management-by-objectives approach viewing subject matter from a Canadian perspective (Ron Duerksen, personal communications, August 31, 2009, and September 25, 2009).

University of Québec at Montreal
www.faccom.uqam.ca

In 2007, UQAM began offering a BA in Marketing Communication. With instruction available only in French, its focus is on the interdependent tools of marketing communications: research, strategic marketing, advertising, media, public relations, and newly emerging marketing communication platforms.

University of Sherbrooke
Baccalaureate and Masters in Marketing Communications
www.usherbrooke.ca/ssp

A innovative approach to advertising education at Sherbrooke integrates Baccalaureate and Masters into a four-year program in marketing communications. Students alternate periods of coursework with paid internships. The Masters level is capped with an advanced work site experience in the student's area of career specialization. Once again, study is conducted in French.

New Brunswick

Mount Allison University
www.mta.ca/calendar/Commerce.html#d0e9400

Through the Ron Joyce Centre for Business Studies, a B.A. program in Commerce is offered that includes an Integrated Marketing Communication course exploring the promotional mix and familiarizing students with Canadian advertising institutions.

University of New Brunswick
www.unb.ca

At the University of New Brunswick's Fredericton campus, students can study toward a Bachelor of Business Administration. Their program also offers an Integrated Marketing Communications course.

New Brunswick Community College
www.nbcc.ca

The New Brunswick Community College has teaching facilities in six provincial towns. At the Moncton and Saint John locations, a Marketing program is available in the Business Administration division. The two-year, full-time diploma program "teaches students how to create superior advertising strategies, produce award winning advertisements, [and] develop competitive strategies." At NBCC's Miramichi campus, the Graphic Design program welcomes students who're "intrigued with advertising." This two-year, full-time diploma program builds expertise and skills in classic design principles, production, and digital for applications in advertising, web and new media design.

Prince Edward Island

The University of Prince Edward Island

The School of Business Administration recognizes advertising's contribution to marketing by way of an Integrated Marketing Communications course, available to students in their third or fourth year as an option in many of the business programs.

Holland College
www.hollandc.pe.ca

The Business Department at Holland College provides a foundation for an advertising management career in its Marketing & Advertising Management program. Courses in marketing basics are teamed with marketing communications courses. Students study the business of advertising and design, examining its management both on the client side and the agency side, as well as key areas of agency function. The two-year program leads to the diploma credential.

Nova Scotia

Acadia University
www.acadiau.ca

The F.C. Manning School of Business offers a four-year Bachelor of Business Administration Marketing, an element of which is a course in Advertising/Promotion Management

Dalhousie University
(School of Business Administration)
www.dal.ca

The Dalhousie business program stresses a hands-on philosophy via a mandatory commerce co-op component. Consistent with that is a Marketing Communication, where students develop a comprehensive integrated campaign.

Mount Saint Vincent University

Department of Business Administration and Tourism and Hospitality Management offers Certificate, Diploma, and Bachelor of Business Administration programs. The Marketing program includes a course in Advertising Theory and Practice.

Nova Scotia College of Art and Design University
www.nscad.ca

Although the faculty emphasizes a breadth that goes beyond training in software and production methods, students who graduate from the four-year Bachelor of Design program "typically take positions in design firms or agencies as junior designers. Many later advance to become art/creative directors."

St. Francis Xavier University
www.stfx.ca

The Gerald Schwartz School of Business and Information Systems offers a Bachelor of Business Administration with major and honors option in marketing, which includes a course in Marketing Communications.

Nova Scotia Community College
www.nscc.ca

In the School of Applied Arts & New Media, an Allied Communication Arts curriculum begins with a one-year Certificate program introducing students to the fields of graphic design, photography, new media, and video/moving image. This provides a foundation for graphic design program that prepares students to design project from concept to production. The School also offers a two-year Diploma program in Interactive & Motion Graphics program combining graphic design, video, photography, animation, type and sound intended to prepares students for careers in fields ranging from advertising to motion pictures.

The Business Administration unit of the School of Business provides a Marketing Concentration where advertising is included as an integral component, represented by an Integrated Marketing Communications course.

Newfoundland and Labrador
Memorial University of Newfoundland
www.mun.ca

While Memorial doesn't offer a complete program in advertising, its Faculty of Business Administration does offer advertising-keyed courses, two at the undergraduate level and one at the graduate level. The graduate level course, Marketing Communications, helps students to "develop analytical and management skills in planning, executing and evaluating advertising and promotional campaigns" (Katherine Gallagher, personal communication, October 15, 2009).

College of the North Atlantic
www.cna.nl.ca

Graduates earn a diploma (two or three year programs) or a certificate (occupational course). Business diploma programs on several campuses emphasize marketing skills, with advertising preparation through a Marketing Communications course.

At the Prince Philip Drive Campus, a two-year Graphic Design diploma program is offered in the School of Applied Arts. In a recent five-year period, students won 25 design awards in provincial, regional and national competitions.

Private Career Schools

Numerous private career schools exist in Newfoundland and Labrador, which are subject to Department of Education approval and oversight. In addition, appropriate regulatory or licensing groups also participate in review and group approval (Department of Education, 2010).

Academy Canada
www.academycanada.com

This private career school offers a six-semester Multimedia Graphic Design program leading to a Diploma of Technology. Two courses are targeted at students with career interests in advertising design: Psychology of Advertising and Advertising Copywriting Fundamentals.

Keyin College
www.keyin.com

The Business Management program at this private career school runs 88 weeks and earns credit toward degree programs at Cape Breton University. The program includes a course in Graphic Design and one in Advertising.

Canadian Territories

Post-secondary education in the three Territories that span Canada's remote northern reaches differs from the provincial models, and are often structured with an eye to preparing students for transfer to a provincial institution. Three programs in two of the Territories are potentially advertising-related.

In the Northwest Territories, Aurora College (www.auroracollege.nt.ca) offers a Marketing Management course as part of a Business Administration Certificate program. In the Yukon Territory, the Yukon College (*www.yukoncollege.yk.ca*) School of Management, Tourism and Hospitality offers a 30-week Multimedia Communication program. Also in the Yukon, KIAC School of the Visual Arts offers a one-year program at Dawson City that earns a Certificate, but also is intended to prepare for transfer to a degree program in the student's career area, such as graphic design.

At Tour's End

The tour of the provinces shows the nature and scope of post secondary advertising education across Canada. By and large, students eager to prepare themselves for a career in advertising head to a college (community college or vocational institute) where advertising programs are at home. There, they find content-rich two and three year programs, some of which rival most university level ad programs in other countries. Any students who wish a traditional university degree can often take advantage of agreements between their college and a university. As a consequence, ad-centric programs at the university level are more rare.

There is, however, a discernible interest in a university level communications-career portal for students, fueled, in part, by advances in communications technologies. The rapid evolution of these technologies has created a need for the chameleon worker, one who can adapt and switch hats within one job or can transition to a new job. Thus, a new broad based communications education framework, which embraces advertising, has emerged at the university level, notably two related instances.

University of Ontario Institute of Technology
Faculty of Criminology, Justice and Policy Studies
www.criminologyandjustice.uoit.ca

Developing a professional communicator is the goal of an undergraduate degree program launched in the Fall. The four-year program, which leads to a Bachelor of Arts (Honors) degree, partners the academic discipline of communication with wide-ranging professional training. Across the first two years, students complete foundation courses in communications and business. Courses in the third and fourth years move the student toward area specialization. A Marketing and Commerce specialization incorporates advertising, and includes courses in Advertising Management, Marketing Strategy, International Marketing, Consumer Behavior, Sales Management, Recruiting and Selection, Management of Change, Human Resource Planning, Developing Management Skills.

UOIT is a completely "laptop" university: all courses are paperless, inside and outside the classroom. Within the Communications Program, the Intercultural Communication course is delivered via Second Life and SKYPE used in the Globalization and International Communication course for conference calls. A strong emphasis is also being placed on enhancing the school's programs through international partnerships. For example, one with the Chinese University of Hong Kong allows UOIT students to take online courses with UOIT professors while enrolled in comparative Western and Chinese values courses with CUHK faculty. Partnering programs are being arranged with universities in Australia, Austria, Ireland, Morocco, and the United States.[60]

Royal Roads University
www.royalroads.ca

The School of Communication and Culture offers a BA in Professional Communication that weds courses about communication, its social role, contexts which shape it, its effects, with its practice in such work environments of communication professionals as public relations, advertising, marketing, journalism, and corporate, technical, or web-based communication. The program also stresses the importance of critical thinking. The Royal Roads program was designed by Dr. Mari Peepre, who later designed UOIT's program, accounting for a trong similarity in the two.

Industry Advocates of Advertising Education in Canada

Industry support of advertising education is a trans-Canada presence and, in some areas, is extraordinarily energetic. With advertising regarded as a profession where training is a huge plus, if not a must, there is both commitment and enthusiasm to the support from current professionals and from industry organizations. Post-secondary education, primarily at the college and institute level, is valued as the shaper of the new blood that renews and invigorates the industry.

The faculty of most advertising programs forge and nurture close ties to their province's advertising community. For many programs, that close tie is essential to the structure of their professional advertising-training program. An internship or field placement is an integral program cap for them, with some programs structured on a co-op basis.

Important, too, is a program's reputation and credibility with advertising professionals. This compels ongoing outreach by ad program faculty to gauge the pulse of ad professionals' opinions on the content and effectiveness of their program. Many programs' promotional information points to the guiding hand of industry professionals, often as part of regular review of program structure.

Strong professional support gives wings to an array of student competitions and events. From the discrete course, to institution-based mega efforts such as DeGroote's Next Top Ad Exec to agency competitions to na-

---

[60] Special thanks to Dr. Anthony B. Chan, Professor and Founding Associate Dean, for information reported in this section (personal communication, September 5, 2009).

tional competitions, professional support is solid. For the 2009 launch of "Advertising Week," with its Youth Day competition, a collection of agencies welcomed student team members into their agencies for the students' shaping of their campaign. Those agencies were: Agency 59, BBDO, Bensimon Byme, Bos, Cossette, Cundari Group, DDB, Due North Communications, Gray Canada, Leo Burnett, Lowe Roche, Quiller and Blake, Ogilvy & Mather, Publicis, Starcom MediaVest Group, TBWA (Canada's First Advertising Week, 2009). Highlights of some of the efforts to support advertising education are identified below.

Institute of Communication Agencies
www.icacanada.ca

The Toronto-based Institute of Communication Agencies is a strong, enduring industry champion. Founded in 1905, it's an untiring industry force coast-to-coast with a roster of top-tier communications and advertising agencies. Among its Canada-based list of high visibility agencies are Cossette, TAXI and Due North Communications along with such international heavyweights as BBDO, Saatchi & Saatchi, DDB, and Dentsu.

ICA's key role in the 2009 launch of the trans-Canada Advertising Week brought the industry front and center to all Canadians. That 2009 industry 'splash' builds on ICA's year-by-year work to help strengthen its member agencies and, thus, "improve their real and perceived value to clients." Through its CASSIES (Canadian Advertising Success Stories} awards, it draws attention to the strategic and creative prowess of Canada's advertising agencies.

ICA's range of agency (and agency employee) programs is extensive. Its Specialist Programs include the highly respected Accreditation Program for Communications Professionals (CAAP, www.caapcanada.ca). Across its 40-plus-year run, it has been completed by over 50,000 professionals. The two-year program builds expertise in marketing communications for ICA members' junior level staff in account and media, media groups' sales representatives, and advertisers' marketing department staffs. Graduates of the program become a Communications and Advertising Accredited Professional and can use the initials 'CAAP' after their name.

Additional specialist programs include a Certification Program for Print Professionals (CPPP), a Broadcast Commercial Production Course (BCPC), and a Creative Portfolio Design Course (CPDC). ICA's collection of workshops zero in on specific skill gains with units such as Managing Creative Development, Writing that Sells and the Art of the Pitch.

Advertisers seeking a new agency find support in ICA's AgencySearch.ca service: confidential access to ICA's database of member agency profiles.

Masters Certificate in Brand Communications

THE ICA, in concert with York University's Schulich Executive Education Centre (SEEC) and with support and input from industry leaders, structured a curriculum to accelerate the readiness of on-the-rise industry leaders as brand communicators. Program participants are ICA member agency employees with at least a ten-year top performance record in marketing communications.

The program strives to maximize its graduates' ability to be adroit, outside-the-box thinkers who can develop strategic solutions for clients' communication needs. It's positioned as an enrichment investment that's of value in creative and media agency areas as well as account-related management. ICA's comments about the program note, "A person who has completed this certification will be expected to be capable of consistently inspiring and leading the highest caliber of brand and communications business solutions by: . . . Enabling a dynamic change environment that stimulates business results and relationship success."

2010 Advertising Week

In January 2010, the ICA-led Advertising Week was the talk of Canada with highlights throughout the week in Toronto, Montreal, Halifax, Vancouver, Edmonton and Calgary. Following its 2009 debut, ICA teamed again with its member agencies along with a range of communications-centered businesses and organizations to celebrate advertising's role in Canada's economic health and the career-enjoyment of those who practice it. Students again got to rub shoulders with professionals, from industry titans to fledgling professionals who were ad program graduates just months ago.

Cossette
www.cossette.com

The name is legendary in Canadian advertising circles. Its roots reach back across nearly four decades of history rich with success to its founding in 1972. Across Canada today, its presence is strong (Halifax, Montreal, Québec city, Toronto, Vancouver) and stretches out internationally to other cities with agency clout, including New York, Los Angeles, London, and Shanghai. It's evolved beyond the more narrow focus of advertising agency and works now to serve clients as a convergent community force.

It also is a powerhouse force in attracting and shaping the talent needed by the industry. Cossette's new Grow-Op Internship Program confers unique visibility for students with talent as well as the coveted opportunity to be tapped for a Cossette internship. In addition to providing career-boosting opportunities for students, the competition also showcases the effectiveness of advertising education. The announcement of Cossette's 2010 Grow-Op competition states:

> In combination with the AEAC (Advertising Educators Association of Canada) the competition concentrates on attracting the best candidates from advertising focused College/University programs. The core quality required within these individuals is a breadth of understanding with regard to all facets of the advertising industry (print/radio/television/interactive/media/ promotions/PR/DR/copywriting/art direction). A convergent understanding is key.

Students across Ontario who're enrolled in an Advertising or Graphic Design program are eligible to compete. Typically, team members are undergraduate students though graduates with a 4-year degree in any discipline can participate if they're concurrently enrolled in an Advertising or Graphic Design program. Cossette urges teams to focus on the strategic thinking needed to tackle the client's (a Cossette client) communications need and, then, let the tactics flow from those strategies.

Each team bundles its recommendation into a compelling selling plan of 32 pages, a 20-minute presentation delivered by a team of six, capped with a challenging 10-minute question-and-answer exchange. The decision on which team gets the first-place nod is reached by a team of industry judges. For many competing students, more coveted than a win is being selected for an internship with Cossette. Following the competition, Cossette handpicks at least four students from any of the teams to intern with the agency (Mark Smyka, personal communication, January 22, 2010).

The Advertising & Design Club of Canada
www.theadcc.ca

Spanning a half-century plus, the Advertising & Design Club of Canada has long championed the visual quests of advertising and design professionals, both current and hopefuls. Its singular mission, since 1948, has been to encourage excellence in Canadian advertising and design. Founded in Toronto, it's now the nationwide hub for a community of creatives where students of kindred spirit are welcome.

The ADCC supports students in two very practical ways. One is through its annual awards show, Directions. Each year, the competition spotlights the 'absolute best' in the fields of Advertising, Graphic Design,

Editorial Design, and Interactive Media. The same categories are covered in ADCC's national student competition. Historically, the student competition centers on students' efforts keyed to a specified brand or product. The rewards of an ADCC win are heady for students: national visibility by being showcased at the Awards show, in the ADCC Awards Annual, and on ADCC's website gallery. At its 60th anniversary awards show, the ADCC introduced a student-level Best in Show Award, tapping one student as rich in promise and who the industry should keep on its radar. Accompanying the extraordinary career boost was a $1500 cash prize.

The second way the ADCC supports students is through a link on its website where post-secondary programs and courses are highlighted. The site makes no attempt to judge any of the programs: "Here you'll see some programs & courses we've heard about that some people like. Have more suggestions? Tell us." Rather, the listing points to a range of options available to students and aids fuller exploration with click-through access. Mentioned on the list are:

> St. Lawrence College
> Alberta College of Art + Design
> Conestoga College
> International Academy of Design and Technology
> Mohawk College of Applied Art & Technologies
> Sheridan College
> Seneca College/Seneca College@York University
> Centennial College
> Humber College
> Ontario College of Art & Design

Association of Québec Advertising Agencies
www.aapq.ca

The quest for top-tier status in the highly competitive international advertising world is unending. A key mission of the Association of Québec Advertising Agencies, founded in 1988, is to support the quest of its member agencies to produce work that exceeds client expectations. Toward that, AQAA (AAPQ in French) has been a leading partner since 2000 with Québec universities in establishing training programs. Part of that leadership has involved engaging key industry professionals both in program design and in providing ongoing instruction support to insure students' experience is both expert and current. Another key form of leadership is the funding that AQAA provides to support these programs:

- HEC Montreal -- Graduate Diploma in Marketing Communications (DESS CM)

- University of Québec at Montreal Baccalaureate in Communication Marketing

- University of Québec at Montreal Diploma of Higher Studies specializing in Creative

Even though AQAA is a relatively young agency association, its role in Québec is strong thanks to its roughly 60-member roster, who "generate more than 80 % of the advertising agency business in Québec." These member agencies benefit directly from AQAA's role in the development and support of university programs in marketing and communications that create a growing talent pool.

In the HEC Montreal DESS CM program, annual membership renewal in AQAA/AAPQ earns the member agency an $800 discount per student. Also for DESS CM students, AQAA awards $5,000 to the graduate with the highest cumulative average.

The importance of career training in Québec is reflected in the province's training tax allowance. "... (E)mployers can take 2% of an employee's salaries for training and deduct it from company taxes. This is unique to Québec and makes training financially easier." (Jani Yates, personal communication, August 21, 2009.)

Advertising Agency Association of British Columbia
www.aaabc.ca

Ad agencies in British Columbia are supported by the AAABC, a non-profit industry association started in 1975 to enhance its member agencies' stature and opportunities. Part of its mission is also "to support and train young people interested in advertising as a career." For this, it works with the Institute of Communications Agencies (ICA) in their CAAP educational program for professionals. AAABC also provides support to British Columbia Institute of Technology students in the marketing communications program through the BCIT Marketing and Advertising Endowment.

Canadian Marketing Association
www.the-cma.org

From its Toronto headquarters, the Canadian Marketing Association serves a robust industry membership of 800 corporate members. Its national outreach as a nonprofit organization links it to affiliate organizations in Alberta, British Columbia, Québec, Manitoba, and Ontario. Since its founding in 1967, the Canadian Marketing Association has pursued it mission to be an advocate of marketers and to serve as their central hub of connection. A third element of its mission, to provide professional development opportunities, is met, in part, through the CMA Student Awards competition.

For this CMA competition, based on case studies uniquely designed for the competition, students develop plans for either a marketing or a creative campaign. Post-secondary students are eligible to enter the competition who are enrolled in direct marketing or programs where it's part of the program. Entering the competition earns a one-year CMA student membership. For winners, there's a cash award, a subscription to Strategy Magazine (along with a profile in it), and visibility on the CMA website.

Career preparation is also supported by the CMA through a professional course program. Core course offerings in the program are:

Advertising & Media
Customer Insight through Research & Analytics
Direct Marketing
E-Marketing
Integrated Branding
Promotions

On its website, the Canadian Advertising Association describes its Advertising and Media course this way: "The Advertising & Media course is designed for both agencies and clients who want to improve their strategies, planning and creative. Participants will learn how to develop an effective advertising plan that will deliver results and align with the business and marketing objectives of your organization."

With assignments and exams to gauge their mastery of course content, those successfully completing a course are awarded certificates. A student who successfully completes four CMA certificate courses and a CMA math seminar is named a Certified Marketing Specialist. This recognition was established by the CMA as an industry designation for marketing professionals.

Advertising Educator's Association of Canada

The Advertising Educator's Association of Canada was born of a shared goal of several advertising professors to unite in a quest for the best, most effective instructional practices. The year was 1990 and the founding group included faculty from Ontario Colleges with strong advertising programs (Ian Fisher, personal communication, May 25, 2010). Among these, a key figure was Professor George Baumann, a professor of advertising at St.

Clair College, Windsor, Ontario (Len Olszewski, personal communication, January 26, 2010).

AEAC works to help members stay abreast of the ever-changing industry through its affiliation with agencies, related industry suppliers, and industry associations such as the Institute of Communications Agencies. Students benefit from those connections through the annual competition AEAC sponsors where students can test their ability in the competition divisions of Creative and IMC (advertising/business planning). For the 2010 competition, Cossette teamed with AEAC and launched the students' work with a live briefing from one of Cossette's clients (www.cossette.com/grow-op). High motivation to win was created by the prize at stake -- internships for highly promising team members with Cossette (Anthony Kalamut, personal communication, May 26, 2010).

Its active visibility in the industry, particularly in Ontario, makes AEAC a go-to resource and ally for professionals. As it builds its reputation as an authority on advertising education, AEAC strives to be sought out as "the expert in identifying the needs of employers and suggesting ways that colleges can respond to these needs with new curriculum" (Len Olszewski, personal communication, January 26, 2010). Colleges whose members and, by extension, students are active in the AEAC are:

Algonquin College	Loyalist College
Cambrian College	Mohawk College
Centennial College	Seneca College
Durham College	Sheridan College
Georgian College	St. Clair College
Humber College	

Canadian Advertising Museum
www.canadianadvertisingmuseum.com

Work is underway for the creation of the Canadian Advertising Museum to showcase Canada's decades of advertising prowess. The museum's unique value to students, not just advertising but students from a broad swath of academic disciplines, is the essence of the project's mission: "The Canadian Advertising Museum will be a resource to inform, educate and inspire a wide range of individuals with a specific focus on young people and educators."

Canada's history as a country, the history of its economic engine, its cultural odyssey – these educational journeys will be powered by exhibits of Canada's progression of advertising. The plan is to show the best campaigns, share the strategies behind them, and feature the people who created them as well as the campaigns' clients.

With its initial online home, the doors to the Canadian Advertising Museum will be open round the clock. Students nationwide will have equal access to Canada's trove of advertising riches. Steering construction of the Museum is a cadre of passionate advertising professionals with oversight and coordination by Humber College Associate Dean, Toby Fletcher.

Afterword

A Klondike-type rush by students worldwide may not be on tap for Canada's colleges and institutes that offer training for an advertising career. Still, the richness of these training opportunities commands attention and praise. From the mid-60s on, an impressive collection of programs has developed that rivals programs anywhere. The variety in both program structure and courses points to innovative, thoughtful planning that strives to keep pace with industry advances.

These education gems are relatively rare in many provinces. The typical experience is a required or optional advertising course in a business program. Advertising also has a presence, often more robust than in business programs, in graphic design programs. And with graphic design programs more prevalent in many provinces than advertising programs, this field opens the door to an ad career for students with artistic and/or computer ability. To a greater or lesser degree, in one form or another, the conduct of advertising is essential subject matter throughout Canada. Among the provinces, as the vignette tour shows, Ontario is where ad education thrives.

Advertising educators around the globe can benefit their own program by selecting a few stellar Canadian programs and bookmarking each program's website. An occasional visit to a site will show what's new and prompt consideration of its value in updating or revising their own program.

One word summarizes the status of advertising education a decade into the twenty-first century: Outstanding. Not only is advertising education a valued player in career preparation across Canada, it's developed a league of superstar programs that merit staying on all ad educators' radar.

References[61]

ACCC: The Association of Canadian Community Colleges. (2009). Retrieved October 12, 2009, from www.accc.ca/english/index.htm

AUCC: The Association of Universities and Colleges of Canada. (2009). Retrieved October 11, 2009, from www.aucc.ca/index_e.html

Canada. (2009). In Encyclopædia Britannica. Retrieved August 20, 2009, from Encyclopædia Britannica Online: www.britannica.com/EBchecked/topic/91513/Canada

Canada's First Advertising Week to Take Place Jan. 26-30. (January 07, 2009). Retrieved October 10, 2009, from www.PubZone.com

Department of Education (Newfoundland and Labrador). (2010). Private Training Institutions. Retrieved April 26, 2010, from www.ed.gov.nl.ca/edu/postsecondary/privatedir.html

Krewen, Nick. (2010). Winners announced in QMAC Sunsilk Challenge. *Media In Canada, Jan 18, 2010*. Retrieved March 29, 2010 from www.mediaincanada.com/articles/mic/20100118/qmac.html?__b=yes

Lloyd, Jeromy. (2009).Ad students ask for global change. *Marketing, October 30, 2009*. Retrieved February 7, 2010 from quote at www.centennialcollege.ca/thecentre/medianews

Soares, Nuno. (January 30, 2009). "Your ticket in is their ticket out" wins Ad Week Youth Day contest. Retrieved October 10, 2009, from www.mediaincanada.com

World Almanac and Book of Facts. (2007). New York: World Almanac Books. pp. 758 - 759, 841 - 842.

---

[61] Numerous approaches led to the gathering of information for this chapter. In late summer 2009, initial queries were sent to faculty and/or the PR director of each university and university college listed as a member institution by the Association of Universities and Colleges of Canada (AUCC). In the Fall, a query was posted by Association of Canadian Community Colleges (ACCC) to its member institutions. Hundreds of post-secondary institutions' websites were explored examining both the institution's self-positioning and history as well as sublinks of promising programs. Government portals, both at the national and provincial levels, were accessed to acquire general historical information as well as ministry-based information on post-secondary education. Input was also sought from advertising association leaders. Usually, parallel examination of these was made using online resources such as Wikipedia with references therein examined where possible. From all, leads were followed which were sometimes richly rewarding . . . sometimes circuitous . . . and sometimes a wash. Content providers are untiringly diligent in their efforts to keep information current or simply to refresh information, so anticipate content differences in future visits to a program's site compared to what you find here from a Fall 2009 through a Spring 2010 info quest.

United States of America

[Extracted from the book *A Century of Advertising Education (2008)*, and the 2011 edition of *Where Shall I Go to Study Advertising & Public Relations?*]

Billy I. Ross
Texas Tech & Louisiana State Universities, USA

Jef I. Richards
Michigan State University, USA

Advertising Education History in America

Advertising education in America dates from 1893; the first course devoted exclusively to advertising and so titled was offered in 1905 at New York University. That course, "Advertising," was taught by the faculty of the University's School of Commerce, Accounts and Finance.

The first undergraduate advertising course taught in a journalism school was "Advertising and Publishing," taught in 1908 by Charles G. Ross at the School of Journalism of the University of Missouri. The University of Missouri also hired Joseph E. Chasnoff as an instructor in advertising in 1911. He was the first faculty member hired specifically to teach advertising in a four-year educational institution.

The first graduate course in advertising was offered in 1921 by the University of Missouri. Two years later, New York University Graduate School of Business started graduate advertising courses.

Psychologists were among the earliest writers on advertising subjects. Some of the pioneer advertising educators included Walter Dill Scott, Harry L. Hollingworth, and Henry F. Adams.

The earliest advertising teachers' organization was the National Association of Teachers of Advertising, founded in 1915. In 1958, the American Academy of Advertising was formed in Dallas, Texas.

Two advertising student organizations, Alpha Delta Sigma, for men, and Gamma Alpha Chi, for women, were founded at the University of Missouri. In 1972 they became the Academic Division of the American Advertising Federation.

Advertising Education Support Organizations

Of six originally advertising education organizations only three exist today. The National Association of Teachers of Advertising, Alpha Delta Sigma and Gamma Alpha Chi no longer exist as such. The NATA eventually became the American Marketing Association while ADS and GAX were merged into the American Advertising Federation. Today, the three major organizations for advertising education include the American Academy of Advertising, the Advertising Division of the Association for Education in Journalism and Mass Communication, and the Academic Division of the American Advertising Federation.

The American Academy of Advertising (the "Three A's") has become the most forceful publishing voice in advertising education, thanks to the increased support of marketing educators who teach advertising. The Advertising Division of the Association for Education in Journalism and Mass Communication has established *The Journal of Advertising Education,* which encourages more articles about the teaching of advertising.

Trends in Advertising Education

The Ford and Carnegie studies in the late 1950s made major changes in where advertising was to be taught. Even though neither of the studies made mention of advertising per se, their recommendations were directed primarily to the reduction of the number of majors in business schools that tended to be "how to" education.

Prior to the studies, many of the major advertising programs were housed in the marketing program of schools of business. By the 1960s many of the programs were either discontinued or moved across campus to journalism programs. Today, about 90 percent of advertising programs are found in journalism and mass communication programs.

In recent years, one of the biggest changes in advertising education, particularly in JMC programs, has been the merging of advertising and public relations programs into a joint program. And, in turn, many programs renamed the programs to Integrated Marketing Communication or Strategic Communication. And, more recently, there emerged a move by many schools toward what has been titled "Media Convergence."

Institutions Offering Advertising Programs

Nationally, there are 165 schools with advertising programs that are listed in the 2011 edition of *Where Shall I Go to Study Advertising & Public Relations?* The programs are listed in 42 states and the District of Columbia. Texas has the largest number of advertising programs, with 13.

Advertising Programs
The most noticeable change has been from the straight advertising programs to joint advertising/public relations programs. Advertising education programs have continued to increase in journalism schools while decreasing in business schools.

Curriculum
Most schools now offer a very general undergraduate advertising curriculum instead of a specialized curriculum. For many years advertising programs offered courses that prepared graduates for work with media. Today's typical curriculum includes a media course that deals with the analysis of media rather than buying or selling advertising for news media. Many advertising educators point out that the curriculum of the 2000s has placed more emphasis on the "why" aspect of advertising rather that the "how," which was prevalent for many years.

The most required courses in advertising have remained about the same for more than two decades. There have been changes in titles such as creative strategy for courses in copy and layout. Another example is in Media Strategy instead of courses in print and broadcasting.

Graduate Advertising Education
In recent years there has been a major change in the number of schools reporting graduate programs for advertising students. One of the major changes most noted currently is the diversity of programs. Most of the change can be attributed to the decrease in programs in marketing and the increase in journalism and mass communication. Another change that is similar to that in the undergraduate curriculum is the merging of advertising and public relations in integrated marketing communication.

Advertising Students
The number of advertising students has grown in recent years. As early at 2005 there were 26,814. One of the major percent of growth has been the number of doctoral students studying advertising. Student growth patterns have continued in the Southeastern and Southwestern states.

Advertising Graduates
The trend of graduates follows the same pattern as that of schools and students. In 1993, 7774 degrees were awarded to advertising students, while more than 9,000 were awarded in 2005. The largest increase came

from master degrees awarded in 1993 to 406 to 650 in 2005.

Faculty
An interesting trend has been the increase in the number of faculty with advanced degrees. In 1993, there were 462 full-time faculty with an increase in 2005 to 589. The most important trend regarding faculty has been the increase in quality. The teachers today have more education; most have doctoral degrees. They spend more time on research than did their counterparts in the 1960s. They have more academic publications available for their research and writings.

Evaluation and Accreditation for Advertising Programs

Formal evaluation of advertising programs has been discussed for many years and no doubt at some time will come about. Today there is no accreditation specifically for advertising education. Three accrediting agencies accredit schools that have advertising programs and are considered as a part of the whole academic unit under which they may serve. The agency that gives a more thorough examination of the advertising program is the Accrediting Council for Education in Journalism and Mass Communication.

Two agencies that accredit business programs that may have an advertising program include the Association of Collegiate Business Schools and Programs and the American Assembly of Collegiate Business Schools and Programs.

Student Organizations and Competitions

Five national organizations offer advertising student competitions. The one most recognized and used is National Student Advertising Competition (NSAC) sponsored by the American Advertising Federation. AAF's web site bills it as "the premier college advertising competition." AAF also offers a Most Promising Minority Students program that recognizes minority students.

The Leonard J. Raymond Collegiate ECHO Competition is sponsored by the Direct Marketing Association. DMA considers it "The Oscar of direct marketing." The International ANDY Awards Student Competition is sponsored by the Advertising Club of New York. The Award recognizes creativity.

The InterAd Competition is sponsored by the International Advertising Association. The international competition is offered for university students from around the world. The Yellow Pages Publishers' Association sponsors the annual Yellow Pages Student Creative Competition.

The Future

In a 1963 article in *Printers' Ink*, Charles H. Sandage foresaw these advancements for advertising education:

> Leading universities will increasingly establish departments of advertising for the purposes of (1) centering responsibility in planning and administering professional advertising programs, (2) giving students who wish to prepare for an advertising career an academic home on the campus with knowledgeable and sympathetic academic counselors, and (3) bringing together qualified teachers as a team with common purpose.

He was right on each count.

References

Ross, Billy I., and Jef I. Richards (2008). A Century of Advertising Education. Beachwood, OH: American Academy of Advertising.

Ross, Billy I., and Jef I. Richards (2011). Where Shall I Go to Study Advertising and Public Relations? Beachwood, OH: American Academy of Advertising.

Sandage, Charles H., (1963) "Too Little for Advertising's Future," *Printers' Ink*, (June 14), 130.

Williams, Sara Lockwood (1929) *Twenty Years for Journalism*, Columbia. MO: E. W. Stephens Publishing CO, 80.

Advertising Education in Australia

Gayle F. Kerr
Queensland University of Technology,
Brisbane, Australia

David S. Waller
University of Technology Sydney,
Australia

In Australia advertising education has had a strong vocational orientation and is taught at technical colleges and at universities that have a heritage as technical institutions. The courses often maintain close industry ties for internships, guest speakers, and full-time, entry-level employment, and encourage a vocational direction.

For many years the main source of advertising talent in Australia was a combination of expatriates (largely from the U.K. and the U.S.A.) and Australians who entered the business immediately after high school or after a few years of working in a related field. Like most of the early advertising practitioners in the U.S., Australians received their advertising education on the job rather than in the classroom. However, over the past 25 years, this has been changing, with undergraduate and postgraduate degree programs being made available across the country.

This chapter will document the development of advertising education in Australia and discuss the current state of advertising education within the tertiary (higher education) sector.

The Development of Advertising Education

The earliest providers of Advertising education are found as far back as World War I, when advertisers were aware of the need for a standard of educational qualification within the industry. At that time private business schools and correspondence courses, such as I.C.S. (International Correspondence Schools) and the Alexander Hamilton Institute, were the only way to study the principles and techniques of the areas of "Advertising and Salesmanship" (Waller 1995).

Advertising agents began to understand the need to improve the image of the advertising industry and thereby build confidence and credibility within the community. Advertising education then became a major interest of professional associations.

Between 1918 and 1931 there were six conventions of Australasian Advertising Men that aimed to recognize advertising as a profession, and the subsequent need for a training system for new entrants to the industry. In 1920, at the Second Convention, the Federal Education Board was established. Students could study for a certificate (1 year) or Diploma (2 years) in Advertising through the State bodies (Waller 1995). It was felt that these would be of the "same value in the commercial world as those issued by the 'Accountancy Institutes' and ... have at least the same standing and value as a University degree" (VIA 1920).

The subjects studied for the Certificate included Advertisement Construction, Media, English, Printing/inks/paper, Commercial Art & Reproduction Processes, and Salesmanship. For the Diploma the subjects were the Certificate level subjects plus Advanced Advertising Construction and Psychology, Planning a Campaign, Management, Advertising Agents and Service Agents, English, General Business and Organization, and General Information. Although it was not necessary to hold a certificate or diploma to enter the advertising industry, by 1935 155 members of the Advertising Association of Australia (AAA) held diplomas, eight of whom were women (AAANZ, 1935).

Also resulting from at the Second Convention was the establishment of the Advertising Institute of Australia, which later becoming the Advertising Institute of Australasia. The objective of this industry body was for all advertising professionals to undertake a course of study and pass what was then called the "Licentiate Exam," that was virtually a license to practice advertising.

Up until the 1960's, the AIA provided the training and conducted the examination of the licentiate. At this point, it had gathered considerable momentum, and it was decided to look for willing and suitable educational partners to deliver advertising education on a broader scale. Since the 1960s the AIA's course has been integrated as part of the TAFE (Technical and Further Education) system as an "Advanced Diploma of Business – Advertising."

The primary Marketing association, the Australian Marketing Institute, was founded 1933, originally as The Institute of Sales Management. The AMI offered seminar programs, guest speakers, and courses, especially during the 1950s and 1960s, and these programs were usually "American-influenced"

(Ellis 1992).

In the early 1950s the AMI became an examining body for courses using commercial and technical colleges as teaching centers. In 1978 it stopped its examiner role, and instead accredited TAFE and university courses. The original AMI Marketing Certificate included a unit on Advertising in the final year. According to Ellis (1992), the "Advertising syllabus, strongly practitioner-oriented, differs little in its general approach from that of the International Correspondence School courses offered some fifty years before."

After World War II, until the 1980s, a number of Technical Colleges taught advertising. For example, Royal Melbourne Institute of Technology (later RMIT University) offered a Certificate of Advertising in the 1950s taught by the Department of Administrative Studies, which required six vocational/professional units in Advertising (but did not require any Marketing units). Other technical colleges that taught advertising subjects included the South Australian School of Mines (later part of the University of South Australia), Sydney Technical College (later the University of Technology, Sydney), Gordon Institute of Technology – Geelong (Gordon Institute of TAFE), Footscray Technical College (later part of the Victoria University), and Perth Technical College (later part of Central Institute of Technology TAFE).

As for advertising being taught at a university level, the first marketing unit taught in Australia was at the University of Melbourne in 1929. The subject "Marketing" was a second year elective offered by the Faculty of Economics and Commerce, and included "Advertising" as one of the topics (Ellis 1992). A Marketing degree was established at the University of New South Wales with the appointment of John Schneider as the Founding Chair of Marketing in 1965. An early review of the course in 1967 pointed out that the UNSW was heavily orientated to Advertising (Liander 1967).

Australia's first advertising degree program was offered in 1974 by the Queensland University of Technology (Kerr, Waller & Patti 2009). The program was as part of the Bachelor of Business (Communication) taught by the School of Communication. The number of advertising degree programs grew in the 1990s, particularly being taught by Business Schools (Table 27-1).

On average, a new comprehensive advertising degree program was introduced every year from 1990-1997. Five of the seven new program providers had recently transformed into universities from technical colleges in 1987 with the missions of curriculum expansion.

An advertising program was perfectly suited to their needs because of the rapid growth of the advertising industry in the 1980s and a demand for skilled entry-level employees. Furthermore, advertising programs could be housed in many different faculties like Arts or Business. The growth and success of the QUT program was a final reassurance (Patti 2006).

Year Commenced	Degree	Institution
1974	Queensland University of Technology	Bachelor of Business-Communication
1985	Queensland University of Technology	Graduate Diploma in Communication
1990	University of Technology, Sydney	Bachelor of Business
1992	RMIT (Royal Melbourne Institute of Technology) University	Bachelor of Arts-Advertising
1994	Charles Sturt University	Bachelor of Arts-Communication
1994	Canberra University	Bachelor of Arts-Communication
1995	Monash University	Bachelor of Communication
1996	Queensland University of Technology	Master of Business-Communication
1997	Curtin University	Bachelor of Business-Advertising & Mktg
1997	Bond University	Bachelor of Communication

Source: Various sources, including Good Universities Guide, University Bulletins, and interviews

Table 27-1: Early Advertising Degree Programs

Undergraduate Advertising Courses

Advertising is popular as a subject and career choice. As an individual subject, it is taught in all but one of the 38 universities in Australia (Waller 2006). There are 12 universities that offer three-year, full-time undergraduate advertising programs. Nine of these are comprehensive advertising programs, i.e., they include an introductory advertising unit, media planning, copywriting, management and a planning, project or campaigns unit. Bond University is the only private university in this group, and more than half of these universities have evolved from other higher education institutions.

Of the remaining, only two (Monash University and University of Queensland) were founded prior to the creation of the National Unified System in 1987. Looking only at those universities that offer a comprehensive advertising education, two-thirds were former institutes of technology. This attests to the original vocational nature and skills-based orientation of comprehensive advertising programs in Australia. A profile of the universities is found in Table 27-2.

Comprehensive advertising programs are typically taught at universities with a large undergraduate population and, often, inadequate facilities, the legacy of past underfunding. These universities must compete with the more traditional, sandstone universities for government funding, creating a drive for research outputs, sometimes at the expense of teaching quality (Ashenden and Milligan 1997, p. 253).

408

University	Year Est.	Year/ Uni Status	Type	Degree	Major	Comprehensive ad program
Bond University	1989	1989	Private-academic, some applied research	BA BComm	1.Arts-Advertising 2.Communication-Adv.	Yes
Charles Sturt University	1990	1990	Public-vocational, distance, ltd. applied res.	BA(Comm-Adv.) BMediaComm	1.Communication-Adv. 2.Media Communication	Yes
Curtin University of Technology	1967	1987	Public-vocational, significant applied res.	BA(MassComm) BCom	1. Creative Adv. Design 2. Commerce-Adv.	Yes
Edith Cowan University	1902	1991	Public-vocational, distance, ltd. applied res.	BMktAdv&PR BComm	1. Marketing, Adv. & Public Relations 2.Communications–Adv.	Yes
Monash University	1958	1958	Public-academic, vocational, distance, res. emphasis	BBus&Com	Business & Commerce - Mktg. Communication	No
Queensland University of Technology	1882	1988	Public-vocational, applied res. emphasis	BBus BMCom	1. Business-Advertising 2. Mass Comm.-Adv.	Yes
RMIT University	1887	1992	Public-vocational, applied res. emphasis	BComm	Advertising	Yes
University of Canberra	1967	1990	Public-vocational, applied res. emphasis	BAdv& MktgComm	Advertising and Mktg. Communication	Yes
University of Queensland	1909	1909	Public-academic, research emphasis	BBus	Business - Advertising & Public Relations	No
University of Technology Sydney	1965	1988	Public-vocational, applied res.	BA(Comm) BBus	1. Public Communication 2. Advertising and Promotion Mgmt.	Yes
University of Western Sydney	1989	1989	Public-vocational, some applied research	BComm	Communication–Adv.	Yes
University of Wollongong	1951	1975	Public-academic, vocational, research emphasis	BC&MSt	Communication & Media Studies-Advertising and Marketing	No

Table 27-2: Profile of Australian Universities offering Undergraduate Adv. Programs

While the advertising program has a traditional vocational focus, today's incarnation includes strategy as well as skills-based content. Most programs offer an introductory advertising subject, an advertising management or strategy subject, and a research subject. Half of the programs teach the more applied areas of copywriting and media planning. Sometimes the absence of the copywriting unit is a reflection of the program's position in the Business School, where creative subjects are the domain of the Arts or Communication Schools. Only six advertising programs conclude with a capstone campaigns course, although others include an advertising project.

Graduate Advertising Courses

As an individual subject, Advertising is taught at the graduate level in more than half of Australian universities (27 of 38). What it is called varies across institutions, most commonly "Integrated Marketing Communications," followed by "Marketing Communications." Most insist on Marketing as a pre-requisite subject.

Advertising as a graduate program is not offered widely in Australia. Queensland University of Technology (QUT) is one exception. Having demonstrated leadership in undergraduate advertising education, QUT was the first university to offer a comprehensive graduate program in advertising. In 1985, it introduced a Graduate Diploma in Communications and then expanded into three coursework Masters programs (Strategic Advertising, Creative Advertising and IMC), a Masters by Research program and PhD studies in 1996. Other universities, such as RMIT, Charles Sturt, and Bond offer Masters by Research programs that include research subjects and a thesis component, without offering specific graduate advertising courses.

Emerging Trends in Advertising Education

In recent years, a number of trends have emerged to challenge the nature and structure of advertising education in Australia. To assist in understanding these trends, an open-ended questionnaire was sent to the course coordinators of those universities that have a comprehensive advertising major. Six of the nine responded, helping identify and expand upon the emerging trends in advertising education in Australia.

Growth in Student Numbers

Student numbers in advertising subjects in Australia are growing in two ways. First, there is evidence of growth in the number of students studying an undergraduate advertising major. Typically there are around 100 students studying in advertising majors in most Australian universities.

University of Technology-Sydney (UTS), for example, has 95 in its Arts Faculty and Edith Cowan has 120. UTS reports an increase from 18 graduates in 2003 to more than 70 who will graduate in 2010. QUT is the largest, graduating around 200 advertising majors per year. Bond, the only private university, has around 30 advertising majors.

Interest is also growing in advertising as an elective subject. There are 200 students taking the introductory advertising unit at Edith Cowan per semester, and around the same number at QUT. At QUT, in any semester, there also are 250 students taking the undergraduate IMC unit.

At the graduate level, continuing to use QUT as an example, enrolment in the Advertising Management subject is around 100 students per semester. Another 100 per semester study the IMC subject. These come from advertising, marketing, and IMC majors. As an elective or a major, at undergraduate or graduate level, students want to study advertising.

Changes in student profile and attitude

Part of this demand for advertising programs comes from other countries. In Australia, international student numbers have increased in response to the need for universities to seek out additional sources of funding.

Large cohorts from China, Taiwan, India, Thailand, Malaysia, and Europe are attracted by the quality of Australia education, athe proximity to home, and the great beaches. This has changed the student mix in many undergraduate and graduate programs. At QUT, for example, around 85% of the graduate advertising management students are international, and 15% domestic. In the undergraduate program, the reverse would be true with domestic students in the majority.

Anecdotal evidence also suggests significant changes in student attendance and attitude. Time-poor students, particularly domestic, full-time undergraduates, balance their university studies with a part-time job and a social life. The introduction of full-fee paying places also changed student mindset, so that university is a service, not a privilege. One course coordinator said, "Attendance at lectures is becoming more and more difficult for many students as the pressures of life and the requirement in many cases to work to self-fund a university education, means that they simply don't have the time to meet the often staggered class times over a week."

The exception here is the private university, Bond, which has an attendance policy of 80% of all lectures and tutorials. There is also suggestion of sliding literacy standards within the student body. A course coordinator noted, "The internet has created problems of copy-and-paste assignments, while mobile texting has created a new generation of students who use jargon and abbreviated language in their assignments."

Extending Advertising Programs

Advertising programs have become more strategic than technical. Most have pushed the boundaries of traditional advertising majors to create new opportunities for thinking spaces, and new applications of advertising knowledge. For example, UTS has redesigned its advertising major to offer greater connectivity with trans-media and cross-platform communication. New subjects in strategic thinking, strategic branding, digital promotion and ethical and social responsibility have populated elective choices. This is remarkable at a time when many universities are cutting back on electives for cost reasons.

Another course coordinator noted, "In our school context, there is funding to develop and enhance programs. However, we do not have the funding to introduce all the technology into the course that is necessary to place us on the cutting edge. In particular, digital is an area of weakness both in terms of equipment and staff capability to present relevant courses."

Most Australian universities invest intellectual capital in IMC. Often it is a stand-alone subject, which may be an elective or even part of the advertising or marketing program. Sometimes, it is a program in itself. QUT for example, offers a suite of six IMC units as an IMC Second Major. Other universities embed an IMC focus into advertising units. As one course coordinator stated, "All advertising courses offered at our university have an IMC perspective, so a subject like Internet Advertising will always have an offline component, a subject like Brand Image an interactive component."

Academics become octopi

One course coordinator summed up the general feeling about the increase in academic workload: "I used to work long hours when I managed an international advertising agency and I never realized that academia is non-stop work of teaching, research, industry engagement, and service to the university (four areas of promotion)! I am like an octopus juggling various roles in my current position."

Another described the main issue for advertising academics as time: "Time and resources to embrace the snowballing effect of technology and the proliferation of communication channels; time to research and publish; time to maintain and develop critical industry relationships and to network with colleagues nationally and internationally; time to think strategically about the on-going development and future of course and program content that exceeds the expectations of our industry employers; time to actually enjoy what we do."

Sense of academic community

While workload might be an issue, at least we all feel the same way. And at long last the academic community has a voice through the Australia and New Zealand Academic Association (ANZAA). ANZAA was formed in 2007, following a special interest session at the national marketing conference. It has a regular newsletter and website, but perhaps best of all, it has identified who teaches advertising in Australia and New Zealand and their main issues and problems.

One of its major initiatives has been to establish a National Student Competition in 2008. Another was to lobby for a change in ranking for two advertising journals. It has also encouraged a number of research partnerships, as well as an annual dinner. In 2011, it co-hosted the AAA Asia Pacific Conference.

Drawing from the historical data, and considering both the current state and emerging trends, the evolution of advertising education in Australia is shown in Figure 27-1.

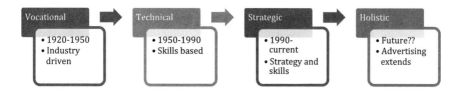

Figure 27-1: Evolution of Advertising Education in Australia

Figure 27-1 documents the evolution from the vocational to the technical to the strategic. It also proposes that advertising education will not stop there. Instead, advertising education will extend into other realms, merging with other disciplines, such as psychology, consumer behavior, etc., and developing into a more holistic communication discipline. Perhaps advertising will be the "everything" that consumers already think it is.

Challenges for the future of Advertising Education in Australia

Kerr, Waller, and Patti (2009) identified six critical issues for advertising education in Australia.

1. What is advertising? – and have we changed as much as the discipline.

2. Funding – international students, off-shore campuses, flexible delivery as surrogates for government funding.

3. Program choices – especially what constitutes an advertising program; how undergraduate and graduate programs are different and how these programs should be delivered.

4. Staffing and workload issues – small pool of qualified staff, low wages and increasing workload.

5. Accreditation – no Australian system of accreditation of advertising programs.

6. Research – university funding and personal promotion tied to research; introduction of national journal ranking scheme.

In asking Australian course coordinators to comment on this list, three priorities emerged. The first was *the need to define what advertising program could be.* This is perhaps very different to what we have traditionally taught or even what we currently teach. It reflects an urgent need to see where the discipline is heading and how we can add value to understanding above and beyond what the industry can provide on-the-job.

The second priority was *the need to understand our students better.* They are quite different to us. Many come from a different cultural background, or from families where English is not the first language. There is also a generational shift to the tech-saavy, information-on-demand, digital natives. How can a university education provide value to someone who can google the information 24/7?

Part of the answer is in inspiring students to think and reason and apply. This is connected with a fundamental drive of many Australian universities to improve generic graduate capabilities, like critical thinking, problem solving, social and ethical understanding and teamwork. While some of this has come from international accreditation requirements such as AACSB and EQUIS, it has also been identified by employers as an on-the-job accelerator.

The third priority is *the need to resource our advertising programs.* Put simply, we need more staff, more money, and fewer things to do. However, given the current climate, this is not likely to happen. Therefore, we need to work smarter, more collaboratively to pool our time and resources to best

414

effect. This spawns research and teaching networks, and the sharing of administration secrets. Of course, all of this cooperation takes time and energy to happen and that is where the problem begins again.

Conclusion

Advertising education is perhaps as complex as advertising itself. Driven by the mandate to educate tomorrow's advertising professionals, it must both keep ahead of the industry and in touch with its needs. In Australia, the educational community has achieved this through evolution, from facilitating the vocational needs, to developing the technical skills, to understanding and implementing the strategic to perhaps a future where advertising education will become more holistic. Ahead, its academics acknowledge a number of key challenges including redefining advertising, understanding the generational and technological shifts within our student population, and resourcing the programs. Time, it would seem, is our most precious and elusive resource.

References

AAANZ (1935) *Advertising Association of Australia and New Zealand Records*, Rare Book and Manuscript Library, National Library of Australia, Canberra (MS1014).

Ashenden D. and S. Milligan (1997). *The Good Universities Guide to Australian Universities*. Western Australia: Ashenden Milligan Publishing.

Ellis, Robert (1992). *"Structural Change in Marketing Education,"* an unpublished paper, Victoria University of Technology, Melbourne.

Kerr, Gayle F., David S. Waller, and Charles Patti (2009). "Advertising Education in Australia: Looking Back to the Future", *Journal of Marketing Education*, 31, 264-274.

Liander, Bertil (ed) (1967). *International Study of Marketing Education.* The International Marketing Federation, Philadelphia, PA.

Patti, Charles (2006). History and Context of Advertising Education in Australia and New Zealand. *Australia New Zealand Marketing Academy Conference (ANZMAC)*, Brisbane, December.

The Good Universities Guide to Australian Universities (2010). Hobsons Australia, Melbourne.

Victoria Institute of Advertising (1920). Report and Recommendations on the Victorian Institute of Advertising Men's Educational Proposals. *Programme of the Second Convention of Advertising Men of Australasia*, Sydney, 1920.

Waller, David S. (2006). Traditional Areas of Study And New Perspectives: An Audit of Current Advertising Education Practice. *Australia New Zealand Marketing Academy Conference (ANZMAC)*, Brisbane, December.

Waller, David S. (1995). Ethics, Education and Self-Regulation: The 1920 Sydney Advertising Convention. *Journal of the Royal Australian Historical Society*, Vol. 81 Part 1, June, 99-107.

Advertising Education in the Philippines[62]

Lulu Rodriguez
Iowa State University, USA

Sela Sar
Iowa State University, USA

According to the *Reader's Digest Asia* (2007), the Philippines ranked third among the seven Asian markets it surveyed in terms of level of support from local consumers. Of the 90 brands that captured the trust of local buyers, 42 were local. Affluent Filipinos were found more supportive of local brands than their counterparts in other Asian countries such as Hong Kong and Singapore, where only 18% of the most trusted brands were home grown.

The preference for the local is more than just an offshoot of nationalistic fervor. The phenomenon is largely a testament to the impact of advertising campaigns that favor the homespun and that resonates with the Filipino culture. Such campaigns are the creative output of advertising practitioners trained to apply concepts that resound with the local ethos.

The emphasis on the local is part of advertising training and curricula that immerse students in a foundation of theory, design and business aspects. In general, advertising programs at the undergraduate level introduce advertising concepts, research, artistic, creative, psychological facets, sales promotional activities, and offers opportunities for the application of advertising principles. This emphasis is on the communicative aspects of the arts. The concentration is on the creative utilization of various media to display Filipino insight.

The common objectives are to help students become more discerning consumers and producers of the media; to develop critical thinkers and ethical communicators; to use practical, innovative experiences and partner-

---

[62] Data for this chapter were gathered through a survey of advertising educators in select programs. Secondary sources of data include published advertising education curricula; listings and descriptions of program objectives, course offerings, and teaching methodologies; vision and mission statements of advertising programs; newspaper articles, journals, graduate theses, books, and government documents.

ships to prepare students for successful communication careers; and to maintain and enhance strong relationships with alumni and community leaders particularly those in the business, government, and the non-profit sectors.

	Institution	Institutional Form of Ownership	Municipality	Program Name	Major
1	Holy Angel Univ.	Private non-sectarian	Angeles City	Bachelor of Arts	Advertising and Public Relations
2	Tarlac State Univ.	State university main campus	City of Tarlac (Capital)	Bachelor of Fine Arts	Advertising
3	Tarlac State Univ.	State university main campus	City of Tarlac (Capital)	Three Year Certificate in Fine Arts	Adv. Design and Illustration
4	Bulacan State Univ.	State university main campus	City of Malolos (Capital)	Bachelor of Fine Arts	Advertising
5	De La Salle Univ.-Dasmariñas	Private sectarian	Dasmariñas	B.S. in Business Administration	Marketing & Adv. Management
6	Manuel S. Enverga Univ. Foundation-Lucena	Private non-sectarian	Lucena City	B.S. in Fine Arts	Advertising
7	Adventist Univ. of the Philippines	Private sectarian	Silang	Associate in Arts	Advertising Arts
8	Univ. of Rizal System-Angono	State university satellite campus	Angono	Bachelor of Fine Arts	Advertising
9	Maryhill College	Private sectarian	Lucena City	Bachelor of Arts	Advertising Management
10	Philippine Cambridge School of Law	Private non-sectarian	Dasmariñas	B.S. in Business Administration	Advertising
11	Batangas State Univ.-Alangilan Campus	State university satellite campus	Batangas City	Bachelor of Science Fine Arts (Advertising)	
12	Aquinas Univ. of Legazpi	Private non-sectarian	Legazpi City	B.S. in Fine Arts	Advertising Arts
13	Central Philippine Univ.	Private sectarian non-stock	Iloilo City	B.S. in Advertising	
14	University of San Agustin	Private non-sectarian	Iloilo City	Bachelor of Fine Arts	Advertising
15	La Consolacion College- Bacolod	Private sectarian	Bacolod City	Bachelor of Fine Arts	Advertising Arts
16	University of Bohol	Private non-sectarian	Tagbilaran City	Bachelor in Fine Arts	Advertising Arts
17	University of San Carlos	Private non-sectarian	Cebu City	Bachelor of Fine Arts	Advertising Arts
18	Philippine Women's College of Davao	Private non-sectarian	Davao City	Bachelor in Fine Arts	Advertising Arts
19	Asia Pacific College	Private non-sectarian	City of Makati	B.S. in Commerce	Marketing and Advertising
20	Asia Pacific College	Private non-sectarian	City of Makati	B.S. in Business Administration	Marketing and Advertising
21	Colegio de San Juan de Letran	Private non-sectarian	Intramuros	B.A. in Advertising	
22	College of the Holy Spirit of Manila	Private non-sectarian	San Miguel	Bachelor of Fine Arts	Advertising
23	College of the Holy Spirit of Manila	Private non-sectarian	San Miguel	Bachelor of Fine Arts	Associate in Advertising

24	Far Eastern University	Private non-sectarian	Sampaloc	Bachelor of Fine Arts	Advertising Arts
25	La Consolacion College Manila	Private sectarian	San Miguel	B.S. in Business Administration	Advertising Management
26	La Consolacion College Manila	Private sectarian	San Miguel	Bachelor of Arts in Mass Communication	Advertising
27	University of Northern Philippines	State university main campus	City of Vigan (Capital)	Bachelor of Fine Arts	Advertising Arts
28	Philippine Women's Univ. System, Manila	Private non-sectarian	Malate	Bachelor of Fine Arts	Advertising
29	Philippine Women's Univ. System, Manila	Private non-sectarian	Malate	Special Advertising Arts Course	
30	Philippine Women's Univ. System, Manila	Private non-sectarian	Malate	Special Advertising Arts Course	
31	St. Scholastica's College	Private sectarian	Malate	B.A. in Mass Communication	Advertising
32	St. Scholastica's College	Private sectarian	Malate	Certificate in Visual Communication/ Advertising Design	
33	De La Salle University	Private sectarian	Malate	B.S. in Commerce	Advertising Management
34	De La Salle University	Private sectarian	Malate	B.S. in Applied Economics and B.S. in Commerce	Advertising Management
35	De La Salle University	Private sectarian	Malate	B.A. in Economics and B.S. in Commerce	Advertising Management
36	De La Salle University	Private sectarian	Malate	B.A. in Behavioral Science and B.S. in Commerce	Advertising Management
37	De La Salle University	Private sectarian	Malate	B.A. in Communication Arts and B.S. in Commerce	Advertising Management
38	De La Salle University	Private sectarian	Malate	B.A in Development Studies and B.S. in Commerce	Advertising Management
39	De La Salle University	Private sectarian	Malate	B.A. in Economics and B.S. in Commerce	Advertising Management
40	De La Salle University	Private sectarian	Malate	B.A. in History and B.S. in Commerce	Advertising Management
41	De La Salle University	Private sectarian	Malate	B.A in Literature and B.S. in Commerce	Advertising Management
42	De La Salle University	Private sectarian	Malate	B.A. in Translation Studies and B.S. in Commerce	Advertising Management
43	De La Salle University	Private sectarian	Malate	B.A. in Int'l. Studies major in American Studies and B.S. in Commerce	Advertising Management
44	De La Salle University	Private sectarian	Malate	B.A. in Int'l. Studies major in Chinese Studies and B.S. in Commerce	Advertising Management
45	De La Salle University	Private sectarian	Malate	B.A. in Int'l. Studies major in European Studies and B.S. in Commerce	Advertising Management

46	De La Salle University	Private sectarian	Malate	B.A. in Int'l. Studies major in Japanese Studies and B.S.in Commerce	Advertising Management
47	De La Salle University	Private sectarian	Malate	B.A. in Organizational Comm. and B.S. in Commerce	Advertising Management
48	De La Salle University	Private sectarian	Malate	B.A. in Philippine Studies major in Filipino in Mass Media and B.S. in Commerce	Advertising Management
49	De La Salle University	Private sectarian	Malate	B.A. in Philosophy and B.S. in Commerce	Advertising Management
50	De La Salle University	Private sectarian	Malate	B.A. in Political Science and B.S. in Commerce	Advertising Management
51	De La Salle University	Private sectarian	Malate	B.A. in Psychology and B.S. in Commerce	Advertising Management
52	Assumption College	Private non-sectarian	City of Makati	Bachelor of Communication	Advertising
53	University of the East, Caloocan	Private non-sectarian	Kalookan City	Bachelor of Fine Arts	Advertising Arts
54	University of Santo Tomas	Private sectarian	Sampaloc	Fine Arts	Advertising Arts
55	Eulogio "Amang" Rodriguez Institute of Science and Tech.	State college main campus	Sampaloc	Bachelor of Fine Arts	Advertising
56	Eulogio "Amang" Rodriguez Institute of Science and Tech.	State college main campus	Sampaloc	Associate in Fine Arts	Advertising
57	St. Paul University, Manila (St. Paul University System)	Private sectarian	Malate	Bachelor of Arts	Advertising
58	Polytechnic University of the Philippines	State university main campus	Santa Mesa	Bachelor in Business Administration	Advertising / Public Relations
59	Polytechnic University of the Philippines	State university main campus	Santa Mesa	Bachelor in Advertising and Public Relations	

Table 28-1. Institutions of higher education in the Philippines that offer advertising and/or advertising-related programs

Advertising Education

As early as 1966, Magsaysay bemoaned the lack of qualified personnel in Philippine advertising. At that time, the Philippine College of Commerce had just offered a full four-year program in advertising in 1963, the first college to do so. Magsaysay lamented the lack of teachers and professional advertising personnel's inability to train new entrants to the job.

In 1982, Javier Calero, chairman and CEO of J. Walter Thompson (Philippines), echoed the same sentiment when he documented the rampant "piracy of qualified personnel" in the advertising industry mainly because of the "lack of trained people" (Concepcion and Yumol, 1989, p. 32). The dearth of skilled manpower was attributed to the late arrival of curricula "that included Marketing Communications as a major subject leading to a bachelor's degree" (p. 32). The paucity in skilled creative personnel, the absence of insights into the Filipino psychology, and poor relationship with clients and the media can be solved, according to the Advertising Board (1989), by offering more Advertising/Marketing Communications especially in state-owned universities.

Today, the Commission on Higher Education, the governing body covering both public and private higher education institutions, as well as degree-granting programs in all tertiary educational institutions in the Philippines, lists 31 colleges and universities that offer 59 advertising programs all over the country (Table 28-1).

Table 28-1 indicates that majority of the advertising programs resides within the Colleges of Fine Arts and offer the Bachelor of Fine Arts degree major in Advertising or Advertising Arts. Graduates of such programs are expected to be skilled in visual presentation, commercial arts techniques and advertising approaches; and to be involved in current technical issues and methods for expressing international trends as well as native traditions and lifestyles.

Another popular home for advertising programs is Journalism and Mass Communication departments, typically lodged within the Colleges of Arts and Sciences. Where before these departments had only three majors (journalism, broadcasting and communication research) one of the most popular majors now is advertising.

Advertising programs can also be found in Communication and Communication Arts departments whose Bachelor of Arts programs typically offer emphasis areas in Advertising and Public Relations. Programs of study that deviate from the norm are rare. Only one institution offers the Bachelor of Arts major in Advertising Management degree and another the Bachelor of Arts in Advertising.

Full-service graduate programs are few and far between. Only one institution offers the Master of Arts in Communication major in Integrated Marketing Communication while another offers both the Master in Marketing Communication and a Master of Science in Marketing. The University of Santo Tomas offers a Master of Science degree in Advertising.

Large advertising programs such as those at De La Salle University, the University of Asia and the Pacific, and Assumption College[63] take in an

---

[63] Assumption College, which offers a holistic advertising program, is an educational institution that caters exclusively to women.

average of 50-60 students per year, with a student body typically composed of 75% females. The University of Santo Tomas, which offers the largest program in the country, enrolls more than 80 students per year. These programs also have an average of 12 full-time faculty members majority of whom hold Master's degrees in advertising, communication, and related disciplines. Many are members of the Philippine Association of Communication Educators Foundation, Inc.

A survey of faculty members of select advertising schools (the University of Santo Tomas, De La Salle University Manila, and University of the Philippines at Diliman, Quezon City), advertising graduates occupying entry-level positions in the top 30 advertising agencies in the country accredited by the Association of Accredited Advertising Agencies of the Philippines (4As-P). Advertising experts from the accounts, creative, and media departments of advertising agencies found the course offerings, program objectives, and program services the three schools offer as moderately measuring up to the requirements of employers despite a wide variance in teaching methodology (Alversado, 2004).

Advertising agency experts also reported two types of skills they require of applicants to entry-level positions: (1) technical skills in computer use, writing, and oral presentation; and (2) behavioral competencies, including "interpersonal skills, resourcefulness, creativity, patience, willingness to learn or be trained, motivation, attention to details, dedication, organization, and flexibility" (Alversado, 2004, p. 92).

Majority of the advertising programs are accredited by the Philippine Association of Colleges and Universities Commission on Accreditation (PACUCOA), a private accrediting agency that gives formal recognition to educational institutions by attesting that their academic programs maintain excellent standards in their operations in the context of their stated aims and objectives. PACUCOA is a member of the Federation of Accrediting Agencies of the Philippines (FAAP).

To be accredited, an educational institution must demonstrate that it satisfies the following requirements:

1. It has formally adopted an appropriate vision and mission;

2. It offers educational programs or curricula consistent with its vision and mission;

3. It has a viable number of students actively pursuing courses at the time of evaluation;

4. It has a charter or legitimate authority to award certificates, diplomas or degrees to each person who has successfully complied with the requirements of an educational program;

5. It has formally designated a chief executive officer or has formally organized and staffed a chief executive office;

6. It has a duly constituted governing board;

7. It has documented its funding base, financial resources and plans for financial development adequate to carry out its stated purposes;

8. It has financial statements that are externally audited on a regular schedule by a certified public accountant or agency;

9. It makes freely available to all interested persons accurate, fair, and substantially complete description of its program, activities and procedures; and

10. It has graduated at least three batches before the evaluation for accredited status (PACUCOA, n.d.).

Employment Opportunities

Traditional career opportunities for advertising graduates are mostly found in the major metropolitan hubs. Those with advertising training are often hired as creative directors, art directors, account managers, advertising artists, graphic artist or designers for the print and television industry, production assistants for advertising agencies, design studios and production companies; marketing assistants, event planners, visual merchandiser artists, and merchandisers for marketing firms, corporate and retail marketing departments and shops, book designers and illustrators for publications and publishing companies, creative and copy writers, and art and advertising teachers.

Those with strategic planning preparation are employed as advertising executives of advertising departments of client companies, advertising agencies, production houses or advertising support service companies, advertising and promotions officers of media companies or as proprietors of their own advertising agencies. They are also easily absorbed in government service and private enterprises as researchers, journalists, publications specialists, personnel managers, human relations supervisors, as well as community and corporate communication officers.

According to the results of a survey of heads of selected advertising programs, over the past five years students most often land jobs as account executives, directors or managers (50%), creative directors (15%), strategic account planners (5%), and media directors (5%). Advertising careers, however, are succumbing to the shrinking job market. Over the past five years, an average of 5,000 mass communication graduates each year compete for a few vacant slots in television and radio stations, newspapers, magazines, advertising agencies and public relations firms.

The problem, according to former economic planning secretary Cielito Habito, is that economic growth is felt only in a few sectors such as finance and telecommunication, which employ only a few thousand people. The Labor Force Survey of 2003-2007 shows that while more than 400,000 students graduate from tertiary educational institutions each year, the number of employed professionals in the Philippines grew by only 31,000 to 1.41 million as of January 2006 from 1.38 million a year earlier (Luo, 2009).

Pioneering Programs

The Philippines boasts of several advertising programs that blaze the trail in advertising education in Asia. The following stand out:

1. In 1999, the *University of Asia and the Pacific* (UA&P) pioneered a five-year program in Integrated Marketing Communication that leads to both a bachelor's and a master's degree. The objective is to equip students with the expertise and skills to design and implement customer-driven marketing and advertising programs through information technology-based promotional tools and competitive marketing strategies.

Its graduates enjoy a high rate of employment after graduation due to the professional residency program that places students in some of the country's major corporations, such as Unilever, Citibank, and in top advertising and communication agencies, including Publicis, Jimenez Basic, Lowe, Ace Saatchi & Saatchi, Starcom, and Arc Worldwide. Many of its alumni now occupy positions where they develop strategies for marketing products and services, spearhead consumer behavior research, and lead in the execution of successful marketing and promotions programs.

This general program is a unique academic plan that allows a student to graduate with a master's degree in five years. The student goes through a three-year liberal education program at the College of Arts and Sciences. The student then seeks admission into the graduate school.

The only program accredited by the International Advertising Association, the UA&P program offers a unique curriculum that combines the fields of marketing, marketing communications (e.g., advertising, public relations, direct marketing, new media), management, and research. It prepares future professionals for a career in cutting edge management communications as they imbibe a holistic and strategic approach to business and brand communications planning that is customer- or audience-focused, data and results-driven, channels-centered, and research-based.

The course offerings include communication, operations management, research, marketing management, advertising agency management, creative strategy, copywriting and public relations. It is the only program in the country that offers finance and accounting as part of the curriculum to complement a strong dosage of communication theory.

The IMC curriculum is divided into three clusters: The first cluster (3rd year) offers introductory courses in communication (business communication and communication theory) and marketing principles. The second cluster (4th year) covers most of the core courses in IMC.

The IMC courses aim to develop an understanding of market segmentation, media selection, marketing communication channels, such as advertising, direct marketing, and public relations, market research and analysis, database management, brand communication management, and global trends in marketing communications. The third cluster (5th year) offers additional courses in IMC, such as financial management, new media message delivery systems, and IMC campaigns.

What sets this curriculum apart is the required fifth year off-campus hands-on training, called the professional residency program, often spent at a major corporation where students work as members of a business unit. Completing this requirement earns the student a Master of the Arts degree with a major in Integrated Marketing Communications. In the fifth year, students are assigned to client organizations or advertising agencies where they work full-time for the entire academic year. Although the hiring of students is not part of the agreement between the sponsoring companies and the university, majority of the students are invited to join the company after graduation.

Similar to a medical residency program, the students are expected to function and perform as legitimate team members. By the time the students start their residency, they have already been through the grind of intensive lectures, discussions, case studies, and projects on IMC, advertising, marketing, public relations, general management, brand management, media strategy and planning, marketing and advertising research, creative strategy, consumer behavior, and database management.

Simultaneous with the residency program, they continue to take a few more courses, such as advanced brand communications management, customer valuation and marketing finance, and IMC campaign development. Each student resident is evaluated by a faculty member through a monthly written report by the resident, an evaluation at the end of each semester by the immediate supervisor-in-charge, an on-site visit by the faculty member assigned, and a final written report by the resident at the end of the program.

2. The Bachelor of Science in Advertising Management at *De La Salle University* is designed for students who intend to pursue a professional career in the advertising-related industry of the Asia-Pacific region. The program of study enhances the managerial, strategic planning, creative and media abilities of students so that they can work in any of the major departments of advertising agencies or within a marketing communications set-up. It aims to supply marketing communications companies, particularly advertising agencies, with a dedicated, properly trained, skilled, and value-oriented advertising professionals who can work in the area of account management, creative, production, media, and marketing services.

The program offers the following core and elective courses typical of many advertising curricula in the country:

Advertising Communication (COMADVE). 3 units[64]. A course that develops the oral communication skills of a would-be advertising executive in situations involving dyadic, small group and public communication interactions. This includes interviewing, presenting advertising proposals to client, negotiating, conducting conferences, and giving speeches on special occasions. The students are required to undergo a company immersion program.

Marketing Management (MARKMAN). 3 units. An in-depth study of the various functions and practices in marketing management from product development, production, pricing, distribution, selling, to various promotional activities. As an application of the principles, the class is grouped into experimental companies that develop new products or services and eventually promote them to specified target markets based on a marketing plan.

Legal Aspects of Advertising and Promotions (LAWADVE) 3. units. A special law subject designed to orient students on the legal aspects of advertising such as intellectual property, trade mark, trade names, sales promotions, and consumer protection.

Principles of Advertising and Marketing Communications (ADPRINS). 3 units. A course that introduces students to the principles and techniques of advertising and related marketing communications activities like sales promotion, public relations, publicity, personal selling, and merchandising. Provides insights into the total marketing communications activities of a client company and the role of the advertising agency in the planning, conceptualization, production and implementation of these activities. A mini-

---

[64] A "unit" is equivalent to a credit in the American educational system.

advertising campaign is produced for experiential learning. Pre-requisite: MARKETI

Advertising, Consumer, and Media Research (ADSERCH). 3 units. Acquaints the student to the methodologies of advertising consumer and media research and its impact on the total development of an advertising campaign plan in particular and the marketing plan in general. Group research projects dealing with consumer and advertising issues are conducted to develop an appreciation of the value of research work in the field of marketing communications. Pre-requisite: ADPRINS

Strategic Planning and Account Management (ADSTRAT). 3 units. Introduces the student to the various strategies and philosophies of developing an advertising campaign or a marketing communications plan. Focuses on the account management function of an advertising agency and the role of the account executive in supervising and advertising campaign. Offers an overview of account and strategic planning. As a requirement, the student prepares an advertising plan covering the facts of the industry or the market, the product, the consumer, sales, advertising and promotional activities. On the basis of the marketing brief, creative and media strategies and tactics are developed and conceptualized into a campaign. Pre-requisite: ADPRINS

Copywriting and Creative Management (ADWRITE). 3 units. Deals with the creative function of the agency with emphasis on copywriting. Exposes the student to the management of the creative department of an advertising agency and the role of the copywriter in the conceptualization of advertising ideas based on strategies. Exercises in tri-media writing are maximized to develop creative abilities in writing for print, radio, and television. Writing for non-traditional media is also explored. Pre-requisite: ADSTRAT

Advertising Visualization and Art Direction (ADVISUA). 3 units. A course that develops visualization, drawing and artistic abilities. Various stages of visualization are discussed and students are allowed to practice drawing skills. Various print ads and television commercials are evaluated in search of the "big idea," the key to an effective advertising campaign. Pre-requisite: ADSTRAT

Print Advertising Production and Management (ADPRINT). 3 units. A production course that deals with the processes and techniques of print advertising from the viewpoints of the print production department of the advertising agency or a print production supplier. A content analysis of print ads currently published by various advertisers is conducted and their strategies evaluated as guidelines in the final print advertising workshop/print campaign presentation. A minimum of 50 hours of practicum is required to complete the course. Pre-requisite: ADWRITE, ADVISUA

Media Planning and Buying (ADMEDIA). 3 units. Focuses on the media function of the advertising agency with emphasis on media planning and buying. Various techniques in planning for various media of mass communication are discussed. The viewpoint of the media sector (i.e., publications, broadcasting companies, and other non-traditional media companies) are investigated for a fuller perspective of the media function. Pre-requisite:

Broadcast Advertising Production and Management (ADBROAD). 3 units. A production course that deals with the process and techniques of broadcast advertising from the viewpoints of the broadcast production department of the advertising agency as well as the production house. A content analysis of radio-television commercials aired by various advertisers is conducted and their strategies evaluated as guidelines in the broadcast advertising workshop/radio-TV campaign presentation. A minimum of 50 hours practicum is required to complete the course. Pre-requisite: ADWRITE, ADVISUA

Advocacy Advertising and Public Relations (ADVOCPR). 3 units. A discussion of the techniques and principles of public relations as a tool of marketing and corporate communications. Advocacy advertising is extensively evaluated as a tool to enhance corporate image and reinforce the role of advertising in the socio-cultural and economic development of the country.

Contemporary Developments in Marketing Communications (ADCONTE). 3 units. A seminar-workshop format to discuss contemporary issues in marketing communications such as telemarketing, advocacy campaigns, account planning, entrepreneurial advertising, advertising ethics, new trends in global advertising and international marketing. Resource speakers on various relevant topics are invited to prepare students for future advertising work. Case studies in marketing communications are likewise deliberated to enhance knowledge of the advertising industry and related fields.

Practicum and Campaign Presentation (ADTICUM). 3 units. A practicum of 300 hours in an advertising agency or an advertising-related industry like production houses, promo agencies, advertising departments of client or media companies. The student develops a full-blown advertising campaign for a particular product, service or idea before a panel of advertising and marketing communications practitioners preferably in a speculative advertising campaign presentation set-up.

Electives
Computer Graphics in Advertising (ADCOMPU). 3 units. A technical course that introduces students to computer graphics in advertising and how computer-generated commercials can convey a creative message. Also orients students to new software developments like storyboarding and presenting ideas using Powerpoint.

Advertising Photography (ADGRAPHY). 3 units. An introduction to black and white and color advertising photography. The intricacies of shooting, developing and printing are discussed via workshops and applications. Animation and cartooning are explored as advertising techniques. A photo exhibit is required.

Direct Response Advertising and Sales Promotion (ADIRECT). 3 units. Acquaints the students with direct marketing communications as a non-traditional tool of advertising. Internal, dealer, and consumer sales promotion activities are also tackled as a means to promote a company's products and services.

3. The Fine Arts curricula at the *University of the East* center on liberal education and studio work linked to the principles of education enhanced by advancements in digital art technology. The curricula offer a specialized field in Advertising Arts whose core courses include the following:

Lettering 1 and 2 (AD. A 111 and AD. A 121). 3 units. A study of the classical and contemporary letters and their application to editorials and advertising layouts. Lecture and studio work.

Mechanical Drawing (AD. A 221). 3 units. Technical drawing with mechanical aids such as T-squares, triangle, drawing instruments, scales. Problems range from sectional, dimensional to more expanded forms and subjects. Lecture and studio work.

Layout 1 (AD. A 212). 3 units. Study of the integration of design theories to the elements of advertising; basic layout procedures and colors. Overview of advertising trends from the conventional to the contemporary. Lecture and studio work. Prerequisite: FA122.

Layout 2 (AD. A 222). 3 units. Continuation of AD. A 212. Advanced study of advertising design for the print media, point-of-sale and promotional materials. Analyses of contemporary trends in advertising copies. Lectures, studio work and research. Prerequisite: AD. A 212.

Illustration 1 (AD. A 213). 3 units. Composition of human, animal and other subjects in various poses and angles from memory. Lecture and studio work. Prerequisite: FA 123.

Illustration 2 (AD. A 223). 3 units. Continuation of Illustration I. Emphasis on advertising production and storyboards. Graphic media in black and white and in color. Lecture and studio work. Prerequisite: AD. A 213.

Cartooning (AD. A 321). 3 units. Developing individual styles in cartooning and caricature for advertising and editorials. Study of comic strips, storyboards and animation for TV and cinema. Lecture and studio work. (3 units)

Design 3: Costume and Fashion Design (AD. A 413). 3 units. A study of the costumes of different races, periods and occasions. Production of designs for contemporary wear. Lecture, studio work and research. Prerequisite: AD. A 213.

Design 4: Textile Design (AD. A 412). 3 units. A study of colors and patterns in creative two-dimensional designs for textile in its various forms. Lecture and studio work.

Design 5: Package Design (AD. A 423). 3 units. Study of packaging design and materials for product containers and sales promotion. Lecture and studio work.

Photography 1 (AD. A 414). 3 units. Study of darkroom techniques, camera operation, negative developing and printing, printing papers and chemicals. Lecture and darkroom work.

Photography 2 (AD. A 424). 3 units. Study of composition, camera angle, lighting, cropping, color printing and mounting, layout for advertising and exhibition, photo essay (photojournalism), visits to photographic laboratories. Lecture and darkroom work. Prerequisite: AD. A414.

Advertising Production (AD. A 416). 3 units. Preparation of advertising materials from conceptualization of designs to final production for various printing processes. Lecture, studio and computer work. Prerequisite: AD. A 222.

Computer-Aided Design 1 (CD 311 A). 3 units. Study and application of computer graphic software for layout, editing, cartooning and other advertising design problems. Lecture and computer work.

Computer-Aided Design 2 (CD 322A). 3 units. Continuation of CD 311 A. Advanced study and application of computer graphic software in 2D animation, webpage design, editing, layout. Prerequisite: CD 311 A.

Workshop (AD. A 425). 6 units. Production of final advertising and editorial art portfolio for graduation. Lecture, studio and computer work. Prerequisite: AD. A 416.

4. Those who graduate with a major in Advertising Design from the *College of the Holy Spirit* are expected to be able to conceptualize and implement advertising concepts in the semi-professional level, show advanced visual skills and conceptual competence both in manual and digital tools and technologies, apply critical and creative thinking skills in forming design solutions, assemble a portfolio of creative works for job search, apply interpersonal skills in dealing with clients in the advertising profession, and use appropriate computer graphic programs in creating advertising designs. The community service component of this program encourage students to teach basic art processes to primary and secondary level students in formal and informal settings, and acquire a clear vision of their role in promoting life values by educating the Filipino consumer.

5. The Bachelor of Arts major in Advertising Arts program at the *Far Eastern University* is a four-year program that trains students to develop their artistic talents in the visual and creative arts, particularly in the field of advertising. Students are trained in graphic art and design, copywriting, branding and identity development, marketing strategies and art direction, among others. A Certificate of Fine Arts Advertising is granted after completion of all prescribed courses until the third year.

6. The Advertising and Public Relations major at the *College of St. Scholastica* provides a foundation for students who will work in a variety of settings. Students are expected to design appropriate messages for specific audiences using a number of media. The interdisciplinary nature of this program reflects the liberal arts focus of the College. The major requires a minimum of 52 credits, including the following 40-credit core: Mass Communication, Intercultural Communication, Computer Graphic Design, Advertising, Public Relations, Mass Media Law and Ethics, Persuasion, Internship, Organizational Behavior, and Introduction to Marketing.

In addition to the core, students must select a concentration in writing or in production and design. The writing concentration requires Newswriting and Reporting, Argumentation, and Feature Writing. The production and design concentration requires Photography I, Publication Design, and either Media Production or Web Design. Graduates are expected to be skilled in creating a variety of messages appropriate for specific audiences in a range of settings and media, creating and evaluating persuasive arguments, and demonstrating a basic understanding of organizations and how advertising and public relations professionals function within them.

Specifically, the program aims to develop the following competencies: mastery of the history, foundations, principles, nature and characteristics of media and communication; critical awareness of and responsiveness to issues related to media and communication; critical awareness of and responsiveness to current and enduring events and issues; advocacy for gender-fairness, ecological harmony, social justice and peace, technical proficiency, resourcefulness and creativity in writing, producing and directing for media and its allied fields, discipline, critical discernment and technical proficiency for media and communication research.

7. The *University of San Carlos'* Department of Fine Arts started with seven faculty members in 1982 with two majors, Advertising Arts and Interior Design. Its program in Advertising Arts is a balance between traditional Fine Arts disciplines and more recent specializations of contemporary advertising design. Students learn from a broad range of skills training—from courses that hone abilities to draw and paint to photography and basic video production. The university also offers an Advertising Certificate.

Training Programs

Colleges and universities with established advertising curricula also offer a number of training and continuing education programs for students and professionals. The more popular ones are as follows:

1. The *Ateneo Center for Continuing Education* and *Blue Blade Technologies, Inc.* jointly offer one-day digital marketing courses called Digital Marketing Made Easy. This program aims to teach marketing and advertising professionals and entrepreneurs how to harness the power of the Inter-

net and mobile technology in reaching and engaging their customers through the most direct and cost-effective strategies.

2. The *College of Saint Benilde at De La Salle University*, in partnership with the Philippine Association of National Advertisers (PANA), offers a post-baccalaureate diploma program in Marketing Communications Management, a series of certificate courses designed to share best practices, update knowledge and enhance the competencies of marketing practitioners. Participants earn a Diploma in Marketing Communications Management upon completion of the required six certificate courses that discuss how to build a brand, public relations and advocacy marketing, relationship marketing, Web advertising and marketing, integrated marketing communications, and market research and media planning.

3. The certificate course in Business and Management at the *Business School of the Harvest Christian School* is designed to equip and train professionals, managers and entrepreneurs with various managerial, leadership and business skills in running and managing enterprises.

4. The *Philippine Marketing Association (PMA)* regularly conducts a series of lectures on "Communicating with Your Customers," designed to help marketing practitioners attain a comprehensive understanding of strategic approaches in advertising. Topics include creative and media planning for advertising campaigns, developing effective sales promotions and public relations strategies, and integrated marketing communication activities.

Other institutions that regularly offer training programs, seminars and symposia are the University of San Carlos, the Institute of Communication at the University of Asia and the Pacific, Assumption College, and the Asian Institute of Management, which specializes in advertising sales promotion and management.

There also are noteworthy agency-based training programs. Among them are:

1. *Lowe Lintas and Partners*, the country's third largest advertising agency, has instituted an in-house training program for its employees, perhaps the first in the industry. Dubbed "Lowe Lintas University (LLU)," the continuing education program offers courses that focus on creatives, accounts, media, and business management. Like a real university, it has two semesters a year, offering six core courses every semester as well as a range of electives. Courses offered include Big Idea Crafting, Accounts Management, Taxation Laws, and Library Science. Classes are held once a week for 12 weeks. Employees shell out nothing except their time and effort.

The faculty roster is composed of the company's senior officers, such as the president and chief executive officer, the chair, and the executive creative director. At LLU, there are also the usual classroom lectures, but laboratory work is given much emphasis. There are no grades. However, the students undergo an evaluation process.

Lowe Lintas has also started a training program for fresh graduates of advertising and marketing. The six-month comprehensive Advertising Training Program (ATP) exposes participants to the "total picture of the advertising business," whether in writing, art direction, strategic account management, brand planning, media planning. Participants undergo inter-department training for two months, and for the rest of the time, they stay where they are going to specialize. There, they handle actual accounts and are asked to design an advertising campaign. Those that pass company standards are hired as regular employees.

2. In its thrust to promote direct marketing as an effective marketing tool and distribution system in the country and to elevate the level of professionalism among industry practitioners, the *Direct Marketing Association of the Philippines (DMAP)* launched in 2004 an annual conference and exhibition that highlight the latest advertising techniques, marketing trends, and directions.

Advertising Competitions and Awards

Professional Level

For the first time in Philippine advertising history, local advertising materials landed top Clio awards in 2002: BBDO Guerrero/Ortega's television commercial for Visa, and Ogilvy & Mather's hotel card key for *The Economist.* Two posters from Ace Saatchi & Saatchi also made it to the short list (Franco-Diyco, 2002).

When a charming campaign with a sprinkling of wisecracks for a mall cafe, an unusual shoe ad that reminded the target to play rather than do house chores on Labor Day, a fabulously art-directed hotel ad, and a print ad that told kids that "bright minds read" won world medals for the Philippines in the 2003 New York Print Advertising Festivals, advertising practitioners seemingly went into an award and international recognition frenzy (Pe, 2003). With a harvest of medals for products ranging from colossal TV productions to very low-budgeted simple print outputs, the quest for more awards continues.

In effect, undergraduate students gear up to be future participants of a host of these local and international advertising competitions at the professional level. On the domestic sphere alone, there are a number of them to prepare for. The more sought-after ones follow:

1. The *Araw Awards* creative competitions are one of the most highly anticipated events of the biennial Philippine Advertising Congress. The awards have become the standard by which Filipino creative excellence in advertising is measured. The judging criteria are 50% creativity, 25% insight or strategy, and 25% results. With the marketing results figuring in the competition, advertising has moved from creative appreciation to effectiveness. Professionals compete for awards in eight categories—film, radio, print, outdoor, ambient and point-of-purchase, digital, direct to consumer, and design.

2. Taking its cues from the American advertising industry's *Effie Awards*, the Marketing Communications Effectiveness Awards (MCEA) are the first of its kind in the country to salute ad campaigns that have given client companies positive financial returns. The winning campaigns are also judged based on their ability to promote excellence and social responsibility without sacrificing creative execution.

The MCEA seeks to promote the practice of accountible marketing communications through analysis and measurement of corporate brand investments and returns. It also recognizes the need to place effectiveness in the context of a campaign's contribution to the promotion of excellence and social responsibility.

The board of judges choose gold, silver, and bronze award winners in six categories: new product, new service, small budget product campaign (below P10 million), small budget service campaign, established product campaign (more than P10 million), and established service campaign. An entry must have used more than one communication channel. That is, the campaign should exhibit a combination of advertising, public relations, customer relationship management, sales promotion, event marketing, and the like to be considered for the awards. The awards are organized by the University of Asia and the Pacific's Institute of Communication, in association with Marketing and Opinion Research Society of the Philippines, and the newspaper *BusinessWorld*.

3. The *Catholic Mass Media Awards* annually selects the best branded outdoor ad, best public service outdoor ad, best public service TV ad, best branded TV ad, best public service radio ad, best public service print ad, and best branded print ad.

4. The Creative Guild chooses the best public service ad of the month for print, radio and television. At the end of the year, these monthly winners automatically become finalists for the *Diwa Ad of the Year Awards*. Began in 1998 with the support of the Ayala Foundation, the Diwa Awards yearly recognizes ads that lift the Filipino spirit by advocating love for country, family, concern for the environment, human life, minority issues, promotion of peace and human rights, civic and social education, philantrophic appeals, respect for law and authority, religious beliefs, and preserving Philippine culture and heritage. It also aims to reward advertising professionals for applying creativity and intellect toward a civic cause.

5. Launched in 1997, the *Ad of the Year Awards* is a project of the 4As-P that gives recognition to member agencies regardless of size or affiliation that have excelled in all areas of advertising. Participating agencies vie for five categories: Best in Creative, Best in Management of Business, Best in Market Performance, Best in Media, and Best in Industry Leadership and Community Leadership.

The advertising professionals and their agencies that often garner the above awards are shown in Table 28-2. That table also lists advertising educators and other advertising personalities often cited in news reports.

Name	Position / affiliation
Mercy Abad	President and general manager, NFO Trends
Jessica Abaya	Senior vice-president and head of marketing, Philamlife; leads the company's initiatives on customer value management, target segmentation, customer and market research, corporate advertising and communications, brand equity building, product strategy development and marketing services.
Emily A. Abrera	Chairperson, McCann World Group Asia-Pacific; branded an "industry maverick" by the 4As-P
Patricia N. Arches	President and chief executive officer, McCann Worldgroup Philippines
Tom Bangis	President, AB Communications
Roger Buhay	Professor of marketing communications, University of Santo Tomas
Ichay Bulaong	Co-founder and managing director, First Direct-Leo Burnett and Arc Worldwide
Javier J. Calero	Chairman and chief executive officer, J. Walter Thompson; chairman, Integrated Marketing Communications Effectiveness Awards (IMCEA) Advisory Board; chairman, Full Circle Communications
Ma. Milagros Formoso Camahort	President, Direct Image Dimensions
Raul Castro	Executive creative director, Lowe Lintas; McCann Erickson Worldgroup
Rosie Chew	Acknowledged "godmother" of market research
Susan Dimacali	Chairperson, DDB Cares, the corporate social responsibility arm of the DDB group in the Philippines
Micky Domingo	Vice president and executive creative director, McCann Erickson Philippines
Jose Faustino	Recipient, Agora Award for outstanding achievement in marketing education, 2006, from the Philippine Marketing Association
David Ferrer	Creative director, JWT Philippines; former creative director, BBDO
Tere Filipinia	President, Basic Advertising
Greg Garcia	Founder and former chairman, Hemisphere-Leo Burnett
Willie Garcia	Chairman, Adformatix and president, International Communicators Agency Network, Inc., a global network of independent advertising and marketing communications agencies
Go Gatchalian	President and CEO, Campaigns & Grey advertising agency

Peter Garrucho	Recipient, Agora Award for outstanding achievement in marketing education, 2006, from the Philippine Marketing Association
David Guerrero	Chairman and executive director, BBDO/Guerrero-Ortega; chair, the Araw Awards creative competitions
Mariles Gustilo	President and chief executive officer, Lowe Lintas
Ernie Hernandez	President, Well Advertising
Merlee Jayme	Vice president and executive creative director, Ace Saatchi & Saatchi; former creative director, DM9 Jayme/Syfu
Abby Jimenez	Founder, Jimenez D'Arcy; immediate past chairman, Publicis JimenezBasic
Mon Jimenez	Joint CEO, JimenezBasic
Jerry Kliatchko	Vice president for corporate communications and executive director, Institute of Communication, University of Asia & the Pacific
Robert Labayen	Managing partner, J. Walter Thompson; past president, Creative Guild
Chiqui Lara	President, Young & Rubicam Philippines
Tommy B. Lopez Jr.	Recipient, Agora Award for outstanding achievement in marketing education, 2006, from the Philippine Marketing Association; professor, Asian Institute of Management (AIM); considered AIM's "guru of services marketing"
Melvin Mangada	Managing partner and executive creative director, TBWA Santiago Mangada Puno; past president, Creative Guild; executive creative director, Ace Saatchi & Saatchi
Louie Morales	Founder, Image Dimensions
Venus Navalta	Senior vice-president and managing director, Universal McCann Erickson
Herminio G. Ordonez	Chief executive officer, Publicis Manila; co-founder, Basic Advertising; chairman emeritus, Publicis JimenezBasic
Jose Ortega	Managing partner, BBDO Guerrero Ortega; former chairman, J. Walter Thompson
Ramon Osorio	Professor of advertising; former president and CEO, Campaigns and Grey
Roger Pe	Executive creative director, DDB Phils.
Socky Pitarque	Past president, Creative Guild
Jaime Puno	Managing partner, TBWA Santiago Mangada Puno; past chairman, president and CEO, Dentsu Young & Rubicam-Alcantara
Marlon Rivera	President and executive creative director, Publicis Manila, Inc.
Eduardo L. Roberto	Research director, Basic Advertising; professor, Asian Institute of Management; recipient, Agora Award for outstanding achievement in marketing education, 2006, from the Philippine Marketing Association; author, two marketing research books and two social marketing books
Jimmy Santiago	Past president, Creative Guild
Dickie Soriano	Managing director, OgilyOne, the direct marketing company of Ogilvy & Mather; founder and president, BCD Pinpoint
Pedro Teodoro, Sr.	One of the founding fathers, 4As-P
Francis Trillana	Chairman, Lowe Lintas
Matec Villanueva	Chairman & CEO, Publicis Manila, Inc.
Ma. Yolanda Villanueva-Ong	Awardee, Ten Outstanding Women in the Nation's Service; founder and chief executive officer, Campaigns & Grey; founding president, Creative Guild of the Philippines; the first female president, 4As-P; gold awardee, Philippine Advertising Congress; first Filipino judge, Clio Awards
Bernardo Villegas	University professor, University of Asia and the Pacific

Table 28-2: Advertising people in the news and those who play a
role in raising the standards and quality of advertising in the country

Student Level

To expose students to the advertising world, professional organizations have launched several coveted student awards. Among them are as follows:

1. Dubbed the "the Junior Olympics" of Philippine advertising, the *Marketing Communications Awards* sponsored by the Philippine Association of National Advertisers (PANA) aims to recognize and reward excellence among competing student groups representing the Department of Education, Culture and Sports, and the Commission on Higher Education Level 3 colleges, universities and state universities. In this competition, young marketing students pitch ideas to some of the country's top advertising executives.

Conducted initially in the National Capital Region, it is envisioned to eventually become a nationwide competition. The contest provides students the opportunity to showcase their marketing skills, particularly in developing strategies that highlight the synergies of integrated marketing communications.

2. Universities and colleges also field entries to the United Kingdom-based *D&AD Awards*. The group, a nonprofit organization that supports and funds training and education for those working in and studying toward creative professions, solicits nominations for the following categories: 3D design, ambient media, print and editorials, broadcast, integrated media, branding, digital media, and the direct sector.

3. The *Student Catholic Mass Media Awards (SCMMA)* for the best student-produced print and TV ads have always received the support of the Department of Education and Culture and the Commission on Higher Education. Each year, entries are received not only from schools within the national capital region, but as far as Central Luzon, the Visayas and Mindanao.

Advertising Organizations

The results of a survey of advertising professors and instructors indicate that educators see advertising agencies and advertising business people as contributing substantially to the content of the advertising curriculum. These professionals also readily offer their service as judges or consultants of advertising competitions and awards.

They are less active, however, in offering scholarships, assistantships and other forms of financial support to students, facilities improvement and other program initiatives. Advertising agencies and advertising business people are typically members of a number of institutions that constitute the Advertising Board of the Philippines (AdBoard).[65]

The AdBoard is a governing body composed of representatives of national organizations involved in advertising practice who have banded together to promote the development of the advertising industry through self-regulation in harmony with industry goals. The AdBoard, in effect, is the umbrella organization of the advertising industry.

The sectoral members of the AdBoard are PANA, 4As-P, the Print Media Organization (PriMO), the Independent Block Timers Association of the Philippines (IBA), the Outdoor Advertising Association of the Philippines, the Cinema Advertising Association of the Philippines (CAAP), the Advertising Suppliers Association of the Philippines (ASAP), and the Marketing and Opinion Research Society of the Philippines (MORES).

The AdBoard, formerly called the "Philippine Board of Advertising," has adopted a code of ethics in 1973 originally drawn up by representatives of the member associations in consultation with the Bureau of Standards for Mass Media. In addition, the AdBoard is guided by the Advertising Content Regulation Manual of Procedures, and the Standards of Trade Practices and Conduct Manuals, that serve to keep advertising within correct, ethical, and wholesome bounds, and to assure professional advertising practice. The Code and Manuals is subject to periodic revisions even as the practices it covers are constantly reviewed and refined.

With respect to education, the AdBoard helps build a reservoir of advertising talent by cooperating with the nation's schools, colleges and universities, and other allied institutions or associations. The AdBoard also holds forums, workshops and seminars on advertising and related arts and sciences. It also encourages the study of the theory and practice of advertising, the improvement of techniques, and serves as a center of information on advertising matters in cooperation with allied institutions and associations.

As a sectoral member of the AdBoard, PANA, launched banner programs designed to prepare current as well as future practitioners in meeting the challenges of the new markets. The first is the post-baccalaureate diploma course in Marketing Communications that the association, through its Education and Research Committee, is undertaking with *De La Salle University's College of St. Benilde*. The course is part of a continuing educa-

---

[65] The AdBoard is a member of the Asian Federation of Advertising Associations (AFAA).

tion program open to all advertising practitioners as well as those interested in pursuing a career in promotions and its related disciplines.

The second is the Marketing Excellence Awards, a school-based initiative designed to introduce the concept and applications of integrated marketing communications among students through inter-school competition. The objective is to provide a more in-depth experience as well as appreciation of marketing communications even before students leave formal education.

The *Tinta Awards* is given by another AdBoard member, the United Print Media Group (UPMG). The awards aim to encourage creativity and excellence in print advertising. UPMG offers experts from the advertising and print media the opportunity to promote themselves by showing their best and most creative work in this unique press awards event.

Another AdBoard sectoral member, the 4As-P, offers the highly coveted "Agency of the Year" award given to the agency which fielded entries in and garnered the highest points in five categories: Best in Creative, Best in Market Performance, Best in Media, Best in Business Management and Best in Industry Leadership and Community Service. The aim of 4As-P is to uphold understanding and cooperation among the agencies in the advertising sector and to encourage acceptable business practices to protect the industry and the consuming public.

The Creative Guild of the Philippines was founded in 1984 to promote Filipino creativity. Since then, it has awarded the best work in advertising and related industries on an annual basis. The Kidlat awards the Guild sponsors are among the most sought-after in the industry. The awards offer opportunity for creative leaders to review the year's best work, network, and learn from the leading professionals in the Asian region.

Advertising Environment

Based exclusively on revenues, the 4As-P has listed the top 35 advertising agencies in the Philippines. These are likely to be multinational companies with local partnerships. These agencies and the revenues they generated, based on 2001 figures, are shown in Table 28-3.[66]

---

[66] Agencies that generate more than P100 million in yearly revenues are considered large scale. Medium scale agencies generate P50M to P100M; those that earn P1 million to P5 million are considered small scale.

Rank	Advertising agency	Revenues (in million pesos)[1]
1	McCann Erickson Philippines	546.584
2	Jimenez-Basic Advertising	418.251
3	Lowe, Inc.	273.251
4	J. Walter Thompson Philippines	252.230
5	Ace-Saatchi and Saatchi	239.310
6	Leo Burnett	201.495
7	Campaigns & Grey	175.054
8	DY&R-Alcantara	145.927
9	Ogilvy and Mather Philippines	133.618
10	DDB Philippines	115.206
11	BBDO-Guerrero Ortega	96.763
12	Adformatix, Inc.	82.121
13	FCB Manila	77.372
14	Image Dimensions	76.850
15	J. Romero & Associates	56.206
16	AB Communications	53.470
17	ASPAC Advertising	40.876
18	PAC-COMM	29.050
19	One Manila	17.597
20	MGM Advertising	15.730
21	Avellana & Associates/Avia	10.206
22	The New Thinkers	9.846
23	Great Wall Advertising	7.804
24	World Impact Communications	7.736
25	Resource Ads	7.144
26	Tactica Ads	7.107
27	PLW, Inc.	6.422
28	Competitivedge, Inc.	6.194
29	Manprom, Inc.	3.986
30	Telenetwork Advertising Center	3.402
31	Admix Inc	1.105
32	Gallardo & Associates	Not available
33	PC&V Communications, Inc.	Not available
34	TBWA Santiago Mangada Puno	Not available
35	Dentsu Philippines	Not available

Source: *The Association of Accredited Advertising Agencies-Philippines, 2001.*
[1] *In 2001, 1 US dollar=51.002 Philippine pesos (PhP).*

Table 28-3. The top 35 advertising agencies in
the Philippines, based on 2000-2001 revenues

The Association of Accredited Advertising Agencies-Philippines also lists the following top 25 advertisers for 2007. In the list below, the ones in bold are local companies:

1. San Miguel Corp.
2. Philippine Long Distance Telephone Co.
3. Unilever, Inc.
4. Procter & Gamble Philippines

5. Jollibee Foods, Inc.
6. McGeorge Food Industries/McDonald's Philippines
7. Coca-Cola Export
8. Colgate-Palmolive Philippines
9. Nestle Philippines, Inc.
10. Globe Telecom, Inc.
11. Johnson & Johnson Philippines
12. Del Monte Philippines
13. Pilipinas Shell Petroleum Corp.
14. Pfizer, Inc.
15. Ayala Land, Inc.
16. Wyeth Philippines, Inc.
17. Pepsi-Cola Products Philippines, Inc.
18. Universal-Robina Corp.
19. Bristol-Myers Squibb Philippines, Inc./Mead-Johnson
20. Bayer Philippines
21. Kraft Foods Philippines, Inc.
22. Kimberly-Clark Philippines, Inc.
23. Toyota Motors Philippines, Inc.
24. California Manufacturing Co.
25. White Hall Pharmaceutical Philippines

As a final note, the people who play, or have played, major roles in elevating the level of advertising in the Philippines are many. Many of those who have made such a mark are listed in Table 28-4, though it certainly is not an exhaustive list.

Name	Position / affiliation
Mercy Abad	President and general manager, NFO Trends
Jessica Abaya	Senior vice-president and head of marketing, Philamlife; leads the company's initiatives on customer value management, target segmentation, customer and market research, corporate advertising and communications, brand equity building, product strategy development and marketing services.
Emily A. Abrera	Chairperson, McCann World Group Asia-Pacific; branded an "industry maverick" by the 4As-P
Patricia N. Arches	President and chief executive officer, McCann Worldgroup Philippines
Tom Bangis	President, AB Communications
Roger Buhay	Professor of marketing communications, University of Santo Tomas
Ichay Bulaong	Co-founder and managing director, First Direct-Leo Burnett and Arc Worldwide
Javier J. Calero	Chairman and chief executive officer, J. Walter Thompson; chairman, Integrated Marketing Communications Effectiveness Awards (IMCEA) Advisory Board; chairman, Full Circle Communications
Ma. Milagros Formoso Camahort	President, Direct Image Dimensions
Raul Castro	Executive creative director, Lowe Lintas; McCann Erickson Worldgroup
Rosie Chew	Acknowledged "godmother" of market research
Susan Dimacali	Chairperson, DDB Cares, the corporate social responsibility arm of the DDB group in the Philippines
Micky Domingo	Vice president and executive creative director, McCann Erickson Philippines
Jose Faustino	Recipient, Agora Award for outstanding achievement in marketing education, 2006, from the Philippine Marketing Association

David Ferrer	Creative director, JWT Philippines; former creative director, BBDO
Tere Filipinia	President, Basic Advertising
Greg Garcia	Founder and former chairman, Hemisphere-Leo Burnett
Willie Garcia	Chairman, Adformatix and president, International Communicators Agency Network, Inc., a global network of independent advertising and marketing communications agencies
Go Gatchalian	President and CEO, Campaigns & Grey advertising agency
Peter Garrucho	Recipient, Agora Award for outstanding achievement in marketing education, 2006, from the Philippine Marketing Association
David Guerrero	Chairman and executive director, BBDO/Guerrero-Ortega; chair, the Araw Awards creative competitions
Mariles Gustilo	President and chief executive officer, Lowe Lintas
Ernie Hernandez	President, Well Advertising
Merlee Jayme	Vice president and executive creative director, Ace Saatchi & Saatchi; former creative director, DM9 Jayme/Syfu
Abby Jimenez	Founder, Jimenez D'Arcy; immediate past chairman, Publicis JimenezBasic
Mon Jimenez	Joint CEO, JimenezBasic
Jerry Kliatchko	Vice president for corporate communications and executive director, Institute of Communication, University of Asia & the Pacific
Robert Labayen	Managing partner, J. Walter Thompson; past president, Creative Guild
Chiqui Lara	President, Young & Rubicam Philippines
Tommy B. Lopez Jr.	Recipient, Agora Award for outstanding achievement in marketing education, 2006, from the Philippine Marketing Association; professor, Asian Institute of Management (AIM); considered AIM's "guru of services marketing"
Melvin Mangada	Managing partner and executive creative director, TBWA Santiago Mangada Puno; past president, Creative Guild; executive creative director, Ace Saatchi & Saatchi
Louie Morales	Founder, Image Dimensions
Venus Navalta	Senior vice-president and managing director, Universal McCann Erickson
Herminio G. Ordonez	Chief executive officer, Publicis Manila; co-founder, Basic Advertising; chairman emeritus, Publicis JimenezBasic
Jose Ortega	Managing partner, BBDO Guerrero Ortega; former chairman, J. Walter Thompson
Ramon Osorio	Professor of advertising; former president and CEO, Campaigns and Grey
Roger Pe	Executive creative director, DDB Phils.
Socky Pitarque	Past president, Creative Guild
Jaime Puno	Managing partner, TBWA Santiago Mangada Puno; past chairman, president and CEO, Dentsu Young & Rubicam-Alcantara
Marlon Rivera	President and executive creative director, Publicis Manila, Inc.
Eduardo L. Roberto	Research director, Basic Advertising; professor, Asian Institute of Management; recipient, Agora Award for outstanding achievement in marketing education, 2006, from the Philippine Marketing Association; author, two marketing research books and two social marketing books
Jimmy Santiago	Past president, Creative Guild
Dickie Soriano	Managing director, OgilyOne, the direct marketing company of Ogilvy & Mather; founder and president, BCD Pinpoint
Pedro Teodoro, Sr.	One of the founding fathers, 4As-P
Francis Trillana	Chairman, Lowe Lintas
Matec Villanueva	Chairman & CEO, Publicis Manila, Inc.
Ma. Yolanda Villanueva-Ong	Awardee, Ten Outstanding Women in the Nation's Service; founder and chief executive officer, Campaigns & Grey; founding president, Creative Guild of the Philippines; the first female president, 4As-P; gold awardee, Philippine Advertising Congress; first Filipino judge, Clio Awards
Bernardo Villegas	University professor, University of Asia and the Pacific

Table 28-4. Advertising people in the news and those who play a role in raising the standards and quality of advertising in the country

441

The Future

Many have observed that Philippine advertising still falls short of international standards in production quality and detail. As they compete in international venues, Philippine advertisers are well aware of the need to achieve world-class production standards.

Indeed, as Alversado (2004) suggests, course offerings and program objectives can stand rigid review to be more directed toward innovative learning and to align intended outcomes with contemporary advertising practices and concepts. In particular, he suggests a re-direction of pedagogy to incorporate more case analyses, projects and classroom presentations, exposure trips and other off-campus activities, and student participation in competitions to supplemental classroom instruction. He also recommends stronger program services by offering more workshops, seminars and symposia, internships, and the provision of more placement services.

What Philippine advertising lacks in technical quality, however, is compensated by a strong national consciousness and the desire to create persuasive messages that are uniquely Filipino. This becomes crucial as the advertising industry is now being summoned to apply its creative and media resources to create awareness for such issues as environmental health, voter education, values formation, women's and children's rights, among others. These attributes also come in handy especially after the global economic meltdown when the industry's focus is on helping clients improve their brands' performance and power their turnaround in the market.

References

Alversado, F. L. (2004). An appraisal of curriculum relevance and receptiveness of selected schools offering advertising programs in relation to the needs of local advertising agencies. Unpublished master's thesis. University of Santo Tomas, Manila, Philippines.

BusinessWorld (1987, Nov. 23). Admen express industry views, p. 2.

BusinessWorld (2009, Aug. 27). ARAW accepts entries, p. S2/6.

BusinessWorld (2005, Mar. 11). AdBoard: Going beyond advertising, p. 27.

BusinessWorld (2001, Sept. 28). Special feature, p. 17.

BusinessWorld (2000, Oct. 11). Briefs: Communication awards.

Catholic Mass Media Awards (2004). Retrieved June 3, 2010, from http://www.cmmafoundation.org/cmma_files/cmma2004winners.pdf.

Commission on Higher Education (CHED), Republic of the Philippines (2009). Directory of Higher Education Institutions and Programs as of November 11, 2009. Retrieved Feb. 2, 2010, from http://www.ched.gov.ph/hei_dir/index.html.

Concepcion, A. V., & N. Yumol (1989). *Profile of the Philippine advertising industry.* Manila: Advertising Board of the Philippines.

Dela Torre, V. (1989). *Advertising in the Philippines.* Manila: National Bookstore.

Feliciano, G., & C. J. Icban, Jr. (1967). *Philippine mass media in perspective*. Quezon City, Philippines: Capitol Publishing House, Inc.

Franco-Diyco, N. (2002, June 14). We're Clio winners! *BusinessWorld*, p. 27.

Lent, J. (1967). Advertising in the Philippines. *Philippine Studies, 16*, 72-96.

Luo, X. (2009). Disparities in labor market performance in the Philippines. *World Bank Policy Research Working Paper Series* No. 5124. Washington, DC: The World Bank.

Madamba, C. R. (2004, July 9). Philippine advertising: Cannes or cannot do? *BusinessWorld*, p. 2.

Magsaysay, J. (1967). Advertising. In G. Feliciano & C. J. Icban, Jr. (Eds.), *Philippine mass media in perspective*. Quezon City, Philippines: Capitol Publishing House, Inc.

Pe, R. (2003, Sept. 1). RP wins awards in New York festival. *Philippine Daily Inquirer*, p. 2.

Philippine Culture and Information (1998). Advertising in the Philippines. Retrieved Sept. 12, 2009.

Philippine Information Agency (1998). Advertising in the Philippines. Retrieved Jan. 26, 2010, from the Philippine Culture and Information website http://www.pia.gov.ph/philinfo/phadv.htm.

Readers Digest (n.d.). The brands you trust. Retrieved Sept. 12, 2009, from http://www.rdtrustedbrands.com/trusted-brands/tb_asia.shtml.

How Brazil's Reputation for Creative Work Influences Its Advertising Higher Education

Alexandra M. Vilela
Towson University, USA

Critics agree that Brazil produces some of the world's most creative and appealing advertising. This chapter explores the cultural, historical, governmental, financial, industrial, and geographical influences of Brazil's advertising education.

> Brazil enjoys an international reputation for producing some of the world's most creative advertising. The mere mention of Brazil to advertising professionals evokes images of innovative, appealing print ads and commercials—many that have taken top prizes at the *Cannes Lions International Advertising Festival* and other international competitions. (O' Barr 2008, p. 3)

> Brazil had begun winning international awards for its advertising as early as the 1970s. This continued through the 1980s and emerged as a major trend in the 1990s.[67] (O' Barr 2008, p. 14)

Few if any will deny the value of world-wide recognition, such as the "Lions." But does advertising recognition reflect business "value?" In Brazil, the answer is a profound "yes," since advertising here, by any measure, is "big business." And advertising higher education is undergoing robust growth to keep pace. With the country's expanding advertising expenditures, especially over the last few decades, a concomitant expansion of bachelor, master's and doctoral degrees, as well as the birth of advertising and communication associations are easily identified. And, in spite of this envi-

---

[67] For instance, in 2010, Brazil won 57 Lions (or 7% of the total Lions distributed in the whole festival) in the *Cannes Lions International Advertising Festival*, in 12 categories (Barbosa, 2010).

444

able blossoming in advertising education, demand for "seats" in advertising classes is extremely competitive.

The activities directly related to Brazilian advertising generated approximately $26.2 billion (in U.S. dollars) in 2007, and represented around 1.85 percent of the country's GDP (2007 = $1.44 trillion). The communication industry in Brazil is comprised of 98,000 companies, employing 612,000 individuals, and paying a salary of $5.3 billion (Abap & IBGE 2007).

Brazilian advertising has been evolving in the past four decades, and is increasingly known by its reputation for originality and creativity. The country began winning international awards for its advertising as early as the 1970s (e.g., it won its first Lion from *Cannes Lions International Advertising Festival* in 1972) (O'Barr 2008). By the 1980s, Brazilian advertisers were "widely recognized as some of the world's most creative and able" (*Advertising Age* 2003, para.17).

At the *Festival Iberoamericano de Publicidad* in 1987, Brazil and Spain won almost 70 percent of the awards. This trend continued through the 1990s, and 2000s. And since 2000, Brazil ranks among the world's most awarded countries (together with the United States, England, Germany, France, and Spain) in the *Cannes Lions International Advertising Festival*, the world's biggest celebration of creativity in communications (*Advertising Age* 2003; Cannes Lions International Advertising Festival 2010; O'Barr 2008). In 2008, Brazil ranked fourth in the advertising after the United States, Germany, and United Kingdom at Cannes (Sampaio 2008).

Yearly, Brazil also participates with its best advertising pieces at other international festivals such as the *London International Awards*, *Clio Awards*, *New York International Advertising Awards*, and also large national competitions such as *Abril Awards*, *Professionals of the Year*, *Gramado Awards*, and the *Outdoor Center Awards*. The success of Brazilian ads coincides with the country's economic growth, media development, and expansion of advertising higher education programs, with Brazil's first advertising school dating to 1951 ("Escola de Propaganda de São Paulo"). Since then, a myriad of advertising and communication courses were established, particularly in the 1960s, 1970s, and 1980s (Durand 2006).

Brazil: The Country and Its Educational System

An overview of Brazil, the country, may help to understand its advertising and related educational program underpinnings. Discovered in 1500 by the Portuguese, Brazil became a colony of Portugal until 1822, when it achieved independence. In 1889, the country became a republic. Brazil remains the only Portuguese-speaking country in the Americas. It is the largest country, both geographically and in population, in South America; and the fifth largest country geographically, and the fifth most populous country in the world (CIA, 2010).

The Federative Republic of Brazil, as it is named on its Constitution (Federative Republic of Brazil, 2010; Mugnier, 2009), is formed by the union of the Federal District, 26 States, and 5,564 Municipalities. The largest cities are São Paulo and Rio de Janeiro (Constituição da República Federativa do Brasil, 1988).

Brazil also is the world's eighth largest economy (GDP), and the ninth largest by purchasing power parity. The country is a founding member of the United Nations, the G20, "Mercosul" (Union of South American Nations market), and it is one of the BRIC Countries (acronym for the related economies of Brazil, Russia, India, and China) (CIA 2010; Clendenning 2008).

Brazilian Educational System, Driven by Federal Government Oversight

The Brazilian educational system is regulated by the federal government through the Ministry of Education and Culture (MEC), which provides the guidelines for all educational programs, both public and private. While the local governments are responsible for establishing state and municipal educational programs, funding usually is provided by the federal government.

Early childhood education is optional. It is mandatory, however, that children between 6 to 14 years old attend school a minimum of nine years. Education in Brazil is divided into three levels: (1) Fundamental education, which is free to everyone, including adults, and mandatory for 6 to 14 year olds; (2) Medium education, which is also free, but not mandatory; (3) Higher education, including graduate degrees, which is free at public universities (Constituição da República Federativa do Brasil 1988; Federative Republic of Brazil 2009; Jones 2006; MEC 2010).

University System or Higher Education.

Secondary education is mandatory for candidates pursuing higher education. Brazil has a mixed higher education system or public and private funded universities. Public-funded universities usually offer the best quality education in Brazil, and they are 100 percent government sponsored. Students pay no tuition.

Public universities can be federally funded (all universities starting with "UF" are federal universities, such as UFMG), state (e.g., USP, UNICAMP, UERJ) or municipal funded (e.g., USCS). Private universities can be either for-profit businesses or nonprofit institutions (e.g., community- or religious-oriented) with tax benefits. Public universities typically run courses all-day long, while private universities offer a mix of day and night-only courses. Some public universities have lately introduced some night-only courses (INEP 2010; Jones 2006; MEC 2009).

Undergraduate Programs in General.

Higher education in Brazil, as in many countries, is divided into both undergraduate and graduate programs. Undergraduate degrees in Brazil (bachelor degrees) vary from four to six years for completion. For example, Social Communication—Journalism, Public Relations, and Advertising—takes around four years, while Law, Architecture, Veterinary Medicine, Psychology and Engineering degrees may take five years, and professional degrees in Medicine requires in turn six years of full-time coursework plus two years of residency.

The bachelor degree is awarded in most fields of Arts, Humanities, Social Sciences, Mathematical Sciences, or Natural Sciences. The degree enables individuals to work in their graduation field. Students who hold a bachelor degree can apply for a graduate program (Federative Republic of Brazil 2009; INEP 2010).

In addition to the bachelor degree, Brazilian universities offer the teaching licensure ("Licenciatura") degree. It is available for students who want to qualify as school teachers. There is also a degree in technological education ("Tecnólogo"), which can be obtained in three years (Brazilian Educational System 2009; INEP 2010; Toscano n.d.).

Graduate Programs in General.

The Coordenação de Aperfeiçoamento de Pessoal de Nível Superior (CAPES) is the division of the Ministry of Education and Culture that manages graduate programs in Brazil. CAPES manages mainly the Master's and doctoral level academic standards and support. Programs are systematically evaluated and awarded points for their quality of performance on a one-to-five-scale with five being the highest.

If a program receives below three, it is disqualified by CAPES, and programs that receive three points can offer only the Master's degree. P rograms that receive four or five points can offer doctoral courses, or partnership programs known as "inter- institutional" Master's or doctoral programs (CAPES 2007; INEP 2009; INEP 2010).

A graduate degree can have two formats: (1) "Lato sensu" degrees are usually in a specific area, and may take from one to two years for completion, with at least 360 hours of course work). It does not require a "thesis" (but may require a monograph), and therefore, it is not a bridge to a doctoral program. Master's of Business Administration (MBA) programs are usually "lato sensu" programs. (2) "Stricto sensu" degrees are normally taken by individuals interested in pursuing an academic career. They include a Master's degree, and are also a first step for the doctoral program.

Both degrees require satisfactory performance in a minimum number of advanced graduate courses. For a "stricto sensu" degree, Master's candidates need to include a Master's thesis (Federative Republic of Brazil 2009; INEP 2010; Jones 2006; MEC 2009).

Similar to the U.S. programs, doctoral degrees require students to complete advanced graduate coursework, pass a doctoral qualifying exam, and submit an extensive doctoral dissertation. A postdoctoral degree is also available (INEP 2010; MEC 2009; Toscano n.d.).

Lastly, following the European model, some Brazilian universities, particularly the public ones, award the title of free docent ("Livre-docente"). It is of higher standing than a doctorate, and is obtained by submitting a second thesis and approval in an examination that includes giving a public lecture before a panel of full professors (Federative Republic of Brazil, 2009; INEP, 2010).

Further, the Brazilian government recognizes distance learning, and hybrid programs that use various communication media. But students and faculty are not required to meet face-to-face (CAPES 2006; Jones 2006).

Higher Education Numbers.
According to the Brazilian higher education census in 2008, there were 2,252 higher education institutions, where 90 percent were private and 10 percent were public (4.1% federal; 3.6% state; and 2.7% municipal). Additionally, there were 24,719 undergraduate courses (requiring students' classroom presence), where 17,947 were offered by private universities. The number of seats available at private and public universities was 2,985,137. Around 5,534,689 candidates competed for a college course in the same year, but only 1,505,819 new students were accepted. Also, 647 online programs were offered by 115 institutions. Approximately 430,259 students were accepted for this type of program (INEP 2009).

In 1995, there were a total of 1,000 master's and 600 doctoral programs serving 60,000 students, with an additional 900 master's and 500 doctoral programs by 2005 (CAPES 2006; Jones 2006).

Admission and Requirements in Brazilian Universities.

Undergraduate Programs.

To get accepted at any public or private Brazilian university, one must pass a competitive entrance examination known as "vestibular," which developed by each school individually and with diverse formats and difficulty levels (Brazilian Educational System, 2009). "Vestibular" usually lasts about two weeks each with at least a two-step process, and varied test topics. The exam takes place once a year, but some private universities may run it twice a year. Universities offer a limited number of seats, and the best qualified candidates, based on the "vestibular," will be selected for entrance.

Grade Point Average is not a factor for university acceptance. The number of candidates competing for a seat at the university level varies per course. For example, the most competitive courses may attract around 30 or 40 candidates per seat at the top public universities. In some courses as many as 200 apply (INEP 2010; Jones 2006; MEC 2009).

Contrary to what happens in the United States, candidates must declare their major during "vestibular" registration. Although it is possible to switch majors after entrance, this is quite rare and difficult to do. Students wishing to change majors usually undergo a second "vestibular." Also, Brazilian undergraduate curricula are usually more rigid than the U.S. curricula (INEP 2010; Toscano n.d.).

Graduate Programs.

Bachelor degrees and professional diplomas or "Licenciatura" are eligible for admission into graduate programs leading to advanced Master's or doctoral degrees. Admission to the Master's and doctoral programs is usually annual, and has several steps and variances based on the program and university.

Some universities require that candidates take entrance exams, where knowledge of the field is usually tested. Others make admission decisions based on undergraduate transcripts, letters of recommendation, and oral interviews. However, in most cases, candidates are required to submit a research proposal, and one faculty member must agree to serve as their advisor. It is also noteworthy to mention that the undergraduate degree needs to be in a field related to the graduate program. For instance, an engineer diploma does not qualify for a Communication graduate program (Federative Republic of Brazil 2009; INEP 2010).

For a master's thesis, the emphasis must be on adding value to the academic knowledge. The thesis is then examined by an oral committee of three faculty members, including one external examiner. Professional Master's degrees on the other hand normally involve taking a larger number of classes, and submitting a final report or completing a project as a company intern (Federative Republic of Brazil 2009; INEP 2010; MEC 2009).

A Master's degree is a prerequisite for a doctorate. With few exceptions (namely, individuals with outstanding research), one may not skip the Master's degree or equivalent. Requirements for a doctoral degree include attending advanced courses, passing an oral exam, and submitting a doctoral dissertation (Federative Republic of Brazil, 2009; INEP, 2010). Communication, and consequently Advertising, degrees follow similar steps as other undergraduate and graduate programs, admissions, and requirements.

Advertising Higher Education Courses in Brazil

The Brazilian Advertising higher education developed at a slow steady pace, but in 2000 the growth of Brazil's advertising market accelerated, with more than 4,000 advertising agencies and 150 advertising courses within 250 Communication schools producing approximately 30,000 professionals with bachelor degrees in Advertising (Gracioso 2001). In 2008, there were 494 private universities, 25 public federal universities, 13 public municipal universities, and 5 public state universities offering higher education in advertising (Editora Abril 2009).

The increase in higher education programs in Brazil by 2000 is justified by the new national education law (Lei de Diretrizes e Bases da Educação Nacional) in 1996. The law is based on "the universal principle right of education opportunities for all." Therefore, after the middle of the 1990s, the number of higher education courses and programs expanded significantly (INEP 2009).

According to the Brazilian higher education census, in 1995 there were 460 seats offered in the country for all Advertising programs. This number jumped to 5,949 in 2007. It is noteworthy that in 1995, the number of seats was measured on the Advertising and Creativity major only, but in 2007 the census classifies Advertising as a subcategory of courses denominated Marketing and Advertising. Thus, the total number of seats in Marketing and Advertising in 2007 was 55,881. Part of this number was classified as Marketing and Propaganda (9,080), Market—Marketing (37,048), Advertising and Propaganda (5,949), and Public Relations (3,804) (INEP 2009).

450

Brazilian graduate programs in Communication are relatively new. There are not specific "Advertising" Master's or doctoral programs. Graduate degrees in this area are usually offered in a broader concept of Social Communication, Communication Science, Communication and Culture, or Communication and Information, and so forth (*see* Table 29-1) to embrace all disciplines, such as Journalism, Advertising, Public Relations, etc., similar to some graduate programs in the United States (CAPES 2007).

The existence of graduate programs, namely Master's and doctoral degrees, depend on the availability of undergraduate courses offered by the same institution. A Master's or doctoral degree in Communication cannot be offered in an institution that does not offer the undergraduate program of the same major (CAPES 2006). Yet, Brazil offers 39 Master's and 15 doctoral Communication programs recommended by the CAPES.

Six master's and doctoral programs received a "5" rating. Ten master's and nine doctoral programs received a "4" rating. And 23 Master's programs received a "3" rating (*see* Table 29-1). The majority of the Communication higher education programs, both undergraduate and graduate, are located in the southeast region mainly São Paulo and Rio de Janeiro, where also the majority of the advertising agencies and media headquarters are located (*see* Tables 29-1 and 29-2).

Programs	Universities Public (PU) vs. Private (PR)	State (UF)*	Rating & Starting Year of Program
1. Communication Science	Universidade Federal do Amazonas—UFAM (PU)	AM	M = 3 (2008) D = ….
2. Communication Science	Universidade de Vale do Rio dos Sinos—UNISINOS (PR)	RS	M = 5 (1994) D = 5 (1999)
3. Communication Science	Universidade de São Paulo —USP (PU)	SP	M = 4 (1972) D = 4 (1980)
4. Communication	Universidade Federal do Ceará —UFC (PU)	CE	M = 3 (2008) D = ….
5. Communication	Universidade de Brasília—UNB (PU)	DF	M = 4 (1974) D = 4 (2003)
6. Communication	Universidade Católica de Brasília—UCB (PR)	DF	M = 3 (2008) D = ….
7. Communication	Universidade Federal de Goiás—UFG (PU)	GO	M = 3 (2007) D = ….
8. Communication	Universidade Federal de Juíz de Fora—UFJF (PU)	MG	M = 3 (2007) D = ….
9. Communication	Universidade Federal de Pernambuco—UFPE (PU)	PE	M = 4 (2001) D = 4 (2007)

10. Communication	Universidade Federal do Paraná ——UFPR (PU)	P R	M = 3 (in process) D = ····
11. Communication	Universidade Estadual de Londrina——UEL (PU)	P R	M = 3 (2008) D = ····
12. Communication	Universidade Federal do Rio de Janei-ro——UFRJ (PU)	R J	M = 5 (1972) D = 5 (1983)
13. Communication	Universidade Federal Fluminense——UFF (PU)	R J	M = 5 (1997) D = 5 (2002)
14. Communication	Universidade do Estado do Rio de Janeiro ——UERJ (PU)	R J	M = 3 (2002) D = ····
15. Communication	Pontifícia Universidade Católica do Rio de Janeiro ——PUC/RJ (PR)	R J	M = 4 (2003) D = ····
16. Communication	Universidade Federal de Santa Maria——UFSM (PU)	R S	M = 3 (2006) D = ····
17. Communication	Universidade Estadual Paulista Júlio de Mesquita Filho/Bauru——UNESP (PU)	S P	M = 3 (2001) D = ····
18. Communication	Faculdade Cásper Líbero——FCL (PR)	S P	M = 3 (2006) D = ····
19. Communication	Universidade de Marília——UNIMAR (PR)	S P	M = 3 (2003) D = ····
20. Communication	Universidade Paulista——UNIP (PR)	S P	M = 3 (1997) D = ····
21. Communication	Universidade Anhembi Morumbi——UAM (PR)	S P	M = 3 (2006) D = ····
22. Communication	Universidade Municipal de São Caetano do Sul——USCS (PU)	S P	M = 3 (2009) D = ····
23. Communication & Culture	Universidade de Sorocaba——UNISO (PR)	S P	M = 3 (2006) D = ····
24. Communication & Contemporary Culture	Universidade Federal da Bahia ——UFBA (PU)	B A	M = 5 (1990) D = 5 (1995)
25. Communication & Cultural Media	Universidade Federal da Paraíba/João Pessoa——UFPB (PU)	P B	M = 3 (2008) D = ····
26. Communication & Information	Universidade Federal do Rio Grande do Sul——UFRS (PU)	R S	M = 4 (1995) D = 4 (2000)
27. Communication & Languages	Universidade Tuiuti do Paraná ——UTP (PR)	P R	M = 4 (1999) D = 4 (in process)
28. Communication & Consumption Practices	Escola Superior de Propaganda & Marketing——ESPM (PR)	S P	M = 3 (2006) D = ····
29. Communication & Semiotics	Pontifícia Universidade Católica de São Paulo——PUC/SP (PR)	S P	M = 4 (1970) D = 4 (1978)
30. Social Communication	Universidade Federal de Minas Gerais——UFMG (PU)	M G	M = 5 (1995) D = 5 (2004)
31. Social Communication	Pontifícia Universidade Católica do Rio Grande do Sul——PUC/RS (PR)	R S	M = 5 (1994) D = 5 (1999)
32. Social Communication	Universidade Metodista de São Paulo——UMESP (PR)	S P	M = 4 (1976) D = 4 (1995)
33. Social Communication: Media Interactions	Pontifícia Universidade Católica de Minas Gerais——PUC/ MG (PR)	M G	M = 3 (2007) D = ····

34. Communication, Culture, & Amazon	Universidade Federal do Pará—UFPA (PU)	P A	M = 3 (in process) D = ...
35. Media Studies	Universidade Federal do Rio Grande do Norte —UFRN (PU)	R N	M = 3 (2009) D = ...
36. Image & Sound	Universidade Federal de São Carlos—UFSCAR (PU)	S P	M = 3 (2008) D = ...
37. Journalism	Universidade Federal de Santa Catari-na—UFSC (PU)	S C	M = 3 (2007) D = ...
38. Audiovisual Means & Process	Universidade de São Paulo— USP (PU)	S P	M = 4 (in process) D = (in process)
39. Multimedia	Universidade Estadual de Campinas—UNICAMP (PU)	S P	M = 4 (1986) D = 4 (1998)

1. M = Master's program, D = Doctoral program
2. Rating on a 3 to 5 score, with 3 being the minimum acceptable for an institution diploma (the program is disqualified if it receive a score below 3) and 5 being the highest score. Programs scored less than 3 are not listed, as they are not authorized and recognized.
* UF = Federative Unit
Source: CAPES (2007)

Table 29-1: Ratings and Start Year of Master's and Doctoral Communication Programs in Brazil

Higher Education in Advertising: Historical Background.

The start of Social Communication higher education in Brazil dates to the end of the 1940s. According to Melo (1991) and Afonso (2006), the first communication courses in this area were implemented in the Southeast, and they were predominantly focused on Journalism. Thus, the first Journalism higher education was established in 1947 by the Cásper Líbero School of Journalism in São Paulo. A year later, the second communication course was available at the Universidade Federal do Rio de Janeiro (UFRJ).

In the beginning of the 20th Century, the Advertising courses offered were informal and diffuse, and known as "courses where individuals learn, but are not taught" (Durand 2006; Durand 2008; Gomes 2008; Martensen 1976). In May 1914, the first advertising agency, named "A Eclética," was established in São Paulo, Brazil (Dias 2003).

Later, in 1926, the advertising department of General Motors was brought to the country for the U.S. advertising experience. The General Motors advertising department was just the beginning of several ad "agencies" establishing in the country around that time, including J. W. Thompson, N. W. Ayer & Son, and Ford's ad department. All were tied to the automobile industry.

These agencies developed "trainee" programs, where individuals would intern in all sections of an advertising agency. The trainee programs extended to all big national and international advertising agencies (e.g., Lintas, McCann Erickson, Grant, Standard, Norton, Interamericana). Indeed, advertising agencies were not enthusiastic about investing to train new personnel, triggering the dispute to get trained professionals from competitive agencies. Advertisers' salaries were skyrocketing by that time (Martensen, 1976).

It was then that the Brazilian Advertising Association ("Associação Brasileira de Propaganda") and the São Paulo Advertising Association ("Associação Paulista de Propaganda") implemented short Advertising specialization courses (Dias 2003; Durand 2006; Durand 2008). It is noteworthy to mention that the press also supported the initiative (particularly the *Diários Associados* of Assis Chateaubriand—a large media conglomerate), as there would be financial gains for their advertising sections (Durand 1989). Thus, advertising agencies needed to recruit professionals of other fields; usually new graduates from Business and Administration, Economy, Architecture, and Law courses (Tarsitano 1999).

In 1951, the *School of Advertising of São Paulo* ("Escola de Propaganda de São Paulo") was funded by Rodolfo Lima Martensen, as a department of the Art Museum of São Paulo ("Museu de Arte de São Paulo—MASP"). The course provided ten basic disciplines such as Psychology, Advertising Techniques, Layout, Comprehensive Layout, Art Graphics and Production, Copywriting, Radio, Cinema and TV, Media, Statistics (Market Research), and Sales Promotion. The course was taught by advertising leaders from ad agencies to provide advertisers with strong professional skills. Four years later, the course grew in size, and separated it from the museum.

In 1961, the School of Advertising of São Paulo became the School of Higher Education in Advertising of São Paulo ("Escola Superior de Propaganda de São Paulo—ESP"). It was Brazil's first "official" advertising higher education school, and the mark for many others to come (Dias 2003; Durand 2006; Durand 2008).

In 1978, the ESP introduced Marketing in its curriculum, gained two extra years to become a four-year academic course, and it was named School of Higher Education in Advertising and Marketing ("Escola Superior de Propaganda e Marketing—ESPM"). The School differentiates itself from other Advertising courses as it proposes to form "advertisers with the marketing mentality," while the Communication schools inserted Advertising into the Communication context (Martensen 1976).

1960s Begin Growth of Social Communication Schools & Advertising Studies

The 1960s is known as the "boom" of the "Social Communication schools." To cite a few, in 1962, the "Universidade Federal de Minas Gerais" (UFMG) and the "Universidade de Brasília" (UNB) funded the School of Mass Communication, which offered the following tracks: (1) Journalism; (2) Radio, TV, and Cinema; and (3) Advertising and Propaganda; and later (4) Public Relations (Dias 2003).

In 1966, the "Universidade de São Paulo" or USP (well ranked internationally)[1], founded the School of Communications and Arts (ECA—for "Escola de Comunicações e Artes"), with eight departments and 21 undergraduate courses, eight of them in Communication[2] (USP 2010). In 1965, the "Pontifícia Universidade Católica de Porto Alegre" (PUC Porto Alegre) changed its Journalism course to School of Media Communication (FAMECOS—for "Faculdade dos Meios de Comunicação"), followed by the "Universidade Federal do Rio de Janeiro (UFRJ), which founded the School of Communication (ECO—for "Escola de Comunicação") in 1967. However, only in 1969 were the Advertising courses regulated (Dias 2003).

In 1972, there were 46 School(s) of Social Communication in Brazil (Pinho 1998), and in 2001, there were 75 different courses in the field of Marketing and Advertising, comprising Marketing and Advertising, Market Research, Advertising and Propaganda, and Public Relations. Additionally, in the field of journalism, there were 300 courses to include Social Communication and Radio and TV (INEP 2001).

As for graduate courses, there were few universities offering Communication Master's and doctoral programs in the 1970s and 1980s. It was not uncommon for students to pursue graduate programs in different fields, or abroad, particularly in European countries (USP n.d.).

Pontifícia Universidade Católica de São Paulo (PUC-SP), a private university, started the first Communication master's program in Brazil in 1970 (CAPES 2007). In 1972, both public universities Universidade de São Paulo (USP) and Universidade Federal do Rio de Janeiro (UFRJ) launched their master's programs a few months apart (CAPES 2007; UFRJ 2010; USP n.d.), followed by Universidade de Brasília (UNB) in 1974 (CAPES 2007; UNB n.d.b). PUC-SP was also the first university to have the first a doctoral program in the field in 1978.

In 1980, USP started its doctoral program, and became responsible in the late 1980s for 48 percent of the academic research production in the country (CAPES 2007; USP n.d.). Table 29-1 provides the start year of each Communication master's and doctoral program.

Since the 1980s, Advertising and Propaganda is the most competitive program at a higher education level to be accepted around the country. The major still carries the perception of a "fantasy," "glamour" lifestyle (Dias 2003; INEP 2001; Souza 1993), particularly with the increase of national and international awards and advertising agency rankings (Durand 2006).

In the 1990s, the attraction was so high that for five consecutive years, the advertising major received an average of 84 to 87 candidates per seat in the University of São Paulo State (USP) (Durand 2006). During the same period, there was a tremendous increase in the number of Advertising courses offered at the undergraduate and graduate levels favored by the new national education law ("Lei de Diretrizes e Bases da Educação Nacional") (INEP 2009).

Rankings Offer Students Selection Assistance

University rankings in Brazil are not as popular as they are in the United States and other countries. The major Brazilian universities are well known by the public, and individuals are likely to attend universities in their own cities or states, or move to a nearby large city. In the 1980s, *Playboy Magazine*, published by Editora Abril (which belongs to the Abril Group, and is the largest publisher in Latin America)[3], released an annual ranking, listing the best courses and higher education institutions. A year later, the *Student Guide* (*"Guia do Estudante"* or *GE*), also an Editora Abril publication (launched in 1984), started releasing similar university rankings.

The purpose is to advise students in the process of taking the "vestibular" on what and where to study, and to provide updated information on the job market and careers (Editora Abril 2008b; Portal da Propaganda 2008). The ranking by the *GE* evolved over the years.

In 1988, for the first time, the guide started classifying the university courses using one to five stars. By 2008, the *GE* listed 203 careers in 13 areas, and 21,367 courses in 1,900 institutions throughout the country (Editora Abril 2008b).

The *GE* evaluates only higher education courses available for at least one year and that offer bachelor and "Licenciatura" degrees. Evaluation criteria of the *GE* ranking include the following: Questionnaires requesting specific information about courses offered, infrastructure (such as labs, equipment, student clubs or junior enterprises) faculty members, and their scientific research production. Evaluator consultants are comprised of faculty members, course coordinators, department chairs and evaluators from MEC. In 2007, the *GE* had 2,040 evaluator consultants. Each evaluator consultant classifies the courses received according to grades that go from excellent (five stars), to good (three stars), to regular, to poor, and to "I prefer not to provide my opinion." Only courses receiving three, four, and five stars are listed in the ranking (Editora Abril 2008a; Editora Abril 2008c).

Some ranked institutions post their classification on their Web sites (e.g., UNB, n.d.c) or publicize their classification in the media (Portal da Propaganda 2008). In 2005 the *GE* and *Banco Real* (bank institution) created the *Best Student Guide and Banco Real Universities' Award* ("Prêmio Melhores Universidades Guia do Estudante e Banco Real") that aims to identify, value, and recognize the best higher education institutions (Editora Abril 2008a; Editora Abril 2008c).

For advertising courses, in 2008, the only two institutions that received five stars from the *GE* were "Escola Superior de Propaganda & Marketing" (ESPM) in Porto Alegre (private university) and Universidade Federal de Santa Maria (public university), both are located at the South of Brazil. *GE* awarded four stars to 25 universities, and three stars to 43 universities. For a complete list of the institutions, their location, classification of private or public universities, and number of stars, see Table 29-2.

Universities—Public (PU) vs. Private (PR)	State (UF)*	Rating
1. Escola Superior de Propaganda & Marketing—Porto Alegre (PR)	RS	*****
2. Universidade Federal de Santa Maria—Santa Maria (PU)	RS	*****

3. Escola Superior de Propaganda & Marketing——São Paulo (PR)	SP	****
4. Escola Superior de Propaganda & Marketing——Rio de Janeiro (PR)	RJ	****
5. Faculdades Integradas Barros Melo——Olinda (PR)	PE	****
6. Universidade Potiguar——Natal (PR)	RN	****
7. Universidade Anhembi Morumbi——São Paulo (PR)	SP	****
8. Universidade Metodista de Piracicaba——Piracicaba (PR)	SP	****
9. Universidade de Fortaleza——Fortaleza (PR)	CE	****
10. Fundação Armando Álavares Penteado——São Paulo (PR)	SP	****
11. Centro Universitário Feevale——Novo Hamburgo (PR)	RS	****
12. Faculdade Cásper Líbero——São Paulo (PR)	SP	****
13. Universidade Federal do Rio Grande do Sul——Porto Alegre (PU)	RS	****
14. Universidade Federal de Pernambuco——Recife (PU)	PE	****
15. Universidade Tiradentes——Aracaju (PR)	SE	****
16. Pontifícia Universidade Católica do Rio de Janeiro——Rio de Janeiro (PR)	RJ	****
17. Universidade Católica de Brasília——Taguatinga (PR)	DF	****
18. Pontifícia Universidade Católica do Rio Grande do Sul——Porto Alegre (PR)	RS	****
19. Universidade de São Paulo——São Paulo (PU)	SP	****
20. Pontifícia Universidade Católica de São Paulo——São Paulo (PR)	SP	****
21. Universidade Metodista de São Paulo——São Bernardo do Campo (PR)	SP	****
22. Universidade de Brasília——Brasília (PU)	DF	****
23. Pontifícia Universidade Católica de Minas Gerais——Belo Horizonte (PR)	MG	****
24. Universidade Presbiteriana Mackenzie——São Paulo (PR)	SP	****
25. Pontifícia Universidade Católica de Campinas——Campinas (PR)	SP	****
26. Universidade do Vale do Rio dos Sinos——São Leopoldo (PR)	RS	****
27. Esamc Campinas——Campinas (PR)	SP	****
28. Faculdade de Tecnologia e Ciências——Salvador (PR)	BA	***
29. Centro Universitário de Brasília——Brasília (PR)	DF	***

458

30. Centro Universitário Luterano de Palmas—Palmas (PR)	TO	***
31. Universidade de Santa Cruz do Sul—Santa Cruz do Sul (PR)	RS	***
32. Universidade Salvador—Salvador (PR)	BA	***
33. Universidade Católica de Goiás—Goiânia (PR)	GO	***
34. Centro Universitário da Bahia—Salvador (PR)	BA	***
35. Universidade Federal do Paraná—Curitiba (PU)	PR	***
36. Centro Universitário Jorge Amado—Salvador (PR)	BA	***
37. Universidade Municipal de São Caetano do Sul—São Caetano do Sul (PR)	SP	***
38. Universidade Anhaguera—Campo Grande (PR)	MS	***
39. Pontifícia Universidade Católica do Parnaná—Curitiba (PR)	PR	***
40. Universidade de Caxias do Sul—Caxias do Sul (PR)	RS	***
41. Faculdades COC Ribeirão Preto—Ribeirão Preto (PR)	SP	***
42. Universidade Federal do Rio de Janeiro—Rio de Janeiro (PU)	RJ	***
43. Faculdade Marista—Recife (PR)	PE	***
44. Universidade Federal de Goiás—Goiânia (PU)	GO	***
45. Iesp Faculdades—Cabedelo (PR)	PB	***
46. Centro de Estudos Superiores de Maceió—Maceió (PR)	AL	***
47. Universidade Católica Dom Bosco—Campo Grande (PR)	MS	***
48. Universidade Paulista—São Paulo (PR)	SP	***
49. Universidade Santa Cecília—Santos (PR)	SP	***
50. Universidade Federal de Minas Gerais—Belo Horizonte (PU)	MG	***
51. Faculdades Integradas Claretianas—Rio Claro (PR)	SP	***
52. Faculdades Nordeste—Fortaleza (PR)	CE	***
53. Faculdades Unime—Lauro de Freitas (PR)	BA	***
54. Universidade Federal do Pará—Belém (PU)	PA	***
55. Universidade de Passo Fundo—Passo Fundo (PR)	RS	***
56. Instituto Baiano de Ensino Superior—Salvador (PR)	BA	***

57. Universidade Católica de Pernambuco—Recife (PR)	PE	***
58. Universidade Regional do Noroeste do Estado do Rio Grande do Sul—Ijuí (PR)	RS	***
59. Centro Universitário do Sul de Minas—Varginha (PR)	MG	***
60. Universidade de Marília—Marília (PR)	SP	***
61. Faculdade do Vale do Ipojuca—Caruaru (PR)	PE	***
62. Faculdade Editora Nacional—São Caetano do Sul (PR)	RS	***
63. Pontifícia Universidade Católica de Minas Gerais—Arcos (PR)	MG	***
64. Universidade do Oeste Paulista—Presidente Prudente (PR)	SP	***
65. Universidade Nove de Julho—São Paulo (PR)	SP	***
66. Universidade Católica do Salvador—Salvador (PR)	BA	***
67. Universidade Católica de Santos—Santos (PR)	SP	***
68. Centro Universitário Fecap—São Paulo (PR)	SP	***
69. Esamc Sorocaba—Sorocaba (PR)	SP	***
70. Centro Universitário Newton de Paiva—Belo Horizonte (PR)	MG	***

*Note. Rating on a three- to five-stars, with three being the lowest and five being the highest number of stars. The universities are listed based on the number of stars received in a descendent order. * UF = Federative Unit. Source: Editora Abril S.A. (2009)*

Table 29-2: Advertising Higher Education Programs: 2008 Ranking

Curriculum of Social Communication

Since Social Communication higher education courses were established in Brazil in the 1960s, there were five minimum curriculum programs added over the years. The latest curriculum for Social Communication, and its tracks, including Advertising and Propaganda, was approved on July 4, 2001, by the Ministry of Education and Culture (MEC) (Moura 2002).

Specifically, the MEC is the government institution that establishes the basic curriculum of undergraduate, graduate, and post-graduate degrees taught in the country. As for the undergraduate courses in Social Communication with tracks in Journalism, Public Relations, Advertising and Propaganda, Cinema, Radio, Editing, and other tracks related to the field of Communication, students are required to take disciplines from basic and specific contents (which varies by track). Specific contents are freely organized by each institution based on the common objectives, profiles, and courses offered (MEC 2001). However, Advertising curriculum programs are similar.

Undergraduate Programs in Social Communication.

Undergraduate programs in Advertising usually take eight semesters or four years for completion. For the undergraduate program, the grid of common disciplines for the Advertising track are the following (may vary by name, but the contents are basically the same):

> (1) *Mandatory disciplines*—Portuguese (Writing and Oral) I, II, and III; Fundaments of Sociology and Communication, Principles of Economy Applied to Communication, Communication Theory, Communication Psychology, Comparative Communication, Philosophy, and Research Theory & Method.

> (2) *Specific disciplines*—Portuguese IV (Advertising Language), Consumers' Right, Advertising Theory and Techniques I and II, Image in Advertising, Ethics and Legislation in Advertising, Marketing and Advertising, Sales Promotion, Ideological Propaganda, Market Analysis and Planning, Research in Advertising, Digital Photography, Visual Programming, Advertising Copywriting (I, II, and III), Graphic/Print Production, Media, Advertising Arts, Advertising Management, Consumer Behavior Study I and II, Audiovisual/Radio/TV Production for Advertising I and II, Advertising/Campaign Planning; Statistics, Experimental Advertising and Propaganda Projects (with a final monograph or project paper worked during the whole semester).

> (3) *Elective disciplines*—vary by institution. They can go from foreign languages such as Spanish or Italian, to Special Topics, or courses such as Environment and Market Communication, Interactive Communication and Electronic/ Digital Text, Visual Communication in Organizations, Political Theory; Institutional Memory and Historical Responsibility, Aspects of the Digital Communication Theory, Brazilian Culture, Art History, Cultural Anthropology, and more. (Dias 2003).

The undergraduate grid of the School of Communications and Arts ("Escola de Comunicações e Artes, ECA-USP") was used as a model for this section (*see* USP 2010). But it is very similar to other courses offered by other universities such as "Universidade de Brasília" (UNB), and "Universidade Federal de Minas Gerais" (UFMG) (*see* UFMG 2010 and UNB n.d.a), including also private universities such as "Pontifícia Universidade Católica" (PUC).

Further, supervised internships and complimentary activities to build the undergraduate academic degree also are available. Such activities may involve special programs with financial assistantship (such as CAPES or CNPq, government assistantships) for research development, teaching assistantship, and extension activities. The hours dedicated to these activities cannot exceed 20% of the total period of class activities (MEC 2001).

Some universities, particularly the private ones, also offer junior enterprises inside their institutions under faculty members' supervision for training purposes. Junior enterprises are nonprofit associations managed exclusively by undergraduate students who provide services and project development for outside business and community (Universia, 2005).

Graduate Programs in Communication.

Course names, tracks, and programs vary among public and private universities around the country. Thus, the curriculum grids are flexible and have variations among them. Based on research topics of the program, and students' thesis and dissertation proposals, students are allowed to take courses outside the department or not related to the field as far as the graduation commission approves them. Some programs allow students to transfer 60 percent of credits of courses already taken in other national or international universities, based on the examination of students' objectives and thesis proposal (UNB, 2005). For this section, Universidade of Brasília was used as a model because of its similarity to other universities (see UFMG, UFRJ, USP).

Master's Programs in Communication

A master's degree in Communication is usually completed in approximately two years or four semesters. It requires a certain amount credits in mandatory courses and another amount of credits in elective courses, where 50 percent of the credits should be taken inside the program. Following the same criteria of a master's degree at any other university program, students are required to take a qualifying exam by no later than the end of the second semester of the program. Next, they need to defend their thesis proposal, and finally present a master's thesis examined by an oral committee of three faculty members, including one external examiner (UNB 2005):

(1) *Mandatory disciplines*—Communication Theories, Research and Methodology and Communication, and Research Seminar I.

(2) *Elective disciplines*—Oriented Teaching I and II, Cultural Studies in Communication, Economic and Political Studies in Communication, Gender and Communication, New Technologies in Communication, Communication Philosophy,

Communication Sociology, Alternative Communication Processes, Communication Planning, Media Studies (Cinema, Video/TV, Print, Photography), and others.

These elective disciplines are the same for the doctoral program at the Universidade de Brasília (UNB 2005).

Doctoral Programs in Communication

The doctoral degree in Communication should be completed, including the period of writing and defending the dissertation, in four years or eight regular semesters. Students are required to complete both mandatory and elective courses, where 50 percent of the credits should be taken inside the program. Similar to the master's program, students are required to take the qualifying exam by no later than the end of the fourth semester. Additionally, students need to defend their dissertation proposal. Lastly, they need to defend their dissertation in a committee formed by at least five faculty members, with at least two external examiners (UNB, 2005):

(1) *Mandatory disciplines*—Communication Theories; Research and Methodology in Communication; Research Seminar I; Research Seminar II.

(2) *Elective disciplines* for the Universidade de Brasília are the same as for the master's program—listed above (UNB, 2005).

Specialization Courses in Communication

Many universities also offer "lato sensu" or specialization courses in Communication, which aim to update professionals in the field or recent graduates. These specializations are either via traditional class format or distance learning (online courses). They are usually one year long, and 360 hours, with an average of 12 disciplines. For example, UFMG (2010), a public university, offers a course in "Communication: Images and Media Cultures," where basic disciplines are Contemporary Communication Thinking and Research and Methodology in Communication.

Another specialization course example is the "Business Communication" offered by the Universidade Metodista de São Paulo, which is 18 months long. The course is addressed to professionals interested in organizational communication, and has core disciplines such as: Media Relations; Internal Communication and New Technologies; Communication, Ethics and Social Responsibility; Research and Methodology, and others (Universidade Metodista de São Paulo n.d.).

Professional advertising and related field associations

There are many Brazilian advertising, marketing, media, and related associations that support professionals and organizations in the communication area. For this section, selected ones that focus on educational and learning are discussed. Specifically, associations that promote and disseminate information on advertising, marketing, communication, and related fields through educational (e.g., conferences, contests, seminars, exhibitions, festivals, books, and research publications), and awards opportunities for practitioners, communication corporations, and students and faculty are emphasized.

For example, the following associations: the Brazilian Association of Advertising ("Associação Brasileira de Publicidade—ABP"), Brazilian Association of Announcers ("Associação Brasileira de Anunciantes—ABA"), Brazilian Association of Business Communication ("Associação Brasileira de Comunicação Empresarial—Aberje"), Brazilian Association of Marketing and Business ("Associação Brasileira de Marketing e Negócios—ABMN"), National Newspapers Association ("Associação Nacional de Jornais—ANJ"), and organizations that focus on communication studies and research, such as the Brazilian Society of Interdisciplinary Studies in Communication ("Sociedade Brasileira de Estudos Interdisciplinares da Comunicação—Intercom"), Forum of Communication Research ("Fórum de Pesquisa de Comunicação—FoPeC"), and the Brazilian Association of Researchers of Organizational Communication and Public Relations ("Associação Brasileira de Pesquisadores de Comunicação Organizacional e Relações Públicas—Abrapcorp") are discussed on Table 29-3.

Associations	About/Activities
Brazilian Association of Advertising ("Associ-ação Brasileira de Pub-licidade—ABP") Founded: July 1937 Location: Rio de Janeiro, RJ	• Oldest advertising association in the country • Goals: motivate the development of ad techniques; and defend the interests of advertisers • Promotes: courses, conferences, seminars, cultural contests, and exhibitions • Established the Brazilian Advertising Self-Regulation Council ("Conselho Nacional de Auto Regulamentação Public-itária—CONAR"), the Executive Council of Standard Norms ("Conselho Executivo das Normas-Padrão—CENP"),[4] the first higher education course in advertising in the country—the School of Higher Education in Advertising and Marketing ("Escola Superior de Propaganda e Marketing—ESPM"), and the International Advertising Festival of Rio de Janeiro [1]
Brazilian Association of Announcers ("Associ-ação Brasileira de	• Group of the biggest announcers responsible for 70% of advertising investment in Brazil • Goals: represent, defend common interests, and contribute

Anunciantes—ABA") Founded: 1959 Location: São Paulo, SP	to the continual evolvement and professionalization of corporate announcers • Affiliated with the World Federation of Advertisers (**WFA**), an organization that has announcers in 55 countries, including corporations responsible for more than 60% of international ad investments • Established with the ABP the Brazilian Advertising Self-Regulation Council ("Conselho Nacional de Auto Regulamentação Publicitária—CONAR"), the Executive Council of Standard Norms ("Conselho Executivo das Normas-Padrão—CENP")[4] • Publishes: "ABA Magazine," which discusses topics related to advertising [2]
Brazilian Association of Business Communication ("Associação Brasileira de Comunicação Empresarial—Aberje") Founded: October 1967 Location: São Paulo, SP	• Actions: focus on information communication and relationships with national and international organizations, institutions, and researchers in the field of business communications • Discusses business communication in terms of educational, administrative, political, cultural, and symbolical strategies • Goals: promote knowledge and initiatives in corporate communications at local and global levels • Promotes: corporate communication forums and courses directed to professionals of the field • Has ten regional chapters distributed around the country • Members: organizations, and corporate employees directly or indirectly related to the area • Publishes: "Business Communications Magazine" (a reference publication in the field) four times a year, and a bimonthly newsletter that covers corporate communication cases • Bookstore: offers books about business communications and related themes • Annually, it awards organizations, personalities, and media that performed relevant work [3]
Brazilian Association of Marketing and Business ("Associação Brasileira de Marketing e Negócios—ABMN") Founded: November 1971 Location: Rio de Janeiro, RJ	• Members: marketing practitioners and professionals of related field • Promotes: the adoption of ethical principles by organizations and other institutional members • Goals: advise, promote, and exchange experiences and techniques among members • Sponsors: contests, conferences, symposia, seminars, research, and awards to practitioners • Publishes: books, manuals, magazines, and bulletins that discuss marketing techniques [4]
Brazilian Society of Interdisciplinary Studies in Communication ("Sociedade Brasileiros de Estudos Interdisciplinares da Comunicação—Intercom") Founded: December 1977 Location: São Paulo, SP	• Among the largest structured institutions that represents the communication field • Goals: gather researchers and communication professionals under interdisciplinary perspectives • Promotes: national and regional conferences, seminars, courses, symposia, and awards • Encourages: the development of communication research • Edits and publishes books and academic journals on communication topics [5]
National Newspapers	• Members: 146 journalism corporations, responsible for more

465

Association ("Associ-ação Nacional de Jornais—ANJ") Founded: August 1979 Location: Brasília, DF	than 90% of the newspaper circulation in the country • Goals: defend the Journalism career, and represent the general interests of its members • Promotes: interchanges of news and information, national and international conferences, seminars, symposia, and national, regional or state meetings • Sponsors: creativity awards for advertisers, advertising students, and advertising agencies • Develops and preserves: cultural projects, and historical communication materials • Affiliated with the World Association of Newspapers (WAN); the Executive Council of Standard Norms ("Conselho Executivo das Normas-Padrão—CENP"),[4] and the Brazilian Advertising Self-Regulation Council ("Conselho Nacional de Auto Regulamentação Publicitária—CONAR) [6]
Forum of Communication Research ("Fórum de Pesquisa de Comunicação—FoPeC") Founded: September 2000 Location: São Paulo, SP	• Based on the U.S. Advertising Research Foundation (ARF), established by the Association of National Advertisers (ANA) and by the American Association of Advertising Agencies (AAAA) • Has similarities with the European Society for Opinion and Marketing Research (ESOMAR) • Members: advertising agencies, announcers, media, research organizations, and academic area [7]
Brazilian Association of Researchers of Organizational Communication and Public Relations ("Associação Brasileira de Pesquisadores de Comunicação Organizacional e Relações Públicas—Abracorp") Founded: May 2006 Location: ECA-USP, São Paulo, SP	• Goals: stimulate and promote advanced studies in the Communication Science • Promotes: conferences, courses, technical and scientific events in the communication area • Interconnects: researchers, professionals, and students for discussions of topics related to corporate organizational communication and public relations • Its "Oganicom Magazine" is an expression of the advanced studies in business communication, public relations, and advertising [8]

Note: [1] (ABP, 2007)   [5] (Intercom, 2010)
[2] (ABA, 2006)   [6] (ANJ, 2010)
[3] (Aberje, 2009)   [7] (FoPec, 2010)
[4] (ABMN, 2007)   [8] (Abracorp, 2009]

Table 29-3: Professional Advertising and
Related Field Associations in Brazil

Final Comments

Brazilian journalism, advertising, and communication, and consequently the higher education programs in these fields are still new, if compared to the United States or European countries. Yet like the United States and Europe, the actual disciplines today are still evolving. Reasons for Brazil's "newness" in these fields lie in the country's history that was predominantly rural until the late 19th and early 20th centuries. That is, Brazil was not an industrial society, and therefore, did not have mass consumptions or demands.

Also, the Brazilian population was only around 14.3 million by the end of the 1800s (Census 1890), and the literacy rate was low. For instance, 99.9 percent of the slaves and 80 percent of the rest of the population were illiterates, providing little condition for the press and advertising to develop (Durand 2008; Goulart 1990).

The initial advertising format that was more towards a simple and "classified" one, started changing with Brazil's economic-socio-cultural transformation, industry arrival (e.g., automotive), and media development (e.g., magazines, radio, TV), by the middle of the 1900s (Durand 2008). Similarly, the Communication higher education was also influenced by these factors.

The first School of Journalism was established in 1947, and four years later, the School of Advertising of São Paulo ("Escola de Propaganda de São Paulo") was founded (Dias 2003; Durand 2006; Durand 2008). However, it is only during the 1960s that Communication schools started opening in the country, with the first master's and doctoral programs in the 1970s, and the predominant number of courses in the 1990s and 2000s.

It is not surprising that the economy drives the Brazilian advertising market and consequently, its education. As the world's eighth largest economy (World Bank, 2010), the country had over 500 public and private universities that offered advertising courses, 39 master's and 15 doctoral Communication programs by 2008 (CAPES 2007; Editora Abril 2010). The majority of them are located in the southeast and south areas, where industries and population are concentrated.

As a field in constant growth with new technologies developing every day, the "glamour" and "creativity" reputation of the advertising festivals and awards, and the early stages of higher education, these numbers are expected to continue to increase in the next couple of years. It is not known whether the job market will be able to absorb all graduates and evolving professionals, despite the economic growth of Brazil in the last few years and relatively promising expectations for the years to come.

Author's Note and Update

Hoping that you find the array of information about Brazil's history and culture compelling enough to learn more or even venture to Brazil. The country offers interests and activities for everyone. You may find the areas that cover the evolution of Brazilian advertising education fascinating, as I have. As with any edu-

cation system, it is a dynamic process. So, consider this chapter a foundation for additional research – a primer or launch pad, if you will. With this in mind, you will need to do additional research particularly on how one gets accepted into Brazilian universities. As of press time, Brazil has moved from what I have described to a more universal exam method (Admission Requirements of Brazilian Universities). That is, more recently, the Brazilian government launched ENEM (Secondary Education Evaluation Exam). Since then, some higher education institutions accept ENEM as part of the admission process. Also, university rankings change regularly. You should find the rankings here to serve as a good initial guideline.

NOTES

1. In the 2009 Performance Ranking of Scientific Papers for World Universities, created by the Higher Education & Accreditation Council of Tawain, the Universidade de São Paulo (USP) was listed in the 78th place. Also, USP was classified in the 35th place, in 2008 survey of the Professional ranking of World Universities (IBGE, 2007) (this list is created by Mines Paris Tech). In 2009, USP is classified as the 38th world's best university, behind University of Pittsburg and ahead of Princeton University (according to the Spain Education Ministry, which examines more than 17 thousand academic universities worldwide—this ranking is updated every six months by the Spanish Education Ministry and takes into consideration the global performance, research index, and quality of scholars and students) ("USP é classificada a 38ª melhor universidade do mundo em ranking" 2009). Additionally, Computer Science students from USP were ranked 14th in the ACM ICP 2010 World Finals, the same rank of MIT. Webometrics classified USP as the best university of the set of countries named BRIC (Higher Education Evaluation & Accreditation Council of Taiwan, 2009).

2. The eight departments of ECA-USP, which are related to the communication field, are the following: (1) Communication & Arts Department (CCA); (2) Journalism & Editing Department (CJE); (3) Public Relations, Advertising, & Tourism Department (CRP); (4) Radio, TV, & Cinema Department (CTR); (5) Library & Documentation Department (CBD); (6) Arts Department (CAP); (7) Music Department (CMU); (8) Theater Department (USP, 2010).

3. Editora Abril is a Brazilian publisher, funded in 1950, and based in São Paulo. It publishes six of ten best-selling titles, and has 58 percent share of Brazilian magazine publishing market. Some of the main magazines are *Veja* (weekly news), *Nova* (teen— *Cosmopolitan Magazine*), *Placar* (sports), *Capricho* (teen), *Quatro Rodas* (automotive), *Estilo de Vida* (in style), *Cláudia, Manequim* (women's mountlies), *Casa Cláudia* (home and gardening), *Boa Forma* (fitness), *Exame* (bussiness), *Superinteressante* (science and culture), *Info* (information and technology), and the Brazilian issue of *Men's Health, Women's Health, Runners,* and *Playboy*. The company also deals with printing, publishing, distribution, and sale of magazines, yearbooks, guidebooks, technical publications, brochures, and CD-ROM. In addition, the publisher engages in sales of advertising and publicity, database marketing, online content and services with various digital portals. It distributes books, inserts, book collection, newspapers, magazines, printed material, periodicals, and consignments. Editora Abril owns the Brazilian MTV and cable company

TVA. The company is the leading pay TV operator in São Paulo (Brazil's largest city) serving more than 300 thousand paid TV subscribers and 45 thousand Internet broadband subscribers. The Ática and Scipione publishing companies lead the Brazilian educational book market with 30 percent of the market share. Naspers acquired 30 percent interest in Editora Abril in 2006. The publisher and its subsidiaries provide informational, cultural, educational, and entertainment services in Latin America (The Abril Group, 2006).

4. The Executive Council of Standard Norms ("Conselho Executivo das Normas-Padrão—CENP") was established in 1998 by the advertising market with the goal of implementing the standard norms of the advertising activities. The basic document defines rules and conducts of the best ethics and commercial practices among the main Brazilian advertising agents. The Executive Council of CENP has 22 representatives of advertising agencies, announcers, media, and federal government (CENP, n.d.).

References

Advertising Age (2003, September 15). Brazil. Retrieved from http://adage.com/article?article_id=98542

Afonso, M. R. T. (2006). Ensino: Sonhos e pesadelos do curso pioneiro. In *Pedagogia d-Comunicação: Matrizes Brasileiras*. São Paulo, SP: Angellara.

Associação Brasileira de Agências de Publicidade—ABAP e Instituto Brasileiro de Geografia e Estatística—IBGE (2007). Números oficiais da indústria da comunicação e seu impacto na econmia brasileira. Retrieved from http://webserver.4me.com.br/wwwroot/abap/ibge.pdf.

Associação Brasileira de Anunciantes—ABA (2006). Sobre a ABA. Retrieved from http://www.aba.com.br/Pagina.aspx?IdSecao=1899,1901

Associação Brasileira de Comunicação Empresarial—Aberje (2009). Uma associação profissional e científica. Retrieved from http://www.aberje.com.br/associacao_quemsomos.asp.

Associação Brasileira de Marketing e Negócios—ABMN (2007). Institucional. Retrieved from http://www.abmn.com.br/abmn/abmn.asp.

Associação Brasileira de Pesquisadores de Comunicação Organizacional e Relações Públicas—Abrapcorp (2009). História. Retrieved from http://www.abrapcorp.org.br/

Associação Brasileira de Publicidade—ABP (2007). Sobre a ABP. Retrieved from http://www.abp.com.br/sobreabp/index.asp.

Associação Nacional de Jornais—ANJ (2010). Quem somos. Retrieved from http://www.anj.org.br/quem-somos.

Barbosa, M. (2010, June 27). Qualidade da propaganda brasileira é questionada em meio a recorde em Cannes. *Folha de São Paulo, Mercado*. Retrieved from http://www1.folha.uol.com.br/mercado/757650-qualidade-da-propaganda-brasileira-e-questionada-em-meio-a-recorde-em-cannes.shtml.

Brazilian Educational System (2009). *Higher Education*. Retrieved from http://www.brasil.gov.br/sobre/education/brazilian-educational-system/higher-education-1.

Cannes Lions International Advertising Festival (2010). Winners Listing. Retrieved from http://www.canneslions.com/lions/previous_winners_shortlists.cfm.

Central Intelligence Agency (CIA) (2010). *The world fact book*. South America: Brazil. Retrieved from https://www.cia.gov/library/publications/the-world-factbook/geos/br.html

Clendenning, A. (2008, April 17). Booming Brazil could be world power soon. *USA Today*. Retrieved from http://www.usatoday.com/money/economy/2008-04-17-310212789 _x.htm.

Conselho Executivo das Normas-Padrão—CENP (n.d.). O que é o CENP. Retrieved from http://www.cenp.com.br/.

Constituição da República Federativa do Brasil (1988). Capítulo 3, artigo 13. Retrieved from http://www.planalto.gov.br/ccivil_03/constituicao/constitui%C3%A7ao.htm.

Coordenação de Aperfeiçoamento de Pessoal de Nível Superior—CAPES (2006). Portal. Retrieved from http://www.capes.gov.br/.

Coordenação de Aperfeiçoamento de Pessoal de Nível Superior—CAPES (2007). Relação de cursos recomendados e reconhecidos. Retrieved from http://conteudoweb.capes.gov.br /conteudoweb/ProjetoRelacaoCursosServlet?acao=pesquisarIes&codigoArea=60900008 &descricaoArea=CI%CANCIAS+SOCIAIS+APLICADAS+&descricaoAreaConhecime nto=COMUNICA%C7%C3O&descricaoAreaAvaliacao=CI%CANCIAS+SOCIAIS+ APLICADAS+I.

Dias, S. C. de S. (2003). A criação da habilitação publicidade e propaganda no Brasil: Seus problemas e soluções. *1° Encontro Nacional da Rede Alfredo de Carvalho – Mídia Brasileira: 2 Séculos de História*. Rio de Janeiro, 1-5 de junho de 2003—Evento promovido pela Rede Alfredo de Carvalho para a Preservação da Memória e a Construção da História da Imprensa no Brasil. Retrieved from http://www.redealcar.jornalismo.ufsc.br /anais/gt6_persuasiva/a%20cria%E7%E3o%20da%20habilita%E7%E3o%20publicida de%20e%20propaganda%20no%20brasil.doc.

Durand, J. C. (1989). *Arte, privilégio e distinção: Artes plásticas, arquitetura e classe dirigente no Brasil, 1855-1985*. São Paulo, SP: Perspectiva.

Durand, J. C. (2006). Educação e ideologia do talento no mundo da publicidade. *Cadernos de Pesquisa, 36* (128), 433-450.

Durand, J. C. (2008). Formação do campo publicitário brasileiro 1930-1970. *Fundação Getúlio Vargas—Escola de Administração e Empresas de São Paulo/GV Pesquisas, 10*, 1-72.

Editora Abril S. A. (2008a). Prêmio melhores universidades—Guia do estudante e Banco Real 2008. Dúvidas sobre o prêmio. Retrieved from http://guiadoestudante.abril.com .br/premio/sobre/conteudo_265362.shtml.

Editora Abril S. A. (2008b). Prêmio melhores universidades—Guia do estudante e Banco Real 2008. História do prêmio. Retrieved from http://guiadoestudante.abril.com .br/premio/sobre/conteudo_132818.shtml.

Editora Abril S. A. (2008c). Prêmio melhores universidades—Guia do estudante e Banco Real 2008. Regulamento. Retrieved from http://guiadoestudante.abril.com.br /premio/sobre/conteudo_132440.shtml.

Editora Abril S. A. (2009). Guia do estudante. Retrieved from www.guiadoestudante .com.br.

Federative Republic of Brazil (2009). Brazilian Educational System. Higher Education. Retrieved from http://www.brasil.gov.br/sobre/education/brazilian-educational-system/hig her-education-1.

Federative Republic of Brazil (2010). Portal. Retrieved from http://www.brasil.gov .br/?set_language=en.

Fórum de Pesquisa de Comunicação (FoPeC) (2010). O que é a FoPeC? Retrieved from http://www.fopec.com.br/html/oque/index.htm

Gomes, N. D. (2008). Publicidade e propaganda. In *O campo da comunicação no Brasil*. Petrópolis, RJ: Vozes.

Goulart, S. (1990). *Sob a verdade oficial. Ideologia, propaganda e censura no Estado Novo.* São Paulo, SP: Marco Zero/CNPq.

Gracioso, F. A. (2001). Contribuição das escolas de propaganda para a formação de jovens profissionais: A experiência da ESPM, *99* (July), 43-50.

Higher Education Evaluation & Accreditation Council of Tawain (2009). *2009 Performance ranking of scientific papers for world universities.* Retrieved from http://ranking.heeact .edu.tw/en-us/2009/TOP/100

Instituto Brasileiro de Geografia e Estatística (IBGE) (n.d.). Países@. Retrieved from http:// www.ibge.gov.br/paisesat/main.php.

Instituto Brasileiro de Geografia e Estatística (IBGE) (2007). Síntese de indicadores sociais. São Paulo, Brazil. Retrieved from ftp://ftp.ibge.gov.br/Indicadores_Sociais/Sintese_de _Indicadores_Sociais_2007/Tabelas.

Instituto Brasileiro de Geografia e Estatística (IBGE) (2008a). Banco de dados agregados. Sistema IBGE de recuperação automatica—SIDRA. Unidades territoriais do nível município. Retrieved fromhttp://www.sidra.ibge.gov.br/bda/territorio/tabunit.asp?n=6&t =2&z=t&o=4.

Instituto Brasileiro de Geografia e Estatística (IBGE) (2008b). Pesquisa Nacional por Amostra de Domicílios (PNAD). Pessoas de 5 anos ou mais de idade por situação, sexo, alfabetização e grupos de idade. Retrieved from http://www.sidra.ibge.gov.br/bda/tabela /protabl.asp?c=271&i=P&sec59=93024&sec59=1023&sec59=1024&nome=on&notar odape=on&tab=271&unit=0&pov=3&opc1=1&poc2=1&orc59=5&OpcTipoNivt=1& opn1=2&nivt=0&poc1=1&sec58=0&orp=7&qtu3=27&opv=1&sec1=0&opc2=1&pop =1&opn2=0&orv=2&orc2=4&opc58=1&qtu2=5&sev=121&sev=1000121&sec2=0&p oc59=2&opp=1&opn3=0&orc1=3&poc58=1&qtu1=1&cabec=on&opc59=1&ascende nte=on&sep=43345&orn=1&qtu7=9&orc58=6&opn7=0&decm=99&pon=1&OpcCa ra=44&proc=1.

Instituto Brasileiro de Geografia e Estatística (IBGE) (2008c). Pesquisa Nacional por Amostra de Domicílios (PNAD). População residente por cor ou raça, situação e sexo. Retrieved from http://www.sidra.ibge.gov.br/bda/tabela/protabl.asp?c=262&i=P&nome =on&notarodape=on&tab=262&unit=0&pov=3&opc1=1&poc2=1&OpcTipoNivt=1 &opn1=2&nivt=0&orc86=3&poc1=1&orp=6&qtu3=27&opv=1&poc86=2&sec1=0& opc2=1&pop=1&opn2=0&orv=2&orc2=5&qtu2=5&sev=93&sev=1000093&opc86=1 &sec2=0&opp=1&opn3=0&sec86=0&sec86=2776&sec86=2777&sec86=2779&sec86 =2778&sec86=2780&sec86=2781&ascendente=on&sep=43344&orn=1&qtu7=9&orc 1=4&qtu1=1&cabec=on&pon=1&OpcCara=44&proc=1&opn7=0&decm=99.

Instituto Nacional de Estudos e Pesquisas Educacionais Anísio Teixeira (INEP) (2001). Sinopse estatística da educação superior 2000. Brasília. Retrieved from http://www.inep .gov.br/.

Instituto Nacional the Estudos e Pesquisas Educacionais Anísio Teixeira (INEP) (2009). Resumo técnico—Censo da educação superior 2008 (dados preliminares)—Ministério da Educação, Brasília, DF. Retrieved from http://www.inep.gov.br/download/censo /2008/resumo_tecnico_2008_15_12_09.pdf. Acesso em 30/01/2010.

Instituto Nacional de Estudos e Pesquisas Educacionais Anísio Teixeira (INEP) (2010). Portal do INEP. Retrieved http://www.inep.gov.br/.

Intercom—Sociedade Brasileira de Estudos Interdisciplinares da Comunicação (2010). Retrieved from http://www.intercom.org.br/.

International Monetary Fund (2009). Report for selected countries and subjects—Brazil. Retrieved from http://www.imf.org/external/pubs/ft/weo/2009/02/weodata/weorept .aspx?sy=2006&ey=2009&scsm=1&ssd=1&sort=country&ds=.&br=1&c=223&s=NG

471

DPD%2CNGDPDPC%2CPPPGDP%2CPPPPC%2CLP&grp=0&a=&pr1.x=61&pr
1.y=8.

Jones, V. (2006). Brazil. *A Global Guide to Management*, 305-311. Retrieved from
http://www.gfme.org/global_guide/pdf/305-312%20Brazil.pdf.

Martensen, R. L. (1976, March 27). O ensino da propaganda no Brasil. *O Estado de São
Paulo.*

Melo, J. M. (1991). Comunicação e modernidade—O ensino e a pesquisa nas escolas de
comunicação. São Paulo, SP: Loyola.

Ministério de Educação e Cultura (MEC) (2001). Conselho Nacional de Educação. Des-
pacho de Ministro em 4/7/2001. *Diário Ofical da União*, Section 1e, 50. Retrieved
from http://portal.mec.gov.br/cne/arquivos/pdf/CES0492.pdf.

Ministério de Educação e Cultura (MEC) (2009). Pós-graduação. Retrieved from http:
//portal.mec.gov.br/index.php?option=com_content&view=article&id=387&Itemid=3
49.

Ministério de Educação e Cultura (MEC) (2010). Consulta de IES/curso. Retrieved from
http://emec.med.gov.br.

Moura, C. P. de (2002). O curso de comunicação social no Brasil: Do currículo mínimo às
novas diretrizes curriculares. Porto Alegre, RS: EDIPUCRS.

Mugnier, C. J. (2009). Federative Republic of Brazil. *Grids & Datums (January)*. Retrieved
from http://www.asprs.org/resources/GRIDS/01-2009-brazil.pdf

O'Barr, W. M. (2008). Advertising in Brazil. *Advertising & Society Review, 9* (2), 1-44.
Retrieved from http://muse.jhu.edu/journals/asr/v009/9.2.o-barr.html#video06s.

Pinho, J. B. (1998). Trajetória e demandas do ensino de graduação em publicidade e propaganda no Brasil. In P. R. Tarsitano (Ed.), *Publicidade: Análise da produção publicitária*
(pp. 156-170). Mauá, SP: Imes/Alaic.

Portal da Propaganda (2008, October 9). Cursos da ESPM-RS conquistam estrelas no *Guia
do Estudante* da Editora Abril. Retrieved from http://www.portaldapropaganda.com
.br/portal/propaganda/6352-cursos-da-espm-rs-conquistam-estrelas-no-guia-do-
estudante-da-editora-abril.html.

Salatiel, J. R. (2009, September 24). *PNAD 2008*—Brasil melhora na economia, mas desig-
ualdade persiste. Retrieved on March 21, 2010 fromhttp://educacao.uol.com.br
/atualidades/pnad-2008.jhtm#direto-ponto.

Sampaio, R. (2008, June 24). Brazil in Cannes 2008: More lions, less points and the fourth
country overall. *Portal da Propaganda*. Retrieved from http://www.portaldapropaganda
.com/cannes/noticias/2008/0080

Souza, S. M. R. de. (1993). A publicidade: Fantasias e realidades. *Revista Propaganda, São
Paulo, 491* (Dezembro), 69-70.

Tarsitano, P. R. (1999). *A EXPOCOM como agente gerador de qualidade no ensino da comunicação social no Brasil* (Doctoral thesis, UMESP, São Bernardo do Campo, SP, Brazil).

The Abril Group (2006). Retrieved from http://www.abril.com.br/arquivo/theabrilgroup.pdf

"The economy of heat" (2007). *The Economist*. Retrieved on from http://www.economist
.com/surveys/displaystory.cfm?story_id=8952496.

Toscano, G. da S. (n.d.). Vestibular: A escolha dos escolhidos (Um estudo sobre a UFRN).
Retrieved from http://74.125.47.132/search?q=cache:onGEEMVjQsgJ:www.histedbr
.fae.unicamp.br/acer_histedbr/seminario/seminario4/trabalhos/trab024.rtf+%22estudo
+sobre+o+vestibular%22+no+brasil&cd=1&hl=pt-BR&ct=clnk&gl=br.

Universia (2005, March 31). Guia de empresas juniors—Conheça como é a estrutura de
uma empresa junior e saiba como montar uma dentro da sua universidade. Retrieved
from http://www.universia.com.br/carreira/materia.jsp?materia=6541.

Universidade de Brasília (UnB) (2005). Faculdade de comunicação—Programa de pós-graduação em comunicação. Regulamento do programa de pós-graduação em comunicação. Retrieved from http://www.fac.unb.br/site/images/stories/Posgraduacao/Pagina_principal/Regulamento_PPG.pdf.

Universidade de Brasília (UnB) (n.d.a). Faculdade de Comunicação. Fluxograma--Publicidade. Retrieved from http://www.fac.unb.br/site/index.php?option=com_content&view=section&id=8&Itemid=72.

Universidade de Brasília (UnB) (n.d.b). Faculdade de Comunicação. Programa de pós-graduação em comunicação. Retrieved from http://www.fac.unb.br/site/index.php?option=com_content&view=article&id=149&Itemid=146.

Universidade de Brasília (UnB) (n.d.c). Tradição no ensino de comunicação. Retrieved from http://www.fac.unb.br/site/index.php?option=com_content&view=article&id=151&Itemid=76.

Universidade de São Paulo (2010). Escola de Comunicações e Artes (ECA). Retrieved from http://www3.eca.usp.br/.

Universidade de São Paulo (USP) (n.d.). Escola de Comunicações e Artes da Universidade de São Paulo (ECA). Pós-graduação—Ciências da Comunicação. Retrieved from http://www.pos.eca.usp.br/index.php?q=pt-br/node/14.

Universidade Federal de Minas Gerais (UFMG) (2010). Departamento de Comunicação Social da Faculdade de Filosofia e Ciências Humanas (Fafich). Estrutura. Retrieved from http://www.fafich.ufmg.br/dcs/strictusensu/t12/departamento/estrutura.

Universidade Federal do Rio de Janeiro (UFRJ) (2010). Escola de Comunicação (ECO). Retrieved from http://www.eco.ufrj.br/.

Universidade Metodista de São Paulo (n.d.). Comunicação empresarial. Pós-graduação lato sensu. Retrieved from http://www.metodista.br/lato/comunicacao-empresarial.

U.S. Department of State (2005). Brazil—International Religious Freedom Report 2005. Bureau of Democracy, Human Rights, and Labor. Retrieved from http://www.state.gov/g/drl/rls/irf/2005/51629.htm.

"USP é classificada a 38ª melhor universidade do mundo em ranking" (2009, January 9). *Folha Online*. Retrieved 2009 from http://www1.folha.uol.com.br/folha/educacao/ult305u617390.shtml.

World Bank (2010). World development indicators database. Retrieved from http://sitereso urces.worldbank.org/DATASTATISTICS/Resources/GDP.pdf.

Advertising Education in Chile

Lucia Castellón
Universidad Mayor, Chile

Maricarmen Estevez
Universidad Mayor, Chile

Origins and Early Years

Advertising education in Chile dates back to 1953, though there were no formal programs at the time. When the School of Journalism at the University of Chile was established, a seminar called *Notions and Techniques for the Advertising Vocation* was offered by Professor Manuel Magallanes, an established advertising professional who co-founded the agency, Magallanes Cori in the 1940s.

A few years later at the same School of Journalism, Julio Ortúzar Prado, a student in the class of 1956 took various courses in the field. Ortúzar went on to become the first professional to create advertising programs in Chile. He was responsible for starting up various institutes and schools to promote education in the field.

In 1962 Ortúzar gave a summer course in advertising at the University of Chile. The course met with such a degree of success and interest that he established the Instituto de Publicidad, Mercado y Ventas/ IPEVE (Institute of Advertising, Marketing and Sales) which he directed until 1968. After leaving the academic world, he held a series of management positions in various companies until 1976 when he returned to academia and opened the School of Advertising of Chile (Escuela de Publicidad de Chile). The school quickly gained prestige and in 1990, after great success, Ortúzar founded the Universidad del Pacífico. He became president of the institution, a position he continues to hold today. Many successful advertising professionals have been trained at this university.

At the same time that advertising courses were offered within journalism programs, the Instituto Pedagógico Técnico at the Universidad de Santiago was training teachers to give courses related to advertising. At the time, these teachers were majoring in "Advertising, Sales and Calligraphy," (Publicidad, ventas y caligrafía) a career that led to a teaching degree but, since most of its graduates went directly into the field of advertising, they later decided to offer the career with two tracks: one for practitioners and the other for teachers who prepared students for a career in the field.

Professionals have been trained in the field of advertising in Chile by some very prominent individuals. One of the most outstanding is Monica Herrera. She received her Ph.D in Education from the Universidad de Sevilla in Spain and is the founder of the Monica Herrera School of Advertising (Escuela de Publicidad Mónica Herrera). In 2000 the school was absorbed into the Universidad Mayor, where Herrera served as Dean of the School of Communication until 2006. Currently she maintains two advertising schools outside Chile, one in Ecuador and the other in El Salvador.

In 1966 Monica Herrera obtained a degree in Journalism from the Universidad de Concepción. Her introduction to the field of advertising began when she was contracted by the advertising firm, McCann Erickson, thus becoming one of the first women in the country to work in the field at the executive level in a prestigious firm. She later became a professor of Communication and Advertising at the Universidad de Concepción in its School of Journalism. This experience opened up a new world for Herrera and she became immersed in the field of advertising. It led her to open the Escuela de Comunicación Mónica Herrera in 1980.

Another outstanding individual who did much to professionalize the field through education is Antonio Freire, a journalist who received his degree from the School of Journalism at the Universidad de Chile. Freire worked in television broadcasting where he directed many successful shows and wrote scripts for documentary programs. He was also a writer for major Chilean newspapers including *El Mercurio* and *La Tercera* where he wrote reviews and commentary. He became a recognized advertising professional widely known for his commercials on Chilean television.

In 1981 Freire formed a partnership with the Guiloff brothers and together they opened the Instituto de Artes, Cultura y Comunicación (IACC). At the time it offered only two careers: Advertising and Visual Communications. After a number of years, IACC became the University of Communications, UNIACC.

Advertising Education in Chile Today

Young people enter the advertising career in Chile after completing their secondary education, generally at the age of 17 or 18 years of age. Before going into detail about the state of advertising education and the profile of its future professionals, it is useful to outline the types of higher education available to students in the country.

Matriculated Students

This type of student is officially matriculated in an academic program at an institution of higher education. The criteria to qualify as an "officially matriculated" student are stipulated by the internal rules and regulations of the educational establishment and include academic requirements, procedures, and other circumstances that a student must fulfill to be considered matriculated.

Undergraduate

Undergraduate studies refer to those required to graduate from an institution of higher learning, and that lead to the first degree or a career. This level includes degrees from technical and professional schools, as well as first degrees awarded by the university.

Advertising education in Chile is offered at the following institutions of higher education:

State-run Universities. State universities are established by law and belong to the Chilean State. As of 2010, there are 16 public universities.

Private Universities with State Support: These private universities were established prior to 1980 or they were formed from those established prior to 1980. As of 2010, there are nine.

Private Universities. Private universities were established after 1980 under the DFL 1 Law or under the 1990 LOCE Law.

Technical Careers: These careers refer to those that lead to a technical degree at the higher education level.

Higher Education Technical Degrees: This degree is awarded to a graduate from a technical training center (centro de formación técnica), a professional institute or a university that has approved a program of study with a minimum duration of 600 hours. These programs develop the knowledge and skills that students need to work in a support capacity at the professional level and/or to become self-employed.

Professional Careers: These lead to a professional degree. They include academic programs such as bachilleratos, basic cycles, or a general studies curriculum, among others, as well as licentiate degree programs (an intermediate degree between that of bachelor and that of doctor).

Professional Degrees: The professional degree is awarded to a graduate from a professional institute or from a university-approved academic program.

In Chile there are 26 educational establishments that offer the advertising career. They are found at the various universities, and the professional and technical institutes, as described above.

Advertising Programs and the Universities that Offer Them

A career in advertising in Chile is offered by all types of institutions of higher education. At the university level, a licentiate degree is awarded. At the professional institutes only a professional degree is awarded. Finally, at the technical institutes, a technical or vocational certificate is awarded. These schools are listed in Tables 30-1, 30-2, and 30-3.

University	Description	Degree Awarded	Academic Level	Duration of academic program
Diego Portales (UDP)	The School of Advertising at the UDP began in 1995 and was based on the experience and tradition of the Instituto Profesional (IPEVE), which was established in 1963. The academic program leads to the licentiate degree in Communication and the title of advertising professional.	Advertising Professional	Licentiate in Communication	9 semesters
Universidad del Pacífico	This degree was first offered in 1990, though education in the field dates back to 1976 when Ortúzar founded the Escuela de Publicidad. The School allows students to choose from majors in Strategic Marketing, Advertising and Creativity and Audiovisual Communication.	Advertising Professional	Licentiate Degree in Communication	8 semesters plus a final project for graduation
Universidad del Desarrollo		Advertising Professional	Licentiate Degree in Advertising	8 semesters (4 year program)
Universidad Mayor		Advertising Professional	Licentiate Degree in Advertising	9 semesters
Universidad de las Américas		Advertising Professional	Licentiate Degree in Communication Sciences	8 semesters
Universidad Central		Advertising Professional	Licentiate Degree in Advertising	8 semesters
Universidad Pedro de Valdivia		Advertising Professional	Licentiate Degree in Advertising	8 semesters
Universidad Andrés Bello		Advertising Professional	Licentiate Degree in Advertising and Communication with a Minor in Creativity and Marketing	9 semesters

	Description	Degree	Academic Level	Duration of Program
Universidad UNIACC		Advertising Professional	Licentiate Degree in Marketing and Communication	9 semesters
Universidad de Santiago de Chile	The only state-run university that offers the career of advertising.	Advertising Professional with a Minor in Creative Management or Business Management	Licentiate Degree in Communication and Advertising	4.5 years on a semester schedule
Universidad del Mar		Advertising Professional with a Minor in Creativity or Business	Licentiate Degree in Persuasion and Communication	8 semesters
Universidad Viña del Mar		Advertising Professional	Licentiate Degree in Persuasion and Communication	9 semesters

Table 30-1: Universities with Advertising Majors

Institute	Description	Degree	Academic Level	Duration of Program
DUOC UC		Advertising Professional		8 semesters
INACAP		Advertising Professional		8 semesters
Inst. Profesional Los Leones		Advertising Specialist		8 semesters
Inst. Profesional de Santiago		Advertising Professional		4 year program
Inst. Profesional AIEP		Advertising Professional		4 year program
Inst. Profesional de Arte y Comunicación ARCOS		Advertising Professional		7 semesters

Table 30-2: Professional Institutes with Advertising Careers

Institute	Description	Degree	Academic Level	Duration of Program
Inst. Profesional Dr. Virginio Gómez G.		Specialist in Public Relations and Advertising		4 semesters
DUOC UC		Advertising Specialist with a Minor in Digital Production		5 semesters
Centro de Formación Técnica La Araucana		Advertising Specialist		5 semesters
Centro de Formación Técnica Osorno		Advertising Specialist		4 semesters
Inst. Profesional La Araucana		Advertising Specialist		5 semesters

Table 30-3: Technical Institutes with Advertising Careers

Links with Professional Associations

In Chile, advertising agencies are grouped into professional organizations. Those that are the most active and supportive in the educational sector are the Asociación Chilena de Agencias de Publicidad/ACHAP (The Chilean Association of Advertising Agencies) and the Asociación Nacional de Avisadores/ANDA (The National Association of Advertisers).

In the case of ACHAP, this organization works closely with schools that have advertising programs. Each November it invites student teams to participate in its creativity contest. Winners are announced in December, at their annual awards ceremony for advertising agencies (www.achap.cl).

Throughout the year ANDA offers seminars and workshops and it extends invitations to students and professors at various educational institutions (www.anda.cl).

The Universidad del Pacífico, the Universidad Mayor, UNIACC, Universidad Diego Portales, and the Instituto Profesional DuocUC are all internationally accredited by the International Advertising Association (IAA). This organization conducts the accreditation process with visits to each university or institute to review the programs and guarantee that the schools comply with their professional requirements. In addition, advertising majors from these accredited institutions are invited to conferences and seminars and they participate in international advertising competitions.

Throughout the academic year in Chile, which extends from March to December, various institutions organize contests for advertising students. The most important ones with the longest traditions include: *La Segunda* newspaper's annual student contest for advertising majors, the All Night Lowe contest organized by the Lowe Porta Advertising Agency, Creaviña sponsored by the Viña del Mar campus of DuocUC, an ACHAP contest for creative youth called Copy Writer, and the Universia contest, among others.

The goal behind each of these contests is to give advertising students an opportunity to compete in real life situations, to foster healthy competition among the advertising schools, and to provide advertising agencies with a venue to observe talented youth and their best ideas. The Lowe Porta Advertising Agency offers internships to the winners of their contest.

For many schools, the prizes and success that their students gain through these contests is an important measure of the success of their respective programs and it serves to foster matriculation. For two consecutive years since 2008, the School of Advertising at the Universidad Mayor won the first prize in the All Night Lowe contest.

Winners from the 2009 All Night Lowe contest, together with the director of the University Mayor School of Advertising

Graphic pieces designed in the campaign for the Municipal Theater of Chile

Winners from the 2008 All Night Lowe contest, and director of
the University Mayor School of Advertising

Advertising Leadership within Educational Institutions

No formal surveys have been conducted in Chile to determine which
advertising schools have the best academic programs. At best, word of
mouth, matriculation numbers, and student performance in national contests serve as some measures of excellence.

	Institution	Vacancies	First-Year Matriculation	Total Matriculation
Advertising	U. del Pacífico	250	263	951
Advertising	I.P Duoc (San Carlos)	180	189	679
Advertising	U. Diego Portales	95	115	483
Advertising	IP Los Leones	263	204	381
Advertising	IP Inacap	148	158	376
Advertising	IP Duoc (Viña del Mar)	100	113	372
Advertising	U. del Desarrollo	110	108	365
Advertising	I.P de Chile	160	145	292
	Uniacc	80	100	266
Advertising	U. de Santiago	60	59	269

Table 30-4: Matriculation of students

As seen in Tables 30-4 and 30-5, the total number of matriculated students, as well as the entering first-year students, show that the highest concentration of students are in Santiago, Chile's capital city. Leading this ranking are: Universidad del Pacífico and the Instituto Profesional DuocUC, followed by Universidad Diego Portales, IP Los Leones, INACAP and the Universidad del Desarrollo.

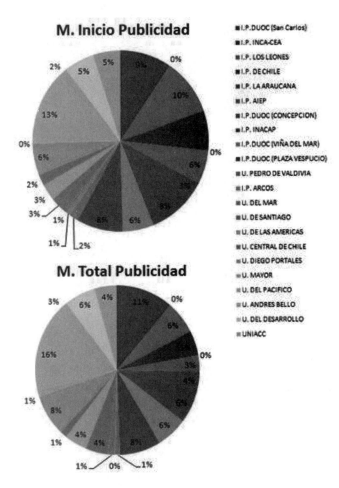

Table 30-5: Distribution of students

Curricula for the Advertising Career in Chile

Although there are many different types of institutions that offer the career of advertising in Chile, it is important to provide a brief summary of the duration of the programs and the course offerings available to students. Overall, schools offer courses to prepare students to work in advertising agencies. They include courses in account management, marketing, market research, consumer behavior and branding.

Many programs also offer a block of courses in advertising media including the design and evaluation of campaigns in the mass media. The creativity area includes seminars on writing, campaigns, art direction, creative workshops and workshops on advertising agencies. The digital area includes courses on the application of software programs used in the field, including Illustrator, Photoshop and Flash. Some programs also require English as a Foreign Language.

All educational institutions offer a degree program that requires an internship in the field and the development of a final project. Requirements vary, but each institution assigns students work on a campaign for a product or service, including the development of a business, or students must do a research project related to the field of communications and marketing.

Graduate Programs:

Currently there is no graduate program in Chile specifically for advertising. As of 2010, only the Universidad Mayor offers a Master of Art degree in Advertising and Communication. There are related programs that include a graduate degree at the Universidad Mayor in Strategic Communication and Branding and another at the Universidad del Desarrollo in Strategic Communication and Business.

Interviews

To conclude the chapter, two interviews follow with key figures who are responsible for developing the first advertising programs in Chile. Both Mónica Herrera and Julio Ortúzar provide relevant data on the early years in the field, as well as their perspectives on the current state of advertising education in the country.

Mónica Herrera, PhD.

The following is extracted from an interview with journalist and advertising professional Mónica Herrera, PhD. Her background includes a Master of Arts in Communication and a Doctorate in Education.

How and when did advertising education begin in Chile?

I don't recall the exact date, but training in vocational schools began in the 1950's. The private institute, IPEVE, was started in the 1960's and at the same time a program in advertising was offered at the Universidad Técnica. Later, in 1975 the Tecnológico opened a two-year program.

The Mónica Herrera School, the Instituto del Pacífico, and UNI-ACC were all established in the 1980's when a new education model for free and open competition was established. I was one of the pioneer's in teaching methodology and for that reason my school quickly gained prestige.

How did you get interested in the field of advertising?

It was by chance. I was a recent graduate of the School of Journalism at the Universidad de Concepción, working as a reporter at El Sur newspaper. I ran into a friend from the university who told me that he was working for McCann Erickson (a transnational ad agency), but they had asked him to move to Santiago. When he turned the offer down, they asked him to recommend someone to take the position. He gave them my name.

When I asked about the remuneration, he said it was three times my salary at the paper. I didn't hesitate to accept. It took a lot for them to offer me a contract because I was a woman. In those days, they could not imagine a woman in an executive position.

I traveled to Santiago to have an interview with the General Manager of the company and then to Valparaíso to speak with the Branch Manager, and that must have convinced them. It was the first time there was a female executive in advertising in Chile. I was a pioneer, both as an executive and later as an educator because my teaching methods were very innovative.

How do you regard advertising education in Chile today?

There are many alternatives today. All institutions of higher learning, including the university and the professional and technical institutes, offer academic programs in advertising. They are homogeneous however, and offer more or less the same programs. A varied curriculum is lacking. The faculty is also the same, teaching simultaneously at various schools. The differences are physical: the size of the buildings varies and the technological infrastructure is at times more advanced in some schools, but nothing more.

The teaching methods have not changed since the last century. Only the contents have changed as a result of the emergence of new communication technologies.

The most important thing is for the advertising professional to know how to do the job and to value his or her creativity, regardless of where he or she works. Graduate degrees in business such as the MBA, are highly valued because advertising and marketing are disciplines that belong to the field of business. Today, the most important programs in the country are at the Universidad del Pacífico given its long tradition and experience, and at UNIACC with its advanced infrastructure.

Changes in content should come as a result of new technologies, the impact of the Internet and innovations that are emerging as a result of Web 2.0 and those that will come with Web 3.0. Other changes should come as a result of new consumer behaviors, the globalization of the marketplace and the ways that (products and services) are bought and sold.

Education for the 21st Century should change regardless of the field, whether it is Advertising, Fine Arts, Medicine, Law or another area. It should change not only with regard to content but also with regard to the social, cultural, political, economic and technological contexts because the world has changed. People have changed. Teachers can no longer continue to enter the classroom and give a lecture. That method is no longer relevant. The methods should change, along with the role of the teacher. Those who refuse are those who continue to survive with the old system, but a crisis will come along that obligates them to change, too.

Concern over quality is universal and occurs at all levels. An excellent education system can't be achieved by simple updates or modifications. They are merely cosmetic changes. A necessary revolution is coming that will affect procedures, paradigms, and beliefs regarding how to teach and how to learn. We are not prepared for this revolution.

Juio Ortúzar Prado

The following is from an interview with Juio Ortúzar Prado, founder of the Universidad del Pacífico, and currently President of its Board of Directors, and considered a key mentor in the field of advertising education in Chile. He is winner of the National Award in Advertising from the International Association of Advertising

How and when did advertising education begin in Chile?

I gave my first seminar in 1961 at the School of Industrial Design at the Universidad Católica. A year later I taught a summer course for a pilot program in advertising. I went on to establish the Instituto de Publicidad de Mercado y Ventas/IPEVE (Advertising, Marketing and Sales Institute) in 1963, and opened a four year academic program. In 1976 I founded the Escuela de Publicidad de Chile (School of Advertising of Chile) with a five-year program for the advertising professional.

How do you regard advertising education in Chile today?

An advertising program should train students not just to practice in the field, but it should prepare them to be ethical professionals and entrepreneurs with a broad culture. Such a background will give them the advantage in their daily performance. The advertising professional today should be connected to other activities in marketing and business in general.

The field of advertising should start with the notion of change. There is no other way for a profession that deals with people and behaviors that change so rapidly. There is a constant need for creativity and innovation, basic elements that are essential to the development of the field.

Given such dynamism, I believe that future developments in the field will be more integrated with the social sciences, and will require a more global understanding that is gained from anthropological, sociological and economic perspectives.

I see advertising as a fundamental bridge to economic activity in societies that have a free and open market. I don't think that it is strictly a commercial activity, but rather the field will influence the environment and other emerging groups. This will require greater training and knowledge and broader understanding of the internationalization of cultures. It will require the professional to be a better researcher and interpreter of the dreams and expectations of people. It will require greater creative abilities that allow for constant innovation in an environment with highly advanced technologies incorporated into daily life and in which the multiple consumption of media will be the norm.

I believe that to look toward the future, one should look to the past. The advertising professional should be a renaissance man or woman, capable of creating and re-creating, global in his or her world vision, and a master at applying his or her knowledge.

Final Thoughts

Based on the research, a few final closing statements are important in evaluation the growth of advertising education in Chile:

Advertising education in Chile has reached a stage of maturity with varied and abundant academic alternatives.

Weaknesses exist within the various alternatives precisely because there is very little difference in the content across programs.

Important technological and content-based changes have yet to occur in the curriculum, in spite of significant global changes as a result of Web 2.0, social networks, and the power of wikis and bloggers.

New media is essential to the field and should be mastered and used by new generations of advertising professionals who will be required to incorporate all of these media into their future advertising campaigns.

Finally, with regard to the presence of advertising agencies in Chile, the large multi-national firms have absorbed the smaller companies. But even in this context, there is a tendency to continue using traditional media when investing in advertising due to a fear of innovation.

Bibliography

Basis, Isidoro (1999). 200 años de la Publicidad en Chile. Holanda comunicaciones S.A. First Edition: February 2000. Printed in Chile. P.204, 205, 206, 207,208.209.210, 211.

www.divesup.cl/sies/ Sistema Nacional de Información de la Educación Superior (Sies), a body under the Chilean Ministry of Education's Division of Higher Education.

INDEX

488

AUTHORS

Akpabio, Eno, BA in English (1987), M.Sc (1991) and a PhD in Mass Communication (2004). In May 2011, he took up an appointment as Professor in the School of Journalism and Mass Communication, University of Dar es Salaam. He was formerly a Lecturer in the Department of Mass Communication at the University of Lagos (1998-2005). He joined the Department of Media Studies, University of Botswana in August 2005 as Senior Lecturer and rose to the position of Associate Professor and Head of Department. Prof. Akpabio has authored two books (*African Communications Systems: An Introductory Text* and *Writing to Win Hearts and Minds*), many chapters in books as well as numerous articles in learned journals. He is a member of the International Council of IAMCR.

Ajami, Joseph, (Ohio University 1982 M.A) and (Ohio University, Ph.d, 1987) is an Associate Professor at Notre Dame University-Lebanon. He has been teaching at NDU since 1994 and assumed the chairmanship of the Department Of Mass Communication three times, the last of which was between 2006-2012. He was also an Assistant professor for five years at Christian Brothers University in Memphis, Tennessee where he also served as the Chair of The Department of Communication and Performing Arts from 1989-1992. His last teaching job in the U.S was at Florida Southern College in 1993. His research areas include Advertising and its potential impact, Public Relations, Political Communication, and Advertising Education in Lebanon, among others. He also wrote a chapter on Public Relations in a book on Advertising and Marketing in the Middle East. He has been both a member of Society of Professional Journalists and Journalism Students Society of America. He has also served as a member of Ohio University's International Understanding Honor Society. His major areas of teaching include: International Communication; Current Issues, Media Ethics, Advertising and Society; Speech Communication, Advertising Creativity and Copywriting, Feature Writing, Media Essentials, and various PR courses, and other courses.

Aslanbay, Yonca, Ph.D (Marmara University, 1992) is Professor of Marketing and Chair of the School of Communication Management, as well as the PhD in Communication at İstanbul Bilgi University. Her recent research focus is new types of networks over cyberspace and sustainable consumption. She has published several articles, and book chapters.

Ayeni, Olugbenga Chris., Ph.D. (University of Southern Mississippi, 1999) is Associate Professor and Coordinator of the Advertising & PR tracks at Eastern Connecticut State University. His research interest include international and political advertising, crisis communication and public relations. He has presented his research work at national and international conferences. He has also published a book on political advertising and series of journal articles and book chapters on his research interests. An award-winning mentor, his students have won top-level awards in state-wide student competitions in integrated marketing communications campaigns. He is a member of American Academy of Advertising and the Public Relations Society of America.

Bhargava, Mukesh, PhD (University of Texas at Austin) was a distinguished professor of marketing at Oakland University, where he taught for 18 years. Born and raised in India, he moved to the United States and began his academic career. Dr. Bhargava passed away before this book was published.

Brioschi, Edoardo Teodoro, Graduated in Economics and Commerce at the Università Cattolica del Sacro Cuore (Milan, Italy) in 1963, he began his academic career in this University in 1965. University professor since the academic year 1971/1972, he became in 1980 the first Chair of "Advertising, Economics and Technique" in the Italian university system and in 1996 the first Chair of "Business Communication Economics and Technique" in the Faculties of Economics of the Italian university. At present he is the President of the Scientific Committee of the Research Laboratory on Business Communication (Labcom) of the Università Cattolica del Sacro Cuore, he established in 1998, and the Scientific Director of the journal *Communicative Business. Italian research review on business communication.* He has written or edited more than 120 publications in both Italian and English. In 2005 he was the only non-American professor to be awarded the "Charles H. Sandage Award for Teaching Excellence" by the American Academy of Advertising, and in 2006 he was also awarded a Medal for Merit by the International Advertising Association. In 2011 he was appointed Grand Officer of the Order of Merit of the Italian Republic for his long dedication to the activity of research and teaching in the Italian University.

Buda, Janusz, B.A.Hons (London University, 1965), is Professor of English and Business Communication at the Faculty of Commerce,

Waseda University in Tokyo, Japan. From 1977 to 1993 he taught English, English Translation, and Area Studies at Otsuma Women's University in Tokyo. His research includes the development and application of course management systems, the role of false memory in second language acquisition, the improvement of university admission programmes, and direct digital publishing. He is a member of the Kipling Society, the Japan-British Society, and has served on the editorial board of the Japan Business Communication Association. Before becoming a teacher he was a professional translator of technical Japanese. His skills include creative writing, proofreading, editing, and typography.

Castellón, Lucía, journalist of Universidad de Chile, teacher of Religion, Hogar Catequístico from Universidad Católica; advance courses in United States, professor in several lectures in Journalism. Founder of the Journalism School, and former Dean of the Faculty of Communication and Information, Universidad Diego Portales. Speaker in different seminars and congresses, both national and international. Articles in Communication magazines. Researcher in subjects on digital divide, communication and education, communication and videogames, among others. Former Vice President of IBERCOM, Asociación Iberoamericana de Investigadores en Comunicación (Latin American and Spanish Association of Communication Researchers), fiscal of ALAIC, Asociación Latinoamericana de Investigadores en Comunicación (Latin American Association of Communication Researchers). Former Head of Chair of Communication in UNESCO Chile. Developer of the National Program Prensa y Educación (Press and Education). Former Director of the Postgraduate Course, Faculty of Communication and Design, Universidad Mayor. Today she acts as Director of a research group on Communication Media, Children and Youth in ALAIC, and works as Dean of the Faculty of Communication, Universidad Mayor.

Chu, Guangzhi, B.A.(Jilin University,1989),M.A.(Beijing Broadcasting Institute, 1994), Ph.D (Renmin University of China, 2001), is Professor of the Department of Advertising at Communication University of China. His research includes advertising management, public service advertising, integrated marketing communication, and digital marketing, and he has published more than 40 articles, books, and book chapters. He is a member of China Advertising Association's Academic Division and a member of China International Public Relations Association.

Clark, Tim, M.A. (University of South Australia), BA (University of Warwick, UK). He is a Senior Lecturer and Deputy Head of the Division of Public and Promotional Communication at Nanyang Technological University in Singapore. His current research interest is the study of the relationship that exists between advertising and art. This is the subject of his latest research paper. Prior to joining NTU, Tim spent 30 years working in advertising. His career began at Ogilvy & Mather in London and New York. After 7 years in London followed by 2 years in South Africa, Tim moved to Singapore and spent over 20 years in S.E. Asia as Regional and Executive Creative Director of various international agencies, from bases in Singapore, Hong Kong, Kuala Lumpur and Tokyo.

D'Souza, Alan, MBA (IIMA), is Dean of the Shanti Business School and Shanti Communication School, Ahmedabad, India. He is the Former Executive Director of Mudra Communications Ltd, (now DDB, India). He is the Founder member MICA, one of the leading Communication Schools in India. He was also for a brief period the Director of the Goa Institute of Management, Goa, India. Mr. D'Souza's area of specialization is Integrated Marketing Communications in which he is currently persuing his Phd. Mr. D'Souza is Visiting Professor at some of the leading Business and Communication Management Schools in India. He is the co-author of a book "Advertising and Promotions, An IMC perspective." He has also authored some working papers and case studies besides contributing to Chapters in various books. He is the winner of the "Outstanding Manager of the year" award by the Ahmedabad Management Association. His work on the new B-C-D model of Management Education has won his Institute the "World Education Award 2012" with a citation signed by the Chairman of the All India Council for Technical Education, the Governing body of Higher Technical Education in India. He is a member of several professional bodies, on the boards of several Institutions and a Consultant in his domain of specialization across the world.

Estevez, María del Carmen, is an Advertising Graduate at Universidad del Pacifico, Chile; currently she is Director of the Advertising Career and also directs both the Bachelor Degree and Postgraduate programs in Advertising and Multimedia Communications at Universidad Mayor. She is Professor at Universidad Andres Bello, teaching Copywriting and Communication courses. She was Academic Coordinator for the Advertising Program at Duoc UC, Chile and professor at

Universidad Santo Tomas. She has more than twenty years of experience in Education, and formerly worked as audiovisual producer for advertising commercials.

Grow, Jean M., Ph.D (University of Wisconsin-Madison, 2001) is Associate Professor of Strategic Communication and Director of the Fine Arts Program at Marquette University in Milwaukee, Wisconsin. She has authored numerous books chapters and articles in journals such as: *Advertising & Society Review*, the *International Journal of Advertising*, the *Journal of Business Ethics*, the *Journal of Consumer Marketing* and *Women's Studies in Communication*. In 2013 Grow co-authored the third edition of *Advertising Creative: Strategy, Copy & Design* (Sage). Her current research addresses the global under-representation of women in advertising creative departments. Prior to joining the academy she worked as an artists' representative. Her corporate clients included: Coca-Cola USA, Kellogg USA, and Zenith; and agency clients included: BBDO, draftfcb, and Leo Burnett. She currently does strategic consulting for clients such as: Flamingo International/London, the National Hemophilia Foundation/New York and Nike.

Hesapçı, Özlem, Ph.D (Bocconi University, 2007), is an Associate Professor of Marketing and Vice Chair of the Department of Management at Bogazici University. She was an Assistant Professor of Marketing at the Department of Advertising in Istanbul Bilgi University, 2007-2011. Her research includes psychological processes that underlie consumers' attitudinal as well as cognitive responses. She has published several articles, and book chapters.

Hwang, Jang-Sun, Ph.D. (University of Tennessee, 2003) is Associate Professor and Chair of the Department of Advertising and Public Relations at Chung-Ang University, Seoul, Korea. He has taught Interactive Brand Communication, Qualitative Research in Advertising, and Marketing Theory in the Chung-Ang University since 2003. His research falls under a combination of new media advertising, consumer behavior, and message strategy. He has published more than 30 articles, books and book chapters including *Journal of Advertising, Journal of Advertising Research, International Journal of Advertising, Journal of Interactive Advertising, Psychology and Marketing*, and other Korean academic journals in advertising field.

Jančič, Zlatko, BSc (1975), MSc (1989), PhD (1993), is Professor and Chair of the Department of Marketing Communications and Public Relations at Faculty for Social Sciences, University of Ljubljana, Slovenia. Previous to his full-time academic career, he created numerous advertising campaigns for major Slovenian companies and governmental bodies. He was the author of the first Code of Slovenian Advertising Practice and the first President of Slovenian Advertising Adjudication Court (1995-2001). His research interests are in marketing and advertising theory, business strategy issues, corporate social responsibility, etc. He is an author/co-author of books, book chapters and scientific articles in a *Journal of Advertising Research, Journal of Marketing Management, Journal of Marketing Communications, European Journal of Marketing, Corporate Communications*, etc.

Keenan, Kevin, Ph.D. (University of Georgia, 1990), is Professor of Journalism and Mass Communication at the American University in Cairo (Egypt). Prior to joining AUC in 1997, he taught at the University of Maryland for 10 years. He is active in a number of academic and professional organizations and has served as an officer for the Advertising Division of the Association for Education in Journalism and Mass Communication and the American Academy of Advertising. Keenan's work has been published in the *International Journal of Advertising, Journal of Advertising Education, Journalism and Mass Communication Educator, Journalism and Mass Communication Quarterly, Public Relations Review, The Global Public Relations Handbook*, and elsewhere. He has presented nearly 100 scholarly papers in North America, Europe, Africa, and Asia and has been cited in popular and trade publications including *Advertising Age, The International Herald Tribune, USA Today, The Washington Post*, and others.

Gayle Kerr (Ph.D., Queensland University of Technology, 2004), is a Professor in Advertising and IMC in the School of Advertising, Marketing and Public Relations, Queensland University of Technology. Kerr worked in the creative side of advertising, before joining academia more than a decade ago to teach and research in advertising and integrated marketing communication (IMC). Her areas of research interest include advertising self-regulation, advertising management, digital and social media, IMC and educational issues in both advertising and IMC. Gayle is the founding President of the Australian and New Zealand Academy of Advertising and the first non-US academic to be honoured with American Academy of Advertising (AAA) Billy I. Ross in 2012. She serves on both the AAA Executive Committee and as Deputy Editor for the Journal of Marketing Communications.

Kline, Mihael/Miro, PhD (1993), is Assistant Professor at the Faculty of Social Sciences of the University of Ljubljana, Department for market communications and public relations. His work focuses mainly on research in the fields of psychology, consumer behavior, management of market brands, market communications, business communications, visual communications and psychology of visual communications. His research papers are published in domestic and foreign magazines: *Teorija in praksa (Theory and Practice), Akademija MM, International journal of technological design education, South medical review*, in different monographs and text books. Besides he is also a co-author in numerous research, communications and strategic projects and he acts as a consultant to different managers in numerous Slovene companies.

Koekemoer, Ludi, C.L. (University of Pretoria, 1969) Ph.D (Rhodes University, 1978) is CEO of AAA School of Advertising in South Africa since 2000. He worked for 3 large advertising agencies between 1972 and 1986, the last 7 years as Managing partner. He was a professor of Marketing of University of Pretoria, 1986 – 1989 and Chairman of the Department of Business Management and Professor of Marketing at Rand Afrikaans University, 1990 – 1999. His research includes advertising brand management and new product development and he has published more than 20 articles, books and book chapters. He serves on the editorial board of Communicare, the Advertising Industry Tribunal of the Advertising Standards Authority; he represents AAA School of Advertising on the board of the Association for Communication & Advertising and has served on many ad. industry bodies in South Africa. He was a visiting professor to Kenan Flagler Business School at University of North Carolina, USA.

Lwin, May O., Ph.D (National University of Singapore, 1997), is Associate Professor of Communication and Associate Dean at the Humanities, Arts and Social Sciences College in Nanyang Technological University (NTU) in Singapore. She was previously with the Marketing Department of the National University of Singapore Business School where she received the Outstanding Educator Award. Her research includes health and societal communication and advertising regulatory issues. May has published more than 100 articles, books/book chapters, reports, and papers in international journals such as the *Journal of Communication, Journal of Health Communication, Journal of Consumer Research, Journal of Public Policy & Marketing, Journal of the Academy of Marketing Science*, and *Journal of Advertising*. She serves on editorial boards of the *Journal of International Advertising* and the *Journal of Consumer Affairs*. She has judged awards like the

International Effies and served on the Singapore National Obesity Task Force, Medical and Dental Board at the Health Promotion Board and the Singapore National Heart Foundation Board. She is also a Senior Fellow at the Asian Consumer Insight Institute.

Micu, Anca C., M.B.A. and Ph.D. (University of Missouri-Columbia, 2001, 2005) is Associate Dean and Associate Professor of Marketing at the John F. Welch College of Business, Sacred Heart University. She worked for BBDO in Europe before her academic career. She was an assistant professor of marketing for 6 years and then became Chairperson of the Department of Marketing and Sport Management at Sacred Heart University. Her research includes measurement of emotions in advertising, examining the effect of synergy between advertising and publicity messages in the Internet environment, and identification of the passive shopping stage. Her work was published in *Management & Marketing, Journal of Advertising Research*, and *Journal of Interactive Advertising*. After BBDO, she worked or consulted for a number of companies including The Estee Lauder Companies, Time Inc. and the Advertising Research Foundation.

Mills, Patrick, BSc (Kings College, London, 1982), is Director of Professional Development at the Institute of Practitioners in ing. Patrick started his career in advertising in 1988 at Generator, the sister agency of Yellowhammer, where he worked on Mitsubishi Motors, Fuji Cameras and Barclays Bank. In 1994 he moved to Hakuhodo to work on NEC computers, then in 1995 he moved to Bates UK to manage the direct marketing and advertising for women's fashion retailer Talbots, Owens Corning and the English Cricket Board. After a spell at the Abbott Mead Vickers design, web and direct arm, The Open Agency, where he launched Demon Internet, Patrick finished his agency career at SOUK, a digital advertising agency, where he worked on travel brands including Flybe, Malta Tourism and Emirates Airlines. Patrick has been at the IPA since September 2008, where he oversees the advertising industry Continuous Professional Development programme, which includes award winning e-learning qualifications and experiential courses.

Moraru, Mădălina E., is a Senior Lecturer of the Faculty of Journalism and Communication Studies, the University of Bucharest, Romania since 2009. She teaches Advertising Agency, Advertising Production, and Advertising Strategies. In 2010 she received a postdoctoral fellowship from Gaylord College, the University of Oklahoma (as a visiting professor too), and in 2012, from Staffordshire University and Buckinghamshire New University (both UK), part of a research project on advertising glocalization funded by the European Union. Her research focuses on the anthropological approach to advertising in her PhD thesis and authored over 10 articles on the topic, as well as a book on the relationship between myth and advertising, storytelling, and global-local influences ("Myth and advertising"). She is also a member of Research Committee of European Institute of Commercials Communication Education (Edcom), representing Romania and University of Bucharest at the international students' competition in advertising field (entitled *Ad Venture)* as well.

Ngu, Teck Hua, Ph.D (Pennsylvania State University, 1996), is Associate Professor of the Department of Advertising at the Mara University of Technology, Shah Alam, Malaysia. His research interest includes advertising regulation and ethics, and public health campaigns.

Nyitse, Gabriel T., Ph. D. (Benue State University, Makurdi Nigeria, 2012) is a seasoned journalism practitioner and administrator. He is the Permanent Secretary in the Governor's Office, Benue State. Prior to that he was the Editor of the state owned newspaper, *The Voice.* He was a senor journalist with *The Concord* news organization before it was proscribed by Nigeria's military government. His research interests are in mediating role of technology in news reporting.

Ogbu, Benjamin Ejuwa, is a Lecturer in the Department of mass communication, Benue State University, Makurdi, Nigeria. He is widely published.

Patti, Charles H., Ph.D. (Illinois, 1975) is Interim Dean and Professor of Marketing in the College of Business at the University of Denver. He is also the inaugural James M. Cox Professor of Customer Experience Management. Prior to joining the University of Denver in 2006, he was Head of the School of Advertising, Marketing, and Public Relations at Queensland University of Technology, Brisbane, Australia. His research covers advertising, marketing communication, and customer experience management and his work includes journal articles, book chapters, and eight books on various aspects of advertising and marketing. His research has appeared in the *Journal of Advertising,* the *Journal of Advertising Research,* the *Journal of Marketing,* the *Journal of Marketing Communications, Industrial Marketing Management,* and others. Dr. Patti serves on a number of editorial boards. He has extensive international experience in teaching and consulting with universities and companies in Italy, New Zealand, Australia, Singapore, Malaysia, France, Finland, Germany, Chile,

Hong Kong, and England. He is a past winner of the Marketing Educator of the Year Award and recently received the James Hershner Free Enterprise Award.

Pennington, Robert, Ph.D. (University of Wisconsin, 1991) has held faculty postions at several universities in the USA and Taiwan in departments of communication, management, and foreign languages and cultures. He specializes in the cultural development implications of communication technology. His general interest concerns consumption and marketing communication as cultural processes for satisfying basic human needs. He has written previously about marketing communication development, advertising and brands within consumer culture, the meanings of consumer brands and psycholinguistic methodology.

Punyapiroje, Chompunuch, Ph.D. (University of Tennessee-Knoxville, 2002) works as an Assistant Professor of the Advertising Major at the Department of Communication Arts, Faculty of Humanities and Social Sciences, Burapha University, Chonburi, Thailand and serves as Head of Advertising Major from 2002 to 2009 and Chair of Marketing Communication Master Program from 2009 to present. Her research relates to advertising cultural values, product placements and consumer protections and has published in *World Communication, Journal of Current Issues & Research in Advertising, Asian Journal of Communication* and *International Journal of Retail and Distribution Management.*

Roca Correa, David, (Universitat Autònoma de Barcelona, 1993), Ph. D (Universitat Autònoma de Barcelona, 2001), is Associate Professor of the Department of Advertising and Public Relations at *Universitat Autònoma de Barcelona.* In 2010 he was a Visiting Professor at Marquette University in Milwaukee, Wisconsin. His research focuses on advertising creativity and gender. He has published in the *International Journal of Advertising, Comunicación & Sociedad, Trípodos* and *Zer.* He also has published chapters related to advertising issues, most recently *Convergences and Divergences Between Advertising and Public Relations* at Palgrave Macmillan (2012). He also consults with the Advertising Research Group (GRP) and has been the recipient of several Government grants including *Is there gender bias when evaluating advertising creativity?*

Rodriguez, Lulu, Ph.D (University of Wisconsin, 1993), is James F. Evans Endowed Professor of Agricultural Communications at the University of Illinois at Urbana-Champaign. She was a Professor at the

Greenlee School of Journalism and Communication and the Biosafety Institute for Genetically Modified Agricultural Products at Iowa State University, 1993-2013. She designs, implements, and evaluates the impact of communication campaigns related to agriculture, renewable energy, the environment, food safety and food security. Her research focuses on the communication of risks related to scientific and technological breakthroughs, investigating people's basic mental models of hazard and their opinions about innovations that cause controversies or may be perceived as risky. She also conducts research on the visual representations of science and risk issues.

Sar, Sela, Ph.D (University of Minnesota, 2006), is an Associate Professor of Advertising at Charles H. Sandage Department of Advertising, University of Illinois. He was an Assistant Professor of Advertising 2006-2012 and an Associate Professor 2012-2013 at Iowa State University. He has published more than 18 refereed journal articles, 4 book chapters, and 12 refereed proceedings for major conferences. His scholarship record also includes more than 30 refereed conference papers presented at different premiere meetings and conventions of the discipline. He serves on editorial boards of the *Journal of Advertising*, and the *International Journal of Advertising*. He also serves as an Associate Editor for the *Asian Journal of Communication*. He is a recipient of the *Journal of Advertising*'s Best Reviewer Award for 2010 and an ad hoc best Reviewer Award for the *Journal of Current Issues & Research in Advertising* for 2012.

Schultz, Don E., BBA (University of Oklahoma), MA and PhD (Michigan State University) is Professor (Emeritus-in-Service) Integrated Marketing Communications, The Medill School, Northwestern University, Evanston, IL. President of Agora, Inc., a global marketing, communication and branding consulting firm. He consults, lectures, and holds seminars on integrated marketing communication, marketing, branding, advertising, sales promotion, and communication management in Europe, South America, Asia/Pacific, the Middle East, Australia, and North America. He is the author/co-author of twenty-seven books and over 150 trade, academic and professional articles. He is a featured columnist in *Marketing News and Marketing Insights*. He was founding editor of the *Journal of Direct Marketing*, and is associate editor, *Journal of Marketing Communications*, co-editor of the *International Journal of Integrated Marketing Communication*, and is on the editorial review board for many trade and scholarly publications. He also holds or has held appointments as an adjunct/visiting professor at the Queensland University of Technology in Australia, Cranfield School of Management in the UK, Tsinghua University and Peking University, China, and the Swedish School of Economics, Finland.

Shaver, Mary Alice, Ph.D (Indiana University, 1984) was most recently the Hamrin Professor of Media Management at the Jonkoping International Business School in Jonkoping, Sweden. Previously she was chair of the Nicholson School of Communication at the University of Central Florida, director of the Advertising Department at Michigan State University, and a Professor at the University of North Carolina. Shaver was President of the American Advertising Association (2002), President of AEJMC (2004-2005), and editor of the Journal of Advertising Education (1999-2004). Her research centered on the effects of advertising in society, on comparative economics in the global environment, on the effects of competition in the media industry and on consumer behavior with regard to influences of economic regulation and standards. She published in the *Journal of Media Economics, Journalism & Mass Communication Quarterly*, the *Newspaper Research Journal* and *Journalism and Mass Communication Educator*.

Shimamura, Kazue, M.A. in Commerce (Waseda University, 1981), is Professor of Advertising of the School of Commerce at Waseda University in Tokyo, Japan. She was a lecturer and Associate Professor at Saitama Women's Junior College from 1989 to 1993, teaching Advertising and Marketing. Her research interests include advertising education in Japan, advertising ethics and regulation, and global advertising creative. She has published numerous articles on these topics in Japan. In addition, she has written and edited several Japanese advertising textbooks. She has served on the board of executive directors of the Japan Academy of Advertising since 1995. In Waseda University she was the Director of the Faculty Development Center from 2008 to 2010, and the Director of the Open Education Center from 2010 to 2012. She is currently the Dean of the School of Commerce.

Taylor, Jonathan, (University of Strathclyde, 1979, 1st Class Honours) is Head of Marketing Communications at the City of London Business School, London Metropolitan University. He was a Visiting Professor in Marketing at the University of Strathclyde from 1990-93, and co-author (with PR Smith) of Editions 3 & 4 of Marketing Communications, the leading UK academic textbook in the subject, adopted by over 40 universities and colleges. He has been the Chief Examiner of CPD Certificates and Diplomas for the Institute of Practitioners in Advertising since the inception of the programs in 2004.

Tena-Parera, Daniel (Universitat Autònoma de Barcelona, 1992), Ph. D (Universitat Autònoma de Barcelona, 1998), is Associate Professor of the Department of Advertising and Public Relations at The Universitat Autònoma de Barcelona. He has been teaching since 1982 and he has specialized in the study of the aspects that affect communication of organizations (advertising, publicity and public relations). He is a specialist in the design and production of visual and audio-visual messages in mass media from the formal and perceptive perspective. His research also includes advertising, publicity and public relations issues, and his publications include Pearson Hall (2004), Palgrave Macmillan (2012), Trípodos (2012), and he is the editor of the *Grafica Journal of Graphic Design*. He is also a member of the Advertising Research Group (GRP) and the Psychology and Advertising Communication Research Group (GRPCP) with a focus on the reception of the communication. Additionally, he is the Director of two Masters programs at the Universitat Autònoma de Barcelona in Journalism and Digital Communication, and Graphic Communication.

Vilela, Alexandra M. (Ph.D. University of Wisconsin-Madison) is an Associate Professor of Advertising and Corporate Communication in the School of Media Arts & Design at James Madison University, in Virginia, USA. Her areas of research focus on cause-related marketing, corporate social responsibility, gender, product placement, and cross-cultural studies in advertising. She worked for more than ten years in advertising, marketing, public relations, and journalism in South America and Europe.

Waller, David S., B.A. (University of Sydney, 1985), M.Com (University of New South Wales, 1988), Ph.D (University of Newcastle, 2000), is a Senior Lecturer in the Marketing Discipline Group, University of Technology Sydney. David has over 20 years' experience teaching marketing subjects at several universities, including University of Newcastle, University of New South Wales and Charles Sturt University-Riverina. His research has included projects on marketing communications, advertising agency-client relationships; controversial advertising; international advertising; marketing ethics; and marketing education. He has published several textbooks and over 60 refereed journal articles, including *Journal of Advertising; Journal of Advertising Research; European Journal of Marketing, Journal of Business Ethics,*

Journal of Business Research; International Journal of Advertising; and *Journal of Marketing Communications.*

Werder, Olaf H., M.S. (University of Illinois, 1994), Ph.D (University of Florida, 2002), is Lecturer of Health Communication and Strategic Public Relations at the University of Sydney, Australia. He was an Associate Professor of Advertising at the University of New Mexico, 2002-2010. Prior to his academic appointment, he has worked in the advertising industry on the media sales and agency side in the USA and Germany for about ten years, during which he was also a member of the respective industry associations, the *American Advertising Federation* (AAF) and the *Gesamtverband Kommunikationsagenturen* (GWA). His research is centered on social marketing and socio-cultural understanding of health in population and media with an emphasis on community collaborative approaches. He has been an investigator on funded research programs in health literacy, obesity prevention and global impacts of infectious diseases and is the author of 30 articles, books, and book chapters. He is an affiliated health communication researcher at Sydney's *Charles Perkins Centre*, a research network member on infectious disease prevention, and an executive board member of the *Australian Association of Social Marketing* (AASM).

Whitlow, S. Scott, Ph.D. (Southern Illinois University at Carbondale, 1975) is ISC Professor in the University of Kentucky' School of Journalism and Telecommunications. Her interest in Canadian approaches to advertising education parallels her overarching interest in academic pedagogy, a thrust that unites her research articles and book chapters as well as service efforts. She structured UK's first Advertising program and also its current integrated program that advanced the program's scope and status from 'sequence' to Major. She initiated the School's coordinator role and served both programs in that capacity. In 1989, she structured the School's first formal internship program, initiating a rigorous application review of businesses to determine eligibility to host an intern.

Ye, Rebecca, MSc (University of Oxford, 2012), is Research Associate at the Institute of Southeast Asian Studies. Her research interests include the sociology of education and work. Beginning fall of 2013, she will be a doctoral candidate at the University of Stockholm, where she will study social networks within the creative industries.

Yu, Jay (Hyunjae), Ph.D. (The University of Georgia, 2007), is an associate professor at the School of Communication, Sogang University,

South Korea. He was an assistant professor at the Manship School of Mass Comm., Louisiana State University, 2007-2010. His research includes diverse issues about advertising/advertising industry (advertising appeals, creativity, cross-cultural perspectives, digital media advertising, privacy and consumers, effects on children, etc.) and Health communication. He has published more than 30 academic articles in the U.S. and Korea including *Journal of Advertising, Journal of Consumer Affairs, International Journal of Consumer Studies, Appetite, Internet Research, Asian Journal of Communication, Journal of Promotion Management, and Korean Journal of Advertising*, etc. He was a copywriter at Cheil Communication, South Korea, before coming to academia (1996-2002).

Žabkar, Vesna, PhD (University of Ljubljana, 1999; Fulbright Grant for 1995/96 in the Marketing PhD program at Northwestern University, Kellogg GSM), is Professor, Chair of the Marketing Academic Unit and Head of the Institute of Marketing at University of Ljubljana, Faculty of Economics (FELU). Her research interests include advertising effectiveness, agency-clients relationships and managerial view of integrated marketing communications. She has published in *Journal of Advertising Research, Journal of Marketing Management, European Journal of Marketing and* serves as editor of the *Economic and Business Review*. She was Vice-President of Advertising Arbitrary Court and supervisor for the National Readership Survey in Slovenia.

EDITORS

Lead Editors

Jef I. Richards

     Jef is Professor and Chair of the Department of Advertising + Public Relations at Michigan State University. He served as 45th President of the American Academy of Advertising in 2008, it's 50th Anniversary. He has worked as a photographer, a sign language interpreter, a lawyer, and an advertising professor. For the past two decades he has taught in The University of Texas Advertising Department, serving as its Chair from 1998 to 2002. He is on the Board of Directors of the Advertising Educational Foundation, and on the Editorial Boards of the *Journal of Public Policy & Marketing*, the *Journal of Advertising*, the *Journal of Interactive Advertising*, the *Journal of Current Issues and Research in Advertising*, the *Journal of Consumer Affairs*, the *International Journal of Electronic Business*, and the *Advertising & Society Review*, as well as being an associate editor of the *International Journal of Internet Marketing & Advertising*. He is author or co-author of two other books and more than 50 articles and book chapters. Dr. Richards holds a Ph.D. from the University of Wisconsin, and a J.D. from Indiana University. And his middle name starts with the same initial as Bill's.

Billy I. Ross

     Bill was one of the founders and the 2nd President of the American Academy of Advertising in 1960. He also has served as Chairman of the National Council of Alpha Delta Sigma (1967-69), President of the Lubbock Advertising Federation (1968-69), President of the American Society of Journalism School Administrators (1976-77), President of Kappa Tau Alpha national honorary journalism society (1984-86), as well as chairman, president, or board member of several other organizations. He is in the Texas Tech University Mass Communications Hall of Fame, as well as in the Louisiana State University, Manship School of Mass Communication Hall of Fame. Having taught at both of those schools (and a couple of other schools) for many years, Bill also was Chair of the Department of Mass Communications at Texas Tech from 1970 to 1987. He has been teaching since the 1950s and writing about advertising education since the 1960s. He has published 8 other books and numerous articles and book chapters. Dr. Ross holds a Ph.D from Southern Illinois University, and also is a retired Colonel in the U.S. Army and a recipient of the "Legion of Merit."

Copy Editors

Tom Bowers

Tom Bowers (BA, MA, PhD, Indiana University) was on the faculty of the School of Journalism and Mass Communication at the University of North Carolina at Chapel Hill from 1971 until his retirement in 2006. He was James L. Knight Professor of Advertising and was senior associate dean from 1979 to 2005 and interim dean in 2005–06. He was president of the Association for Education in Journalism and Mass Communication (AEJMC) in 1988–89 and editor of Journalism Educator from 1983 to 1988. He was on the Accrediting Committee of the Accrediting Council for Education in Journalism and Mass Communication for six years and chair of the committee for two years. He was a member of the Academic Committee of the American Advertising Federation and the National Advertising Review Board.

He was the author of Making News: 100 Years of Journalism and Mass Communication at Carolina in 2009, and he co-authored (with Alan Fletcher) Fundamentals of Advertising Research, which was printed in four editions and widely used throughout the United States and other countries. He published articles in numerous other scholarly and trade publications. From 1988 to 1995, he was co-director of The Freedom Forum Seminar for Advertising Teachers, a program that brought advertising teachers to UNC-Chapel Hill for an intensive week of sessions on course content and teaching styles.

He won the Silver Medal Award from the Triangle Advertising Federation (North Carolina) in 1994, the John L. Sanders Award for Distinguished Undergraduate Teaching and Service from UNC-Chapel Hill in 1997, and Distinguished Advertising Educator from the American Advertising Federation in 2007.

Joe Pisani

Joseph R. Pisani is Professor Emeritus and former Chairman of the Department of Advertising at the University of Florida. Pisani, a New York City native, earned his B.S. in marketing from Fordham University (1960), M.B.A. from UCLA (1961) and Ph.D. in Economics and Business Administration from the University of Maryland, College Park (1972).

He joined the University of Florida advertising faculty in 1973 and headed the Department for 19 years before stepping down in 2001. Previously he taught marketing and business administration at the College of Business Administration at the University of Maryland, College Park (1964-69), and advertising in the College of Communications at the University of Texas at Austin (1969-73). In 1978, he was a visiting professor at the College of Communications, University of Kentucky.

Professionally, Pisani worked for Goodwin, Dannenbaum, Littman & Wingfield Advertising and Public Relations in Houston, Texas. Since 1972 he has served as a part-time consultant to businesses, government agencies, advertising agencies, media and educational institutions. In 1991-92 he served as President of the Gainesville Advertising Federation and in 1995, the GAF awarded him the AAF Silver Medal. Pisani served as the 2003 President of the American Academy of Advertising, a national organization of advertising educators.

He published articles, book chapters and case studies in multi-media instruction, media planning and advertising management. He retired on May 31, 2005 and became an independent consultant.

In July 2013, Pisani returned to UF to serve as Interim Chairman of the Department of Advertising. He and his wife of 42 years Philomena D'Agostino of Washington, D.C. have two sons: Joe, 39, a senior project manager for Accenture lives in St. Petersburg, FL with his wife Lacy and daughter Sophia and Vincent, 35, a film, TV and stage actor/teacher based in Atlanta.